The Measurement of Productive Efficiency

THE
MEASUREMENT
OF PRODUCTIVE
EFFICIENCY
Techniques and Applications

Edited by

HAROLD O. FRIED
Union College

C. A. KNOX LOVELL
University of North Carolina

SHELTON S. SCHMIDT
Union College

New York   Oxford
OXFORD UNIVERSITY PRESS
1993

Oxford University Press

Oxford   New York   Toronto
Delhi   Bombay   Calcutta   Madras   Karachi
Kuala Lumpur   Singapore   Hong Kong   Tokyo
Nairobi   Dar es Salaam   Cape Town
Melbourne   Auckland   Madrid

and associated companies in
Berlin   Ibadan

Library of Congress Cataloging-in-Publication Data
The Measurement of productive efficiency : techniques and applications /
edited by Harold O. Fried, C.A. Knox Lovell, Shelton S. Schmidt.
p. cm.   Includes bibliographical references and index.
ISBN 0-19-507218-9
1. Efficiency, Industrial—Measurement.
2. Industrial productivity—Measurement.   I. Fried, Harold O.
II. Lovell, C. A. Knox.   III. Schmidt, Shelton S.
HD56.25.M436   1993
658.5′036—dc20   92-9385

1 3 5 7 9 8 6 4 2

Printed in the United States of America
on acid-free paper

To The Kids . . .

Claire
Clara
Ian
Lee Ann
Stephanie

PREFACE

In this book, we are concerned with measuring and explaining producer performance. We view performance as a function of the state of technology and economic efficiency. The former defines a frontier relation between inputs and outputs; the latter incorporates waste and misallocation relative to this frontier. Improvements in firm performance can occur through both technology and efficiency avenues.

The measurement of performance is tied to the economic objective of the producing unit. We allow the producer to pursue any of a wide variety of objectives, subject to any of a similarly wide variety of constraints. This enables us to study performance of private or public producers of goods and services at all levels of aggregation from individual plants to national economies. Moreover, performance can be measured with a variety of econometric and mathematical programming techniques as well.

Assuming that high levels of economic efficiency and productivity, and high rates of productivity growth, are desirable goals, then it is important to define and measure efficiency and productivity in ways that respect economic theory and provide useful information to managers and policy makers. Although much of traditional analysis studies productivity under the assumption that all producers are efficient, in our view there exists far too much evidence to the contrary. By ignoring inefficiency, the conventional framework is misspecified and estimates of productivity are contaminated with variation in efficiency. We believe that important insights can be gained by allowing for the possibility of a divergence between the economic objective and actual performance, and by associating this economic inefficiency with causal variables that might be subject to managerial or policy influence. This new paradigm leads to a richer understanding of the sources of improvements in producer performance.

The origins of this book date back to late 1989, when Hal and Shelton asked Knox, then basking in the warm Adelaide summer sun, to assist in the organization of a series of workshops on efficiency and productivity, to be held at Union College in Schenectady, N.Y. The workshops were generously funded by The New Liberal Arts Program of the Alfred P. Sloan Foundation. The objective was to encourage faculty to introduce quantitative methods into undergraduate courses on public policy and technology.

We began with a series of five weekend faculty workshops on the set of techniques and tools for studying producer performance. These workshops were held during the first half of 1990 and were presented by Knox Lovell, Bill Greene, Agha Iqbal Ali and Larry Seiford, Shawna Grosskopf, and Knox again. An outgrowth was Chapters 1 to 4, the "techniques" half of this book. Next, we built upon this foundation with a series of three additional workshops that focused on applications. In October 1990, Finn Førsund and Henry Tulkens visited, and their presentations became Chapters 14 and 12, respectively. In August and December 1991, we held workshops on applications to education and to the public and service sectors.

These workshops have had a major impact on faculty and students at Union College. Since the techniques can be applied to a wide variety of issues, these workshops attracted faculty in fields ranging from economic history to macroeconomics to public finance and so on. An undergraduate course was developed on the efficient management of technology. All economics majors at Union write a senior thesis that is equivalent to two courses; one-third of these theses are on the measurement of efficiency. Chapter 6 of this book is a revision of Dennis Baldwin's senior thesis directed by Linda Cavalluzzo. Faculty have individual and joint research projects in the area. Examples include Chapter 10, an analysis of performance of New Jersey school districts by Therese McCarty and Suthathip Yaisawarng, and Chapter 13, an analysis of U.S. Veterans Administration hospitals by Jim Burgess and Paul Wilson. Issues of efficiency and productivity have become a common bond that unites the faculty, as complementarities across fields have been created. And the economics major at Union College is exposed to a quantitative framework for the study of important public policy issues as envisioned by the designers of the Sloan Foundation Program.

The organization of this book is patterned after the Union College workshops. The techniques chapters (Chapters 1–4) contain up-to-date expositions by scholars who are among the founders of these empirical methods and continue to be at the forefront of research in efficiency and productivity measurement. The first chapter is an overview, followed by treatments of the econometric, nonparametric, and productivity approaches. Chapters 5 to 16 provide a wide range of interesting applications to policy issues, authored by experts from around the world. These applications are grouped according to technique. We believe that this book is unique in its eclectic approach to methodologies and applications in this important area.

We are grateful to the Alfred P. Sloan Foundation, to Bill Fairchild, director of the Sloan Program at Union College, to the Union College Internal Education Fund, to Household International Corporation, and to Herb Addison, Mary Sutherland and Dolores Oetting at Oxford, who are a pleasure to work with. And then none of this would have been possible without the late night discussions of productivity, with Horace Silver first in the background, and then as the dawn approached, Horace took over and productivity faded away.

CONTENTS

CONTRIBUTORS

Agha Iqbal Ali
School of Management,
The University of Massachusetts,
  Amherst, Mass.

Dennis Baldwin
School of Industrial and Labor
  Relations,
Cornell University, Ithaca, N.Y.

Paul W. Bauer
Federal Reserve Bank of Cleveland,
Cleveland, Ohio

Allen N. Berger
Board of Governors of the Federal
  Reserve System,
Washington, D.C.

James F. Burgess
Graduate Management Institute, Union
  College,
Schenectady, N.Y.

Linda Cavalluzzo
Department of Economics, Union
  College,
Schenectady, N.Y.

B. Kelly Eakin
Department of Economics, University
  of Oregon,
Eugene, Ore.

Fabienne Fecher
Department of Economics, Université
  de Liège,
Belgium

Finn R. Førsund
Department of Economics, University
  of Oslo,
Oslo, Norway

William Greene
Graduate School of Business
  Administration, New York
  University,
New York, N.Y.

Shawna Grosskopf
Department of Economics, Southern
  Illinois University,
Carbondale, Ill.

Lennart Hjalmarsson
Department of Economics, University
  of Gothenburg,
Göteborg, Sweden

David B. Humphrey
College of Business, Florida State
  University,
Tallahassee, Florida

Janet C. Hunt-McCool
Fu Associates, Ltd.,
Arlington, Va.

Marie-Astrid Jamar
CORE, Université Catholique de
  Louvain,
Louvain-la-Neuve, Belgium

Subal C. Kumbhakar
Department of Economics, University
  of Texas,
Austin, Tex.

Hyunok Lee
U.S. Department of Agriculture,
Washington, D.C.

Young Hoon Lee
Hanshin Economic Research Institute,
Seoul, Korea

C.A. Knox Lovell
Department of Economics, University
   of North Carolina,
Chapel Hill, N.C.

Therese A. McCarty
Department of Economics, Union
   College,
Schenectady, N.Y.

Pierre Pestieau
Department of Economics, Université
   de Liège,
Liège, Belgium

Peter Schmidt
Department of Economics, Michigan
   State University,
East Lansing, Mich.

Lawrence M. Seiford
IEOR, The University of
   Massachusetts,
Amherst, Mass.

Agapi Somwaru
U.S. Department of Agriculture,
Washington, D.C.

Henry Tulkens
CORE, Université Catholique de
   Louvain,
Louvain-la-Neuve, Belgium

Philippe Vanden Eeckaut
CORE, Université Catholique de
   Louvain,
Louvain-la-Neuve, Belgium

Ronald S. Warren, Jr.
Department of Economics, University
   of Georgia,
Athens, Ga.

Paul W. Wilson
Department of Economics, University
   of Texas,
Austin, Tex.

Suthathip Yaisawarng
Department of Economics, Union
   College,
Schenectady, N.Y.

I
TECHNIQUES

1

PRODUCTION FRONTIERS AND PRODUCTIVE EFFICIENCY

C. A. Knox Lovell

1.1 Introduction

When discussing the performance of production units, it is common to describe them as being more or less "efficient," or more or less "productive." In this chapter[1] I discuss the relationship between these two concepts, and I consider some hypotheses concerning the determinants of producer performance as measured by efficiency and productivity. I then turn to an analysis of some of the techniques that have been developed for measuring efficiency and productivity. Since these techniques are discussed in detail in the next three chapters, and illustrated in subsequent chapters, my analysis of them is brief and nontechnical. It focuses on the differences among the techniques, and on their relative strengths and weaknesses.

By the productivity of a production unit I mean the ratio of its output to its input. This ratio is easy to compute if the unit uses a single input to produce a single output. In the more likely event that the unit uses several inputs to produce several outputs, the outputs in the numerator must be aggregated in some economically sensible fashion, as must the inputs in the denominator, so that productivity remains the ratio of two scalars. Productivity varies due to differences in production technology, differences in the efficiency of the production process, and differences in the environment in which production occurs. I am interested in isolating the efficiency component and measuring its contribution to productivity.

[1] This chapter draws on ideas that I have developed over a period of several years, usually in the company of exceptionally talented coauthors and frequently with the generous financial support of the U.S. National Science Foundation. I am fortunate to have had access to extensive and helpful comments on a previous draft of this chapter from Rolf Färe, Bill Greene, Shawna Grosskopf, K. P. Kalirajan, Larry Seiford, Philippe Vanden Eeckaut, and, most importantly, Hal Fried.

By the efficiency of a production unit I mean a comparison between observed and optimal values of its output and input. The comparison can take the form of the ratio of observed to maximum potential output obtainable from the given input, or the ratio of minimum potential to observed input required to produce the given output, or some combination of the two. In these two comparisons the optimum is defined in terms of production possibilities, and efficiency is technical. It is also possible to define the optimum in terms of the behavioral goal of the production unit. In this event efficiency is economic and is measured by comparing observed and optimum cost, revenue, profit, or whatever the production unit is assumed to pursue, subject, of course, to the appropriate constraints on quantities and prices.

Even at this early stage three problems arise: How many, and which, outputs and inputs should be included in the analysis, how should they be weighted in the aggregation process, and how should the potential of the production unit be determined? Many years ago Knight (1933, pp. 9–10) addressed the first two questions by noting that if all outputs and inputs are included, then since neither matter nor energy can be created or destroyed, all units would achieve the same unitary productivity score. In this circumstance Knight proposed to redefine productivity as the ratio of useful output to input. Extending Knight's redefinition to the ratio of useful output to useful input, and representing usefulness with weights incorporating market prices, generates a modern economic productivity measure. As a practical matter, however, the first problem is not what to do when all outputs and inputs are included, but rather what to do when not enough outputs and inputs are included. As Stigler (1976, pp. 213–214) has observed, measured inefficiency may be a reflection of a failure to incorporate the right variables and the right constraints and to specify the right economic objective, of the production unit. An excellent illustration of Stigler's point is provided by Kopp, Smith, and Vaughan (1982), who demonstrate the adverse consequences for efficiency measurement of the failure to account for residual discharge constraints in steel production.

Nonetheless such partial productivity and efficiency measures are sometimes useful, and sometimes necessary. They are useful when the objectives of producers, or the constraints facing producers, are either unknown or unconventional or subject to debate. In this case a popular research strategy has been to model producers as unconstrained optimizers of some conventional objective and to test the hypothesis that inefficiency in this environment is consistent with efficiency in the constrained environment. An illustration of this strategy is provided in Section 1.6.2. The use of such partial measures has proved necessary in a number of contexts for lack of relevant data. One example of considerable policy import occurs when the production of desirable (and measured and priced) outputs is recorded but the generation of undesirable (and frequently unmeasured and more frequently unpriced) byproducts is not. Another occurs when the use of government capital services is unrecorded. In each case the measure of efficiency or productivity that is obtained may be very different from the measure one would like to have. Even when all relevant outputs and inputs are included, there remains the difficulty that market prices may not exist, and if they do exist they may not provide an appropriate measure of usefulness. This complicates the problem of determining what is meant by "relevant."

The third problem makes the first two seem easy. It is as difficult for the analyst to determine empirically the potential of a production unit as it is for the producer to achieve that potential. It is perhaps for this reason that for many years the productivity literature ignored the efficiency component. Only recently, with the development of a separate efficiency literature, has the problem of determining productive potential been seriously addressed. Resolution of this problem makes it possible to integrate the two literatures. Such an integration is important for policy purposes since action taken to enhance productivity performance requires an accurate attribution of observed performance to its three components.

Why the interest in measuring efficiency and productivity? I can think of two reasons. First of all, they are success indicators, performance measures, by which production units are evaluated. Second, only by measuring efficiency and productivity, and separating their effects from the effects of the production environment, can we explore hypotheses concerning the sources of efficiency or productivity differentials. Identification of sources is essential to the institution of public and private policies designed to improve performance. Moreover, macro performance depends on micro performance, and so the same reasoning applies to the study of the growth of nations and to the concern about growth retardation in the West, both absolutely and relative to economic growth in Japan over the same period.

In some cases measurement enables us to quantify differentials that are predicted qualitatively by theory. An example is provided by the effect of market structure on performance. There is a common belief that productive efficiency is a survival condition in a competitive environment, and that its importance diminishes as competitive pressure subsides. Hicks (1935, p. 8) gave eloquent expression to this belief by asserting that producers possessing market power ". . . are likely to exploit their advantage much more by not bothering to get very near the position of maximum profit, than by straining themselves to get very close to it. The best of all monopoly profits is a quiet life." Alchian and Kessel (1962) proposed to replace the narrow profit maximization hypothesis with a broader utility maximization hypothesis, in which case monopolists and competitors might be expected to be equally proficient in the pursuit of utility. The ostensible efficiency differential is then explained by the selection of more (observed) profit by the competitor and more (unobserved) leisure by the monopolist, which of course recalls the analyst's problem of determining the relevant outputs and inputs of the production process. Alchian and Kessel offer an alternative explanation for the apparent superior performance of competitive producers. This is that monopolies are either regulated, and thereby constrained in the pursuit of efficiency, or unregulated but threatened by regulation and consequently similarly constrained. If these units are capable of earning more than the regulated profit, and if their property right to the profit is attenuated by the regulatory environment, then inefficiency becomes a free good to the unit subject to, or threatened by, regulation. Or, as Alchian and Kessel (1962, p. 166) put it, "(t)he cardinal sin of a monopolist . . . is to be too profitable."

Thus competition is expected to enhance performance either because it forces the unit to concentrate on "observable" profit-generating activities at the expense of Hicks' quiet life, or because it frees producers from the actual or potential constraints imposed by the regulatory process. One interesting illustration of the market structure hypothesis is the measurement of the impact of international trade barriers on domestic industrial performance. Carlsson (1972) found a statistically significant inverse relationship between the productive efficiency of Swedish industries and various measures of their protection from international competition. Similar results have been obtained by many other writers, including Bergsman (1974) for a set of six developing countries, Bloch (1974) for Canada, and Caves and Barton (1990) for the United States.

A second situation in which measurement enables the quantification of efficiency or productivity differentials predicted fairly consistently by theory is in the area of economic regulation. The most commonly cited example is rate-of-return regulation, to which many utilities have been subjected for many years, and for which there exists a familiar and tractable analytical paradigm developed by Averch and Johnson (1962). Access to a tractable model and to data supplied by regulatory agencies has spawned innumerable studies, virtually all of which have found rate-of-return regulation to have had an adverse effect on performance. Another regulatory context in which theoretical predictions have been quantified by empirical investigation is the impact of environmental controls on producer efficiency [Färe, Grosskopf, and Pasurka (1986) and Bernstein, Feldman, and Schinnar (1990)] and productivity [Gollop and Roberts (1983) and Conrad and Morrison (1989)]. In this example, however, the private costs of reduced efficiency or productivity must next be compared with the social benefits of environmental protection. Once again the problem of specifying the relevant variables crops up.

A third situation in which measurement can quantify theoretical propositions is the effect of ownership on performance. Alchian (1965) noted that the inability of public sector owners to influence performance by buying and selling shares in public sector units means that public sector managers worry less about bearing the costs of their decisions than do their private sector counterparts. Hence they are contractually constrained in their decision-making latitude, given less freedom to choose, so to speak. "Because of these extra constraints—or because of the 'costs' of them—the public arrangement becomes a higher cost (in the sense of 'less efficient') than that for private property agencies" [Alchian (1965, p. 828)]. Most public/private comparisons are conducted using regulated utility data, because public and private firms frequently compete in these industries, and because the regulatory agencies collect data. Surveys are provided by De Alessi (1980), Borcherding, Pommerhene, and Schneider (1982), and Pestieau and Tulkens (1990). The Pestieau-Tulkens paper is noteworthy for its admonition that such comparisons should be narrowly based on the criterion of productive efficiency, the only objective shared by both types of producer and the only objective not in conflict with other goals of the public producer.

In some cases theory provides no guidance, or provides conflicting signals, concerning the impact of some phenomenon on performance. In such cases empirical measurement provides qualitative as well as quantitative evidence. Three examples illustrate the point. Is the profit-maximizing firm more efficient/productive than the sharing firm? Is one form of sharecropping more efficient/productive than another? Is slavery an efficient way of organizing production? The answer to all three questions seems to be "it depends," and so empirical measurement is called for. Recent empirical work illustrating the above answer is summarized by Côté and Desrochers (1990) for the ownership issue, and by Otsuka and Hayami (1988) for sharecropping. New results on sharecropping are provided by Laffont and Matoussi (1990) and Lee and Somwaru (1992), and on slavery by Grabowski and Pasurka (1989a,b) and Hofler and Folland (1991).

Of course it is not necessary to conduct the comparisons mentioned in the previous paragraph, or indeed any of the comparisons mentioned in the previous several pages, in a frontier context. If the question is whether producers in one category outperform producers in another category, then OLS with dummy variables will do just fine. However dummy variable techniques categorize producers prior to estimation, and frontier techniques do not. Thus frontier techniques can be more informative, since they can show which producers in one category outperform which producers in another category. Moreover, since the categories can be defined after estimation, they can be selected so as to maximize the performance differential, and thereby to refine the original hypothesized categorization. Yet another strategy is to combine the two techniques by using dummy variables in frontier models. This allows the comparison of performance across categories, and also permits a determination of the ability of members of each category to keep up with best practice in their own category. Moroney and Lovell (1991) use this technique to compare the performance of groups of planned and market economies.

Finally, the ability to quantify efficiency and productivity provides management with a control mechanism with which to monitor the performance of production units under its control. The economics, management science, and public administration literatures contain numerous examples of the use of efficiency/productivity measurement for this purpose, and a few of the more interesting recent applications are referenced in Table 1.1. In each of these applications interesting issues concerning relevant variables and variable measurement arise. These applications also illustrate the rich variety of analytical techniques that can be used in making efficiency and productivity comparisons.

Table 1.1   Management-Oriented Applications of Efficiency Analysis

Applications	Authors
Air Force Maintenance Units	
Israel	Roll, Golany, and Seroussy (1989)
United States	Charnes, Clark, Cooper, and Golany (1985)
	Bowlin (1987)
Bank Branches	
Belgium	Tulkens and Vanden Eeckaut (1990)
Canada	Parkan (1987)
Greece	Vassiloglou and Giokas (1990)
Norway	Berg, Førsund and Jansen (1991a,b)
United States	Sherman and Gold (1985)
Child Care	
United Kingdom	Hughes (1988)
United States	Cavalluzzo and Yanofsky (1991)
Courts	
Belgium	Jamar and Tulkens (1990)
Norway	Førsund and Kittelsen (1992)
United States	Lewin, Morey, and Cook (1982)
Developmentally Disabled Care Facilities	
United States	Dusansky and Wilson (1989, 1991)
Education—Primary and Secondary	
United Kingdom	Jesson, Mayston, and Smith (1987)
	Smith and Mayston (1987)
United States	Bessent, Bessent, Kennington and Reagan (1982)
	Charnes, Cooper and Rhodes (1981)
	Desai and Schinnar (1990)
	Färe, Grosskopf and Weber (1989)
	Lovell, Walters and Wood (1990)
	McCarty and Yaisawarng (1990, 1992)
	Ray (1991)
	Wyckoff and Lavigne (1991)
Education—Tertiary	
Australia	Cameron (1989)
Canada	Jenkins (1991)
United States	Ahn, Arnold, Charnes, and Cooper (1989)
	Ahn, Charnes, and Cooper (1988)
	Goudriaan and de Groot (1991a,b)
Employment Offices	
United States	Cavin and Stafford (1985)
Fast-Food Outlets	
United States	Banker and Morey (1986)
Health Clinics	
United States	Huang and McLaughlin (1989)
	Johnson and Lahiri (1992)

Table 1.1 Continued

Applications	Authors
Highway Maintenance	
Canada	Cook, Kazakov, and Roll (1989)
United States	Deller and Nelson (1991)
Hospitals	
United States	Banker, Das, and Datar (1989)
	Byrnes and Valdmanis (1990)
	Grosskopf and Valdmanis (1987)
	Register and Bruning (1987)
	Sexton et al. (1989)
Military Recruiting Units	
United States	Charnes, Cooper, Divine, Klopp, and Stutz (1985)
	Lovell and Morey (1991)
	Lovell, Morey and Wood (1991)
Municipalities	
Belgium	Vanden Eeckaut, Tulkens, and Jamar (1992)
	De Borger, Kerstens, Moesen, and Vanneste (1991)
China	Charnes, Cooper, and Li (1989)
United States	Ali, Lerme, and Nakosteen (1992)
National Parks	
United States	Rhodes (1986)
Post Offices	
Belgium	Deprins (1983)
	Deprins, Simar, and Tulkens (1984)
	Tulkens (1986)
United States	Register (1988)
Rates Departments	
United Kingdom	Dyson and Thanassoulis (1988)
	Thanassoulis, Dyson, and Foster (1987)
Refuse Collection	
Switzerland	Burgat and Jeanrenaud (1990)
United Kingdom	Cubbin, Domberger, and Meadowcroft (1987)
Urban Transport	
Belgium	Tulkens, Thiry, and Palm (1988)
	Thiry and Tulkens (1992)
Republic of China	Chang and Kao (1992)

1.2 Definitions and measures of productive efficiency

Productive efficiency has two components. The purely technical, or physical, component refers to the ability to avoid waste by producing as much output as input usage allows, or by using as little input as output production allows. Thus the analysis of technical efficiency can have an output augmenting orientation or an input-conserving orientation. The allocative, or price, component refers to the ability to combine inputs and outputs in optimal proportions in light of prevailing prices.

Koopmans (1951, p. 60) provided a formal definition of technical efficiency: a producer is technically efficient if an increase in any output requires a reduction in at least one other output or an increase in at least one input, and if a reduction in any input requires an increase in at least one other input or a reduction in at least one output. Thus a technically inefficient producer could produce the same outputs with less of at least one input, or could use the same inputs to produce more of at least one output.

Debreu (1951) and Farrell (1957) introduced a measure of technical efficiency. Their measure is defined as one minus the maximum equiproportionate reduction in all inputs that still allows continued production of given outputs. A score of unity indicates technical efficiency because no equiproportionate input reduction is feasible, and a score less than unity indicates the severity of technical inefficiency. In some circumstances it is desirable to convert the Debreu-Farrell measure to equiproportionate output expansion with given inputs; the conversion is straightforward.

In order to relate the Debreu-Farrell measure to the Koopmans definition, and to relate both to the structure of production technology, it is useful at this point to introduce some notation and terminology. [2] Let producers use inputs $x = (x_1, \ldots, x_n) \in R_+^n$ to produce outputs $y = (y_1, \ldots, y_m) \in R_+^m$. Production technology can be represented with an input set

$$L(y) = \{x : (y, x) \quad \text{is feasible}\} \tag{1.1}$$

which for every $y \in R_+^m$ has isoquant

$$\text{Isoq}L(y) = \{x : x \in L(y), \quad \lambda x \notin L(y), \lambda \in [0, 1)\} \tag{1.2}$$

and efficient subset

$$\text{Eff}L(y) = \{x : x \in L(y), \quad x' \notin L(y), \quad x' \leq x\} \tag{1.3}$$

For future reference I note that $\text{Eff}L(y) \subseteq \text{Isoq}L(y)$. Shephard (1953, 1970) introduced the input distance function to provide a functional representation of a multiple output technology. The input distance function is

$$D_I(y, x) = \max\{\lambda : (x/\lambda) \in L(y)\} \tag{1.4}$$

---

[2] For two vectors $a = (a_1, \ldots, a_l)$ and $b = (b_1, \ldots, b_l)$, $a^T b = \sum_{i=1}^{l} a_i b_i$. $a > b$ means $a_i > b_i$ for all $i = 1, \ldots, l$. $a \geq b$ means $a_i \geqq b_i$ for all $i = 1, \ldots, l$, but $a \neq b$. $a \geqq b$ means $a_i \geqq b_i$ for all $i = 1, \ldots, l$.

Clearly $D_I(y, x) \gtreqless 1$, and it follows from (1.2) that

$$\text{Isoq}L(y) = \{x : D_I(y, x) = 1\} \tag{1.5}$$

The Debreu-Farrell input-oriented measure of technical efficiency can now be given a somewhat more formal interpretation as

$$\text{DF}_I(y, x) = \min\{\lambda : \lambda x \in L(y)\} \tag{1.6}$$

$\text{DF}_I(y, x) \lesseqgtr 1$, and it follows from (1.4) that

$$\text{DF}_I(y, x) = \frac{1}{D_I(y, x)} \tag{1.7}$$

and from (1.5) that

$$\text{Isoq}L(y) = \{x : \text{DF}_I(y, x) = 1\} \tag{1.8}$$

Since so much technical efficiency measurement is oriented toward output augmentation, it is useful to replicate the above development in that direction. Production technology can also be represented with an output set

$$P(x) = \{y : (x, y) \quad \text{is feasible}\} \tag{1.9}$$

which for every $x \in R_+^n$ has isoquant

$$\text{Isoq}P(x) = \{y : y \in P(x), \theta y \notin P(x), \theta \in (1, +\infty)\} \tag{1.10}$$

and efficient subset

$$\text{Eff}P(x) = \{y : y \in P(x), y' \notin P(x), y' \geq y\} \tag{1.11}$$

having the property that $\text{Eff}P(x) \subseteq \text{Isoq}P(x)$. Shephard's (1970) output distance function

$$D_0(x, y) = \min\{\theta : (y/\theta) \in P(x)\} \tag{1.12}$$

provides another functional representation of production technology. $D_0(x, y) \lesseqgtr 1$ and it follows from (1.10) that

$$\text{Isoq}P(x) = \{y : D_0(x, y) = 1\} \tag{1.13}$$

The Debreu-Farrell output-oriented measure of technical efficiency is defined as

$$\text{DF}_0(x, y) = \max\{\theta : \theta y \in P(x)\} \tag{1.14}$$

$DF_0(x, y) \gtreqqless 1$, and it follows from (1.12) that

$$DF_0(x, y) = \frac{1}{D_0(x, y)} \tag{1.15}$$

and consequently

$$\mathrm{Isoq}P(x) = \{y : DF_0(x, y) = 1\} \tag{1.16}$$

The two technical efficiency measures are illustrated in Figure 1.1. In the input-oriented upper panel, input vectors x^A and x^B can be contracted radially and still

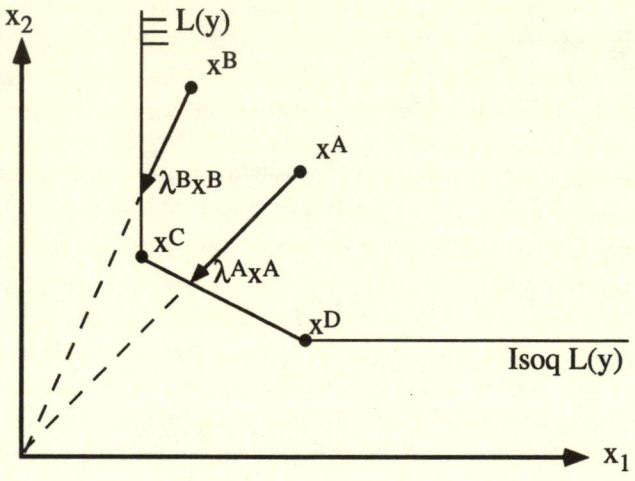

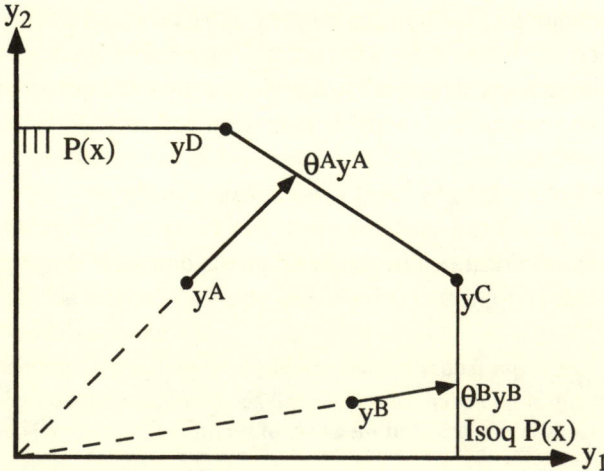

Fig. 1.1   Debreu-Farrell technical efficiency measurement

remain capable of producing output vector y, but input vectors x^C and x^D cannot be contracted radially and still remain capable of producing output vector y. Consequently, $\mathrm{DF}_I(y, x^C) = \mathrm{DF}_I(y, x^D) = 1 > \max\{\mathrm{DF}_I(y, x^A), \mathrm{DF}_I(y, x^B)\}$. Note also that input vector $(\lambda^B x^B)$ cannot be contracted radially and still remain capable of producing output vector y, even though it contains slack in input x_2, and there may be some hesitancy in describing input vector $(\lambda^B x^B)$ as technically efficient in the production of output vector y. No such problem occurs with input vector $(\lambda^A x^A)$. Thus $\mathrm{DF}_I(y, \lambda^A x^A) = \mathrm{DF}_I(y, \lambda^B x^B) = 1$ even though $(\lambda^A x^A) \in \mathrm{Eff}L(y)$ but $(\lambda^B x^B) \notin \mathrm{Eff}L(y)$. Similar remarks apply to the output-oriented lower panel. Of course $\mathrm{DF}_I(y, x) \neq 1/\mathrm{DF}_0(x, y)$ in general. Färe and Lovell (1978) and Deprins and Simar (1983) have shown that $\mathrm{DF}_I(y, x) = 1/\mathrm{DF}_0(x, y)$ if, and only if, technology exhibits constant returns to scale.

The Debreu-Farrell measure of technical efficiency is widely used. Since it is the reciprocal of a distance function, the measure satisfies several nice properties [as noted originally by Shephard (1970) and, in an efficiency measurement context, by Färe and Lovell (1978), Bol (1986, 1988), and Russell (1985, 1988, 1990)], including

1. $\mathrm{DF}_I(y, x)$ is homogeneous of degree -1 in inputs and $\mathrm{DF}_0(x, y)$ is homogeneous of degree -1 in outputs.
2. $\mathrm{DF}_I(y, x)$ is weakly monotonically decreasing in inputs and $\mathrm{DF}_0(x, y)$ is weakly monotonically decreasing in outputs.
3. $\mathrm{DF}_I(y, x)$ and $\mathrm{DF}_0(x, y)$ are invariant with respect to changes in units of measurement.

On the other hand, it is not perfect. A notable feature of the Debreu-Farrell measure of technical efficiency is that it does not coincide with Koopmans' definition of technical efficiency. Koopmans' definition is stringent, requiring simultaneous membership in both efficient subsets, while the Debreu-Farrell measure, being the reciprocal of a distance function, only requires membership in an isoquant. Thus the Debreu-Farrell measure correctly identifies all Koopmans-efficient producers as being technically efficient, and also identifies as being technically efficient any other producers located on an isoquant outside the efficient subset. Consequently Debreu-Farrell technical efficiency is necessary, but not sufficient, for Koopmans technical efficiency. Both possibilities are illustrated in Figure 1.1, where $(\lambda^B x^B)$ and $(\theta^B y^B)$ satisfy the Debreu-Farrell condition but not the Koopmans condition, and $(\lambda^A x^A)$ and $(\theta^A y^A)$ satisfy the Debreu-Farrell condition and perhaps the Koopmans condition as well.

Much has been made of this "flaw" in the Debreu-Farrell measure, but I am inclined to think that the problem is exaggerated. The practical significance of the problem depends on how many observations lie outside the cone spanned by the relevant efficient subset. Hence the problem disappears in much econometric analysis, in which the parametric form of the function used to represent production technology (e.g., Cobb-Douglas) imposes equality between isoquants and efficient subsets, and

eliminates slack by assuming it away. The problem may be important in the mathematical programming approach discussed in Section 1.5, in which the nonparametric
form of the frontier used to represent the boundary of production possibilities imposes
slack by assumption. If the problem is deemed significant in practice, then it is always
possible to report Debreu-Farrell technical efficiency scores and slacks separately,
side by side. This is rarely done. Instead, much effort has been directed toward finding
a "solution" to the problem. At least three remedies have been proposed.

1. Replace the radial Debreu-Farrell measure with an additive measure that takes
    up slack in all $(m + n)$ dimensions [Charnes, Cooper, Golany, Seiford, and
    Stutz (1985)]. This technique has the great virtue of guaranteeing that a pro-
    ducer is called efficient if, and only if, it belongs to the efficient subset. On the
    other hand, since slacks are denominated differently for different variables,
    the efficiency measure is not invariant to changes in units of measurement,
    and the ranking of producers on the basis of this measure is therefore arbitrary
    [Färe, Grosskopf, and Lovell (1987a)]. An "extended" additive model that
    is units-invariant has been developed by Charnes, Cooper, Rousseau, and
    Semple (1987).
2. Replace the radial Debreu-Farrell measure with a nonradial multiplicative
    measure [Färe and Lovell (1978)]. This technique also guarantees that a
    producer is called efficient if, and only if, it belongs to the efficient subset.
    This measure has its own problems [Bol (1986, 1988), Russell (1985, 1988,
    1990)].
3. Measures that combine the Debreu-Farrell radial measure and any remaining
    slacks into a single measure of technical efficiency have been proposed
    [Charnes, Cooper and Rhodes (1978), Ali (1989, 1991)] and widely used.
    However the various combination measures have flaws of their own [Boyd
    and Färe (1984), Färe and Hunsaker (1986), Färe, Grosskopf, and Lovell
    (1987a)].

None of these attempts to eliminate the difference between the Koopmans definition
and the Debreu-Farrell measure of technical efficiency has been an overwhelming
success. The two most popular options seem to be to report the radial Debreu-Farrell
measure and ignore possible slack, or to report a combination measure. If prices are
available and economic efficiency can be calculated, two more options are available.
They are mentioned below.

Happily, there is no such distinction between the definition and the measure
of economic efficiency. Defining and measuring economic efficiency requires the
specification of an economic objective and information on market prices. If the
objective of the production unit (or the objective assigned to it by the analyst) is
cost minimization, then a measure of cost efficiency is provided by the ratio of
minimum cost to observed cost. This measure is input price dependent. It attains a

value of unity if the producer is cost efficient, and a value less than unity indicates the degree of cost inefficiency. A measure of price or allocative efficiency in input markets is obtained residually as the ratio of the measure of cost efficiency to the Debreu-Farrell input-oriented measure of technical efficiency. The modification of this Farrell (1957) decomposition of cost efficiency to the output-oriented problem of decomposing revenue efficiency is straightforward. Modifying the procedure to accommodate alternative behavioral objectives is sometimes straightforward and occasionally challenging. So is the inclusion of regulatory and other nontechnological constraints that impede the pursuit of some economic objective.

Suppose producers face input prices $w = (w_1, \ldots, w_n) \in R^n_{++}$ and output prices $p = (p_1, \ldots, p_m) \in R^m_{++}$. Then a minimum cost function, or a cost frontier, is defined as

$$c(y, w; \beta) = \min_x \{w^T x : D_I(y, x; \beta) \geq 1\} \qquad (1.17)$$

and a maximum revenue function, or a revenue frontier, is defined as

$$r(x, p; \beta) = \max_y \{p^T y : D_0(x, y; \beta) \leq 1\} \qquad (1.18)$$

where in each equation β is a vector of parameters describing the structure of production technology. The measurement and decomposition of cost efficiency and revenue efficiency is illustrated in Figure 1.2. In the input-oriented upper panel x^E minimizes the cost of producing y at input prices w, and so $w^T x^E = c(y, w; \beta)$. The cost efficiency of x^A is given by the ratio $w^T x^E / w^T x^A = c(y, w; \beta) / w^T x^A$. The Debreu-Farrell measure of the technical efficiency of x^A is given by the ratio $\lambda^A = \lambda^A x^A / x^A = w^T(\lambda^A x^A) / w^T x^A$. The allocative efficiency of x^A is determined residually as the ratio of cost efficiency to technical efficiency, or by the ratio $w^T x^E / w^T(\lambda^A x^A)$. This measure of cost efficiency is bounded by zero and one, as are its two components. A producer is cost efficient if, and only if, it is technically and allocatively efficient. The magnitudes of technical, allocative, and cost inefficiency are all measured by ratios of price-weighted input vectors. The direction of allocative inefficiency is revealed by the input vector difference $(x^E - \lambda^A x^A)$. The measurement and decomposition of revenue efficiency in the lower panel of Figure 1.2 follows exactly the same steps.

The measurement and decomposition of cost efficiency and revenue efficiency is illustrated again in Figure 1.3, for the case in which efficient subsets are proper subsets of isoquants. In this event for some observations, such as x^A in the input-oriented upper panel and y^A in the output-oriented lower panel, economic efficiency has three components. The cost efficiency of x^A has a Debreu-Farrell technical component $[w^T(\lambda^A x^A) / w^T x^A]$, a slack component $[w^T x^B / w^T(\lambda^A x^A)]$, and an allocative component $(w^T x^E / w^T x^B)$. With input price data all three components

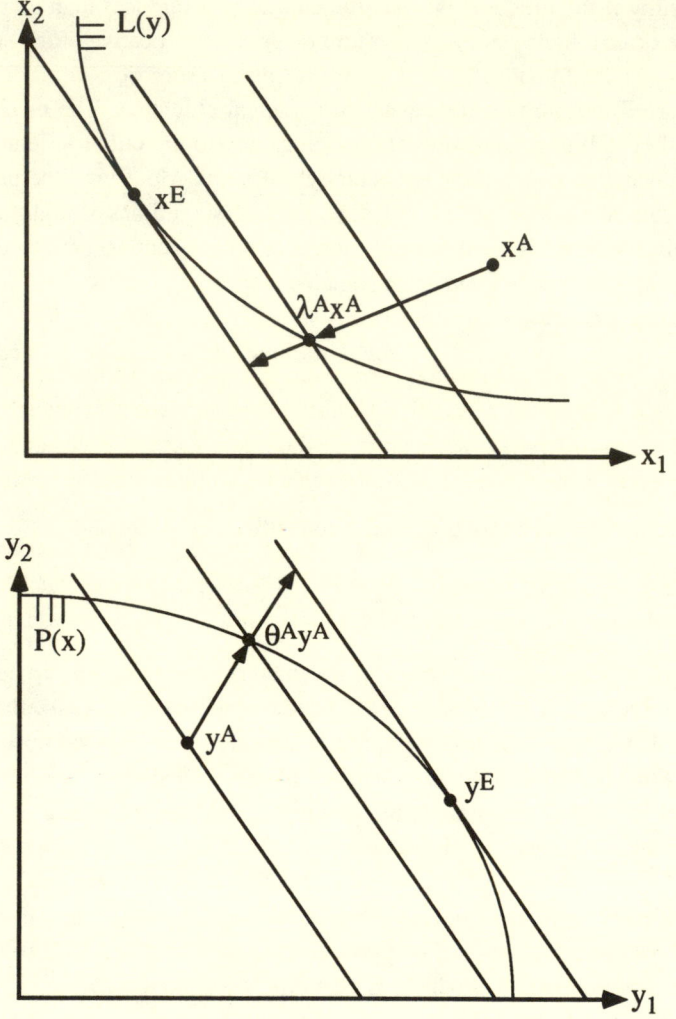

Fig. 1.2 The measurement and decomposition of cost efficiency and revenue efficiency

can be identified, although they almost never are. The slack component is routinely assigned to either the technical or the allocative component. The same story is told in the output-oriented lower panel.

At some point in the definition/measurement/implementation process it is worth thinking about the likely sources of variation in efficiency. I have alluded to a few general hypotheses in Section 1.1, including the strength of competitive pressure, the regulatory environment, and the form of ownership. In addition, there exists the possibility that measured inefficiency is partly a reflection of an inability to completely and accurately measure quantity and quality of all relevant variables, and

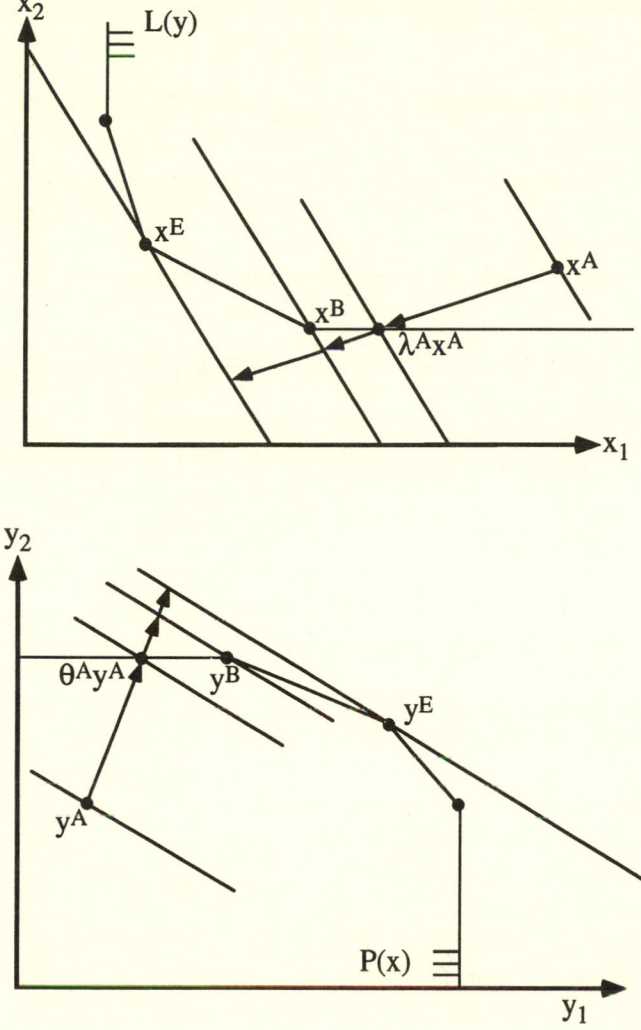

Fig. 1.3 The measurement and decomposition of cost efficiency and revenue efficiency in the presence of slack

to model objectives and constraints correctly. Somewhat more specifically, variation in technical efficiency has been attributed to variation in factors under the control of the producers, although the search for these factors rarely proceeds very far beyond the allegation of variation in the (usually unmeasured) managerial input. In contrast, variation in allocative efficiency has been attributed to numerous sources, including a divergence between expected and actual prices, a persistent under- or overvaluation of prices, discrimination or nepotism [Boehm and Hofler (1987) and Robinson and

Wunnava (1989)], and satisficing behavior. Two important elements are missing, and need to be addressed.

1. To date there has been very little effort directed toward integrating the literature on the theory of production under uncertainty (about technology or prices) into the efficiency measurement literature. But if producers are uncertain about productivities and prices, they are bound to make decisions that appear to be inefficient.
2. There has also been little effort directed toward making use of the literature on the internal organization of the firm in developing hypotheses on efficiency variation. For years Williamson (1975, 1985), Leibenstein (1976, 1987), Aoki (1984), and others have been developing models of intrafirm organization, hierarchy, and performance. More or less concurrently a huge literature on principals and agents and incentives and tournaments has developed. To date this literature has hardly made a dent in the efficiency measurement literature, despite its obvious relevance to the problem of measuring producer performance. It will.

1.3   Techniques for efficiency measurement

The economic theory of production is based on efficient subsets of production sets, on value duals such as minimum cost functions and maximum revenue or profit functions, and on envelope properties yielding cost-minimizing input demand functions, revenue maximizing output supply functions, and profit-maximizing output supply and input demand functions. Emphasis is placed on efficient production and its consequences, and the evocative term "frontier" is applied to these bounding functions. However for over 60 years, at least since Cobb and Douglas started running regressions, the empirical analysis of production has been based on a least squares statistical methodology by which estimated functions of interest pass through the data. Thus the frontiers of theory have become the functions of analysis, interest in surrounding data has been replaced with the practice of intersecting data, and unlikely efficient outcomes have been neglected in favor of less efficient but more likely outcomes, all as attention has shifted from extreme values to central tendency.

If econometric analysis is to be brought to bear on the investigation of the structure of economic frontiers, and on the measurement of productive efficiency relative to these frontiers, then conventional econometric techniques require modification. The modifications that have been developed and implemented in the last 10 to 15 years run the gamut from trivial to sophisticated. They are introduced in the next section of this chapter, developed in considerable detail in Chapter 2, and applied in Part II.

In sharp contrast to econometric techniques, mathematical programming techniques are inherently bounding techniques, and so they require little or no modification to be employed in the analysis of production frontiers. (In fact, modifying programming techniques to incorporate the statistical noise that drives conventional econometric analysis is a nontrivial task.) These techniques are introduced in section 1.5 of this chapter, developed further in Chapter 3, and applied in Part II.

The econometric approach to the construction of production frontiers and the measurement of efficiency relative to the constructed frontiers differs from the mathematical programming approach. The two approaches use different techniques to envelop data more or less tightly in different ways. In so doing they make different accommodations for random noise and for flexibility in the structure of production technology. It is these two different accommodations that generate the strengths and weaknesses of the two approaches. In my judgment neither approach strictly dominates the other, although not everyone agrees with this opinion; there still remain some true believers out there. The two approaches differ in many ways, but the essential differences, and the sources of the advantages of one approach or the other, boil down to two characteristics.

1. The econometric approach is stochastic, and so attempts to distinguish the effects of noise from the effects of inefficiency. The programming approach is nonstochastic, and lumps noise and inefficiency together and calls the combination inefficiency.
2. The econometric approach is parametric, and confounds the effects of misspecification of functional form (of both technology and inefficiency) with inefficiency. The programming approach is nonparametric and less prone to this type of specification error.

Obviously it would be desirable to make the programming approach stochastic, and to make the econometric approach more flexible in its parametric structure. Limited progress has been achieved in both areas; some of this progress is mentioned in Chapters 2 and 3, and illustrated in Part II. The introductory analysis of the two techniques in Sections 1.4 and 1.5 largely ignores these advances, and focuses on the widely used basic models. In addition to the excellent treatments to be found in Chapters 2 and 3, I recommend surveys of the econometric approach by Schmidt (1985–1986) and Bauer (1990b), and of the programming approach by Banker, Charnes, Cooper, Swarts, and Thomas (1989), Adolphson, Cornia, and Walters (1990), and Seiford and Thrall (1990).

1.4 The econometric approach to efficiency measurement

Econometric models can be categorized according to the type of data they use (cross section or panel), the type of variables they use (quantities only, or quantities and prices), and the number of equations in the model. By far the most widely used model is the single equation cross-sectional model.

1.4.1 Single equation cross-sectional models

Suppose producers use inputs $x \in R^n_+$ to produce scalar output $y \in R_+$ with technology

$$y_i = f(x_i; \beta) \exp\{v_i + u_i\} \tag{1.19}$$

where β is a vector of technology parameters to be estimated and $i = 1, \ldots, I$ indexes producers. The random disturbance term v_i is intended to capture the effects of statistical noise and is assumed to be independently and identically distributed as $N(0, \sigma_v^2)$. The disturbance term u_i is assumed to be distributed independently of v_i and to satisfy $u_i \lesseqgtr 0$. The deterministic production frontier is $f(x_i; \beta)$, and the stochastic production frontier is $[f(x_i; \beta) \exp\{v_i\}]$. The nonpositive error component u_i represents technical inefficiency. The degree of technical efficiency of a producer is given by the ratio of observed to maximum feasible output, where maximum feasible output is given by the stochastic production frontier. The stochastic production frontier is in turn determined by the structure of production technology—the deterministic production frontier—and by external events, favorable and unfavorable, beyond the control of the producer. The econometric version of the Debreu-Farrell output-oriented technical efficiency (TE) measure is actually the reciprocal of $DF_0(x_i, y_i)$, and is written

$$TE_i = \frac{y_i}{[f(x_i; \beta) \exp\{v_i\}]} = \exp\{u_i\} \tag{1.20}$$

The problem is to calculate TE_i, which requires estimation of (1.19), which is relatively easy, and which also requires a decomposition of the residuals into separate estimates of noise and technical inefficiency, which is not so easy. Estimation was first accomplished, at the same time on three different continents, by Aigner, Lovell, and Schmidt (1977), Battese and Corra (1977), and Meeusen and van den Broeck (1977). However because they were unable to solve the decomposition problem, none of these teams was able to obtain estimates of technical efficiency for each observation. All they were able to do was to calculate the mean technical efficiency over all observations, a relatively easy task. A solution to the decomposition problem was first proposed by Jondrow, Lovell, Materov, and Schmidt (1982), who specified the functional form of the distribution of the one-sided inefficiency component and derived the conditional distribution $(u_i | v_i + u_i)$. Either the mean or the mode of this distribution provides a point estimate of u_i, which can be inserted in (1.20) to obtain estimates of TE_i.

If $y \in R_{++}$ and $x \in R^n_{++}$ the model (1.19) can be written in logarithmic form. This makes the interpretation of u_i easy. A restriction of the logarithmic form to first-order terms, that is, the assumption that technology is Cobb-Douglas, makes

| Chapter One |

③ → Productivity = ratio of
output to its input
(easy if production process
uses 1 input and produces
1 output) ∿> not normal
→ numerator (output) aggregated
in some econ sensible fashion
+ too must denominators so
prod = ratio of 2 scalars.
→ productivity varies due to
differences in production technologies,
differences in efficiencies of
prod process + env production
occurs.

④ efficiency of production unit,
means comparison btwn
observed + optimal values
(ratio observed to max potential
output from given input
or // min potential input
to produce given output)

Chapter 4

- many consider productivity growth + technical progress as synonymous.

 BUT new mindset

- productivity growth = net change in output due to change in efficiency and technically chang
 • former is understood to be change in how far observation is from frontier of technology
 • latter is understood to be shifts in production frontier

(162) - TFP — index of output / index of **total** input usage

interesting ←

69 — in Nishimizu + Page (1982
pp. 920 - 921)

    ↳ productivity growth =
    "when we define technological
progress as change in best
practice frontier — all

②
①

other productivity change —
ex. learning by doing, diffusion
of new technological knowledge,
improved managerial practice
as well as short run adjustment
to shocks external to the enterprise—
as tech efficiency change

Chapter 14

(352) — Key concepts when studying production over time are productivity, efficiency + technological change.

- productivity $\frac{\text{index of outputs}}{\text{index of inputs}}$

- efficiency defined as production unit's "success in producing as large as possible an output from a given set of inputs"

- technical change is the change in the transformation functions btwn inputs + outputs.

(370) — prices generally used in forming weights.

(375) — frontier vs index # approach
  └ big difference (in one assumption):
    • existence of an unobservable function (production frontier) corresponding to the set of max attainable output levels for a given combination of inputs

estimation easy. It also forces restrictive scale and substitution properties on the frontier, and so risks the specification error of confusing a nonconstant scale elasticity and nonunitary substitution elasticities with inefficiency. Nonetheless Cobb-Douglas is the functional form of choice in the overwhelming majority of single equation econometric production frontier models.

If it is assumed that $u_i = 0$, the problem simplifies to one of OLS estimation of the parameters of a production function with no technical inefficiency, while if it is assumed that $v_i = 0$ the problem simplifies to one of estimating the parameters of a deterministic production frontier with no noise. In the former case there is no efficiency measurement problem to worry about. In the latter case there is no decomposition problem to worry about, although in my opinion the benefit of having no decomposition problem is more than offset by the cost of assuming away noise.

Two basic estimation strategies exist. The simpler strategy is to assume that $v_i = 0$ and estimate a deterministic production frontier, using any of three techniques. The slightly more complicated strategy is to allow $v_i \neq 0$ and estimate a stochastic production frontier, using two of the three deterministic frontier techniques. I prefer the second strategy, despite its greater difficulty. My objection to the first strategy is that it combines the bad features of the econometric and programming approaches to frontier construction: it is deterministic and parametric. Nonetheless, it refuses to go away, and so needs an introduction.

I refer to the three variants of the first strategy as "corrected" ordinary least squares (COLS), "modified" or "displaced" ordinary least squares (MOLS), and maximum likelihood (MLE), respectively. COLS was first proposed by Winsten (1957), although Gabrielsen (1975) is usually credited with its discovery. It makes no assumption concerning the functional form of the nonpositive efficiency component u_i. It estimates the technology parameters of (1.19) by OLS, and corrects the downward bias in the estimated OLS intercept by shifting it up until all corrected residuals are nonpositive and at least one is zero. Corrected residuals are then used in (1.20) to calculate TE_i, which by construction satisfy $0 < TE_i \leqq 1$.

MOLS was introduced by Richmond (1974). It makes an assumption about the functional form of the nonpositive efficiency component u_i. The most popular assumption is half normal, which requires estimation of one additional parameter, the variance of the normal distribution that is truncated above at zero. Another single-parameter distribution that has been widely used is the exponential. Two-parameter distributions that have been used include the truncated normal [Stevenson (1980)] and the gamma [Greene (1980)]. An empirical comparison of the gamma, the Weibull, the lognormal and the log-logistic is provided by Deprins (1989). MOLS proceeds by estimating the technology parameters of (1.19) by OLS, and modifies the estimated OLS intercept by shifting it up by minus the estimated mean of u_i, which is extracted from the moments of the OLS residuals. The OLS residuals are modified in the opposite direction, and used in (1.20) to calculate TE_i. There is no guarantee that this technique shifts the estimated intercept up far enough to cover all the observations, however, and if an observation has a sufficiently large positive OLS residual, it is possible that $TE_i > 1$.

MLE was suggested by Afriat (1972) and apparently first used by Greene (1980) and Stevenson (1980). MLE is implemented by assuming a functional form for the nonpositive efficiency component u_i and simultaneously estimating all the technology parameters and the parameter(s) of the distribution of u_i. The MLE frontier envelops all observations, and the MLE residuals are inserted in Equation (1.20) to provide estimates of TE_i, which by construction satisfy $0 < TE_i \leqq 1$.

OLS, COLS, MOLS, and MLE are illustrated in Figure 1.4. COLS, MOLS, and MLE are all suspect because they make no accommodation for noise and so attribute all deviation from the production frontier to technical inefficiency. COLS and MOLS are further deficient in that both adjust the OLS estimate of the intercept, leaving the remaining elements of β unchanged from their OLS estimates. As a result, the structure of efficient frontier technology (e.g., scale and substitution characteristics) is the same as the structure of technology of less efficient producers. Consequently MOLS and COLS assign the same efficiency ranking as OLS does, so a justification of MOLS or COLS techniques must be made on the ground that the magnitudes, as well as a ranking, of efficiency scores are of interest. Moreover, this structural similarity rules out the possibility that efficient producers are efficient precisely because they exploit available economies and substitution possibilities. MLE allows for structural dissimilarity between OLS and frontier technology. I should add that the desirability of allowing frontier technology to differ from technology down there in the middle of the data is not a new idea. It is the central hypothesis of a study by Klotz, Madoo, and Hansen (1980), who, in a nonfrontier model, sought to determine if high and low

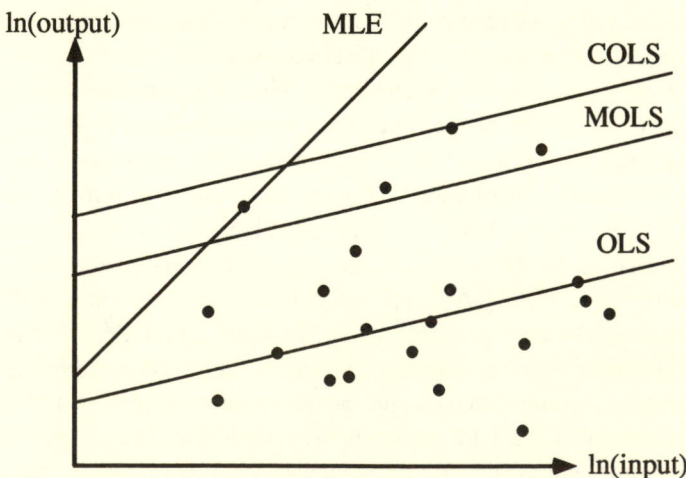

Fig. 1.4   MOLS, COLS, and MLE deterministic production frontiers

productivity plants had different scale and substitution possibilities. Moreover, many frontier studies which report both OLS and MLE frontier estimates reveal striking differences in the structure of the two technologies. None of this is available with COLS or MOLS.

The second strategy is to allow $u_i \neq 0$ and estimate a stochastic production frontier. COLS is not a feasible technique, but MOLS and MLE are. MOLS and MLE proceed roughly as in the deterministic frontier strategy, beginning with an assumption on the functional form of the distribution of the nonpositive efficiency term u_i. MOLS adjusts the OLS intercept by minus the mean of u_i, which is extracted from the moments of the OLS residuals. MLE estimates technology and efficiency parameters simultaneously. Unlike in the deterministic frontier case, however, the resulting residuals obtained from MOLS and MLE contain both noise and inefficiency, and must be decomposed using the technique suggested by Jondrow, Lovell, Materov, and Schmidt (1982). The conditional estimates of u_i are inserted in Equation (1.20) to obtain estimates of TE_i, which satisfy $0 < TE_i \leqq 1$ since inclusion of noise allows the stochastic frontier to envelop all observations.

Before leaving this subsection I wish to point out that the restriction to a single output is commonplace but unnecessary. Multiple outputs can be accommodated in three ways. First, a single- input–multiple-output input requirements frontier can be estimated in place of a single-output–multiple-input production frontier, as in Bjurek, Hjalmarsson and Førsund (1990), Kumbhakar and Hjalmarsson (1991), and Gathon and Perelman (1992). In this case the measure of technical efficiency that results is an econometric approximation to $DF_I(y, x)$. Second, a distance frontier can be estimated in place of a production frontier, as in Lovell, Richardson, Travers, and Wood (1990). In this case use of $D_I(y, x)$ or $D_0(x, y)$ leads to econometric approximations to $DF_I(y, x)$ or $DF_0(x, y)$, respectively. Third, a value dual frontier, such as a cost or revenue or profit frontier, can be estimated in place of a production frontier to estimate cost or revenue or profit efficiency, as in Hughes (1988). A measure of technical efficiency can then be extracted from the measure of economic efficiency using a decomposition technique first proposed by Kopp and Diewert (1982) and later simplified by Zieschang (1983). The drawback to the third alternative is that estimation of a single value dual frontier sacrifices statistical efficiency relative to estimation of a value dual system, an idea to which we now turn.

1.4.2 Multiple-equation cross-sectional models

Work on this type of model is in its infancy, and much remains to be done. This type of model is potentially very valuable, for three reasons. First, it easily accommodates functional forms for production technology more flexible than Cobb-Douglas, but which would be plagued by multicollinearity problems if estimated in a single-equation format. Second, it easily accommodates multiple outputs. Third, it incorporates a behavioral assumption and so allows for the possibility of estimating both technical and allocative, and hence economic, efficiency. I illustrate the basic idea behind this approach with one example that should be recognizable to those familiar with the standard translog cost and input share system introduced by Christensen and Greene (1976). The modification of this approach to revenue maximization or profit maximization contexts is straightforward.

Suppose producers use input vector $x \in R^n_{++}$, available at fixed prices $w \in R^n_{++}$, to produce output vector $y \in R^m_{++}$. Observed cost is $w^T x \gtreqless c(y, w; \beta)$ and observed input shares are $w_j x_j / w^T x \gtreqless s_j(y, w; \beta), j = 1, \ldots, n$, where $c(y, w; \beta)$ is the minimum total cost function and $s_j(y, w; \beta)$ are cost-minimizing input share equations, respectively, and β is a vector of technology parameters. These inequalities can be converted into the following system of equations suitable for estimation:

$$\ln(w^T x)_i = c(\ln y_i, \ln w_i; \beta) + v_{0i} + T_i + A_i$$

$$\left(\frac{w_j x_j}{w^T x}\right)_i = s_j(\ln y_i, \ln w_i; \beta) + v_{ji} + u_{ji} \qquad j = 1, \ldots, n-1$$

(1.21)

where i indexes producers and j indexes inputs. In keeping with the terminology of Section 1.4.1, $c(\ln y_i, \ln w_i; \beta)$ is the deterministic cost frontier and the $s_j(\ln y_i, \ln w_i; \beta)$ are its associated deterministic input shares, while $[c(\ln y_i, \ln w_i; \beta) + v_{oi}]$ is the stochastic cost frontier and the $[s_j(\ln y_i, \ln w_i; \beta) + v_{ji}]$ are its associated stochastic input shares. The terms v_{oi} and v_{ji} represent statistical noise and are assumed to be distributed as multivariate normal with zero mean. This is the Christensen-Greene model, which is transformed into a frontier model by the additional terms T_i, A_i, and u_{ji}. $T_i \gtreqless 0$ captures the cost increase attributable to technical inefficiency. Since technical inefficiency is measured radially, it is neutral with respect to inputs and has no impact on input share equations. $A_i \gtreqless 0$ captures the cost increase attributable to allocative inefficiency. Since allocative inefficiency represents an inappropriate input mix, its cost must be linked with the input share equations, in this model with the terms $u_{ji} \gtreqless 0$. The linkage must respect the fact that cost is raised by allocative errors in either direction. The formidable problem is to estimate the technology parameters β and the efficiency measures (T_i, A_i, u_{ji}) for each producer.

There are two basic solutions to the estimation problem. One is to extend COLS or MOLS techniques to a system of equations, an approach that has been referred to as CITSUR or MITSUR, since it involves correcting or modifying estimates obtained from an iterated seemingly unrelated regressions procedure. This generates estimates of $(T_i + A_i)$, which are decomposed into separate estimates of T_i and A_i by means of the Kopp-Diewert-Zieschang algorithm mentioned above. A second approach is to use MLE techniques, in which functional forms must be specified for T_i (half normal, usually), u_{ji} (either merged with v_{ji} or merged with the share equation intercepts), and a linkage relationship between A_i and the u_{ji}. For details see Bauer (1990b), Kumbhakar (1991), and Chapter 2.

1.4.3 Panel data models

In Sections 1.4.1 and 1.4.2 each producer is observed once. If each producer is observed over a period of time, panel data techniques may be brought to bear on the problem. At the heart of the approach is the association of the "firm effect" from the panel data literature with a one-sided inefficiency term from the frontier literature. How this association is formulated and how the model is estimated are what distinguish one model from another. Whatever the model, the principal advantage of having panel data is the ability to observe each producer more than once; it should be possible to parlay this ability into "better" estimates of efficiency for each producer than can be obtained from a single cross section.

Schmidt and Sickles (1984) specified a production frontier model as

$$y_{it} = f(x_{it}; \beta) \exp\{v_{it} + u_i\} \tag{1.22}$$

where $t = 1, \ldots, T$ indexes time periods. Note that statistical noise varies over producers and time, but technical inefficiency varies only over producers. The firm-specific inefficiencies can be merged with the constant intercepts to obtain a conventional panel data model in which there is no time effect, and the firm effect is one-sided. Estimation of (1.22) does not require an assumption on the functional form of the firm effects $u_i \leqq 0$, and if there are no time-invariant inputs it is not necessary to assume that u_i is distributed independently of the inputs. Both of these assumptions are required in a single cross-sectional stochastic frontier framework, whether estimation is by MOLS or MLE, and the ability to relax these assumptions is another benefit of having access to panel data. Schmidt and Sickles consider three ways of estimating (1.22). The "within" estimator makes no distributional assumption on the u_i and makes no independence assumption between the u_i and the inputs. A generalized least squares (GLS) estimator makes no distributional assumption on the u_i, but assumes that the u_i are uncorrelated with the inputs so as to allow for the inclusion of time-invariant regressors in the model. An MLE estimator makes both distributional and independence assumptions. In the first two cases the estimated one-sided firm effects are normalized so that the most efficient observation has $TE_i = 1$. The three estimators are compared in a Monte Carlo study by Gong and Sickles (1989).

In long panels it is desirable to allow technical inefficiency to vary over time, and to test the invariance hypothesis. Cornwell, Schmidt, and Sickles (1990) show how to do the former, simply by replacing the one-sided firm effects of (1.22) with quadratic functions of time having firm-specific coefficients. Battese and Coelli (1988) use MLE techniques to estimate a model of the form of (1.22) in which u_i is independently distributed as truncated normal, and Battese, Coelli, and Colby (1989) also allow the panel to be unbalanced. An additional specification, in which technical efficiency is allowed to vary over time, in which the time-invariance hypothesis is testable, and in which MLE techniques are used, is provided by Battese and Coelli (1992) in a single-equation format similar to (1.22) above.

Extensions of panel data frontier models like (1.22) to equation systems like (1.21), that incorporate behavioral objectives and allow for the estimation of both technical and allocative efficiency, have been considered by Kumbhakar (1990, 1991) and Seale (1990).

1.5 Mathematical programming models

The mathematical programming approach to the construction of production frontiers and the measurement of efficiency relative to the constructed frontiers frequently goes by the descriptive title of data envelopment analysis (DEA). It truly does envelop a data set; it makes no accommodation for noise, and so does not "nearly" envelop a data set the way most econometric models do. Moreover, subject to certain assumptions about the structure of production technology, it envelops the data as tightly as possible.

The programming approach can be categorized according to the type of data available (cross section or panel), and according to the type of variables available (quantities only, or quantities and prices). With quantities only, technical efficiency can be calculated, while with quantities and prices economic efficiency can be calculated and decomposed into its technical and allocative components, just as in the econometric approach. However DEA was developed in a public sector, not-for-profit environment, in which prices were suspect at best and missing at worst. Consequently the vast majority of DEA models use quantity data only and calculate technical efficiency only, despite the fact that the procedure is easily adapted to the calculation of economic efficiency in a situation in which prices are available and reliable.

A spirited defense of the focus on technical efficiency is offered by Pestieau and Tulkens (1990). Their defense is in the context of public sector production, and more particularly in the context of public versus private provision of services, although some of their arguments apply to purely private production as well. Whereas proponents of DEA argue that focus on technical efficiency measurement is "safer" because of the difficulty of measuring public sector prices accurately and because of the undesirability of weighting variables prior to the analysis, the Pestieau-Tulkens argument is different. They just want a level playing field. They argue that public providers have objectives and constraints (e.g., equity and fiscal balance considerations) different from those of private providers, and so the only common ground on which to compare their performance is on the basis of their technical efficiency.

In the rest of this section I lead off with a brief analysis of the simplest, most restrictive variant of DEA. I then show how the model can be generalized in three economically distinct ways. I then present one DEA model of economic efficiency. I conclude with a brief indication of how a simple DEA model might be made stochastic, so as to account for the effects of noise.

1.5.1 A simple DEA model

As before, producers use input vector $x \in R_+^n$ to produce output vector $y \in R_+^m$. The research objective is to measure the performance of each producer relative to the best observed practice in the sample of I producers. To this end weights are attached to each producer's inputs and outputs so as to solve the problem

$$\min_{u,v} \frac{v^T x_o}{u^T y_o} \tag{1.23}$$

subject to

$$\frac{v^T x_i}{u^T y_i} \geqq 1 \qquad i = 1, \ldots, 0, \ldots, I$$

$$u, v \geqq 0,$$

where (x_o, y_o) is the input-output vector of the producer being evaluated and (x_i, y_i) is the input-output vector of the ith producer in the sample. That is, a set of nonnegative weights is desired which, when applied to every producer's inputs and outputs, minimizes the weighted input-to-output ratio for the producer being evaluated, subject to the constraint that no producer in the sample have a ratio less than unity. This nonlinear ratio model can be converted to the linear programming "multiplier" problem

$$\min_{u,v} v^T x_o \tag{1.24}$$

subject to

$$u^T y_o = 1$$
$$v^T x_i \geqq u^T y_i \qquad i = 1, \ldots, 0, \ldots, I$$
$$u, v \geqq 0$$

the dual to which is the linear programming "envelopment" problem

$$\max_{\theta, \lambda} \theta \tag{1.25}$$

subject to

$$X\lambda \lesseqgtr x_o$$
$$\theta y_o \lesseqgtr Y\lambda$$
$$\lambda \gtreqless 0$$

where X is an n by I input matrix with columns x_i, Y is an m by I output matrix with columns y_i, and λ is an I by 1 intensity vector. Problem (1.25) is solved I times, once for each producer being evaluated, to generate I optimal values of (θ, λ). The data matrices X and Y are assumed to satisfy the Karlin (1959) conditions requiring strictly positive row sums and column sums.

In the DEA envelopment problem the performance of a producer is evaluated in terms of the ability of that producer to expand its output vector subject to the constraints imposed by best observed practice. If radial expansion is possible for a producer, its optimal $\theta > 1$, while if radial expansion is not possible, its optimal $\theta = 1$. Noting the output orientation of problem (1.25), it follows that θ is the DEA variant of $DF_0(x, y)$. Noting that θ is a radial measure of technical efficiency, and recalling the divergence between Koopmans' definition of technical efficiency and the Debreu-Farrell measure of technical efficiency, it follows directly that optimal $\theta = 1$ is necessary but not sufficient for technical efficiency since $(\theta y_o, x_o)$ may contain slack in any of its $m + n$ dimensions. At optimum, $\{\theta = 1, X\lambda = x_0, y_0 = Y\lambda\}$ characterizes technical efficiency in the sense of Koopmans.

For the producer being evaluated the positive elements of the optimal λ identify the set of dominating producers located on the constructed production frontier, against which the producer is evaluated. The efficient producers so identified are similar to, and a linear combination of them is better than, an inefficient producer being evaluated.

The DEA envelopment problem (1.25) is output-oriented, just like the econometric problem (1.20) is. It is a simple matter to obtain an analogous input-oriented envelopment problem, by replacing equation (1.23) with a maximization problem, equation (1.24) with a maximization multiplier problem, and equation (1.25) with a minimization envelopment problem. Although exogeneity is not a statistical issue in DEA in the same sense that it is in the econometric approach, the choice between output-oriented and input-oriented models turns on similar considerations. Thus, for example, if producers are required to meet market demands, and if they can freely adjust input usage, then an input-oriented model seems appropriate.

The DEA model above is known as the CCR model, after Charnes, Cooper, and Rhodes (1978). Input-oriented and output-oriented versions are illustrated in Figure 1.1. The CCR model imposes three restrictions on frontier techology prior to solving the envelopment problem for each producer. These restrictions are constant returns-to-scale, strong disposability of inputs and outputs, and convexity of the set of feasible input-output combinations. Each of these restrictions can be relaxed.

[Another restriction of the CCR model, as I have written it, is the suppression of slacks. I do not relax this restriction, partly for expositional convenience, but primarily because I do not like the idea of aggregating slacks, and I like even less the idea of combining aggregated slacks with a radial efficiency score. Two expositions of the CCR and related models that do incorporate slacks are Charnes and Cooper (1985) and Ali (1991). See also the analysis in Chapter 3.]

Constant returns-to-scale is the restriction that is most commonly relaxed. Nonincreasing returns-to-scale is modeled by adding to Equation (1.25) the constraint $e^T \lambda \overset{\leq}{=} 1$, where e is an I by 1 vector of ones. Variable returns-to-scale is modeled by adding to (1.25) the constraint $e^T \lambda = 1$. The variable returns-to-scale formulation is frequently referred to as the BCC model, after Banker, Charnes, and Cooper (1984). The differences among the three DEA frontiers are illustrated in Figure 1.5. It is apparent from the relationships among the three frontiers that output-oriented efficiency scores calculated relative to each of them can be ordered, and that for each producer the ordering may provide information concerning the existence of potential scale economies available at any observed input vector. Consider the producer labeled (y^*, x^*) in Figure 1.5. The output-oriented efficiency measures for this producer are the same for the nonincreasing returns-to-scale and variable returns-to-scale technologies, but lower for the constant returns-to-scale technology. This ordering suggests that the constant returns-to-scale technology does not envelop the data as closely as the other two technologies at input vector x^*, and so returns-to-scale are decreasing at scale x^*. Note the association of scale with the size of the input vector.

The same two constraints $e^T \lambda \overset{\leq}{=} 1$ and $e^T \lambda = 1$ are added to the input-oriented model to model nonincreasing returns-to-scale and variable returns-to-scale. This procedure generates information concerning the existence of potential scale economies

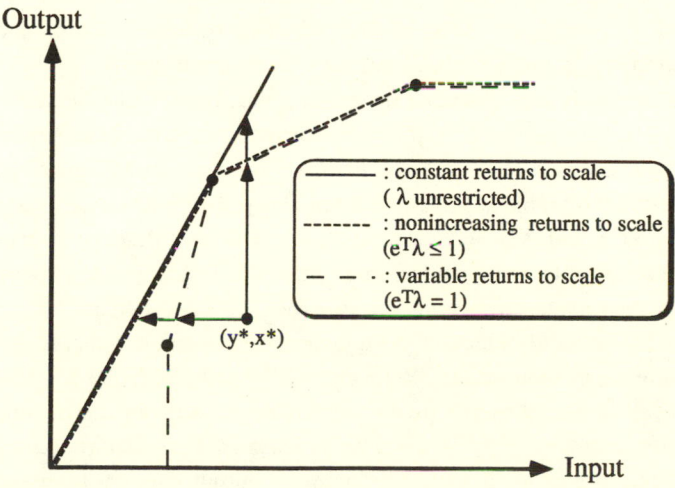

Fig. 1.5 Returns-to-scale in DEA

available at any observed output vector. Consider again the producer labeled (y^*, x^*) in Figure 1.5. The input-oriented efficiency measures for this producer are the same relative to the constant returns-to-scale and nonincreasing returns-to-scale technologies, but higher relative to the variable returns-to-scale technology. This ordering suggests that the variable returns-to-scale technology envelops the data more closely than the other two technologies at output vector y^*, and so returns-to-scale are increasing at y^*. Note the association of scale with the size of the output vector.

Obviously the output-oriented approach and the input-oriented approach can provide different signals concerning scale economies. The different signals are not inconsistent, because they are based on different conceptions of the scale of production and because they are obtained by looking in different directions toward different points on the production frontier. Each approach is based on an ordering of efficiency scores, and the ordering provides only qualitative information on the nature of returns-to-scale. No cardinally useful quantitative information comparable to the economic notion of a scale elasticity or a cost elasticity is provided. This use of an ordering relationship to uncover the nature of scale economies was first proposed by Afriat (1972), and then implemented in a deterministic parametric frontier context by Førsund and Hjalmarsson (1979a). In a piecewise linear DEA context the information so revealed is not unambiguous, however, as Chang and Guh (1991) and Banker and Thrall (1991) have shown.

Note the shape of the variable returns-to-scale production frontier in Figure 1.5. Requiring strictly positive input to produce nonzero output is a consequence of not allowing for the possibility of inactivity, and of imposing convexity on the production possibilities set. This creates a somewhat strained notion of variable returns-to-scale, one that is well removed from the classical S-shaped production frontier that reflects Frisch's (1965) "regular ultra passum" law. Petersen (1990) has attempted to introduce more flexibility into the DEA approach to measuring scale economies by dropping the assumption of convexity of the set of production possibilities while maintaining the assumption of convexity of input sets $L(y)$ and output sets $P(x)$.

Strong disposability is rarely relaxed, despite the obvious interest in testing the free disposability of surplus inputs or unwanted outputs. Nonetheless it is easy to relax strong disposability in a DEA context. Weak disposability of outputs and inputs is modeled by replacing the constraints $\theta y_0 \leqq Y\lambda$ and $X\lambda \leqq x_0$ in (1.25) with $\theta y_0 = \alpha Y\lambda$ and $X\lambda = \beta x_0, \alpha, \beta, \in (0, 1]$. The difference between strong and weak disposability is illustrated in Figure 1.6. In the lower panel output y_1 is not freely disposable throughout the positive orthant relative to the output set $P^{WDO}(x)$. Any desired reduction in y_1 beneath y_1^* requires either a reduction in y_2 or an increase in input usage. Both are costly, and so disposal is not free. In the upper panel input x_1 is not freely disposable throughout the positive orthant relative to the input set $L^{WDI}(y)$. Any increase in x_1 either reduces output or requires an increase in x_2 in order to maintain output. Notice the association of weak disposability with upward-sloping segments of $\text{Isoq}P(x)$ and $\text{Isoq}L(y)$. Since

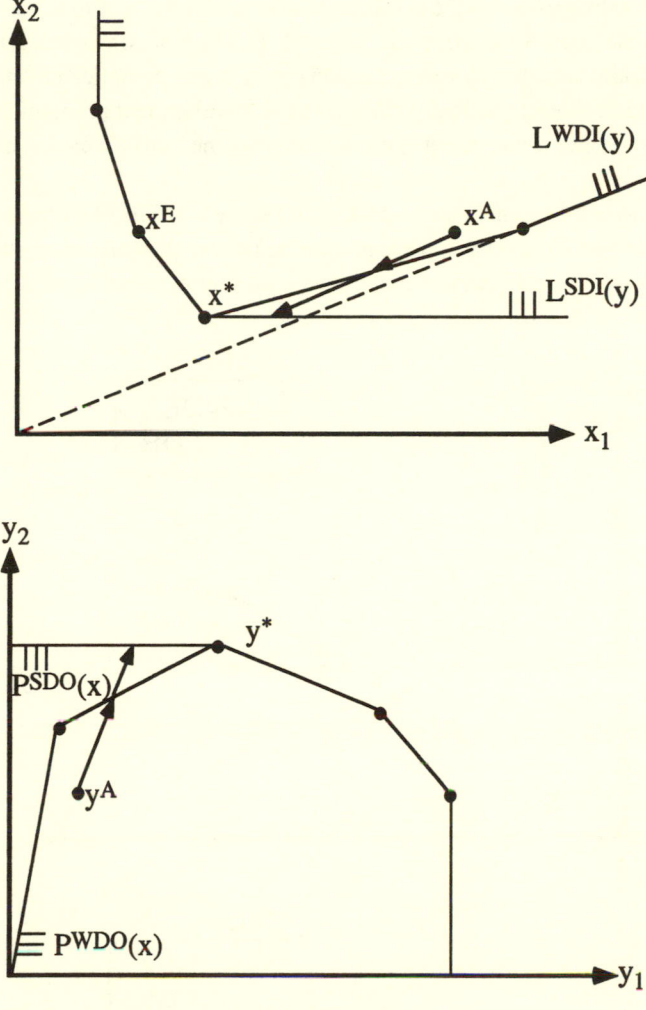

Fig. 1.6   Strong and weak disposability in DEA

$P^{WDO}(x) \subseteq P^{SDO}(x)$, and $L^{WDI}(y) \subseteq L^{SDI}(y)$, a comparison of efficiency scores calculated relative to frontiers that impose strong and weak disposability can reveal the nature of disposability of outputs and of inputs. This strategy is the same as the strategy for revealing the nature of scale economies. Both output disposability and input disposability are analyzed in Färe, Grosskopf, and Lovell (1985, 1987b).

Convexity of output sets $P(x)$ and input sets $L(y)$ is also rarely relaxed, despite the belief of many, expressed by McFadden (1978, pp. 8–9), that its importance lies more in its analytical convenience than in its technological realism. A "free disposal hull" (FDH) that relaxes convexity of $P(x)$ and of $L(y)$, but maintains strong disposability of outputs and inputs as well as variable returns-to-scale, is modeled by adding to (1.25) the additional constraints $e^T \lambda = 1$ to allow for variable returns-to-scale, and $\lambda_i \in \{0, 1\}, i = 1, \ldots, I$, to relax convexity. Although this added constraint appears to convert (1.25) to a more complicated mixed-integer programming problem, it actually simplifies the envelopment problem to be solved. In fact, linear programming is not even used to solve the FDH efficiency measurement problem.

DEA and FDH frontiers are compared in Figure 1.7. The FDH frontier envelops the data more tightly, and has a more restrictive notion of domination, than the DEA frontier does. A producer is FDH-dominated by a single observed efficient producer,

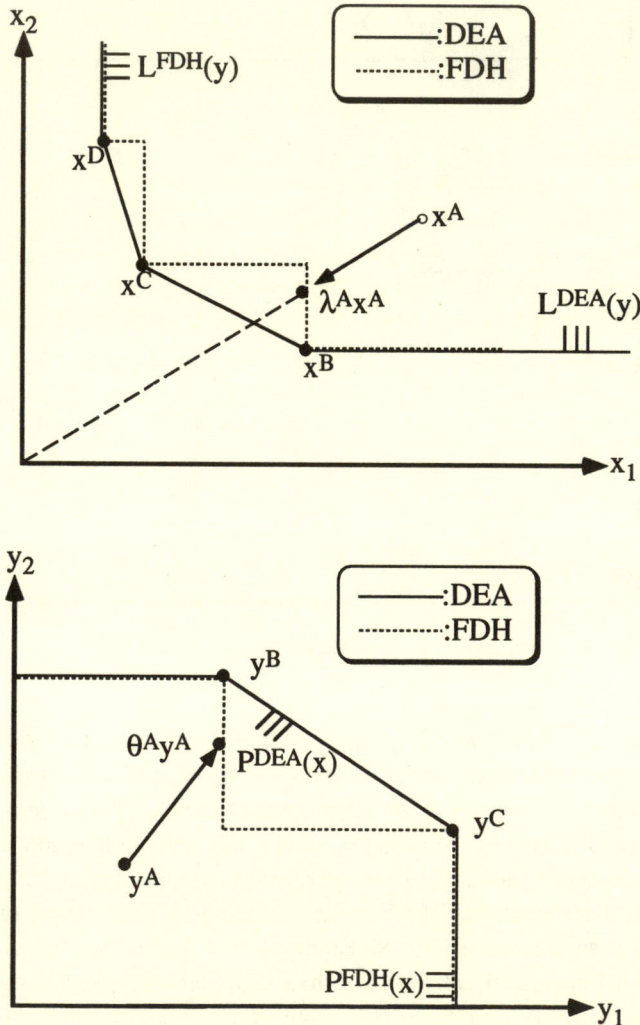

Fig. 1.7   Technical efficiency measurement relative to DEA and FDH frontiers

since $e^T \lambda = 1$ and $\lambda_i \in \{0, 1\}$, whereas a producer is DEA-dominated by a fictitious observation defined as a linear (convex if $e^T \lambda = 1$ is imposed) combination of a set of efficient producers. In the input-oriented upper panel $L^{\text{FDH}}(y) \subseteq L^{\text{DEA}}(y)$, and $\text{Eff} L^{\text{FDH}}(y)$ consists of the input vectors x^B, x^C and x^D. Inefficient input vector x^A is dominated by x^B, and has Debreu-Farrell technical efficiency score λ^A with slack in input x_2. A similar story is told in the output-oriented lower panel. Note that slack is a much more serious problem in FDH than in DEA. Although FDH is an old idea, it was introduced into the frontier literature by Deprins, Simar, and Tulkens (1984); for more details see Tulkens (1990).

1.5.2 A DEA model of economic efficiency

All DEA models in Section 1.5.1 use quantity data only, and so capture technical efficiency and some of its features such as slack, scale efficiency, and departures from disposability and convexity. In this section I show how to extend the DEA model to provide a measure of economic efficiency.

Producers are assumed to use inputs $x \in R_+^n$ to produce outputs $y \in R_+^m$, for sale at prices $p \in R_{++}^m$. Their objective is assumed to be the maximization of revenue, subject to the constraints imposed by output prices, input supplies, and the structure of production technology. Assuming constant returns to scale, strong disposability of inputs and outputs, and convexity, all of which can be relaxed, this problem has linear programming structure

$$\max_y p^T y \tag{1.26}$$

subject to

$$X\lambda \leqq x_o$$
$$y_o \leqq Y\lambda$$
$$\lambda \geqq 0$$

The revenue maximization problem is solved separately for each producer in the sample. The problem is illustrated in the lower panel of Figure 1.3. Revenue efficiency, the ratio of observed to maximum possible revenue, decomposes into the product of output-oriented technical efficiency and output mix allocative efficiency. Revenue efficiency is obtained from the solution to Equation (1.26), output-oriented technical efficiency is obtained as the solution to Equation (1.25), and output mix allocative efficiency is derived residually.

Alternative objectives and alternative or additional constraints can be entertained within the same general linear programming framework. All that is required is the requisite data and the ability to write down a linear programming problem analogous to (1.26) that captures the objective and the constraints of the economic problem of interest. Examples can be found in Färe and Grosskopf (1990).

1.5.3 Stochastic DEA

A shortcoming of all models discussed previously in this section is that they are nonstochastic. Consequently efficiency scores are contaminated by omitted variables, measurement error, and other sources of statistical noise. This puts a lot of pressure on users of these techniques to collect all relevant variables and to measure them accurately. Alternatively, it makes the development of a stochastic DEA an important research objective. Recently much effort has been devoted to the development of a stochastic DEA. One stochastic DEA model, due to Land, Lovell, and Thore (1988, 1990), is sketched in this section. Similar models have been developed by Desai and Schinnar (1987), Sengupta (1987), Petersen and Olesen (1989), and Olesen and Thore (1990). Empirical experience with each of these models is sufficiently limited to lead me to characterize them as potentially useful rather than established and reliable. Time will tell.

Consider the no-frills output-oriented DEA model (1.25). The conversion of this model to a stochastic DEA model begins by allowing the evaluator to be uncertain about the accuracy of the data. This suggests the application of chance-constrained programming techniques developed by Charnes, Cooper, and Symonds (1958) and Charnes and Cooper (1959, 1962, 1963), in which the constraints of (1.25) have a chance of being violated, and (1.25) becomes

$$\max_{\theta,\lambda} \theta \tag{1.27}$$

subject to

$$\Pr\left(\sum_{i=1}^{I} x_{is}\lambda_i \overset{\leq}{=} x_{os}\right) \overset{\geq}{=} P_s \qquad s = 1,\ldots,n$$

$$\Pr\left(\theta y_{ot} \overset{\leq}{=} \sum_{i=1}^{I} y_{it}\lambda_i\right) \overset{\geq}{=} P_t \qquad t = 1,\ldots,m$$

$$\lambda \overset{\geq}{=} 0$$

where P_s and P_t are probabilities. Problem (1.27) is to radially expand the output vector of the producer being evaluated as far as possible, subject to the constraint that at optimum $(\theta y_o, x_o)$ "probably" will be feasible relative to the production frontier constructed from the sample data. Because of uncertainty about the accuracy of the data, however, the evaluator is uncertain about the correct placement of the frontier, and so allows for the possibility that an extremely productive producer might violate the feasibility constraints.

If it is assumed that each input x_{is} is a normally distributed random variable with expected value Ex_{is} and variance-covariance matrix $Vx_{is}x_{js}$, and each output y_{it} is a normally distributed random variable with expected value Ey_{it} and variance-covariance matrix $Vy_{it}y_{jt}$, then (1.27) can be rewritten in modified certainty-equivalent form as

$$\max_{\theta,\lambda} \theta \tag{1.28}$$

subject to

$$x_{os} \geq \sum_{i=1}^{I} x_{is}\lambda_i + \sum_{i=1}^{I}(Ex_{is} - x_{is})\lambda_i + F^{-1}(P_s)(\sum_{i=1}^{I}\sum_{j=1}^{I} \lambda_i\lambda_j Vx_{is}x_{js})^{1/2}$$
$$s = 1 \ldots, n$$

$$\theta y_{ot} \leq \sum_{i=1}^{I} y_{it}\lambda_i + \sum_{i=1}^{I}(Ey_{it} - y_{it})\lambda_i - F^{-1}(P_t)(\sum_{i=1}^{I}\sum_{j=1}^{I} \lambda_i\lambda_j Vy_{it}y_{jt})^{1/2}$$
$$t = 1,\ldots, m$$

$$\lambda \geq 0$$

This is a nonlinear programming problem to be solved I times, once for each producer in the sample. The goal is to radially expand outputs of the producer being evaluated, subject to constraints imposed by observed data and by the evaluator's confidence in the data. If $Ex_{is} - x_{is} = Ey_{it} - y_{it} = Vx_{is}x_{js} = Vy_{it}y_{jt} = 0$ for all i, j, s, t, equation (1.28) collapses to the original DEA problem (1.25). However if the evaluator has reason to believe that a sample data point departs from its expected value, due perhaps to unusually good weather or unexpected input supply disruption, then this information is fed into the chance-constrained efficiency measurement equation (1.28). The desired outcome is that, unlike (1.25), good and bad fortune for a producer do not distort efficiency measures for any producer. Similarly, if the evaluator has reason to believe that one variable is measured with less accuracy than another, the greater likelihood of measurement error can also be fed into the chance-constrained efficiency measurement equation (1.28). The desired outcome is that measurement error in one variable does not contaminate the efficiency measure of any producer.

The data requirements of chance-constrained efficiency measurement are severe. In addition to the data matrices Y, X, it is necessary for the evaluator to supply information on expected values of all variables, variance-covariance matrices for all variables, and probability levels at which feasibility constraints are to be satisfied. Lunch is not free.

1.6 Two other approaches to efficiency measurement

The category of models considered in Section 1.4 is parametric and (more or less) stochastic, and uses econometric techniques. The category of models considered in Section 1.5 is nonparametric and (largely) nonstochastic, and uses mathematical programming techniques. Alternative approaches can be found, although they do not readily fit into either of these two categories. Two of the more popular approaches are discussed briefly in this section.

1.6.1 Goal programming

In an early and influential study Aigner and Chu (1968) considered a production relationship of the form

$$y_i \overset{<}{=} f(x_i; \beta) \tag{1.29}$$

where the production frontier was assumed to be Cobb-Douglas. Their problem was to obtain "estimates" of the parameters β describing the structure of the production frontier. One solution was to solve the problem

$$\min_{\beta} \sum_{i=1}^{I} [f(x_i; \beta) - y_i] \tag{1.30}$$

subject to

$$[f(x_i; \beta) - y_i] \overset{>}{=} 0, \qquad i = 1, \dots, I$$
$$\beta \overset{>}{=} 0$$

and another was to solve the problem

$$\min_{\beta} \sum_{i=1}^{I} [f(x_i; \beta) - y_i]^2 \tag{1.31}$$

subject to the same constraints. The first problem is a linear programming problem, the second is a quadratic programming problem, and both fall under the general category of goal programming problems, where the goal is to select a nonnegative parameter vector that minimizes the sum of deviations (or squared deviations) beneath the parametric frontier, and the method is mathematical programming. Variants on this technique, maintaining the Cobb-Douglas assumption, have been employed by Førsund and Hjalmarsson (1979b, 1987), Førsund and Jansen (1977), and Albriktsen and Førsund (1990). A translog frontier with additional subsidiary constraints appended has been constructed using these techniques by Nishimizu and Page (1982) (a production frontier), by Charnes, Cooper, and Sueyoshi (1988) (a cost frontier), and by Färe, Grosskopf, Lovell, and Yaisawarng (1990) (an output distance frontier).

The resemblance of (1.31) and, to a lesser extent (1.30), to least squares estimation of the parameter vector β is strong. The deviations are one-sided, and no assumption is made about their distribution. Schmidt (1976) first explained the relationship. He showed that the goal programming problem (1.30) is equivalent to maximum likelihood estimation of the deterministic production frontier $f(x_i; \beta)$ if the nonnegative deviations have an exponential distribution. He also showed that the goal programming problem (1.31) is equivalent to maximum likelihood estimation of the deterministic production frontier $f(x_i; \beta)$ when the nonnegative deviations have a half-normal distribution.

This remarkable result appears to lend some respectability to goal programming frontiers. Since goal programming techniques calculate rather than estimate frontier parameters, these calculations do not come with standard errors attached. Linking frontiers calculated by goal programming methods with frontiers estimated by maximum likelihood methods might seem to provide them with a statistical foundation. However Schmidt dashed that hope by noting that the statistical properties of the maximum likelihood estimators themselves are uncertain in this context, since the range of y_i depends on β, which violates a regularity condition for maximum likelihood estimation. Later Greene (1980) showed that a deterministic frontier model with deviations assumed to follow a gamma distribution satisfies all regularity conditions for maximum likelihood estimation. This result is comforting to those who use MLE to estimate deterministic frontiers with technical inefficiency distributed as gamma, but it is of no apparent value to those who use goal programming to construct frontiers. This is because neither Schmidt nor anyone since has managed to identify the goal programming problem that would be equivalent to Greene's MLE problem. Thus the two goal programming models that have known MLE counterparts have unknown statistical properties, and the MLE model that has nice statistical properties has no known goal programming counterpart. Further work on this problem might pay dividends.

A related problem that has attracted some attention is the development of a chance-constrained goal programming efficiency measurement model. All that is required is to rewrite the constraints in equations (1.30) or (1.31) as probability statements and then convert to certainty equivalents, just as in the case of chance-constrained DEA. The desired outcome is a stochastic goal programming model. An interesting application of this technique to efficiency measurement in Indian cotton production is provided by Satish (1986).

Another approach to the development of a stochastic goal programming efficiency measurement model has been followed by Banker (1989), Vassdal (1989), and Banker, Datar, and Kemerer (1991). This model can be formulated as

$$\min_{\gamma} \quad \gamma v_i + (1 - \gamma)u_i \qquad (1.32)$$

subject to

$$[f(x_i; \beta) - y_i] + v_i - u_i = 0, \qquad i = 1, \ldots, I$$
$$v_i, u_i \geqq 0$$
$$\beta \geqq 0$$

In this model the objective is to minimize a weighted sum of deviations from the production frontier. The v_i's represent deviations above the frontier and are due to noise only. The u_i's represent deviations beneath the frontier and are due to noise and technical inefficiency. The parameter γ, which influences the attribution of deviations to noise and inefficiency, is specified by the evaluator. No distributional assumptions are required for the components v_i and u_i. This stochastic goal programming model is structurally similar to an "asymmetric criterion funtion" approach to the econometric estimation of production frontiers developed by Aigner, Amemiya, and Poirier (1976). It has been compared to the stochastic DEA model discussd above by Retzlaff-Roberts and Morey (1991).

1.6.2 Nonfrontier efficiency measurement methods

The techniques described in Sections 1.4, 1.5, and 1.6.1 are all enveloping techniques. Each of them treats technical efficiency in terms of distance to a production frontier, economic efficiency in terms of distance to an appropriate economic frontier, and allocative efficiency as a ratio of economic efficiency to technical efficiency. They are in rough concordance on the fundamental notions of frontiers and distance, with distance being represented with one-sided deviations from the frontier. They differ mainly in the techniques they employ to construct frontiers and to measure distance.

There is a literature that seeks to measure efficiency without explicit recourse to frontiers, and indeed it contains many papers in which the word "frontier" never appears. In this literature almost no attempt is made to envelop data or to associate efficiency with distance from an enveloping surface. Unlike much econometric efficiency analysis and most mathematical programming efficiency analysis, the focus is on allocative efficiency. The method used is econometric.

The literature seems to have originated with Hopper (1965), who found subsistence agriculture in India to attain a high degree of allocative efficiency. He reached this conclusion by using OLS to estimate Cobb-Douglas production functions (not frontiers), then to calculate the value of the marginal product for each input, and then to make two comparisons: the value of an input's marginal product across outputs, and the value of an input's marginal product with its price. In each comparison equality implies allocative efficiency, and the sign and magnitude of any inequality indicate the direction and severity (and the cost, which can be calculated since the production function parameters have been estimated) of the allocative inefficiency. Hopper's work was heavily criticized, and enormously influential.

In a nutshell, the nonfrontier efficiency models that have followed have simply parameterized Hopper's comparisons, with inequalities being replaced with parameters to be estimated. Thus, following Lau and Yotopoulos (1971) and Yotopoulos and Lau (1973), suppose producers use inputs $x \in R_+^n$ available at prices $w \in R_{++}^n$ to produce output $y \in R_+$ for sale at price $p \in R_{++}$. Then the inequality

$$y_i \lesseqgtr f(x_i; \beta) \qquad (1.33)$$

is parameterized as

$$y_i = A_i f(x_i; \beta) \qquad (1.34)$$

and the hypothesis of equal technical efficiency is tested by testing the hypothesis that $A_i = A_j$ for two producers i and j. Notice that there is no notion of a production frontier here, since in moving from (1.33) to (1.34) the obvious requirement that $\max\{A_i, A_j\} \lessgtr 1$ is ignored. Indeed, so far this model is just a Hoch (1955)–Mundlak (1961) management bias production function model, in which different intercepts are intended to capture the effects of variation in the (unobserved) management input. But it gets better.

If producers seek maximum profit, then the inequalities

$$\frac{\partial A_i f(x_i; \beta)}{\partial x_{ij}} \gtreqless \frac{w_j}{p} \qquad j = 1, \ldots, n \qquad (1.35)$$

are parameterized as

$$\frac{\partial A_i f(x_i; \beta)}{\partial x_{ij}} = B_{ij} \left(\frac{w_j}{p} \right) \qquad (1.36)$$

and a host of hypotheses can be tested. Cost minimization for producer i is tested by testing the hypothesis that $B_{ij} = B_{ik}$ for $j, k = 1, \ldots, n$. Profit maximization for producer i is tested by testing the hypothesis that $B_{ij} = B_{ik} = 1$ for $j, k = 1, \ldots, n$. Equal relative and absolute allocative efficiency with respect to the cost minimization and the profit maximization goals across producers are tested in an analogous fashion. All that is required to implement the model is specification of a functional form for the production function and the derivation of a set of estimating equations similar to (1.36) that allow estimation of the technology parameters β and the efficiency parameters (A_i, B_{ij}). The methodology is described in considerable detail, and supported with an international array of applications, in Yotopoulos and Lau (1979).

The technique is illustrated in Figure 1.8. In the upper panel a producer producing y^A and facing input price ratio (w_1/w_2) is located at x^A, which is allocatively inefficient. The technique estimates the structure of technology and the parameter (B_{i1}/B_{i2}), which generates a shadow price ratio $(B_{i1}/B_{i2})(w_1/w_2)$ for which x^A

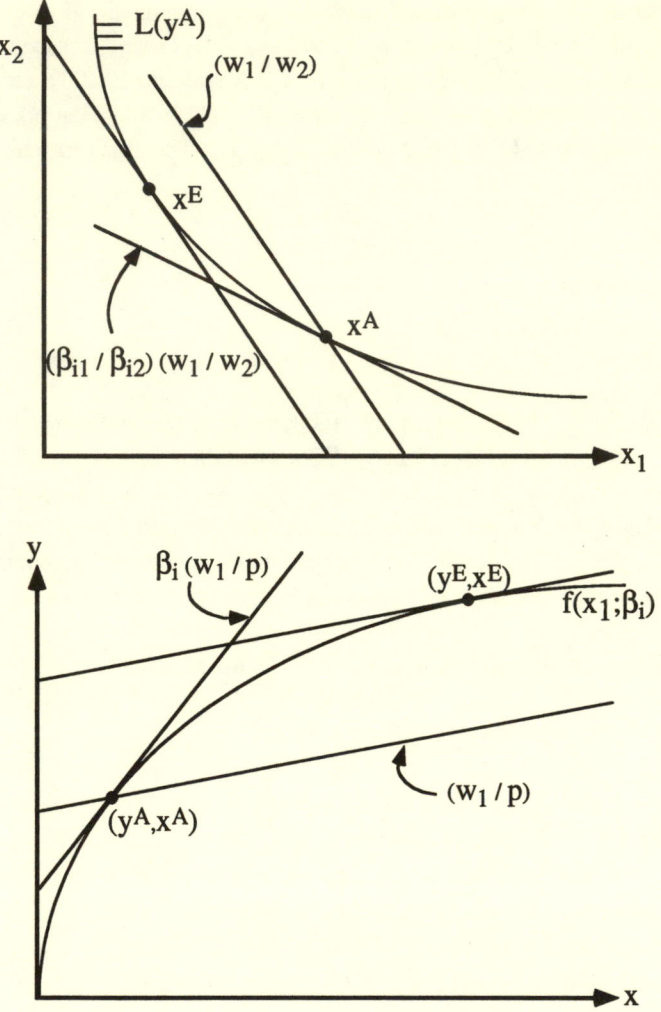

Fig. 1.8   Using shadow prices to measure allocative efficiency

would be allocatively efficient. In this case since $(B_{i1}/B_{i2}) < 1$ the shadow input price ratio is less than the observed input price ratio, and so (x_1/x_2) is larger at x^A than at the cost-efficient point x^E. In the lower panel a producer facing price ratio (w_1/p) is located at allocatively inefficient point (y^A, x^A). In this case $B_i > 1$, the shadow price ratio is greater than the observed price ratio, and so (y^A, x^A) is smaller than the allocatively efficient point (y^E, x^E).

A parametric illustration is provided by the model of Toda (1976), as extended by Lovell and Sickles (1983). Producers use inputs $x \in R_+^n$ available at prices $w \in R_{++}^n$ to produce outputs $y \in R_+^m$ for sale at prices $p \in R_{++}^m$. Production technology is represented by the generalized Leontief profit frontier (with $m = n = 2$ for simplicity)

$$\pi(p, w) = A_{11}p_1 + A_{12}p_1^{1/2}p_2^{1/2} + A_{13}p_1^{1/2}w_1^{1/2} + A_{14}p_1^{1/2}w_2^{1/2} \qquad (1.37)$$
$$+ A_{21}p_2^{1/2}p_1^{1/2} + A_{22}p_2 + A_{23}p_2^{1/2}w_1^{1/2} + A_{24}p_2^{1/2}w_2^{1/2}$$
$$+ A_{31}w_1^{1/2}p_1^{1/2} + A_{32}w_1^{1/2}p_2^{1/2} + A_{33}w_1 + A_{34}w_1^{1/2}w_2^{1/2}$$
$$+ A_{41}w_2^{1/2}p_1^{1/2} + A_{42}w_2^{1/2}p_2^{1/2} + A_{43}w_2^{1/2}w_1^{1/2} + A_{44}w_2$$

where $A_{ij} = A_{ji}$ for all $j \neq i$. Hotelling's lemma yields the profit-maximizing output supply and input demand equations

$$y_1(p, w) = A_{11} + A_{12}\left(\frac{p_1}{p_2}\right)^{-1/2} + A_{13}\left(\frac{p_1}{w_1}\right)^{-1/2} + A_{14}\left(\frac{p_1}{w_2}\right)^{-1/2}$$

$$y_2(p, w) = A_{22} + A_{21}\left(\frac{p_1}{p_2}\right)^{1/2} + A_{23}\left(\frac{p_2}{w_1}\right)^{-1/2} + A_{24}\left(\frac{p_2}{w_2}\right)^{-1/2}$$

$$\qquad (1.38)$$

$$-x_1(p, w) = A_{33} + A_{31}\left(\frac{p_1}{w_1}\right)^{1/2} + A_{32}\left(\frac{p_2}{w_1}\right)^{1/2} + A_{34}\left(\frac{w_1}{w_2}\right)^{-1/2}$$

$$-x_2(p, w) = A_{44} + A_{41}\left(\frac{p_1}{w_2}\right)^{1/2} + A_{42}\left(\frac{p_2}{w_2}\right)^{1/2} + A_{43}\left(\frac{w_1}{w_2}\right)^{1/2}$$

In the spirit of Hopper, and Lau and Yotopoulos, allocative inefficiency is modeled by allowing producers to adjust output supplies and input demands to the "wrong" prices. Also, technical inefficiency is modeled by shifting the intercepts of the output supplies and input demands. This approach to parameterizing inefficiency leads to actual output supply and input demand equations

$$y_1 = (A_{11} - B_{11}) + A_{12}\left[B_{12}\left(\frac{p_1}{p_2}\right)\right]^{-1/2} + A_{13}\left[B_{13}\left(\frac{p_1}{w_1}\right)\right]^{-1/2}$$
$$+ A_{14}\left[B_{14}\left(\frac{p_1}{w_2}\right)\right]^{-1/2}$$

$$y_2 = (A_{22} - B_{22}) + A_{12}\left[B_{12}\left(\frac{p_1}{p_2}\right)\right]^{1/2} + A_{23}\left[B_{23}\left(\frac{p_2}{w_1}\right)\right]^{-1/2}$$
$$+ A_{24}\left[B_{24}\left(\frac{p_2}{w_2}\right)\right]^{-1/2}$$

$$\qquad (1.39)$$

$$-x_1 = (A_{33} - B_{33}) + A_{13}\left[B_{13}\left(\frac{p_1}{w_1}\right)\right]^{1/2} + A_{23}\left[B_{23}\left(\frac{p_2}{w_1}\right)\right]^{1/2}$$

$$+ A_{34}\left[B_{34}\left(\frac{w_1}{w_2}\right)\right]^{-1/2}$$

$$-x_2 = (A_{44} - B_{44}) + A_{14}\left[B_{14}\left(\frac{p_1}{w_2}\right)\right]^{1/2} + A_{24}\left[B_{24}\left(\frac{p_2}{w_2}\right)\right]^{1/2}$$

$$+ A_{34}\left[B_{34}\left(\frac{w_1}{w_2}\right)\right]^{1/2}$$

and to actual profit

$$p^T y - w^T x = \sum_{i=1}^{4}(A_{ii} - B_{ii})q_i$$

$$+ \sum_{i=1}^{3}\sum_{j=2}^{4} A_{ij}(B_{ij}^{-1/2} + B_{ij}^{1/2})q_i^{1/2}q_j^{1/2} \qquad j > i \qquad (1.40)$$

where $q = (p_1, p_2, w_1, w_2)$. Technical inefficiency is captured by the terms $B_{ii} \geqq 0$; it is variable-specific and nonradial, unlike the Debreu-Farrell measure, which is both radial and either input-oriented or output-oriented. Allocative inefficiency is captured by the terms $B_{ij} \gtreqless 1$. Comparing (1.40) with (1.37), it is clear that profit is maximized if, and only if, $B_{ii} = 0$ for all i and $B_{ij} = 1$ for all $i \neq j$.

In the model above there is no requirement that allocative inefficiency be consistent. The model has $(m + n)$ market prices, and $(m + n - 1)$ independent market price ratios, but $[(m + n)(m + n - 1)/2]$ parameters B_{ij} to capture the allocative inefficiency. Consistency can be imposed on the model by adding the parametric restrictions $B_{ik} = B_{ij} * B_{jk}$ for all $i < j < k$. This reduces the number of independent allocative inefficiency parameters to be estimated to $(m + n - 1)$, the same as the number of independent price ratios. Of course it is not clear why allocatively inefficient producers should be consistent in their misallocations, but at least it is a testable hypothesis.

When modeling the behavior of producers who are constrained in their pursuit of a conventional objective, or who pursue an unconventional objective, researchers have two choices. The preferred choice is to model objective and constraint(s) correctly, derive the first-order conditions, and construct an estimating model based on the assumption that producers are efficient. This can be hard work, as Färe and Logan (1983) have demonstrated for the case of the profit-seeking rate-of-return regulated firm. An easier alternative approach is to model such producers as being unconstrained in their pursuit of a conventional objective, allow for failure to satisfy first order conditions, and check to see if the direction of the allocative inefficiency is consistent with what one would expect if in fact the producers were constrained or pursued some other objective. That is, use a model that is inappropriate but familiar, and look for allocative inefficiency by comparing calculated shadow prices with observed prices.

In a related situation the researcher does not know the constraints or the objective of producers, perhaps because there are competing paradigms at hand. In this case it is feasible to use the familiar model and use calculated shadow prices to provide an indirect test of the competing paradigms.

These are the two purposes which the nonfrontier efficiency measurement models described in this section most frequently serve. Thus, allocative inefficiency in the unconstrained pursuit of cost minimization or profit maximization suggests allocative efficiency in a more complicated environment, and departures of shadow prices from observed prices provide the basis for hypothesis tests. The model has been used by Atkinson and Halvorsen (1980, 1984) to test the Averch-Johnson (1962) hypothesis that rate-of-return regulation induces overcapitalization in electric utilities. It has also been used by Atkinson and Halvorsen (1986) to compare allocative efficiency in private and public electric utilities, and by Hollas and Stansell (1988) to compare allocative efficiency in proprietary, cooperative, and municipal electric utilities. It has also been used by Eakin and Kniesner (1988) to examine the allocative efficiency of input use in hospitals.

1.7 Efficiency and productivity

I noted in Section 1.1 that productivity, the ratio of output to input, varies due to differences in production technology, differences in the efficiency of the production process, and differences in the environment in which production takes place. The problem is to attribute productivity variation to these sources and an unattributed residual—Abramovitz's (1956) famous "measure of our ignorance."

In Figure 1.9 it is apparent that productivity has increased from period t to period $t + 1$; in the upper panel (y/x) has increased, and in the lower panel $(w^T x/y)$ has declined. The challenging problem is to tell a story that connects the dots, or better yet one that does not.

Until very recently virtually all the stories that have been told have ignored the potential contribution of efficiency change to productivity change. Solow (1957) sought to attribute output growth to input growth and technical change by distinguishing movements along a production frontier from shifts in the frontier. Economies of scale were added to the story by Brown and Popkin (1962). David and van de Klundert (1965) allowed technical change to be biased. The effects of scale economies and

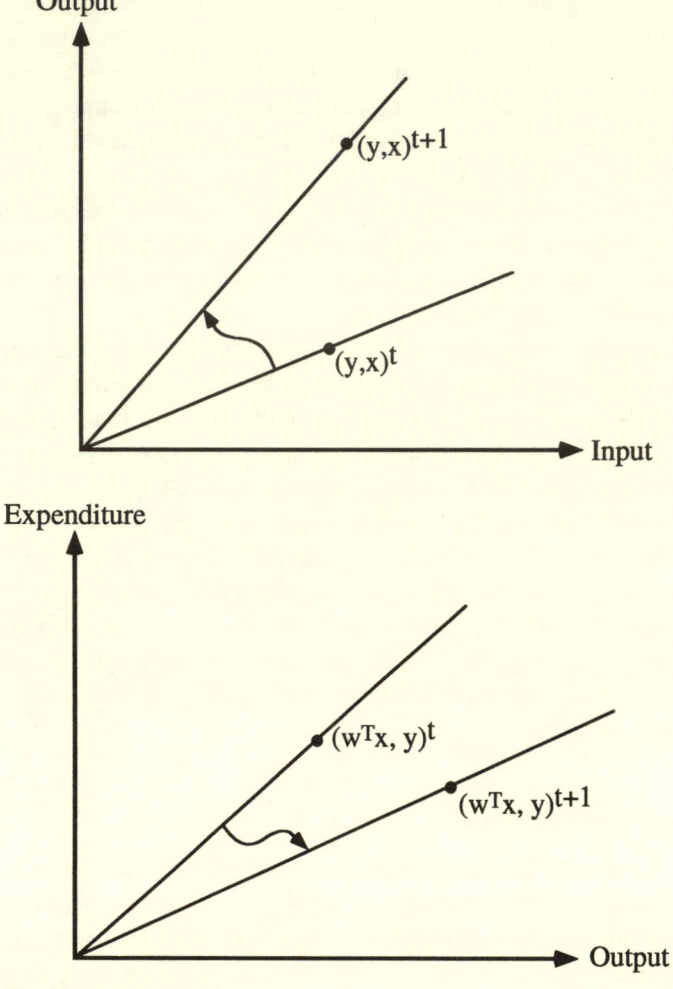

Fig. 1.9   Productivity change

technical change on productivity growth were translated into their effects on production cost by Ohta (1974) and Binswanger (1974). A full-blown model of productivity change decomposed into movements along a cost frontier (scale economies), shifts in the cost frontier (technical change), and nonmarginal cost pricing was developed by Denny, Fuss, and Waverman (1981) and Gollop and Roberts (1981). Only Nishimizu and Page (1982), who decomposed productivity growth into shifts in the production frontier and movements toward or away from it, attempted to incorporate efficiency change into a model of productivity change. I will return to their model shortly.

If efficiency variation contributes anything to variation in output across producers in a cross-sectional context or in a panel data context, then it stands to reason that efficiency change might have something to offer in a temporal context. If efficiency change can contribute to productivity growth, it ought to be incorporated into models of productivity growth. Despite the fact that some econometric panel data models cited in Section 1.4.3 assume that efficiency is time-invariant, I believe that the efficiency of a producer can vary over time as surely as it can vary across producers during a period of time, and my belief strengthens as the time period lengthens. Consequently in this section, I consider conditions in which efficiency can usefully be incorporated into a productivity growth model, and I consider several ways in which this task might be accomplished.

The ability to include efficiency change as a component of productivity change depends on the data one has to work with, and the assumptions one is willing to make. Data can be either a single time series or a panel, and can consist of quantities only or quantities and prices. Assumptions can be strong or weak. With sufficiently strong assumptions (e.g., constant returns to scale and no change in technology) it is possible to use a single time series on quantity data only to tell a story about the contribution of efficiency change to productivity change. But the story would not be very persuasive. Weakening the assumptions requires more data, and adding time series price data to time-series quantity data is probably not sufficient. I believe that a persuasive story about the role of efficiency change in productivity change requires panel data. The panel data can include quantities only if the efficiency change is technical only, but must include quantities and prices if the efficiency change is to be technical and allocative.

1.7.1 The econometric approach

The econometric approach to incorporating efficiency change into a model of productivity growth is due to Bauer (1990a), who built upon previous work of Christensen and Greene (1976) and Denny, Fuss, and Waverman (1981). The basic idea is to begin with a cross-sectional translog cost and input share equation system with technical and allocative inefficiency allowed, as in equation (1.21) in Section 1.4.2. Then convert the cross section to a panel and add a time subscript to the producer subscript. Finally, allow for technical change by adding time as an argument in the cost frontier and the efficient shares. This leads to a system suitable for estimation that looks like

$$\ln(w^T x)_{it} = c(\ln y_{it}, \ln w_{it}, t; \beta) + v_{oit} + T_{it} + A_{it} \qquad (1.41)$$

$$\left(\frac{w_j x_j}{w^T x}\right)_{it} = s_j(\ln y_{it}, \ln w_{it}, t; \beta) + v_{jit} + u_{jit} \qquad j = 1, \ldots, n-1$$

where $i = 1, \ldots, I$ indexes producers and $t = 1, \ldots, T$ indexes time. This system is a bear to estimate, even (especially?) when technical change is assumed to be neutral so that time does not appear in the efficient shares. But in principle at least the formulation allows productivity change, as reflected by dual cost change, to occur as a result of scale economies, technical change, and changes in technical and allocative efficiency.

After estimation, the desired decomposition of productivity change is obtained by means of the relationship

$$\text{MFP} = (1 - \sum \epsilon_{cy_k})\dot{y}^* + \dot{c} + \dot{T} + \dot{A} + \sum \left[\left(\frac{w_j x_j}{w^T x} \right) - s_j \right] \dot{w}_j + (\dot{y}^{**} - \dot{y}^*) \quad (0.1)$$

where a dot over a variable indicates a rate of growth, ϵ denotes an elasticity, and

$$\dot{y}^* = \sum [\epsilon_{cy_k} / \sum \epsilon_{cy_k}] \dot{y}_k$$
$$\dot{y}^{**} = \sum (p_k y_k / p^T y) \dot{y}_k$$

Here multifactor productivity growth, MFP, is decomposed into six elements. The first is scale economies, which captures one aspect of the shape of the cost frontier and makes no contribution if the cost elasticity is unity. The second is technical change, captured by the shift in the cost frontier over time. The third and fourth are changes in technical and allocative efficiency over time, which show up as separate movements toward or away from the cost frontier, respectively. The fifth term, which Bauer calls a "price effect" term, reinforces the contribution of allocative inefficiency and makes no contribution if producers are allocatively efficient, or if input prices change equiproportionately. The final term captures the effect of nonmarginal cost pricing on productivity growth and disappears under marginal cost pricing or equiproportionate markup pricing.

The complexity of the model has made the estimation problem sufficiently daunting to slow implementation of the econometric approach to date. However empirical work can be expected to spread as larger panels and faster computers appear, and perhaps also as those who employ the econometric approach with panel data to measure efficiency become aware of how close they are to the productivity change decomposition problem. Recall from Section 1.4.3 that the Schmidt and Sickles (1984) panel data frontier model assumed time-invariant efficiency and no technical change. Later Cornwell, Schmidt and Sickles (1990), Kumbhakar (1990, 1991), and others succeeded in allowing efficiency to vary over time. But none of these models incorporates technical change, and none of them investigates productivity change. Just as long panels make time-invariant efficiency a tenuous assumption, they also make time-invariant technology a tenuous assumption, and they make an investigation of productivity change and its decomposition a tempting exercise. I predict a merger between econometric panel data frontier models and econometric productivity growth models in the near future.

1.7.2 The DEA window analysis approach

The data envelopment analysis literature has not produced a full-scale model of productivity change and its decomposition into efficiency change and other sources. Nonetheless it does have a technique, dubbed "window analysis" by Charnes, Clark, Cooper, and Golany (1985), Charnes, Cooper, Dieck-Assad, Golany, and Wiggins (1985), and Charnes, Cooper, Divine, Klopp, and Stutz (1992), for analyzing efficiency change over time in a panel data context. The technique could be used in an econometric approach as well, for it amounts to nothing more than partial pooling of a panel data set.

Suppose we have panel data on input quantities and output quantities only, and we wish to solve the output-oriented envelopment problem (1.25) in Section 1.5.1. If the panel is large enough it is possible to break it up into a series of shorter overlapping panels, each having I producers and S time periods. Thus the first pooled panel would consist of I producers and time periods $\{1, \ldots, S\}$, the second would consist of I producers and time periods $\{2, \ldots, S + 1\}$, and so on until the final pooled panel would consist of I producers and time periods $\{T - S + 1, \ldots, T\}$. The widths of the "windows" are equal and arbitrarily chosen. The procedure is to solve the envelopment problem (1.25) on each pooled panel. The result is that each producer gets one efficiency score in the first time period, with a comparison set consisting of all producers in time periods $\{1, \ldots, S\}$; two efficiency scores in the second time period, with the first comparison set consisting of all producers in time periods $\{1, \ldots, S\}$ and the second comparison set consisting of all producers in time periods $\{2, \ldots, S + 1\}$; three efficiency scores in the third time period, with comparison sets consisting of all producers in time periods $\{1, \ldots, S\}, \{2, \ldots, S+1\}$, and $\{3, \ldots, S + 2\}$; and so on.

One purpose of window analysis is to relieve degrees-of-freedom pressure when $(m + n)$ is large relative to I. As such, it provides a compromise between the two extreme options of running DEA T times on T small cross sections and running DEA once on one large $I * T$ pooled panel. The cost of relieving degrees-of-freedom pressure is computational: many more linear programming problems must be solved. A second purpose of window analysis is to reveal trends in efficiency scores. In fact, each of the three procedures generates information on the trend in efficiency for each producer, although it must be kept in mind that the comparison sets are different in the three procedures. As Charnes, Clark, Cooper, and Golany (1985, p. 106) note, another virtue of window analysis is that it "... can also be used to examine stability and other properties of the efficiency evaluations across as well as within windows." They also use it as an outlier diagnostic.

1.7.3 The sequential FDH approach

The FDH approach to productivity change and efficiency change is very different from the econometric and DEA window analysis approaches. Although productivity change is not the main focus of FDH, it can be inferred from information on efficiency change and technical change that is revealed by FDH. The technique was developed by Tulkens (1986), and goes by the name "sequential" FDH. Although it has been used in a single-time-series context [Thiry and Tulkens (1992), Tulkens, Thiry, and Palm (1988)], I discuss one of its panel data variants.

Suppose input quantity data and output quantity data for I producers are observed over T time periods. Sequential FDH proceeds as follows. First, perform FDH on the first cross section, construct a period 1 production frontier, and calculate the efficiency of each producer in time period 1 relative to the period 1 production frontier. Next, perform FDH on the second cross section, construct a period 2 production frontier, and calculate the efficiency of each producer in time period 2 relative to the outer boundary of the period 1 and period 2 production frontiers. Depending on how a producer's inputs and outputs change over time, and depending on how the frontier grows over time, the efficiency of a producer can improve or deteriorate over time. Outward shifts in the production frontier that do not dominate previously efficient observations are interpreted as new evidence on the structure of unchanged production possibilities. Outward shifts in the production frontier that do dominate previously efficient observations are interpreted as local technical progress. The production frontier is constructed sequentially, and it can never shift inward, so technical regress cannot occur.

Sequential FDH is illustrated in Figure 1.10. In time period 1 producers A, B, and C are efficient, and the period 1 frontier is a step function through these three points. In time period 2 producers D, E, and F are efficient, and the period 2 sequential frontier is a new step function through points D, A, E, B, C, and F. In time

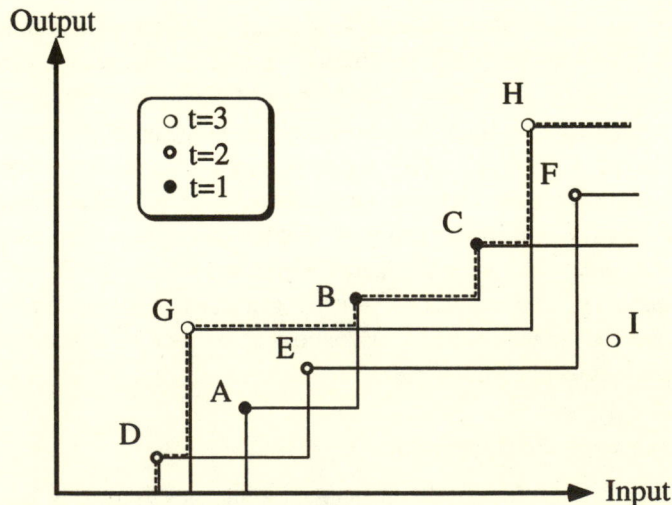

Fig. 1.10   Sequential FDH

period 3 producers G and H are efficient and producer I is inefficient, and the period 3 sequential frontier is a new step function through points D, G, B, C, and H. No technical progress has occurred between periods 1 and 2, since no previously efficient producers became dominated. New efficient observations D, E, and F merely add new information on the structure of the production frontier. Technical progress has occurred between periods 2 and 3, however, since previously efficient producers A and E became dominated by new producer G, and previously efficient producer F became dominated by new producer H. Technical progress is measured in the same way as efficiency is, either in terms of output augmentation or in terms of input reduction, relative to dominated (in the case of technical progress) or dominating (in the case of efficiency) producers. Of course producers D, E, and F can be producers A, B, and C observed in the second time period, and producers G, H, and I can be producers A, B, and C observed in the third time period, and so on, as would be the case in a typical panel data set.

The econometric approach uses the entire panel once. The DEA window analysis approach uses several overlapping subpanels, and so discards old data as it adds new data. Sequential FDH uses single cross sections in order of their temporal appearance, but creates new production frontiers each time period on the basis of new and previously accumulated data. It measures efficiency relative to current and past production possibilities only. It allows technical progress to be local, occurring at a certain time period or at a specific input mix or over a specific output size class, for example. This localized nature of technical progress is a nice feature not shared by most econometric models of technical change. On the other hand, the distinction between efficient new producers that do not embody technical progress and those who do seems a bit arbitrary.

1.7.4 The intertemporal goal programming approach

This approach has been developed by Nishimizu and Page (1982) in a single-output production frontier context, but it can easily be modified to a multiple-output distance frontier context or, data permitting, to a multiple-output cost frontier context

Suppose we have an $I * T$ panel of observations on quantities of outputs and inputs. If production technology has translog structure, then the goal programming problem (1.30) in Section 1.6.1 becomes

$$\min \sum_{i=1}^{I} \sum_{t=1}^{T} [(\alpha_0 + \alpha_t t + 0.5\alpha_{tt} t^2) + \sum_j (\alpha_j + \alpha_{jt} t) \ln x_{jit}$$

$$+ 0.5 \sum_j \sum_k \alpha_{jk} \ln x_{jit} \ln x_{kit} - \ln y_{it}] \quad (1.43)$$

subject to

$$[(\alpha_0 + \alpha_t t + 0.5\alpha_{tt}t^2) + \sum_j (\alpha_j + \alpha_{jt}t) \ln x_{jit}$$
$$+ 0.5 \sum_j \sum_k \alpha_{jk} \ln x_{jit} \ln x_{kit}] \geqq \ln y_{it} \quad (1.44)$$

and whatever other restrictions are deemed appropriate, such as monotonicity or concavity or homogeneity.

Problem (1.43) may be described as one of fitting a translog production frontier closely above a panel data set. An output-oriented Debreu-Farrell technical efficiency measure can be calculated for each producer in each time period, and the trend in efficiency can be calculated for each producer. In addition, the production frontier shifts over time, with the rate of technical change being given by the expression $[\alpha_t + \alpha_{tt}t + \sum_j \alpha_{jt} \ln x_{jit}]$.

Like the econometric approach, this approach uses the entire panel one time, parameterizes production possibilities, and allows for shifts in technology by adding time as an additional variable. Like the DEA and FDH approaches, it is nonstochastic and can be made stochastic using techniques sketched in Sections 1.5.3 and 1.6.1.

1.7.5   The nonparametric Malmquist approach

This approach to the decomposition of productivity change into technical change and efficiency change uses linear programming techniques to decompose what Caves, Christensen and Diewert (1982) refer to as a Malmquist (1953) productivity index. The technique has been developed by Färe and Grosskopf and their associates as a way of decomposing productivity growth, and has been used to analyze productivity growth in Swedish hospitals [Färe, Grosskopf, Lindgren, and Roos (1989)], in Swedish pharmacies [Färe, Grosskopf, Lindgren, and Roos (1992)], in U.S. electric utilities [Färe, Grosskopf, Yaisawarng, Li, and Wang (1990) and Klein, Schmidt, and Yaisawarng (1991)], and in Norwegian banks [Berg, Førsund, and Jansen (1991b)]. The data requirement is a panel of output quantities and input quantities. The basic idea is illustrated in Figure 1.11. Technical progress has occurred between time periods t and $t + 1$, since $P^t(x) \subseteq P^{t+1}(x)$, although the improvement in technology has not been output-neutral. The technical efficiency of producer A appears to have improved from time period t to time period $t + 1$ as well. Note that $y^{A,t} \in P^t(x)$ and $y^{A,t+1} \in P^{t+1}(x)$, but that $y^{A,t+1} \notin P^t(x)$. Note also that neither production frontier can be constructed without a cross section, so that implementation of the model requires panel data. Note finally that the fact that the input vector is the same in both time periods is for expository convenience only.

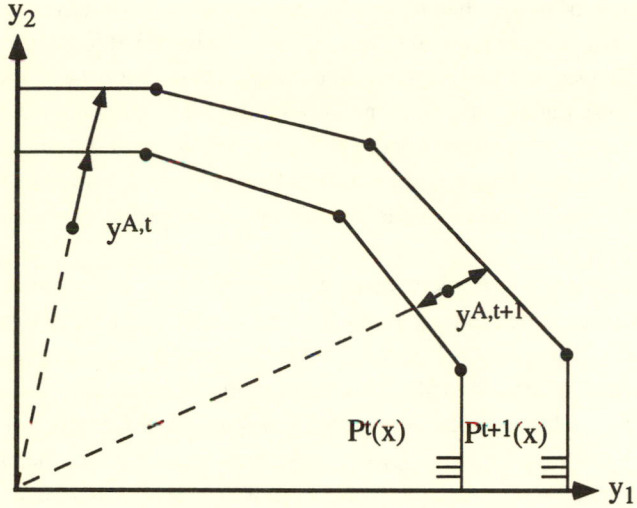

Fig. 1.11   The nonparametric Malmquist approach

A Malmquist output-oriented productivity index is defined as

$$M_0^{t+1}(x^{t+1}, y^{t+1}, x^t, y^t) = \left[\frac{D_0^t(x^{t+1}, y^{t+1})}{D_0^t(x^t, y^t)} \frac{D_0^{t+1}(x^{t+1}, y^{t+1})}{D_0^{t+1}(x^t, y^t)}\right]^{1/2} \quad (1.45)$$

This productivity index is the geometric mean of a pair of ratios of output distance functions. The first ratio compares the performance of data from periods t and $t + 1$ relative to production possibilities existing in period t, and the second compares the performance of the same data relative to production possibilities existing in period $t + 1$.

The right side of (1.44) can be rewritten as

$$M_0^{t+1}(x^{t+1}, y^{t+1}, x^t, y^t) = \frac{D_0^{t+1}(x^{t+1}, y^{t+1})}{D_0^t(x^t, y^t)}$$

$$\left[\frac{D_0^t(x^{t+1}, y^{t+1})}{D_0^{t+1}(x^{t+1}, y^{t+1})} \frac{D_0^t(x^t, y^t)}{D_0^{t+1}(x^t, y^t)}\right]^{1/2} \quad (1.46)$$

Expression (1.45) decomposes the Malmquist output-oriented productivity index into the product of two terms. The first term is the ratio of two output distance functions involving data and technology from periods $t + 1$ and t, respectively. Recall from equation (1.15) in Section 1.2 that these output distance functions are reciprocals of Debreu-Farrell output-oriented technical efficiency measures. Consequently the first term has a value of unity when there is no change in technical efficiency, and has a value greater than or less than unity according as technical efficiency has improved or declined. The second term remains a geometric mean, but now of the shift in the production frontier along two rays, one through the first-period data (x^t, y^t) and the other through the second-period data (x^{t+1}, y^{t+1}). The second term has a value of unity when technical change has not occurred along either ray, and has a value greater than or less than unity according as technical change has on balance been progressive or regressive.

All that remains is to implement the procedure. This is accomplished by solving four sets of linear programming problems. All are of the general form given by equation (1.25) in Section 1.5.1. [Recall that technology described in equation (1.25) satisfies constant returns to scale. This assumption is apparently indispensable in the Malmquist problem. The assumption is discussed in Chapter 4.] Calculation of $D_0^t(x^t, y^t)$ and $D_0^{t+1}(x^{t+1}, y^{t+1})$ is straightforward, involving the calculation of technical efficiency scores for each producer in a time period in comparison with all producers in the same time period. Calculation of $D_0^t(x^{t+1}, y^{t+1})$ and $D_0^{t+1}(x^t, y^t)$ is a bit unconventional, since it involves calculation of technical efficiency scores for each producer in a time period in comparison with all producers, including itself, in the other time period. Once these four linear programming problems are solved, efficiency scores are inverted and substituted into equation (1.45) to obtain a decomposition of productivity change into efficiency change and technical change, for each producer. Then the entire procedure is repeated for the same set of producers in time periods $t + 1$ and $t + 2$, and so on through time periods $T - 1$ and T.

The procedure is similar to DEA window analysis in three respects: it uses linear programming, it uses less than the full panel at each stage in the process, and it discards old data and old information concerning production possibilities as it adds new data and looks for new information about production possibilities. It is also similar to DEA and DEA window analysis, as I have described them, in that it ignores slacks, and so is capable of a misallocation of productivity change to technical change and efficiency change. At the same time, it has a close relationship with both the econometric approach and the goal programming approach, and thus with the index number approach to the measurement of productivity growth. I do not intend to explore these relationships here. I do note, however, that the econometric approach and the goal programming approach can be based on translog specifications of technology. I also note that Caves, Christensen and Diewert (1982, p. 1401, theorem 2) have shown that if the distance functions in equation (1.44) above are translog, then under certain conditions the Malmquist output-oriented productivity index coincides with the widely used Törnqvist (1936) output index. This establishes a link between the superlative index number approach to productivity growth measurement and what I have called the nonparametric Malmquist approach. Whereas the superlative index number approach requires quantity and price data, but no information on the structure of production technology, the Malmquist approach requires only quantity data but requires information on the structure of technology. Moreover, if panel data are available, the Malmquist approach can decompose productivity change into efficiency change and technical change.

1.8. "Explaining" efficiency scores

In Section 1.1 I suggested two reasons for measuring productive efficiency. Efficiency scores are performance indicators, like won-lost percentages, and so they are of considerable interest in their own right. However there remains an interest in explaining the distribution of efficiency scores, and so the scores make attractive dependent variables in a second-stage regression analysis. Results of this second-stage analysis can help guide public policy [Caves and Barton (1990)], assist managerial decision making [Sexton, Sleeper, and Taggart (1991)], and even help settle sports arguments [Porter and Scully (1982)].

The two-stage procedure works as follows. In the first stage, use any of the techniques mentioned above. Employ data on inputs and outputs to generate a vector of efficiency scores. In the second stage, regress the efficiency scores against a set of explanatory variables. Then use the results of the second-stage analysis to guide public policy or managerial decision making. The two-stage procedure has been around for a long time, at least since Timmer (1971) used it in an attempt to explain interstate variation in technical efficiency in U.S. agriculture. The procedure is by now common practice and has been put to particularly good use when sufficiently rich data have been available. To cite but one example, variation in agricultural performance, at the farm level, has been associated with such policy-sensitive variables as education, tenure status, off-farm earnings, and timely availability of credit to permit on-time planting and fertilizing [see, for example, Ali and Flinn (1989) and Kalirajan (1990)].

Three cautionary notes are in order, however. First, and perhaps least important, efficiency scores are bounded, either by zero and one or below by one. Consequently they must be transformed prior to use as a dependent variable in the second stage [as in Kalirajan and Shand (1988)], or appropriate limited dependent variable regression techniques must be employed [as in Goudriaan and de Groot (1991b)]. Second, it is worth thinking hard about what variables are inputs and outputs that belong in the first stage, and what variables are explanatory variables that belong in the second stage. This must be done on a case-by-case basis, of course. The only general guideline I have to offer is that variables under the control of the decision maker during the time period under consideration belong in the first stage. Variables over which the decision maker has no control during the time period under consideration belong in the second stage. Candidates for second-stage variables include quasi-fixed variables, site-specific characteristics, socioeconomic and demographic characteristics, the weather, and so on.

The third cautionary note concerns the nature of the production paradigm underlying the two-stage model. In this formulation, explanatory variables influence the efficiency with which inputs generate outputs; they do not influence the transformation process itself. The note is easily illustrated using a simple stochastic production frontier model in the first stage; the principle carries over to all types of first-stage models. Let the first-stage production relationship be characterized by

$$y_i = f(x_i; \beta) \exp\{v_i + u_i\} \qquad i = 1, \ldots, I \qquad (1.47)$$

which is identical to (1.19). Next let the second-stage explanatory relationship be expressed as

$$\exp\{u_i\} = g(z_i; \gamma) \exp\{e_i\} \qquad i = 1, \ldots, I \qquad (1.48)$$

where $\exp\{u_i\} = \text{TE}_i$ from equation (1.20) is to be explained with a vector of variables z_i, and $e_i \sim N(0, \sigma_e^2)$ captures statistical noise. This is a sensible formulation when z_i and x_i are uncorrelated. However when z_i and x_i are correlated, estimates of β are biased, and presumably so too are the estimates of TE_i that are to be explained in the second stage. This problem has led Deprins (1989) and others to propose a one-stage model of the form

$$y_i = h(x_i, z_i; \delta) \exp\{v_i + u_i\} \qquad i = 1, \ldots, I \qquad (1.49)$$

in which z_i influences y_i directly, rather than indirectly through u_i. This does not resolve the problem of correlation between z_i and x_i, however; it simply replaces an omitted variables problem with a multicollinearity problem. The important point is that the paradigm is different. In the one-stage model efficiency is measured while controlling for the influence of exogenous variables, whereas in the two-stage model variation in efficiency is attributed to variation in the exogenous variables.

The principles involved in the two-stage versus one-stage formulation apply equally well to noneconometric efficiency measurement models; on collinearity in DEA models, see Olesen and Petersen (1991). The single-stage DEA model is perhaps most clearly described in Adolphson, Cornia, and Walters (1990), and Ray (1988) offers a thoughtful treatment of the two-stage DEA model. Empirical applications of each approach are numerous. An interesting comparison of the two-step and one-step approaches by McCarty and Yaisawarng (1992) shows little difference between the two approaches in the overall effect of student socioeconomic status on education performance of school districts.

1.9 Concluding remarks

Even a cursory reading of business publications around the world suffices to convince one that productive inefficiency is a widespread problem. That being the case, it is incumbent upon the economics and management science professions to develop an apparatus for characterizing, quantifying, and explaining productive (in)efficiency. In this chapter I have endeavored to capture the essence of the literature that has developed over the past three decades. The literature appears to be growing exponentially and is surveyed more completely in the next three chapters.

REFERENCES

Abramovitz, M. (1956), "Resource and Output Trends in the United States Since 1870," National Bureau of Economic Research Occasional Paper 52.

Adolphson, D. L., G. C. Cornia, and L. C. Walters (1990), "A Unified Framework for Classifying DEA Models," in H. E. Bradley, ed., *Operational Research '90*. New York: Pergammon Press.

Afriat, S. N. (1972), "Efficiency Estimation of Production Functions," *International Economic Review* 13(3) (October): 568–598.

Ahn, T., V. Arnold, A. Charnes, and W. W. Cooper (1989), "DEA and Ratio Efficiency Analyses for Public Institutions of Higher Learning in Texas," in J. L. Chan, ed., *Research in Governmental and Nonprofit Accounting,* Vol. 5. Greenwich, Conn.: JAI Press.

Ahn, T., A. Charnes, and W. W. Cooper (1988), "Some Statistical and DEA Evaluations of Relative Efficiencies of Public and Private Institutions of Higher Learning," *Socio-Economic Planning Sciences* 22(6): 259–269.

Aigner, D. J., and S-F Chu (1968), "On Estimating the Industry Production Function," *American Economic Review* 58(4) (September): 826–839.

Aigner, D. J., T. Amemiya, and D. J. Poirier (1976), "On the Estimation of Production Frontiers: Maximum Likelihood Estimation of the Parameters of a Discontinuous Density Function," *International Economic Review* 17(2) (June): 377–396.

Aigner, D. J., C. A. K. Lovell, and P. Schmidt (1977), "Formulation and Estimation of Stochastic Frontier Production Function Models," *Journal of Econometrics* 6(1) (July): 21–37.

Albriktsen, R. O., and F. R. Førsund (1990), "A Productivity Study of the Norwegian Building Industry," *Journal of Productivity Analysis* 2(1) (December): 53–66.

Alchian, A. A. (1965), "Some Economics of Property Rights," *Il Politico* 30(4) (December): 816–829.

Alchian, A. A., and R. A. Kessel (1962), "Competition, Monopoly, and the Pursuit of Money," in *Aspects of Labor Economics*. Princeton, N.J.: Princeton University Press for the National Bureau of Economic Research, pp. 157–175.

Ali, A. I. (1989), "IDEAS: Integrated Data Envelopment Analysis System," Technical Report, Department of General Business and Finance, University of Massachusetts, Amherst, Mass.

Ali, A. I. (1991), "Data Envelopment Analysis: A Unifying Perspective," Working Paper, School of Management, University of Massachusetts, Amherst, Mass.

Ali, A. I., C. S. Lerme, and R. A. Nakosteen (1992), "Assessment of Intergovernmental Revenue Transfers," Working Paper, School of Management, University of Massachusetts, Amherst, Mass.

Ali, M., and J. C. Flinn (1989), "Profit Efficiency Among Basmati Rice Producers in Pakistan Punjab," *American Journal of Agricultural Economics,* 71(2) (May): 303–310.

Aoki, M. (1984), *The Co-operative Game Theory of the Firm*. New York: Oxford University Press.

Atkinson, S. E., and R. Halvorsen (1980), "A Test of Relative and Absolute Price Efficiency in Regulated Utilities," *Review of Economics and Statistics* 62(1) (February): 81–88.

Atkinson, S. E., and R. Halvorsen (1984), "Parametric Efficiency Tests, Economies of Scale, and Input Demand in U.S. Electric Power Generation," *International Economic Review* 25(3) (October): 647–662.

Atkinson, S. E., and R. Halvorsen (1986), "The Relative Efficiency of Public and Private Firms in a Regulated Environment: The Case of U.S. Electric Utilities," *Journal of Public Economics* 29(3) (April): 281–294.

Averch, H., and L. L. Johnson (1962), "Behavior of the Firm Under Regulatory Constraint," *American Economic Review* 52(5) (December): 1052–1069.

Banker, R. D. (1989), "Stochastic Data Envelopment Analysis," Working Paper, Carnegie Mellon University, Pittsburgh, Pa.

Banker, R. D., A. Charnes, and W. W. Cooper (1984), "Some Models for Estimating Technical and Scale Inefficiencies in Data Envelopment Analysis," *Management Science* 30(9) (September): 1078–1092.

Banker, R. D., and R. C. Morey (1986), "Efficiency Analysis for Exogenously Fixed Inputs and Outputs," *Operations Research* 34(4) (July–August): 513–521.

Banker, R. D., A. Charnes, W. W. Cooper, J. Swarts, and D. A. Thomas (1989), "An Introduction to Data Envelopment Analysis with Some of its Models and Their Uses," in J. L. Chan, ed., *Research in Governmental and Nonprofit Accounting,* vol. 5. Greenwich, Conn.: JAI Press.

Banker, R. D., S. Das, and S. M. Datar (1989), "Analysis of Cost Variances for Management Control in Hospitals," in J. L. Chan, ed., *Research in Governmental and Nonprofit Accounting,* vol. 5. Greenwich, Conn.: JAI Press.

Banker, R. D., S. M. Datar, and C. F. Kemerer (1991), "A Model to Evaluate Variables Impacting the Productivity of Software Maintenance Projects," *Management Science* 37(1) (January): 1–18.

Banker, R. D., and R. M. Thrall (1991), "Estimation of Returns to Scale Using Data Envelopment Analysis," *European Journal of Operational Research,* to appear.

Battese, G. E., and T. J. Coelli (1988), "Prediction of Firm-Level Technical Efficiencies with a Generalized Frontier Production Function and Panel Data," *Journal of Econometrics* 38:387–399.

Battese, G. E., and T. J. Coelli (1992), "Frontier Production Functions, Technical Efficiency and Panel Data: With Application to Paddy Farmers in India," *Journal of Productivity Analysis* 3(1/2) (June): 153–169.

Battese, G. E., T. J. Coelli, and T. C. Colby (1989), "Estimation of Frontier Production Functions and the Efficiencies of Indian Farms Using Panel Data from ICRISAT's Village Level Studies," *Journal of Quantitative Economics* 5(2) (July): 327-348.

Battese, G. E., and G. S. Corra (1977), "Estimation of a Production Frontier Model: With Application to the Pastoral Zone of Eastern Australia," *Australian Journal of Agricultural Economics* 21(3) (December): 169-179.

Bauer, P. W. (1990a), "Decomposing TFP Growth in the Presence of Cost Inefficiency, Nonconstant Returns to Scale, and Technological Progress," *Journal of Productivity Analysis* 1(4) (June): 287–300.

Bauer, P. W. (1990b), "Recent Developments in the Econometric Estimation of Frontiers," *Journal of Econometrics* 46(1/2) (October/November): 39–56.

Berg, S. A., F. R. Førsund, and E. S. Jansen (1991a), "Technical Efficiency of Norwegian Banks: The Non-Parametric Approach to Efficiency Measurement," *Journal of Productivity Analysis,* 2(2) (July): 127–142.

Berg, S. A., F. R. Førsund, and E. S. Jansen (1991b), "Malmquist Indices of Productivity Growth During the Deregulation of Norwegian Banking 1980–1989," Working Paper,

Research Department, Bank of Norway, Oslo; to appear in *Scandinavian Journal of Economics*.

Bergsman, J. (1974), "Commercial Policy, Allocative Efficiency, and 'X-efficiency'," *Quarterly Journal of Economics* 88(3) (August): 409–433.

Bernstein, M. A., S. L. Feldman, and A. P. Schinnar (1990), "Impact of Pollution Controls on the Productivity of Coal-Fired Power Plants," *Energy Economics* 12(1) (January): 11–17.

Bessent, A., W. Bessent, J. Kennington, and B. Reagan (1982), "An Application of Mathematical Programming to Assess Productivity in the Houston Independent School District," *Management Science* 28(12) (December): 1355–1367.

Binswanger, H. P. (1974), "The Measurement of Technical Change Biases with Many Factors of Production," *American Economic Review* 64(6) (December): 964–976.

Bjurek, H., L. Hjalmarsson and F. R. Førsund (1990), "Deterministic Parametric and Nonparametric Estimation of Efficiency in Service Production: A Comparison," *Journal of Econometrics*. 46(1/2)(October/November): 213–227.

Bloch, H. (1974), "Prices, Costs, and Profits in Canadian Manufacturing: The Influence of Tariffs and Concentration," *Canadian Journal of Economics* 7(4) (November): 594–610.

Boehm, T. P., and R. A. Hofler (1987), "A Frontier Approach to Measuring the Effect of Market Discrimination: A Housing Illustration," *Southern Economic Journal* 54(2) (October): 301–315.

Bol, G. (1986), "On Technical Efficiency Measures: A Remark," *Journal of Economic Theory* 38(2) (April): 380–385.

Bol, G. (1988), "On the Definition of Efficiency Measures: A Note," in W. Eichhorn, ed., *Measurement in Economics: Theory and Applications of Economic Indices*. Heidelberg: Physica-Verlag.

Borcherding, T. E., W. W. Pommerhene, and F. Schneider (1982), "Comparing the Efficiency of Private and Public Production: The Evidence from Five Countries," *Zeitschrift für Nationalökonomie* 42 (Suppl. 2): 127–156.

Bowlin, W. F. (1987), "Evaluating the Efficiency of U.S. Air Force Real-Property Maintenance Activities," *Journal of the Operational Research Society* 38(2): 127–135.

Boyd, G., and R. Färe (1984), "Measuring the Efficiency of Decision Making Units: A Comment," *European Journal of Operational Research* 15 (March): 331–332.

Brown, M., and J. Popkin (1962), "A Measure of Technological Change and Returns to Scale," *Review of Economics and Statistics* 44(4) (November): 402–411.

Burgat, P., and C. Jeanrenaud (1990), "Mesure de l'Efficacite Productive et de l'Efficacite-cout: Cas des Dechets Menagers en Suisse," Working Paper No. 9002, Institut de Recherches Economiques et Regionales, Université de Neuchatel, Neuchatel, Switzerland.

Byrnes, P., and V. Valdmanis (1990), "DEA and Hospital Management: Analyzing Technical and Allocative Efficiency," Working Paper, School of Public Policy and Management, The Ohio State University, Columbus, Ohio; in A. Charnes, W. W. Cooper, A. Y. Lewin, and L. M. Seiford, eds., *Data Envelopment Analysis: Theory, Method and Process*. IC^2 Management and Management Science Series. New York: Quorum Books (forthcoming).

Cameron, B. (1989), "Higher Education Efficiency Measurement Using DEA," Working Paper, Darling Downs Institute of Advanced Education, Toowoomba, Australia.

Carlsson, B. (1972), "The Measurement of Efficiency in Production: An Application to Swedish Manufacturing Industries, 1968," *Swedish Journal of Economics* 74(4) (December): 468–485.

Cavalluzzo, L., and C. Yanofsky (1991), "The Effect of Subsidies on Quality and Production Efficiency of Daycare Centers," working paper, Department of Economics, Union College, Schenectady, N.Y.

Caves, D. W., L. R. Christensen, and W. E. Diewert (1982), "The Economic Theory of Index Numbers and the Measurement of Input, Output and Productivity," *Econometrica* 50(6) (November): 1393–1414.

Caves, R. E., and D. R. Barton (1990), *Efficiency in U.S. Manufacturing Industries*. Cambridge, Mass.: The MIT Press.

Cavin, E. S., and F. P. Stafford (1985), "Efficient Provision of Employment Service Outputs: A Production Function Analysis," *Journal of Human Resources* 20: 484–503.

Chang, K-P, and Y-Y Guh (1991), "Linear Production Functions and the Data Envelopment Analysis," *European Journal of Operational Research,* 52(2) (May): 215–223.

Chang, K-P, and P-H Kao (1992), "The Relative Efficiency of Public versus Private Municipal Bus Firms: An Application of Data Envelopment Analysis," *Journal of Productivity Analysis* 3(1/2) (June): 67–84.

Charnes, A., W. W. Cooper, and G. H. Symonds (1958), "Cost Horizons and Certainty Equivalents: An Approach to Stochastic Programming of Heating Oil," *Management Science* 4(3) (April): 235–263.

Charnes, A., and W. W. Cooper (1959), "Chance-Constrained Programming," *Management Science* 5: 73–79.

Charnes, A., and W. W. Cooper (1962), "Chance Constraints and Normal Deviates," *Journal of the American Statistical Association* 57: 134–148.

Charnes, A., and W. W. Cooper (1963), "Deterministic Equivalents for Optimizing and Satisficing Under Chance Constraints," *Operations Research* 11(1): 18–39.

Charnes, A., W. W. Cooper, and E. Rhodes (1978), "Measuring the Efficiency of Decision-Making Units," *European Journal of Operational Research* 2(6): 429–444.

Charnes, A., W. W. Cooper, and E. Rhodes (1981), "Evaluating Program and Managerial Efficiency: An Application of Data Envelopment Analysis to Program Follow Through," *Management Science* 27(6) (June): 668–697.

Charnes, A., C. T. Clark, W. W. Cooper, and B. Golany (1985), "A Developmental Study of Data Envelopment Analysis in Measuring the Efficiency of Maintenance Units in the U.S. Air Forces," *Annals of Operations Research* 2: 95–112.

Charnes, A., W. W. Cooper, M. Dieck-Assad, B. Golany, and D. E. Wiggins (1985), "Efficiency Analysis of Medical Care Resources in the U.S. Army Health Services Command," Research Report CCS 516, Center for Cybernetic Studies, University of Texas, Austin, Tex.

Charnes, A., W. W. Cooper, D. Divine, G. A. Klopp, and J. Stutz (1985), "An Application of Data Envelopment Analysis to U.S. Army Recruitment Districts," Research Report CCS 436, Center for Cybernetic Studies, University of Texas, Austin, Tex.

Charnes, A., W. W. Cooper, B. Golany, L. Seiford and J. Stutz (1985), "Foundations of Data Envelopment Analysis for Pareto-Koopmans Efficient Empirical Production Functions," *Journal of Econometrics* 30(1/2) (October/November): 91–107.

Charnes, A., W. W. Cooper, J. Rousseau and J. Semple (1987), "Data Envelopment Analysis and Axiomatic Notions of Efficiency and Reference Sets," Research Report CCS 558, Center For Cybernetic Studies, University of Texas, Austin, Tex.

Charnes, A., W. W. Cooper, and T. Sueyoshi (1988), "A Goal Programming/ Constrained Regression Review of the Bell System Breakup," *Management Science* 34(1) (January): 1–26.

Charnes, A., W. W. Cooper, and S. Li (1989), "Using Data Envelopment Analysis to Evaluate Efficiency in the Economic Performance of Chinese Cities," *Socio-Economic Planning Sciences* 23(6): 325–344.

Christensen, L. R., and W. H. Greene (1976), "Economies of Scale in U.S. Electric Power Generation," *Journal of Political Economy* 84(4) (Part 1): 655–676.

Conrad, K., and C. J. Morrison (1989), "The Impact of Pollution Abatement Investment on Productivity Change: An Empirical Comparison of the U.S., Germany, and Canada," *Southern Economic Journal* 55(3) (January): 684–698.

Cook, W. D., A. Kazakov, and Y. Roll (1989), "On the Measurement and Monitoring of Relative Efficiency of Highway Maintenance Patrols," in A. Charnes, W. W. Cooper, A. Y. Lewin and L. M. Seiford, eds., *Data Envelopment Analysis: Theory, Method and Process*. IC^2 Management and Management Science Series. New York: Quorum Books (forthcoming).

Cornwell, C., P. Schmidt, and R. C. Sickles (1990), "Production Frontiers with Cross-Sectional and Time-Series Variation in Efficiency Levels," *Journal of Econometrics* 46(1/2) (October/November): 185–200.

Côté, D., and S. Desrochers (1990), "L'Efficacite des Organisations Participatives: Propositions Theoriques et Etudes Empiriques," *Coopératives et Developpement* 22(1) (November).

Cubbin, J., S. Domberger, and S. Meadowcroft (1987), "Competitive Tendering and Refuse Collection: Identifying the Sources of Efficiency Gains," *Fiscal Studies* 8(3) (August): 49–58.

David, P. A., and Th. van de Klundert (1965), "Biased Efficiency Growth and Capital-Labor Substitution in the U.S., 1899–1969," *American Economic Review* 55(3) (June): 357–394.

De Alessi, L. (1980), "The Economics of Property Rights: A Review of the Evidence," *Research in Law and Economics* 2: 1–47.

De Borger, B., K. Kerstens, W. Moesen, and J. Vanneste (1991), "Explaining Differences in Productive Efficiency: An Application to Belgian Municipalities," working paper, Center For Economic Studies, Katholieke Universiteit Leuven, Leuven, Belgium.

Debreu, G. (1951), "The Coefficient of Resource Utilization," *Econometrica* 19(3) (July): 273–292.

Deller, S. C., and C. H. Nelson (1991), "Measuring the Economic Efficiency of Producing Rural Road Services," *American Journal of Agricultural Economics* 73(1) (February).

Denny, M., M. Fuss, and L. Waverman (1981), "The Measurement and Interpretation of Total Factor Productivity in Regulated Industries, with an Application to Canadian Telecommunications," in T. G. Cowing and R. E. Stevenson, eds., *Productivity Measurement in Regulated Industries*. New York: Academic Press, pp. 179–218.

Deprins, D. (1983), "Estimation de Frontiere et Mesure d'Efficacite: Approches Descriptive et Econometrique," *Revue Belge de Statistique, D'Informatique et de Recherche Operationelle* 23(1) (March): 19–62.

Deprins, D. (1989), *Estimation de Frontieres de Production et Mesures de l'Efficacite Technique*. Université Catholique de Louvain, Faculte des Sciences Economiques, Sociales et Politiques, Nouvelle Serie No. 186. Louvain-la-Neuve, Belgium: CIACO.

Deprins, D., and L. Simar (1983), "On Farrell Measures of Technical Efficiency," *Recherches Economiques de Louvain* 49(2) (June): 123–137.

Deprins, D., L. Simar, and H. Tulkens (1984), "Measuring Labor-Efficiency in Post Offices," in M. Marchand, P. Pestieau, and H. Tulkens, eds., *The Performance of Public Enterprises: Concepts and Measurement*. Amsterdam: North-Holland.

Desai, A., and A. P. Schinnar (1987), "Stochastic Data Envelopment Analysis," Working Paper WPS 87-23, College of Business, Ohio State University, Columbus, Ohio.

Desai, A., and A. P. Schinnar (1990), "Technical Issues in Measuring Scholastic Improvement due to Compensatory Education Programs," *Socio-Economic Planning Sciences* 24(2): 143–153.

Dusansky, R., and P. W. Wilson (1989), "On the Relative Efficiency of Alternative Modes of Producing Public Sector Output: The Case of the Developmentally Disabled," Working Paper, Department of Economics, University of Texas, Austin, Tex.; forthcoming in *European Journal of Operational Research.*

Dusansky, R., and P. W. Wilson (1991), "Technical Efficiency in the Decentralized Care of the Developmentally Disabled," Working Paper, Department of Economics, University of Texas, Austin, Tex.

Dyson, R. G., and E. Thanassoulis (1988), "Reducing Weight Flexibility in Data Envelopment Analysis," *Journal of the Operational Research Society* 39(6): 563–576.

Eakin, B. K., and T. J. Kniesner (1988), "Estimating a Non-minimum Cost Function for Hospitals," *Southern Economic Journal* 54(3) (January): 583–597.

Färe, R., and C. A. K. Lovell (1978), "Measuring the Technical Efficiency of Production," *Journal of Economic Theory* 19(1) (October): 150–162.

Färe, R., and J. Logan (1983), "The Rate-of-Return Regulated Firm: Cost and Production Duality," *Bell Journal of Economics* 14(2) (Autumn): 405–414.

Färe, R., S. Grosskopf, and C. A. K. Lovell (1985), *The Measurement of Efficiency of Production.* Boston: Kluwer-Nijhoff Publishing.

Färe, R., and W. Hunsaker (1986), "Notions of Efficiency and their Reference Sets," *Management Science* 32(2) (February): 237–243.

Färe, R., S. Grosskopf, and C. Pasurka (1986), "Effects on Relative Efficiency in Electric Power Generation due to Environmental Controls," *Resources and Energy* 8(2) (June): 167–184.

Färe, R., S. Grosskopf, and C. A. K. Lovell (1987a), "Some Observations on the New DEA," Working Paper 87-4, Department of Economics, University of North Carolina, Chapel Hill, N.C.

Färe, R., S. Grosskopf, and C. A. K. Lovell (1987b), "Nonparametric Disposability Tests," *Zeitschrift für Nationalökonomie* 47(1):77–85.

Färe, R., S. Grosskopf, and W. Weber (1989), "Measuring School District Performance," *Public Finance Quarterly* 17(4) (October): 409–428.

Färe, R., S. Grosskopf, B. Lindgren, and P. Roos (1989), "Productivity Developments in Swedish Hospitals: A Malmquist Output Index Approach," Working Paper, Department of Economics, Southern Illinois University, Carbondale, Ill. in A. Charnes, W.W. Cooper, A. Y. Lewin, and L. M. Seiford, eds., *Data Envelopment Analysis: Theory, Method and Process. IC* [2] Management and Management Science Series. New York: Quorum Books (forthcoming).

Färe, R., and S. Grosskopf (1990), *Cost and Revenue Constrained Production*, Bilkent University Lecture Series. Berlin: Springer-Verlag (forthcoming).

Färe, R., S. Grosskopf, C. A. K. Lovell, and S. Yaisawarng (1990), "Derivation of Virtual Prices for Undesirable Outputs: A Distance Function Approach," Working Paper 90-3, Department of Economics, University of North Carolina, Chapel Hill, N.C. (forthcoming in *Review of Economics and Statistics*).

Färe, R., S. Grosskopf, S. Yaisawarng, S. K. Li, and Z. Wang (1990), "Productivity Growth in Illinois Electric Utilities," *Resources and Energy* 12: 383–398.

Färe, R., S. Grosskopf, B. Lindgren, and P. Roos (1992), "Productivity Changes in Swedish Pharmacies 1980–89: A Nonparametric Malmquist Approach," *Journal of Productivity Analysis* 3(1/2) (June): 85–101.

Farrell, M. J. (1957), "The Measurement of Productive Efficiency," *Journal of the Royal Statistical Society* Series A, General, 120(3): 253–281.

Førsund, F. R., and E. S. Jansen (1977), "On Estimating Average and Best Practice Homothetic Production Functions via Cost Functions," *International Economic Review* 18(2) (June): 463–476.

Førsund, F. R., and L. Hjalmarsson (1979a), "Generalized Farrell Measures of Efficiency: An Application to Milk Processing in Swedish Dairy Plants," *Economic Journal* 89(354) (June): 294–315.

Førsund, F. R., and L. Hjalmarsson (1979b), "Frontier Production Functions and Technical Progress: A Study of General Milk Processing in Swedish Dairy Plants," *Econometrica* 47(4) (July): 883–900.

Førsund, F. R., and L. Hjalmarsson (1987), *Analyses of Industrial Structure: A Putty Clay Approach*. Stockholm: Almqvist and Wiksell International.

Førsund, F. R., and S. A. C. Kittelsen (1992), "Efficiency Analysis of Norwegian District Courts," *Journal of Productivity Analysis* 3(3) (September): 277–306.

Frisch, R. (1965), *Theory of Production*. Chicago: Rand McNally and Company.

Gabrielsen, A. (1975), "On Estimating Efficient Production Functions," Working Paper No. A-35, Chr. Michelsen Institute, Department of Humanities and Social Sciences, Bergen, Norway.

Gathon, H-J, and S. Perelman (1992), "Measuring Technical Efficiency in European Railways: A Panel Data Approach," *Journal of Productivity Analysis* 3(1/2) (June): 135–151.

Gollop, F. M., and M. J. Roberts (1981), "The Sources of Economic Growth in the U.S. Electric Power Industry," in T. G. Cowing and R. E. Stevenson, eds., *Productivity Measurement in Regulated Industries*. New York: Academic Press, pp. 107–143.

Gollop, F. M., and M. J. Roberts (1983), "Environmental Regulations and Productivity Growth: The Case of Fossil-Fueled Electric Power Generation," *Journal of Political Economy* 91(4) (August): 654–674.

Gong, B-H, and R.C. Sickles (1989), "Finite Sample Evidence on the Performance of Stochastic Frontier Models Using Panel Data," *Journal of Productivity Analysis* 1(3) (December): 229–261.

Goudriaan, R., and H. de Groot (1991a), "Internal Regulation in the Public Sector with an Application to American Public Universities," Discussion Paper No. 9013/P, Institute for Economic Research, Erasmus University, Rotterdam, The Netherlands.

Goudriaan, R., and H. de Groot (1991b), "Regulation and the Performance of American Research Universities," Working Paper, Department of Economics, Erasmus University, Rotterdam, The Netherlands.

Grabowski, R., and C. Pasurka (1989a), "The Relative Efficiency of Slave Agriculture: An Application of a Stochastic Production Frontier," *Applied Economics* 21(5) (May): 587–595.

Grabowski, R., and C. Pasurka (1989b), "The Relative Technical Efficiency of Slave and Non-Slave Farms in Southern Agriculture: 1860," *Eastern Economic Journal* 15(3) (July–September): 245–258.

Greene, W. H. (1980), "Maximum Likelihood Estimation of Econometric Frontier Functions," *Journal of Econometrics* 13(1) (May): 27–56.

Grosskopf, S., and V. Valdmanis (1987), "Measuring Hospital Performance: A Non-parametric Approach," *Journal of Health Economics* 6: 89–107.

Hicks, J. R. (1935), "The Theory of Monopoly: A Survey," *Econometrica* 3(1) (January): 1–20.

Hoch, I. (1955), "Estimation of Production Function Parameters and Testing for Efficiency," *Econometrica* 23(3) (July): 325–326.

Hofler, R. A., and S. T. Folland (1991), "The Relative Efficiency of Slave Agriculture: a Comment," *Applied Economics* 23: 861–868.

Hollas, D. R., and S. R. Stansell (1988), "An Examination of the Effect of Ownership Form on Price Efficiency: Proprietary, Cooperative and Municipal Electric Utilities," *Southern Economic Journal* 55(2) (October): 336–350.

Hopper, W. D. (1965), "Allocation Efficiency in a Traditional Indian Agriculture," *Journal of Farm Economics* 47(August): 611–624.

Huang, L. Y-G, and C. P. McLaughlin (1989), "Relative Efficiency in Rural Primary Health Care: An Application of Data Envelopment Analysis," *Health Services Research* 24(2) (June): 143–158.

Hughes, M. D. (1988), "A Stochastic Frontier Cost Function for Residential Child Care Provision," *Journal of Applied Econometrics* 3: 203–214.

Jamar, M. A., and H. Tulkens (1990), "Mesure de l'efficacite de l'activite des tribunaux et evaluation de l'arriere judiciare," Working Paper No. 90/1, CORE, Université Catholique de Louvain, Louvain-la-Neuve, Belgium.

Jenkins, L. (1991), "Using Data Envelopment Analysis to Evaluate the Relative Efficiency of Academic Departments," Working Paper, Department of Engineering Management, Royal Military College, Kingston, Ontario, Canada.

Jesson, D., D. Mayston, and P. Smith (1987), "Performance Assessment in the Education Sector: Educational and Economic Perspectives," *Oxford Review of Education* 13: 249–266.

Johnson, S. C., and K. Lahiri (1992), "A Panel Data Analysis of Productive Efficiency in Freestanding Health Clinics," *Empirical Economics* 17(1): 141–151.

Jondrow, J., C. A. K. Lovell, I. S. Materov, and P. Schmidt (1982), "On the Estimation of Technical Inefficiency in the Stochastic Frontier Production Function Model," *Journal of Econometrics* 19(2/3) (August): 233–238.

Kalirajan, K. P. (1990), "On Measuring Economic Efficiency," *Journal of Applied Econometrics* 5: 75–85.

Kalirajan, K. P., and R. T. Shand (1988), "Testing Causality Between Technical and Allocative Efficiencies," Working Paper No. 88/6, Research School of Pacific Studies," Australian National University, Canberra, Australia.

Karlin, S. (1959), *Mathematical Methods and Theory in Games, Programming, and Economics*. Reading, Mass.: Addison-Wesley Publishing Co.

Klein, D., S. Schmidt, and S. Yaisawarng (1991), "Productivity Changes in the U.S. Electric Power Industry," Working Paper, Department of Economics, Union College, Schenectady, N.Y.

Klotz, B., R. Madoo, and R. Hansen (1980), "A Study of High and Low 'Labor Productivity' Establishments in U.S. Manufacturing," in J. W. Kendrick and B. N. Vaccara, eds., *New Developments in Productivity Measurement and Analysis*. National Bureau of Economimc Research Conference on Research in Income and Wealth, Studies in Income and Wealth, vol. 44. Chicago: The University of Chicago Press, pp. 239–286.

Knight, F. H. (1933[1965]), *The Economic Organization*. New York: Harper & Row.

Koopmans, T. C. (1951), "An Analysis of Production as an Efficient Combination of Activities," in T. C. Koopmans, ed., *Activity Analysis of Production and Allocation*, Cowles Commission for Research in Economics, Monograph No. 13. New York: John Wiley and Sons, Inc.

Kopp, R. J., and W. E. Diewert (1982), "The Decomposition of Frontier Cost Function Deviations into Measures of Technical and Allocative Efficiency," *Journal of Econometrics* 19(2/3) (August): 319–332.

Kopp, R. J., V. K. Smith, and W. J. Vaughan (1982), "Stochastic Cost Frontiers and Perceived Technical Inefficiency," in V. K. Smith, ed., *Advances in Applied Micro-economics*, vol. 2. Greenwich, Conn.: JAI Press.

Kumbhakar, S. C. (1990), "Production Frontiers, Panel Data, and Time-Varying Technical Inefficiency," *Journal of Econometrics* 46(1/2) (October/November): 201–211.

Kumbhakar, S. C. (1991), "The Measurement and Decomposition of Cost-Inefficiency: The Translog Cost System," *Oxford Economic Papers* 43: 667–683.

Kumbhakar, S. C., and L. Hjalmarsson (1991), "Labour-Use Efficiency in Swedish Social Insurance Offices," Memorandum No. 152, Department of Economics, Gothenburg University, Goteborg, Sweden; forthcoming in *European Journal of Operational Research.*

Laffont, J-J, and M. S. Matoussi (1990), "Moral Hazard, Financial Constraints and Share-cropping in El Oulja," Cahier No. 90c, GREMAQ, Université des Sciences Sociales de Toulouse, Toulouse, France.

Land, K. C., C. A. K. Lovell, and S. Thore (1988), "Chance-Constrained Efficiency Analysis," Working Paper, Department of Economics, University of North Carolina, Chapel Hill, N.C.

Land, K. C., C. A. K. Lovell, and S. Thore (1990), "Chance-Constrained Data Envelopment Analysis," Working Paper, The IC^2 Institute, University of Texas, Austin, Tex.

Lau, L. J., and P. A. Yotopoulos (1971), "A Test for Relative Efficiency and Application to Indian Agriculture," *American Economic Review* 61(1) (March): 94–109.

Lee, H., and A. Somwaru (1992), "Share Tenancy and Efficiency in U.S. Agriculture," pp. xx–xx (this volume).

Leibenstein, H. (1976), *Beyond Economic Man*. Cambridge, Mass.: Harvard University Press.

Leibenstein, H. (1987), *Inside the Firm*. Cambridge, Mass.: Harvard University Press.

Lewin, A. Y., R. C. Morey, and T. J. Cook (1982), "Evaluating the Administrative Efficiency of Courts," *Omega* 10(4): 401–411.

Lovell, C. A. K., and R. C. Morey (1991), "The Allocation of Consumer Incentives to Meet Simultaneous Sales Quotas: An Application to U.S. Army Recruiting," *Management Science* 37(3) (March): 350–367.

Lovell, C. A. K., R. C. Morey, and L. L. Wood (1991), "Cost-Efficient Military Recruiting: An Econometric Approach," *Defence Economics* 2: 339–351.

Lovell, C. A. K., S. Richardson, P. Travers, and L. L. Wood (1990), "Resources and Function-ings: A New View of Inequality in Australia," Working Paper No. 90-8, Department of Economics, University of North Carolina, Chapel Hill, N.C.

Lovell, C. A. K., and R. C. Sickles (1983), "Testing Efficiency Hypotheses in Joint Production: A Parametric Approach," *Review of Economics and Statistics* 65(1) (February): 51–58.

Lovell, C. A. K., L. C. Walters, and L. L. Wood (1990), "Stratified Models of Education Production Using DEA and Regression Analysis," Working Paper No. 90-5, Department of Economics, University of North Carolina, Chapel Hill, N.C. in A. Charnes, W. W. Cooper, A. Y. Lewin, and L. M. Seiford, eds., *Data Envelopment Analysis: Theory, Method and Process*. IC^2 Management and Management Science Series. New York: Quorum Books (forthcoming).

Malmquist, S. (1953), "Index Numbers and Indifference Surfaces," *Trabajos de Estatistica* 4: 209–242.

McCarty, T. A., and S. Yaisawarng (1990), "A Strategy for Effective School Finance Reform," Working Paper, Department of Economics, Union College, Schenectady, N.Y.

McCarty, T. A., and S. Yaisawarng (1992), "Technical Efficiency in New Jersey School Districts," pp. xx–xx (this volume).

McFadden, D. (1978), "Cost, Revenue and Profit Functions," in M. Fuss and D. McFadden, eds., *Production Economics: A Dual Approach to Theory and Applications*. Amsterdam: North-Holland Publishing Company, pp. 3–109.

Meeusen, W., and J. van den Broeck (1977), "Efficiency Estimation from Cobb-Douglas Production Functions with Composed Error," *International Economic Review* 18(2) (June): 435–444.

Moroney, J. R., and C. A. K. Lovell (1991), "The Performance of Market and Planned Economies Revisited," Working Paper, Department of Economics, University of North Carolina, Chapel Hill, N.C.

Mundlak, Y. (1961), "Empirical Production Function Free of Management Bias," *Journal of Farm Economics* 43(1) (February): 44–56.

Nishimizu, M., and J. M. Page, Jr. (1982), "Total Factor Productivity Growth, Technological Progress and Technical Efficiency Change: Dimensions of Productivity Change in Yugoslavia, 1965–78," *Economic Journal* 92(368) (December): 920-936.

Ohta, M. (1974), "A Note on the Duality Between Production and Cost Functions: Rate of Return to Scale and Rate of Technical Progress," *Economic Studies Quarterly* 25(3) (December): 63–65.

Olesen, O. B., and S. Thore (1990), "Two-Stage DEA Under Uncertainty," Working Paper, IC^2 Institute, University of Texas, Austin, Tex.

Olesen, O. B., and N. C. Petersen (1991), "Collinearity in Data Envelopment Analysis: An Extended Facet Approach," Working Paper No. 1/1991, Department of Management, Odense University, Denmark.

Otsuka, K., and Y. Hayami (1988), "Theories of Share Tenancy: A Critical Survey," *Economic Development and Cultural Change* 37(1): 31–68.

Parkan, C. (1987), "Measuring the Efficiency of Service Operation: An Application to Bank Branches," *Engineering Costs and Production Economics* 12: 237–242.

Pestieau, P., and H. Tulkens (1990), "Assessing the Performance of Public Sector Activities: Some Recent Evidence from the Productive Efficiency Viewpoint," Discussion Paper No. 9060, CORE, Université Catholique de Louvain, Louvain-la-Neuve, Belgium.

Petersen, N. C. (1990), "Data Envelopment Analysis on a Relaxed Set of Assumptions," *Management Science* 36(3) (March): 305–314.

Petersen, N. C., and O. Olesen (1989), "Chance Constrained Efficiency Evaluation," Working Paper No. 9/1989, Department of Management, Odense University, Odense, Denmark.

Porter, P. K., and G. W. Scully (1982), "Measuring Managerial Efficiency: The Case of Baseball," *Southern Economic Journal,* 48(3) (January): 542–550.

Ray, S. C. (1988), "Data Envelopment Analysis, Nondiscretionary Inputs and Efficiency: An Alternative Interpretation," *Socio-Economic Planning Sciences* 22(4): 167–176.

Ray, S. C. (1991), "Resource-Use Efficiency in Public Schools: A Study of Connecticut Data," *Management Science* 37(12) (December), 1620–1628.

Register, C. A. (1988), "Technical Efficiency Within the U.S. Postal Service and the Postal Reorganization Act of 1970," *Applied Economics* 20: 1185–1197.

Register, C. A., and E. R. Bruning (1987), "Profit Incentives and Technical Efficiency in the Production of Hospital Care," *Southern Economic Journal* 53(4) (April): 899–914.

Retzlaff-Roberts, D. L., and R. C. Morey (1991), "A Comparison of Stochastic Allocative DEA Methods," Working Paper, College of Business and Economics, Memphis State University, Memphis, Tenn.

Rhodes, E. L. (1986), "An Exploratory Analysis of Variations in Performance Among U.S. National Parks," in R. H. Silkman, ed., *Measuring Efficiency: An Assessment of Data Envelopment Analysis*. San Fransisco: Jossey-Bass, pp. 47–71.

Richmond, J. (1974), "Estimating the Efficiency of Production," *International Economic Review* 15(2) (June): 515–521.

Robinson, M. D., and P. V. Wunnava (1989), "Measuring Direct Discrimination in Labor Markets Using a Frontier Approach: Evidence from CPS Female Earnings Data," *Southern Economic Journal* 56(1) (July): 212–218.

Roll, Y., B. Golany, and D. Seroussy (1989), "Measuring the Efficiency of Maintenance Units in the Israeli Air Force," *European Journal of Operational Research* 43(2) (November): 136–142.

Russell, R. R. (1985), "Measures of Technical Efficiency," *Journal of Economic Theory* 35(1) (February): 109–126.

Russell, R. R. (1988), "On the Axiomatic Approach to the Measurement of Technical Efficiency," in W. Eichhorn, ed., *Measurement in Economics: Theory and Applications of Economic Indices*. Heidelberg, Physica-Verlag.

Russell, R. R. (1990), "Continuity of Measures of Technical Efficiency," *Journal of Economic Theory* 51(2) (August): 255–267.

Satish, S. (1986), "Relative Economic Efficiencies in Indian Agriculture: A Case Study of Cotton in Karnatake," *Indian Journal of Quantitative Economics* 2(1): 45–55.

Schmidt, P. (1976), "On the Statistical Estimation of Parametric Frontier Production Functions," *Review of Economics and Statistics* 58(2) (May): 238–239.

Schmidt, P. (1985–1986), "Frontier Production Functions," *Econometric Reviews* 4(2): 289–328.

Schmidt, P., and R. C. Sickles (1984), "Production Frontiers and Panel Data," *Journal of Business and Economic Statistics* 2: 367–374.

Seale, J. L., Jr. (1990), "Estimating Stochastic Frontier Systems with Unbalanced Panel Data: The Case of Floor Tile Manufactories in Egypt," *Journal of Applied Econometrics* 5(1): 59–74.

Seiford, L. M., and R. M. Thrall (1990), "Recent Developments in DEA: The Mathematical Programming Approach to Frontier Analysis," *Journal of Econometrics* 46(1/2) (October/November): 7–38.

Sengupta, J. K. (1987), "Data Envelopment Analysis for Efficiency Measurement in the Stochastic Case," *Computers and Operations Research* 14(2): 117–129.

Sexton, T. R., A. M. Leiken, A. H. Nolan, S. Liss, A. Hogan, and R. H. Silkman, (1989), "Evaluating Managerial Efficiency of Veterans Administration Medical Centers Using Data Envelopment Analysis," *Medical Care* 27(12) (December): 1175–1188.

Sexton, T. R., S. Sleeper and R. E. Taggart, III (1991), "Data Envelopment Analysis For Nonhomogeneous Units: Pupil Transportation Budgeting in North Carolina," Working Paper, The W. Averill Harriman School for Management and Policy, The State University of New York, Stony Brook, N.Y.

Shephard, R. W. (1953), *Cost and Production Functions*. Princeton, N.J.: Princeton University Press.

Shephard, R. W. (1970), *Theory of Cost and Production Functions*. Princeton, N.J.: Princeton University Press.

Sherman, H. D., and F. Gold (1985), "Branch Bank Operating Efficiency: Evaluation with Data Envelopment Analysis," *Journal of Banking and Finance* 9(2) (June): 297–315.

Smith, P., and D. Mayston (1987), "Measuring Efficiency in the Public Sector," *Omega* 15(3): 181–189.

Solow, R. M. (1957), "Technical Change and the Aggregate Production Function," *Review of Economics and Statistics* 39(3) (August): 312–320.

Stevenson, R. E. (1980), "Likelihood Functions for Generalized Stochastic Frontier Estimation," *Journal of Econometrics* 13(1) (May): 58–66.

Stigler, G. J. (1976), "The Xistence of X-Efficiency," *American Economic Review* 66(1) (March): 213–216.

Thanassoulis, E., R. G. Dyson, and M. J. Foster (1987), "Relative Efficiency Assessments Using Data Envelopment Analysis: An Application to Data on Rates Departments," *Journal of the Operational Research Society* 38(5): 397–411.

Thiry, B., and H. Tulkens (1992), "Allowing for Technical Inefficiency in Parametric Estimation of Production Functions for Urban Transit Firms," *Journal of Productivity Analysis* 3(1/2) (June): 45–65.

Timmer, C. P. (1971), "Using a Probabilistic Frontier Production Function to Measure Technical Efficiency," *Journal of Political Economy* 79(4) (July/August): 776–794.

Toda, Y. (1976), "Estimation of a Cost Function When the Cost Is Not Minimum: The Case of Soviet Manufacturing Industries, 1958– 1971," *Review of Economics and Statistics* 58(3) (August): 259–268.

Törnqvist, L. (1936), "The Bank of Finland's Consumption Price Index," *Bank of Finland Monthly Bulletin* 10: 1–8.

Tulkens, H. (1986), "La performance productive d'un service public: Definition, methodes de mesure et application a la Regie des Postes en Belgique," *L'Actualite Economique, Revue d'Analyse Economique* 62(2) (June): 306–335.

Tulkens, H. (1990), "Non-parametric Efficiency Analyses in Four Service Activities: Retail Banking, Municipalities, Courts and Urban Transit," Discussion Paper No. 9050, CORE, Université Catholique de Louvain, Louvain-la-Neuve, Belgium.

Tulkens, H., B. Thiry, and A. Palm (1988), "Mesure d'efficacite productive: methodologies et applications aux societes de transports intercommunaux de Liege, Charleroi et Verviers," in B. Thiry and H. Tulkens, eds., *La Performance Economique Des Societes Belges de Transports Urbains*. Liege: CIRIEC.

Tulkens, H., and P. Vanden Eeckaut (1990), "Productive Efficiency Measurement in Retail Banking in Belgium," Document de Travail from the Fonds de Documentation Statistique et Economique sur les Services Publics Belges, CORE, Université Catholique de Louvain, Louvain-la-Neuve, Belgium (forthcoming).

Vanden Eeckaut, P., H. Tulkens and M-A Jamar (1992), "Cost Efficiency in Belgian Municipalities," pp. xxx–xxx (this volume).

Vassdal, T. (1989), "A Method to Compare Average and Deterministic Frontier Functions," Working Paper, University of Tromsø, Norway.

Vassiloglou, M., and D. Giokas (1990), "A Study of the Relative Efficiency of Bank Branches: An Application of Data Envelopment Analysis," *Journal of the Operational Research Society* 41(7) (July): 591–597.

Williamson, O. E. (1975), *Markets and Hierarchies*. New York: The Free Press.

Williamson, O. E. (1985), *The Economic Institutions of Capitalism*. New York: The Free Press.

Winsten, C. B. (1957), "Discussion on Mr. Farrell's Paper," *Journal of the Royal Statistical Society* Series A, General, 120(3): 282–284.

Wyckoff, J. H., and J. Lavigne (1991), "The Technical Inefficiency of Public Elementary Schools in New York," Working Paper, Graduate School of Public Affairs, The State University of New York, Albany, N.Y.

Yotopoulos, P. A., and L. J. Lau (1973), "A Test for Relative Economic Efficiency: Some Further Results," *American Economic Review* 63(1) (March): 214–223.

Yotopoulos, P. A., and L. J. Lau, eds. (1979), "Resource Use in Agriculture: Applications of the Profit Function to Selected Countries," *Food Research Institute Studies* 17(1): 1–120.

Zieschang, K. D. (1983), "A Note on the Decomposition of Cost Efficiency into Technical and Allocative Components," *Journal of Econometrics* 23(3) (December): 401–405.

2

THE ECONOMETRIC APPROACH TO EFFICIENCY ANALYSIS

William H. Greene

As described in Chapter 1, two very distinct methods of estimating efficiency in production have developed in the literature. This chapter will survey the econometric approach and provide a summary of the received techniques. Little attempt will be made to survey the received empirical literature. Not only is the list already prohibitively large, but it continues to grow, partly with the latter chapters of this volume.[1] Section 2.8 will present some estimates based on the U.S. airline industry in order to illustrate some of the basic, more accessible techniques.

2.1 Introduction

The literature on frontier production and cost functions and the calculation of efficiency measures begins with Farrell (1957). He suggested that we could usefully analyze technical efficiency in terms of realized deviations from an idealized, frontier isoquant. This approach falls naturally into an econometric approach in which the inefficiency is identified with disturbances in a regression model.

The empirical estimation of production functions had begun long before Farrell's paper, essentially around 1928 with the papers of Cobb and Douglas (1928). However, until the 1950s, production functions were largely used as devices for studying the functional distribution of income between capital and labor at the macroeconomic level. [Consider, as well, the celebrated contribution of Arrow, Chenery, Minhas, and Solow (1961).] The origins of empirical analysis of microeconomic production structures can be more reasonably identified with the work of Dean (1951), John-

---

[1] A survey of empirical applications in agricultural economics is given by Battese (1991). Schmidt (1985) gives a cursory review of the econometrics literature, but a substantial amount of new work on technique and application has appeared in the last five years. Bauer (1990) provides a brief, but current survey of econometric developments.

ston (1959), and, in his seminal work on electric power, Nerlove (1963). Interestingly enough, all these focus on costs rather than production per se, though Nerlove, following on Samuelson (1938) and Shephard (1953), highlighted the relationship between the two. Nonetheless, empirical attention to production functions at disaggregated levels has been a fairly recently developed literature.[2]

The empirical literature on production and cost developed largely independently of the discourse on production frontiers. Least squares, or some variant, was routinely used to pass a function through the middle of a cloud of points, and residuals of both signs were, as in other areas of study, not singled out for special treatment, given a name and face as it were. An argument could (indeed, has been) made that these "averaging" estimators were estimating the "average" rather than the "best practice" technology, but this just rationalizes the least squares techniques after the fact. Farrell's arguments provide an intellectual basis for redirecting attention from the production function specifically to the deviations from that function, and respecifying the regression and the techniques accordingly.

The literature on production frontiers represents a reconciliation of these strands of literature. This chapter presents a survey of the econometric methods that have been employed. Section 2.2 lays out some of the formalities of the analysis and defines the terms used later. Section 2.3 discusses some studies of "deterministic frontiers." These represent an orthodox approach to Farrell's model, and are predecessors to the current methodology. Section 2.4 discusses the central pillar of the extant and ongoing literature, the stochastic production frontier. The stochastic frontier represents a solution to dealing with theoretical propositions while simultaneously allowing for variation in real-world data that obviously falls outside the confines of our idealized economy. Section 2.5 extends Section 2.4 into a particular analytical framework, that of panel data. Section 2.6 returns to the subject of cost functions, and discusses implications of the production frontier approach for the specification of models of production costs. Section 2.7 considers methods of incorporating information about systems of demand equations into the estimation of the production or cost function. This has posed some formidable problems of specification and estimation. Section 2.8 illustrates a number of the econometric techniques with a data set from the U.S. domestic airline industry. Some conclusions are drawn in Section 2.9.

2.2 Econometric Framework and Definitions

The theoretical underpinnings of a general model of production were given in Chapter 1. This chapter will take as given the specification of a well-defined production structure, characterized by a smooth, continuous, continuously differentiable, quasi-concave production or transformation function.[3] Producers are assumed to be price

---

[2] For example, Hildebrand and Liu (1965).

[3] These assumptions might be more stringent than necessary, but relaxing them in the current context would add little generality at the expense of considerable complexity.

takers in their input markets, so input prices may be treated as exogenous. It is an interesting question as to how one should view price behavior in the output markets. Strictly speaking, an orthodox reading of microeconomics rules out Farrell's interpretation. A competitive market in equilibrium would not tolerate inefficiency of the sort considered here. Resolving that conflict is beyond the scope of this study.

Throughout this chapter, the production process is modeled with a single- output production frontier,

$$Q_i = f(x_i, \beta) \tag{2.1}$$

where Q denotes output, x denotes a set of inputs, β is a set of parameters that is the object of estimation, and i denotes producers. The assumption of a single output is largely for convenience. The frontiers literature contains results for multiple-output technologies, though in these cases, it is necessary to work with cost, revenue, and profit functions. Here, it is necessary to make some further clarification of the assumptions and relationships among the variables in the models. All the usual assumptions about smoothness, curvature, and continuity of the production function and optimizing behavior of producers are also made at this point.

In nearly all applications, after transformation, the functional form of the model to be estimated is linear in the logs of output and a set of independent variables, so, at least in the context of this literature, little generality is lost by writing the production frontier as

$$y_i = \ln Q_i = \alpha + \beta' x_i \tag{2.2}$$

This does not restrict the model to the Cobb-Douglas functional form, since the translog, generalized Leontief, generalized Cobb-Douglas, and a number of other functions are also linear in the parameters. Since the focus of this survey is efficiency measurement, and not the production frontier itself, the form above will be assumed and the question of functional form will not be reconsidered.

Technical inefficiency is assumed to enter the production model multiplicatively, or additively after taking logarithms, so, in general terms,

$$\ln Q_i = \alpha + \beta' x_i + \epsilon_i \tag{2.3}$$

In what follows, various models for ϵ are discussed. A common feature is that the model for ϵ_i has a nonzero mean which reflects the systematic deviation of actual output from the theoretical norm.

The subject of this study is the specification and estimation of models of ϵ. As such, the estimation of α and β as characteristics of the production process is of only secondary interest. Estimates of such features as elasticities of substitution, economies of scale, and technical change may well be byproducts, but they are not of any direct concern. Also, only limited attention is paid to the statistical properties of estimators of α and β. Where statements can be made at all, it is usually true that the estimator employed is the most efficient available, one of ordinary least squares, generalized least squares, or maximum likelihood. Estimates of ϵ are of interest. Here, as will be clear shortly, perhaps the best that can be hoped for is consistency, and even this is lacking in some cases.

One assumption which is common throughout most of the analysis is that ϵ is a random variable with a constant mean. As such, the model can be rewritten as

$$y_i = \alpha + E[\epsilon_i] + \beta' x_i + \epsilon_i - E[\epsilon_i] = \alpha^* + \beta' x_i + \epsilon_i^* \tag{2.4}$$

Since this is a regression model with all of the characteristics of the classical model, its parameters can be estimated consistently by ordinary least squares. But, the model for ϵ, even in the context above, may be fairly involved. As such, much of the work to follow is concerned with either how to make use of the consistent least squares estimates or how to modify the estimation technique to account for the special nature of the disturbance.

2.3 Deterministic Production Frontiers

The development of the current econometric methodology has two distinct stages. In the early applications, a strict interpretation of Farrell's propositions produced some interesting, but less than completely satisfactory attempts to force the model specification to conform exactly to the underlying theory. In current terminology, these specifications have been denoted "deterministic frontiers." The second stage brought a more flexible approach to the specification of the frontier model, the "stochastic frontier" model, which is the subject of Section 2.4.

2.3.1 Programming Estimators

Following Farrell's initiative, Aigner and Chu (1968) suggested a log-linear (Cobb-Douglas) production function,

$$Q_i = A X_{1i}^{\beta_1} X_{2i}^{\beta_2} U_i = Q_i^* U_i \tag{2.5}$$

in which U_i is a random disturbance between 0 and 1. Taking logs produces

$$
\begin{aligned}
y_i &= \alpha + \sum_k \beta_k x_{ki} + \epsilon_i \\
&= \alpha + \sum_k \beta_k x_{ki} - u_i
\end{aligned} \tag{2.6}
$$

where $\alpha = \ln A$, $x_{ki} = \ln X_{ki}$, $\epsilon_i = \ln U_i$, and $u_i = -\epsilon_i$. The last of these is defined for consistency with the formulations of the model defined in the material to follow.

The nonstochastic part of the right-hand side is viewed as the frontier. It is labeled "deterministic" because the stochastic component of the model is entirely contained in the (in)efficiency term, u_i. The Farrell measure of technical inefficiency is, then,

$$\frac{Q_i}{Q_i^*} = U_i = e^{-u_i} \tag{2.7}$$

Aigner and Chu suggested two estimation methods that would constrain the residuals ϵ_i to be negative: linear programming;

$$\min_{\beta} \ \sum_i \left| y_i - \alpha - \sum_k \beta_k x_{ki} \right| \tag{2.8}$$

subject to

$$\epsilon_i = y_i - \alpha - \sum_k \beta_k x_{ki} \overset{\le}{=} 0 \qquad \forall i$$

and quadratic programming;

$$\min_{\beta} \sum_i [y_i - \alpha - \sum_k \beta_k x_{ki}]^2 \tag{2.9}$$

subject to

$$- \ \epsilon_i = y_i - \alpha - \sum_k \beta_k x_{ki} \overset{\le}{=} 0 \qquad \forall i$$

While these procedures did, indeed, produce "estimates," they had the notable disadvantage that they did not produce standard errors for the estimates, so inference was precluded. The efficiency of these "estimators" is questionable, though expressions for their asymptotic covariance matrices have, in fact, never been devised. For present purposes, their main disadvantage is that without a more detailed specification, consistency of the estimates cannot be verified nor, as such, can consistency of the estimates of u_i. The programming estimators may have the virtue of robustness to specification errors (e.g., the distribution of u_i), though this, too, remains to be verified. Indeed, one might argue that this consideration would be compelling were it not for the problem of measurement error discussed below.

2.3.2 Maximum Likelihood Estimation

Schmidt (1976) observed that the Aigner-Chu optimization criteria could be interpreted as the log-likelihood functions for models in which one sided residuals were distributed as exponential,

$$l(\alpha, \beta, \sigma) = -N \ln \sigma - \sum_i \frac{|y_i - \alpha - \beta' x_i|}{\sigma} \qquad (2.10)$$

and half-normal,

$$l(\alpha, \beta, \sigma) = \frac{-N}{2}(\ln \sigma^2 + \ln 2\pi + 2\ln \frac{1}{2}) - \frac{1}{2}\sum_i \frac{(y_i - \alpha - \beta' x_i)^2}{\sigma^2}. \qquad (2.11)$$

This would appear to endow the programming estimators with a statistical pedigree. However, a peculiar problem arises in that the gradients of both log-likelihoods have nonzero expectations, and the Hessians of both log-likelihoods are singular.

It is clear that the Aigner-Chu approach does satisfy the original objective. Having computed the programming estimators in this fashion, one can compare the individual residuals,

$$\hat{u}_i = \hat{\alpha} + \hat{\beta}' x_i - y_i \qquad (2.12)$$

to each other or to an absolute standard to assess the degree of technical (in)efficiency represented in the sample. A summary measure which could characterize the entire sample would be the

$$\text{Average inefficiency} = \frac{1}{N}\sum_i \hat{u}_i \qquad (2.13)$$

(The DEA approach discussed in Chapter 3 is essentially based on this approach to efficiency measurement.) For a Cobb-Douglas or other log-linear function, the counterpart to the Farrell measure would be $\exp(e_i)$, so another useful statistic would be

$$\text{Average proportional inefficiency} = \frac{1}{N}\sum_i \exp(-\hat{u}_i) \qquad (2.14)$$

The statistical problem with Schmidt's estimators appears to be a violation of one of the familiar regularity conditions, that the range of the observed dependent variable y_i is dependent upon the parameters being estimated. Greene (1980a) showed, however, that this interpretation was too narrow. The violation of the regularity conditions in the Aigner-Chu/Schmidt formulations is that for those likelihoods, the interchange of integration and differentiation of the gradient needed to obtain the asymptotic distribution by the familiar methods is impermissible. But, this leaves the possibility that for other distributions, the conditions might be met and, consequently, a well-behaved likelihood function for a one-sided disturbance might still be definable. Greene proposed a model based on the gamma distribution,

$$f(u_i) = \frac{\theta^P}{\Gamma(P)} u_i^{P-1} e^{-\theta u_i} \qquad u_i > 0, \theta > 0, P > 2 \qquad (2.15)$$

The gamma frontier model does produce a bona fide MLE, with all the familiar properties. In principle, the log-likelihood can be maximized by familiar methods (subject to the constraints on P and λ).[4] Inference can then proceed as in more conventional problems. There have, in fact, been a few such applications, including Greene (1980a, b), Stevenson (1980), Aguilar (1988), and Hunt, Kim, and Warren (1986). Further discussion appears in Deprins and Simar (1986) and Deprins (1986).

2.3.3 Adjustments to Ordinary Least Squares

As noted in Section 2.2, the slope parameters in all the frontier models can be estimated consistently by ordinary least squares. A side result in Greene's study, which has since proved useful in subsequent work on panel data, is that the constant term in a deterministic frontier model can be consistently estimated simply by shifting the least squares line upward sufficiently so that the largest residual is zero.[5] The corrected constant term is "$a + \max(e_i)$." The resulting efficiency measures are

$$\hat{\epsilon}_i = e_i - \max_i(e_i) \qquad (2.16)$$

Thus, absolute estimators of the efficiency measures in this model are directly computable using nothing more elaborate than ordinary least squares. In the gamma frontier model, "a," the OLS estimate of α converges to

$$\mathrm{plim} a = \alpha - E[u_i] = \alpha - \frac{P}{\theta} \qquad (2.17)$$

so another approach, if possible, would be to correct the constant term using estimates of P and θ. This possibility is considered below.

The gamma model produces individual estimates of technical efficiency. A summary statistic, which might also prove useful, is

$$E[u_i] = \frac{P}{\theta} = \mu \qquad (2.18)$$

which can be estimated with the corrected residuals shown above. Likewise, an estimate of

$$\mathrm{Var}[u_i] = \frac{P}{\theta^2} = \sigma_u^2 \qquad (2.19)$$

[4] The restriction that all sample residuals must be kept strictly negative for the estimator to be computable turns out to be a persistent complication for iterative search methods.

[5] The result also appears in an earlier paper by Gabrielsen (1975).

is produced with the least squares residual variance. Combining the two produces a standardized mean

$$\frac{\mu}{\sigma_u} = \sqrt{P} \tag{2.20}$$

It is worthwhile to note in passing that here, as elsewhere, functions of the OLS estimates can be used to obtain estimates of the underlying structural parameters. In particular, consistent estimates of

$$\theta = \frac{P}{\mu} \tag{2.21}$$

and

$$P = \theta\mu \tag{2.22}$$

are easily computed. Using this correction to the least squares constant term produces what has come to be known as the COLS estimator. The counterparts for several of the other models are examined below. For present purposes, another useful parameter to estimate is

$$E[e^{-u_i}] = \left(\frac{\theta}{\theta + 1}\right)^P \tag{2.23}$$

2.3.4 Methodological Problems

A fundamental practical problem with the gamma and, to be sure, all other deterministic frontiers is that any measurement error, and any other source of stochastic variation in the dependent variable, must be embedded in the one- sided disturbance. As such, in any sample, a single errant observation can have profound effects on the estimates. It is important to note that, unlike measurement error in y, this outlier problem is not alleviated by resorting to large-sample results.

There have been a number of other contributions to the econometric literature on specification and estimation of deterministic frontier functions. Two important papers which anticipated the stochastic frontier model discussed in the next section are Timmer (1971), which proposed a probabilistic approach to frontier modeling that allowed some residuals to be positive, and Aigner, Amemiya, and Poirier (1976), who, in a precursor to Aigner, Lovell, and Schmidt (1977), focused on asymmetry in the distribution of the disturbance as a reflection of technical inefficiency. But, it is reasonable to say that for practical purposes, econometricians have largely abandoned the deterministic frontier as a useful model for efficiency measurement. The technical problems are quite surmountable, as shown by Schmidt (1976) and Greene (1980a), but the inherent problem with the stochastic specification and the implications of measurement error render it extremely problematic.

2.4 The Stochastic Production Frontier

2.4.1 The Model

The stochastic production frontier [Aigner, Lovell, and Schmidt (1977), Battese and Corra (1977), and Meeusen and van den Broeck (1977)] is motivated by the idea that deviations from the production "frontier" might not be entirely under the control of the agent being studied. Under the interpretation of the deterministic frontier of the preceding section, for example, an unusually high number of random equipment failures, or even bad weather, might ultimately appear to the analyst as inefficiency. Worse yet, any error or imperfection in the specification of the model could likewise translate into increased inefficiency measures. This is an unattractive consequence of the deterministic frontier specification. A more reasonable interpretation is that any particular producer faces their own production frontier, and that frontier is randomly placed by the whole collection of stochastic elements which might enter the model outside the control of the producer. An appropriate formulation in terms of a general production function h^* is

$$
\begin{aligned}
y_i &= h^*(\mathbf{x}_i, \boldsymbol{\beta}) - u_i \\
    &= \alpha + \boldsymbol{\beta}' \mathbf{x}_i + v_i - u_i
\end{aligned}
\tag{2.24}
$$

$$
y_i = \alpha + \boldsymbol{\beta}' \mathbf{x}_i + \epsilon_i
\tag{2.25}
$$

where $u_i \overset{\geq}{=} 0$ and v_i is unrestricted.

2.4.2 Specification and Estimation

The counterpart to the one-sided disturbance in the deterministic frontier model is u_i. However, the compound disturbance in this model, while asymmetrically distributed, is otherwise well-behaved, and maximum likelihood estimation is generally straightforward. The one-sided part of the compound disturbance (u_i) is typically assumed to be the absolute value of a normally distributed variable, though several other specifications have been considered. For a half-normally distributed inefficiency term, the log-likelihood function for this model is

$$
l(\alpha, \boldsymbol{\beta}, \sigma, \lambda) = -N \ln \sigma - \text{constant} + \sum_i \left[\ln \Phi \left(\frac{-\epsilon_i \lambda}{\sigma} \right) - \frac{1}{2} \left(\frac{\epsilon_i}{\sigma} \right)^2 \right]
\tag{2.26}
$$

where $\lambda = \sigma_u/\sigma_v$, $\sigma^2 = \sigma_v^2 + \sigma_u^2$, and $\Phi(.)$ is the cumulative distribution function (cdf) of the standard normal distribution. Details may be found in Aigner, Lovell, and Schmidt (1977). The parameter λ embodies the model of inefficiency. The simple regression model results from $\lambda = 0$. The implication would be that every firm operates on its frontier. This does not imply, however, that one can "test" for inefficiency by the usual means, because the polar value, $\lambda = 0$, is on the boundary of the parameter space, not in the interior. As such, standard sorts of tests, such as the Lagrange multiplier (LM) test are likely to be problematic.[6]

One additional point should be noted for the practitioner. The model above is parameterized in terms of λ and σ^2. It might seem that the variance ratio σ_u^2/σ^2 would be a useful indicator of the influence of the inefficiency component in the overall variance. But, the variance of the truncated normal random variable u_i is $[(\pi/2)-1]\sigma_u^2$, not σ_u^2. In the decomposition of the total variance into two components, the contribution of u_i is $[(\pi/2) - 1]\sigma_u^2/\{\sigma_v^2 + [(\pi/2) - 1]\sigma_u^2\}$. In addition, for estimation purposes, it is sometimes convenient to use a different parameterization altogether, as in Battese (1991) and Greene (1991, chap. 47). The interpretation of the ancillary variance parameters is a source of some ambiguity in this literature, which could easily be remedied.

As in the case of the gamma model, there are corrections to least squares which can be computed based on the OLS residuals. In particular, using the second and third moments of the OLS residuals, m_2 and m_3, the moment equations are

$$\left(\frac{2}{\pi}\right)^{1/2}\left[1 - \left(\frac{4}{\pi}\right)\right]\sigma_u^3 = m_3 \tag{2.27}$$

$$\left[\left(\frac{\pi}{2}\right) - 1\right]\sigma_u^2 + \sigma_v^2 = m_2$$

Since $E[u_i] = (2/\pi)^{1/2}\sigma_u$, the correction to the OLS constant term is

$$\hat{\alpha} = a - \hat{\sigma}_u\left(\frac{2}{\pi}\right)^{1/2} \tag{2.28}$$

These corrected least squares estimators are consistent, but inefficient in comparison to the maximum likelihood estimators. The degree to which they are inefficient remains to be determined.

Waldman (1982) has pointed out an intriguing quirk in the half-normal model. Normally, there are two roots of the log-likelihood function, one at the ordinary least squares estimates and another at the MLE. In theory, the distribution of the compound

---

[6] The statistics, LM, Wald, etc. are quite well-defined, even at $\lambda = 0$, which presents something of a conundrum in this model. There is, in fact, no problem computing a test statistic, but problems of interpretation are sure to arise. For related commentary, see Breusch and Pagan (1980). The corresponding argument as regards testing for a one-sided term would be the same. In this case, the parametric "restriction" would be $\lambda \to +\infty$ which, of course, would be difficult to test formally.

disturbance is skewed to the left. But, if the model is badly specified, it can occur that the OLS residuals are skewed in the opposite direction. In this instance, the OLS results are the MLE's, and consequently, one must estimate the one-sided terms as 0.0. (Note that if this occurs, the COLS estimate of σ_u^2 is undefined.) One might view this as a built-in diagnostic, since the phenomenon is likely to arise in a badly specified model or in an inappropriate application.

As in many other settings, the assumption of half-normality has brought some criticism, and several alternatives have been suggested. Meeusen and van den Broeck (and Aigner, Lovell, and Schmidt (1977)) presented the log-likelihood and associated results for an exponentially distributed disturbance.

$$f(u_i) = \theta e^{-\theta u_i} \tag{2.29}$$

and

$$l(\alpha, \beta, \sigma_v, \theta) = N \left[\ln \theta + \frac{1}{2}(\theta \sigma_v)^2 \right] + \sum_i \left[\ln \Phi \left(\frac{-\epsilon_i}{\sigma_v} - \theta \sigma_v \right) + \theta \epsilon_i \right] \tag{2.30}$$

The corrected least squares estimators are computed using

$$\text{plim } m_2 = \sigma_v^2 + \frac{1}{\theta^2}$$
$$\text{plim } m_3 = \frac{-2}{\theta^3} \tag{2.31}$$

so

$$\hat{\theta} = \left(\frac{-2}{m_3} \right)^{1/3} \tag{2.32}$$

$$\hat{\sigma}_v^2 = m_2 - \frac{1}{\hat{\theta}^2} \tag{2.33}$$

and

$$\hat{\alpha} = a - \frac{1}{\hat{\theta}} \tag{2.34}$$

Stevenson (1980) argued that the zero mean assumed in the Aigner, Lovell, and Schmidt model was an unnecessary restriction. He produced results for a truncated as opposed to half-normal distribution. That is, the one-sided error term u_i is taken to be the variable obtained by truncating at zero the distribution of a variable with possibly nonzero mean. The relevant log-likelihood is

$$l(\alpha, \beta, \sigma, \lambda, \mu) = - \sum_i \left[\ln \sigma + \frac{1}{2} \ln 2\pi + \frac{1}{2} \left(\frac{\epsilon_i}{\sigma} \right)^2 \right.$$

$$\left. - \ln \left\{ 1 - \Phi \left[\frac{\epsilon_i \lambda}{\sigma} + \frac{\mu}{(\sigma \lambda)} \right] \right\} + \ln \Phi \left(\frac{-\mu}{\sigma_u} \right) \right] \quad (2.35)$$

In terms of the previous parameterization, $\mu/\sigma_u = \mu(1+\lambda^2)^{1/2}/(\lambda\sigma)$. For purposes of interpreting the model, the parameter μ is not, in and of itself, particularly informative. The reason is that the scaling of the underlying variable is arbitrary; the units of μ are those of σ_u, not natural units. The normalized value μ/σ_u should be reported if this variant of the model is used.[7] There does not appear to be a convenient method of moments estimator for the truncated normal model, but maximum likelihood estimation presents no unusual difficulty. The obvious starting value for the iterations would be the estimates for a half-normal model and 0 for μ. Whether this additional level of generality is warranted remains to be explored. The benefit is obviously the relaxation of a possibly erroneous restriction. Within the author's limited experience, the cost appears to be that the log-likelihood is relatively flat in the dimension of μ. As such, estimation of a nonzero μ often inflates the standard errors of the other parameters considerably, and quite frequently impedes or prevents convergence of the iterations. There are virtually no applications of the truncated normal model in the received literature outside of the present one, so it is difficult to draw any general conclusions on these issues. It is also unclear how the restriction of μ to zero, as is usually done, would affect efficiency estimates.

Stevenson also produced a few results for the gamma/normal distribution, but limited his attention to the Erlang form (integer values of P), which greatly restricts the model. Beckers and Hammond (1987) first derived the log-likelihood for the convolution of a normal and a gamma variate. Greene (1990) produced an alternative formulation which highlights the relationship of the gamma model to the exponential model considered above,

$$l(\alpha, \beta, \sigma_v, \theta, P) = N \left[P \ln \theta - \ln \Gamma(P) + \frac{1}{2}(\theta\sigma_v)^2 \right]$$

$$+ \sum_i \left[\ln \Phi \left(\frac{-\epsilon_i}{\sigma_v} - \theta\sigma_v \right) + \theta\epsilon_i + \ln h(P - 1, \epsilon_i) \right]$$

$$= l_{\text{exponential}} + N[(P - 1) \ln \theta - \ln \Gamma(P)]$$

$$+ \sum_i \ln h(P - 1, \epsilon_i) \quad (2.36)$$

---

[7] The precise value obtained by one's software may be relevant here. The log-likelihood function is, in fact, more conveniently formulated in terms of μ/σ_u rather than in terms of μ separately.

where $h(r, \epsilon_i) = E[z^r | z > 0, \epsilon_i]$ when $z \approx$ normal with mean $-(\epsilon_i + \theta \sigma_v^2)$ and variance σ_v^2. The additional terms drop out if P equals 1, producing the exponential model. The corrected least squares estimators are

$$\hat{\theta} = \frac{-3m_3}{m_4 - 3m_2^2} \tag{2.37}$$

$$\hat{P} = \frac{-\hat{\theta}^3 m_3}{2}$$

$$\hat{\sigma}_v^2 = m_2 - \frac{\hat{P}}{\hat{\theta}^2}$$

$$\hat{\alpha} = a - \frac{\hat{P}}{\hat{\theta}}$$

The exponential and truncated normal models are no more difficult to fit than the half-normal model.[8] Greene's formulation of the gamma model brought some substantial differences from the half-normal specification in an empirical application. However, the greatly increased complexity of the procedure seems likely to outweigh its benefits.[9] Beckers' and Hammond (1987) formulation may prove to be more practical, but this remains to be demonstrated. If so, the increased flexibility of the gamma density for the inefficiency should be beneficial. For better or worse, though, the normal/half-normal model has dominated the received empirical studies.

Finally, Kopp and Mullahy (1989) have derived generalized method of moments[10] (GMM) estimators for the stochastic frontier model which require only that the distribution of v_i be symmetric, that the distribution of u_i be defined over the positive half of the real line, and that moments of u_i and v_i up to order six be finite. This provides a high level of generality, but at the very high cost that the method produces no definable estimate of u_i. Under the assumptions made thus far, ordinary least squares estimates of the model with an adjusted constant term $(\alpha + E[u_i])$ satisfies the assumptions of the Gauss-Markov theorem. As such, the appeal of a GMM estimator of the slope parameters is intellectual at best.

2.4.3 Estimation of the Inefficiency Component of the Disturbance

The inefficiency component u_i must be observed indirectly. The residual, $(y_i - \alpha - \beta' x_i)$, estimates ϵ_i, not u_i. Jondrow, Lovell, Materov, and Schmidt (1982) present an explicit form for the half-normal model,

---

[8] All are available as regression options in LIMDEP [Greene (1991)].

[9] The difficulty lies in computing the fractional moment of the truncated normal distribution [the $h(.,.)$ function]. This is difficult to obtain with much accuracy. An equally complex model which has also not been used empirically is Lee's (1983) four-parameter Pearson family of distributions.

[10] See Hansen (1982).

$$E[u_i|\epsilon_i] = \frac{\sigma\lambda}{(1+\lambda^2)}\left[\frac{\phi(\epsilon_i\lambda/\sigma)}{\Phi(-\epsilon_i\lambda/\sigma)} - \frac{\epsilon_i\lambda}{\sigma}\right] \tag{2.38}$$

where $\phi(.) =$ the density of the standard normal distribution. For the truncated normal model, the counterpart is obtained by replacing $\epsilon_i\lambda/\sigma$ with

$$\mu_i^* = \frac{\epsilon_i\lambda}{\sigma} + \frac{\mu}{\sigma\lambda} \tag{2.39}$$

The expressions for the exponential and gamma models are

$$E[u_i|\epsilon_i] = (\epsilon_i - \theta\sigma_v^2) + \frac{\sigma_v\phi[(\epsilon_i - \theta\sigma_v^2)/\sigma_v]}{\Phi[(\epsilon_i - \theta\sigma_v^2)/\sigma_v]} \tag{2.40}$$

and

$$E[u_i|\epsilon_i] = \frac{h(P, \epsilon_i)}{h(P-1, \epsilon_i)} \tag{2.41}$$

respectively.[11] These enable unbiased, but not consistent estimation of u_i. (They are inconsistent because regardless of N, the variance of the estimate remains nonzero, not because they converge to some other quantity.)

The inconsistency of the estimator of u_i is unfortunate in view of the fact that the purpose of the exercise to begin with is to estimate inefficiency. It would appear, however, that no improvement on this measure for the single-equation, cross-sectional framework considered here is forthcoming. The problem is analogous to that of predicting the dependent variable in a linear regression model. The regression prediction has minimum mean-squared error given the information in hand, but that is no assurance that the forecast is good in an absolute sense. The same logic applies here. We can write

$$u_i = E[u_i|\epsilon_i] + \zeta_i \tag{2.42}$$

Now, whether the "systematic" part of this regression is a "good" predictor in an absolute sense hinges on the correlation measure,

$$\rho^2 = \frac{\mathrm{var}[E(u_i|\epsilon_i)]}{\mathrm{var}[u_i]} \tag{2.43}$$

This may be large or small. The precise form of the expression remains to be derived, and, in any event, the outcome is doubtless data-dependent. Matters do improve in a panel data setting. Viewed in the context of the previous equation, in a panel data

---

[11] For the gamma model, $E[u_i^r|\epsilon_i] = h(P + r - 1, \epsilon_i)/h(P - 1, \epsilon_i)$.

setting, we are, essentially, able to average the noise out of the expression for u_i. This leaves, in a large enough sample, an observation on u_i plus a term which tends to zero. Further discussion appears in Section 2.5.

Finally, for models in which the log of output appears on the left hand side, Battese and Coelli's (1988) result for the panel data random effects model specializes in the case of a single observation to

$$E[e^{-u_i}|\epsilon_i] = \frac{\Phi[\mu_i^*/\sigma_* - \sigma_*]}{\Phi[\mu_i^*/\sigma_*]} e^{-\mu_i^* + \frac{1}{2}\sigma_*^2} \tag{2.44}$$

where $\mu_i^* = \gamma\mu + (1 - \gamma)(-\epsilon_i)$, $\sigma_*^2 = \gamma\sigma_u^2$, and $\gamma = 1 / (1 + \lambda^2)$.

Either of these estimates can be based on the (consistent) corrected least squares estimates as well as the maximum likelihood estimates of the parameters. As such, they can be computed even in the absence of the specialized software needed for efficient estimation of the frontier models. In particular, for stochastic frontier models of Aigner, Lovell, and Schmidt and of Meeusen and van den Broeck, if all one had in hand were a set of ordinary least squares residuals, one could easily obtain the method of moments estimators of α, β, σ_v, and either σ_u for the half-normal model or θ for the exponential model using the formulas given earlier. The estimation of $E[u_i|\epsilon_i]$ or $E[e^{-u_i}|\epsilon_i]$ now requires only the ability to compute the density and cdf of the standard normal distribution. Whether this method of proceeding is as effective as using the full MLEs is an open question. Whatever consistency properties are enjoyed by the estimator based on the MLEs would carry over to these OLS-based estimates. (But, see above on the general question of consistency.) The MLEs do use the asymmetry of the distribution in estimation of the parameters, however. But, as noted, how this influences the estimated efficiencies remains to be investigated.[12]

2.5 Panel Data

When producers are observed at several points in time, there are some potential improvements to be made on the preceding. In particular, three shortcomings can be handled explicitly:[13]

1. The assumption that the firm-specific level of inefficiency is uncorrelated with the input levels may be unwarranted.
2. The assumption of normality, while probably relatively benign, is yet one more assumption that one might prefer not to make. A few alternatives are noted in the preceding. Nonetheless, under certain assumptions, more robust panel data treatments are likely to bring improvements in the estimates.

---

[12] This seems to be an interesting enough question to merit further exploration. On the other hand, the computation of the full MLEs and the Jondrow, Lovell, Materov, and Schmidt estimator is completely automated in LIMDEP [Greene (1991)] and FRONTIER [Coelli (1989)], so the issue may well be moot.
[13] These observations were made by Schmidt and Sickles (1984).

3. The need to compute the firm-specific inefficiency in the stochastic frontier model with an estimator (Jondrow, Lovell, Materov, and Schmidt) which does not converge to the true value is a particularly nettlesome problem in view of the fact that this estimation is arguably the focus of the whole exercise.

Consider once again, a simple production model,

$$y_{it} = \alpha + \boldsymbol{\beta}' \boldsymbol{x}_{it} + v_{it} - u_{it} \tag{2.45}$$

There are N firms and T_i observations on each. (It is customary to assume that T_i is constant across firms. But, this is not necessary, and it does not hold in the application in Section 2.8.) If observations on u_{it} and v_{it} are independent over time as well as across individuals, then the preceding is no different from the models which have preceded it; the panel nature of the data set is irrelevant. But, if one is willing to make further assumptions about the nature of the inefficiency, a number of new possibilities arise.

If u_{it} is constant over time, the model becomes

$$y_{it} = \alpha + \boldsymbol{\beta}' \boldsymbol{x}_{it} + v_{it} - u_i \tag{2.46}$$

which lends itself to several familiar "panel data" treatments.

2.5.1 A Fixed Effects Approach

If the the $u_i's$ are treated as firm-specific constants, the model may be estimated by ordinary least squares, as a "fixed effects" model (using the "within groups" transformation if the number of firms is extremely large). In this case, estimates of the individual effects are extracted as follows: The least squares dummy variable (LSDV) estimator produces either a set of firm-specific constants α_i or an overall constant and $N - 1$ contrasts, $\alpha_i^* = \alpha_i - \alpha$, depending on the software employed. In either case, relying on the Gabrielsen/Greene [14] argument, we may use the estimated constants in the expression

$$\hat{u}_i = \hat{\alpha}_i - \max_i(\hat{\alpha}_i) \tag{2.47}$$

(Note that if an overall constant term $\hat{\alpha}_1$ has been computed, $\hat{\alpha}_i$ will have to be computed for the remaining $N - 1$ firms by adding this to the estimated differences.) By this construction, one of the firms meets the benchmark value (zero), and the remaining firms have positive inefficiency estimates. This approach has the distinct

---

[14] Both papers contain proofs of the proposition that shifting the estimated regression up or down so that exactly one residual is zero and the rest have the desired sign produces a consistent estimate of the constant.

advantage that it dispenses with the assumption that the firm inefficiencies are uncorrelated with the input levels. Moreover, no assumption of normality is needed. Finally, this approach shares the consistency property of the deterministic frontier model in the estimation of u_i. This estimate is consistent in T_i, which may, in practice, be quite small. For example, the several panel studies of the airline industry (including the one in Section 2.8) use only 15 or so years of data. Thus, the consistency argument may be of largely theoretical appeal. Still, a mean T_i observations is still $\sqrt{T_i}$ times better than one observation.

One obstacle to this approach is the presence of time-invariant attributes of the firms. If the model is conditioned on firm attributes such as the capital stock, location, or some other characteristics, and if these do not vary over time, then the LSDV estimator cannot be computed as shown above. Worse yet, if these effects are simply omitted from the model, then they reappear in the fixed effects, masquerading as inefficiency (or lack of), when obviously they should be classified otherwise. The question is one of identification. Hausman and Taylor (1981) have discussed conditions for identification of such effects and methods of estimation which might prove useful. But, alternative treatments such as the random effects model might prove more effective.

2.5.2 Random Effects Models

If the assumption of independence of the inefficiencies and input levels can be maintained, then a random effects approach might be preferable. One immediate advantage of the random effects model is that it allows time-invariant firm- specific attributes, such as the capital stock of a firm which is not growing, to enter the model. In this case, two approaches are available, generalized least squares and maximum likelihood.

For the first of these, rewrite the model as

$$y_{it} = \alpha - E[u_i] + \beta' x_{it} + v_{it} - (u_i - E[u_i])$$
$$= \alpha^* + \beta' x_{it} + v_{it} + r_i \tag{2.48}$$

Note that α^* does not depend on "i" because $E[u_i]$ is (a positive) constant. This model conforms exactly to the familiar random effects model (REM) widely discussed in the panel data literature. The displacement of the constant term notwithstanding, it is amenable to the usual two-step generalized least squares treatment. At the first step, least squares estimates of all parameters are computed. The variance components, var$[v_{it}]$ and var$[r_i]$, can be computed by any of the several methods documented in the literature. Then, finally, estimates of $[\alpha^*, \beta]$ are computed by feasible generalized least squares.

In order to derive an estimate of the inefficiency component, subsequent calculations are required. The simplest approach is to compute

$$\hat{\alpha}_i = \frac{1}{T_i} \sum_t (y_{it} - a^* - \boldsymbol{b}' \boldsymbol{x}_{it}) = \hat{r}_i = \hat{u}_i - \hat{E}[u_i] \tag{2.49}$$

This estimator is consistent in T_i, and requires consistency of $\boldsymbol{b}$, which, in turn, is consistent in N. A second estimator, which shares this characteristic, is the best linear unbiased predictor,

$$r_i^* = \frac{-T_i \sigma_u^2 \bar{e}_i}{T_i \sigma_u^2 + \sigma_v^2} = -\left(\frac{\lambda T_i}{1 + \lambda T_i}\right) \bar{e}_i \tag{2.50}$$

where $\bar{e}_i = \hat{\alpha}_i = \hat{r}_i = (1/T_i) \sum_t e_{it}$ and $\lambda = \sigma_u^2 / \sigma_v^2$.

Note, once again, that neither of these actually estimates u_i. In order to do so, it is necessary to obtain an estimate of $E[u_i]$, which, in turn, necessitates a fuller specification of the distribution of u_i. If, for example, the truncated normal model [Stevenson (1980)] is assumed, then

$$E[u_i] = \mu - \sigma_u \left[\frac{\phi(-\mu/\sigma_u)}{\Phi(-\mu/\sigma_u)}\right] = \sigma_u(\eta - \gamma) \tag{2.51}$$

in which ϕ and Φ denote the standard normal density (pdf) and cdf, respectively, and where σ_u is the variance of the underlying normal distribution. This is not identified in terms of $\bar{r}$, which equals 0 by construction.[15] For what it is worth, there are other ways to proceed. The parameters are identified in terms of the second and third moment of v, or the second moment of r and any sample cumulative frequency, assuming that N is large enough.[16]

Readers should note a possible conflict in the notation. The symbol σ_u^2 is used in the preceding expression for r_i^* to signify the variance of the disturbance, $r_i = u_i - E[u_i]$. The literature on stochastic frontiers uniformly uses this same symbol to indicate the variance of the underlying normal distribution. (See, as well, Section 2.4.) But, in this model, the variance of the one-sided variable, u_i or r_i would be $[(\pi/2) - 1]\sigma_u^2$, not σ_u^2 based on the original specification. The difference is little more than a question of notation, but analysts interested in isolating estimates of the specific structural parameters in the model should keep this distinction in mind. The issue is reconsidered in Section 2.8.

---

[15] If the more conventional case of $\mu = 0$, the "half-normal" model, is assumed, then $E[u_i] = 2\sigma_u/(2\pi)^{1/2} = .79788\sigma_u$, $\text{var}[u_i] = [(\pi/2) - 1]\sigma_u^2$, both of which can be estimated from the estimated variance of r_i.

[16] See Greene (1990, pp. 719–720).

Some efficiency is gained by using maximum likelihood if it is available. The relevant log-likelihood for this random effects model with a *half-normal* distribution has been derived by Pitt and Lee (1981) and discussed further by Battese and Coelli (1988). The *truncated* normal model of Stevenson (1980) is adopted here for generality and in order to maintain consistency with Battese and Coelli (1988) who provide a number of interesting results for this model. The half-normal model can be produced simply by restricting μ to equal 0. The structural model is, then,

$$y_{it} = \alpha + \boldsymbol{\beta}' \boldsymbol{x}_{it} + v_{it} - |u_i| \tag{2.52}$$

where u_i is distributed as normal, with mean μ, and variance σ_u^2. As before, there are T_i observations on the ith firm. The log-likelihood function in Aigner, Lovell, and Schmidt's model is reparameterized slightly to obtain[17]

$$
\begin{aligned}
l = \sum_i & \left\{ -\frac{1}{2} \left[T_i \ln 2\pi - \ln 2 + T_i \ln \sigma_v^2 + \ln(1 + \lambda T_i) - 2 \ln \Phi \left(\frac{\mu}{\sigma_v} \right) \right] \right\} \\
& + \sum_i \left(-\frac{1}{2} \left\{ \frac{-\lambda}{(1 + \lambda T_i)} \left[\sum_t \frac{(\epsilon_{it} - \mu)}{\sigma_v} \right]^2 + \sum_t \left[\frac{(\epsilon_{it} - \mu)}{\sigma_v} \right]^2 \right\} \right) \\
& + \sum_i \ln \Phi \left\{ \left(\frac{\lambda}{1 + \lambda T_i} \right)^{1/2} \frac{1}{\sigma_v} \left[\sum_t (\epsilon_{it} - \mu) + T_i \mu \left(1 - \frac{1}{\lambda} \right) \right] \right\}
\end{aligned}
\tag{2.53}
$$

with $\lambda = \sigma_u^2 / \sigma_v^2$ and $\epsilon_{it} = y_{it} - \boldsymbol{\beta}' \boldsymbol{x}_{it}$. With the parameter estimates in hand, once again, estimation can proceed based on Aigner, Lovell, and Schmidt. Battese and Coelli (1988) have extensively analyzed this model, with Stevenson's extension to the truncated normal distribution for u_i. They provide the counterpart to the Jondrow, Lovell, Materov, and Schmidt estimator of u_i. With the reparameterization, their result is

$$E[u_i | \epsilon_{i,1}, \dots, \epsilon_{i,t_i}] = \mu_i^* + \sigma_{*i} \left[\frac{\phi(\mu_i^* / \sigma_{*i})}{\Phi(-\mu_i^* / \sigma_{*i})} \right] \tag{2.54}$$

where $\mu_i^* = \gamma_i \mu + (1 - \gamma_i)(-\bar{\epsilon}_i)$, $\gamma_i = 1/(1 + \lambda/T_i)$, and $\sigma_{*i}^2 = \sigma_u^2/(1 + \lambda T_i)$. Note that as $T_i \to \infty$, $\gamma_i \to 0$, and the entire expression collapses to $\bar{\epsilon}_i$, which, in turn, converges to u_i, as might be expected. As Schmidt and Sickles (1984) observe, this can be interpreted as the advantage of having observed u_i N times. Taking the mean averages out the noise contained in v_{it}, which only occurs once. It is worth noting that the preceding, perhaps with the simplifying assumption that $\mu = 0$, could be

---

[17]For this specification, the parameterization of $\lambda = (\sigma_u/\sigma_v)^2$ and σ_u^2 as opposed to $\lambda = \sigma_u/\sigma_v$ and $\sigma = [(\sigma_v)^2 + (\sigma_u)^2]^{1/2}$ (Aiger, Lovell, and Schmidt (1977)) is more convenient.

employed after estimation of the random effects model by GLS, rather than maximum likelihood. The aforementioned corrections to the moment-based variance estimators would be required, of course.

If the model is logarithmic, e^{u_i} gives more accurately the Farrell measure of inefficiency. Battese and Coelli have also derived the panel data counterpart to the measure $E[e^{u_i}|\epsilon_i]$,

$$E[e^{u_i}|\epsilon_{i1}, \ldots, \epsilon_{iT_i}] = \frac{\Phi[\mu_i^*/\sigma_{*i} - \sigma_{*i}]}{\Phi[\mu_i^*/\sigma_{*i}]} e^{-\mu_i^* + \frac{1}{2}\sigma_{*i}^2} \tag{2.55}$$

Cornwell, Schmidt, and Sickles (1990) and Kumbhakar (1990) suggest that it might be useful to relax the assumption of fixed inefficiencies over time. One possibility is a two-way effects model,

$$u_{it} = u_i + r_t \tag{2.56}$$

as if a similar effect hits every firm in each particular period. This can be treated as a fixed or random effects model. In either case, it is necessary to compensate for the presence of the time effect in the model. This does relax the assumption of time invariance of the inefficiency, but it is questionable whether it really adds much substance to the specification of the model. As before, an estimate of the unique component u_i can be based either on the best linear unbiased predictor or on the conditional mean approach of Battese and Coelli.

An alternative is to allow the individual effect to evolve over time, as in

$$u_{it} = \gamma_i + \delta_i t + \theta_i t^2 \tag{2.57}$$

Cornwell, Schmidt, and Sickles analyze the estimation problem in this model at some length. For large N, this presents a fairly cumbersome problem of estimation. But, for settings of the size in their applications and the one below, this enhanced fixed effects model can comfortably be estimated by simple, unadorned least squares. (For example, their model involved 14 basic coefficients and a $[\gamma, \delta, \theta]$ for each of eight firms, for a total of 38 coefficients. This is well within the reach of any modern regression package, even on a PC.)[18] Alternative approachs are suggested by Kumbhakar (1991), Kumbhakar and Heshmati (1991), and Kumbhakar and Hjalmarsson (1991).

Obviously, there is no single right way to formulate the model in this context. On the other hand, it is clear from the preceding, having a panel of data opens up a number of possibilities.

---

[18] The point is that there are few practical obstacles to computing estimators for the various frontier models given the current state of computer software.

2.6 The Costs of Production and Other Formulations

Thus far, little mention has been made of alternative representations of the technology, including the cost, profit, revenue, and distance functions. Consider, for example, a stochastic cost frontier,

$$C_i = C(y_i, \boldsymbol{w}_i) + v_i + u_i \qquad (2.58)$$

The same logic as appears in Sections 2.4 and 2.5 and discussed in Chapter 1 leads to a composed error model. Any errors in production decisions would have to translate into costs of production higher than the theoretical norm. Likewise, in the context of a profit or revenue function, any error of optimization would necessarily translate into lower profits or revenues for the producer. But, at the same time, the stochastic nature of the production frontier would imply that the theoretical minimum cost frontier would also be stochastic.

The interpretation of the inefficiency terms is complicated a bit by the dual approach to estimation. Suppose that on the production side of the model, the representation of a one-sided error term as reflective purely of technical inefficiency is appropriate. The computation is *conditional* on the inputs chosen, so whether the choice of inputs is itself *allocatively* efficient is a side issue, albeit an important one. On the cost side, however, any errors in optimization, technical or allocative, must show up as higher costs. As such, a producer that we might assess as operating technically efficiently by a production function measure might still appear inefficient viz-a-viz a cost function. Some recent applications which have been based on cost functions have made this explicit by further decomposing the stochastic term in the cost function to produce

$$C_i = C(y_i, \boldsymbol{w}_i) + v_i + u_i + A_i \qquad (2.59)$$

where A_i is strictly attributable to allocative inefficiency. This decomposition is examined in the next section.

In the absence of constant returns-to-scale, even with allocative efficiency, there is an ambiguity in the interpretation of the one-sided error on the cost side. Take a Cobb-Douglas production function with no allocative inefficiency as a simple illustration. [This derivation appears in detail in Schmidt (1986), so it is omitted here.] If the production function is Cobb-Douglas,

$$y_i = \alpha + \sum_k \beta_k \ln x_k + v_i - u_i \qquad (2.60)$$

Then,

$$\ln c_i = K + \frac{1}{r}\ln y_i + \sum_k \gamma_k \ln w_{ik} - \frac{1}{r}(v_i - u_i) \tag{2.61}$$

$$\text{where } r = \sum_k \beta_k$$

$$\text{and } \gamma_k = \beta_k/r.$$

Thus, economies of scale ($r > 1$) tend to dampen the effect of technical inefficiency. Evidently, the simple interpretation of the one-sided error on the cost side as a Farrell measure of inefficiency is inappropriate *unless the measure is redefined in terms of costs, rather than output*. That is, one might choose to make costs, rather than output, the standard against which efficiency is measured. At least in this context, this is nothing more than a matter of interpretation. On the other hand, it is equally clear that by some further manipulation, the estimated inefficiency obtained in the context of a cost function can be translated into a Farrell measure of technical inefficiency, that is, just by multiplying it by r.

For the simple case above in which the production function is linearly homogeneous, the effect of economies of scale can be removed by rescaling the estimated disturbance. A corresponding adjustment may be possible in more involved models such as the translog model. Suppose that the production function is homothetic, but not homogeneous, and, as before, that

$$Q_i = Q_i^* U_i \tag{2.62}$$

Then,[19]

$$\ln C_i = \ln c(w_i) + \ln H(Q_i) \tag{2.63}$$

Schmidt's formulation above is clearly a special case. Unless $\ln H(.)$ is linear in $\ln Q_i$, as it is when the production function is homogeneous, the technical inefficiency may be carried over to the cost function in a very complicated manner. For example, in the translog model with homothetic production frontier,

$$\ln H(Q_i) = \gamma_Q \ln Q_i + \frac{1}{2}\gamma_{QQ}(\ln Q_i)^2 \tag{2.64}$$

The substitution of $Q_i = Q_i^* U_i$ produces

$$\ln H(Q_i) = \gamma_Q \ln Q_i^* + \frac{1}{2}\gamma_{QQ}(\ln Q_i^*) + \ln U_i(\gamma_Q + \gamma_{QQ}\ln Q_i^* + \frac{1}{2}\gamma_{QQ}\ln U_i)$$
$$= \gamma_Q \ln Q_i^* + \frac{1}{2}\gamma_{QQ}(\ln Q_i^*)^2 + u_i. \tag{2.65}$$

[19] See Christensen and Greene (1976).

The latter term would appear is the "inefficiency" term. Other models might be expected to appear similarly. As such, the usual assumption that u_i in the cost frontier function can vary independently of y_i may be problematic. (This merely reinforces the problem.) The issue of the exogeneity of y_i in estimation of a cost function was raised as early as 1963, by Nerlove (1963).

Similar arguments apply to a profit function. This does not preclude either formulation, but one should bear in mind the possible ambiguities in interpretation in these alternative models. It might make more sense, then, to relabel the result on the cost side as "cost inefficiency." The strict interpretation of technical inefficiency in the sense of Farrell may be problematic, but it seems counterproductive to let this be a straightjacket. The argument that there is a cost frontier that would apply to any given producer would have no less validity. Deviations from the cost frontier could then be interpreted as the total of technical and allocative inefficiency. At the same time, both inefficiencies have a behavioral interpretation, and whatever effect is carried over to the production side is induced, instead. The same logic would carry over to a profit function. The upshot of this argument is that estimation techniques which seek to decompose cost inefficiency into an allocative and a true Farrell measure of technical inefficiency may neglect to account for the direct influence of output, itself, on the residual inefficiency once allocative inefficiency is accounted for. The Kopp and Diewert (1982) approach is an attempt to deal with this issue.

2.7   Measuring Allocative Efficiency

It is clear from the preceding that measurement of allocative efficiency, that is, the extent to which input choices fail to satisfy the marginal equivalences for cost minimization, is outside the reach of the production frontier model. Several approaches to measuring allocative inefficiency have been suggested.

The cost function provides a convenient framework for analyzing allocative inefficiency. It is a convenient specification for multiple-output technologies. Second, Shephard's lemma provides directly a set of input choices which are both technically and allocatively efficient.

Kopp and Diewert (1982) approach the problem by analyzing the cost-minimizing demands implied by Shephard's lemma (see Figure 2.1). The efficient isoquant is labeled SS' while the actual input choice is labeled x^A. The technically efficient input vector, *relative to* x^A is labeled x^B so the Farrell measure of the technical efficiency of x^A is $\| x^B \| / \| x^A \|$, where $\| z \|$ denotes the length of the vector z, $(z'z)^{1/2}$. The line WW' shows the observed price ratio. The technically *and* allocatively efficient input point, given output, Q, and the observed input price vector, w^A, is x^E. The costs of producing at point x^C are the same as at x^E, so the measure of allocative efficiency is $\| x^C \| / \| x^B \|$. Note that x^B is merely a benchmark. The measure gives the increase in costs solely attributable to a suboptimal

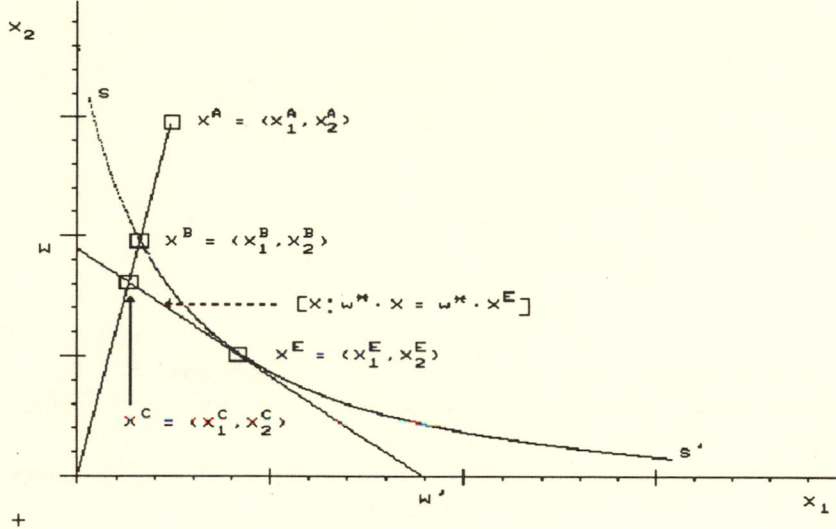

Fig. 2.1 Technical and allocative efficiency

input mix. By construction, the *mix* of inputs at x^A is the same as that at x^B. The "total efficiency," or "cost efficiency," is then $\| x^C \| / \| x^A \|$.

These efficiency measures can be computed if the two input vectors, x^B and x^C, can be deduced from known information. Kopp and Diewert suggest the following approach: Obtain an estimate of the minimum cost function, say $C(y, w^A)$, where w_A denotes the observed input price vector. Denote by C_*^A the implied minimum cost of production of y at w^A. The components of the vector x^C can be deduced with the following equations:

1. The input mix (factor input ratios) of x^A and x^C are the same.

$$\frac{x_i^C}{x_N^C} = \frac{x_i^A}{x_N^A} \qquad \forall \quad i = 1, \ldots, N - 1 \tag{2.66}$$

2. The total costs of production at x^C are the same as those at x^E.

$$w^{A'} x^C = C_*^A \tag{2.67}$$

The right-hand sides of all N equations are observed, the last as the predicted cost from the estimated cost frontier. Recall that the ratio $x_i^A/x_N^A = a_i$ is known. The solution for x^C is contained in

$$
\begin{bmatrix}
1 & 0 & 0 & \cdots & 0 & \dfrac{-x_1^A}{x_N^A} \\[1ex]
0 & 1 & 0 & \cdots & 0 & \dfrac{-x_2^A}{x_N^A} \\[1ex]
0 & 0 & 1 & \cdots & 0 & \dfrac{-x_3^A}{x_N^A} \\[1ex]
\cdots & \cdots & \cdots & \cdots & \cdots & \cdots \\[1ex]
w_1 & w_2 & w_3 & \cdots & & w_N
\end{bmatrix}
\begin{bmatrix}
x_1^C \\ x_2^C \\ x_3^C \\ \vdots \\ x_N^C
\end{bmatrix}
=
\begin{bmatrix}
0 \\ 0 \\ 0 \\ \vdots \\ C_*^A
\end{bmatrix}
$$

The solution vector is C_*^A times the last column of the inverse of the matrix on the left, which, consequently, gives the column vector of S_j/w_*^A, where S_j is the factor cost share and w_*^A is an element of the input price vector at which x^C minimizes costs.

This produces the wherewithal to compute the total efficiency. To compute the allocative efficiency component, the vector x^B is required. Kopp and Diewert observe that there is some price vector w^B for which x^B is allocatively efficient. They suggest, therefore, deriving simultaneously the $N-1$ relative prices in w^B and the N elements of x^B by employing

1. Equality of the factor input mix of x^B and x^A

$$
\frac{x_i^B}{x_N^B} = \frac{x_i^A}{x_N^A} \qquad i = 1, \ldots, N-1 \tag{2.68}
$$

2. The demand system implied by Shephard's lemma:

$$
x_i^B = \frac{\partial C(y, w^B)}{\partial w_i^B} \qquad i = 1, \ldots, N \tag{2.69}
$$

This provides a set of $N-1$ linear equations and N nonlinear equations for obtaining the N factor demands and $N-1$ relative input prices. With x^B in hand, the allocative efficiency component of the total efficiency can be computed.

Kopp and Diewert illustrate their technique with a Cobb-Douglas and with a nonhomothetic translog cost function.[20] For purposes of illustration, it is worthwhile to lay out in detail the calculations involved in their method: For a Cobb-Douglas technology, the problem is actually rather simple. The elements of the solution for $x_i^B/_N^B$ obey the same proportionality relationship as $x_i^C/_N^C$, that is, 1. above. To

---

[20]Zeischang (1983) shows how the latter system may be reduced from a $(2N-1)$ order problem to an N-order problem. The original methodology is presented in detail purely for pedagogical reasons; it is simpler to interpret. In practical terms, N is rarely more than 4, so the computational savings of the Zeischang method could be overestimated. On the other hand, as Zeischang observed, setting up the nonlinear solution, the effort for which is independent of N, may be simpler with his method.

solve for the remaining element, it is possible, with a Cobb-Douglas cost function, to go back to the production function. Schmidt and Lovell (1979) give the explicit relationship,

$$C = K\,Q^{1/r}\prod_i w_i^{\gamma_i},$$

$$Q = a\prod_i x_i^{\alpha_i}$$

(2.70)

where $r = \sum_i \alpha_i, \gamma_i = \alpha_i/r,$ and $\ln K = \ln r - (\ln a)/r - (1/r)\sum_i \alpha_i \ln \alpha_i.$

From the parameters of the cost function, it is possible to deduce directly the parameters of the production function. The system for the unscaled elements of x^B is then closed by substituting $x_i^B = (x_i^A/x_N^A)x_N^B$ into the production function, and inverting with the known value of Q to produce the Nth equation,

$$x_N^B = \left[\frac{Q}{a\prod_{i=1}^{N-1}(x_i^A/x_N^A)^{\alpha_i}}\right]^{1/r}$$

(2.71)

The cost frontier used by Kopp and Diewert is an extension of Christensen and Greene's (1976) nonhomothetic cost function,

$$\ln C_t = \alpha_0 + \sum_{i=1}^N \alpha_i \ln w_{it} + \frac{1}{2}\sum_{i=1}^N\sum_{j=1}^N \gamma_{ij}\ln w_{it}\ln w_{jt}$$
$$+ \sum_{i=1}^N \rho_i t \ln w_{it} + \psi + \sum_{i=1}^N \delta_{Qi}\ln w_{it}\ln Q_t$$
$$+ \gamma_Q \ln Q_t + \frac{1}{2}\gamma_{QQ}\ln^2 Q_t + u_t,$$

(2.72)

where "t" indexes time periods—they used aggregate time-series data.[21] The various parametric restrictions needed to impose homogeneity of degree zero in the input prices are assumed to be in place. The demand system is

$$m_i = \frac{\partial \ln C_t}{\partial \ln w_{it}} = \alpha_i + \sum_{j=1}^N \gamma_{ij}\ln w_{jt} + \delta_{Qi}\ln Q_t + \rho_i t.$$

(2.73)

The parameters of the cost function are estimated first, in their case by using an iterative seemingly unrelated regressions technique. The cost function is then used in

---

[21] The incorporation of nonneutral technical change is achieved by the terms involving t. It is not clear whether the remaining translog terms, the cross terms involving t and $\ln y$, were omitted from the study or merely from the text.

the two steps discussed above. The second set of equations to be solved (iteratively, by Newton's method) is

$$x_i - \left[\frac{C}{w_i}\right]\left[\alpha_i + \sum_{j=1}^{N} \gamma_{ij} \ln w_j + \delta_{yi} \ln y + \rho_i t\right] = 0 \qquad i = 1,\ldots,N-1$$

$$x_N - \left[\frac{C}{w_N}\right][1 - m_1 - m_2 - \cdots - m_{N-1}] = 0 \qquad (2.74)$$

$$x_i - a_i x_N = 0 \qquad i = 1,\ldots,N-1$$

The $2N - 1$ equation system can obviously be reduced to one of N equations by substituting the last $N - 1$ into the left-hand side of the first $N - 1$. The unknowns become the $N - 1$ relative prices and x_N. It can be reduced further to $N - 1$ equations by dividing x_i in the first $N - 1$ equations by x_N to obtain a_i and then dividing the cost term not by x_N but by $\partial C(..)/\partial w_N$, which equals x_N by Shephard's lemma. Of course, this is merely a substitution of the Nth equation in the first $N - 1$.[22]

Kopp and Diewert argued that the technique was only applicable to deterministic frontier cost functions, though this seems a bit strong. If the cost function were a stochastic frontier, instead, the only difference in the computations would be the addition of an estimate of v_i to C_*^A. A footnote in Kopp and Diewert suggests that this point was made at the time by Knox Lovell. Note, also, that the outcome of this exercise hangs crucially on the value used for C_*^A. This, in turn, depends on how the "frontier" nature of the cost function is handled. Since their model was estimated by a variant of least squares, some correction was necessary. In the authors' words, "To transform the resulting average practice cost function into a frontier, we have altered several higher order parameters and the intercept. The result is a non-neutrally displaced function which has the characteristics of [a] full frontier" (p. 328). Without dwelling on the issue, it is worth emphasizing the importance of the adjustment of the cost function in the final estimates. Note, for example, that the proportional adjustment in C_*^A translates unit for unit into the estimated technical efficiency estimate. The Kopp and Diewert method is a creative solution to the problem of measuring technical and allocative inefficiency, but there is a very serious loose end to be tied up. Further research is clearly warranted.

---

[22]Zeischang (1983) suggested this as well. His statement (p. 404) that the equation system be further reduced to one of $N - 1$ equations in $N - 1$ unknowns is a bit misleading, however, since one way or another, the system must be closed with an estimate of the numeraire input. His result does serve to show that the system can be solved recursively. That is, x_N can be obtained residually, after the input vector is obtained, and only $N - 1$ equations need be solved iteratively. His point that one need not solve the $(2N - 1)$-order system iteratively is, of course, clear upon inspection.

A second possibility is to estimate, directly, the demand system and the measurement of technical efficiency. For a simple example, Schmidt (1977) reports the following demand system derived from a stochastic frontier model:

$$\ln x_k^* = B_k + \frac{1}{r} \ln y_i + g_k(w_i) - \frac{1}{r}(v_i - u_i) \qquad (2.75)$$

The implication is that factor demands are all bounded from below by the cost-minimizing factor demand associated with output on the stochastic frontier. This is, in itself, a rather unsatisfactory result, in that it implies that factor *ratios* are efficient. On the other hand, it also confirms the earlier observation, that allocative inefficiency should be modeled apart from technical inefficiency.

An alternative approach is to posit the cost minimizing demands,

$$x_{ik} = x_i^*(\boldsymbol{w}_i, y_i) + \eta_{ik} \qquad (2.76)$$

where the deterministic part on the RHS right-hand side is the cost-minimizing factor demand, and η_i represents the deviation, or allocative inefficiency. Given the formulation, it might be more convenient to model x_i/x_j. Schmidt (1986) extended the Cobb-Douglas model above to include a demand system:

$$\ln \frac{x_N}{x_j} = \ln \left(\frac{\beta_N/w_N}{\beta_j/w_j} \right) + \eta_j = B_j + \eta_j \qquad (2.77)$$

where $(\eta_1, \ldots, \eta_{N-1})$ has a multivariate normal distribution. The demand system can then be estimated jointly with the cost frontier. The difficulty with this approach, which is recurrent, is that the relationship between η_j and the disturbance in the cost frontier model makes estimation exceedingly complicated in even the simplest of models.

A number of studies have posited cost functions and associated demand systems:

$$\ln C = h(\boldsymbol{w}, y) + v + u' \qquad (2.78)$$
$$S_j = \frac{\partial \ln C}{\partial \ln w_j} = m(\boldsymbol{w}, y) + \eta_j$$

where S_j is the cost share of the jth factor. Examples include Greene (1980b), Kumbhakar (1991), and Ferrier and Lovell (1990). Greene raised the issue of the connection that must exist between η and u', but his model treated them as independent (and omitted v). Subsequent modelers have attempted to formulate such a relationship. Ferrier and Lovell imposed the restriction

$$u' = u_* + \sum_j F_j \eta_j^2 \qquad (2.79)$$

with u_* and $F_j > 0$, which ostensibly solves the problem. But they also assumed that the allocative inefficiencies were the same for all observations, which rather limits the generality of the technique.[23]

Kumbhakar extends Ferrier and Lovell by imposing the conditions of Shephard's lemma on the disturbances in the cost function. He imposes the relationship $\eta = \partial u' / \partial \ln w_j$, then determines the implications for u' and formulates the log-likelihood. His results are specific to a translog cost function corresponding to a nonhomothetic production function, but throughout this literature, this model appears to have proved quite general enough for the analyses. [See Christensen and Greene (1976).]

Several recent studies have couched inefficiency in terms of a profit maximizing firm using either a production function and the first-order conditions for profit maximization or a profit function and, through Hotelling's lemma, the implied demand system. The former is illustrated by Kalirajan (1990), whose estimating system consisted of a translog production function,

$$\ln Q = \alpha + \sum_k \beta_k \ln x_k + \frac{1}{2} \sum_k \sum_l \gamma_{kl} \ln x_k \ln x_l + v - u \qquad (2.80)$$

and a set of "marginal productivity conditions,"

$$C_k = \frac{p_k x_k}{p_y y} = \beta_k + \sum_l \gamma_{kl} \ln x_l + w_k. \qquad (2.81)$$

The inefficiency terms are u, the technical component, and the vector w, the allocative components. A log-likelihood function is formulated based on a joint normal distribution for w and an independent convolution of v and u. [This is the same approach taken in Greene (1980b).] The second approach is illustrated by Kumbhakar (1987), who formulates and estimates a profit function based on a Cobb-Douglas production function and a set of demand equations which are essentially the same as Kalijaran's. Other references which are based on this approach include Kumbhakar (1989), Seale (1990), and Kumbhakar and Bhattacharyya (1991). The latter takes a novel approach based on a shadow profit function which deviates from the "frontier" profit function when the producer is inefficient.

Questions of how to integrate the primary function and the demand system apply equally to profit, cost, and production functions. The specification of a demand system containing two-sided disturbances *derived by differentiation* from a cost func-

---

[23] Panel data allow the allocative inefficiency to vary over observations if either F_j or η_j are assumed to be time-invariant.

tion which contains an aggregated one-sided disturbance presents a sticky problem. Consider the formulation suggested by Kumbhakar:

$$\ln C = \ln C^* + v + u + \mathbf{a}' \mathbf{Fa} \tag{2.82}$$

where $\mathbf{a}$ is the set of allocative inefficiency terms also appearing in the factor share equations,[24]

$$S_i = \frac{\partial \ln C}{\partial \ln \mathbf{w}} \tag{2.83}$$

The difficult issue seems to be how to justify the *quadratic* form in $\mathbf{a}$ in the cost function and the *linear* form in $\mathbf{a}$ in the share equations without assuming that $\mathbf{a}$ is just a linear function of $\ln \mathbf{w}$.[25] *The differentiation is with respect to* $\ln \mathbf{w}$, *not* $\mathbf{a}$.

A specification which is consistent with Shephard's lemma and which allows *independent* variation of the allocative inefficiency and the input prices remains to be operationalized. Consider the following candidate: Let $\mathbf{a}$ be an $N \times 1$ vector of disturbances, distributed normally with mean $\mathbf{0}$ and covariance matrix , where N is the number of factors of production. Let the cost function be

$$\ln C = \alpha_0 + \sum_i \alpha_i \ln w_i + \cdots + v + u + e^{\sum_i a_i \ln w_i} \tag{2.84}$$

$$= \alpha_0 + \sum_i \alpha_i \ln w_i + \cdots + v + u + A$$

where

$$v = \text{stochastic variation in the frontier}$$
$$u = \text{technical inefficiency, } u \gtrless 0$$
$$A = \text{allocative inefficiency, } A \gtrless 0$$

By Shephard's lemma,

$$S_i = \frac{\partial \ln C}{\partial \ln w_i} = \alpha_i + \cdots + a_i A \tag{2.85}$$

Since the factor shares must sum to 1, it follows that $\sum_i a_i = 0$ and that

$$A = \prod_{i=1}^{N-1} \left(\frac{w_i}{w_N} \right)^{a_i} \tag{2.86}$$

---

[24] Since the variances and covariances of the inefficiency terms are unconstrained, the positive definite matrix F is superfluous and will generally be unidentified.

[25] This is, in fact, explicitly derived as such in Kumbhakar (1991).

which might have been expected given that the cost function and the shares are fully determined by the $N - 1$ relative prices. The characteristics of A are fairly straightforward. Write

$$A = \prod_i e^{z_i} \qquad (2.87)$$

where $z_i = a_i \ln w_i \approx N[0, (\ln w_i)^2]$.

The exponent of a normally distributed variable has a log-normal distribution, and the product of log-normals is distributed log-normally. Collecting some terms, we find that $A|\mathbf{w}$ has a log-normal distribution with mean

$$E[A|\boldsymbol{w}] = e^{\frac{1}{2}(\ln \boldsymbol{w})' \boldsymbol{\Sigma}(\ln \boldsymbol{w})}, \qquad (2.88)$$

and variance

$$\text{var}[A|\boldsymbol{w}] = E^2[A](E^2[A] - 1)$$

This captures the flavor of Schmidt's and Kumbhakar's formulations, but still allows the inefficiency **a** and the factor prices **w** to vary independently. Among the costs are that A is heteroskedastic, an aspect which proves problematic below.

There are a number of problems to be solved before this could be made operational. Looking only at the cost function, the compound disturbance is the sum of a normal, a log-normal, and whatever distribution is assumed for u, usually truncated normal. The relationship between the disturbance in the cost function, A, and the share equations, $a_i A$, remains to be established. Conditioned on w,

$$E[a_i A] = E_{a_i}[E[a_i A|a_i]] = E_{a_i}[a_i E[A|a_i]] \qquad (2.89)$$

The inner expectation is

$$E[A|a_i] = w_i^{a_i} E[e^{\sum_{j \neq i} a_j \ln w_j}] \qquad (2.90)$$

The variable in brackets is log-normally distributed. The mean is the counterpart to the expression given earlier, but omitting a_i. Denote this mean $\sigma_{(i)}$. Collecting terms,

$$E[a_i A] = \sigma_{(i)} E[a_i e^{a_i \ln w_i}] = \sigma_{(i)} E[a_i (w_i)^{a_i}] \qquad (2.91)$$

The sign of this is indeterminate, as it is a function of w_i as well as the normally distributed a_i.[26] With this expectation denoted as μ_i, the share equation is

---

[26] The results in Beckers and Hammond (1987) may prove useful in evaluating the expression.

$$S_i = (\alpha_i + \mu_i) + \cdots + (a_i A - \mu_i) \qquad (2.92)$$

This completes the specification. Obviously, estimation procedures remain a difficult problem. Joint estimation of the share equations by SURE procedures is unlikely to provide consistent estimates of the parameters. Although the disturbance has mean zero, the constant term $(\alpha_i + \mu_i)$ is a function of w, which differs across observations. Least squares estimation of the cost function alone is likewise inconsistent. Unlike the more familiar cases, the effect of the inefficiency term A is dependent on w. Thus, since A has a nonconstant mean, it does not appear that least squares will merely displace the constant term in this model. The formulation of a full information maximum likelihood estimator appears to be a particularly intricate problem, but may provide the only way out of these constraints. It does appear that difficulties on the order of the preceding must inevitably accompany a fully internally consistent specification. On the other hand, the problem does not appear to be unsurmountable. The translog system is especially convenient for this specification because of the tractability of the distribution of functions of the log-normal distribution.

Yet another approach to estimating allocative inefficiency is to examine the observed demands to ascertain whether they are the cost-minimizing demands consistent with the observed prices. Alternatively, one might attempt to ascertain the set of prices which would make the observed factor demands cost minimizing. Deviations of these "perceived prices" from the actual observed prices are taken as evidence of allocative inefficiency. Examples include Sickles, Good, and Johnson (1986), and Eakin and Kniesner (1988). Eakin and Kniesner estimate a translog cost function and demand system of the form

$$\ln C = \ln C[y, \ln(w_1 + \theta_1), \ldots] \qquad (2.93)$$
$$S_j = \frac{\partial \ln C}{\partial \ln(w_j + \theta_j)}$$

The parameters θ_j represent the deviations of shadow prices from actual prices, so they are the inefficiency measures in this model.

The simultaneous estimation of technical and allocative inefficiency remains a relatively lightly trodden path in this literature. Kumbhakar's results suggest that it may be possible to operationalize a joint estimator. But, there remains the problem of reconciling the allocative inefficiency estimate produced by an estimated cost function with the original Farrell measure. If the production function is nonhomothetic, this relationship remains obscure.

2.8 Application

The latter chapters of this volume contain several applications of frontier and efficiency estimation. They are part of a voluminous and growing literature on this subject. In order to illustrate the techniques described above, this section presents a study based on a previously used [by Kumbhakar (1991)] panel data set from the U.S. domestic airline industry.[27] The purpose is not to study the airline industry as such, but merely to show how different assumptions and specifications affect the estimates one obtains and the inferences one might make.

2.8.1 Computer Software and Some Methodological Issues

All the analysis is carried out using the LIMDEP (Greene, 1991) computer program. Some of the panel data techniques are available in many other packages (e.g., SAS, TSP, Rats, Gauss), and, of course, least squares and variants thereon can be handled with any econometrics program. Battese (1991) describes a program by Coelli (1989) which also handles the random effects model for the stochastic frontier. The cross-sectional version of the stochastic frontier model is actually quite straightforward, and, for example, easily programmed with Gauss or Fortran (e.g., in conjunction with GQOPT). There do not appear to be any general-purpose packages other than LIMDEP which include both the stochastic frontier models and the various panel data estimators (nor, surprisingly enough, any others which even include the cross-sectional variants of the stochastic frontier models). The gamma/normal mixture model remains to be operationalized. Greene's (1990) formulation is quite cumbersome. Beckers and Hammond's may prove to be the more practical, and an implementation may (as of this writing) be in process.[28] If so, this could also be a useful and interesting extension of the stochastic frontier model.

There are no general-purpose econometric packages which specifically contain maximum likelihood estimators for deterministic frontier models, though there are any number of programs with which the linear and quadratic programming "estimators" can be computed. The log-likelihood function for the gamma model is extremely simple. However, estimation of this model is quite difficult for iterative search methods based on gradient techniques. The fact that the signs of the residuals must be constrained often requires some adjustment of the parameter estimates when the constraint is violated. Any ad hoc method of doing so will almost certainly introduce discontinuities in the function being maximized. The Kopp and Diewert method requires some rather specialized programming. Once the methodological issue of how best to handle the frontier versus average practice issue in this area is settled—see the earlier description of Kopp and Diewert's ad hoc adjustment of the model—a general program which "hardwired" the Kopp and Diewert technique would be a very useful addition to the analyst's tool kit.

The preceding are all single-equation methods and estimators. Simultaneous estimation of a cost function and a demand system based on a multivariate normal

---

[27] The present data set contains several additional years of data.
[28] Personal correspondence from Hammond to the author.

distribution for all disturbances presents no particular obstacle with modern software (once again, TSP, LIMDEP, RATS, Gauss). But, there is no general-purpose program yet available for handling a properly specified system of cost and demand equations which would estimate both technical and allocative inefficiency. A difficult methodological issue remains to be sorted out before this can be done.

2.8.2 The Data Set

This application is based on the U.S. domestic airline industry. The data are an extension of Trethaway and Windle (1983). The raw data set is a balanced panel of 25 firms observed over 15 years. After removing observations because of strikes, mergers, and missing data, the panel becomes an unbalanced one of a total of 194 observations on 15 firms. A summary appears in Table 2.1.

In a few cases, the time series contain gaps. If this study were to involve fitting models of stochastic processes, this would be problematic, and it might be preferable to omit these firms. But the fixed and random effects models are not affected by gaps in the series, since the ordering of observations within a group (firm) is not used in fitting the models. One of the models, that proposed by Cornwell, Schmidt, and Sickles (1990), does involve quadratic functions of time t, which are computed *before* selecting out these observations. This has some effect on the estimates for these firms, since it involves interpolating the missing interior points. But the gaps will not invalidate the techniques as long as the time variable is properly constructed.

Production and cost frontiers are fit for a five-input production process—labor, fuel, flight equipment, ground property, and materials. Labor is an index of 15 types of employees, and fuel is an index based on total consumption. The remaining variables are types of capital. It might be preferable to aggregate these into a single index,

Table 2.1 Summary of Data Set

Airline	Years	Observations
American	1970–1984	15
Braniff	1970–1982	13
Continental	1970–1981	12
Delta	1970–1984	15
Eastern	1970–1979, 1981–1984	14
National	1971–1973, 1976–1979	7
Northwest	1971, 1973–1977, 1979–1981, 1983–1984	11
PanAm	1970–1979	10
TWA	1970–1972, 1974–1984	14
United	1970–1978, 1980–1984	14
Western	1970–1984	15
USAir	1970–1984	15
Frontier	1970–1984	15
AirWest	1970, 1971, 1973–1978, 1980	9
Piedmont	1970–1984	15

but for present purposes, little would be gained. Output aggregates four types of service—regular passenger service, charter service, mail, and other freight. Costs are also conditioned on two control variables—average stage length, which may capture an economy of scale not reflected directly in the output variable, and load factor, which partly reflects the capital utilization rate. A simple log-linear (Cobb-Douglas) specification is used, partly to exploit the self duality of the production and cost functions. The translog or some other function might be preferable, but, as noted, specification is not at issue in the current context.[29]

2.8.3 Least Squares Estimation

Ordinary least squares estimates of the production and cost frontiers using the pooled data set appear in Tables 2.2 and 2.3. The OLS coefficients, themselves, are of somewhat limited usefulness. But it will be worthwhile to note how different assumptions and estimators sometimes produce only minor variation on the OLS estimates. As noted earlier, the presence of economies of scale has implications for the measurement of technical inefficiency with a cost function. Based on the OLS results for the cost function, the estimate of scale economies for these data is $1.14\pm$, which is actually quite substantial by the usual measures. Under most of the assumptions made here, the OLS slope estimates are consistent. Corrections to the OLS estimates for several different possible specifications are shown in the succeeding tables.

The negative coefficient on labor in the production frontier is unexpected. But, it persists in nearly all alternative specifications. This could be due to any of several causes, including specification problems and measurement error.

---

[29] Obviously, the estimates will partly depend on the extent to which the Cobb-Douglas function misspecifies the technology. A more detailed analysis would doubtless consider this issue more closely. As noted, the purpose here is merely to illustrate the estimation techniques.

Table 2.2   Ordinary Least Squares Estimates of the Production Frontier

Dependent variable	=	lnOUTPUT
Observations	=	194
Standard deviation of residuals	=	.1501687
Sum of squares	=	4.23952
R-squared	=	.9818345

Variable	Coefficient	Standard Error	t-Ratio
Constant	−.12802	.05055	−6.231
LnFUEL	.29405	.07305	4.025
LnMTL	.76259	.08146	9.361
LnEQUIP	.15567	.07909	1.968
LnLABOR	−.35542	.06396	−5.557
LnPROPERTY	.22510	.03334	6.751

Table 2.3 Ordinary Least Squares Estimates of the Cost Frontier

Dependent variable	$= \ln COST/w_P$
Observations	= 194
Standard deviation of residuals	= .123126
Sum of squares	= 2.04609
R-squared	= .9839330

Variable	Coefficient	Standard Error	t-Ratio
Constant	1.9646	.1628	12.068
$\ln w_F/w_P$	.015670	.02329	.673
$\ln w_M/w_P$	.67444	.1341	5.031
$\ln w_E/w_P$	.10369	.09134	1.135
$\ln w_L/w_P$	.11964	.1223	.978
$\ln OUTPUT$	.87605	.01492	58.700
STAGE	−.00020136	.4998E-04	−4.029
LOADFCTR	−.77334	.2490	−3.106
POINTS	.0023915	.4101E-03	5.832
Economies of scale $= 1/\gamma_y = 1.14$			

2.8.4 Deterministic Frontier Models

If a deterministic frontier model applies, a direct approach is to use the results of Gabrielsen/Greene and just shift the estimated function up or down, as appropriate, so as to obtain a set of residuals all of which contain the right sign. In the case of the production frontier,

$$\hat{u}_i = \max_i (e_i) - e_i \tag{2.94}$$

while for a cost frontier,

$$\hat{u}_i = e_i - \min_i (e_i) \tag{2.95}$$

The extreme residuals for the two sets of OLS estimates given in Tables 2.2 and 2.3 appear in Table 2.4. If the production function is homogeneous of degree "r," then the inefficiency term estimated with a cost function is $1/r$ times the counterpart from the production function. The necessary correction is shown at the end of Table

Table 2.4 Extreme Residuals—Shift Factor for Estimated Function

Production frontier:	Maximum residual	= .3614
Cost frontier:	Negative of minimum residual	= .2370

To be comparable to the value for the production frontier, the shift factor for the cost frontier should be scaled up by the economies of scale measure of $1/\Sigma_{k\gamma k} = 1.14$, to give .2702.

Table 2.5 Average Proportional Efficiency for Deterministic Frontier
Models

Computed as $(1/N)\ \Sigma_i e^{-\hat{u}_i}$	
Production frontier	.7043
Cost frontier	.7941
Cost, corrected	.7689

The correction for economies of scale is $(E\,[\exp(-\mu)])^r$

2.4. Table 2.5 presents the average of the sample estimates of the Farrell measures of
technical efficiency based on these deterministic frontiers. Once again, a correction is
needed to account for the fact that there are nonconstant returns-to-scale. The rather
high estimated residuals and low efficiency indices are noteworthy. As will be clear
below, the deterministic frontier appears to be including a considerable amount of
random variation in the efficiency term.

Table 2.6 gives a set of method of moments estimators for the parameters of the
distribution of u based on the moments of the OLS residuals. The formulas for these

Table 2.6 Estimated Efficiency Distributions for Deterministic Frontier
Models

	Production	**Cost**
Exponential		
θ	2.763	4.205
$E\,[u]$	.3619	.2378
$S.D.[u]$	.3619	.2378
$E\,[u]$ corrected for scale economies		.2710
$E\,[\exp(-u)]$	.7343	.8079
$E\,[\exp(-u)]$ corrected		.7841
Gamma		
θ	2.3705	3.3487
P	.8567	.7945
$E\,[u]$	.3614	.2373
$S.D.[u]$	.3905	.2662
$E\,[u]$ corrected for scale economies		.2704
$E\,[\exp(-u)]$	.7397	.8125
$E\,[\exp(-u)]$ corrected		.7893
Half-normal		
σ_u	.4529	.1898
$E\,[u]$	.3613	.1514
$S.D.[u]$	.2730	.1144
$E\,[u]$ corrected for scale economies		.1726

calculations follow directly from the expressions for the moments of the distributions. In particular, for the gamma distribution,

$$E[u] = \frac{P}{\theta} \quad \text{and} \quad \text{var}[u] = \frac{P}{\theta^2} \tag{2.96}$$

The exponential is obtained by setting P to 1. Then,

$$E[\exp(-u)] = \left\{ \left[\frac{\lambda}{(1+\lambda)} \right]^P \right\}^r \tag{2.97}$$

(On the production side, r is ignored in the preceding.) Further discussion appears in Section 2.3.3.

The deterministic frontier models, in general, suggest a quite high degree of technical inefficiency. The individual estimates tend to be around .35. The Farrell measure, likewise, is only on the order of .75 to .8.

As might be expected, the gamma and exponential models produce similar results. But, on the cost side, both estimates of $E[u]$ deviate quite substantially from the half-normal model, and the estimated standard deviation of u is substantially lower in both production and cost frontiers for the half-normal model. The substantially lower inefficiency estimates produced by the cost frontier, which in principle reflects both technical and allocative inefficiency, is unexpected. No obvious cause stands out, but the possibility that measurement error might be unduly affecting the deterministic frontier models seems plausible.

2.8.5 Stochastic Frontier Models

Table 2.7 presents method of moments estimators for the parameters of the stochastic frontier models. The basis for the calculations appears in Section 2.4.2 above. Although there is some variation across the specifications, all show a dramatic reduction in the amount of the unexplained variation which is attributed to inefficiency. In particular, $E[u]$ ranges from 5 to 10 percent here as opposed to 30 to 40 percent in the deterministic models. This seems consistent with the proposition that attributing the entire deviation from the frontier to inefficiency instead of partly to random variation leads to quite considerable distortions.

Table 2.8 presents the airline-specific measures of technical inefficiency for the cost and production functions. For the deterministic frontier models, these are just the individual residuals, corrected as described earlier. To save space, only the airline-specific means are given—there is a considerable amount of within airline variation being masked by this calculation. For the stochastic frontier, these are the Jondrow, Lovell, Materov, and Schmidt measures based on corrected least squares. That is, the intercept of the model is adjusted before the residual is computed and the Jondrow,

Table 2.7 Indirect Estimates of Distribution of μ for Stochastic Frontier Models

	Production	Cost
Exponential		
θ	16.072	19.666
σ_v	.1341	.1090
E [u]	.0622	.0508
$S.D.$[u]	.0622	.0508
E [u] corrected for scale economies		.0579
Gamma		
θ	5.987	7.189
P	.5167	.4889
σ_v	.1429	.1162
E [u]	.0863	.0680
$S.D.$[u]	.1201	.0973
E [u] corrected for scale economies		.0775
Half-normal		
σ_u	.1120	.1148
σ_v	.1212	.1083
E [u]	.0894	.0917
$S.D.$[u]	.0407	.0417
E [u] corrected for scale economies		.1045

Table 2.8 Airline-Specific Means of Estimated Inefficiencies, E[u/ϵ] Stochastic Frontier

	Production Frontier		Cost Frontier	
Airline	**Derterministic Frontier**	**Stochastic Frontier**	**Deterministic Frontier**	**Stochastic Frontier**
All airlines	.3746	.0896	.2885	.0729
American	.4049	.1302	.3354	.0754
Braniff	.3908	.0622	.1788	.0725
Continential	.3908	.0519	.1271	.0604
Delta	.3091	.0721	.2085	.0600
Eastern	.4062	.0968	.2741	.0772
National	.4075	.0442	.1045	.0837
Northwest	.3657	.0492	.9229	.0787
Pan Am	.4487	.0972	.2707	.0857
TWA	.3797	.1364	.3514	.0725
United	.3278	.0902	.2502	.0629
Western	.1669	.0481	.1173	.0441
US Air	.5125	.1668	.3995	.1025
Frontier	.2559	.0500	.1322	.0525
Air West	.4600	.1414	.3573	.0920
Piedmont	.3918	.1072	.2979	.0733

Value are computed using the Jondrow, Lovell, Materov, and Schmidt result. Cost frontier estimates are not corrected for scale economies.

Lovell, Materov, and Schmidt transformation is applied. The stark difference between the deterministic and stochastic frontier is clearly visible once again.

Tables 2.9 and 2.10 give the maximum likelihood estimates (MLEs) of the stochastic production and cost frontier models under the assumption of half-normal and exponential disturbances.[30] It is interesting to note that save for the constant terms, the MLEs differ only marginally from the OLS estimates. This is to be expected, since both are consistent. On the other hand, the fact that the MLE of θ in the exponential model is identical to the OLS estimate is striking.

Estimation of a cost frontier as opposed to a production frontier requires a minor change in the log-likelihood function, its derivatives, and the calculation of estimates of u_i. A simple formulation which encompasses both cases is simply to replace ϵ_i and μ (for Stevenson's truncated regression model) with $q\epsilon_i$ and $q\mu$, where $q = +1$ for a production frontier and -1 for a cost frontier, wherever they appear.

Table 2.11 is the counterpart to the right-hand column of each pair in Table 2.8. We also compare the predictions of the exponential and half-normal models in this table. The differences between the two models are substantial. A specification test for one against the other might be useful at this point, but we are not aware of one which could be used. On the other hand, the rankings of the group means is roughly preserved by the two models, so the major difference is actually the more pessimistic assessment produced by the half-normal model.

[30] The truncated normal model routinely defied convergence and, as often as not, produced nonsense estimates. For these data, the assumption of $\mu = 0$ seems warranted.

Table 2.9   Maximum Likelihood Estimates of Stochastic Production Frontiers

Dependent   = lnOUTPUT
Observations = 194

	Half-Normal Model			Exponential Model		
Variable	**Coefficient**	**Std. Error**	**t-Ratio**	**Coefficient**	**Std. Error**	**t-Ratio**
Constant	$-.03459$	.05439	-0.636	$-.06246$	.03197	-1.953
LnFUEL	.30092	.07853	4.832	.30334	.07757	3.911
LnMTL	.75183	.09404	7.995	.73402	.09474	7.748
LnEQUIP	.16064	.08530	1.883	.17864	.08858	2.017
LnLABOR	$-.36598$	.07478	-4.894	$-.37717$	.07461	-5.055
LnPROPERTY	.23005	.03872	5.942	.23256	.03661	6.352
λ	.90561	.63350	1.429			
θ	—	—	—	16.072	5.610	2.865
σ	.17501	.02714	6.449	.13296	.01345	9.885
σ_u	.11747					
σ_ν	.12973					
$E[u]$		.09327			.06222	
S.D.[u]		.07081			.06222	
Log $-$ L		95.899			96.405	

Table 2.10 Maximum Likelihood Estimates of Stochastic Cost Frontiers

Dependent variable = lnCOST/w_P
Observations = 194

	Half-Normal Model			Exponential Model		
Variable	Coefficient	Std. Error	t-Ratio	Coefficient	Std. Error	t-Ratio
Constant	1.84810	.19520	9.470	1.92135	.21560	8.913
Lnw_F/w_P	.01038	.02824	.368	.01417	.02847	.498
Lnw_M/w_P	.72424	.14240	4.752	.68969	.15223	4.531
Lnw_E/w_P	.09508	.09990	.952	.10157	.09945	1.021
Lnw_L/w_P	.07859	.12870	.611	.10761	.12941	.831
LnOUTPUT	.87840	.01950	46.104	.87659	.01952	44.905
STAGE	−.00020	.00007	−3.026	−.00020	.00007	−2.919
LOADFCTR	−.73133	.24423	−2.995	−.76231	.24270	−3.141
POINTS	.00256	.00044	5.860	.00242	.00046	5.304
λ	1.35143	.48970	2.760			
θ				26.720	48.750	.548
σ	.15723	.02797	5.621	.11437	.02304	4.964
σ_u	.12641					
σ_ν	.09354					
$E[u]$	.10086			.03742		
S.D.[u]	.04593			.03742		
Log − L	136.09			135.79		

Table 2.11 Airline-Specific Means of Estimated Inefficiencies, $E[u/\epsilon]$, by MLE Stochastic Frontier

	Production		Cost	
Airline	Half-Normal Frontier	Exponential Frontier	Half-Normal Frontier	Exponential Frontier
All airlines	.0936	.0632	.1011	.0373
American	.0987	.0634	.1399	.0462
Braniff	.0962	.0623	.0729	.0307
Continental	.0801	.0542	.0623	.0279
Delta	.0794	.0511	.0827	.0330
Eastern	.1003	.0646	.1037	.0381
National	.1083	.0788	.0549	.0263
Northwest	.1008	.0828	.0587	.0268
Pan Am	.1111	.0726	.1050	.0382
TWA	.0945	.0609	.1466	.0473
United	.0829	.0583	.0987	.0366
Western	.0586	.0390	.0587	.0272
US Air	.1312	.0942	.1794	.0583
Frontier	.0697	.0456	.0591	.0278
Air West	.1180	.0824	.1524	.0495
Piedmont	.0971	.0642	.1194	.0406

Values are computed using the Jondrow, Lovell, Materov, and Schmidt result. *Note:* Cost frontier estimates are not corrected for scale economies.

Table 2.12 gives the Farrell measures of technical efficiency based on the half-normal model. These are translations of the values in Table 2.11, using Battese and Coelli's result in Section 2.4.3.

2.8.6 Models Based on Panel Data

Table 2.13 contains the OLS estimates of fixed effects models for the production and cost functions. The estimated fixed effects from the estimated cost function provide firm-specific estimates of technical inefficiency. As suggested by Schmidt and Sickles (1984) and Cornwell, Schmidt, and Sickles (1990), these are interpreted as observations from a deterministic frontier model. Table 2.14 contains the implied estimates. It is worth noting the apparent problems of the deterministic frontier model at this point. These estimates, based on the same calculations underlying Tables 2.4 and 2.5, are likely to be somewhat problematic. It is probably more useful to compare them to each other, rather than to an absolute benchmark, such as 0. The effect of noise is to drive the estimated efficiencies away from zero. If it can be assumed even roughly that the distortion is similar across firms, then a comparison of firms to each other will be much more informative than a simple comparison of all firms to the fixed benchmark.

A comparison of Tables 2.14 and 2.6 produces an important difference. The estimates in Tables 2.6 and 2.14 are roughly similar, but, in contrast to those in Table 2.6, the values in Table 2.14 are consistent with the notion that the estimated cost inefficiency contains both allocative and technical components while the estimated productive inefficiency contains only the latter.

Table 2.12 Estimated Farrell Measures of Technical Efficiency Computed as $E[\exp(-u)]$ (raised to r power if cost function)

Airline	Production	Cost
American	.908	.856
Braniff	.910	.922
Continental	.925	.933
Delta	.925	.912
Eastern	.907	.891
National	.900	.940
Northwest	.908	.937
Pan Am	.897	.890
TWA	.912	.850
United	.922	.896
Western	.944	.936
US Air	.880	.819
Frontier	.934	.936
Air West	.891	.844
Piedmont	.909	.875

Based on group means of residuals from models fit by ML.

Table 2.13   Fixed Effects Estimators for the Production and Cost Frontiers

			Production	Cost		
R-squared			.99041	.99679		
F test for group effects			11.120	48.932		
Standard dev. of residual			.11340	.05742		
	Coefficient	S.E.	t-Ratio	Coefficient	S.E.	t-Ratio
Fuel	.085621	.09897	.865	.10257	.01631	6.288
Materials	.95995	.09090	10.560	.52795	.07873	6.706
Equipment	.30006	.1060	2.830	.25701	.04490	5.724
Labor	−.18482	.1359	−1.360	.02579	.06711	.384
Property	.05253	.03591	1.463			
ln Output	—	—	—	.79356	.02161	36.729
Stage Length	—	—	—	−.000245	.000091	−2.691
Load Factor	—	—	—	−.96603	.1493	−6.469
Points	—	—	—	−.000381	.000377	−1.011

Table 2.14   Derived Estimates of Parameters of $f(u)$ Based on Fixed Effects

	Production	Cost
Sample mean	.26526	.24155
Sample standard deviation	.13888	.19014
σ_u	.18382	.25167
$E[u]$	.14667	.20080
$E[u]$ corrected for economies of scale	—	.25304
σ_u corrected for economies of scale	—	.31713

Table 2.15 gives the GLS estimates of the random effects model. MLEs are given in Table 2.16. Derived estimates of the variance parameters in Table 2.15 are consistent with the earlier observations. This model produces a direct estimate of the variance of "v." What is normally produced as the variance of the common disturbance, "u," would, in the current setting, have to be modified according to

$$\text{var}[u] = \left[\left(\frac{\pi}{2}\right) - 1\right] \sigma_u^2 \tag{2.98}$$

The estimates of $E[u]$ produced by this method are nearly the same as those in Table 2.14 for the fixed effects model.

As noted in Section 2.5, panel data allow one to handle explicitly the possibility that the effects might be correlated with the inputs in the production function. Table

Table 2.15 Random Effects Estimators of Production and Cost Frontiers

	Production	Cost
Standard deviation of v		
OLS	.1134	.0572
GLS	.1145	.0577
Standard deviation of u		
OLS	.0802	.1399
GLS	.1426	.2427
σ_u based on GLS	.1886	.3213
$E[u]$	.1505	.2249
Sum of squared residuals	4.8672	4.9600
Sum of squares/total SS	.9791	.9716

	Coefficient	S.E.	t-Ratio	Coefficient	S.E.	t-Ratio
Constant	−.15045	.03298	−4.562	2.3105	.1261	18.327
Fuel	.17651	.08133	2.170	.08233	.01468	5.606
Materials	.93724	.08047	11.647	.59204	.07532	7.860
Equipment	.25257	.09108	2.773	.23792	.04450	5.346
Labor	−.30572	.08800	−3.474	.00816	.06659	.122
Property	.08862	.03179	2.788			
Output	—	—	—	.81239	.02000	40.616
Stage length	—	—	—	−.000147	.000078	−1.884
Load factor	—	—	—	−1.0062	.1470	−6.846
Points	—	—	—	−.0000452	.000360	−.125

Table 2.16 Random Effects Models Estimated by MLE for Half-Normal Model

	Production	Cost
σ_v	.2558	.2827
σ_u	.1124	.0561
Log-likelihood	121.25	244.63

	Production			Cost		
	Coefficient	S.E.	t-Ratio	Coefficient	S.E.	t-Ratio
Constant	.07428	.05458	1.361	2.1048	.2028	10.380
Fuel	.14496	.1154	1.256	.09329	.02374	3.930
Materials	.96951	.07251	13.371	.56303	.3035	1.855
Equipment	.27485	.1300	2.115	.24699	.1493	1.654
Labor	−.28959	.1010	−2.867	.01252	.3101	.040
Property	.06304	.02273	2.773			
Output	—	—	—	.80070	.01550	51.650
Stage Length	—	—	—	−.000208	.00016	−1.290
Load Factor	—	—	—	−.95715	.4468	−2.142
Points	—	—	—	−.0001159	.000444	−.261

Table 2.17   Test Statistics for Fixed vs. Random Effects

	Production	Cost
Hausman test	20.264	14.733
LM test	120.845	475.218

2.17 gives the Hausman test and Lagrange multiplier test statistics for testing the specifications of the fixed and random effects models. The LM statistic in both cases is extremely large, which should rule out any variant of simple least squares. The LM test suggests that there is considerable heterogeneity across the airlines. The several tables above and below which give airline-specific estimates would seem to bear this out. The Hausman statistic bears on the question of which estimator, random or fixed effects, is to be preferred. The Hausman statistic for the production frontier is larger than the critical value—$\chi^2[6]_{.95} = 12.59$. For the cost frontier, the critical value, with 9 degrees of freedom, is 16.92, which presents something of a dilemma. From the point of view of the underlying model, the fixed effects approach would seem to have much less to recommend it. But, the large value for the production frontier weighs in favor of the fixed effects approach in spite of that.

Estimates of the airline-specific average inefficiency terms, u_i, computed by adjusting the fixed effects, are given in Table 2.18. The Farrell measures, computed using Battese and Coelli's formula and the MLE's are given in Table 2.19.

Table 2.18   Estimated Inefficiencies for the LSDV and Random Effects Estimators

	Production			Cost		
Airline	Fixed[1]	REM[2]	MLE/REM[2]	Fixed[1]	REM[2]	MLE/REM[2]
American	.3820	.1404	.2232	.4659	.1782	.1615
Braniff	.2007	.0576	.1391	.1300	.0181	.0557
Continental	.0407	.0093	.1992	.0704	.0143	.0452
Delta	.2256	.0275	.1175	.3032	.0646	.1073
Eastern	.4215	.0203	.2436	.4431	.1723	.1475
National	.2164	.0806	.1359	.0000	.0176	.0395
Northwest	.2617	.0961	.1712	.0807	.0148	.0457
Pan Am	.3741	.1474	.2026	.5399	.1825	.1359
TWA	.3865	.1431	.2257	.4488	.1539	.1479
United	.3069	.0583	.1532	.4629	.1681	.1516
Western	.0000	.0050	.0412	.0525	.0109	.0425
US Air	.4498	.2537	.3163	.3071	.1136	.1170
Frontier	.1208	.0153	.0949	.0588	.0140	.0453
Air West	.3909	.2109	.2501	.1857	.0496	.0641
Piedmont	.2011	.0651	.1539	.0742	.0172	.0508

[1]Adjusted by subtracting maximum for production, minimum for cost. Maximum estimated effect for production was .14576. Value is .14576-a_i. Minimum estimated effect for cost was 2.14608. Value is a_i-2.14608.

[2]Computed by applying Battese and Coelli's formula to group means.

Table 2.19   Farrell Measures of Technical Efficiency Based on MLE

Airline	Production	Cost*
American	.8011	.8182
Braniff	.8716	.9334
Continental	.8209	.9455
Delta	.8904	.8755
Eastern	.7851	.8327
National	.8748	.9525
Northwest	.8443	.9451
Pan Am	.8184	.8460
TWA	.7993	.8322
United	.8593	.8284
Western	.9602	.9488
US Air	.7300	.8651
Frontier	.9106	.9455
Air West	.7805	.9238
Piedmont	.8587	.9391

*Cost measures are corrected for economies of scale.

The final set of estimates for this section is based on Cornwell, Schmidt, and Sickels' model,

$$u_{it} = \theta_{1i} + \theta_{2i}t + \theta_{3i}t^2 \tag{2.99}$$

As noted earlier, the elaborate matrix results in their paper notwithstanding, for a moderately sized data set, the most expeditious way to handle this model is brute force, OLS. In the interest of saving space, the parameter estimates are not given. (The models had, in addition to the previous specification, 45 firm-specific parameters.) The fixed effects for each firm can be computed simply by evaluating the quadratic at the firm-specific coefficients.[31] The first five columns of Table 2.20 give these values for the production frontier for the first five firms. The second set of figures gives the estimated technical inefficiencies for these five firms. Figure 2.2 plots the quadratic function for these firms for the production frontier. (The estimates for the cost frontier appear similar, and are omitted for brevity.) Cornwell, Schmidt, and Sickels suggest that in order to account for the one-sided nature of the disturbance, the estimated disturbances be normalized according to

$$\hat{u}_{it} = \max_i(e_{it}) - e_{it}$$

or

$$\tag{2.100}$$

$$\hat{u}_{it} = e_{it} - \min_i(e_{it})$$

---

[31] This, in turn, is easily automated by gathering coefficients in an $N \times 3$ matrix, Θ, and postmultiplying by a $3 \times T$ matrix, containing a row of 1s, time, and time squared.

Table 2.20 Estimated Firm Effects for Five Firms, Time-Varying Effects

Year	Fixed Effects from Model					After Correction, $Max_i e_{it} - e_{it}$				
	Amer	Bran	Cont	Delta	East	Amer	Bran	Cont	Delta	East
1970	−.333	−.395	−.272	−.333	−.392	.187	.249	.125	.186	.246
1971	−.276	−.359	−.182	−.266	−.334	.159	.241	.064	.149	.216
1972	−.221	−.320	−.101	−.205	−.279	.171	.270	.051	.156	.229
1973	−.168	−.279	−.029	−.151	−.228	.179	.290	.040	.162	.239
1974	−.117	−.235	.034	−.102	−.181	.183	.301	.032	.167	.246
1975	−.067	−.189	.088	−.058	−.137	.181	.303	.026	.172	.251
1976	−.020	−.141	.134	−.021	−.097	.176	.297	.022	.176	.252
1977	.026	−.090	.170	.011	−.060	.165	.281	.021	.180	.251
1978	.070	−.037	.197	.037	−.027	.164	.271	.037	.197	.261
1979	.112	.019	.216	.058	.002	.211	.304	.107	.265	.320
1980	.152	.076	.225	.072	.028	.268	.343	.195	.348	.392
1981	.190	.137	.226	.081	.050	.336	.390	.301	.445	.476
1982	.227	.200	.217	.084	.068	.415	.442	.424	.558	.574
1983	.261	.266	.200	.081	.083	.505	.502	.566	.685	.684
1984	.294	.332	.174	.073	.094	.606	.568	.726	.828	.806

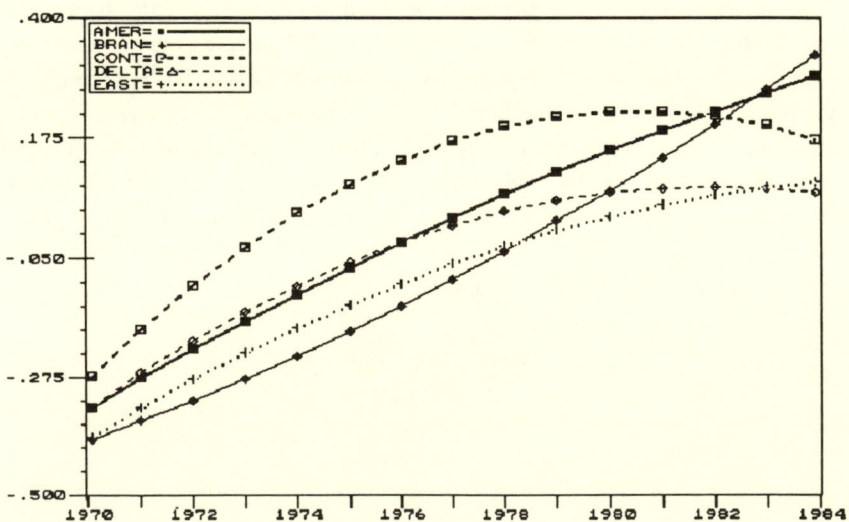

Fig. 2.2 Estimates of u_{it} from fixed effects model

a cost frontier. Since the maximum or minimum is period-specific, and need not apply to the same firm in each period, this correction may upset the quadratic relationship between time and the estimated inefficiencies. Figure 2.3 shows the transformed disturbances from the production frontier for the same five firms.

2.9   Conclusions

As noted at the outset of this discussion, current practice includes two approaches to efficiency measurement, the programming approach and the econometric approach. The deterministic frontier models presented in Section 2.3 represent something of a hybrid of these two approaches. Although it is difficult to draw general conclusions from a single study, the results of this one concur with the common perception that the main advantage of the econometric approach lies in its ability to shift the deleterious effect of measurement error away from estimates of efficiency. The values produced by the deterministic estimators in Table 2.6 seem not only to be implausibly large, but also to distort the expected relationship between cost and production frontiers.

The stochastic frontier approach has a number of virtues, notably its internal consistency and its ease of implementation. For single-equation, cross-sectional analysis, with modern computer software, the stochastic frontier model is not appreciably more complex than a linear regression model. Among the several specifications, half-normal, exponential, and gamma, the only obvious selection criterion seems to be the complexity of the latter, which, in spite of its useful characteristics, rules it out at this time. The possibility of adding a shift parameter to it, and the numerous interesting

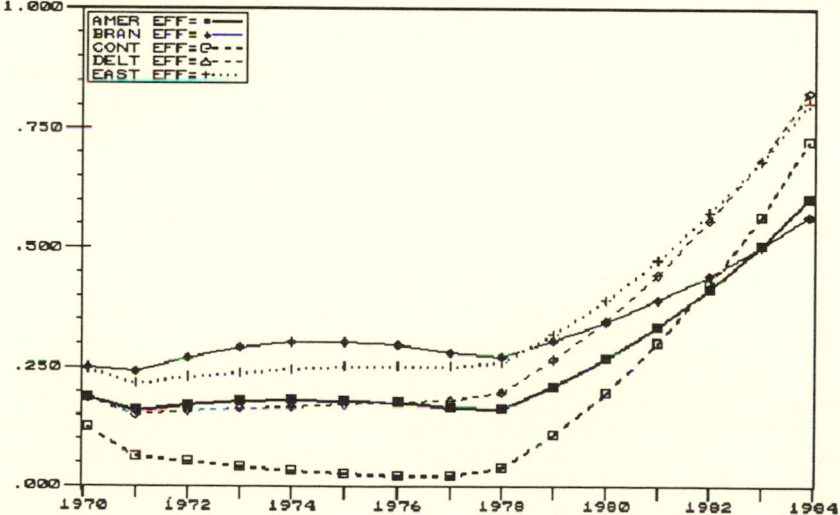

Fig. 2.3   Estimated technical inefficiencies

ancillary calculations derived by Jondrow, Lovell, Materov, and Schmidt and Battese and Coelli suggest that the half-normal model is the most useful formulation.

Panel data obviously open up numerous interesting possibilities. Approaches based on regression analysis of the fixed and random effects models have the appeal of robustness and the potential for a consistent estimator of inefficiency. Unfortunately, the fixed effects model carries with it the necessity that the analyst revert back, essentially, to the deterministic frontier model. The random effects model, on the other hand, has the appeal of the single-equation stochastic frontier. But, as in other settings, the drawback to this approach is that the effects must be assumed to be uncorrelated with the regressors (factors). This is likely to be minor in this context. It is routinely assumed in any event. A remaining drawback to the regression approach is that GLS ignores any additional information that might be available about the distribution of the inefficiency component in the disturbance. Once again, the half-normal model is available as an alternative for which there is a full information MLE available. Whether one is willing to accept the risk of misspecification (the half-normal distribution) in return for the efficiency gain of the MLE over GLS is an issue that the analyst must settle for themselves. The received literature is silent on the issue, perhaps because it is only recently that both random effects estimators have been operationalized in an accessible fashion. This seems to be an issue that might be usefully analyzed in future research.

The truly difficult issue in this context remains how to estimate allocative inefficiency in the context of a properly specified, internally consistent model. The single-equation approach is obviously inadequate. The identification problem is transparent. The construction of a set of demand equations which incorporate allocative inefficiency and which are properly integrated with a cost or production frontier will solve a longstanding and very interesting problem. It appears to this author that the problems of specifying and estimating single-equation models of technical inefficiency are largely solved, and that this is the direction to which methodological research should now turn.

REFERENCES

Aguilar, R. (1988), "Efficiency in Production: Theory and an Application on Kenyan Small-holders," Ph.D. Dissertation, Department of Economics, University of Goteborg, Sweden.

Aigner, D., and S. Chu (1968), "On Estimating the Industry Production Function," *American Economic Review* 58: 826–839.

Aigner, D., T. Amemiya, and D. Poirier (1976), "On the Estimation of Production Frontiers," *International Economic Review* 17: 377–396.

Aigner, D., K. Lovell, and P. Schmidt (1977), "Formulation and Estimation of Stochastic Frontier Production Function Models," *Journal of Econometrics* 6: 21–37.

Arrow, K., H. Chenery, B. Minhas, and R. Solow (1961), "Capital Labor Substitution and Economic Efficiency," *Review of Economics and Statistics* 45: 225–247.

Battese, G. (1991), "Frontier Production Functions and Technical Efficiency: A Survey of Empirical Applications in Agricultural Economics," Department of Econometrics, University of New England, Armedale, Australia (mimeographed).

Battese., G., and G. Corra (1977), "Estimation of a Production Frontier Modeli With Application to the Pastoral Zone of Eastern Australia," *Australian Journal of Agricultural Economics* 21(3) (December): 167–179.

Battese, G., and T. Coelli (1988), "Prediction of Firm-Level Technical Efficiencies with a Generalized Frontier Production Function and Panel Data," *Journal of Econometrics* 38: 387–399.

Bauer, P. (1990), "A Survey of Recent Econometric Developments in Frontier Estimation," Journal of Econometrics 46: 21–39.

Beckers, D., and C. Hammond (1987), "A Tractable Likelihood Function for the Normal-Gamma Stochastic Frontier Model," *Economics Letters* 24: 33–38.

Breusch, T., and A. Pagan (1980), "The LM Test and Its Applications of Model Specification in Econometrics," *Review of Economic Studies* 47: 239–254.

Christensen, L., and W. Greene (1976), "Economies of Scale in U.S. Electric Power Generation," *Journal of Political Economy* 84(4): 655–676.

Cobb, S., and P. Douglas (1928), "A Theory of Production," *American Economic Review* 18: 139–165.

Coelli, T. (1989), "Estimation of Frontier Production Functions: A Guide to the Computer Program FRONTIER," Working Papers in Econometrics and Applied Statistics, No. 34, Department of Econometrics, University of New England, Armidale, Australia.

Cornwell, C., P. Schmidt, and R. Sickles (1990), "Production Frontiers with Cross-Sectional and Time Series Variation in Efficiency Levels," *Journal of Econometrics* 46: 185–200.

Dean, J. (1951), *Managerial Economics.* Englewood Cliffs, N.J.: Prentice Hall.

Deprins, D. (1986), "Maximum Likelihood Estimation of Production Functions with Gamma Residuals and Exogenous Factors of Inefficiency," C.O.R.E., Catholic University of Louvain, Brussels, Belgium, (mimeographed).

Deprins, D., and L. Simar (1986), "Modified Least-Squares Estimators for Deterministic Frontier Functions," C.O.R.E., Catholic University of Louvain, Brussels, Belgium (mimeographed).

Eakin, K., and T. Kniesner (1988), "Estimating a Non-minimum Cost Function for Hospitals," *Southern Economic Journal* 54(3): 583–597.

Farrell, M. (1957), "The Measurement of Productive Efficiency," *Journal of the Royal Statistical Society* (A, general) 120(pt. 3): 253–281.

Ferrier, G., and K. Lovell (1990), "Measuring Cost Efficiency in Banking: Econometric and Linear Programming Evidence," *Journal of Econometrics* 46: 229–245.

Gabrielsen, A. (1975), "On Estimating Efficient Production Functions," Working Paper, No. A-85, Chr. Michelsen Institute, Department of Humanities and Social Sciences, Bergen, Norway.

Greene, W. (1980a), "Maximum Likelihood Estimation of Econometric Frontier Functions," *Journal of Econometrics* 13(1): 27–56.

Greene, W. (1980b), "On the Estimation of a Flexible Frontier Production Model," *Journal of Econometrics* 13(1): 101–115.

Greene, W. (1990), "A Gamma-Distributed Stochastic Frontier Model," *Journal of Econometrics* 46: 141–163.

Greene, W. (1991), "LIMDEP Computer Program: Version 6.0," Econometric Software, Bellport, N.Y.

Hansen, L. (1982) "Large Sample Properties of Generalized Method of Moments Estimators," *Econometrica* 50: 1029–1054.

Hausman, J., and W. Taylor (1981), "Panel Data and Unobservable Individual Effects," *Econometrica* 49: 1377–1398.

Hildebrand, G., and T. Liu (1965), *Manufacturing Production Functions in the United States.* Ithaca, N.Y.: Cornell University Press.

Hunt, J., Y. Kim, and R. Warren (1986), "The Effect of Unemployment Duration of Re-employment Earnings: A Gamma Frontier Approach," Department of Economics, University of Georgia, Athens, Ga University of Georgia (mimeographed).

Johnston, J. (1959), *Statistical Cost Analysis* New York: McGraw-Hill.

Jondrow, J., C. Lovell, I. Materov, and P. Schmidt (1982), "On the Estimation of Technical Inefficiency in the Stochastic Frontier Production Function Model," *Journal of Econometrics* 19(2/3): 233–238.

Kalirajan, K. (1990), "On Measuring Economic Efficiency," *Journal of Applied Econometrics* 5(1): 75–86.

Kopp, R., and W. Diewert (1982), "The Decomposition of Frontier Cost Function Deviations into Measures of Technical and Allocative Efficiency," *Journal of Econometrics* 19(2/3): 319–332.

Kopp, R., and J. Mullahy (1989), "Moment-Based Estimation and Testing of Stochastic Frontier Models," Resources for the Future, Discussion Paper No. 89-10.

Kumbhakar, S. (1987), "The Specification of Technical and Allocative Inefficiency in Stochastic Production and Profit Frontiers," *Journal of Econometrics* 34(3): 335–348.

Kumbhakar, S. (1989), "Modelling Technical and Allocative Inefficiency in Translog Production Function," *Economics Letters* 31(2): 119–124.

Kumbhakar, S. (1990), "Production Frontiers and Panel Data, and Time Varying Technical Inefficiency," *Journal of Econometrics* 46(1/2): 201–211.

Kumbhakar, S. (1991), "Estimation of Technical Inefficiency in Panel Data Models with Firm- and Time-Specific Effects," *Economics Letters* 36(2): 43–48.

Kumbhakar, S., and A. Bhattacharyya (1991), "Price Distortions and Resource-Use Efficiency in Indian Agriculture: A Restricted Profit Function Approach," Department of Economics, University of Texas, Austin, Tex. June (forthcoming in *Review of Economics and Statistics*).

Kumbhakar, S., and A. Heshmat (1991), "Efficiency Measurement Using Rotating Panel Data: An Application to Swedish Dairy Farms, 1976–1988," Department of Economics, University of Texas at Austin (mimeographed).

Kumbhakar, S., and L. Hjalmarsson (1991), "Labor Use Efficiency in Swedish Social Insurance Offices," Department of Economics, University of Texas at Austin (mimographed).

Lee, L. (1983), "A Test for Distributional Assumptions for the Stochastic Frontier Function," *Journal of Econometrics* 22(3): 245–267.

Meeusen, W., and J. van den Broeck (1977), "Efficiency Estimation from Cobb-Douglas Production Functions with Composed Error," *International Economic Review* 18(2): 435–444.

Nerlove, M. (1963), "Returns to Scale in Electricity Supply," in C. Christ, ed., *Measurement in Economics.* Stanford, Calif.: Stanford University Press.

Pitt, M., and L. Lee (1981), "The Measurement and Sources of Technical Inefficiency in the Indonesian Weaving Industry," *Journal of Development Economics* 9: 43–64.

Samuelson, P. (1938), "Foundations of Economic Analysis. Cambridge, Mass.: Harvard University Press.

Schmidt, P. (1976), "On the Statistical Estimation of Parametric Frontier Production Functions," *Review of Economics and Statistics* 58: 238–239.

Schmidt, P. (1977), "Estimating Technical and Allocative Inefficiency Relative to Stochastic

Production and Cost Frontiers," Workshop Paper No. 7702, Department of Economics, Michigan State University, East Lansing, Mich.

Schmidt, P. (1984), "An Error Structure for Systems of Translog Cost and Share Equations," Workshop Paper No. 8309, Department of Economics, Michigan State University, East Lansing, Mich.

Schmidt, P. (1985), "Frontier Production Functions," *Econometric Reviews* 4(2): 289–328.

Schmidt, P. (1986), "Frontier Production Functions," *Economic Reviews* 4: 289–328.

Schmidt, P., and K. Lovell (1979), "Estimating Technical and Allocative Inefficiency Relative to Stochastic Production and Cost Frontiers," *Journal of Econometrics* 9(3): 343–366.

Schmidt, P., and R. Sickles (1984), "Production Frontiers and Panel Data," *Journal of Business and Economic Statistics* 2(4): 367–374.

Seale, J. (1990), "Estimating Stochastic Frontier Systems with Unbalanced Panel Data: The Case of Floor Tile Manufactories in Egypt," *Journal of Applied Econometrics* 5(1): 59–74.

Shephard, R. (1953), *Cost and Production Functions.* Princeton, N.J.: Princeton University Press.

Sickles, R., D. Good, and R. Johnson (1986), "Allocative Distortions and the Regulatory Transition of the Airline Industry," *Journal of Econometrics* 33: 143–163.

Stevenson, R. (1980), "Likelihood Functions for Generalized Stochastic Frontier Estimaton," *Journal of Econometrics* 13(1): 58–66.

Timmer, P. (1971), "Using a Probabilistic Frontier Production Function to Measure Technical Efficiency," *Journal of Political Economy* 79: 776–794.

Trethaway, M., and R. Windle (1983), "U.S. Airline Cross Section: Sources of Data," Department of Economics, University of Wisconsin, Madison (mimeographed).

Waldman, D. (1982), "A Stationary Point for the Stochastic Frontier Likelihood," *Journal of Econometrics* 18: 275–279.

Waldman, D. (1984), "Properties of Technical Efficiency Estimators in the Stochastic Frontier Model," *Journal of Econometrics* 25: 353–364.

Zeischang, K. (1983), "A Note on the Decomposition of Cost Efficiency into Technical and Allocative Components," *Journal of Econometrics* 23(3): 401–405.

Zellner, A., J. Kmenta, and J. Dreze (1966), "Specification and Estimation of Cobb-Douglas Production Functions," *Econometrica* 34 October: 784–795.

3

THE MATHEMATICAL PROGRAMMING APPROACH TO EFFICIENCY ANALYSIS

Agha Iqbal Ali and Lawrence M. Seiford

In his classic paper, M. J. Farrell (1957) argues that the measurement of productive efficiency is of theoretical and practical importance; a satisfactory efficiency measure allows both empirical testing of theoretical arguments and economic planning to improve the productivity of particular industries. Farrell's approach, largely inspired by Koopmans (1951), was based on a production possibility set consisting of the conical hull of input-output vectors. This framework was generalized to multiple outputs and reformulated as a mathematical programming problem by Charnes, Cooper, and Rhodes (1978, 1979, 1981) thus initiating the mathematical programming approach to efficiency measurement known as data envelopment analysis (DEA).

In their original study Charnes, Cooper, and Rhodes (1978) described the DEA methodology as a "mathematical programming model applied to observed data [that] provides a new way of obtaining empirical estimates of extremal relationships such as the production functions and/or efficiency production possibility surfaces that are the cornerstones of modern economics." Since this seminal paper, numerous data envelopment analysis models have appeared in the literature as well as a host of studies employing the technique. Seiford (1990a) lists over 400 articles in a comprehensive bibliography. Introductory surveys are given in Banker, Charnes, Cooper, Swarts, and Thomas (1989) and Seiford and Thrall (1990).

At present DEA with its various models actually encompasses a number of alternate approaches to efficiency measurement. In the discussion to follow we classify these different models with respect to the type of envelopment surface, efficiency measurement, orientation or focus, and the effect of scale changes.

The plan of this chapter is as follows. Section 3.1 discusses two basic envelopment surfaces and presents two pairs of DEA models. Solutions to these models provide efficiency characterizations. Efficiency measurement relative to an envelopment surface is discussed in Section 3.2, and the effects of input and output orientations are examined in Section 3.3. Scale invariance is addressed in Section 3.4. Section 3.5 highlights selected extensions to the basic DEA methodology. Summary and conclusions are given in Section 3.6.

3.1. Envelopment Surfaces

In standard microeconomic theory, the production function can be interpreted as forming the basis for a description of input-output relationships in a firm. Alternatively, the production function constitutes a frontier for the production possibility set. Efficiency computations can be made relative to this frontier *if it is known*. However, in practice, one has only data—a set of observations for each decision-making unit (DMU) corresponding to achieved output levels for given input levels. Thus, the initial task is to determine which of the set of DMUs, as represented by observed data, form an *empirical* production function or envelopment surface.

We assume that there are n DMUs to be evaluated. Each DMU consumes varying amounts of m different inputs to produce s different outputs. Specifically, decision-making unit l consumes amount $x_{il} > 0$ of input i and produces amount $y_{rl} > 0$ of output r. On occasion we will employ the more compact notation, X_l and Y_l, which denote, respectively, the vectors of input and output values for DMU_l. [1]

Each of the various models for data envelopment analysis (DEA) seeks to determine which of the n decision-making units determine an *envelopment surface*. This envelopment surface is referred to as the *empirical production function* or the *efficient frontier*. DEA provides a comprehensive analysis of relative efficiency for multiple input–multiple output situations by evaluating each DMU and measuring its performance relative to an envelopment surface composed of other DMUs. Units that lie on (determine) the surface are deemed *efficient* in DEA terminology. Units that do not lie on the surface are termed *inefficient* and the analysis provides a measure of their relative efficiency.

An examination of the 11-DMU example data set in Table 3.1 reveals that both DMU_5 and DMU_{10} are clearly dominated by other units. That is, other units (e.g., DMU_1 or DMU_8) simultaneously have both higher levels of output and lower levels of inputs and are thus more efficient. Obviously, these dominated units (DMU_5 and DMU_{10}) should not form part of any envelopment surface.

Figure 3.1 provides a three dimensional plot of the 11-DMU example data set. Since the envelopment surfaces to be examined partially obscure a number of

---

[1] As the discussion indicates, in data envelopment analysis each data component is classified as either an input or an output. DEA can be applicable, however, in scenarios where the data components cannot be strictly interpreted as inputs or outputs and there is no direct functional relationship between the measures. In such situations a general guideline for the classification is that inputs are components for which lower levels are better while outputs are those measures for which higher levels are more desired. Of course, any analysis assumes at least moderate relationships exist between the measures.

TECHNIQUES

Table 3.1   Example Data Set

DMU	Output 1	Input 1	Input 2
Unit 1	12.	5.	13.
Unit 2	14.	16.	12.
Unit 3	25.	16.	26.
Unit 4	26.	17.	15.
Unit 5	8.	18.	14.
Unit 6	9.	23.	6.
Unit 7	27.	25.	10.
Unit 8	30.	27.	22.
Unit 9	31.	37.	14.
Unit 10	26.5	42.	25.
Unit 11	12.	5.	17.

the points, this figure and those to follow consist of both top-front and bottom-rear perspectives.

There are two basic types of envelopment surfaces in DEA, referred to as *constant returns-to-scale* (CRS) and *variable returns-to-scale* (VRS) surfaces. As the names indicate, an implicit assumption concerning returns-to-scale is associated with each type of surface. [2] Thus, the appropriateness of a particular envelopment surface is frequently determined (dictated) by economic and other assumptions regarding the data set to be analyzed. As discussed in the following sections, this choice of envelopment surface for an analysis is implicit in the selection of the particular DEA mathematical programming model.

[2] Hybrid envelopment surfaces which model nondecreasing returns-to-scale or nonincreasing returns-to-scale are also possible. For complete details the reader is referred to Seiford and Thrall (1990).

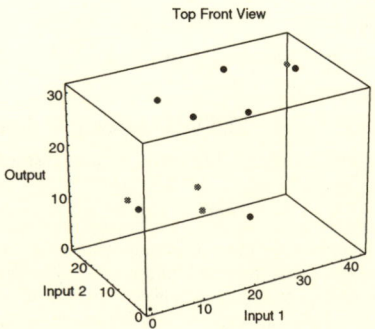
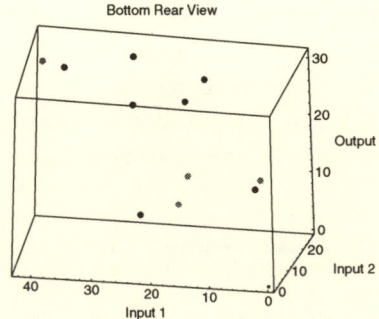
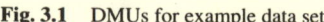

Fig. 3.1   DMUs for example data set

3.1.1   Variable Returns to Scale

As illustrated in Figure 3.2, a VRS envelopment surface consists of portions of supporting hyperplanes in R^{m+s} that form particular facets of the convex hull of the points (Y_j, X_j), $j = 1, \ldots, n$.

The general equation for a hyperplane in R^{m+s} with normal $(\mu_1, \mu_2, \ldots, \mu_s,$ $-\nu_1, -\nu_2, \ldots, -\nu_m)$ is given by $\sum_{r=1}^{s} \mu_r y_r - \sum_{i=1}^{m} \nu_i x_i + \omega = 0$. Such a hyperplane is a supporting hyperplane (and forms a facet of the envelopment surface) if and only if all the points (Y_j, X_j) lie on or beneath the hyperplane and, additionally, the hyperplane passes through at least one of the points. These conditions may be stated as

$$\sum_{r=1}^{s} \mu_r y_{rj} - \sum_{i=1}^{m} \nu_i x_{ij} + \omega \leq 0 \qquad \text{for all } j = 1, \ldots, n$$

$$\sum_{r=1}^{s} \mu_r y_{rk} - \sum_{i=1}^{m} \nu_i x_{ik} + \omega = 0, \qquad \text{for some } k$$

Note that the first condition identifies that portion of the convex hull that demonstrates high-output and/or low-input values while the second condition assures that the hyperplane passes through at least one of the points.

The preceding conditions are reflected in the following linear programming problem[3] for DMU$_l$. (Recall that x_{ij} and y_{rj} are the observed values for the DMUs and are constant; the variables are μ_r, ν_i, and ω.) For a feasible solution (μ_r, ν_i, ω), DMU$_j$ always lies on or below the hyperplane $\sum_{r=1}^{s} \mu_r y_r - \sum_{i=1}^{m} \nu_i x_i + \omega = 0$, by virtue of the jth constraint. Thus the set of constraints ensure that all points lie on or below this hyperplane. The objective function measures the distance from DMU$_l$ to

---

[3] The VRS model is also referred to in the literature as the additive model and was originally presented in Charnes, Cooper, Golany, Seiford, and Stutz (1985).

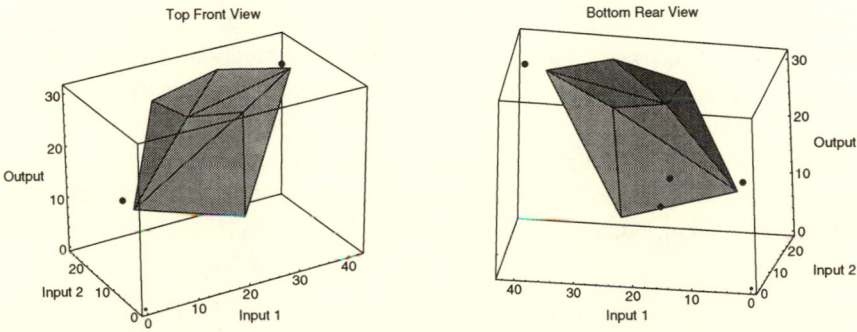

Fig. 3.2   VRS envelopment surface for example data set

this hyperplane. Maximization of the objective function selects a hyperplane which minimizes this distance. Note that the objective function value is nonpositive; hence an optimal value of zero indicates that DMU_l lies *on* this hyperplane. Inefficient DMUs lie *below* the closest supporting hyperplane and thus correspond to nonzero objective function values.

$VRS_M(Y_l, X_l)$:

$$\max_{\mu_r, \nu_i, \omega} \quad \sum_{r=1}^{s} y_{rl}\mu_r - \sum_{i=1}^{m} x_{il}\nu_i + \omega$$

$$\sum_{r=1}^{s} y_{rj}\mu_r - \sum_{i=1}^{m} x_{ij}\nu_i + \omega \leq 0 \qquad \text{for } j = 1, \ldots, n$$

$$\mu_r \geq 1 \qquad \text{for } r = 1, \ldots, s$$

$$\nu_i \geq 1 \qquad \text{for } i = 1, \ldots, m$$

Observe that performing a DEA analysis actually requires the solution of n linear programming problems of the above form, one for each decision making unit l. The optimal solution to each program, $VRS_M(Y_l, X_l)$, is given by the s-vector μ^l, the m-vector ν^l, and the variable ω^l. In the literature, these values have been interpreted as virtual multipliers. As such, the linear programming problem, VRS_M, has been referred to as the *multiplier* side. The program directly addresses the underlying *characterization of efficiency:* A decision-making unit, l, is efficient if it lies on a facet-defining hyperplane $\mu^l \mathbf{y} - \nu^l \mathbf{x} + \omega^l = 0$ of the envelopment surface.

Each of the n sets of values obtained, $\{\mu^l, \nu^l, \omega^l\}$, $l = 1, 2, , \ldots, n$, are the coefficients or normals for supporting hyperplanes that define facets of the envelopment surface. Readers should not assume that each of the n programs $VRS_M(Y_l, X_l), l = 1, \ldots, n$, yields a distinct hyperplane; in fact, supporting hyperplanes for efficient DMUs serve as the *closest* supporting hyperplane for an inefficient DMU.

The preceding multiplier problem provides a partial identification of the underlying facet structure. In particular, the efficient DMUs which lie on the supporting hyperplane are associated with binding (tight, active) constraints. A more accessible representation of this facet, however, (as a convex combination of these reference DMUs) is given by the solution to the following linear programming dual[4] of the multiplier problem.

Derivation of the dual problem to VRS_M proceeds as follows. Rewriting the lower bound constraints as "less than or equal to" constraints, the program VRS_M is in canonical form. Associating dual variables $(\lambda_j, j = 1, \ldots, n; s_r, r = 1, \ldots, s;$

---

[4] Another desirable feature of this dual problem (VRS_E) is that it has $s + m + 1$ constraints, in contrast to the n constraints for the multiplier problem, VRS_M. In practice $n \gg s + m + 1$, thus making VRS_E the preferred problem to solve.

$e_i, i = 1, \ldots, m$) with the three sets of constraints, the dual linear program to VRS_M consists of $s + m + 1$ equality constraints since the variables of VRS_M are unconstrained. (Note that the $s + m + 1$ variables in VRS_M correspond to the $s + m + 1$ constraints in VRS_E. In particular, the first s constraints correspond to the s outputs, the next m constraints correspond to the m inputs, and the last "convexity" constraint, $\sum_{j=1}^{n} \lambda_j = 1$, is associated with the variable ω.) Finally, the variables in the dual program VRS_E are nonnegative since the primal constraints are "$\leq$."

Thus the linear programming dual to the preceding multiplier problem is given by

$\text{VRS}_E(Y_l, X_l)$:

$$\min_{\lambda_j, s_r, e_i} \; - \left(\sum_{r=1}^{s} s_r + \sum_{i=1}^{m} e_i \right)$$

$$\sum_{j=1}^{n} y_{rj}\lambda_j - s_r = y_{rl} \qquad r = 1, \ldots, s$$

$$-\sum_{j=1}^{n} x_{ij}\lambda_j - e_i = -x_{il} \qquad i = 1, \ldots, m$$

$$\sum_{j=1}^{n} \lambda_j = 1$$

$$\lambda_j \geq 0 \qquad j = 1, \ldots, n$$

$$s_r \geq 0, \qquad r = 1, \ldots, s$$

$$e_i \geq 0, \qquad i = 1, \ldots, m.$$

The optimal solution to $\text{VRS}_E(Y_l, X_l)$ for DMU_l consists of the s-vector of output slacks, s^l, the m-vector of excess inputs, e^l, and the n-vector λ^l. A closer examination of the optimal solution for DMU_l reveals whether it is efficient and lies on the envelopment surface. We know, from the duality theory of linear programming, that for each of these $\lambda_j^l > 0$, the corresponding j^{th} dual constraint is binding, that is, $\mu^l Y_j - \nu^l X_j + \omega^l = 0$. Since each point (Y_j, X_j), for which $\lambda_j^l > 0$ lies on the hyperplane with normal (μ^l, ν^l), we also have

$$\mu^l \left(\sum_{j=1}^{n} \lambda_j^l Y_j \right) - \nu^l \left(\sum_{j=1}^{n} \lambda_j^l X_j \right) + \omega^l = 0$$

Thus, each associated decision making unit $j \in \Lambda = \{j \mid \mu^l Y_j - \nu^l X_j + \omega^l = 0\}$ is efficient and lies on the hyperplane $\mu^l \mathbf{y} - \nu^l \mathbf{x} + \omega^l = 0$ which defines a facet of the envelopment surface.

The vector λ^l defines a point

$$(\widehat{Y_l}, \widehat{X_l}) = \left(\sum_{j=1}^{n} \lambda_j^l Y_j, \sum_{j=1}^{n} \lambda_j^l X_j \right)$$

which is a *convex* combination ($\sum_{j=1}^{n} \lambda_j^l = 1$) of units that lie on a facet of the envelopment surface. If $\lambda_l^l = 1, \lambda_j^l = 0$ for $j \neq l$ then clearly DMU_l lies on the envelopment surface and is efficient. Thus $(\widehat{Y_l}, \widehat{X_l}) = (Y_l, X_l)$ for an *efficient* DMU_l. For a DMU_l that is inefficient, that is, does not lie on the envelopment surface, the point $(\widehat{Y_l}, \widehat{X_l})$ is referred to as the *projected point*. Note that the solution of VRS_E for DMU_l actually identifies a subset of efficient DMUs since λ_j^l is nonzero only if unit j is efficient. [5]

As is clear from the constraints, the projected point can be equivalently expressed as

$$(\widehat{Y_l}, \widehat{X_l}) = \left(\sum_{j=1}^{n} \lambda_j^l Y_j, \sum_{j=1}^{n} \lambda_j^l X_j \right) = (Y_l + \mathbf{s}^l, X_l - \mathbf{e}^l)$$

This explains our previous reference to the vector $\mathbf{s}^l$ as the vector of *output slacks* and the m-vector $\mathbf{e}^l$ as the vector of *excess inputs*. These vectors ($\mathbf{s}^l$ and $\mathbf{e}^l$) gauge the distance between an inefficient DMU (Y_l, X_l) and its projected point $(\widehat{Y_l}, \widehat{X_l})$ on the envelopment surface.[6] Because problem VRS_E expresses the projected point as a combination of DMUs on the envelopment surface (an efficient reference set) this linear programming problem has been labeled as the *envelopment* form.

The relationship between the values of output slacks and excess inputs and the multipliers is given by the following complementary slackness conditions from linear programming duality theory:

$$s_r^l > 0 \quad \Rightarrow \quad \mu_r^l = 1 \qquad r = 1, \ldots, s$$

$$e_i^l > 0 \quad \Rightarrow \quad \nu_i^l = 1 \qquad i = 1, \ldots, m$$

For future reference we note that the term $-\mu^l \mathbf{s}^l - \nu^l \mathbf{e}^l$ is the optimal objective value $-(\mathbf{1}\mathbf{s}^l + \mathbf{1}\mathbf{e}^l)$. This optimal value for the sum of the slacks is denoted by $\Sigma^l \equiv \mathbf{1}\mathbf{s}^l + \mathbf{1}\mathbf{e}^l$.

Example   To illustrate these concepts we employ the example data set previously given in Table 3.1 and investigate the efficiency of DMU_2. The efficiency or ineffi-

---

[5] The complete set of efficient units (the efficient reference set) for unit l is given by $\Lambda = \{j \mid \mu^l Y_j - \nu^l X_j + \omega^l = 0\}$.

[6] As discussed in Sections 3.3 and 3.4, alternative projections onto the envelopment surface are possible.

ciency of DMU_2 is not immediately obvious from Table 3.1. (Recall that DMU_5 and DMU_{10} were immediately identified as being inefficient.) DMU_2 produces 14 units of output and consumes 16 units of input 1 and 12 units of input 2. The VRS_E and VRS_M problems for unit $l = 2$ can be stated as:

$VRS_E(Y_2, X_2)$:

$$
\min_{\lambda_1,\ldots,\lambda_{11},s_1,e_1,e_2} - \left(s_1 + \sum_{i=1}^{2} e_i \right)
$$

$$
12\lambda_1 + 14\lambda_2 + 25\lambda_3 + 26\lambda_4 + 8\lambda_5 + 9\lambda_6
$$
$$
+ 27\lambda_7 + 30\lambda_8 + 31\lambda_9 + 26.5\lambda_{10} + 12\lambda_{11} - s_1 = 14
$$
$$
- 5\lambda_1 - 16\lambda_2 - 16\lambda_3 - 17\lambda_4 - 18\lambda_5 - 23\lambda_6
$$
$$
- 25\lambda_7 - 27\lambda_8 - 37\lambda_9 - 42\lambda_{10} - 5\lambda_{11} - e_1 = -16
$$
$$
- 13\lambda_1 - 12\lambda_2 - 26\lambda_3 - 15\lambda_4 - 14\lambda_5 - 6\lambda_6
$$
$$
- 10\lambda_7 - 22\lambda_8 - 14\lambda_9 - 25\lambda_{10} - 17\lambda_{11} - e_2 = -12
$$
$$
\lambda_1 + \lambda_2 + \lambda_3 + \lambda_4 + \lambda_5 + \lambda_6 + \lambda_7 + \lambda_8 + \lambda_9 + \lambda_{10} + \lambda_{11} = 1
$$
$$
\lambda_1, \ldots, \lambda_{11} \geq 0
$$
$$
s_1 \geq 0
$$
$$
e_1, e_2 \geq 0
$$

$VRS_M(Y_2, X_2)$:

$$
\max_{\mu_1,\nu_1,\nu_2,\omega} \quad 14\mu_1 - 16\nu_1 - 12\nu_2 + \omega
$$
$$
12\mu_1 - 5\nu_1 - 13\nu_2 + \omega \leq 0
$$
$$
14\mu_1 - 16\nu_1 - 12\nu_2 + \omega \leq 0
$$
$$
25\mu_1 - 16\nu_1 - 26\nu_2 + \omega \leq 0
$$
$$
26\mu_1 - 17\nu_1 - 15\nu_2 + \omega \leq 0
$$
$$
8\mu_1 - 18\nu_1 - 14\nu_2 + \omega \leq 0
$$
$$
9\mu_1 - 23\nu_1 - 6\nu_2 + \omega \leq 0
$$
$$
27\mu_1 - 25\nu_1 - 10\nu_2 + \omega \leq 0
$$
$$
30\mu_1 - 27\nu_1 - 22\nu_2 + \omega \leq 0
$$
$$
31\mu_1 - 37\nu_1 - 14\nu_2 + \omega \leq 0
$$
$$
26.5\mu_1 - 42\nu_1 - 25\nu_2 + \omega \leq 0
$$
$$
12\mu_1 - 5\nu_1 - 17\nu_2 + \omega \leq 0
$$
$$
\mu_1 \geq 1
$$
$$
\nu_1, \nu_2 \geq 1
$$

The optimal solution (λ^l, s^l, e^l) to $VRS_E(Y_2, X_2)$ is given by $\lambda^2 = (\frac{2}{3}, 0, 0, 0, 0, 0, \frac{1}{3}, 0, 0, 0, 0)$ with output slack $s_1^2 = 3$ and excess input values $e_1^2 = 4.33, e_2^2 = 0$.

Table 3.2   Optimal Solutions to VRS Model

| DMU | Multiplier Problem | | | | | Envelopment Problem | | |
	μ_1	ν_1	ν_2	ω	Σ^l	λ	s	e
Unit 1	1.000	1.000	1.000	6.00	0.0	$\lambda_1 = 1$	0	(0,0)
Unit 2	1.000	1.000	1.677	14.67	7.33	$\lambda_1 = \frac{2}{3}$	3	(4.33,0)
						$\lambda_7 = \frac{1}{3}$		
Unit 3	67.000	78.000	1.000	−401.00	0.0	$\lambda_3 = 1$	0	(0,0)
Unit 4	1.000	1.000	1.000	6.00	0.0	$\lambda_4 = 1$	0	(0,0)
Unit 5	1.000	1.000	1.000	6.00	18.0	$\lambda_1 = \frac{1}{2}$	11	(7,0)
						$\lambda_4 = \frac{1}{2}$		
Unit 6	1.000	1.000	4.000	38.00	0.0	$\lambda_6 = 1$	0	(0,0)
Unit 7	3.000	1.000	1.000	−46.00	0.0	$\lambda_7 = 1$	0	(0,0)
Unit 8	5.000	1.300	1.000	−92.90	0.0	$\lambda_8 = 1$	0	(0,0)
Unit 9	4.000	1.000	1.000	−73.00	0.0	$\lambda_9 = 1$	0	(0,0)
Unit 10	3.000	1.000	1.000	−46.00	33.5	$\lambda_4 = \frac{1}{2}$	0	(21,12.5)
						$\lambda_7 = \frac{1}{2}$		
Unit 11	1.000	1.000	1.000	6.00	4.0	$\lambda_1 = 1$	0	(0,4)

Unit 2 is clearly inefficient. The projected point $(\widehat{Y}_l, \widehat{X}_l)$ with $\widehat{Y}_2 = 17$ and $\widehat{X}_2 = (11.67, 12)$ indicates that production of 17 units of output is possible with 11.67 units of input 1 and 12 units of input 2. Thus DMU_2 should have produced an additional 3 units of output and consumed 4.33 fewer units of input 1 to be judged efficient. The projected point $(\widehat{Y}_2, \widehat{X}_2)$ is a convex combination of units 1 and 7 ($\lambda_1^2 = \frac{2}{3}, \lambda_7^2 = \frac{1}{3}$) and lies on the facet determined by units 1 and 7. Units 1 and 7 thus form an efficient reference set for DMU_2, that is, a peer group against whom the performance of DMU_2 is evaluated.

The optimal solution (μ^l, ν^l, ω^l) for $VRS_M(Y_2, X_2)$ is given by $\mu^2 = 1, \nu^2 = (1, 1.667)$, and $\omega = 14.67$. Note that both units 1 and 7 lie on the facet of the envelopment surface that is defined by the hyperplane $y_1 - x_1 - 1.667x_2 + 14.67 = 0$ determined by these coefficients.[7] This is a consequence of our earlier observation that the dual constraints are binding for positive λ_j^l, that is, $\lambda_1^2 = 2/3$ and $\lambda_7^2 = 1/3$. Thus, units 1 and 7 form the efficient reference set for DMU_2. Finally, the optimal values for the two dual linear programs for DMU_2 are, of course, the same and equal to $-7.33 = -(3 + 4.33) = (14 - 36 + 14.67)$.

Table 3.2 lists solutions[8] for the multiplier and the envelopment problems for each of the 11 units. As is readily ascertained by the value of Σ^l, units 1,3,4,6,7,8, and 9 lie on the envelopment surface and are therefore efficient. The value Σ^l for the inefficient units (2, 5, 10, and 11) measures the proximity of the inefficient unit to the envelopment surface.

[7] Of course the projected point $(\widehat{Y}_2, \widehat{X}_2)$ also lies on this facet of the envelopment surface.
[8] The reader should note that alternative optimal solutions may exist; the optimal objective function value, however, is unique. In this and the solution tables to follow, we list *an* optimal solution. Use of the term "the solution" in discussion is not meant to imply uniqueness.

3.1.2 Constant Returns to Scale

A CRS envelopment surface consists of hyperplanes in R^{m+s} that form particular facets of the *conical* hull of the points (Y_j, X_j), $j = 1, \ldots, n$. Such a surface is illustrated in Figure 3.3. (While the two hyperplanes actually continue to infinity, they have been clipped at the top of the bounding box for visual clarity.)

In contrast to the previous surface, all supporting hyperplanes for a CRS envelopment pass through the origin. Thus, $\omega = 0$, and the equation for a hyperplane reduces to $\sum_{r=1}^{s} \mu_r y_r - \sum_{i=1}^{m} \nu_i x_i = 0$. Such a hyperplane forms a facet of the CRS envelopment surface if and only if

$$\sum_{r=1}^{s} \mu_r y_{rj} - \sum_{i=1}^{m} \nu_i x_{ij} \le 0 \qquad \text{for all } j = 1, \ldots, n$$

$$\sum_{r=1}^{s} \mu_r y_{rk} - \sum_{i=1}^{m} \nu_i x_{ik} = 0 \qquad \text{for some } k$$

The statement of the CRS multiplier program which follows is a direct consequence of the above conditions for the CRS envelopment surface.

$\text{CRS}_M(Y_l, X_l)$:

$$\max_{\mu_r, \nu_i} \quad \sum_{r=1}^{s} y_{rl} \mu_r - \sum_{i=1}^{m} x_{il} \nu_i$$

$$\sum_{r=1}^{s} y_{rj} \mu_r - \sum_{i=1}^{m} x_{ij} \nu_i \le 0 \qquad \text{for } j = 1, \ldots, n$$

$$\mu_r \ge 1 \qquad \text{for } r = 1, \ldots, s$$

$$\nu_i \ge 1 \qquad \text{for } i = 1, \ldots, m$$

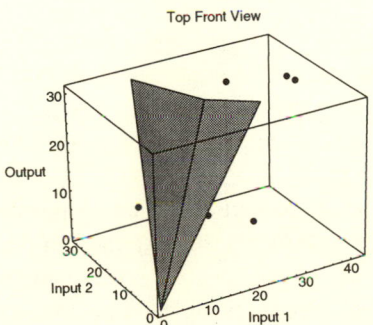 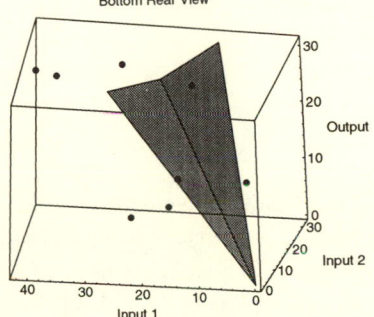

Fig. 3.3   CRS envelopment surface for example data set

Again, performing a DEA analysis actually requires the solution of n linear programming problems of the above form, one for each decision-making unit l. The optimal solution to the multiplier problem for DMU_l is given by the s-vector μ^l and the m-vector ν^l. For a CRS envelopment, DMU_l is efficient if it lies on a facet-defining hyperplane, $\mu^l \mathbf{y} - \nu^l \mathbf{x} = 0$,[9] of the envelopment surface. Each of the n solutions given by the sets of values $\{\mu^l, \nu^l\}$, $l = 1, 2, \ldots, n$, is the set of coefficients (or normal) for a hyperplane which defines a facet of the envelopment surface.

The CRS envelopment form, which is the linear programming dual to the above multiplier program, is given by

$CRS_E(Y_l, X_l)$:

$$
\min_{\lambda_j, s_r, e_i} \; -\left(\sum_{r=1}^{s} s_r + \sum_{i=1}^{m} e_i \right)
$$

$$
\sum_{j=1}^{n} y_{rj}\lambda_j - s_r = y_{rl} \qquad r = 1, \ldots, s
$$

$$
-\sum_{j=1}^{n} x_{ij}\lambda_j - e_i = -x_{il} \qquad i = 1, \ldots, m
$$

$$
\lambda_j \geq 0 \qquad j = 1, \ldots, n
$$

$$
s_r \geq 0 \qquad r = 1, \ldots, s
$$

$$
e_i \geq 0 \qquad i = 1, \ldots, m
$$

The optimal values of variables for the (CRS_E) envelopment problem for DMU_l are denoted by the s-vector of output slacks $\mathbf{s}^l$, the m-vector of excess inputs $\mathbf{e}^l$, and the n-vector λ^l. Again, from complementary slackness, for each $\lambda_j^l > 0$, the corresponding dual constraint is binding, that is, $\mu^l Y_j - \nu^l X_j = 0$. Thus, the decision making units $j \in \Lambda = \{j \mid \mu^l Y_j - \nu^l X_j = 0\}$ are efficient and lie on the hyperplane, $\mu^l \mathbf{y} - \nu^l \mathbf{x} = 0$. This hyperplane, which passes through the origin, defines a facet of the envelopment surface. Note that DMU_l, if efficient, must also lie on this facet.

As before, the vector λ^l defines a point

$$
(\widehat{Y}_l, \widehat{X}_l) = \left(\sum_{j=1}^{n} \lambda_j^l Y_j, \sum_{j=1}^{n} \lambda_j^l X_j \right)
$$

which lies on the envelopment surface. However in the case of a CRS envelopment the point $(\widehat{Y}_l, \widehat{X}_l)$ is a *linear* combination of efficient units that lie on a facet of the envelopment surface. [Recall that for the VRS envelopment, $(\widehat{Y}_l, \widehat{X}_l)$ was a <u>convex</u> combination.] For a DMU_l that is inefficient, that is, does not lie on the envelopment

---

[9] Note that this hyperplane passes through the origin since $\omega \equiv 0$.

surface, the point $(\widehat{Y}_l, \widehat{X}_l)$ is referred to as the *projected point*.[10] The projected point can be equivalently represented in terms of the vector of *output slacks* $\mathbf{s}^l$ and the vector of *excess inputs* $\mathbf{e}^l$, as

$$(\widehat{Y}_l, \widehat{X}_l) = \left(\sum_{j=1}^{n} \lambda_j^l Y_j, \sum_{j=1}^{n} \lambda_j^l X_j \right) = (Y_l + \mathbf{s}^l, X_l - \mathbf{e}^l)$$

Before examining the preceding discussion in terms of our example data set, we pause to compare the VRS and CRS problem formulations. In matrix notation, the statements of the programs employ the $s \times n$ matrix of outputs, $\mathbf{Y}$, and the $m \times n$ matrix of inputs, $\mathbf{X}$.

The VRS formulations can be stated as[11]

$\mathrm{VRS}_M(Y_l, X_l):$ $\qquad\qquad\qquad$ $\mathrm{VRS}_E(Y_l, X_l):$

$$\max_{\mu,\nu,\omega} \quad \mu Y_l - \nu X_l + \omega$$
$$\mu \mathbf{Y} - \nu \mathbf{X} + \mathbf{1}\omega \leq \mathbf{0}$$
$$\mu \geq \mathbf{1} \qquad \nu \geq \mathbf{1}$$

$$\min_{\lambda,s,e} \quad -(\mathbf{1s} + \mathbf{1e})$$
$$\mathbf{Y}\lambda - \mathbf{s} = \quad Y_l$$
$$-\mathbf{X}\lambda - \mathbf{e} = -X_l$$
$$\mathbf{1}\lambda = 1$$
$$\lambda \geq \mathbf{0} \qquad \mathbf{e} \geq \mathbf{0} \qquad \mathbf{s} \geq \mathbf{0}$$

while the CRS formulations are given by

$\mathrm{CRS}_M(Y_l, X_l):$ $\qquad\qquad\qquad$ $\mathrm{CRS}_E(Y_l, X_l):$

$$\max_{\mu,\nu} \quad \mu Y_l - \nu X_l$$
$$\mu \mathbf{Y} - \nu \mathbf{X} \leq \mathbf{0}$$
$$\mu \geq \mathbf{1} \qquad \nu \geq \mathbf{1}$$

$$\min_{\lambda,s,e} \quad -(\mathbf{1s} + \mathbf{1e})$$
$$\mathbf{Y}\lambda - \mathbf{s} = \quad Y_l$$
$$-\mathbf{X}\lambda - \mathbf{e} = -X_l$$
$$\lambda \geq \mathbf{0} \qquad \mathbf{e} \geq \mathbf{0} \qquad \mathbf{s} \geq \mathbf{0}$$

Three subtle differences in the above formulations which have major consequences are the following. The convexity constraint, $\mathbf{1}\lambda = 1$, present in VRS_E, restricts attention to convex combinations of DMUs (in contrast to the linear combinations allowed in CRS_E). The associated variable, ω, in VRS_M removes the restriction (in CRS_M) that supporting hyperplanes must pass through the origin. Since the constraint set for CRS_E is less restrictive (the convexity constraint is absent), lower efficiency scores are possible; thus, as we would expect, fewer DMUs are declared

---

[10] For an efficient DMU_l, $(\widehat{Y}_l, \widehat{X}_l) = (Y_l, X_l)$.

[11] We require the vector inequality to be satisfied componentwise, that is, $\mu \geq \mathbf{1} \Leftrightarrow \mu_r \geq 1$ for all $r = 1, \ldots, s$.

efficient for a CRS envelopment.[12] The reader should verify these differences in the following example.

Example For the example data set in Table 3.1 the envelopment form of the CRS model for unit $l = 3$ is given by

$\text{CRS}_E(Y_3, X_3):$

$$\min_{\lambda_1,\dots,\lambda_{11},s_1,e_1,e_2} -\left(s_1 + \sum_{i=1}^{2} e_i\right)$$

$$12\lambda_1 + 14\lambda_2 + 25\lambda_3 + 26\lambda_4 + 8\lambda_5 + 9\lambda_6$$
$$+27\lambda_7 + 30\lambda_8 + 31\lambda_9 + 26.5\lambda_{10} + 12\lambda_{11} - s_1 = 25$$
$$-5\lambda_1 - 16\lambda_2 - 16\lambda_3 - 17\lambda_4 - 18\lambda_5 - 23\lambda_6$$
$$-25\lambda_7 - 27\lambda_8 - 37\lambda_9 - 42\lambda_{10} - 5\lambda_{11} - e_1 = -16$$
$$-13\lambda_1 - 12\lambda_2 - 26\lambda_3 - 15\lambda_4 - 14\lambda_5 - 6\lambda_6$$
$$-10\lambda_7 - 22\lambda_8 - 14\lambda_9 - 25\lambda_{10} - 17\lambda_{11} - e_2 = -24$$
$$\lambda_1,\dots,\lambda_{11} \geq 0$$
$$s_1 \geq 0$$
$$e_1, e_2 \geq 0$$

while the multiplier form of the CRS problem for unit 3 is stated as

$\text{CRS}_M(Y_3, X_3):$

$$\max_{\mu_1,\nu_1,\nu_2} \quad 25\mu_1 - 16\nu_1 - 26\nu_2$$

$$12\mu_1 - 5\nu_1 - 13\nu_2 \leq 0$$
$$14\mu_1 - 16\nu_1 - 12\nu_2 \leq 0$$
$$25\mu_1 - 16\nu_1 - 26\nu_2 \leq 0$$
$$26\mu_1 - 17\nu_1 - 15\nu_2 \leq 0$$
$$8\mu_1 - 18\nu_1 - 14\nu_2 \leq 0$$
$$9\mu_1 - 23\nu_1 - 6\nu_2 \leq 0$$
$$27\mu_1 - 25\nu_1 - 10\nu_2 \leq 0$$
$$30\mu_1 - 27\nu_1 - 22\nu_2 \leq 0$$
$$31\mu_1 - 37\nu_1 - 14\nu_2 \leq 0$$
$$26.5\mu_1 - 42\nu_1 - 25\nu_2 \leq 0$$
$$12\mu_1 - 5\nu_1 - 17\nu_2 \leq 0$$
$$\mu_1 \geq 1$$
$$\nu_1, \nu_2 \geq 1$$

The optimal solution (λ^l, s^l, e^l) to the CRS envelopment form for unit 3, is $\lambda_1 = .1216216$, $\lambda_4 = .9054054$, and $\lambda_j = 0$, otherwise, with output slack $s^3 = 0$ and input

[12] See Ahn, Charnes, and Cooper (1988a) for a characterization of this and other efficiency relationships between models.

slacks $e_1^3 = 0$ and $e_2^3 = 10.84$. Thus, DMU_3 is *not* efficient for the CRS envelopment surface and the projected point $(\widehat{Y}_l, \widehat{X}_l)$ has $\widehat{Y}_3 = 25$ and $\widehat{X}_3 = (16, 15.16)$. An optimal multiplier solution (μ^l, ν^l) is given by $\mu^3 = 1.973, \nu^3 = (2.135, 1.0)$. It is easily verified that both units 1 and 4 form the efficient reference set and lie on the facet defined by the hyperplane $1.973y_1 - 2.135x_1 - x_2 = 0$. This hyperplane with normal $(\mu^l, -\nu^l) = (1.973, -2.135, -1)$ differs from the one obtained previously for the VRS formulation since it must pass through the origin.

Table 3.3 reports optimal solutions for the CRS model for each DMU. Note, as previously discussed, that only three units are efficient for the CRS envelopment surface. [These efficient units (1, 4, and 7) were also efficient for the VRS envelopment.]

3.1.3   Other Envelopment Surfaces

As illustrated in the preceding sections, the VRS and CRS envelopments result in piecewise *linear* envelopment surfaces. However, other piecewise envelopment surfaces are possible.

For example, instead of the additive combinations of inputs and outputs of the previous sections, one can utilize multiplicative combinations of the inputs and outputs. The resulting envelopments are piecewise log linear or piecewise Cobb-Douglas with multiplicative measures of relative efficiency; these can prove advantageous in applications, interpretations, and extensions of other theories as described in Charnes, Cooper, Seiford, and Stutz (1982, 1983).

As is easily verified, the following multiplicative model of Charnes, Cooper, Seiford, and Stutz (1983) results from the direct application of the VRS model to the

Table 3.3   Optimal Solutions to CRS Model

| DMU | Multiplier Problem | | | Envelopment Problem | | | |
	μ_1	ν_1	ν_1	Σ^l	λ	s	e
Unit 1	1.973	2.135	1.000	.00	$\lambda_1 = 1$	0	(0,0)
Unit 2	1.231	1.000	1.000	10.77	$\lambda_4 = .538$	0	(6.85,3.92)
Unit 3	1.973	2.135	1.000	10.84	$\lambda_1 = .122$	0	(0,10.84)
					$\lambda_4 = .905$		
Unit 4	1.231	1.000	1.000	.00	$\lambda_4 = 1$	0	(0,0)
Unit 5	1.231	1.000	1.000	22.15	$\lambda_4 = .307$	0	(12.77,9.38)
Unit 6	1.231	1.000	1.000	17.92	$\lambda_4 = .346$	0	(17.12,.81)
Unit 7	1.414	1.000	1.317	.00	$\lambda_7 = 1$	0	(0,0)
Unit 8	1.231	1.000	1.000	12.08	$\lambda_4 = 1.15$	0	(7.38,4.69)
Unit 9	1.414	1.000	1.317	11.61	$\lambda_4 = .469$	0	(11.61,0)
					$\lambda_7 = .697$		
Unit 10	1.231	1.000	1.000	34.38	$\lambda_4 = 1.019$	0	(24.67,9.71)
Unit 11	1.973	2.135	1.000	4.00	$\lambda_1 = 1$	0	(0,4)

logarithms of the original data values. The envelopment surface determined by this model is piecewise Cobb-Douglas.[13]

$\text{MULT}_E(Y_l, X_l):$

$$\min_{\lambda,s,e} - \left(\sum_{r=1}^{s} s_r + \sum_{i=1}^{m} e_i \right)$$

$$\sum_{j=1}^{n} \log(y_{rj})\lambda_j - s_r = \log(y_{rl}) \qquad r = 1,\ldots,s$$

$$-\sum_{j=1}^{n} \log(x_{ij})\lambda_j - e_i = -\log(x_{il}) \qquad i = 1,\ldots,m$$

$$\sum_{j=1}^{n} \lambda_j = 1$$

$$\lambda_j \geq 0 \qquad j = 1,\ldots,n$$
$$s_r \geq 0 \qquad r = 1,\ldots,s$$
$$e_i \geq 0 \qquad i = 1,\ldots,m$$

$\text{MULT}_M(Y_l, X_l):$

$$\max_{\mu,\nu,\omega} \sum_{r=1}^{s} \log(y_{rl})\mu_r - \sum_{i=1}^{m} \log(x_{il})\nu_i + \omega$$

$$\sum_{r=1}^{s} \log(y_{rj})\mu_r - \sum_{i=1}^{m} \log(x_{ij})\nu_i + \omega \leq 0 \qquad j = 1,\ldots,n$$

$$\mu_r \geq 1 \qquad r = 1,\ldots,s$$
$$\nu_i \geq 1 \qquad i = 1,\ldots,m$$

We do not examine this model in detail since the discussion would, in essence, be identical to that for the VRS model. Similarly, application of the CRS model to the logarithms of the data results in the piecewise log-linear envelopment model of Charnes, Cooper, Seiford, and Stutz (1982). [14]

In the next section we return to the CRS and VRS (piecewise linear) envelopment surfaces and examine more fully the issue of efficiency measurement.

3.2. A Basis for Measuring Efficiency.

Recall that a DEA analysis requires the solution of n linear programming (LP) problems, one for each DMU. In the evaluation of unit l we solve the LP problem

---

[13] Thus, this model allows one to estimate piecewise Cobb-Douglas production functions directly from empirical data.

[14] Banker and Maindiratta (1986) discuss piecewise log-linear envelopments with oriented (radial) efficiency measures similar to the oriented models discussed in Section 3.3.

for the particular envelopment surface [either $\text{VRS}_E(Y_l, X_l)$ or $\text{CRS}_E(Y_l, X_l)$], and obtain

1. A facet-defining hyperplane of the envelopment surface
2. A projected point $(\widehat{Y}_l, \widehat{X}_l)$ that lies on the facet-defining hyperplane

Measures of efficiency for DMU_l address the discrepancy between the point (Y_l, X_l) and the projected point $(\widehat{Y}_l, \widehat{X}_l)$ on the envelopment surface.

Since $(\widehat{Y}_l, \widehat{X}_l)$ lies on the facet defining plane $\mu^l \mathbf{y} - \nu^l \mathbf{x} + \omega^l = 0$, we have

$$\mu^l Y_l - \nu^l X_l + \omega^l = [\mu^l Y_l - \nu^l X_l + \omega^l] - [\mu^l \widehat{Y}_l - \nu^l \widehat{X}_l + \omega^l]$$
$$= -\mu^l(\widehat{Y}_l - Y_l) - \nu^l(X_l - \widehat{X}_l)$$

Thus the points $(\widehat{Y}_l, \widehat{X}_l)$ and Y_l, X_l lie on parallel planes that differ by the constant

$$\Delta^l = -\mu^l(\widehat{Y}_l - Y_l) - \nu^l(X_l - \widehat{X}_l) = -\mu^l \mathbf{s}^l - \nu^l \mathbf{e}^l$$

The distance measure Δ^l reflects the magnitude of the discrepancy between the observed point (Y_l, X_l) and the projected point $(\widehat{Y}_l, \widehat{X}_l)$ with respect to the evaluation represented by μ^l, ν^l, ω^l and, as discussed in Section 3.1.1, is the optimal (minimum) value for the objective function.

For VRS and CRS envelopments, we have examined one possible path to the envelopment surface, that is, moving from (Y_l, X_l) to $(\widehat{Y}_l, \widehat{X}_l)$ along the vector $(\mathbf{s}^l, -\mathbf{e}^l)$. Figure 3.4 illustrates this projection path for the VRS model. However, alternative paths and projected points can be constructed for inefficient units. The incentive for producing these alternative points rests in the particular set of variables (inputs or outputs) upon which one focuses. Two such alternative projected points were originally developed by Charnes, Cooper, and Rhodes (1978) and correspond to either an input or an output orientation. In an input orientation the focus is on input reduction while an output orientation concentrates on output augmentation. Thus, an essential concept for input/output orientation is that of proportional reduction/augmentation which we now discuss.

For the VRS and CRS models of Sections 3.1.1 and 3.1.2, the relation between the observed point (Y_l, X_l) and the projected point $(\widehat{Y}_l, \widehat{X}_l)$ is completely given by the vector $(\mathbf{s}^l, \mathbf{e}^l)$. The output augmentation and input reduction prescribed by $(\mathbf{s}^l, \mathbf{e}^l)$, however, might consist of an overall proportional augmentation/reduction component which could be applied first[15] and then additional residual output augmentation and input reduction beyond the proportional component to achieve efficiency.

---

[15] The proportional components are frequently examined separately since they keep the mix ratios, that is, the basic technological recipes, approximately unchanged.

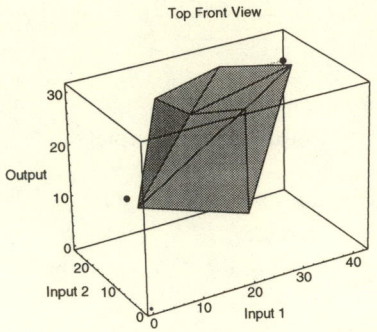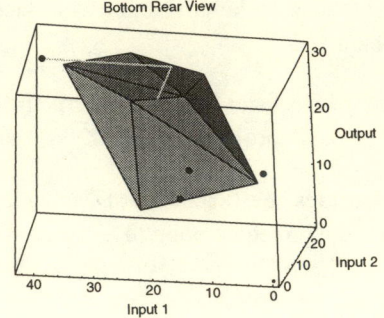

Fig. 3.4 VRS projection of inefficient unit

These proportional components can be determined by introducing the scalar ρ to represent the intrinsic proportional augmentation and the scalar γ to represent the intrinsic proportional reduction and writing

$$\mathbf{s}^l = \rho Y_l + \delta_{\mathbf{s}}^l \qquad \mathbf{e}^l = \gamma X_l + \delta_{\mathbf{e}}^l$$

Thus, the output vector can be increased proportionally by a factor of ρ and the individual additional residual increases are given by $\delta_{\mathbf{s}}^l$. (Note that at least one element of this vector is zero.) Similarly, the input vector for unit l can be decreased proportionally (in each component) by a factor of γ. The residual decreases in each of the individual input variables are given by $\delta_{\mathbf{e}}^l$. (Note that at least one element of this vector is zero.) The amount of proportional increase of outputs (ρ) and the amount of proportional decrease of inputs (γ) possible for the obtained projected point is given by

$$\rho = \min_{r=1,\ldots,s} \frac{\hat{y}_{rl} - y_{rl}}{y_{rl}} \geq 0$$

$$\gamma = \min_{i=1,\ldots,m} \frac{x_{il} - \hat{x}_{il}}{x_{il}} \geq 0$$

ρ and γ determine the extent to which inefficiency can be improved by proportional output augmentation and proportional input reduction. Specifically, the intrinsic proportional increases and decreases serve to *partly* explain the total discrepancy between the observed point (Y_l, X_l) and a projected point $(\widehat{Y}_l, \widehat{X}_l)$. We have

$$\Delta^l = -\rho(\mu^l Y_l) - \gamma(\nu^l X_l) - \mu^l \delta_{\mathbf{s}}^l - \nu^l \delta_{\mathbf{e}}^l$$

Thus the total discrepancy consists of a component due to proportional augmentation in outputs, a component due to proportional reduction in inputs, and components due to residual (nonproportional) augmentation in outputs and residual (nonproportional) reductions in input. The projected point or path to the frontier can be thought of as being obtained by first identifying an intermediate point $[(1 + \rho)Y_l, (1 - \gamma)X_l]$ (obtained by proportional reduction/augmentation) and then obtaining the projected point $(\widehat{Y}_l, \widehat{X}_l)$ from the residual (δ_s^l, δ_e^l).

3.3. Oriented Models.

The preceding discussion of proportional reduction/augmentation is in the framework of the VRS and CRS envelopments of Section 3.1. In these models output slack and input excess are considered comparable in that neither should preempt or receive greater scrutiny than the other. In oriented models the envelopment surface remains the same—either VRS or CRS. However, one set of variables (inputs or outputs) preempts the other in that proportional (radial) movement toward the frontier is first achieved in that space. For an input-oriented projection, one is seeking a projection such that the proportional reduction in inputs, γ, is maximized. Similarly, for the output-oriented projection, one is seeking a projection such that the proportional augmentation in outputs, ρ, is maximized. Such oriented projections require *first* determining the maximum value for γ *or* the maximum value for ρ. This identifies an intermediate point $[Y_l, (1 - \gamma)X_l]$ for the input orientation *or* an intermediate point $[(1 + \rho)Y_l, X_l]$ for the output orientation.

Instead of considering the amount of proportional increase or decrease, one could equivalently characterize input and output orientations in terms of the resultant proportion of the input or output vector after the increase or decrease has been effected. Since this characterization results in a more compact formulation and also has been prevalent in the literature we employ the notation

$$\phi = 1 + \rho \qquad \theta = 1 - \gamma$$

That is, maximizing γ is equivalent to minimizing $\theta = 1 - \gamma$ and maximizing ρ is equivalent to maximizing $\phi = 1 + \rho$.

The input and output constraints (in matrix form) can be rewritten in the following manner:

$$\mathbf{Y}\lambda - \phi Y_l - \delta_s^l = 0 \tag{3.1a}$$

$$-\mathbf{X}\lambda + \theta X_l - \delta_e^l = 0 \tag{3.1b}$$

Orientations which focus on input variables or output variables are discussed in the following two sections. Oriented models employ either $(3.1a)$ or $(3.1b)$ and identify efficiency in two stages. For an input orientation this identification consists of two steps; the intermediate point $(Y_l, \theta^l X_l)$ is first obtained and then the subsequent projection point is obtained by solving $\text{CRS}_E(Y_l, \theta^l X_l)$, or $\text{VRS}_E(Y_l, \theta^l X_l)$. For output orientation the two-step approach first determines the intermediate point $(\phi^l Y_l, X_l)$ from which the subsequent projection point is obtained by solving $\text{VRS}_E(\phi^l Y_l, X_l)$ or $\text{CRS}_E(\phi^l Y_l, X_l)$. As will be discussed, the preemption effected in the first stage produces a projected point that can differ from that obtained in Section 3.1 for the standard VRS or CRS model.

The model formulations which have appeared in the literature represent this two-stage procedure by a single one-step non-Archimedean model in which preemption is achieved via an infinitesimal. Implicit in these one-step non-Archimedean models is the two-stage approach. While the one-step non-Archimedean approach may have value as a modeling construct, the explicit two-stage approach avoids computational difficulties as described in Ali and Seiford (1989).

3.3.1 Input Orientation

It is possible to create models that yield input-oriented projections for both the VRS and CRS envelopments of Sections 3.1.1 and 3.1.2. These input-oriented models strive to maximize the proportional decrease in input variables while remaining within the envelopment space (production possibility set). Clearly, a proportional decrease is possible until at least one of the excess input variables is reduced to zero. As discussed above this maximal proportional decrease is accomplished in the first-stage problem. The resulting intermediate point is employed in the second-stage program (VRS_E or CRS_E) to obtain the projected point.

The input reduction models for CRS and VRS envelopment are stated below. Note that the first-stage model formulations are not valid for efficiency determination when used by themselves; they must be used as the first step in a two-step approach since the intermediate point which results from the first stage may not lie on the efficient frontier.

Solving the (two-stage) CRS input orientation yields a CRS envelopment while the (two-stage) VRS input orientation determines a VRS envelopment.

CRS Input Orientation

First Stage	Second Stage
$\text{CRS}'(Y_l, X_l)$:	$\text{CRS}_E(Y_l, \theta^l X_l)$:
$\min_{\theta, \lambda, s, e} \theta$	$\min_{\lambda, s, e} -(\mathbf{1}s - \mathbf{1}e)$
$Y\lambda - s = Y_l$	$Y\lambda - s = Y_l$
$-X\lambda + \theta X_l - e = 0$	$-X\lambda + \theta^l X_l - e = 0$
$\lambda \geq 0 \quad e \geq 0 \quad s \geq 0$	$\lambda \geq 0 \quad e \geq 0 \quad s \geq 0$

VRS Input Orientation

First Stage	Second Stage
$\text{VRS}^I\,(Y_l, X_l)$:	$\text{VRS}_E\,(Y_l,\, \theta^l X_l)$:
$\min_{\theta,\lambda,s,e}\ \theta$	$\min_{\lambda,s,e}\ -(\mathbf{1s} + \mathbf{1e})$
$Y\lambda - s = Y_l$	$Y\lambda - s = Y_l$
$-X\lambda + \theta X_l - e = 0$	$-X\lambda + \theta^l X_l - e = 0$
$1\lambda = 1$	$1\lambda = 1$
$\lambda \geqslant 0 \quad e \geqslant 0 \quad s \geqslant 0$	$\lambda \geqslant 0 \quad e \geqslant 0 \quad s \geqslant 0$

In the two-step approach, the above input reduction models (CRS^I and VRS^I) yield the intermediate point $(Y_l, \theta^l X_l)$.[16] The subsequent projections are obtained by solving $\text{CRS}_E(Y_l, \theta^l X_l)$ or $\text{VRS}_E(Y_l, \theta^l X_l)$.

For example, when $\text{VRS}_E(Y_l, \theta^l X_l)$ is solved, the projected point obtained is

$$\widehat{Y_l} = Y_l + \mathbf{s}^l \qquad \widehat{X_l} = \theta^l X_l - \mathbf{e}^l$$

Note that $\mathbf{e}^l$ corresponds to $\delta_{\mathbf{e}}^l$ (the nonproportional slack) in Equation (3.1b).

An input-oriented DEA analysis requires solving the two-stage procedures for each DMU. The reader should also note that the only item of interest from the solution of the first-stage model is the optimal value of θ, the maximal proportional input reduction. This specific optimal value, θ^l, is used in the second-stage formulation; the adjusted input values for the second-stage being $\theta^l X_l$. Thus, θ^l in the second-stage model is *not* a variable. Since proportional input reduction has already been accomplished via θ^l, the second-stage solution determines a projected point which lies on the frontier.

The (one-step) non-Archimedean models for input orientation employ a non-Archimedean constant ϵ as a modeling construct[17] for expressing the sequential (two-stage) solution of a pair of models.

These models are presented below.[18]

---

[16]The intermediate point $(Y_l, \theta^l X_l)$ is not necessarily on the efficient frontier. It is, however, always a boundary point of the convex hull of the data. See Seiford and Thrall (1990) for a discussion of this distinction between boundary points and efficient points.

[17]The scalar ϵ is an infinitesimal, that is, satisfies $0 < \epsilon < 1/N$ for all positive integers N.

[18]These models have been identified with the authors of the papers in which they originally appeared. Our labels reflect this tradition: CCR [Charnes, Cooper, and Rhodes (1978)] and BCC [(Banker, Charnes, and Cooper (1984)]. The superscripts indicate an input orientation (I) while the subscripts indicate either the primal (P) or dual (D) formulation of the linear program.

$\text{CCR}_P^I:$

$\min_{\theta,\lambda,s,e} \quad \theta - \epsilon(1s + 1e)$
$Y\lambda - s = Y_l$
$\theta X_l - X\lambda - e = 0$
$\lambda \geq 0 \quad e \geq 0 \quad s \geq 0$

$\text{CCR}_D^I:$

$\max_{\mu,\nu} \quad \mu Y_l$
$\nu X_l = 1$
$\mu Y - \nu X \leq 0$
$\mu \geq \epsilon 1 \quad \nu \geq \epsilon 1$

$\text{BCC}_P^I:$

$\min_{\theta,\lambda,s,e} \quad \theta - \epsilon(1s + 1e)$
$Y\lambda - s = Y_l$
$\theta X_l - X\lambda - e = 0$
$1\lambda = 1$
$\lambda \geq 0 \quad e \geq 0 \quad s \geq 0$

$\text{BCC}_D^I:$

$\max_{\mu,\nu,\omega} \quad \mu Y_l + \omega$
$\nu X_l = 1$
$\mu Y - \nu X + 1\omega \leq 0$
$\mu \geq \epsilon 1 \quad \nu \geq \epsilon 1$

In the initial implementations of DEA it was not recognized that the non-Archimedean models should be solved in two stages. It has since been recognized that attempts to solve these non-Archimedean models as a single linear program with an explicit numerical value for the infinitesimal frequently creates computational inaccuracies and leads to erroneous results.

The above models also clearly indicate the effect of single-stage formulations which use zero for lower bounds on the multipliers, or, equivalently, use θ as the sole measure of efficiency ignoring residual nonproportional output slack and input excess. It is true that such models accurately identify θ. However, by focusing solely on θ they improperly classify units as efficient when θ is one even if output slack and/or input excess is present. In contrast, the above formulations of the non-Archimedean models as single linear programs do properly classify these inefficient units in the absence of computational inaccuracies.

The comparison between the CRS and VRS models made in Section 3.1.2 applies here for the above input-oriented formulations. In particular, the effect of the convexity constraint $(1\lambda = 1)$ and the variable ω (present in the VRS^I model and absent in the CRS^I model) on the envelopment surface is the same as before.

Example   Recall that the data values for unit 2 are $Y_2 = 14.00$ and $X_2 = (16, 12)$. The solution of the (first-stage) input reduction model BCC^I yields $\theta^l = .86999$. The optimal solution to $\text{VRS}_E(Y_l, \theta^l X_l)$ for unit 2 (after $\theta^l = .87$ has been determined) is $\lambda_1 = .5255878, \lambda_7 = .1901798, \lambda_6 = .2842324$, and $\lambda_j = 0$ otherwise. Thus, the projected point has $\widehat{Y}_2 = 14.00$, $\widehat{X}_2 = (13.92, 10.44)$ with output slack $s_1 = 0$ and input slacks $e_1 = 0, e_2 = 0$.

The optimal solution for unit 5 after proportional reduction of inputs has been determined is $\lambda_1 = .5661376, \lambda_7 = 0, \lambda_6 = .4338624$, and $\lambda_j = 0$ otherwise. Thus, the projected point has $\widehat{Y}_5 = 10.70$, $\widehat{X}_5 = (12.81, 9.96)$ with output slack $s_1 = 2.70$

Table 3.4 Solutions for VRS Input-Oriented Model

DMU	θ^l	Σ^l	$\hat{Y}_l$	$\hat{X}_l$
Unit 1	1.00000	.000	12	(5,13)
Unit 2	.86999	.000	14	(13.92,10.44)
Unit 3	1.00000	.000	25	(16,26)
Unit 4	1.00000	.000	26	(17,15)
Unit 5	.71164	2.698	10.7	(12.81,9.96)
Unit 6	1.00000	.000	9	(23,6)
Unit 7	1.00000	.000	27	(25,10)
Unit 8	1.00000	.000	30	(27,22)
Unit 9	1.00000	.000	31	(37,14)
Unit 10	.50000	.000	26.5	(21,12.5)
Unit 11	1.00000	4.000	12	(5,13)

and input slacks $e_1 = 0, e_2 = 0$. A comparison of the reported statistics in Table 3.4 with those in Table 3.2 reveals the effect of input orientation. The inefficient and efficient DMUs and the envelopment surface remain the same for the VRS input-oriented model as for the standard VRS model. However, as Figure 3.5 illustrates, efficiency scores, projected points, and therefore the total distance from (Y_l, X_l) to $(\hat{Y}_l, \hat{X}_l)$ are different.[19] [Note that the values of Σ^l given in Table 3.4 are the slack values for the intermediate point $(Y_l, \theta^l X_l)$, i.e., the slack values from the second-stage problem.]

3.3.2 Output Orientation

Output-oriented models maximize the proportional increase in the output vector while remaining within the envelopment space. Thus, an output orientation finds interme-

[19] The reader should compare Figures 3.4 and 3.5.

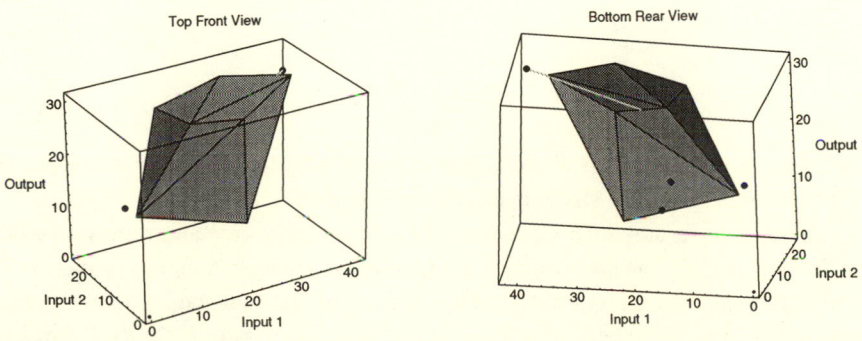

Fig. 3.5 VRS input oriented projection of inefficient unit

diate points $(\phi^l Y_l, X_l)$ from which subsequent projections are obtained. Clearly, a proportional increase is possible until at least one of the output slack variables is reduced to zero. The output-oriented models for CRS and VRS envelopment are stated below.

CRS Output Orientation

First Stage	Second Stage
$\mathrm{CRS}^O (Y_l, X_l)$:	$\mathrm{CRS}_E (\phi' Y_l, X_l)$:
$\max_{\phi,\lambda,s,e} \phi$	$\min_{\lambda,s,e} - (\mathbf{1s} - \mathbf{1e})$
$\mathbf{Y\lambda - \phi Y_l - s = 0}$	$\mathbf{Y\lambda - \phi' Y_l - s = 0}$
$\mathbf{X\lambda + e = X_l}$	$\mathbf{X\lambda + e = X_l}$
$\mathbf{\lambda \geqslant 0 \quad e \geqslant 0 \quad s \geqslant 0}$	$\mathbf{\lambda \geqslant 0 \quad e \geqslant 0 \quad s \geqslant 0}$

VRS Output Orientation

First Stage	Second Stage
$\mathrm{VRS}^O (Y_l, X_l)$:	$\mathrm{VRS}_E (\phi' Y_l, X_l)$:
$\max_{\phi,\lambda,s,e} \phi$	$\min_{\lambda,s,e} - (\mathbf{1s} - \mathbf{1e})$
$\mathbf{Y\lambda - \phi Y_l - s = 0}$	$\mathbf{Y\lambda - \phi' Y_l - s = 0}$
$\mathbf{X\lambda + e = X_l}$	$\mathbf{X\lambda + e = X_l}$
$\mathbf{1\lambda = 1}$	$\mathbf{1\lambda = 1}$
$\mathbf{\lambda \geqslant 0 \quad e \geqslant 0 \quad s \geqslant 0}$	$\mathbf{\lambda \geqslant 0 \quad e \geqslant 0 \quad s \geqslant 0}$

The first-stage output augmentation models yield an intermediate point $(\phi^l Y_l, X_l)$. As before, the subsequent projections are obtained by solving $\mathrm{VRS}_E(\phi^l Y_l, X_l)$ or $\mathrm{CRS}_E(\phi^l Y_l, X_l)$.

The reader should again note that the specific optimal value ϕ^l which appears in the second-stage formulation is not a variable; it is the maximal proportional output augmentation determined from the first-stage problem.

For example, when $\mathrm{VRS}_E(\phi^l Y_l, X_l)$ is solved, the obtained projection is given by

$$\widehat{Y}_l = \phi^l Y_l + \mathbf{s}^l \qquad \widehat{X}_l = X_l - \mathbf{e}^l$$

and $(\widehat{Y}_l - Y_l) = (\phi^l - 1)Y_l + \mathbf{s}^l$ and $(X_l - \widehat{X}_l) = \mathbf{e}^l$. Again, note that $\mathbf{s}^l$ corresponds to $\delta_\mathbf{s}^l$ (the nonproportional slack) in Equation (3.1a).

The one-stage non-Archimedean models for output orientation are given below. In both models, the non-Archimedean construct allows output augmentation to preempt the maximization of slacks. Thus the sequential two-stage process can be expressed as a single model. The labeling of the models is as before; the CCR^O model yields a CRS envelopment while the BCC^O model yields a VRS envelopment.

$\text{CCR}_P^O:$

$$\max_{\phi,\lambda,s,e} \quad \phi + \epsilon(1\mathbf{s} + 1\mathbf{e})$$
$$\phi Y_l - \mathbf{Y}\lambda + \mathbf{s} = 0$$
$$\mathbf{X}\lambda + \mathbf{e} = X_l$$
$$\lambda \geq 0 \quad \mathbf{e} \geq 0 \quad \mathbf{s} \geq 0$$

$\text{CCR}_D^O:$

$$\min_{\mu,\nu} \quad \nu X_l$$
$$\mu Y_l = 1$$
$$-\mu\mathbf{Y} + \nu\mathbf{X} \geq 0$$
$$\mu \geq \epsilon 1 \quad \nu \geq \epsilon 1$$

$\text{BCC}_P^O:$

$$\max_{\phi,\lambda,s,e} \quad \phi + \epsilon(1\mathbf{s} + 1\mathbf{e})$$
$$\phi Y_l - \mathbf{Y}\lambda + \mathbf{s} = 0$$
$$\mathbf{X}\lambda + \mathbf{e} = X_l$$
$$1\lambda = 1$$
$$\lambda \geq 0 \quad \mathbf{e} \geq 0 \quad \mathbf{s} \geq 0$$

$\text{BCC}_D^O:$

$$\min_{\mu,\nu,\omega} \quad \nu X_l + \omega$$
$$\mu Y_l = 1$$
$$-\mu\mathbf{Y} + \nu\mathbf{X} + 1\omega \geq 0$$
$$\mu \geq \epsilon 1 \quad \nu \geq \epsilon 1$$

Example Table 3.5 lists the solutions for the VRS output-oriented program. A comparison of the values with those in Tables 3.4 and 3.2 illustrates the effect of model orientation. Units 2, 5, 10, and 11 remain inefficient but now projection (improvement) is in the output direction as illustrated in Figure 3.6. To avoid confusion the reader should note that the slack value Σ^l given in Tables 3.2, 3.4, and 3.5 are for (intermediate) points, (Y^l, X^l), $(Y^l, \theta^l X^l)$, and $(\phi^l Y^l, X^l)$, respectively.

We stress that the envelopment surface and the sets of inefficient and efficient DMUs remain the same for the standard VRS model of Section 3.1, the input-oriented VRS model of Section 3.3.1, and the output-oriented VRS model of Section 3.3.2; only the actual efficiency scores and the projected points may change. Similarly, the standard CRS, input-oriented CRS, and output-oriented CRS models yield identical envelopment surfaces and identical sets of efficient and inefficient DMUs. Table 3.6 classifies models by type of envelopment surface and variable set focus.

Table 3.5   Solutions for VRS Output-Oriented Model

DMU	ϕ^l	Σ^l	$\hat{Y}_l$	$\hat{X}_l$
Unit 1	1.00000	.000	12	(5,13)
Unit 2	1.50752	.000	21.11	(16,12)
Unit 3	1.00000	.000	25	(16,26)
Unit 4	1.00000	.000	26	(17,15)
Unit 5	3.20295	.000	25.63	(18,14)
Unit 6	1.00000	.000	9	(23,6)
Unit 7	1.00000	.000	27	(25,10)
Unit 8	1.00000	.000	30	(27,22)
Unit 9	1.00000	.000	31	(37,14)
Unit 10	1.16981	16.000	31	(37,14)
Unit 11	1.00000	4.000	12	(5,13)

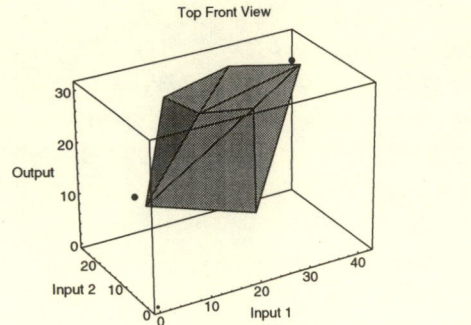
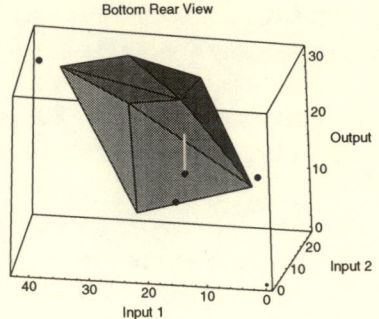

Fig. 3.6   VRS output oriented projection of inefficient unit

Table 3.6   Summary of Models

Type of Envelopment Surface	Variable Set Focus		
	Inputs & Outputs	**Inputs**	**Outputs**
Constant returns-to-scale	(Standard) CRS model	CRS^I	CRS^O
Variable returns-to-scale	(Standard) VRS model	VRS^I	VRS^O

3.4. Units of Measurement

As discussed in earlier sections, the envelopment surface is determined by the set of efficient DMUs. These DMUs are efficient because of relative spatial relationships. A change in the units of measurement stretches or shrinks this envelopment surface but leaves the relative spatial relationships and hence the efficiency/inefficiency classifications unchanged. A change in the units, however, can have a considerable impact on the projections produced in the CRS and VRS models. In typical linear programming problems, if a constraint is scaled (multiplied by a nonzero scalar), the solution is not altered. In data envelopment analysis, when the data is scaled (each input or output value is multiplied by a nonnegative scalar), the results may change.[20] Projections and efficiency scores that are obtained depend on the units of measurement precisely because of the relationship between nonzero slacks and multipliers described in Section 3.1. Thus the change in projections and efficiency scores when different units of measurement are used for data is directly tied to the lower bounds on multipliers (which are specified) since these lower bounds form the coefficients for the objective function of the dual linear program.

---

[20] In DEA models the slack variables (s and e) appear with nonzero coefficients in the objective function in contrast to other linear programming models.

The term $\mu^l \mathbf{s}^l + \nu^l \mathbf{e}^l$ is exactly $\mathbf{1}\mathbf{s}^l + \mathbf{1}\mathbf{e}^l$ for the CRS and VRS envelopment models, a quantity which obviously depends on the units of measurement of the data. This dependence of $(\mathbf{1}\mathbf{s} + \mathbf{1}\mathbf{e})$ on units of measurement alters both projections and efficiency score evaluation when different units of measurement are employed.

In the standard envelopment models, the lower bounds of 1 for the multipliers (in CRS_M and VRS_M) implicitly assume that the marginal worth of each of the nonzero output slacks and nonzero excess inputs for a DMU are identical. In addition, the marginal worth of nonzero output slacks for a particular output (or nonzero excess for a particular input) are the same across all decision-making units.

If one has prioritized the variables and the units reflect this prioritization, the standard models have the distinct advantage of establishing a common baseline for evaluation. That is, a unit of slack is worth exactly the same amount to each DMU.

In contrast to the standard envelopment models with multiplier lower bounds of one, the *units-invariant* models have lower bounds defined by

$$\mu_r \geq \frac{1}{y_{rl}} \qquad r = 1, \ldots, s$$
$$\nu_i \geq \frac{1}{x_{il}} \qquad i = 1, \ldots, m \tag{3.2}$$

These units-invariant models allow each DMU the additional flexibility to select a base of evaluation that is determined by its own particular relative mix of inputs and outputs. In particular, these models implicitly assume that the marginal values of nonzero output slack and excess input variables are not identical. The relative worth of each output slack or input excess is gauged with respect to the level of the output or input. This not only distinguishes the relative worth among the inputs and outputs for a particular decision making unit but also distinguishes the relative worth of a particular output or input across decision-making units.

As an example, a units-invariant VRS envelopment model[21] is given by the following dual linear programs:

$$\max_{\mu_r, \nu_i, \omega} \sum_{r=1}^{s} y_{rl}\mu_r - \sum_{i=1}^{m} x_{il}\nu_i + \omega$$
$$\sum_{r=1}^{s} y_{rj}\mu_r - \sum_{i=1}^{m} x_{ij}\nu_i + \omega \leq 0 \qquad j = 1, \ldots, n$$
$$\mu_r \geq \frac{1}{y_{rl}} \qquad r = 1, \ldots, s$$
$$\nu_i \geq \frac{1}{x_{il}} \qquad i = 1, \ldots, m$$

[21] This units invariant model is the extended additive model of Charnes, Cooper, Rousseau, and Semple (1987) for discretionary inputs and outputs. (See Section 3.5.1.)

$$\min_{\lambda_j, s_r, e_i} \; - \left[\sum_{r=1}^{s} \left(\frac{1}{y_{rl}} \right) s_r + \sum_{i=1}^{m} \left(\frac{1}{x_{il}} \right) e_i \right]$$

$$\sum_{j=1}^{n} y_{rj} \lambda_j - s_r = y_{rl} \qquad r = 1, \ldots, s$$

$$- \sum_{j=1}^{n} x_{ij} \lambda_j - e_i = -x_{il} \qquad i = 1, \ldots, m$$

$$\sum_{j=1}^{n} \lambda_j = 1$$

$$\lambda_j \geq 0 \qquad j = 1, \ldots, n$$
$$s_r \geq 0 \qquad r = 1, \ldots, s$$
$$e_i \geq 0 \qquad i = 1, \ldots, m$$

The term $\mu^l s^l + \nu^l e^l$ is exactly $\sum_{r=1}^{s}(1/y_{rl}) s_r^l + \sum_{i=1}^{m}(1/x_{il}) e_i^l$ for units-invariant models. Thus, the units-invariant models produce (dimensionless) efficiency scores and projections that are invariant to the units in which the data are expressed. The reader should note that while the projections obtained from units-invariant models can differ from projections obtained from the corresponding standard models of Sections 3.1.1 and 3.1.2, the envelopment surface and the efficient/inefficient classification remain the same for both standard and units-invariant formulations.

The non-Archimedean (input/output-oriented) models discussed in Section 3.2 produce *efficiency scores* which are invariant to units of measurement since nonzero input excess values and output slack values are overwhelmed by the infinitesimal ϵ, that is, $\epsilon(1s^l + 1e^l) \equiv \epsilon$. However, while the optimal objective function value is units-invariant, the projection point itself for these non-Archimedean models remains units-dependent.

The property of units invariance discussed in this section is invariance with respect to scalar *multiplication* and, as has been demonstrated, requires lower bounds as given above in Equations (3.2). In contrast, Ali and Seiford (1990) have shown that translation invariance (invariance with respect to *addition* of a scalar) is determined by the presence of the convexity constraint.

Example   For the example data set in Table 3.1 the units invariant VRS models for unit $l = 2$ are given by

$$\max_{\mu_1, \nu_1, \nu_2, \omega} \quad 14\mu_1 - 16\nu_1 - 12\nu_2 + \omega$$

$$12\mu_1 - 5\nu_1 - 13\nu_2 + \omega \leq 0$$
$$14\mu_1 - 16\nu_1 - 12\nu_2 + \omega \leq 0$$
$$25\mu_1 - 16\nu_1 - 26\nu_2 + \omega \leq 0$$
$$26\mu_1 - 17\nu_1 - 15\nu_2 + \omega \leq 0$$
$$8\mu_1 - 18\nu_1 - 14\nu_2 + \omega \leq 0$$

$$9\mu_1 - 23\nu_1 - 6\nu_2 + \omega \leq 0$$
$$27\mu_1 - 25\nu_1 - 10\nu_2 + \omega \leq 0$$
$$30\mu_1 - 27\nu_1 - 22\nu_2 + \omega \leq 0$$
$$31\mu_1 - 37\nu_1 - 14\nu_2 + \omega \leq 0$$
$$26.5\mu_1 - 42\nu_1 - 25\nu_2 + \omega \leq 0$$
$$12\mu_1 - 5\nu_1 - 17\nu_2 + \omega \leq 0$$
$$\mu_1 \geq 1/14$$
$$\nu_1 \geq 1/16$$
$$\nu_2 \geq 1/12$$

and

$\text{VRS}_E(Y_2, X_2)$:

$$\min_{\lambda_1,\ldots,\lambda_{11},s_1,e_1,e_2} -(\frac{1}{14}s_1 + \frac{1}{16}e_1 + \frac{1}{12}e_2)$$

$$12\lambda_1 + 14\lambda_2 + 25\lambda_3 + 26\lambda_4 + 8\lambda_5 + 9\lambda_6$$
$$+27\lambda_7 + 30\lambda_8 + 31\lambda_9 + 26.5\lambda_{10} + 12\lambda_{11} - s_1 = \quad 14$$
$$-5\lambda_1 - 16\lambda_2 - 16\lambda_3 - 17\lambda_4 - 18\lambda_5 - 23\lambda_6$$
$$-25\lambda_7 - 27\lambda_8 - 37\lambda_9 - 42\lambda_{10} - 5\lambda_{11} - e_1 = -16$$
$$-13\lambda_1 - 12\lambda_2 - 26\lambda_3 - 15\lambda_4 - 14\lambda_5 - 6\lambda_6$$
$$-10\lambda_7 - 22\lambda_8 - 14\lambda_9 - 25\lambda_{10} - 17\lambda_{11} - e_2 = -12$$
$$\lambda_1 + \lambda_2 + \lambda_3 + \lambda_4 + \lambda_5 + \lambda_6 + \lambda_7 + \lambda_8 + \lambda_9 + \lambda_{10} + \lambda_{11} = \quad 1$$
$$\lambda_1,\ldots,\lambda_{11} \geq \quad 0$$
$$s_1 \geq \quad 0$$
$$e_1, e_2 \geq \quad 0$$

Table 3.7 lists solutions for both multiplier and envelopment forms for the units-invariant VRS model. The reader should contrast these solutions with the solutions given in Table 3.2 for the standard VRS model. While the same units remain efficient the projection for inefficient units has changed to reflect the different marginal worth. For example, unit 2, which previously had an input excess in Table 3.2, now has all its slack in output as a result of the change in relative worth from $(1 : 1)$ to $(\frac{1}{14} : \frac{1}{16})$.

3.5.   Extensions

A number of extensions to the basic DEA models have appeared in the literature. Many of these enhancements were originally proposed in the course of a particular study and may have been (1) necessary to take into account managerial or organizational factors or stipulations, (2) proposed as a solution to overcome inconsistencies in or incompleteness of the data, and/or (3) developed as refinements to a particular model. Regardless of their origin, these extensions are now accepted as valuable additions to the methodology of data envelopment analysis. While a comprehensive treatment of all extensions is outside the scope of this chapter, we briefly examine

Table 3.7 Optimal Solutions to Units-Invariant VRS Model

DMU	Multiplier Problem				Envelopment Problem			
	μ_1	v_1	v_2	ω	Σ^1	λ	s	e
Unit 1	.08333	.20000	.07692	1.000	0.0	$\lambda_1 = 1$	0	(0,0)
Unit 2	.07143	.06767	.09398	.703	.508	$\lambda_1 = .382$	7.11	(0,0)
						$\lambda_4 = .171$		
						$\lambda_7 = .447$		
Unit 3	2.57690	3.00000	.03846	-15.423	0.0	$\lambda_3 = 1$	0	(0,0)
Unit 4	.05994	.05882	.06667	.441	0.0	$\lambda_4 = 1$	0	(0,0)
Unit 5	.12500	.11842	.16447	1.230	2.204	$\lambda_1 = .039$	17.63	(0,0)
						$\lambda_4 = .776$		
						$\lambda_7 = .184$		
Unit 6	.11111	.14729	.42636	4.946	0.0	$\lambda_6 = 1$	0	(0,0)
Unit 7	.03704	.04000	.10000	1.000	0.0	$\lambda_7 = 1$	0	(0,0)
Unit 8	.22727	.05909	.04545	-4.223	0.0	$\lambda_8 = 1$	0	(0,0)
Unit 9	.15251	.02703	.07143	-2.728	0.0	$\lambda_9 = 1$	0	(0,0)
Unit 10	.03774	.02381	.04000	$-.024$	1.024	$\lambda_7 = 1$	.50	(17,15)
						$\lambda_7 = \frac{1}{2}$		
Unit 11	.08333	.20000	.05882	.765	.235	$\lambda_1 = 1$	0	(0,4)

three of the more important extensions to illustrate the richness and adaptability of the basic DEA methodology. The three extensions we examine can be viewed as modifications of the reference set, the variable set, and the possible range for multipliers, respectively.

3.5.1 Categorical Variables

Frequently, an input or output variable may have a natural representation as discrete levels (e.g., population categories) or may reflect the presence or absence of a particular capability (e.g., a drive-in facility). Banker and Morey (1986b) discuss the problems associated with attempting to estimate the resources (such as labor or capital) that a branch bank should require to obtain a given level of deposits, given a population base of 100,000 with specific demographic characteristics. As discussed in the preceding sections, DEA will compare the DMU (branch) under examination with combinations of efficient DMUs, some of which might have a population base considerably larger than the DMU being examined. Thus it would be less controversial if the comparison group of DMUs, consisted only of branches with a population of 100,000 or less. Similar considerations would hold if some branches of a bank have a drive-in capability while others do not. In such situations, one may wish to ensure that a branch is compared with branches which are in the same category or possibly with those operating in an even more difficult or unfavorable situation. The use of categorical (input or output) variables allows the incorporation of such discrete or binary factors and can improve the construction of an efficient reference set.

Consider an input variable that may take on one of the values $1, 2, \ldots, C$. These C values effectively partition the set of DMUs into categories. Specifically, the set of decision-making units $D = \{1, 2, \ldots, n\} = D_1 \cup D_2 \cup \cdots \cup D_C$ where $D_a = \{i \mid i \in D$ and input value is $a\}$ and $D_a \cap D_b = \emptyset, a \neq b$. The following model specification allows the evaluation of a decision-making unit l with respect to the envelopment surface determined for the units comprising its and all preceding categories.[22] Here we consider the basic VRS model; however, it should be obvious that the inclusion of such variables is possible for any DEA model.

$\mathrm{CAT}_P(Y_l, X_l)$:

$$
\begin{aligned}
\min_{\lambda, s, e} \quad & -(\mathbf{1s} + \mathbf{1e}) \\
& \sum_{j \in \cup_{k=1}^{K} D_k} Y_j \lambda_j - \mathbf{s} = \quad Y_l \\
& - \sum_{j \in \cup_{k=1}^{K} D_k} X_j \lambda_j - \mathbf{e} = -X_l \\
& \mathbf{1}\lambda = \quad 1 \\
& \lambda \geq \quad \mathbf{0} \\
& e \geq \quad \mathbf{0} \\
& s \geq \quad \mathbf{0}
\end{aligned}
$$

The above specification provides an explanation of how the implied hierarchy of evaluation in the categories can be addressed via data envelopment analysis. A decision-making unit $l \in D_K, K \in \{1, \ldots, C\}$ may be evaluated with respect to the units in $\cup_{k=1}^{K} D_k$. Thus, one can evaluate all units $l \in D_1$ with respect to the units in D_1, all units $l \in D_2$ with respect to the units in $D_1 \cup D_2, \ldots,$ all units $l \in D_C$ with respect to the units in $\cup_{k=1}^{C} D_k$. For a more thorough discussion the reader is referred to Banker and Morey (1986b) and Kamakura (1988).

Example   Consider the example data set from Table 3.1. Suppose units 1 to 4 are in category 1 while units 5 to 11 are in category 2, that is, $D_1 = \{1, 2, 3, 4\}$ and $D_2 = \{5, 6, \ldots, 11\}$.

The following model formulation for evaluation of unit 2 clearly illustrates that the evaluation is with respect to only those units in category 1.

---

[22] Implicit in this development is the assumption that there is a natural nesting or hierarchy of the categories. Otherwise, one should perform a separate analysis for each category.

$CAT_P(Y_2, X_2)$:

$$\min_{\lambda_1,\ldots,\lambda_4,s_1,e_1,e_2} \quad -\left(s_1 + \sum_{i=1}^{2} e_i\right)$$

$$12\lambda_1 + 14\lambda_2 + 25\lambda_3 + 26\lambda_4 - s_1 = 14$$
$$-5\lambda_1 - 16\lambda_2 - 16\lambda_3 - 17\lambda_4 - e_1 = -16$$
$$-13\lambda_1 - 12\lambda_2 - 26\lambda_3 - 15\lambda_4 - e_2 = -12$$
$$\lambda_1 + \lambda_2 + \lambda_3 + \lambda_4 = 1$$
$$\lambda_1, \ldots, \lambda_4 \geq 0$$
$$s_1 \geq 0$$
$$e_1, e_2 \geq 0$$

Table 3.8 reports the optimal solutions for all 11 units. Since DMUs in category 2 are evaluated with respect to categories 1 and 2 (all DMUs) the solutions for units 5 to 11 remain the same as in Table 3.2. Since units 1 to 4 are evaluated against only those units of category 1, their solutions could change. However, unit 2 is the only DMU which exhibits a different solution; units 1, 3, and 4 were previously efficient and remain so.

3.5.2 Nondiscretionary Variables

Nondiscretionary[23] variables are variables over which a DMU has no control. For example, snowfall or number of competitors are inputs for which information about the extent to which excess input may be reduced is not meaningful. An example of

---

[23] Banker and Morey (1986a) originally introduced this concept as exogenously fixed inputs and outputs. See also Ray(1988).

Table 3.8   Optimal Solutions to Categorical (VRS) Model

DMU	Multiplier Problem				Envelopment Problem			
	μ_1	v_1	v_2	ω	Σ^1	λ	s	e
Unit 1	1.000	1.000	1.000	6.00	0.0	$\lambda_1 = 1$	0	(0,0)
Unit 2	1.000	1.000	9.000	110.00	0.0	$\lambda_2 = 1$	0	(0,0)
Unit 3	67.000	78.000	1.000	−401.00	0.0	$\lambda_3 = 1$	0	(0,0)
Unit 4	1.000	1.000	1.000	6.00	0.0	$\lambda_4 = 1$	0	(0,0)
Unit 5	1.000	1.000	1.000	6.00	18.0	$\lambda_1 = \frac{1}{2}$	11.0	(7,0)
						$\lambda_4 = \frac{1}{2}$		
Unit 6	1.000	1.000	4.000	38.00	0.0	$\lambda_6 = 1$	0	(0,0)
Unit 7	3.000	1.000	1.000	−46.00	0.0	$\lambda_7 = 1$	0	(0,0)
Unit 8	5.000	1.300	1.000	−92.90	0.0	$\lambda_8 = 1$	0	(0,0)
Unit 9	4.000	1.000	1.000	−73.00	0.0	$\lambda_9 = 1$	0	(0,0)
Unit 10	3.000	1.000	1.000	−46.00	33.5	$\lambda_4 = \frac{1}{2}$	0	(21,12.5)
						$\lambda_7 = \frac{1}{2}$		
Unit 11	1.000	1.000	1.000	6.00	4.0	$\lambda_1 = 1$	0	(0,4)

a nondiscretionary output would be the check-cashing transactions in a bank where this output is a purely gratis service function.

Banker and Morey (1986a), in their analysis of a 60-DMU network of fast food restaurants, consider six inputs: expenditures for supplies and materials, expenditures related to labor, age of store, advertising expenditures allocated to store by headquarters, presence/absence of drive-in window, and location in urban versus rural area. Only the first two inputs are under the control of the individual restaurant manager. Thus, information concerning reduction in these expenditures would be useful. The other four inputs are beyond the discretionary control of the DMU manager. As such, the marginal worth of nondiscretionary input excesses (and similarly output slacks) should not enter into the evaluation of inefficiency.

We limit our discussion to the VRS envelopment. Suppose that the input and output variables may each be partitioned into subsets of discretionary and nondiscretionary variables. Thus $I = \{1, 2, \ldots, m\} = I_D \cup I_N, I_D \cap I_N = \emptyset$ and $O = \{1, 2, \ldots, s\} = O_D \cup O_N, O_D \cap O_N = \emptyset$. The basic model formulation for a VRS envelopment surface is given by

$\text{VRS}_E(Y_l^D, Y_l^N, X_l^D, X_l^N)$:

$$\min_{\lambda_j, s_r, e_i} - \left(\sum_{r \in O_D} s_r + \sum_{i \in I_D} e_i \right)$$

$$\sum_{j=1}^{n} y_{rj} \lambda_j - s_r = y_{rl} \qquad r = 1, \ldots, s$$

$$-\sum_{j=1}^{n} x_{ij} \lambda_j - e_i = -x_{il} \qquad i = 1, \ldots, m$$

$$\sum_{j=1}^{n} \lambda_j = 1$$

$$\lambda_j \geq 0 \qquad j = 1, \ldots, n$$

$$s_r \geq 0 \qquad r = 1, \ldots, s$$

$$e_i \geq 0 \qquad i = 1, \ldots, m$$

Essentially, the above model omits non-discretionary input excesses and output slacks from the objective function as they are beyond the control of the DMU manager.

In the case of oriented models the treatment of non-discretionary inputs and outputs is similar. Thus, for the input orientation, it is not relevant to maximize the proportional decrease in the entire input vector. Such minimization should occur only with respect to the subvector that comprises discretionary inputs. Similarly, the maximization of proportional increase in the output orientation is only for the subvector that comprises discretionary outputs. Viewed as a two-step procedure, after the value of θ^l (or ϕ^l) is determined for the discretionary inputs (or outputs), one then solves the appropriate envelopment, that is, $\mathrm{VRS}_E(Y_l^D, Y_l^N, \theta^l X_l^D, X_l^N)$ or $\mathrm{VRS}_E(\phi^l Y_l^D, Y_l^N, X_l^D, X_l^N)$.

Example   Consider the standard VRS model (Section 3.1.1) and the example data of Table 3.1 where the second input is assumed to be nondiscretionary. The model formulation for unit $l = 2$ is given by

$$\mathrm{VRS}_E(Y_2^{\{1\}}, Y_2^{\emptyset}, X_2^{\{1\}}, X_2^{\{2\}}):$$

$$\min_{\lambda_1,...,\lambda_{11},s_1,e_1,e_2} -(s_1 + e_1)$$

$$12\lambda_1 + 14\lambda_2 + 25\lambda_3 + 26\lambda_4 + 8\lambda_5 + 9\lambda_6$$
$$+27\lambda_7 + 30\lambda_8 + 31\lambda_9 + 26.5\lambda_{10} + 12\lambda_{11} - s_1 = 14$$
$$-5\lambda_1 - 16\lambda_2 - 16\lambda_3 - 17\lambda_4 - 18\lambda_5 - 23\lambda_6$$
$$-25\lambda_7 - 27\lambda_8 - 37\lambda_9 - 42\lambda_{10} - 5\lambda_{11} - e_1 = -16$$
$$-13\lambda_1 - 12\lambda_2 - 26\lambda_3 - 15\lambda_4 - 14\lambda_5 - 6\lambda_6$$
$$-10\lambda_7 - 22\lambda_8 - 14\lambda_9 - 25\lambda_{10} - 17\lambda_{11} - e_2 = -12$$
$$\lambda_1 + \lambda_2 + \lambda_3 + \lambda_4 + \lambda_5 + \lambda_6 + \lambda_7 + \lambda_8 + \lambda_9 + \lambda_{10} + \lambda_{11} = 1$$
$$\lambda_1,...,\lambda_{11} \geq 0$$
$$s_1 \geq 0$$
$$e_1, e_2 \geq 0$$

Table 3.9 lists the solutions for the above model. Notice that the only change in terms of Σ^l is for units 10 and 11. Thus for our example data the projected point remains the same for units 1 to 9.[24]

3.5.3 Constrained Multiplers

In particular applications,[25] it may be desirable to perform an analysis with additional restrictions on the variables $\mu_j, j = 1, ..., s$ and $\nu_r, r = 1, ..., m$. Cook, Kazakov, and Roll (1991) in their study of highway maintenance patrols in Ontario, Canada, examined the efficiency with which maintenance operations were carried out in various parts of the province in order to determine what accomplishments could be expected within a given budget limit. Early in their study they realized that the regular DEA models may yield efficiency ratings that tend to credit patrols with a higher level of performance than may be justified. When complete flexibility in the choice of multipliers is allowed, the model often assigns unreasonably low or excessively high values to the multipliers in an attempt to drive the efficiency rating for a particular

---

[24] Because of the existence of alternative optimal solutions, the optimal values of the multipliers may differ for units 1 to 9, that is, the prices may change but the projected point remains the same.

[25] See, for example, Charnes, Cooper, Huang, and Sun (1990), Dyson and Thanassoulis (1988), and Thompson, Singleton, Thrall, and Smith (1986).

Table 3.9 Optimal Solutions to Nondiscretionary (VRS) Model

DMU	Multiplier Problem				Envelopment Problem			
	μ_1	v_1	v_2	ω	Σ^1	λ	s	e
Unit 1	1.000	1.181	0	−6.09	0.00	$\lambda_1 = 1$	0	(0,0)
Unit 2	1.000	1.000	1.667	14.67	7.33	$\lambda_1 = \frac{2}{3}$	3	(4.33,0)
						$\lambda_7 = \frac{1}{3}$		
Unit 3	1.000	1.000	0	−9.00	0.00	$\lambda_3 = 1$	0	(0,0)
Unit 4	1.000	1.000	0	−9.00	0.00	$\lambda_4 = 1$	0	(0,0)
Unit 5	1.000	1.000	1.000	6.00	18.00	$\lambda_1 = \frac{1}{2}$	11.0	(7,0)
						$\lambda_4 = \frac{1}{2}$		
Unit 6	1.000	1.000	4.000	38.00	0.00	$\lambda_6 = 1$	0	(0,0)
Unit 7	3.833	1.000	.833	−70.17	0.00	$\lambda_7 = 1$	0	(0,0)
Unit 8	2.500	1.000	0	−48.00	0.00	$\lambda_8 = 1$	0	(0,0)
Unit 9	10.000	1.000	0	−273.00	0.00	$\lambda_9 = 1$	0	(0,0)
Unit 10	2.500	1.000	0	−48.00	23.75	$\lambda_4 = .875$	0	(23.75,9.12)
						$\lambda_8 = .125$		
Unit 11	1.000	1.181	0	−6.09	0.00	$\lambda_{11} = 1$	0	(0,0)

patrol as high as possible. Moreover, the multiplier value for a particular input (capital expenditures, for example) for one patrol may differ drastically from that for another patrol. In order to exercise a reasonable level of control, Cook, Kazakov, and Roll imposed additional restrictions on the values that the multipliers can assume.

Such restrictions can increase the power and flexibility of DEA and thus yield sharper efficiency estimates by incorporating ancillary managerial information into the analysis. Additional restrictions can be enforced by incorporating inequality constraints of the following kind in the multiplier form problem:

$$\mu \mathbf{a}_k^o + v \mathbf{a}_k^i \leq 0 \qquad k = 1, \ldots, K$$

where $\mathbf{a}_k^o$ is the s-vector of coefficients for the variables μ and $\mathbf{a}_k^i$ is the m-vector of coefficients for the variables v.

Such constraints may be included in any of the DEA models. Here we consider their inclusion in the basic VRS envelopment model.

$\mathrm{CON}_M(Y_l, X_l)$:

$$\max_{\mu, v, \omega} \quad \mu Y_l - v X_l + \omega$$
$$\mu \mathbf{Y} - v \mathbf{X} + 1\omega \leq \mathbf{0}$$
$$\mu \mathbf{A}^o + v \mathbf{A}^i \leq \mathbf{0}$$
$$\mu \geq 1$$
$$v \geq 1$$

Each of these introduced constraints corresponds to a variable z_k in the (dual) envelopment program CON_E. The K-vector of variables corresponding to the additional constraints is denoted $\mathbf{z}$. The coefficients of each of the K constraints are given by columns of the (s, k) matrix $\mathbf{A}^o$ and the (m, k) matrix $\mathbf{A}^i$.

$\text{CON}_E(Y_l, X_l)$:

$$
\begin{aligned}
\min_{\lambda,s,e,z} \quad & -(\mathbf{1s} + \mathbf{1e}) \\
\mathbf{Y}\lambda - \mathbf{s} + \mathbf{A}^o\mathbf{z} = \quad & Y_l \\
-\mathbf{X}\lambda - \mathbf{e} + \mathbf{A}^i\mathbf{z} = \quad & -X_l \\
\mathbf{1}\lambda = \quad & 1 \\
\lambda \geq \quad & 0 \\
\mathbf{e} \geq \quad & 0 \\
\mathbf{s} \geq \quad & 0
\end{aligned}
$$

We refer to the elements of the vectors $\mathbf{A}^o\mathbf{z}$ and $\mathbf{A}^i\mathbf{z}$ as *residues*. Introducing such restrictions on the multipliers has the effect of altering the envelopment surface as explained in the following example.

Example For the example data of Table 3.1 and the standard VRS model, upon introducing the additional constraints[26]

$$
\begin{aligned}
.75\mu_1 - \nu_1 &\leq 0 \\
\mu_1 - \nu_2 &\leq 0 \\
\nu_2 - \nu_1 &\leq 0
\end{aligned}
$$

the envelopment surface is reduced to the plane with coefficients $\mu_1 = 1$, $\nu_1 = 1, \nu_2 = 1, \omega = 6$. As illustrated in Figure 3.7, only two units are efficient (units 1 and 4). An intuitive explanation for this reduced efficient frontier is that the constraints on the multipliers (normals of the hyperplanes) prevent the supporting hyperplanes from tilting far enough to pick up additional units.

Table 3.10 lists solutions for the constrained multiplier model for the example data. The optimal solution for unit 2 has $\lambda_1 = .2857143, \lambda_4 = .7142857$, and $\lambda_j = 0$, otherwise. Thus, the projected point has $\widehat{Y}_2 = 22.00, \widehat{X}_2 = (13.57, 14.43)$ with output slack $s_1 = 8$ and the input slacks $e_1 = 0, e_2 = 0$. However, the residues are nonzero for the input variables, -2.43 and 2.43, respectively.

Note that a previously efficient unit can be rendered inefficient with the new evaluation scheme imposed by the additional constraints on the multipliers. For

---

[26] We assume that these restrictions reflect managerial information as to acceptable ranges of multiplier ratios which should be incorporated in the analysis.

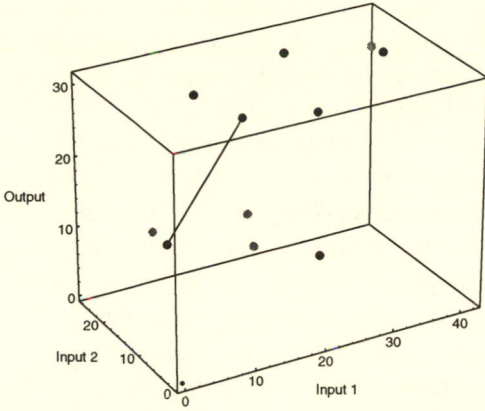

Fig. 3.7   Envelopment surface for constrained multipler example

example, unit 3 is efficient in Table 3.2 for the standard VRS model. In contrast, unit 3 is inefficient for the constrained multiplier model. The optimal solution has $\lambda_1 = .0833333, \lambda_4 = .9166667$, and $\lambda_j = 0$, otherwise with a projected point of $\widehat{Y}_3 = 24.83, \widehat{X}_3 = (16.00, 14.83)$. The only nonzero slack/excess is for input 2 with value 11.00. However, the residues are nonzero for both the output, .17, and the second input, −.17.

3.6. Conclusions

DEA actually encompasses a variety of alternative (but as we have demonstrated) related models for evaluating performance. Because of the widespread use of the

Table 3.10   Optimal Solutions for Constrained Multiplier (VRS) Model

DMU	Multiplier Problem					Envelopment Problem		
	μ_1	v_1	v_2	ω	Σ^1	λ	s	e
Unit 1	1.0	1.0	1.0	6.0	0	$\lambda_1 = 1$	0	(0,0)
Unit 2	1.0	1.0	1.0	6.0	8	$\lambda_1 = .286$	8	(0,0)
						$\lambda_4 = .714$		
Unit 3	1.0	1.0	1.0	6.0	11	$\lambda_1 = .083$	0	(0,11)
						$\lambda_4 = .917$		
Unit 4	1.0	1.0	1.0	6.0	0	$\lambda_4 = 1$	0	(0,0)
Unit 5	1.0	1.0	1.0	6.0	18	$\lambda_1 = \frac{1}{2}$	11	(7,0)
						$\lambda_4 = \frac{1}{2}$		
Unit 6	1.0	1.0	1.0	6.0	14	$\lambda_1 = 1$	3	(11,0)
Unit 7	1.0	1.0	1.0	6.0	2	$\lambda_4 = 1$	0	(2,0)
Unit 8	1.0	1.0	1.0	6.0	13	$\lambda_4 = 1$	0	(10,3)
Unit 9	1.0	1.0	1.0	6.0	14	$\lambda_4 = 1$	0	(14,0)
Unit 10	1.0	1.0	1.0	6.0	34.5	$\lambda_4 = 1$	0	(25,9.5)
Unit 11	1.0	1.0	1.0	6.0	4	$\lambda_1 = 1$	0	(0,4)

methodology, however, the models have appeared in journals spanning a number of fields. The discussion in this chapter brings together a number of developments and presents them in a standard unifying framework which facilitates interdisciplinary communication and collaboration.

The preceding sections illustrate the effects of envelopment surface, efficiency measurement, orientation, and scale changes. For the models examined, there are two possible envelopment surfaces (VRS or CRS), three possible orientations (equal, input, or output), and either standard or units-invariant forms. Selection of a model thus consists of choosing (1) an envelopment surface, (2) an orientation, and (3) the form of invariance (multiplier lower bounds). Each of these 12 possible models can be further extended to incorporate categorical variables, nondiscretionary variables, and/or constrained multipliers as discussed in Section 3.5.

However, the DEA models presented here do not exhaust the topic. Other models are available including the input-oriented multiplicative model of Banker and Maindiratta (1986) and the cone ratio model of Charnes, Cooper, Huang, and Sun (1990). Likewise the extensions of Section 3.5 are not exhaustive. A number of additional theoretical extensions to the basic DEA models have appeared in the literature. These range from the window analysis technique of Charnes, Clark, Cooper, and Golany (1985) for analyzing a DMU's performance over time to the recent results of Ali, Cook, and Seiford (1991) which allow the inclusion of ordinal relationships on the multipliers for modeling diminishing or lag effects over time. The extensions of Section 3.5 further indicate the ready adaptability of the basic DEA methodology as illustrated by the modifications to the reference set, the variable set, and the multiplier set. This results in an extremely flexible and applicable methodology which has seen rapid growth and widespread acceptance (see Seiford 1990b).

DEA's empirical orientation and absence of a priori assumptions have resulted in its use in a number of studies involving efficient frontier estimation in the nonprofit sector, in the regulated sector, and in the private sector. Researchers in a number of fields have quickly recognized that DEA is an excellent methodology for measuring productive efficiency and our expectation is that future theoretical developments will draw DEA and the more traditional econometric approaches ever closer together.

REFERENCES

Adolphson, D. L., G. C. Cornia, and L. C. Walters (1989), "Railroad Property Valuation Using Data Envelopment Analysis," *Interfaces* 19(3): 18–26.

Ahn, Taesik, A. Charnes, and W. W. Cooper (1988a), "A Note on the Efficiency Characterizations Obtained in Different DEA Models," *Socio-Economic Planning Sciences* 6: 253–257.

Ahn, Taesik, A. Charnes, and W. W. Cooper (1988b), "Some Statistical and DEA Evaluations of Relative Efficiencies of Public and Private Institutions of Higher Learning," *Socio-Economic Planning Sciences* 22(6): 259–269.

Ahn, Taesik, A. Charnes, and W. W. Cooper (1988c), "Using Data Envelopment Analysis to Measure the Efficiency of Not-for-Profit Organizations: A Critical Evaluation—Comment," *Managerial and Decision Economics* 9: 251–253.

Ali, Agha Iqbal (1989), "Computational Aspects of Data Envelopment Analysis," Technical Report, Department of General Business and Finance, University of Massachusetts at Amherst, Amherst. (Presented at the NSF Conference on DEA in Austin, Tex., September 1989.)

Ali, Agha Iqbal (1991), "Data Envelopment Analysis: A Unifying Perspective," Technical Report, Department of General Business and Finance, University of Massachusetts at Amherst, Amherst.

Ali, Agha Iqbal, and Lawrence M. Seiford (1989), "Computational Accuracy and Infinitesimals in Data Envelopment Analysis," Technical Report, University of Massachusetts at Amherst, Amherst.

Ali, Agha Iqbal, and Lawrence M. Seiford (1990), "Translation Invariance in Data Envelopment Analysis," *Operations Research Letters* 9(5): 403–405.

Ali, Agha Iqbal, Wade D. Cook, and Lawrence M. Seiford (1991), "Strict vs. Weak Ordinal Relations for Multipliers in Data Envelopment Analysis," *Management Science* 37(6): 733–738.

Banker, R. D., A. Charnes, and W. W. Cooper (1984), "Some Models for Estimating Technical and Scale Inefficiencies in Data Envelopment Analysis," *Management Science* 30(9): 1078–1092.

Banker, R. D., and A. Maindiratta (1986), "Piecewise Loglinear Estimation of Efficient Production Surfaces," *Management Science* 32(1): 126–135.

Banker, R. D., and R. C. Morey (1986a), "Efficiency Analysis for Exogenously Fixed Inputs and Outputs," *Operations Research* 34(4): 513–521.

Banker, R. D., and R. C. Morey (1986b), "The Use of Categorical Variables in Data Envelopment Analysis," *Management Science* 32(12): 1613–1627.

Banker, R. D., A. Charnes, W. W. Cooper, J. Swarts, and D. A. Thomas (1989), "An Introduction to Data Envelopment Analysis with Some of its Models and Their Uses," *Research in Governmental and Nonprofit Accounting* 5: 125–163.

Bessent, A., W. Bessent, A. Charnes, W. W. Cooper, and N. Thorogood (1983), "Evaluation of Educational Program Proposals by Means of Data Envelopment Analysis," *Educational Administration Quarterly* 19(2): 82–107.

Borden, J. P. (1988), "An Assessment of the Impact of Diagnosis Related Group (DRG)-Based Reimbursement on the Technical Efficiency of New Jersey Hospitals Using Data Envelopment Analysis," *Journal of Accounting and Public Policy* 7(2): 77–96.

Byrnes, P., R. Färe, and S. Grosskopf (1984), "Measuring Productive Efficiency: An Application to Illinois Strip Mines," *Management Science* 30(6): 671–681.

Byrnes, P., R. Färe, S. Grosskopf, and C. A. K. Lovell (1988), "The Effect of Unions on Productivity: U.S. Surface Mining of Coal," *Management Science* 34(9): 1037–1053.

Charnes, A., W. W. Cooper, and E. Rhodes (1978), "Measuring the Efficiency of Decision Making Units," *European Journal of Operational Research* 2(6): 429–444.

Charnes, A., W. W. Cooper, and E. Rhodes (1979), "Short Communication: Measuring the Efficiency of Decision Making Units," *European Journal of Operational Research* 3(4): 339.

Charnes, A., W. W. Cooper, and E. Rhodes (1981), "Evaluating Program and Managerial Efficiency: An Application of Data Envelopment Analysis to Program Follow Through," *Management Science* 27(6): 668–697.

Charnes, A., W. W. Cooper, L. Seiford, and J. Stutz (1982), " A Multiplicative Model for Efficiency Analysis," *Socio-Economic Planning Sciences* 16(5): 223–224.

Charnes, A., W. W. Cooper, L. Seiford, and J. Stutz (1983), "Invariant Multiplicative Efficiency and Piecewise Cobb-Douglas Envelopments," *Operations Research Letters* 2(3): 101–103.

Charnes, A., C. T. Clark, W. W. Cooper, and B. Golany (1985), "A Developmental Study of Data Envelopment Analysis in Measuring the Efficiency of Maintenance Units in the U.S. Air Forces," in R. Thompson and R. M. Thrall, eds., *Annals of Operation Research* 2: 95–112.

Charnes, A., W. W. Cooper, B. Golany, L. Seiford, and J. Stutz (1985), "Foundations of Data Envelopment Analysis for Pareto-Koopmans Efficient Empirical Production Functions," *Journal of Econometrics* 30(12): 91–107.

Charnes, A., W. W. Cooper, J. Rousseau, and J. Semple (1987), "Data Envelopment Analysis and Axiomatic Notions of Efficiency and Reference Sets," Research Report CCS 558, Center for Cybernetic Studies, The University of Texas at Austin, Tex.

Charnes, A., W. W. Cooper, Z. M. Huang, and D. B. Sun (1990), "Polyhedral Cone-Ratio DEA Models with an Illustrative Application to Large Commercial Banks," *Journal of Econometrics* 46: 73–91.

Cook, W. D., A. Kazakov, and Y. Roll (1991), "On the Measurement and Monitoring of Relative Efficiency of Highway Maintenance Patrols," in A. Charnes, W. W. Cooper, Arie Y. Lewin, and Lawrence M. Seiford, eds., *Data Envelopment Analysis: Theory, Methodology and Applications* (forthcoming).

Desai, Anand, and J. Stephen Henderson (1988), "Natural Gas Prices and Contractual Terms," *Energy Systems and Policy* 12: 255–271.

Dyson, R. G., and E. Thanassoulis (1988), "Reducing Weight Flexibility in Data Envelopment Analysis," *Journal of the Operational Research Society* 39(6): 563–576.

Epstein, M. K., and J. C. Henderson (1989), "Data Envelopment Analysis for Managerial Control and Diagnosis," *Decision Sciences* 20(1): 90–119.

Farrell, M. J. (1957), "The Measurement of Productive Efficiency," *Journal of the Royal Statistical Society*, A, 120: 253–281.

Kamakura, W. A. (1988), "A Note on the Use of Categorical Variables in Data Envelopment Analysis," *Management Science* 34(10): 1273–1276.

Koopmans, T. C. (1951), *Activity Analysis of Production and Allocation.* New York: Wiley.

Lewin, A. Y., R. C. Morey, and T. J. Cook (1982), "Evaluating the Administrative Efficiency of Courts," *Omega* 10(4): 401–411.

MacMillan, W. D. (1986), "The Estimation and Application of Multi-Regional Economic Planning Models Using Data Envelopment Analysis," *Papers of the Regional Science Association* 60: 41–57.

MacMillan, W. D. (1987), "The Measurement of Efficiency in Multiunit Public Services," *Environment and Planning A* 19: 1511–1524.

Ray, S. C. (1988), "Data Envelopment Analysis, Nondiscretionary Inputs and Efficiency: An Alternative Interpretation," *Socio-Economic Planning Sciences* 22(4): 167–176.

Seiford, Lawrence M. (1990a), "A Bibliography of Data Envelopment Analysis (1978–1990)," Working Paper, Department of IEOR, University of Massachusetts at Amherst (Version 5.0).

Seiford, Lawrence M. (1990b), "Models, Extensions, and Applications of Data Envelopment Analysis: A Selected Reference Set," *Computers, Environment, and Urban Systems* 14(2): 171–175.

Seiford, Lawrence M., and R. M. Thrall (1990), "Recent Developments in DEA: The Mathematical Programming Approach to Frontier Analysis," *Journal of Econometrics* 46: 7–38.

Sengupta, J. K. (1989), *Efficiency Analysis by Production Frontiers: The Nonparametric Approach* . Dordrecht, The Netherlands: Kluwer Academic Publishers.

Sherman, H. David (1988), *Service Organization Productivity Measurement,* Hamilton, Ontario: The Society of Management Accountants of Canada.

Thompson, R. G., F. D. Singleton Jr., R. M. Thrall, and B. A. Smith (1986), "Comparative Site Evaluations for Locating a High-Energy Physics Lab in Texas," *Interfaces* 16(6): 35–49.

4

EFFICIENCY AND PRODUCTIVITY

S. Grosskopf[1]

4.1 Introduction

The purpose of this chapter is to provide an overview of productivity measurement. This overview is selective: productivity measurement has a long history, much of which is not touched on here. Instead, the focus here is on relatively recent developments; especially those dealing with the measurement of total factor productivity and the relationship between productivity and efficiency. The goal is to sketch the empirical options with special emphasis on those which explicitly include consideration of efficiency.

By worrying about efficiency as a component of productivity I obviously have a particular definition of productivity in mind. Although many consider productivity growth and technical progress as synonymous, I belong to a small but growing group who distinguish the two concepts. I define productivity growth as the net change in output due to change in efficiency and technical change, where the former is understood to be the change in how far an observation is from the frontier of technology and the latter is understood to be shifts in the production frontier.

To motivate the discussion, this chapter begins with a section called "thinking about productivity." Here the notation used throughout this chapter is introduced. Included is a graphical description of what I mean by productivity, technical change, and change in efficiency. This section is intended to clarify the difference between

[1] I would like to thank Rolf Färe for his encouragement and many comments. He suggested what is now Section 4.2. Much of the material covered in section 4 is a summary of his work on productivity and efficiency. Knox Lovell patiently read several earlier versions of this chapter; his suggestions and comments improved both style and substance. Finn Førsund's comments are also appreciated. I am also grateful to the participants of the Union College workshop on efficiency and productivity; their interaction contributed significantly to this chapter.

nonfrontier and frontier approaches to productivity measurement. The frontier approaches explicitly incorporate inefficiency and account for changes in efficiency.

Section 4.3 includes a brief survey of some of the more familiar nonfrontier approaches, beginning with nonparametric, nonfrontier approaches. Under the umbrella of nonparametric, nonfrontier approaches I include the growth accounting models as well as various index number approaches. I then turn to econometric (parametric), nonfrontier approaches to productivity measurement.

The discussion of frontier approaches to productivity measurement in Section 4.4 begins with what I am most familiar with: nonparametric models. Here I summarize recent work which extends and shows how to calculate Malmquist type indexes of productivity introduced by Caves, Christensen, and Diewert (1982a,b). This work [first undertaken by Färe, Grosskopf, Lindgren, and Roos (FGLR) (1989)] exploits the fact that Malmquist indexes of total factor productivity are defined as ratios of distance functions. Recognizing that the distance functions are reciprocal to Farrell measures of technical efficiency[2] allows calculation of these indexes using nonparametric programming techniques familiar from the efficiency measurement literature. The FGLR group also showed that a Malmquist-type index could be decomposed into changes in efficiency and changes in frontier technology.

Also included in this section are the nonparametric models used in the literature on testing for regularity conditions. This work also relies on programming methods to identify technical change, and, in that sense, also identifies technical change as a change in the frontier of (best practice) technology.

The last part of Section 4.4 takes up the parametric, frontier approach to total factor productivity measurement. The earliest examples of this approach were "deterministic," that is, they also relied on programming models with no explicit attempt to model error other than that due to inefficiency. Included in this group is perhaps the first study which attempted to explicitly decompose productivity growth into technical change and change in efficiency [Nishimizu and Page (1982)].[3] This decomposition was largely ignored until the nonparametric work by FGLR using a Malmquist-type index, and work in a parametric, econometric framework beginning with Bauer (1987) and Perelman and Pestieau (1988). Current work in this area has extended these earlier deterministic, parametric frontier models to the estimation of parametric, stochastic frontiers which allow identification of change in technology and change in efficiency. A brief discussion of strengths and weaknesses of these various approaches to productivity measurement concludes.

---

[2] I follow Färe, Grosskopf and Lovell (1985) and define Farrell technical efficiency as reciprocal to the corresponding input or output distance function.

[3] The intellectual foundations of this idea go back much farther, at least to the literature on "best" and "average" practice, see Salter (1966). Leif Johansen's (1972) contributions are also relevant here, particularly his "complete growth equation." I would like to thank Finn Førsund for pointing this out to me. For a more complete historical overview, see Førsund (1991) and Førsund and Hjalmarsson (1987).

4.2 Thinking About Productivity Measurement

The earlier chapters of this monograph have dealt primarily with ways to gauge the efficiency of production in a given period. In this chapter the focus is on how performance changes over time. The particular notion of performance used here is total factor productivity. By total factor productivity I mean an index of output divided by an index of total input usage. Thus total factor productivity is a generalization of single-factor productivity measures such as labor productivity which is the ratio of (an index of) output to a single input, labor. Total factor productivity growth refers to the change in productivity over time.

Consider the simplest case. Let there be two periods, t and $t + 1$. Denote output[4] in each period by y^t, y^{t+1}, assumed to be of constant quality in the two periods. Denote inputs employed in the two periods by x^t, x^{t+1}. For each time period let the production set S^t model the transformation of inputs $x^t \in \Re_+^N$ into output $y^t \in \Re_+$

$$S^t = \{(x^t, y^t) : x^t \text{ can produce } y^t\} \tag{4.1}$$

and similarly for S^{t+1}. Thus the set S describes all feasible input-output pairs at a given time. Technology may also be described with a production function in each period

$$y^t = \max\{\hat{y}^t : (x^t, \hat{y}^t) \in S^t\} \tag{4.2}$$

and similarly for period $t + 1$. If we assume disembodied (that is, independent of inputs) Hicks neutral technical change[5] the production functions at t and $t + 1$ can be rewritten as

$$\begin{aligned} y^t &= A(t)f(x^t) \\ y^{t+1} &= A(t+1)f(x^{t+1}) \end{aligned} \tag{4.3}$$

Note that the structure of technology $f(x)$ does not change over time; nevertheless, the production function may shift between t and $t + 1$ through the parameter A.

Now define total factor productivity (TFP) at t as the ratio of output produced at t to total input used at t as

---

[4] For the moment I am assuming scalar output. This facilitates definition of a production function. Note, however, that this assumption may be relaxed, as I shall do presently.

[5] By this I mean that technical change leads to proportional reductions in all inputs, leaving the input mix unchanged. Alternatively, following Hicks (1932), technical change is Hicks neutral if the ratio of marginal products remains unchanged for any given input mix. For a recent overview of definitions of neutral technical change, see Färe and Chambers (1991) who extend these definitions to the case of multiple outputs. The definition here assumes away the possibility of technical change occurring through the introduction of new goods, clearly a restrictive assumption.

$$\text{TFP}(t) = \frac{y^t}{f(x^t)} = A(t) \tag{4.4}$$

and similarly for $\text{TFP}(t+1)$, that is, total factor productivity is a measure of "average" product. Total factor productivity growth may then be defined as the change in total factor productivity between periods t and $t + 1$

$$\begin{aligned} \frac{\text{TFP}(t + 1)}{\text{TFP}(t)} &= \frac{y^{t+1}/f(x^{t+1})}{y^t/f(x^t)} \\ &= \frac{y^{t+1}/y^t}{f(x^{t+1})/f(x^t)} \\ &= \frac{A(t + 1)}{A(t)} \end{aligned} \tag{4.5}$$

In this form TFP consists of ratios of "aggregator functions," that is, an index number. In fact, if $y^t = A(t)x^t$ and $y^{t+1} = A(t + 1)x^{t+1}$, where both input and output are scalar, the index in (4.5) becomes $\text{TFP}(t + 1)/\text{TFP}(t) = (y^{t+1}/y^t)(x^{t+1}/x^t)$, which is a very simple index number form of total factor productivity.

Figure 4.1 illustrates for the very simple case: a single output is produced via a single input for a constant returns-to-scale technology. In Figure 4.1 there are two observations of input and output, (x^t, y^t) and (x^{t+1}, y^{t+1}) which are on the "frontier" or boundary of S^t and S^{t+1}, respectively, that is, production is technically efficient in the sense of Farrell (1957). $A(t + 1)$ and $A(t)$ represent average productivity in their respective time periods; they are also equal to the slope of the frontier technology. In this diagram, productivity growth is equal to the ratio of the slopes of the boundaries of S^{t+1} and S^t. More generally, productivity growth is the change in average product. Notice that in the special case where observed production occurs on the production frontier, productivity growth and technical change (the shift in the production frontier) are identical.[6]

One may also restate this index of total factor productivity growth in terms of percentage changes as[7]

---

[6] If technology does not satisfy constant returns-to-scale, but rather exhibits the textbook total product curve consistent with increasing, constant then decreasing returns-to-scale, the ratio of average products will only approximate the shift in technology even if production occurs on the production frontier. Approximation error can be reduced for the discrete case by taking the geometric mean of the shift in technology at t and $t + 1$. This is consistent with several of the index numbers used to calculate total factor productivity growth, including the Malmquist-type index introduced in Section 4.4.

[7] Here we are defining percentage change in the following way: $\Delta\text{TFP}/(\Delta_t\text{TFP}) = [\text{TFP}(t + 1) - \text{TFP}(t)]/\text{TFP}(t)$, where $\Delta t = 1$.

$$\frac{A(t+1) - A(t)}{A(t)} = \frac{y^{t+1} - y^t}{y^t}$$

$$-\frac{f(x^{t+1}) - f(x^t)}{f(x^t)} \qquad (4.6)$$

which looks like a discrete form of the growth accounting approach to total factor productivity measurement associated with Solow (1957), among others. Referring again to Figure 4.1, this definition can be interpreted as the percent change in output, $(y^{t+1} - y^t)/y^t$, less the percent change in inputs. In terms of distance along the y axis, percentage change in input usage between $t + 1$ and t corresponds to the percent difference $(y' - y^t)/y^t$. Thus productivity growth would be equivalent to the y distance, $(y^{t+1} - y')/y'$.

This formulation also corresponds to the following definition by Jorgenson and Griliches (1967, p. 249):

> The rate of growth of total factor productivity is the difference between the rate of growth of real product and the rate of growth of real factor input.

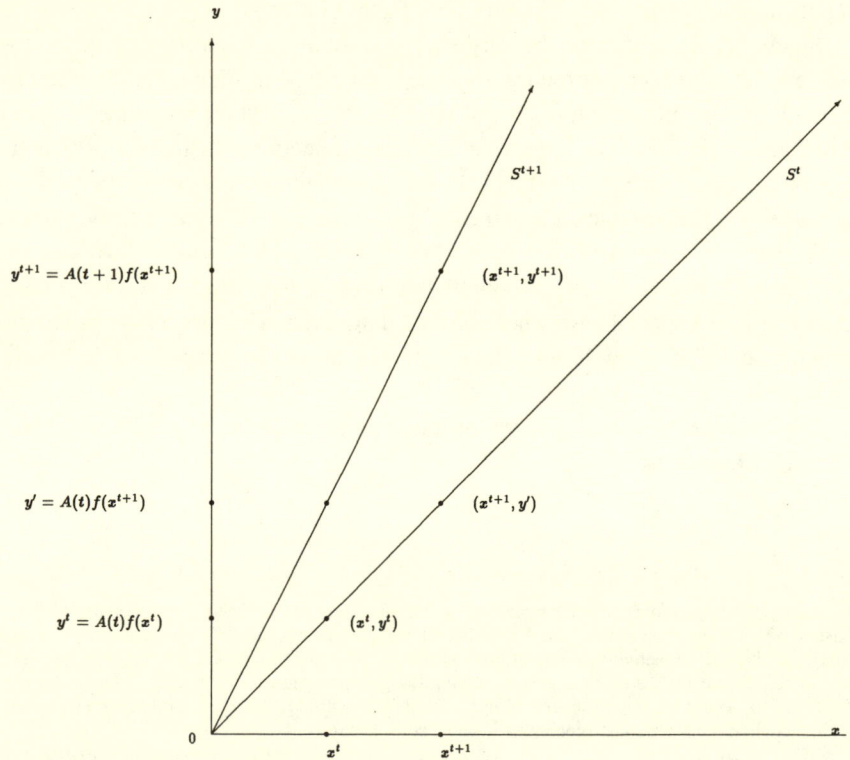

Fig. 4.1 Productivity change: No technical inefficiency

Thus total factor productivity growth may be thought of as change in output net of change in input usage [see Equation (4.6)], or equivalently as the shift in technology between t and $t + 1$, that is, $A(t + 1)/A(t)$.[8] More generally, technical change and productivity growth are synonomous in the special case when production is technically efficient.

Next, suppose that, instead of observed input output bundles appearing on the boundary of technology, they fall short of the boundary of technology in both period t and $t + 1$. Such a situation is shown in Figure 4.2. Under the traditional nonfrontier approaches to productivity measurement, it is assumed that observed production in periods t and $t + 1$ is equivalent to frontier production, that is, the boundaries of S^t and S^{t+1} are assumed to go through those observed points.[9]

[8] I have not addressed the issue of accurately measuring inputs, which was one of the major contributions of the exchange between Denison (1967) and Jorgenson and Griliches (1967). Clearly, given the formulation of TFP in Equations (4.5) and (4.6), the accurate measurement of inputs is critical to accurate measurement of TFP as residual growth. Again, much of the growth accounting literature is devoted to reducing the residual through adjustment of quantity and quality of inputs.

[9] In the nonfrontier regression approach, the boundary of S^t and S^{t+1} is estimated through the mean of the observed data.

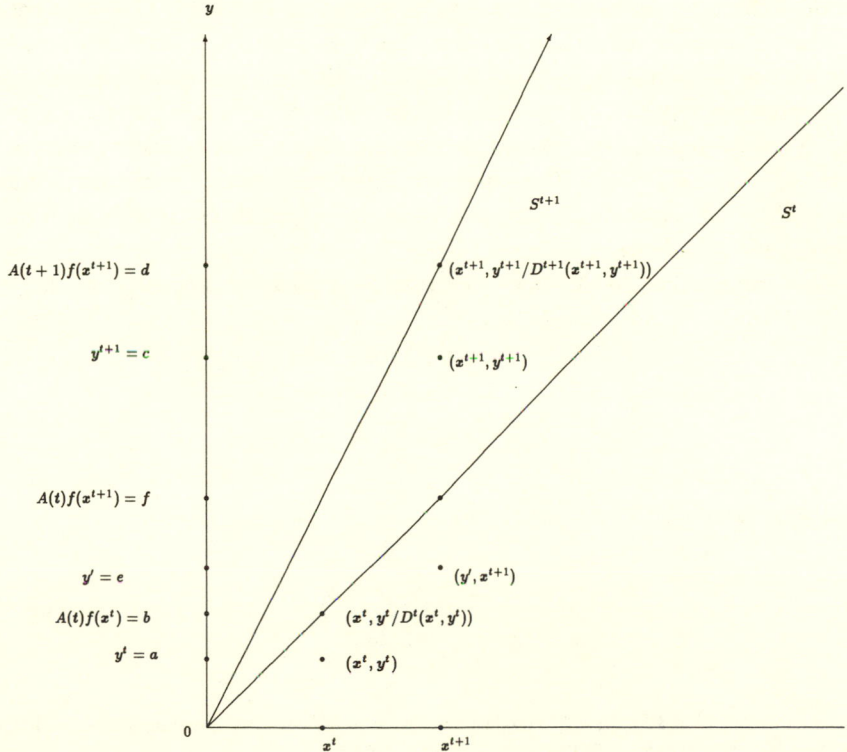

Fig. 4.2 Productivity change in the presence of technical inefficiency

In Figure 4.2, there is a discrepancy between observed output and maximum potential output in each period, that is,

$$y^t < A(t)f(x^t) \tag{4.7}$$

and

$$y^{t+1} < A(t+1)f(x^{t+1}). \tag{4.8}$$

In order to account for that discrepancy, it is necessary to correct observed output to bring it up to the frontier technology in each period, that is, we need to correct for technical inefficiency. The appropriate tool to use in this context is the output distance function. Following Shephard (1970) or Färe (1988) the output distance function is defined at t as[10]

$$D_o^t(x^t, y^t) = \inf\{\theta : (x^t, y^t/\theta) \in S^t\} \tag{4.9}$$

and similarly for $D_o^{t+1}(x^{t+1}, y^{t+1})$. This function completely describes (multiple output) technology and is equal to the reciprocal of the Farrell (1957) output-based measure of technical efficiency. Referring back to Figure 4.2, maximum feasible output is derived by increasing output as much as possible northward, while remaining in the appropriate period's production set. In terms of distances along the y axis, $D_o^t(x^t, y^t) = 0a/0b$. Since maximum potential output exceeds observed output in period t, $D_o^t(x^t, y^t) < 1$. The value of the distance function equals unity if and only if observed output equals maximum potential output, that is, if and only if there is no technical inefficiency.[11]

In order to relate the distance function to the production function, consider

$$D_o^t(x^t, y^t) = \inf\{\theta : y^t/\theta \leq A(t)f(x^t)\}$$

$$= \frac{y^t}{A(t)f(x^t)} \tag{4.10}$$

Similarly

$$D_0^{t+1}(x^{t+1}, y^{t+1}) = \frac{y^{t+1}}{A(t+1)f(x^{t+1})} \tag{4.11}$$

---

[10]We assume that S^t and S^{t+1} satisfy certain axioms which suffice to define meaningful output distance functions. See Shephard (1970) or Färe (1988) for such axioms.

[11]More precisely, $D_o(x, y) = 1$ if and only if y is an element of the isoquant of the technology.

Thus maximum potential output in year t is equal to

$$\frac{y^t}{D_o^t(x^t, y^t)} = A(t)f(x^t) \tag{4.12}$$

and maximum potential output in year $t + 1$ is equal to

$$\frac{y^{t+1}}{D_o^{t+1}(x^{t+1}, y^{t+1})} = A(t+1)f(x^{t+1}) \tag{4.13}$$

Note that the right-hand sides of (4.12) and (4.13) are identical to the right-hand sides of the production functions in Equation (4.3), which is in accord with the assumption that the production function yields maximum feasible output. The left-hand sides of (4.12) and (4.13) may also be thought of as output corrected for technical inefficiency since the output distance function is equal to the reciprocal of the Farrell output-based measure of technical efficiency.

If we continue to define total factor productivity as the ratio of output to input usage, we have from (4.12)

$$\text{TFP}(t) = \frac{y^t}{f(x^t)} = A(t)D_o^t(x^t, y^t) \tag{4.14}$$

and similarly for $\text{TFP}(t + 1)$ from (4.13). Total factor productivity growth becomes

$$\begin{aligned} \frac{\text{TFP}(t + 1)}{\text{TFP}(t)} &= \frac{y^{t+1}/f(x^{t+1})}{y^t/f(x^t)} \\ &= \frac{A(t+1)D_o^{t+1}(x^{t+1}, y^{t+1})}{A(t)D_o^t(x^t, y^t)} \\ &= \frac{A(t+1)/A(t)}{D_o^{t+1}(x^{t+1}, y^{t+1})/D_o^t(x^t, y^t)} \end{aligned} \tag{4.15}$$

that is, total factor productivity growth is a composite of the shift in the production frontier, $A(t + 1)/A(t)$ and the change in efficiency between t and $t + 1$ as captured in the distance function terms.

In terms of Figure 4.2, the interpretion of the ratio $A(t + 1)/A(t)$ is as before: the change in the slope of technology between the two periods. Note that this is given a "frontier" interpretation, since the slope of technology is determined at the point on the boundary where output is projected by the distance function, that is, at the efficiency-corrected output levels in each period.[12] Put differently, $A(t + 1)/A(t)$

[12]Note that there are actually two observations of $A(t + 1)/A(t)$ here, one at x^t and one at x^{t+1}. Given constant returns-to-scale and disembodied Hicks neutral technical change, these are identical. Nonetheless, under other circumstances they may differ. One solution is to take the (geometric) mean of the shifts in technology at these two input levels. As we shall see, this is exactly how technical change is calculated in the Malmquist-type productivity index in Section 4.4.

captures the vertical shift in technology between t and $t+1$, that is, technical change, which is defined as frontier technical change.

The ratio of the distance functions has a different interpretation. In Figure 4.2, $D_o^t(x^t, y^t)$ is equivalent to the ratio of y^t to $A(t)f(x^t)$. In terms of distances on the y axis, $D_o^t(x^t, y^t) = 0a/0b$ and $D_o^{t+1}(x^{t+1}, y^{t+1}) = 0c/0d$. Thus the ratio of the two distance functions is the change in how far output was from the frontier of technology between period t and $t+1$, that is, the change in technical efficiency over time.

The Malmquist-type productivity index to be introduced in Section 4.4 is equivalent to Equation (4.15), that is, it is a composite of technical change (shifts in the production frontier) and change in efficiency. It is also defined in terms of output distance functions.

Substituting for $A(t+1)$ and $A(t)$ from Equations (4.12) and (4.13), respectively, the expression for technical change in percentage change terms yields

$$\frac{A(t+1) - A(t)}{A(t)} = \frac{y^{t+1} - y^t}{y^t} \tag{4.16}$$

$$- \frac{f(x^{t+1}) - f(x^t)}{f(x^t)}$$

$$- \frac{D_o^{t+1}(x^{t+1}, y^{t+1}) - D_o^t(x^t, y^t)}{D_o^t(x^t, y^t)}$$

The formulation in (4.16) resembles the standard growth accounting formulation of productivity growth, albeit adjusted for change in efficiency. Equation (4.16) shows the percentage change formulation of *technical change*, which now contains a distance function (efficiency) term to evaluate technical change at the frontier. Technical change and productivity change are no longer identical. Notice that moving the distance function term to the left-hand side yields the percentage change equivalent of Equation (4.15), since the terms remaining on the right-hand side of (4.16) are equivalent to the percentage change definition of total factor productivity growth.

This is also closely related to the decompostion of productivity growth proposed by Nishimizu and Page (1982). In terms of Figure 4.2, productivity growth in percentage change terms is equivalent to $(0c - 0e)/0e$ in terms of distances along the y axis. This is also equal to the observed change in output $(0c - 0a)/0a$ less the change in usage of inputs, in y terms, $(0e - 0a)/0a$. Note that $0e$ represents the amount of output y' which could have been produced with inputs at x^{t+1} and the technology *and the same degree of technical inefficiency* prevailing at period t. Following Nishimizu and Page, this measure of total factor productivity growth may be decomposed into technical change $(0d - 0f)/0f$ and change in efficiency (evaluated at x^{t+1}) as $(0f - 0e)/0e - (0d - 0c)/0c$.[13]

---

[13] Nishimizu and Page (1982) use a parameterized production function to calculate their decomposition.

The traditional growth accounting definition of the rate of total factor productivity growth is the difference between the rate of growth in output and the rate of growth of inputs, that is, the difference between the first two bracketed terms on the right-hand side of Equation (4.16). In the presence of inefficiency, that is no longer synonomous with technical change, where technical change is understood to be the change in frontier of technology.

Notice that measures of total factor productivity growth based on the original formulation which ignores efficiency [see Equations (4.5) and (4.6)], can no longer be interpreted as technical change unless there is no technical inefficiency or unless technical efficiency does not change over time. That is, if $D_o^{t+1}(x^{t+1}, y^{t+1}) = D_o^t(x^t, y^t) \leqq 1$, then the two measures in (4.5) and (4.6) equal (4.15) and (4.16), respectively. As I shall show in the next section, however, in calculating total factor productivity using the growth accounting approach, input shares are typically used to aggregate inputs into an input index $f(x)$. This entails assuming that there is no allocative inefficiency. Thus even if there is no technical inefficiency, or no change in technical efficiency, in practice, the growth accounting approach may yield biased estimates of TFP growth if the input shares do not represent cost-minimizing shares, that is, if allocative inefficiency exists.

To summarize, in a world in which inefficiency exists, total factor productivity growth is defined as the net effect of changes in efficiency and shifts in the production frontier, the latter being technical change.[14] We would argue that the distinction is important. If inefficiency exists and is ignored, productivity growth no longer necessarily tells us about technical change. This may be quite important from a policy perspective; a slowdown in productivity growth due to increased inefficiency suggests different policies than a slowdown due to lack of technical change. Slow productivity growth due to inefficiency may be due to institutional barriers to diffusion of innovations, for example. In this case, policies to remove these barriers may be more effective in improving productivity than policies directed at innovation.

Others have recognized that productivity is affected both by changes in efficiency and shifts in the production frontier. In particular, Nishimizu and Page (1982, pp. 920–921) used just such a definition of productivity growth:

> We define technological progress as the change in the best practice frontier.
> ... all other productivity change—for example, learning by doing, diffusion of new technological knowledge, improved managerial practice as well as short run adjustment to shocks external to the enterprise—as technical efficiency change.

---

[14] For the moment I ignore other factors which may affect measures of total factor productivity including deviations from constant returns-to-scale, excess capacity, effects of regulation, etc. Many of these issues are addressed in Morrison and Diewert (1990). For issues related to regulation, see Cowing and Stevenson (1981).

4.3 Approaches to Total Factor Productivity Measurement
Which Ignore Inefficiency

The traditional approaches to productivity measurement generally (implicitly) assume that observed output is best practice or frontier output. In this context, then, it is (again implicitly) assumed that observed output in every period is technically efficient in the sense of Farrell (1957). These approaches have been summarized by a number of authors; for a detailed overview I recommend Diewert's (1989) survey or Link (1987). A nice short overview of alternative approaches in the nonfrontier framework is found in Diewert (1980). Morrison and Diewert (1990) provide a good update on the nonfrontier approaches, including adjustments for terms of trade, fixity of factors of production, capacity utilization, and imperfect competition. What follows relies heavily on the aforementioned sources.

This section contains two subsections. In Section 4.3.1, I first summarize models which ignore inefficiency and measure productivity growth using nonparametric or index number methods. This includes the familiar growth accounting models. In Section 4.3.2, a second set of models (which also ignore inefficiency) is discussed. These are the parametric models of productivity growth, that is, those which use econometric techniques to identify productivity growth, but ignore inefficiency.

4.3.1 Nonparametric (Index Number) Models Which Ignore Inefficiency

I begin the overview of nonparametric models which ignore inefficiency with a discussion of Solow's (1957) model, which provides a convenient summary of the conceptual underpinnings of the measurement of total factor productivity, including the growth accounting approach.

Solow's goal was to provide an "elementary way of segregating variations in output per head due to technical change from those due to changes in the availability of capital per head" (1957, p. 312). He defines technical change as "a shorthand for *any kind of shift* in the production function" (1957, p. 312).

Suppose that $y^t \in \Re_+$ represents output in period t and $x^t \in \Re_+^N$ represents the vector of inputs used in period t to produce scalar output y^t. Following Solow, assume continuous time, Hicks neutral technical change, and no technical inefficiency. Thus the production function can be written as

$$y^t = A(t)f(x^t) \tag{4.17}$$

where $A(t)$ captures shifts in the production function over time. The goal is to calculate $A(t)$. Again following Solow, assume that $f(x^t)$ is homogeneous of degree one, and that inputs are paid the value of their marginal products, that is, $\partial f/\partial x_n^t = w_n^t/p^t$, where $w^t \in \Re_{++}^N$ is the vector of input prices in period t and $p^t \in \Re_{++}$ is output price in period t. This last assumption presumes that producers maximize profit, implying no technical nor allocative inefficiency. Total differentiation of (4.17) with respect to time and division by y^t yields

$$
\begin{aligned}
\frac{\dot{y}}{y} &= \frac{\dot{A}}{A} + \sum_{n=1}^{N} \left(\frac{\partial f}{\partial x_n^t} \right) \left[\frac{x_n}{f(x^t)} \right] \left(\frac{\dot{x}_n}{x_n} \right) \\
&= \frac{\dot{A}}{A} + \sum_{n=1}^{N} s_n \left(\frac{\dot{x}_n}{x_n} \right)
\end{aligned}
\tag{4.18}
$$

where dots indicate time derivatives and

$$
\begin{aligned}
s_n &= \left(\frac{\partial y}{\partial x_n} \right) \left(\frac{x_n}{y} \right) \\
&= \frac{w_n x_n}{py} \\
&= \frac{w_n x_n}{\sum\limits_{n=1}^{N} w_n x_n}
\end{aligned}
\tag{4.19}
$$

I have suppressed the t's to simplify notation. Rearranging (4.18) gives the desired result

$$
\frac{\dot{A}}{A} = \frac{\dot{y}}{y} - \sum_{n=1}^{N} s_n \left(\frac{\dot{x}_n}{x_n} \right)
\tag{4.20}
$$

This leads to the growth accounting definition of productivity as the residual growth in output not accounted for by growth in inputs associated with Solow (1957), Denison (1972), Kendrick (1961), and Jorgenson and Griliches (1967).[15]

In order to calculate (4.20), Solow made the assumption that the time derivatives could be approximated by discrete changes, much like the two-period example in percentage change terms in Equation (4.6) in Section 4.2. Notice that this results in what might be called a nonparametric index of productivity growth. In fact, in its continuous time formulation (4.20) is equivalent to a Divisia index of productivity growth.[16] If the continuous growth rates in (4.20) are replaced by the discrete difference in the logarithms, that is, $\dot{y}/y = \ln y^{t+1} - \ln y^t$, and the input shares are calculated as

[15] Jorgenson and Griliches (1967) also show that this relationship may be derived from the basic income accounting identity.

[16] The Divisia index of total factor productivity may be written as the line integral $DI(t) = \exp\{ \int \dot{y}/y - [\sum_{n=1}^{N} s_n(\dot{x}_n/x_n)] \}$. See Hulten (1973).

arithmetic means, the index in (4.20) becomes equivalent to the Törnqvist (1936) index (TI) of total factor productivity growth[17]

$$\ln \text{TI} = \ln y^{t+1} - \ln y^t - \sum_{n=1}^{N} \frac{1}{2}[s_n(t+1) + s_n(t)](\ln x_n^{t+1} - \ln x_n^t) \qquad (4.21)$$

The Törnqvist index has been shown to be "exact" if the technology in Equation (4.17) is of the translog form [Diewert (1976)].[18] This means that starting with a translog specification of the production function in Equation (4.17), derivations like those in (4.18) and (4.19) lead to the Törnqvist index (4.20), after applying the discrete approximation mentioned above. Since the (linearly homogeneous) translog production function is flexible, that is, it is a second-order approximation to any arbitrary twice continuously differentiable (linearly homogeneous) production function, the Törnqvist index is also a "superlative" index, see Diewert (1976).[19]

Thus the Solow model provides the basic underpinnings for what may be called the nonfrontier, nonparametric approach to productivity measurement, which includes both the index number approach (an example of which is the Törnqvist index) as well as the growth accounting approach to total factor productivity measurement. Note that in the discrete form of Equation (4.10) as well as for the Törnqvist index, everything required to calculate $\dot{A}/A$ is observable—no estimation is required. In addition, Diewert's (1976) results show that the natural discrete approximation of productivity growth (the Törnqvist index) not only captures multifactor productivity, but it is exact for translog technology. Furthermore, this index is superlative since the translog functional form is flexible. Thus these nonparametric approaches are very appealing in terms of ease of calculation and flexible modeling of underlying technology, good reasons for their popularity.

Note, however, that no account is taken of possible inefficiency. As was shown in Section 4.2, calculating total factor productivity growth as the residual between observed output and input use may lead to bias in the presence of inefficiency. In the standard growth accounting model (as well as in the corresponding nonparametric

---

[17] It is also possible to define a multiple output version of this index by introducing output revenue shares.

[18] The continuous form consistent with a Divisia index as in (4.20) is exact for any technology satisfying general "regularity" conditions; see Solow (1957), Richter (1966), and Hulten (1973). See Chambers, Färe, and Grosskopf (1991) for a synthesis of efficiency, productivity, and index numbers.

[19] There is a large literature concerned with the properties satisfied by various forms of index numbers which goes back to Fisher (1922) and Frisch (1936) among others. More recently, Eichhorn and his colleagues and students at Karlsruhe have contributed to this literature. Examples of the properties (or tests) which index numbers might be expected to satisfy include independence of unit of measurement, the time reversal test, the factor reversal test, the circular test, etc. What Diewert refers to as the "test approach" to index numbers seeks what Fisher called "ideal" index numbers, that is, those that satisfy as many of these properties or tests as possible. [With the exception perhaps of the circular test. Fisher himself ultimately rejected the circular test as "theoretically unsound," see Fisher (1922, 3d ed., p. $xiii$)]. See Diewert (1992) for a very nice overview of various index number and econometric approaches to productivity measurement.

index number approaches including the Törnqvist index) technical inefficiency is typically ignored. Note, too, that by using input shares to aggregate inputs, it is assumed that input prices are "correct," that is, there is no allocative inefficiency. This too may cause bias, suggesting that researchers should use shadow prices[20] when aggregating, or employ alternative measures of productivity which do not require price information, such as the Malmquist index.

4.3.2 Econometric Approaches Which Ignore Inefficiency

As mentioned in Section 4.3.1, the Solow model yields the basic growth accounting equation and is also equivalent to various nonparametric productivity indexes. These approaches have the advantage of computational simplicity (there are no parameters to be estimated), but that is achieved at some cost. That cost includes the fact that they do not account for measurement or sampling error, nor do they account for departures from efficient production. Thus the resulting measures of productivity growth may be biased, and there is no notion of the precision with which productivity growth is measured.

An alternative approach is to parameterize the production function and estimate

$$y^t = f(x^t, t) + \epsilon \tag{4.22}$$

for $t = 1, 2, \ldots, T$. The estimated parameters are then used to solve for technical change as $\partial \ln f(x^t, t)/\partial t$, for example. Given no change in technical inefficiency, this is equivalent to total factor productivity growth. Alternatively, the estimated parameters can be used to derive an estimate of the marginal products of the inputs. In turn, the estimated marginal products and the input and output quantity data can be used to calculate a Törnqvist index, for example.

This econometric approach has the advantage of allowing for measurement error, but may introduce specification error. The number of parameters to be estimated may also pose problems, which is obviously avoided in nonparametric approaches.

As pointed out by Ohta (1975), the duality between cost and production functions can be exploited to formulate technical progress using the cost function, which has proven useful in the econometric approach to productivity measurement. Obviously, one of the difficulties of the production function approach is that output is scalar.[21]

---

[20] One of the more interesting applications of this idea is due to Pittman (1983) who calculated shadow prices of undesirable outputs to construct an enhanced Törnqvist index of total factor productivity which explicitly accounts for (joint) production of desirable and undesirable outputs. He did not, however, explicitly address the issue of allocative inefficiency. In the context of distance functions, Färe and Grosskopf (1990a) show how to use a dual Shephard's lemma to retrieve firm-specific shadow prices of inputs and outputs. Färe, Grosskopf, Lovell, and Yaisawarng (1990) apply this technique to Pittman's data on paper and pulp mills.

[21] This "problem" can be circumvented, however. Alternatives include estimation of an input distance function, estimation of Equation (4.22) by including only one output on the left-hand side and the others on the right-hand side, or by aggregating outputs using an output quantity index.

The cost function, which is dual to the production function, readily allows for multiple outputs, providing a useful complement to the production function. To see this, note that if technical and allocative efficiency are assumed,

$$C^t = C(y^t, w^t, t)$$
$$= \sum_{n=1}^{N} w_n^t x_n^t \qquad (4.23)$$

where inputs x_n^t are chosen to minimize cost at t given outputs $y^t \in \Re_+^M$, input prices w^t, and technology.

Assuming that constant returns-to-scale characterize technology, scalar output, and Hicks neutral technical change, the cost function may be written as

$$C^t = B(t)C(w^t)y^t \qquad (4.24)$$

where $B(t)$ is the efficiency function which captures technical change. Totally differentiating (4.24) and using Shephard's lemma yields

$$\frac{\dot{C}}{C} = \frac{\dot{y}}{y} + \frac{\dot{B}}{B} + \sum_{n=1}^{N} s_n \left(\frac{\dot{w}_n}{w_n} \right) \qquad (4.25)$$

or

$$\frac{\dot{B}}{B} = \frac{\dot{C}}{C} - \frac{\dot{y}}{y} - \sum_{n=1}^{N} s_n \left(\frac{\dot{w}_n}{w_n} \right) \qquad (4.26)$$

Thus technical change is the residual change in average cost ($\dot{C}/C - \dot{y}/y$) not accounted for by the change in the index of input prices. Note also that under constant returns-to-scale $\dot{B}/B = -\dot{A}/A$, that is, in the case in which there is no technical or allocative inefficiency technical change is again synonymous with total factor productivity growth. Again, if technical or allocative inefficiency is present, then (4.26) yields a biased measure of total factor productivity growth.

Other representations of technology such as the revenue function may also be estimated and used to derive a measure of total factor productivity growth econometrically. As long as inefficiency is ignored, however, the possibility of bias remains.

4.4 Frontier Approaches to Productivity Measurement

Included in this section are two types of frontier approaches to productivity measurement, that is, approaches which explicitly allow for inefficiency. The first subsection covers nonparametric frontier approaches, the second subsection covers parametric frontier approaches.

4.4.1 Nonparametric Frontier Approaches to Productivity Measurement

This section focuses on nonparametric approaches to productivity measurement which explicitly allow for inefficiency. Almost all of this section is devoted to a discussion of recent work initiated by Färe, Grosskopf, Lindgren, and Roos using a Malmquist-type index total factor productivity. This emphasis reflects the fact that it is what I know best, as well as the fact that it is probably not familiar to a very general audience. This section is designed to convince the reader that this Malmquist-type productivity index is potentially very useful in calculating productivity growth in the presence of inefficiency. It is constructed from distance functions, allowing explicit calculation (and isolation of) changes in efficiency. It does not require price or share data, allowing applications where outputs or inputs may not be marketable. It can also be calculated easily by exploiting the fact that the component distance functions are reciprocal to Farrell measures of technical efficiency. Isolation of changes in efficiency and technical change does, however, require panel data.

Malmquist firm-specific productivity indexes were introduced by Caves, Christensen, and Diewert (1982a). They named these indexes after Malmquist, who had earlier proposed constructing input quantity indexes as ratios of distance functions [see Malmquist (1953)]. Indeed, these Malmquist indexes are constructed from ratios of distance functions, which are a natural way of modeling the production frontier as well as deviations from and shifts in that frontier, that is, technical inefficiency and technical change. Although not recognized by Caves, Christensen, and Diewert at the time,[22] the formulation of these indexes in terms of distance functions also leads to straightforward calculation by exploiting the relation between distance functions and Farrell measures of technical efficiency.

To define an output-based Malmquist productivity index, assume that for each time period $t = 1, \ldots, T$, the production technology S^t models the transformation of inputs $x^t \in \Re_+^N$ into outputs $y^t \in \Re_+^M$. It is also assumed that S^t is sufficiently regular to define meaningful output distance functions.[23]

Recall from Equation (4.9) that

$$D_o^t(x^t, y^t) = \inf\{\theta : (x^t, y^t/\theta) \in S^t\} \tag{4.27}$$

Note that $D_o^t(x^t, y^t) \leq 1$ if and only if $(x^t, y^t) \in S^t$. It follows from the definition of the distance function that it is homogeneous of degree $+1$ in outputs. In addition,

---

[22] They treated the Malmquist index as a theoretical index. They showed that, under certain conditions, the Törnqvist index (which is readily computable) can be derived from this theoretical index.

[23] See Shephard (1970) or Färe (1988) for details concerning axioms on S^t.

it is reciprocal to Farrell's (1957) output-oriented measure of technical efficiency. This last observation permits decomposition of productivity change into two parts, one measuring changes in technical efficiency and one which captures the shift in the production frontier.

To define a Malmquist index requires definition of distance functions with respect to two different time periods such as

$$D_o^t(x^{t+1}, y^{t+1}) = \inf\{\theta : (x^{t+1}, y^{t+1}/\theta) \in S^t\} \qquad (4.28a)$$

and

$$D_o^{t+1}(x^t, y^t) = \inf\{\theta : (x^t, y^t/\theta) \in S^{t+1}\} \qquad (4.28b)$$

The first distance function, in (4.28a), measures the maximum proportional change in outputs required to make (x^{t+1}, y^{t+1}) feasible in relation to the technology at the previous period t. Similarly, the second mixed-period distance function, in (4.28b), measures the maximum proportional change in output required to make (x^t, y^t) feasible in relation to the technology at $t + 1$, which we call $D_o^{t+1}(x^t, y^t)$. In both these mixed-period cases, the value of the distance function may exceed unity. This can occur if the observation being evaluated is not feasible in the other period.

Caves, Christensen, and Diewert (1982a) define an output-based Malmquist productivity index relative to a single technology t as[24]

$$M_o^t = \frac{D_o^t(x^{t+1}, y^{t+1})}{D_o^t(x^t, y^t)} \qquad (4.29a)$$

and for $t + 1$ as

$$M_o^{t+1} = \frac{D_o^{t+1}(x^{t+1}, y^{t+1})}{D_o^{t+1}(x^t, y^t)} \qquad (4.29b)$$

Färe, Grosskopf, Lindgren, and Roos (1989) employed the geometric mean of the two output-based Malmquist indexes defined above to yield the following Malmquist-type measure of productivity:

$$M_o(x^{t+1}, y^{t+1}, x^t, y^t) = \left[\frac{D_o^t(x^{t+1}, y^{t+1})}{D_o^t(x^t, y^t)} \frac{D_o^{t+1}(x^{t+1}, y^{t+1})}{D_o^{t+1}(x^t, y^t)}\right]^{1/2} \qquad (4.30)$$

----

[24] They define the index generally, so that it could compare two firms, or one firm over two periods. For the moment, I assume that we are looking at one firm over two periods.

Following Färe, Grosskopf, Lindgren, and Roos (1989) an equivalent way of writing this index is

$$M_o(x^{t+1}, y^{t+1}, x^t, y^t) = \frac{D_o^{t+1}(x^{t+1}, y^{t+1})}{D_o^t(x^t, y^t)} \left[\frac{D_o^t(x^{t+1}, y^{t+1})}{D_o^{t+1}(x^{t+1}, y^{t+1})} \frac{D_o^t(x^t, y^t)}{D_o^{t+1}(x^t, y^t)} \right]^{1/2}$$

$$(4.31)$$

where the ratio outside the bracket measures the change in the output-oriented measure of Farrell technical efficiency between years t and $t + 1$. The geometric mean of the two ratios inside the bracket captures the shift in technology between the two periods evaluated at the input level x^{t+1} and at the input level realized at x^t.[25] Recall from Section 4.2 that the simple index of total factor productivity in the presence of technical inefficiency includes a change in efficiency term and a term capturing shifts in the frontier of technology [see Equation (4.15)].

Thus the two terms in (4.31) correspond to

$$\text{Efficiency change} = \frac{D_o^{t+1}(x^{t+1}, y^{t+1})}{D_o^t(x^t, y^t)}$$

$$\text{Technical change} = \left[\frac{D_o^t(x^{t+1}, y^{t+1})}{D_o^{t+1}(x^{t+1}, y^{t+1})} \frac{D_o^t(x^t, y^t)}{D_o^{t+1}(x^t, y^t)} \right]^{1/2}$$

The efficiency change term is equivalent to the ratio of Farrell technical efficiency in period $t + 1$ divided by Farrell technical efficiency in period t. The technical change term is the geometric mean of the shift in technology as observed at x^{t+1} (the first ratio inside the bracket) and the shift in technology observed at x^t (the second ratio inside the bracket).

This decomposition is illustrated in Figure 4.3, where technical advance has occurred in the sense that $S^t \subset S^{t+1}$. Note that $(x^t, y^t) \in S^t$ and $(x^{t+1}, y^{t+1}) \in S^{t+1}$, however, (x^{t+1}, y^{t+1}) does not belong to S^t. In terms of the distances along the y axis, the index (4.31) becomes

$$M_o(x^{t+1}, y^{t+1}, x^t, y^t) = \frac{Oc}{Od} \frac{Ob}{Oa} \left[\frac{Od}{Of} \frac{Oe}{Ob} \right]^{1/2} \qquad (4.32)$$

The ratios inside the square bracket measure shifts in technology at input levels x^t and x^{t+1}, respectively, and so technical change is measured as the geometric mean of those two shifts. The terms outside the bracket measure technical efficiency at t and $t + 1$, capturing changes in efficiency over time. We note that improvements yield

---

[25] More precisely, the shift in the frontier is evaluated at the two different observed input levels, holding the mix of observed outputs constant as well. Since these are output distance functions, the level of outputs is not held constant, but rather is expanded radially as much as is feasible given technology.

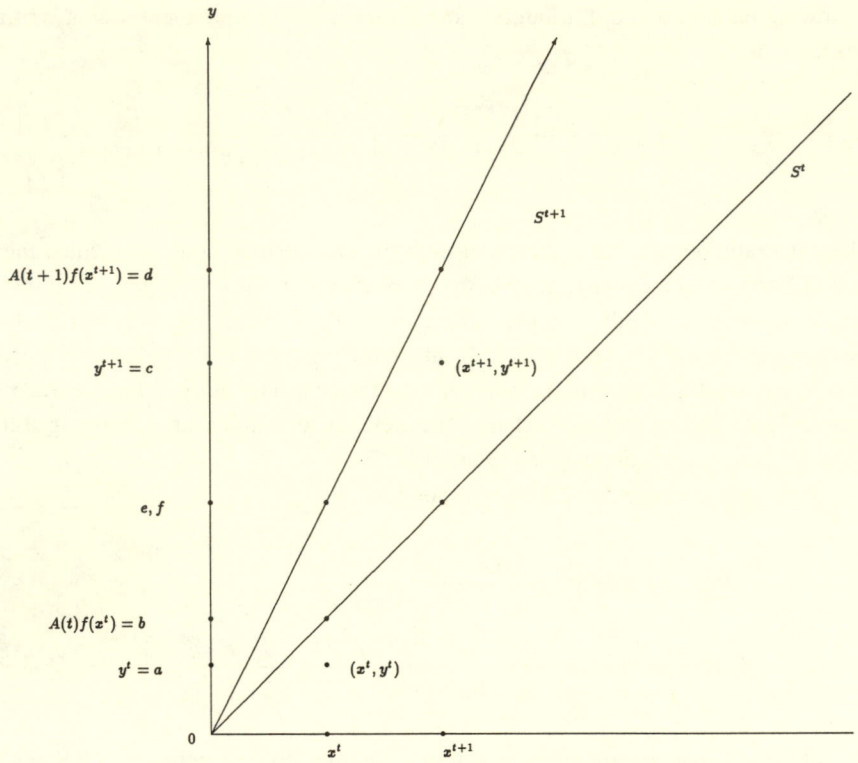

Fig. 4.3   The Malmquist output-based index of total factor productivity

Malmquist indexes with values greater than unity. Deterioration in performance over time is associated with a Malmquist index with value less than unity. The efficiency change and technical change components have the same interpretation. Note, however, that productivity growth may involve technical regress (if gains in efficiency dominate the regress) or a fall in efficiency (if technical progress dominates the loss in efficiency). Similar possibilities hold for the case of declines in productivity.

One may calculate Malmquist-type indexes in several ways. Caves, Christensen, and Diewert (1982a) showed that if the distance functions are of translog form with identical second-order terms, and if $D_o^t(x^t, y^t)$ and $D_o^{t+1}(x^{t+1}, y^{t+1})$ are each equal to unity (that is, they assume away any technical inefficiency), and firms maximize profits (that is, input and output shares are cost-minimizing and revenue-maximizing, respectively), then Equation (4.30) can be computed as the quotient of Törnqvist indexes.[26] Assuming away inefficiency implies that the Törnqvist index cannot be decomposed into technical change and change in efficiency, and the resulting index will be biased if inefficiency exists and is not constant over time.

---

[26] Färe and Grosskopf (1990b, 1992) show that if there is no allocative inefficiency, Malmquist-type indexes may be calculated as a quotient of Fisher ideal indexes.

Färe, Grosskopf, Lindgren, and Roos (1989) calculate the distance functions which make up the Malmquist-type index in Equation (4.30) by applying the linear programming approach outlined by Färe, Grosskopf, and Lovell (1985). Another possibility is to use the free disposal hull (FDH) approach introduced by Deprins, Simar, and Tulkens (1984), which is discussed in more detail later in this section. One could also calculate the component distance functions using the Aigner-Chu (1968) parametric linear programming approach. Another alternative is to estimate the component distance functions using stochastic frontier techniques and construct a Malmquist index from those estimates.[27]

Here I follow Färe, Grosskopf, Lindgren, and Roos (1989), and show how to calculate the Malmquist productivity index using nonparametric programming techniques. Assume that there are $k = 1, \ldots, K^t$ observations using $n = 1, \ldots, N$ inputs $x_n^{k,t}$ at each time period $t = 1, \ldots, T$. These inputs are used to produce $m = 1, \ldots, M$ outputs $y_m^{k,t}$.

The frontier technology in period t is constructed from the data as

$$S^t = \{(x^t, y^t) : y_m^t \leq \sum_{k=1}^{K} z^{k,t} y_m^{k,t}, m = 1, \ldots, M,$$

$$\sum_{k=1}^{K} z^{k,t} x_n^{k,t} \leq x_n^t, n = 1, \ldots, N,$$

$$z^{k,t} \geq 0, k = 1, \ldots, K\} \tag{4.33}$$

where $z^{k,t}$ is an intensity variable indicating at what intensity a particular activity (or observation) may be employed in production.[28] This technology exhibits constant returns-to-scale (the intensity variable is constrained to be nonnegative)[29] and strong disposability of inputs and outputs,[30] see Färe, Grosskopf, and Lovell (1985) or Grosskopf (1986) for details. Note that the technology, and consequently the asso-

---

[27] This is closely related to the approach taken by Perelman, Pestieau, and others at Liège and CORE. See the discussion later in this section.

[28] These variables serve to construct the reference technology from the data by taking linear combinations, as well as radial contractions and expansions of the data.

[29] This assumption may be relaxed by restricting the sum of the intensity variables to unity, which allows technology to exhibit increasing, constant, and decreasing returns-to-scale. This introduces the possibility, however, that no solution to the mixed-period problems may exist. Assuming constant returns-to-scale or nonincreasing returns-to-scale (the sum of the intensity variables is restricted to sum to less than or equal to unity) eliminates that problem in this case. In the case of Malmquist input-based productivity indexes, assuming nonincreasing returns may not be sufficient to guarantee existence of mixed-period problems; in that case constant returns-to-scale is, however, sufficient. See Färe, Grosskopf, Lindgren, and Roos (1989).

[30] The constraints are inequalities allowing for linear combinations of observed data, such as $\sum_{k=1}^{K} z^{k,t} y^{k,t}$, or output levels less than or equal to those linear combinations, that is, output is freely disposable. Input levels may be greater than or equal to linear combinations of observed input, that is, producers may freely dispose of inputs as well.

ciated distance functions, are independent of unit of measurement. (The technology for period $t + 1$ is constructed similarly using data from period $t + 1$.)

Before turning to the calculation of the distance functions used to construct the Malmquist productivity index, I would like to spend a little time discussing the piecewise linear technology used in this approach. In order to better see that Equation (4.33) readily describes a multiple-output technology, consider the following similarly constructed output set:

$$P^t(x^t) = \{y^t : y_m^t \leqq \sum_{k=1}^{K} z^{k,t} y_m^{k,t}, m = 1, \ldots, M,$$

$$\sum_{k=1}^{K} z^{k,t} x_n^{k,t} \leqq x_n^t, n = 1, \ldots, N,$$

$$z^{k,t} \geqq 0, k = 1, \ldots, K\},$$

where $P^t(x^t)$ is the production possibilities set. Notice that the set of inequalities here is identical to those in Equation (4.33); however, here I consider the set of feasible outputs rather than the set of feasible input-output bundles. As before, technology satisfies free disposability and constant returns-to-scale. The output set for period $t + 1$ may be constructed by substituting $t + 1$ for t above.

In order to demonstrate that the assumption of constant returns is fairly unrestrictive, consider Figure 4.4 where there are two outputs, and the output sets for periods t and $t + 1$ appear. The boundaries of the respective output sets are determined by the extremal points in the data; these are typically the kinks in the frontiers. Here constant returns and strong disposability are imposed on each period's technology. Strong disposability is reflected in the vertical and horizontal segments intersecting the horizontal and vertical axes, respectively. Although constant returns to scale is imposed in each period, each period is allowed to have a completely *different* constant returns-to-scale technology. An extreme case is illustrated here: the t and $t + 1$ frontiers intersect. This illustrates the fact that technical regress is entirely possible, and that technical change is in no way necessarily neutral over time, even under constant returns-to-scale.

In order to calculate the productivity of observation k' between t and $t + 1$ based on Equation (4.30), it is necessary to solve four different sets of linear programming problems. Noting that the output distance function is equal to the reciprocal of the Farrell output-oriented measure of technical efficiency, compute for each $k = 1, \ldots, K$

$$\left[D_o^t(x^{k',t}, y^{k',t})\right]^{-1} = \max \theta \qquad (4.34)$$

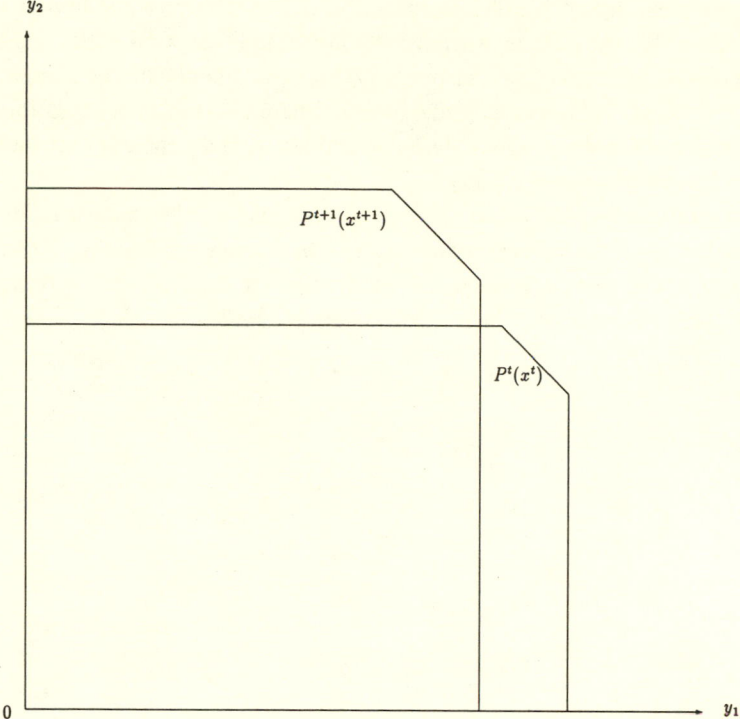

Fig. 4.4   Output sets under constant returns-to-scale

subject to

$$\theta y_m^{k',t} \leqq \sum_{k=1}^{k} z^{k,t} y_m^{k,t} \qquad m = 1, \ldots, M$$

$$\sum_{k=1}^{K} z^{k,t} x_n^{k,t} \leqq x_n^{k',t} \qquad n = 1, \ldots, N$$

$$z^{k,t} \geqq 0 \qquad k = 1, \ldots, K$$

The solution value of θ^* in (4.34) is equal to $\|\theta^* y^{k',t}\| / \|y^{k',t}\|$, that is, maximum potential output divided by observed output. Accordingly, the output distance function is the ratio of observed to maximum potential output.[31] This problem is also equivalent to the standard output-oriented DEA linear programming problem. Notice that as long as the observation being evaluated is a member of the reference set [the summed terms

---

[31] This verbal interpretation is, of course, strictly valid only for the scalar output case. The interpretation as ratios of sizes of vectors is general, however.

in (4.34)], the value of the distance function is less than or equal to unity for that observation This must occur whenever the time superscript on $D_o(.)$ and the time superscript on the x and y arguments in $D_o(x, y)$ are identical. The computation of $D_o^{t+1}(x^{k',t+1}, y^{k',t+1})$ is exactly like (4.34), where $t + 1$ is substituted for t. Since technology and the observation to be evaluated are from the same period, the solution value is less than or equal to unity.

Two of the distance functions used to construct the Malmquist index require information from two different periods, that is, the reference technology is constructed from data in one period, whereas the observation to be evaluated is from another period. One of these is computed for observation k' as

$$\left[D_o^t(x^{k',t+1}, y^{k',t+1})\right]^{-1} = \max \theta \qquad (4.35)$$

subject to

$$\theta y_m^{k',t+1} \leqq \sum_{k=1}^{K} z^{k,t} y_m^{k,t} \qquad m = 1, \ldots, M$$

$$\sum_{k=1}^{K} z^{k,t} x_n^{k,t} \leqq x_n^{k',t+1} \qquad n = 1, \ldots, N$$

$$z^{k,t} \geqq 0 \qquad k = 1, \ldots, K$$

In (4.35), observations from both period t and period $t + 1$ are involved. The reference technology relative to which $(x^{k',t+1}, y^{k',t+1})$ is evaluated is constructed from observations in period t. In contrast in Equation (4.34), $(x^{k',t}, y^{k',t}) \in S^t$ and therefore $D_o^t(x^{k',t}, y^{k',t}) \leq 1$. However, in (4.35), $(x^{k',t+1}, y^{k',t+1})$ need not belong to S^t, and so $D_o^t(x^{k',t+1}, y^{k',t+1})$ may take values greater than one.

The last linear programming problem required to construct the Malmquist index is also a mixed-period problem. It is specified as in (4.35), but the t and $t + 1$ superscripts are reversed.

The (reciprocals of the) solutions to these linear programming problems may be substituted into Equation (4.30) to derive Malmquist productivity indexes for each observation for every adjacent pair of periods for which data are available. In addition, firm-specific efficiency change and technical change components may be calculated as long as the researcher has access to panel data. If only time series data are available, the solutions to $D_o^t(x^t, y^t)$ and $D_o^{t+1}(x^{t+1}, y^{t+1})$ (which only include data from period t and $t + 1$, respectively) must be unity; and in this case productivity change is identical to technical change.[32]

---

[32] On the other hand if one includes the history of data up to the period to be evaluated, that is, if $D_o^t(x^t, y^t)$ is calculated using data from period t as well as periods preceding t in the reference technology, one could calculate what Tulkens (1991) calls sequential efficiency. This is also close to the technique suggested by Diewert (1980), both of which are discussed in more detail below. One problem with this approach is that the number of observations in the reference set changes over time. This problem could be addressed using DEA window-type techniques.

The Malmquist output-based index of total factor productivity and its components have been calculated using the programming problems outlined above by Färe,
Grosskopf, Lindgren, and Roos (1989) for a sample of Swedish hospitals, and Färe,
Grosskopf, Norris, and Zhang (1991) for a sample of O.E.C.D. economies. Notice
that one may interpret the component output distance function measures as taking
input quantities as given, and seeking the greatest feasible proportional expansion of
outputs given technology. No behavioral assumption concerning revenue maximization, cost minimization, or profit maximization is required.[33] Nor is any information
required with respect to input or output prices, which is very useful in cases where
outputs are not marketed as in the case of Swedish hospitals.

One may also calculate a Malmquist input-based measure of total factor productivity, which is constructed from ratios of input distance functions. Färe, Grosskopf,
Lindgren, and Roos (1991) have calculated these input-based Malmquist productivity
measures for a sample of Swedish pharmacies. They chose the input-based measure
to reflect the fact that these pharmacies are under obligation to the government to
meet demand at minimum cost. That is consistent with the input distance function,
which takes output as given and seeks to reduce inputs (proportionally) as much as
possible given technology.[34] Berg, Førsund, and Jansen (1991) have also employed
input-based Malmquist productivity measures to analyze the effects on productivity
of deregulation in the Norwegian banking industry. Färe, Grosskopf, Yaisawarng,
Li, and Wang (1990) applied the Malmquist input-based productivity measures to
evaluate productivity growth in Illinois electric utilities.

The examples cited above suggest that this index may prove especially useful
where productivity is most difficult to measure, in those cases where data are limited,
or where the assumption of profit maximization or efficiency is unlikely to hold.
Along those lines, Färe, Grosskopf, and Lovell (1990) have developed "indirect"
Malmquist productivity indexes. These are based on revenue- or cost-restricted models of technology. For example, the cost-indirect Malmquist productivity index is
based on cost-indirect output distance functions, which are defined as

$$ID_o(p/C, y) = \min\{\theta : y/\theta \in IP(p/C)\} \qquad (4.36)$$

where $IP(p/C) = \{y : y \in P(x), \sum p_n x_n \leqq C\}$ and $P(x)$ is the production possibilities set.[35] Instead of input quantities taken as given as in $D_o(x, y)$, the budget
C is given. The producer is allowed to choose any input bundle as long as it satisfies the budget, given input prices. This type of indirect model would be especially
appropriate in modeling local government behavior, for example, or not-for-profit

---

[33] A necessary condition for revenue maximization, however, is that $D_o(x, y) = 1$.

[34] $D_i(y, x) = 1$ is a necessary condition for cost minimization.

[35] This distance function is indirect in the same way as an indirect utility function is indirect: both are
budget constrained. For a nice discussion of indirect distance functions, see Färe and Primont (1990).

producers.[36] Analogously, one can also construct an indirect input-based productivity index consisting of revenue-indirect input distance functions, see Färe, Grosskopf, and Lovell (1990, 1991), and Färe and Grosskopf (1991).

There are other examples of frontier, nonparametric approaches to measuring total factor productivity growth. One group of these is related to the general literature on nonparametric tests of regularity conditions of production. In this literature, tests of consistency of a data set with some hypothesis (e.g., cost minimization) are constructed. These typically require computing a series of inequalities which often may be restated as linear programming problems. Examples include Afriat (1972), Hanoch and Rothschild (1972), Diewert and Parkan (1983), and Varian (1984). Early examples of linear programming tests of technical change include Diewert and Parkan (1983) and Diewert (1980). More recently, Chavas and Cox (1988, 1990) and Cox and Chavas (1990) have provided tests of biased and neutral technical change using linear programming methods.[37]

Computationally, this approach is very similar to the calculations of the component distance functions of the Malmquist index described above. For example, in his 1980 paper [which relies on an earlier 1979 working paper which ultimately appeared as Diewert and Parkan (1983)], Diewert points out that the efficiency hypothesis that $y^t = f(x^t)$ (where y is scalar and $t = 1, \ldots, T$) could be tested for a time series of data (that is, $K = 1$) by calculating the solution to the following linear programming problem

$$\tilde{f}^t(x) = \max \sum_{i=1}^{t} z_i y^i \tag{4.37}$$

subject to

$$\sum_{i=1}^{t} z_i x_{in} \leqq x_{tn} \qquad n = 1, \ldots, N$$

$$\sum_{i=1}^{t} z_i = 1$$

$$z_i \geqq 0 \qquad i = 1, \ldots, t,$$

[36] For a more detailed discussion of indirect models, see Färe and Grosskopf (1991) and Färe, Grosskopf, and Lovell (1991). Basic indirect efficiency measures were proposed and illustrated by Färe, Grosskopf, and Lovell (1988). Indirect productivity indexes are derived in Färe, Grosskopf, and Lovell (1990).

[37] Chavas and Cox do not explicitly identify technical inefficiency, thus they do not attempt to disentangle technical change and changes in technical efficiency. Their tests are all conditional on hypotheses of either profit maximization or cost minimization. Technical change is modeled as a translation (that is, additive change) in output in their model.

where the summation occurs over the history of data up through the period t of the data to be evaluated. If the solution value $\theta^t = 1$, then $y^t = f(x^t)$ for that period. That is, production in period t is judged relative to previous periods, and, as long as there is no technical regression, a solution value $\theta^t = 1$ implies production occurs on the production frontier in that period.[38] If the solution value of θ^t is greater than unity, then production was not consistent with the efficiency hypothesis in that period. If data from period t are then compared to data up to and including $t + 1$, then Diewert (1980, p. 264) suggests that a "reasonable measure of the shift in the true production function going from period" t to $t + 1$ is the ratio of the solution values $\tilde{f}^{t+1}(x^t)/\tilde{f}^t(x^t)$. Diewert also suggests how this might be generalized to the multiple output case by setting up a cost minimization problem. The work of Chavas and Cox builds on this general approach.

One disadvantage of these approaches is that the hypothesis (cost minimization, technical change, etc.) is rejected if even one observation in the sample violates the hypothesis. Varian (1985) suggested extending ideas from Afriat (1972) to allow for "small" violations of the hypothesis. This allows one to test whether any violation is significant in a statistical sense. This technique entails identifying the degree of the violation of the hypothesis. In later work, Varian (1990) also proposes a goodness-of-fit test which is employed by Chavas and Cox (1990).

Another nonparametric frontier approach to total factor productivity measurement has been pioneered by Tulkens. See Tulkens (1990, 1991), and Thiry and Tulkens (1989, 1992) for examples of this approach which is very much in the spirit of that proposed by Diewert discussed above. The Tulkens approach differs from that described above (and that used in calculation of the Malmquist index using the programming approach) in that the technology is not restricted to satisfy convexity. Instead, the smallest freely disposable hull (FDH) which spans the data serves as technology [see Deprins, Simar, and Tulkens (1984) and Tulkens (1986) for examples of efficiency measurement using this technique]. The programming version of output efficiency using their approach may be written for each $k' = 1, \ldots, K$ as

$$\text{Eff}^t(x^{k',t}, y^{k',t}) = \max \ \theta \tag{4.38}$$

subject to

$$\theta y_m^{k',t} \leqq \sum_{k=1}^{K} z^{k,t} y_m^{k,t} \qquad m = 1, \ldots, M$$

[38] In the nonparametric test jargon, this implies that the data "are consistent with the efficiency hypothesis (that is, the firm produces a maximal amount of output for a given input vector) and with the hypothesis of no technological regress for some family of production functions $\{f^t : t = 1, 2, \ldots, T\}$ where f^t is continuous, nondecreasing, and concave over the domain set $S(x^1, x^2, \ldots, x^t)$" [Diewert (1980, p. 263)].

$$\sum_{k=1}^{K} z^{k,t} x_n^{k,t} \leq x_n^{k',t} \qquad n = 1, \ldots, N$$

$$z^{k,t} \in \{0,1\} \qquad k = 1, \ldots, K$$

$$\sum_{k=1}^{K} z^{k,t} = 1$$

Efficiency is first calculated sequentially, that is, relative to the FDH technology constructed only from observations up to and including the year to be evaluated. Local technical change is said to occur when a sequentially efficient observation dominates earlier sequentially efficient observations. This can be measured in an input-saving or output-increasing direction, just as in the case of Farrell technical efficiency measurement. In a later paper Tulkens and Vanden Eeckaut (1991) generalize this approach to better exploit panel data. Here they characterize efficiency relative to three different kinds of FDH frontiers: a contemporaneous frontier (constructed from the K firms in one period), an intertemporal frontier (includes all years), and a sequential frontier (includes years up to and including t). This allows them to derive a local measure of technical change (as above, which does not allow for regression) as well as what they call benchmark technical change which allows for regression or progression.

The FDH approach, due to its very unrestrictive assumptions concerning technology, provides a "tighter" fit around the data than the programming models used by Diewert or FGLR (or DEA).[39] This implies that observations are more likely to be judged efficient relative to the FDH technology than to a DEA technology allowing for variable returns-to-scale and strong disposability.

To sum up, these nonparametric, frontier techniques all allow for inefficiency. None imposes a specific functional form on technology, minimizing specification error. These approaches are sensitive to measurement error, and typically do not allow for statistical inference.[40] In order to identify technical efficiency as well as technical change, they also typically require panel data.

4.4.2 Parametric Frontier Approaches to Productivity Measurement

This section gives a selective overview of parametric frontier approaches to productivity measurement. The intention is to give the reader some helpful references to this small, but ambitious literature.

---

[39] This is strictly true as long as strong disposability is imposed in these other approaches. If weak disposability is allowed, this may no longer be true.

[40] Here again, one might mention Varian's work. Some other very interesting work addresses some of these problems. Wilson (1991) and Seaver and Triantis (1989) have considered means of statistically testing for outliers in these nonparametric models. Simar (1991) and Wilson (1991) address the issue of precision of these models by employing bootstrapping methods. Resampling has also been employed in these types of programming models by Färe, Grosskopf and Weber (1989) and Grosskopf and Yaisawarng (1990).

To my knowledge, the first efforts devoted to calculating technical change using a parametric frontier model are due to Førsund and Hjalmarsson (1979). They applied a linear programming approach developed by Aigner and Chu (1968) to calculate a production frontier. They generalized the production frontier to the homothetic case, and by using panel data on Swedish dairy farms, they were able to include time trends which allowed them to identify frontier technical change. They also derived the associated reductions in average cost due to frontier technical change.[41]

They solved a linear programming problem of the following general form:

$$\min \sum_{t=1}^{T} \sum_{k=1}^{K} [\ln A + \gamma_t t + \gamma_{lt} t \ln L_k(t) + \gamma_{kt} t \ln K_k(t) - \gamma_{yt} t \ln y_k(t)] \quad (4.39)$$

subject to

$$\ln A + \gamma_t t + \gamma_{lt} t \ln L_k(t) + \gamma_{kt} t \ln K_k(t) - \gamma_{yt} t \ln y_k(t) \geqq 0$$
$$t = 1, \dots, T \qquad k = 1, \dots, K$$

subject also to nonnegativity constraints and homogeneity constraints. L and K represent labor and capital, respectively. Note that the objective is to minimize the sum of the deviations of frontier from observed output, and that the restrictions require that all deviations be nonnegative, that is, the estimated production relationship is indeed a frontier. Thus all deviations from the frontier are due to inefficiency, that is, the model constructs a deterministic, parametric frontier with no allowance for other types of error.

Another early study which also used this type of frontier is due to Nishimizu and Page (1982). Their frontier is much like that due to Førsund and Hjalmarsson, except that they specify technology as translog. Whereas the focus in Førsund and Hjalmarsson was on isolating frontier technical change, Nishimizu and Page focus on identifying productivity growth, which they define as the sum of frontier technical change and change in efficiency, much like that developed for the Malmquist index above. In contrast to the Nishimizu and Page approach, the Malmquist approach is nonparametric, avoiding problems due to specification error. On the other hand, this approach shares with the nonparametric frontier approaches a lack of statistical underpinnings.

An interesting extension of the Nishimizu and Page decomposition has been contributed by Perelman and Pestieau (1988). In their work they specify a parametric production function, which they estimate as a deterministic frontier using what they call displaced ordinary least squares, or corrected ordinary least squares. Included

---

[41] They also decomposed those cost savings due to technological advance into proportional technical advance (including change in optimal scale, proportional change due to bias, and Hicks neutral advance) and factor bias advance.

in the specification is a time trend. The time trend is then used to identify technical change. They also calculate technical efficiency in each year. Following Nishimizu and Page, they use these two components to define a productivity index. This index and decomposition is the parametric, continuous counterpart of the Malmquist index and decomposition described above.[42] This approach has been generalized to a stochastic frontier and applied to a wide variety of data, see, for example, Fecher and Perelman (1989), Fecher (1990), Fecher and Perelman (1991), and Fecher and Pestieau (1991).

All the papers just mentioned used frontier production functions to calculate technical change and productivity growth. This implies that output is scalar. In order to explicitly include multiple outputs one could employ other function representations of technology including distance functions, revenue function, profit function, and, of course, the cost function. A good example of such an approach is that due to Bauer (1990), who calculates total factor productivity using a stochastic, cost frontier. He begins with the traditional definition of total factor productivity in a continuous time framework as follows:

$$\text{T\dot{F}P} = \dot{y} - (\dot{F}) \tag{4.40}$$

where dots are time derivatives and F is an index of input usage, where F is usually proxied by $\sum_{n=1}^{N}(w_n x_n/C)\dot{x}_n$, and C is total cost. In a world in which allocative and technical efficiency exist, this measure of TFP leads to bias. To address both types of inefficiency, Bauer starts with the Farrell cost efficiency (CE) measure

$$\text{CE} = \frac{C(y,p)}{C} \tag{4.41}$$

which can be decomposed into CE = TE · AE, or

$$\dot{\text{CE}} = \dot{\text{TE}} + \dot{\text{AE}} \tag{4.42}$$

where TE and AE are Farrell input-based measures of technical and allocative efficiency, respectively. Total differentiation of (4.40) and some substitution yields the following modified measure of total factor productivity growth:

$$\text{T\dot{F}P} = [1 - \epsilon_{cy}(y,w,t)]\dot{y} + \dot{\text{TE}} + \dot{\text{AE}} - \dot{C}(y,w,t) + \sum_{n=1}^{N}[s_n - s_n(y,w,t)]\dot{x}_n \tag{4.43}$$

---

[42] There are some minor differences in addition to the fact that Nishimizu and Page and Perelman and Pestieau use parametric models of technology. First of all, these parametric production frontier models are restricted to the case of scalar output. Second, technical change differs since the parametric models calculate technical change as the derivative of the production frontier with respect to time evaluated at some year t. The Malmquist approach described in the previous section calculates technical change as the geometric mean of the shift in technology at two consecutive time periods; it is a discrete measure of technical change.

where $-\dot{C}(y, w, t)$ is technical progress, ϵ_{cy} is output cost elasticity, s_n is the observed cost share, and $s_n(y, w, t)$ is the minimal cost share of the nth input. This is a much more general version of the econometric cost function approach to total factor productivity discussed in Section 4.2.[43]

In order to calculate (4.44), Bauer uses a translog system of cost and input share equations, estimated as frontiers

$$\ln C = \ln C(y, w, t) + u + v \qquad (4.44)$$
$$s_n = s_n(y, w) + w_n \qquad n = 1, \ldots, N$$

where u is a one-sided disturbance term which captures the cost of inefficiency (both allocative and technical), v is a two-sided noise disturbance, and w_n is a two-sided disturbance which allows for noise as well as allocative inefficiency (since that allocative inefficiency could result in shares greater than or less than cost minimizing shares). After imposing the appropriate homogeneity and symmetry restrictions, Bauer estimates this system of equations using maximum likelihood based on a panel of data on U.S. airlines.[44]

Clearly, other representations of technology (revenue function, distance function[45]) could be estimated as stochastic frontiers to derive similar decompositions of total factor productivity. This approach is best pursued with panel data, particularly if one wishes to allow for identification of firm specific or time specific efficiency effects.

4.5 Concluding Remarks

The purpose of this chapter was to provide a brief overview of approaches to productivity measurement, particularly those which explicitly account for inefficiency. Another way of thinking about this taxonomy is to divide these approaches into two groups: frontier and nonfrontier. Within each group I have further subdivided into parametric and nonparametric models, where the latter is understood to include the programming approaches, and the former includes both stochastic and deterministic models. At this point, I would like to look back and try to make an overall assessment of the strengths and weaknesses of these alternative approaches, beginning where I left off—with stochastic, parametric frontier approaches.

---

[43] This may be further generalized to the case of multiple outputs. In that case one sums over the outputs in the first bracketed term and another term would be introduced to capture any deviations from marginal cost pricing. See Denny, Fuss, and Waverman (1981).

[44] Bauer (1990) also includes multiple outputs as well as a vector of network characteristics.

[45] In fact, the distance function has much to commend it in this approach. Since the distance function embodies technical, but not allocative, efficiency, the connection between the error terms on the distance function and the error terms for the associated share equations (which would capture allocative efficiency, but as before, that implies that shares could be greater than or less than observed shares) would be simpler than in the case of the cost function or revenue function.

How does the stochastic parametric frontier approach compare to the other frontier approaches to total factor productivity measurement? Relative to the deterministic parametric frontier approach it has the advantage of allowing for random shocks and measurement error. Both frontier parametric approaches are subject to specification error, although that can be minimized by choosing a flexible functional form. The number of parameters to be estimated may become a problem in the stochastic frontier approach, however, especially in cases where there are large numbers of inputs and outputs. Specification of the error structure in the stochastic frontier approach is not straightforward, indeed, such specification introduces another potential source of error.

Relative to the stochastic parametric frontier approach, nonparametric frontier approaches have the advantage of minimal specification error, but do not allow for measurement error or random shocks.[46] The nonparametric, frontier models discussed here have the advantage of being suitable for analysis of discrete data. This avoids the approximation error introduced in the parametric models which presume continuity. Computationally, they are probably less demanding than the stochastic frontier approaches, although the number of programming problems to be solved in the nonparametric frontier approach can be quite large.[47] A consequence is that the nonparametric approach provides an enormous amount of disaggregated information: producer-specific efficiency measures in each period and producer-specific efficiency change and technical change components for every adjacent pair of periods.[48] In addition, there is producer-specific information in each period on dual solution values, basic solutions, slacks, etc.

And how do the frontier approaches compare to the nonfrontier approaches to total factor productivity measurement? The nonfrontier nonparametric approaches (including the growth accounting and index number approaches) have the distinct advantage of familiarity and computational ease. There are no parameters to estimate and no linear programming problems to run. They are amenable to calculation in the face of large numbers of inputs and outputs. The Törnqvist index is even consistent with a flexible functional form of technology. On the other hand, they are vulnerable to bias; these approaches are based on assumptions of technical and allocative efficiency. Insofar as these are violated, the resulting productivity indexes will be biased. The nonparametric nonfrontier approaches have the advantage relative to their parametric

---

[46] Again, one may mention Varian's test approach as an attempt to address this problem. One might also use outlier tests or jackknifing or bootstrapping techniques to ameliorate the deterministic nature of these approaches. See the references mentioned in footnote 39.

[47] For example, to calculate Malmquist indexes between period t and $t + 1$ for K observations requires solving $4K$ linear programming problems. Calculating Malmquist indexes for t to $t + 1$ and $t + 1$ to $t + 2$ for the same panel requires solving $7K$ linear programming problems.

[48] In fact, summarizing this information is not straightforward. The FGLR specification of the Malmquist index does not satisfy the circular test. One may specify a chained version of the Malmquist index in this case if desired.

nonfrontier counterparts of avoidance of specification error, albeit at the cost of ignoring measurement error.

To conclude, I would argue that measurement of total factor productivity can and has benefited from an interface with the efficiency measurement (or frontier) literature. The major current contribution is in making explicit the possible bias arising from ignoring inefficiency. As shown here, this literature is beginning to provide computational alternatives to the traditional nonfrontier approach as well. There is, however, much to be done.

REFERENCES

Afriat, S. (1972), "Efficiency Estimation of Production Functions," *International Economic Review* 13(3) (October): 568–598.

Aigner, D. J. and S. F. Chu (1968), "On Estimating the Industry Production Function," *American Economic Review* 58: 226–239.

Bauer, Paul W. (1990), "Decomposing TFP Growth in the Presence of Cost Inefficiency, Nonconstant Returns to Scale, and Technological Progress," *Journal of Productivity Analysis* 1(4): 287–301.

Berg, S. A., F. R. Førsund, and E. S. Jansen (1991), "Malmquist Indices of Productivity Growth During the Deregulation of Norwegian Banking 1980–89," *Scandinavian Journal of Economics* (forthcoming).

Caves, D., L. Christensen, and W. E. Diewert (1982a), "The Economic Theory of Index Numbers and the Measurement of Input, Output, and Productivity," *Econometrica* 50(6): 1393–1414.

Caves, D., L. Christensen, and W. E. Diewert (1982b), "Multilateral Comparisons of Output, Input, and Productivity Using Superlative Index Numbers," *The Economic Journal* 92: 73–86.

Chambers, R., R. Färe, and S. Grosskopf (1991), "Efficiency, Quantity Indexes and Productivity Indexes: A Synthesis," *Bulletin of Economic Research* (forthcoming).

Chavas, J-P., and T. L. Cox (1988), "A Nonparametric Analysis of Agricultural Technology," *American Journal of Agricultural Economics* 70: 303–310.

Chavas, J-P., and T. L. Cox (1990), "A Non-Parametric Analysis of Productivity: The Case of U.S. and Japanese Manufacturing," *American Economic Review* 80(30) (June): 450–464.

Cowing, T. G., and R. E. Stevenson, eds., (1981), *Productivity Measurement in Regulated Industries*, New York: Academic Press.

Cox, T. L., and J-P. Chavas (1990), "A Nonparametric Analysis of Productivity: The Case of U.S. Agriculture," *European Review of Agricultural Economics* 17: 449–464.

Denison, E. F. (1967), *Why Growth Rates Differ*, Washington, D.C.: Brookings.

Denison, E. F. (1972), "Classification of Sources of Growth," *Review of Income and Wealth* 18: 1–25.

Denny, M., M. Fuss, and L. Waverman (1981)," The Measurement of Total Factor Productivity in Regulated Industries, with an Application to Canadian Telecommunications," in T. G. Cowing and R. E. Stevenson, eds., *Productivity Measurement in Regulated Industries*, New York: Academic Press.

Deprins, D., L. Simar, and H. Tulkens (1984), "Measuring Labor Efficiency in Post Offices," in M. Marchand, P. Pestieau, and H. Tulkens, eds., *The Performance of Public Enterprises: Normative, Positive and Empirical Issues*, Amsterdam: North Holland, chap. 10, pp. 243–267.

Diewert, W. E. (1976), "Exact and Superlative Index Numbers," *Journal of Econometrics* 4: 115–145.

Diewert, W. E. (1979), "The Economic Theory of Index Numbers: A Survey," Discussion Paper No. 79-09, Department of Economics, University of British Columbia, March.

Diewert, W. E. (1980), "Capital and the Theory of Productivity Analysis," *American Economic Review* 79(5) (December): 260–267.

Diewert, W. E. (1989), "The Measurement of Productivity," Discussion Paper No. 89-04, Department of Economics, University of British Columbia, January.

Diewert, W. E. (1992), "Fisher Ideal Output, Input and Productivity Indexes Revisited" *Journal of Productivity Analysis* 3:3, 211–249.

Diewert, W. E. and C. Parkan (1983), "Linear Programming Tests of Regularity Conditions for Production Frontiers," in W. Eichhorn, R. Henn, K. Neumann, and R. Shephard, eds. *Quantitative Studies of Production and Prices*, Würzburg and Vienna: Physica-Verlag.

Färe, R. (1988), *Fundamentals of Production Theory*, Berlin: Springer-Verlag.

Färe, R., S. Grosskopf, and C. A. K. Lovell (1985), *The Measurement of Efficiency of Production*, Boston: Kluwer-Nijhoff.

Färe, R., S. Grosskopf, and C. A. K. Lovell (1988), "An Indirect Approach to the Evaluation of Producer Performance," *Journal of Public Economics* 37: 71–89.

Färe, R., S. Grosskopf, and W. Weber (1989), "Measuring School Disrict Performance," *Public Finance Quarterly* 17(4): 409–428.

Färe, R., S. Grosskopf, B. Lindgren, and P. Roos (1989), "Productivity Developments in Swedish Hospitals: A Malmquist Output Index Approach," Discussion Paper 89-3, Department of Economics, Southern Illinois University, Carbondale (forthcoming in Charnes, Cooper, Lewin, and Seiford, eds.).

Färe, R., and S. Grosskopf (1990a), "A Distance Function Approach to Measuring Price Efficiency," *Journal of Public Economics* 43: 123–126.

Färe, R., and S. Grosskopf (1990b), "The Fisher Ideal Index and the Indirect Malmquist Productivity Index: A Comparison," *New Zealand Economic Papers* 24: 66–72.

Färe, R., and S. Grosskopf (1990c), "Theory and Calculation of Productivity Indexes: Revisited," Department of Economics, Southern Illinois University, Carbondale (mimeo graphed).

Färe, R., and D. Primont (1990), "A Distance Function Approach to Multioutput Technologies," *Southern Economic Journal* 56(4): 879–891.

Färe, R., S. Grosskopf, and C. A. K. Lovell (1990), "Cost Indirect Productivity Measurement," Working Paper No. 90-4, Department of Economics, University of North Carolina, Chapel Hill (forthcoming in *Journal of Productivity Analysis*).

Färe, R., S. Grosskopf, C. A. K. Lovell, and S. Yaisawarng (1990), "Derivation of Virtual Prices for Undesirable Outputs: A Distance Function Approach," *Review of Economics and Statistics* (forthcoming).

Färe, R., S. Grosskopf, S. Yaisawarng, S. K. Li, and Z. Wang (1990), "Productivity Growth in Illinois Electric Utilities," *Resources and Energy* 12: 383–398.

Färe, R., and R. Chambers (1991), "Hicks Neutrality and Multiple Outputs" (mimeographed).

Färe, R., and S. Grosskopf (1991a), *"Cost and Revenue Constrained Production"* Bilkent University Lecture Series, Springer Verlag, Berlin (forthcoming).

Färe, R., and S. Grosskopf (1991b), " Nonparametric Tests, Goodness-of-Fit and Farrell Efficiency" (mimeographed).

Färe, R., S. Grosskopf, and C. A. K. Lovell (1991), *Production Frontiers*, Cambridge: Cambridge University Press (forthcoming).

Färe, R., S. Grosskopf, B. Lindgren, and P. Roos (1991), "Productivity in Swedish Pharmacies: A Malmquist Input Index Approach," Southern Illinois University, Carbondale, IL (mimeographed) (forthcoming in *Journal of Productivity Analysis*).

Färe, R., S. Grosskopf, M. Norris, and Z. Zhang (1991), "Decomposition of Productivity Growth in Industrialized Countries into Technical Change and Change in Performance," Department of Economics, Southern Illinois University, Carbondale (mimeographed).

Färe, R., and S. Grosskopf (1992), "Malmquist Productivity Indexes and Fisher Ideal Indexes," *Economic Journal* 102(4): 158–160.

Farrell, M. J. (1957) "The Measurement of Productive Efficiency," *Journal of the Royal Statistical Society*, Series A, General, 120(3): 253–281.

Fecher, F. (1990), "Productivity Growth, Catching-Up and Innovation in OECD Manufacturing Sectors," paper presented at the Fifth Annual Congress of the EEA, Lisbon.

Fecher, F., and S. Perelman (1989), "Productivity Growth, Technological Progress and R & D in OECD Industrial Activities," *Public Finance and Steady Economic Growth*, Proceedings of the 45th Congress of the International Institute of Public Finance, G. Krause-Junk, ed., The Hague: The Public Finance Foundation, pp. 231-249.

Fecher, F., and S. Perelman (1991), "Productivity Growth and Technical Efficiency in OECD Industrial Activities," University of Liege, Belgium (mimeographed).

Fecher, F., and P. Pestieau (1991), "Efficiency and Competition in Financial Services," presented at the conference for Public versus Private Enterprises: In Search of the Real Issues, CIRIEC, University of Liege, Belgium.

Fisher, I. (1922), *The Making of Index Numbers*, Boston: Houghton-Mifflin.

Førsund, F. R. (1991), "The Malmquist Productivity Index," Memorandum, No. 28, Department of Economics, University of Oslo, Norway.

Førsund, F. R. and L. Hjalmarsson (1979), "Frontier Production Functions and Technical Progress: A Study of General Milk Production in Swedish Dairy Plants," *Economic Journal* 89: 294–315.

Førsund, F. R., and L. Hjalmarsson (1987), *Analyses of Industrial Structure: A Putty-Clay Approach*, The Industrial Institute for Economic and Social Research, Stockholm: Almqvist and Wiksell International.

Frisch, R. (1936), "Annual Survey of General Economic Theory: The Problem of Index Numbers," *Econometrica* 50: 1393–1414.

Grosskopf, S. (1986), "The Role of the Reference Technology in Measuring Technical Efficiency," *Economic Journal* 96: 499–513.

Grosskopf, S., and S. Yaisawarng (1990), "Economies of Scope in the Provision of Local Public Services," *National Tax Journal* 43: 61–74.

Hanoch, G., and M. Rothschild (1972), "Testing the Assumptions of Production Theory: A Nonparametric Approach," *Journal of Political Economy* 89(4): 878–892.

Hicks, J. R. (1932), *Theory of Wages*. London: MacMillan.

Hulten, C. R. (1973), "Divisia Index Numbers," *Econometrica* 41: 1017–1025.

Johansen, L. (1972), *Production Functions*, Amsterdam: North Holland.

Jorgenson, D. W., and Z. Griliches (1967), "The Explanation of Productivity Change," *Review of Economic Studies* 34(3) (July): 249–282.

Kendrick, J. W. (1961), *Productivity Trends in the United States*, Princeton: National Bureau of Economic Research.

Link, A. N. (1987), *Technological Change and Productivity Growth*, London: Harwood Academic Publishers.

Malmquist, S. (1953), "Index Numbers and Indifference Surfaces," *Trabajos de Estatistica* 4: 209–242.

Morrison, C., and W. E. Diewert (1990), "New Techniques in the Measurement of Multifactor Productivity," *Journal of Productivity Analysis* 1(4) (June): 267–286.

Nishimizu, M., and J. M. Page (1982), "Total Factor Productivity Growth, Technological Progress and Technical Efficiency Change: Dimensions of Productivity Change in Yugoslavia 1965-78," *Economic Journal* 92: 920–936.

Ohta, M. (1975), "A Note on the Duality Between Production and Cost Functions: Rate of Returns to Scale and Rate of Technical Progress," *Economic Studies Quarterly* 25: 63–65.

Perelman, S., and P. Pestieau (1988), "Technical Performance in Public Enterprise: A Comparative Study of Railways and Postal Services," *European Economic Review* 32: 432–441.

Pittman, R. (1983), "Multilateral Productivity Comparisons with Undesirable Outputs," *Economic Journal* 93(372): 883–891.

Richter, M. K. (1966), "Invariance Axioms and Economic Indexes," *Econometrica* 34: 739–755.

Salter, W. E. G. (1966), *Productivity and Technical Change*, 2d ed. Cambridge: Cambridge University Press.

Shephard, R. W. (1970), *Theory of Cost and Production Functions*. Princeton: Princeton University Press.

Shephard, R. W. (1974), *Indirect Production Functions*. Meisenheim Am Glan: Verlag Anton Hain.

Seaver, B. L., and K. P. Triantis (1989), "The Implications of Using Messy Data to Estimate Production-Frontier-Based Technical Efficiency Measures," *Journal of Business and Economic Statistics* 7(1): 49–59.

Simar, L. (1991), "Estimating Efficiencies from Frontier Models with Panel Data: A Comparison of Parametric, Nonparametric and Semi-parametric Methods with Bootstrapping," *Journal of Productivity Analysis* (forthcoming).

Solow, R. A. (1957), "Technical Change and the Aggregate Production Function," *Review of Economics and Statistics* 39: 312–320.

Thiry, B., and H. Tulkens (1989), "Productivity, Efficiency and Technical Progress: Concepts and Measurement," *Annales de L'Economie Publique Sociale et Coopérative* 60(1): 9–42.

Thiry, B., and H. Tulkens (1992), "Allowing for Technical Inefficiency in Parametric Estimates of Production Functions," *Journal of Productivity Analysis* 3(1/2)(June): 45–65.

Tinbergen, J. (1942), "Zur Theorie der langfristigen Wirtschaftsentwicklung," *Weltwirtschaft liches Archiv* 55(1): 511–549.

Törnqvist, L. (1936), "The Bank of Finland's Consumption Price Index," *Bank of Finland Monthly Bulletin* 10: 1–8.

Tulkens, H. (1986), "La Performance Productive d'un Service Public: Définitions, Méthodes de Mesure et Application à la Régie des Postes en Belgique," *L'Actualité Economique, Revue d'Analyse Economique* 62(2) (June): 306–335.

Tulkens, H. (1990), "Non-Parametric Efficiency Analyses in Four Service Activities: Retail Banking, Municipalities, Courts and Urban Transit," CORE Discussion Paper 9050, Louvain-la-Neuve, Belgium (submitted to *Journal of Productivity Analysis*).

Tulkens, H. (1991), "Non-Parametric Efficiency Measurment for Panel Data: Methodologies and an FDH Application to Retail Banking," CORE, 34 Voie du Roman Pays, B-1348 Louvain-La-Neuve, Belgium (mimeographed).

Tulkens, H., and Vanden Eechart (1991), "Non-Frontier Measures of Efficiency, Progress and Regress," CORE, Lourain-la-Neuve, Belgium (mimeographed).

Varian, H. (1984), "The Nonparametric Approach to Production Analysis," *Econometrica* 52(3)(May): 579–597.

Varian, H. (1985), "Nonparametric Analysis of Optimizing Behavior with Measurement Error," *Journal of Econometrics* 30(1/2): 445–458.

Varian, H. (1990), "Goodness-of-Fit in Optimizing Models," *Journal of Econometrics* 30(1/2): 445–458.

Wilson, P. (1991), "A Bootstrap Methodology for Estimating Production Efficiency with Multiple Outputs," Department of Economics, University of Texas, Austin (mimeographed).

II
APPLICATIONS

5

EARNINGS FRONTIERS AND LABOR MARKET EFFICIENCY

Janet C. Hunt-McCool and Ronald S. Warren, Jr.[1]

5.1 Introduction

The rhetoric of human capital theory borrows heavily from the neoclassical theories of investment and production. Investments in human capital in the form of schooling, on-the-job training, and work experience represent inputs to an earnings production function, which is usually given empirical expression by the semilogarithmic earnings equation popularized by Becker and Chiswick (1966), Mincer (1974), and Heckman and Polachek (1974). With a few very recent exceptions, however, the stochastic specifications of empirical earnings equations have not been faithful to the theoretical concept of a production function as giving "... the maximum scalar output as a function of the inputs ..." [Varian (1984), p. 10]. In particular, the specification and estimation of human capital earnings functions have not kept pace with developments in the theory and estimation of econometric production frontiers, which envelop the technically efficient combinations of input sets and outputs.

The purpose of this chapter is to provide evidence concerning the extent of inefficiency in the transformation of human capital into earned income.[2] The estimation of potential, rather than average, earnings functions not only provides an opportunity for estimating the extent of labor market inefficiency but also suggests a reinterpretation of the typically weak explanatory power of average earnings functions. Specifically, our empirical results imply that a large part of the unexplained variance in earnings across individuals that is usually attributed to incomplete model

[1] We thank the U.S. Department of Labor for financial support under contract #41USC252C3 and Volker Pollman for expert research assistance.

[2] See van den Broek, Førsund, Hjalmarsson, and Meeusen (1980) for a similar study of technical inefficiency in the context of production frontiers.

specification or worker heterogeneity may be more properly ascribed to earnings inefficiency.

Two distinct earnings frontiers are estimated, using stochastic specifications that were originally devised for the case of production frontiers. In one specification, proposed by Greene (1980), the earnings frontier is deterministic, and differences between observed and (estimated) potential earnings are attributed to individual-specific ignorance (informational inefficiency) about rental rates for particular types of human capital. In the other approach, developed independently by Aigner, Lovell, and Schmidt (1977) and Meeusen and van den Broeck (1977), the earnings frontier is stochastic and deviations from the frontier represent not only informational deficiencies but also errors of model specification and data measurement. Under the maintained assumption that the disturbance distribution is correctly specified, the maximum likelihood (ML) estimators of the slope parameters of the earnings frontier will be asymptotically efficient relative to the ordinary least squares (OLS) estimator, since the former incorporates a priori information about the asymmetry of the distribution of the deviations from the frontier.

Data are taken from the Panel Study on Income Dynamics on male household heads who were unemployed at some time in 1980 but who were previously employed in 1979 and reemployed by 1981. Maximum potential earnings obtainable upon reemployment are specified to be a function of prior human capital investments, race, union membership, and variables which proxy the depreciation of general and specific skills occasioned, respectively, by time spent unemployed and by changes in occupation between jobs. The deterministic and stochastic earnings frontiers are estimated by ML methods and the results are compared with those obtained by OLS. We find that potential earnings are increased by schooling and by work experience, the latter at a diminishing rate. They are higher for whites than for nonwhites and for individuals who joined, left, or again found jobs with unionized employers after a spell of unemployment, compared with those who remained in the nonunion sector. Of special interest are our findings that time spent unemployed and a change of occupation between jobs reduce potential earnings. These results suggest that both general on-the-job skills and occupation-specific human capital are important determinants of the reward structure in the labor market.

The ML estimates of the slope parameters of the frontier are numerically very similar to each other and to the OLS estimates, as expected in light of the consistency of the OLS estimator and the large sample size. However, the gain in (asymptotic) efficiency of the deterministic frontier estimator relative to OLS is approximately 20 percent. The mean of the one-sided disturbance in the stochastic frontier is significantly different from the value (zero) imposed by OLS. Moreover, a decomposition of the error variance provided by estimates of the stochastic frontier implies that approximately one-fourth of the residual variance is due to earnings inefficiency and the rest is attributed to statistical noise.

The chapter is organized in the following way: Section 5.2 contains the deterministic and stochastic specifications of an earnings frontier and a discussion of appropriate estimation techniques. In Section 5.3, we describe the model of reemployment earnings and present the empirical results. Section 5.4 provides a summary of our findings and some concluding remarks.

5.2 The Model and Estimation Techniques

Following Becker and Chiswick (1966), Mincer (1974), and Heckman and Polachek (1974), let maximum potential earnings for the ith individual be given by the semilogarithmic human capital production function

$$\log_e E_i = \alpha + \beta^T X_i - \epsilon_i \qquad i = 1, \ldots, K \tag{5.1}$$

where E_i is observable earnings for the ith individual, X is a vector of explanatory variables, ϵ_i is a random disturbance, α is a fixed but unknown population intercept, β is a vector of fixed but unknown slope coefficients of the frontier, and K is the size of the sample. The systematic part of the model determines potential earnings for a given endowment of human capital (proxied by schooling, work experience, and the like), the depreciation of this capital caused by unemployment and changes in occupation, and the receipt of union or other rents. Hofler and Polachek (1985) argued that the random component differs from zero because of individual-specific deficiencies in the acquisition and utilization of labor market information. Since actual earnings cannot, by definition, exceed potential earnings, the disturbances are nonpositive, $-\epsilon_i \leq 0$. Conceptually, then, the potential earnings function defines a frontier which envelops the technically feasible (or informationally efficient) earnings associated with varying amounts of human capital inputs. As a consequence, the earnings frontier for an individual is analogous to a production frontier, introduced by Farrell (1957) to describe the efficient technology of a firm.

The earnings function specified in (5.1) has typically been interpreted as a reduced-form equation to be estimated by OLS. Indeed, even if the theoretical earnings equation is interpreted to be a "frontier" function, OLS provides a best linear unbiased and consistent estimate of the vector of slope coefficients, β. Moreover, the OLS estimator of β is asymptotically normally distributed and the conventionally calculated standard errors are correct so that hypothesis testing can be carried out in the usual manner. However, the OLS estimator of α is biased and inconsistent, since the mean of ϵ_i is nonzero.[3] Moreover, the OLS estimator of β will, in general, be less efficient than an alternative estimator that incorporates the a priori information that the distribution of ϵ is asymmetric.

Greene (1980) proposed the gamma distribution as a characterization of the

---

[3] As Schmidt (1976) demonstrated, however, the OLS estimator of α is the best linear unbiased estimator of $[\alpha + E(\epsilon)]$.

disturbance term of the frontier model. If ϵ is assumed to be a gamma-distributed random variable, then the probability density function is

$$f(\epsilon) = G(\lambda_1, P) = \frac{\lambda_1^P}{\Gamma(P)} \epsilon^{P-1} e^{-\lambda_1 \epsilon} \tag{5.2}$$

where $\epsilon \geq 0$, and $\lambda_1 > 0$ is the "scale" parameter. The "shape" parameter (P) of the gamma density is restricted to be greater than 2 in order to satisfy the regularity conditions established by Greene (1980). Since the gamma distribution is asymmetric, ML estimation of the parameters of the log-likelihood function

$$\begin{aligned}
\log_e L = {} & KP \log_e \lambda_1 - K \log_e \Gamma(P) \\
& + (P-1) \sum_i \log_e (\log_e E_i - \alpha - \beta^T X_i) \\
& - \lambda_1 \sum_i (\log_e E_i - \alpha - \beta^T X_i)
\end{aligned} \tag{5.3}$$

is more efficient than estimation with OLS, which does not incorporate the asymmetry. In particular, the gain in efficiency obtained by using ML rather than OLS is a function of the degree of skewness of the distribution of the error term, which is an empirical matter. Since the coefficient of skewness for the gamma distribution is $2P^{-1/2}$, the efficiency of ML relative to OLS increases as $P \to 2$. Indeed, the value of the statistic $p = P/(P-2)$ is a measure of the relative (asymptotic) efficiency of ML over OLS in the gamma frontier model. When P is large, the error distribution is almost symmetric and $p \to 1$, which implies that ML offers little gain in efficiency relative to OLS. In this case, the ML estimates of β will be similar to the OLS estimates in magnitude and efficiency and the OLS estimator of α is consistent. Alternatively, as $P \to 2, p \to \infty$ and the observations on earnings tend to be grouped near the frontier, implying that the distribution of the error term is highly skewed. In this situation, the ML estimator of the slope coefficients will be efficient relative to OLS. Finally, in the limiting (and inadmissible) case of $P = 2$, the matrix of second derivatives of the likelihood function is singular and asymptotic standard errors cannot be calculated.

The assumption that the disturbance in the earnings frontier has a gamma distribution constrains the observations on individual earnings to lie on or below the frontier. This feature of Greene's (1980) model accords with the *theoretical* concept of a frontier as an upper bound for the actual values of the dependent variable. As a practical framework for modeling the observed values of labor market earnings, however, this approach is rather restrictive since the underlying frontier is assumed to be deterministic. As a consequence, deviations of observed from estimated potential earnings are attributed entirely to earnings (informational) inefficiency. Of course, econometric models in general and earnings functions in particular are typically underspecified, and earnings data suffer from errors of measurement. Thus, a deterministic earnings frontier like Equation (5.1) may confound earnings inefficiency arising from incomplete labor market information with the effects of specification and measurement errors.

Aigner, Lovell, and Schmidt (1977) proposed a composite disturbance structure for the frontier model in which one normally distributed component represents specification and measurement errors and the other, half-normally distributed disturbance term captures inefficiency. This "stochastic frontier" model has been implemented previously in an earnings function context by Hofler and Polachek (1985), Herzog, Hofler, and Schlottmann (1985), and Robinson and Wunnava (1989). The stochastic earnings frontier may be written

$$\log_e E_i = \alpha + \beta^T X_i + \nu_i - \mu_i \qquad i = 1, \ldots, K \tag{5.4}$$

where ν is assumed to be a normally distributed random variable with mean zero and variance σ_ν^2, while μ has the half-normal distribution

$$f(\mu) = \frac{\sqrt{2}}{\sigma_\mu \sqrt{\pi}} e^{-\mu^2/2\sigma_\mu^2} \tag{5.5}$$

where $\mu \geq 0$ and $\sigma_\mu^2 > 0$. Thus, the earnings frontier itself is stochastic (and given by $\alpha + \beta^T X + \nu$), in recognition of the effects of specification and measurement errors which cause the location of the deterministic kernel ($\alpha + \beta^T X$) of the frontier to vary across individuals. Deficiencies in labor market information relative to this stochastic earnings frontier are then captured by the one-sided error component $\mu \geq 0$. Estimation of the parameters of this model can be accomplished by maximizing the likelihood function

$$\log_e \mathcal{L} = K \log_e \frac{\sqrt{2}}{\sqrt{\pi}} + K \log_e \sigma^{-1} + \sum_i \log_e[1 - F^*(\eta \lambda_2 \sigma^{-1})]$$

$$- \frac{1}{2\sigma^2} \sum_i (\log_e E_i - \alpha - \beta^T X_i)^2 \tag{5.6}$$

where $F^*(\cdot)$ is the standard normal distribution function, $\sigma^2 \equiv \sigma_\eta^2 = \sigma_\nu^2 + \sigma_\mu^2$, $\lambda_2 = \sigma_\mu/\sigma_\nu$, and $\eta = \nu - \mu$.

Although the stochastic earnings frontier represents a useful generalization of the deterministic framework, it has three shortcomings. First, since the stochastic frontier model does not constrain the observations to lie on or below the estimated frontier (so that large positive sample values of ν can be accommodated), the theoretical concept of *potential* earnings as an upper bound for *observed* earnings is compromised.[4] Second, there is no one preferred method for obtaining individual-specific estimates of labor market ignorance in this model since the composite residual for each observation cannot be uniquely decomposed.[5] Finally, for applications such as potential earnings functions in which the systematic component of the model is typically underspecified (and the explained variance in earnings is therefore low), the two-sided residuals will dominate the one-sided residuals in absolute magnitude. In this situation, existing algorithms may have difficulty identifying the one-sided component and, within standard tolerance levels, OLS may be maximum likelihood. Fortunately, for the data and model specification used in the present study, the stochastic frontier method was computationally feasible. In general, feasibility is a feature of both the model and the data.

In short, both the deterministic and stochastic frontier models have strengths and weaknesses as frameworks for the estimation of potential earnings functions. As a result, empirical evidence is required to shed light on their relative performance.

5.3 Empirical Results

Specification of the earnings frontier equation (5.1) follows the standard human capital approach, augmented by variables which capture changes in union status and changes in occupation, as well as a proxy for the depreciation of general skills occasioned by time spent unemployed. The vector of explanatory variables (X) is composed of proxies for individual productivity, years of schooling completed (SCH) and work experience (EXP), and a variable (RACE) that captures black-white differences in potential earnings associated with labor market discrimination and unobserved heterogeneity in the quality of human capital investments. The variable EXP is also entered in quadratic form (EXPSQ) in order to allow for diminishing returns to work experience. Separate dichotomous variables indicate whether an individual became a union member (UJOIN), left union membership (ULEAVE), or remained a member of a union (USTAY) as a result of his change of job. The omitted category contains those individuals who remained in the nonunion sector. A dichotomous variable (MAR) is included to control for marital status which, according to Becker (1981) and Kenny (1983), may proxy the degree of specialization in market

---

[4] Polachek and Yoon (1987) developed a model of earnings in which both employee and *employer* ignorance is allowed. With this "two-tiered" approach, one-sided disturbances representing informational inefficiencies on the supply and demand sides of the labor market are combined with a two-sided error that captures specification and measurement errors. However, in this three-component model of the error structure, the analogy between production frontiers (maximum output) and earnings frontiers (potential earnings) breaks down.

[5] Jondrow, Lovell, Materov, and Schmidt (1982) proposed estimating the inefficiency associated with each observation by the expectation of μ, conditional on $(\nu - \mu)$. Waldman (1984) provided evidence that this (nonlinear) estimator is preferred to two linear estimators with respect to measuring the relative inefficiency of the observations. However, the variance of the distribution of this estimator does not vanish as sample size increases, so the estimator is inconsistent.

work relative to home production and therefore affect potential (market) earnings. Human capital accumulated on a previous job may be specific to an occupation so that changes in occupation may result in the loss of potential earnings. Accordingly, a dummy variable (OCCH) is included to represent a change in occupation across one-digit classifications. Finally, to capture the notion that time spent unemployed depreciates general workplace skills and, thus, potential earnings, a variable measuring hours of unemployment between jobs (DUR) is included in the potential earnings equation.[6]

The systematic component of the earnings frontier model can be written

$$\log_e \text{POSTE} = \alpha + \beta_1 \text{SCH} + \beta_2 \text{EXP} + \beta_3 \text{EXPSQ} + \beta_4 \text{RACE}$$
$$+ \beta_5 \text{UJOIN} + \beta_6 \text{ULEAVE} + \beta_7 \text{USTAY}$$
$$+ \beta_8 \text{MAR} + \beta_9 \text{OCCH} + \beta_{10} \text{DUR} \tag{5.7}$$

where POSTE denotes average hourly reemployment earnings. Years of schooling completed and years of full-time work experience are, of course, expected to be positively related to potential earnings so the coefficients of these variables (β_1 and β_2, respectively) should be positive. If, as expected, additional years of work experience have a diminishing effect on potential earnings, then the coefficient on EXPSQ (β_3) will be negative. The RACE variable is defined to be equal to 1 if the individual is white and O otherwise. Whites are hypothesized to have higher potential earnings than blacks, even after controlling for observable differences in earnings-enhancing attributes, because of labor market discrimination and unmeasured racial heterogeneity in the quality of human capital investments. The coefficient on the RACE variable (β_4) is, therefore, expected to be positive. Persons who become union members (UJOIN) are expected to have higher potential earnings relative to those who were not in a union in their previous jobs and are not now union members (the reference group). This may arise either because of the monopoly rents accruing to individuals in unionized jobs or because unionized employers compensate their workers for skills unobserved by the researcher [Mellow (1981)], or both. As a consequence, the coefficient on UJOIN (β_5) is expected to be positive. Following this line of argument, then, one might expect individuals who leave union membership (ULEAVE) to have their potential earnings reduced, relative to those who join unions (UJOIN) or retain union status upon reemployment (USTAY). There is evidence [Mellow (1981)], however, that prior union premiums (whether rents or productivity payments) are not completely extinguished upon reemployment in the nonunion sector. Therefore, in comparison with persons in the reference group who remained in nonunion jobs, we would expect that those who have left union employment would have higher potential earnings so that β_6 would be positive. Of course, relative to this same reference group, individuals who were union members

[6] Lazear (1976), Kiker and Roberts (1984), Mincer and Ofek (1982), and Madden (1987).

prior to unemployment are expected to have higher potential earnings, implying that β_7 will be positive. Married males have higher labor market earnings than single males, other things equal, so that the coefficient on MAR (β_8) should be positive. This empirical phenomenon may reflect a combination of assortive mating [Becker (1981)]—that is, the better labor market prospects are more likely to be married at any age—and the greater incentive that married men have to accumulate human capital on the job [Kenny (1983)]. Individuals who change occupations suffer a reduction in potential earnings associated with the human capital investment that was specific to the previous occupation. Consequently, the coefficient on the OCCH variable (β_9) is expected to be negative. Finally, human capital theory predicts that time spent unemployed reduces potential earnings on the subsequent job, as a result of the deterioration of general workplace skills. Thus, the coefficient on DUR is expected to be negative.

Data for this study were taken from the Panel Study of Income Dynamics (PSID) on male household heads who were unemployed at some time during 1980 but who were employed in both 1979 and 1981. After deleting individuals from the sample for whom missing values of one or more of the variables existed, we were left with 337 observations. Sample means and definitions of the variables are given in Table 5.1. Approximately 59 percent of the household heads in the sample are white. On average, they have completed about $11\frac{1}{2}$ years of schooling and have accumulated almost 12 years of full-time work experience; 31 percent are married and approximately 37 percent experienced a change in occupation upon reemployment. While 32 percent of the previously unionized individuals in the sample were able to renter the union sector, 8 percent who were union members moved to nonunion jobs, and the same proportion found union jobs after a previous stint of nonunion employment. The mean duration of the unemployment experienced between jobs was approximately 10 weeks. Average hourly earnings on the post-unemployment job was $7.35.

Table 5.1 Means and Definitions of Variables

Variable	Mean	Definition*
SCH	11.41	Number of grades in school completed.
EXP	11.81	Full-time work experience in years.
RACE	.59	Equals 1 if white; 0 otherwise.
UJOIN	.08	Equals 1 if union member in 1981 and not a union member in 1979; 0 otherwise.
UNLEAVE	.08	Equals 1 if not a union member in 1981 and union member in 1979; 0 otherwise.
USTAY	.32	Equals 1 if union member in 1981 and union member in 1979; 0 otherwise.
MAR	.31	Equals 1 if married and wife present; 0 otherwise.
OCCH	.37	Equals 1 if one-digit occupation in 1981 is different from that of 1979; 0 otherwise.
DUR	397.34	Hours of unemployment.
POSTE	7.35	Income from wages and salaries divided by annual hours of work, 1981.

*Observations were recorded for the year 1980, unless otherwise indicated.

Table 5.2 contains the estimates of the earnings frontier (5.7) obtained by OLS and the two ML (deterministic and stochastic frontier) methods. The OLS results are reported in column 1 and are broadly consistent with theoretical expectations. Potential earnings are higher for whites than nonwhites,[7] enhanced by additional schooling and work experience, and diminished both by time spent unemployed between jobs and by a change in occupation upon reemployment. The return to experience is non-linear, declining with additional years of work. Relative to individuals who worked in nonunion jobs before and after unemployment, those who joined, left, or remained with unionized employers had higher potential earnings. Married individuals had higher earnings than their single counterparts, but the sample size is not large enough to estimate this effect precisely. As a consequence, potential earnings cannot be distinguished by marital status with these data. Finally, the overall goodness-of-fit of the model (as indicated by $\bar{R}^2 = .43$) is quite satisfactory, given the unobserved heterogeneity that characterizes earnings potential across individuals.

Maximum likelihood estimates of the earnings frontiers are presented in columns 2 and 3 of Table 5.2. Column 2 reports the results of estimating the deterministic model, based on the assumption that the (one-sided) error term has a gamma distribution. Column 3 records the parameter estimates based on the stochastic frontier model in which the composite disturbance has a two-sided, normally distributed (noise) component and a one-sided, half-normally distributed (inefficiency) term. The estimated slope coefficients obtained with the two ML procedures are strikingly similar to those generated by OLS, a result which is not entirely surprising in view of the consistency of the OLS estimator of β and the relatively large size of the sample. However, the OLS estimator of the intercept is inconsistent and that partly explains the divergence between the OLS and ML point estimates of α.[8]

The principal statistical advantage of ML estimation of the earnings frontier is an expected gain in efficiency, since both the gamma and composite specifications of the error distribution incorporate a priori information regarding the asymmetry of the disturbances. Evidence on the efficiency, relative to OLS, of the ML estimator based on the gamma-distributed error term can be gleaned from the sample value of the test statistic $p = P/(P - 2)$. Since $\hat{P} = 9.726$, $\hat{p} = 1.259$ so there is approximately a 21 percent gain in efficiency from using the gamma-distributed error assumption rather than the normally distributed disturbance of the OLS model. An assessment of the ML estimator of the stochastic frontier relative to OLS can proceed as follows. The estimated mean of the one-sided disturbance, $E(\mu)$, is .196 with an associated estimated t-statistic of 2.607, implying a rejection of the OLS estimator for which $E(\mu) \equiv 0$. Similarly, the sample estimate of $\lambda_2 = \sigma_\mu/\sigma_\nu$ is .803 with an estimated t-statistic of 2.059, suggesting $\sigma_\mu > 0$ and the conclusion that ML is relatively

---

[7] This estimated racial differential in potential earnings is comparable in magnitude to the differentials in observed earnings reported by Hoffman and Link (1984).

[8] Note that the OLS estimate of α plus the mean of ϵ equals the ML estimate of α in the deterministic frontier. Also, as expected, $\hat{\alpha}_{OLS} < \hat{\alpha}_{ALS} < \hat{\alpha}_\Gamma$.

Table 5.2 Empirical Results*

Variable**	(1) OLS	(2) ML Deterministic	(3) ML Stochastic
Constant	1.180 (9.759)	2.253 (11.101)	1.360 (9.879)
SCH	.040 (4.662)	.041 (5.240)	.042 (4.597)
EXP	.015 (4.538)	.015 (5.096)	.015 (3.795)
EXPSQ	-1.574×10^{-4} (3.438)	-1.407×10^{-4} (3.443)	-1.593×10^{-4} (2.171)
RACE	.168 (4.122)	.168 (4.623)	.168 (3.857)
UJOIN	.408 (5.668)	.399 (6.129)	.402 (4.896)
ULEAVE	.247 (3.459)	.247 (3.877)	.246 (3.911)
USTAY	.445 (10.080)	.445 (11.290)	.439 (9.257)
MAR	.041 (0.801)	.041 (0.901)	.043 (0.837)
OCCH	$-.095$ (2.306)	$-.095$ (2.584)	$-.095$ (2.350)
DUR	-1.899×10^{-4} (3.320)	-1.906×10^{-4} (4.302)	-1.887×10^{-4} (3.774)
R^2	.428		
λ_1		9.038 (4.972)	
P		9.726 (2.823)	
$E(\epsilon)$		1.076 (6.192)	
σ_ϵ^2		.119 (11.484)	
σ_η^2			.153 (10.689)
λ_2			.083 (2.059)
$E(\mu)$			.196 (2.607)
σ_μ^2			.060 (1.304)

*Absolute values of estimated (asymptotic) t-ratios are in parentheses.

**The dependent variable is $\log_e$ POSTE

efficient. However, the confidence with which these inferences are made should be tempered by Greene's observation in Section 2.4.2 that the usual t-tests of statistical significance are suspect here since the value of $E(\mu)$ and λ_2 under the null hypothesis (zero) is at the boundary of the parameter space.

It is difficult to make a rigorous comparison of the statistical performances of the two ML estimators, based on the results reported in Table 5.2, since their likelihood functions are not nested.[9] On theoretical grounds, however, the stochastic frontier would seem to have one important advantage over the deterministic specification, since the latter confounds (two-sided) noise arising from specification and measurement error with (one-sided) deviations from the fitted frontier attributed to earnings inefficiency. Evidence of the extent to which the deterministic approach overstates average inefficiency in this way can be obtained by comparing the estimated means of the one-sided errors reported in Table 5.2.[10] The estimated mean of the gamma-distributed error in the deterministic frontier model is $\hat{E}(\epsilon) = 1.076$, which translates into an average inefficiency of \$2.93 per hour. Evaluated as a percentage of mean potential earnings (\$10.28 = \$7.35 + \$2.93), the inefficiency attributed to labor market ignorance is approximately 28 percent. In contrast, the estimated mean of the half-normally distributed error in the stochastic frontier model is $\hat{E}(\mu) = .196$, which represents an average inefficiency of \$1.22 per hour or about 14 percent below estimated potential earnings (\$8.57 = \$7.35 + 1.22). From these results, we infer that the deterministic approach overestimates the average extent of labor market inefficiency (or, equivalently, mean potential earnings) by \$1.71 per hour, relative to the stochastic frontier specification.

At one extreme, of course, the OLS estimator embodies the implicit assumption that labor market inefficiency is nonexistent and that all deviations of observed earnings from predicted earnings can be ascribed to errors of model specification or data measurement. At the other extreme, the deterministic frontier model attributes all deviations from the estimated frontier to inefficiency. It is instructive, therefore, to examine the variance decomposition provided by estimates of the stochastic frontier, since the latter allows for both noise and inefficiency. The estimated variance of the composite error (σ_η^2) is .153 and, under the maintained assumption of the independence of the one-sided and two-sided error components, the estimate of the variance of the noise is .093. However, the variance of the one-sided disturbance is not $\sigma_\mu^2 = \sigma_\eta^2 - \sigma_\nu^2$ but rather $[(\pi/2) - 1]\sigma_\mu^2$, as Greene points out in Section 2.4.2. Hence, the contribution of the variance of μ to the total variance is $[(\pi/2) - 1]\sigma_\mu^2/\{\sigma_\nu^2 + [(\pi/2) - 1]\sigma_\mu^2\}$. As a consequence, approximately 27 percent

---

[9] One possible criterion for comparative evaluation would be extra-sample predictive power but that is beyond the scope of the present chapter. Another approach is the use of non-nested hypothesis testing procedures of the sort discussed by McAleer and Pesaran (1986). However, Judge, Hill, Griffiths, Lutkepohl, and Lee (1988, p. 852) conclude that these procedures should not be used for the purpose of model selection until more is known about the sampling properties of the resulting estimation rules.

[10] Alternatively, one may compare the estimated values of the intercepts, since $\alpha_{ALS} - \alpha_\Gamma = E(\epsilon) - E(\mu)$. Similarly, since $E(\upsilon) = 0$, $\alpha_{OLS} - \alpha_{ALS} = E(\mu)$.

of the estimated variance of the composite error is assigned to earnings inefficiency, while the remaining 73 percent represents unexplained variability. One interpretation of these results is that a substantial portion of the unexplained variance in estimated earnings functions—heretofore ascribed to model underspecification, unobserved heterogeneity, and data mismeasurement—may be due to information deficiencies in the labor market.

5.4 Concluding Remarks

This chapter has provided evidence on the extent of technical inefficiency in the transformation of human capital into earned income. Two stochastically distinct earnings frontiers were estimated by maximum likelihood, and the results were compared with ordinary least squares estimates of an average earnings equation. The ML estimates exhibit statistically significant (asymptotic) efficiency gains relative to OLS. Moreover, the estimated mean levels of earnings inefficiency are substantial in magnitude, ranging from 14 to 28 percent of estimated potential earnings. Estimates of the stochastic earnings frontier imply that approximately one-fourth of the unexplained variance in earnings across individuals may be ascribed to earnings inefficiency.

Several alternative specifications of frontiers merit consideration for application in an earnings function context. For example, one of the estimators described by Schmidt and Sickles (1984) might be used for the earnings frontier problem when panel data are available. This approach would be especially valuable if individual effects arising from heterogeneity are deemed important. Moreover, other specifications of inefficiency, such as the gamma, exponential and truncated-normal distributions discussed by Greene (1990) and in Section 2.4.2, could be explored in a stochastic frontier framework. It might then be worthwhile to examine the sensitivity of estimates of earnings inefficiency to different parameterizations. These possible extensions merely illustrate the myriad avenues for obtaining improved estimates of earnings potential and earnings inefficiency with advanced methods of frontier analysis.

REFERENCES

Aigner, D. J., C. A. K. Lovell, and P. Schmidt (1977), "Formulation and Estimation of Stochastic Frontier Production Function Models," *Journal of Econometrics* 6(1)(July): 21–37.

Becker, G. S. (1981), *A Treatise on the Family*. Cambridge: Harvard University Press.

Becker, G. S., and B. R. Chiswick (1966), "Education and the Distribution of Earnings," *American Economic Review* 56(2)(May): 358–369.

Farrell, M. J. (1957), "The Measurement of Productive Efficiency," *Journal of the Royal Statistical Society* Series A, General, 120: 253–281.

Greene, W. H. (1980), "Maximum Likelihood Estimation of Econometric Frontier Functions," *Journal of Econometrics* 13(1)(May): 27–56.

Greene, W. H. (1990), "A Gamma Distributed Stochastic Frontier Model," *Journal of Econometrics* 46(1/2)(October/November): 141–163.

Heckman, J., and S. Polachek (1974), "Empirical Evidence on the Functional Form of the Earnings-Schooling Relationship," *Journal of the American Statistical Association* 69(2)(June): 350–354.

Herzog, H. W., Jr., R. A. Hofler, and A. M. Schlottmann (1985), "Life on the Frontier: Migrant Information, Earnings and Past Mobility," *Review of Economics and Statistics* 67(3)(August): 373–382.

Hoffman, S. D., and C. R. Link (1984), "Selectivity Bias in Male Wage Equations: Black-White Comparisons," *Review of Economics and Statistics* 66(2)(May): 320–324.

Hofler, R. A., and S. Polachek (1985), "A New Approach for Measuring Wage Ignorance in the Labor Market," *Journal of Economics and Business* 37(3)(August): 267–276.

Jondrow, J., C. A. K. Lovell, I. S. Materov, and P. Schmidt (1982), "On the Estimation of Technical Inefficiency in the Stochastic Frontier Production Function Model," *Journal of Econometrics* 19(2/3)(August): 233–238.

Judge, G. G., R. C. Hill, W. E. Griffiths, H. Lutkepohl, and T.-C. Lee (1988), *Introduction to the Theory and Practice of Econometrics*, 2d ed. New York: John Wiley & Sons.

Kenny, L. W. (1983), "The Accumulation of Human Capital During Marriage by Males," *Economic Inquiry* 21(2)(April): 223–231.

Kiker, B. F., and R. B. Roberts (1984), "The Durability of Human Capital: Some New Evidence," *Economic Inquiry* 22(2)(April): 269–281.

Lazear, E. (1976), "Age, Experience, and Wage Growth," *American Economic Review* 66(4) (September): 548–558.

Madden, J. F. (1987), "Gender Differences in the Cost of Displacement: An Empirical Test of Discrimination in the Labor Market," *American Economic Review* 77(2)(May): 246–251.

McAleer, M., and M. H. Pesaran (1986), "Statistical Inference in Non-nested Econometric Models," *Applied Mathematics and Computation* 20(3/4)(November): 271–311.

Meeusen, W., and J. van den Broeck (1977), "Efficiency Estimation from Cobb-Douglas Production Functions with Composed Error," *International Economic Review* 18(2)(June): 435–444.

Mellow, W. (1981), "Unionism and Wages: A Longitudinal Analysis," *Review of Economics and Statistics* 63(1)(February): 43–52.

Mincer, J. (1974), *Schooling, Experience and Earnings*. New York: Columbia University Press.

Mincer, J., and H. Ofek (1982), "Interrupted Work Careers: Depreciation and Restoration of Human Capital," *Journal of Human Resources* 17(1)(Winter): 3–24.

Polachek, S. W., and B. J. Yoon (1987), "A Two-Tiered Earnings Frontier Estimation of Employer and Employee Information in the Labor Market," *Review of Economics and Statistics* 69(2)(May): 296–302.

Robinson, M. D., and P. V. Wunnava (1989), "Measuring Direct Discrimination in Labor Markets Using a Frontier Approach: Evidence from CPS Female Earnings Data," *Southern Economic Journal* 56(2)(July): 212–218.

Schmidt, P. (1976), "On the Statistical Estimation of Parametric Frontier Production Functions," *Review of Economics and Statistics* 58(2)(May): 38–239.

Schmidt, P., and R. C. Sickles (1984), "Production Frontiers and Panel Data," *Journal of Business and Economic Statistics* 21(4)(October): 367–374.

van den Broeck, J., F. R. Førsund, L. Hjalmarsson, and W. Meeusen (1980), "On the Estimation of Deterministic and Stochastic Frontier Production Functions: A Comparison," *Journal of Econometrics* 13(1)(May): 117–138.

Varian, H. R. (1984), *Microeconomic Analysis*, 2d ed. New York: W. W. Norton.

Waldman, D. M. (1984), "Properties of Technical Efficiency Estimators in the Stochastic Frontier Model," *Journal of Econometrics* 25(3)(July): 353–364.

6

UNIONIZATION AND PRODUCTIVE EFFICIENCY[1]

Linda Cavalluzzo and Dennis Baldwin

The theoretical definition of a production function expressing the maximum amount of output obtainable from given input bundles with fixed technology has been accepted for many decades. And for almost as long, econometricians have been estimating average production functions.

Aigner, Lovell, and Schmidt (1977, p. 21)

6.1 Introduction

Wage premiums that accrue to unionized workers are well established in the empirical literature [Lewis (1963, 1986)]. By contrast, no clear consensus has emerged on the role played by unions in improving productivity. Freeman and Medoff (1984) report that productivity is generally (though not always) higher in unionized establishments. More recently, Addison and Hirsch (1989), sorted through statistical pitfalls and selected empirical works to conclude that the evidence on union productivity is mixed. Productivity advantages seem to be greatest in competitive settings and in industries where wage differentials are largest. But on average, they conclude, unions do not significantly raise productivity.

One drawback of the existing literature on union–nonunion productivity differentials is the pervasive attention to average rather than best-practice production processes. This focus may systematically understate the output obtainable from a given set of inputs. Moreover, productivity differentials heretofore reported in the literature reflect differences in union–nonunion performance among average production units in each sector. But measurements of average differences in cross-sectional studies may provide misleading indicators of potential marketwide differences, since

[1] We are grateful to Steven Allen, who generously provided us with his data, and William Greene, who provided many useful comments.

the least efficient production units can be expected to drop out of competitive markets [Addison and Hirsch (1989, p.100)]. Both these difficulties can be addressed by estimating a production frontier.

The present chapter analyzes differences in productivity across union and nonunion projects in office building construction. These data were originally examined by Allen (1986), who used OLS estimators. We successfully replicate Allen's results and provide evidence that the OLS residuals are negatively skewed, rather than normally distributed. This result is consistent with the presence of inefficient projects in the data sample and suggests that the production function is more properly specified as a stochastic frontier. In subsequent work, we specify a compound error and assume that the inefficient component of the error follows a half-normal distribution. We then compare our results to OLS estimates for several alternative specifications of the model.

It is well known that estimates of the intercept derived from the OLS estimator are biased downward if the disturbance has a negative expected value. Consequently, predictions from the model will underestimate the production potential of any given input bundle. Our results bear this out. In every model examined, we obtain larger point estimates of the intercept using the frontier model. Moreover, the estimated union effect obtained via maximum likelihood exceeds the OLS estimate in each case. Remaining estimates of the production function parameters are generally similar. We note, however, that under the maintained assumption regarding the error distribution, the maximum likelihood estimator is generally more efficient than OLS [Greene (1990, p.328)].

Decomposition of the residuals allows us to separate estimates of white noise in the data from estimates of the one-sided disturbances that act to prevent projects from reaching their productive potential. Sources of the one-sided disturbances are not accounted for elsewhere in the model and are generally taken as estimates of the level of managerial or organizational inefficiency in production. Of course, other factors may help to explain the inefficiency estimates and we examine several possibilities.

Like Allen, we find that unions do indeed enhance productivity in construction. Further, we find that the productivity advantage is more pronounced when a stochastic frontier model is specified. Estimates of the union advantage rise from 28 to 38 percent when we move from the OLS to the stochastic frontier model. Our estimates of average proportional efficiency in building construction range from .65 to .82, depending on the distribution selected to describe the inefficient component of the error and from .73 to .89, when differences in the characteristics of each project are taken into account.

Section 6.2 discusses factors that may lead to union productivity differentials in construction. We discuss the empirical specification of the model and describe our data in Section 6.3. We report empirical results in Section 6.4 and conclude in Section 6.5.

6.2 Union Productivity Differentials in Construction

Price-theoretic causes of union productivity differentials arise from union wage premiums. Specifically, if union workers are to receive a wage premium, then profit-maximizing employers, operating on their demand curve in competitive environments, must raise the value of marginal product of labor to match the higher wage. This may be done by raising the capital-labor ratio or by hiring higher-quality labor. In other words, even if unionization has no intrinsic benefits in production, we may observe productivity differences across sectors [Reynolds (1986)]. If we are to gain insights into union-caused productivity effects, we first need to control for these price-theoretic differences.

Allen (1984) presents five institutional factors that may lead to productivity differences between union and open-shop contractors in the construction industry. These include union hiring halls, apprenticeship programs, and managerial shock effects, each of which should raise union productivity, and work rules and craft jurisdictions, which should reduce it.

Construction is characterized by volatile labor demand. More important than the macroeconomic effects of the business cycle, individual construction projects proceed in a sequence that creates fluctuations in demand for workers with specific types of skills over the life of a project. As a result, demand by individual employers tends to be brief and sporadic. The building trades unions, through a mechanism known as the hiring hall, benefit both unionized workers and contractors by sharply reducing search costs. In addition, confidence in the ability to obtain skilled labor on demand allows contractors to tighten schedules and tailor labor hours to the needs of the project. Tighter scheduling can lead in turn to reduced costs for renting heavy equipment, material inventories, and interest expense [Allen (1987)]. These forces may act to improve productivity and cost efficiency within the unionized sector.

Because most of the benefits of on-the-job training in construction are easily transported to other employers, human capital models predict that the full cost of training will be borne by the employee. Apprenticeship programs spread costs among labor, contractors, and government [Allen (1984, p.253)]. This cost-sharing mechanism creates training incentives that should raise productivity in the unionized sector. Because apprenticeship programs provide well-rounded training within a trade, union contractors may also require fewer supervisors, which should further stimulate productivity.

A third potential source of union productivity advantage comes from improved management practices which are thought to attend unionization. Presented with increased labor costs and the prospect of reduced profits, managers operating in competitive environments are "shocked" into more efficient behavior, according to this theory. If the theory is correct, technical inefficiency may well be lower in the union sector.

By contrast, craft jurisdictions and work rules are two widely publicized institutions that act to reduce labor productivity in the union sector. Union work rules may include excessive crew size requirements or restrictions on the use of labor-saving devices like prefabricated components. Jurisdictional rules, which restrict tasks to specific trade unions, may add unnecessary labor hours to projects as laborers from one craft union wait for laborers from another to complete a possibly simple task that overlaps into another jurisdiction. Taken together, these two institutions may reduce labor productivity and increase technical inefficiency in production. The net effect of unionization on productivity, then, is an empirical question.

6.3 Empirical Specification

Following Allen (1986), we begin with a Cobb-Douglas production function,

$$Q_i = AK_i^\alpha L_i^\beta \qquad i = 1, \ldots, 83 \tag{6.1}$$

where Q_i is square feet, A is a constant reflecting organizational factors and other controls, K_i measures capital input, L_i is labor input, α is the elasticity of output with respect to capital, β is the elasticity of output with respect to labor, and $(\alpha + \beta)$ measures returns-to-scale. We divide (6.1) by L_i and take logarithms to get

$$\ln \frac{Q_i}{L_i} = \ln A + \alpha \ln \frac{K_i}{L_i} + (\alpha + \beta - 1) \ln L_i \tag{6.2}$$

Allen controls for labor quality with the addition of W_i, the predicted annual income for the labor force on a particular project. Price-theoretic effects of unionization are measured in terms of changes in K_i/L_i and adjustments to labor quality. Organizational and labor relations impacts of unionization are captured through the variable U_i, equal to 1 for unionized projects and 0 otherwise. The estimating equation becomes

$$\ln \frac{Q_i}{L_i} = \ln A_n + \alpha \ln \frac{K_i}{L_i} + (\alpha + \beta - 1) \ln L_i$$
$$+ \delta \ln W_i + b_1 U_i + e_i \tag{6.3}$$

where δ is the elasticity of productivity with respect to labor quality, $\ln A_n$ is the intercept for nonunion projects, $(\ln A_n + b_1)$ is the intercept for union projects, and $e_i \sim N(O, \sigma_e^2)$.

In order to use the standard errors that result from OLS estimation for accurate tests of statistical significance, one must assume that the error is distributed independently and identically (iid) normal. If the data contain inefficient projects, however, the error is likely to be negatively skewed, causing the assumption of normality to be violated.

Following Aigner, Lovell, and Schmidt (1977), we redefine the error structure e_i as the sum of two components,

$$e_i = u_i + v_i \qquad (6.4)$$

where $v_i \sim N(o, \sigma_v^2)$ and u_i, the inefficiency component, is assumed to be distributed independently of v_i and the regressors and to be drawn from a normal distribution with mean zero and constant variance (σ_u^2) truncated from above at zero.

This more general specification of the error has several advantages. The model provides a better description of the underlying theory that it is intended to represent. Rather than focusing on estimates of the average relationship between inputs and outputs, the frontier model redirects our attention to the best-practice relationship between inputs and outputs. Projects that fall below the frontier are considered to be technically inefficient and the *degree* of their inefficiency can be estimated under appropriate assumptions. With this information in hand, one may return to the data to investigate the *sources* of inefficiency. But even if no subsequent investigation takes place, use of the compound error structure incorporates a priori information into the model that will improve the efficiency of the parameter estimates.

We use data originally compiled by the U.S. Census Bureau as part of the Bureau of Labor Statistics (BLS) Construction Labor and Materials Requirements series to test the models. The BLS sample contains projects completed between May 1, 1973 and August 1, 1974 that are valued at $100,000 or more. The sample is stratified by geographic location and cost class.

Among the 83 projects contained in the sample, 64 are unionized and 19 are not. We define a unionized project as one that used 50 percent or more union labor. Buildings range in size from 3000 to 1.7 million square feet. The 30 smallest projects, those 16,000 square feet or less, are evenly split between union and nonunion labor. Each of the 16 biggest projects is unionized.

In addition to information on building characteristics, the data set contains information on capital expenditures, labor hours, and a number of factors that may influence productivity. Capital inputs are based on on-site expenditures and include depreciation or rental cost plus interest expense incurred on money borrowed for the contract. Labor inputs are given by total on-site hours. Virtually all these hours are for production workers. Off-site hours and off-site capital expenditures are unobserved.

6.4 Empirical Tests

We successfully replicate Allen's original results in column 1 of Table 6.1. Our initial interest is in the distribution of the residuals that result from the OLS model. Following Schmidt and Lin (1984), we conduct a simple test for existence of technical inefficiency that can be carried out on the second (m_2) and third (m_3) moments of

Table 6.1   Production Function Estimates*

		Model			
		(1)	**(2)**	**(3)**	**(4)**
Variable	**Parameter**	**OLS**	**ALS**	**OLS**	**ALS**
Intercept	$\ln A_n$	−6.86	−1.84	−6.98	−1.63
		(.75)	(.18)	(.75)	(.15)
$\ln (K/L)$	α	.194	.204	.198	.195
		(2.58)	(3.57)	(2.55)	(2.70)
$\ln$ (LHRS)	$\alpha + \beta - 1$	−.118	−.127	−.122	−.130
		(3.45)	(3.41)	(3.49)	(3.50)
Union	b_1	.308	.373	.305	.369
		(2.35)	(2.68)	(2.27)	(2.54)
$\ln W$	δ	.916	.393	.936	.375
		(.874)	(.329)	(.88)	(.30)
Weather	b_2	—	—	.085	−.044
				(.78)	(.36)
Building codes	b_3	—	—	.082	.091
				(.55)	(.58)
Strikes	b_4	—	—	.078	.083
				(.52)	(.55)
	R^2	0.416	—	.426	
	λ		1.82		1.87
			(1.41)		(1.27)
	σ		.566		.57
			(4.62)		(4.05)
	$\hat{\sigma}_u$		.496		.503
	$\hat{\sigma}_v$		.273		.268
	Log-likelihood		−41.67		−41.10

Note: Equation 1 replicates Allen (1986; p. 193, table 2, col. 3). Each equation includes three region dummies, SMSA, and a control for percent interior completed.

*t-statistics are reported in parentheses.

the OLS residuals. The test statistic is based on the skewness coefficient and is given by $\sqrt{b_1} = m_3/m_2^{3/2}$.

The OLS residuals have second and third moments equal to .163 and −.144, respectively, yielding a value of −2.185 for $\sqrt{b_1}$. The null hypothesis, that the combined error $(v_i + u_i)$ is iid normal, is rejected well beyond the 1 percent significance level, and the direction of skewness (negative) is consistent with a production frontier.

The frontier model appears to be a superior characterization of both the theory and the data. Even so, OLS yields consistent estimates of all the parameters except the intercept [Richmond (1974), Schmidt (1985–1986)]. But, this is important if we hope to capture union productivity effects through intercept adjustments. Moreover, inclusion of *a priori* information about the disturbance should improve the efficiency of point estimates for the remaining parameters of the model. Turning to column 2 of Table 6.1, we see that the ALS estimator yields a statistically significant union coefficient of .373, an amount that is 21 percent higher than its OLS counterpart. This difference is striking and suggests that the union–nonunion productivity gap is wider between efficient projects than at the mean.

Continuing the comparison of OLS and ALS estimates, we find, as expected, that the frontier function lies above the average function, though both estimates of the intercept are insignificant in this specification of the model. Output elasticities and returns-to-scale are robust to the estimation technique. Point estimates for the labor quality index are less similar, though neither estimate is significant. Finally, $\lambda = \sigma_u / \sigma_v$ has a t-statistic that exceeds one, but which is insignificant at conventional levels, providing weak support for the frontier model.

Allen points out that incorporation of relevant factors into the model serves to isolate the causes of the union advantage and to reduce the size of the union coefficient. We begin by including controls for weather, building codes, and strikes. Each of these factors is arguably outside of the control of management and is intended to reduce the random variation in performance due to luck. Interestingly, as seen in column 4 of Table 6.1, inclusion of these variables causes a slight decline in the estimated variance of the two-sided disturbance. Since luck can be good or bad, this is precisely what we should observe. Because none of the coefficients are remotely significant, either individually or as a group, we do not consider them further.

The BLS survey includes a set of questions about the production process that might be helpful in determining the sources of the estimated union productivity premium. "For each factor, the contractor reported whether it raised, lowered or had no effect on the number of employee hours required to construct the project as contrasted to any similar projects in which he participated during the previous two years" [Allen (1986, p.196)]. In successive models, we include the proportion of supervisors and dummy variables (equal to 1 if the factor helped, and 0 otherwise), for standardized components, apprenticeship programs, prefabricated materials, and supply of skilled workers. The inclusion of apprenticeship programs, prefabricated materials, and supply of skilled workers added no explanatory power to the model. Both standardized components and the proportion of supervisors proved to be important, however.

Results reported in column 1 of Table 6.2 reveal that, for those reporting that standardized components helped, the output per labor hour increases by an estimated 40 percent.[2] Rather than reducing the size of the union coefficient, however, it has the surprising effect of raising this value. It appears that omission of this variable masks the contribution of other beneficial attributes of unionization that are not included in the model. The result is also notable in that it departs from the conclusion derived from its OLS counterpart, reported in column 4 of Table 6.2. Relying on OLS estimates, we find that the coefficient on standardized components is positive but insignificant. Moreover, its inclusion has virtually no effect on the union coefficient.

---

[2] ln (Q/L) is .1168 at the mean of the data, yielding antilog values of 1.576 and 1.124 with and without standardized components, respectively. The ratio of these two values is 1.40.

Table 6.2   Systematic Factors That May Affect Union Productivity Premiums*

	Model					
	ALS			OLS		
Variable	(1)	(2)	(3)	(4)	(5)	(6)
Intercept	3.80	−18.29	−9.13	−5.75	−20.47	−19.59
	(.36)	(1.58)	(.71)	(.625)	(1.93)	(1.86)
ln (K/L)	.180	.251	.254	.186	.245	.237
	(2.76)	(3.55)	(3.71)	(2.46)	(3.22)	(3.12)
ln (LHRS)	−.148	−.140	−.168	−.120	−.137	−1.41
	(3.46)	(4.14)	(4.49)	(3.53)	(4.03)	(4.14)
Union	.419	.268	.323	.307	.249	.247
	(3.18)	(.184)	(2.13)	(2.35)	(1.92)	(1.91)
ln W	−.224	2.28	1.88	.789	2.50	2.40
	(.185)	(1.74)	(.88)	(.752)	(2.06)	(1.99)
Standardized components	.338	—	.366	.183	—	.199
(helped = 1)	(2.06)		(2.24)	(1.18)		(1.32)
Proportion supervisors	—	−2.09	−2.07	—	−2.12	−2.17
		(2.02)	(1.91)		(2.38)	(2.45)
R^2	—	—	—	.43	.46	.47
λ	3.40	1.04	3.63			
	(1.72)	(.867)	(1.82)			
σ	.634	.474	.617			
	(6.93)	(3.36)	(6.83)			
$\hat{\sigma}_u$	.608	.342	.595			
$\hat{\sigma}_v$	.179	.329	.164			
Log-likelihood	−39.25	−38.81	−36.21			

*t-statistics are reported in parentheses.

It is apparent from column 2 of Table 6.2 that the ratio of supervisor hours to total hours is an important factor in explaining the union productivity advantage. Although this ratio is only 0.2 percentage points higher in the nonunion setting, the variable is statistically significant at the 1 percent level and its inclusion in the ALS model (Table 6.2, column 2) reduces the union coefficient (Table 6.1, column 2) by 28 percent.

The final model presented in Table 6.2 includes both standardized components and the proportion of supervisors. Based on a likelihood-ratio test, this model provides our best description of production. The model reveals a union effect that is estimated to raise productivity by 38 percent. We note also that $\lambda = 3.63$ and that this value is statistically significant at the 10 percent level. This result provides empirical support for the frontier specification.

A broad comparison of results derived from the two estimation methods reveals that the union coefficients and the intercepts of the OLS model are always smaller than their ALS counterparts. While both methods lead us to conclude that unions increase productivity, the OLS model (column 6) reveals a more modest 28 percent productivity premium among average performers.

We use the Jondrow, Lovell, Materov, and Schmidt (1982) decomposition technique to isolate estimates of the one-sided disturbances for individual projects. The expected value of the resulting series, $E(\hat{u}) = \hat{\sigma}_u \sqrt{2/\pi}$ is 0.47 for our preferred model [Column 3, Table 6.2]. Although the statistical significance of this value is of interest, we note that the usual t-statistic is suspect and do not compute it here (Greene, Chapter 2).[3] Using the average proportional efficiency measure suggested by Greene in Chapter 2, equal to $\frac{1}{N}[\Sigma_i \exp(-\hat{u}_i)]$, we obtain a value of 0.65 for our preferred model [Column 3, Table 6.2]. This value is interpreted in a manner analogous to Farrell (1957) and suggests that projects are only obtaining 65 percent of their potential output with given inputs.

Our estimate of inefficiency is rather substantial and likely embodies a variety of causes in addition to managerial or organizational differences among projects. Since efficiency estimates derive from the unexplained component of the model, they are necessarily sensitive to the selection of functional form for the deterministic kernel, assumed distribution of the residuals, and variable measurement and selection.

If we assume that the inefficiency component of the error is distributed exponentially as suggested by Meeusen and van den Broeck (1977), rather than half-normal, our estimate of average proportional efficiency is 0.82, and continues to suggest that a substantial amount of inefficiency exists among projects examined.[4] A likely source of some share of inefficiency measured by our preferred model comes from differences in characteristics of the buildings under construction. Guided by results presented in Allen (1983), we attempt to explain the sources of estimated inefficiency by an OLS regression of the Jondrow, Lovell, Materov, and Schmidt efficiency measures against building attributes. Our initial regressions included 15 variables. We eliminated variables whose t-statistics fell below 1. This procedure left us with 8 (9) variables that may help to explain the residuals generated by the half-normal (exponential) model. The resulting set of building characteristics includes three controls for type of frame (concrete, masonry, and steel), two for type of roof base (steel and concrete) and one each for air conditioning, type of heat, and type of roof cover. The model of exponential residuals also includes a control for concrete floor base.

As shown in Table 6.3, the coefficients of determination obtained from the OLS analysis are 0.25 and 0.27, for the two models. In other words, about one-quarter of the total variation in estimated inefficiency among projects can be explained by differences in the characteristics of the projects. Steel frame construction and type of roof cover are associated with greater efficiency and air conditioning and heat type

---

[3] If $E(u) = 0$, the compound error collapses to the normal distribution.

[4] Individual estimates of proportional efficiency generated by the half-normal and exponential models have a .93 correlation. Efficiency estimates from the top and bottom quartiles of the distribution range from .93 to .80 and from .49 to .21, respectively, for half-normal models 3 and 1, Table 6.2. The exponential counterparts are .92 to .88 and .78 to .43.

Table 6.3 Building Characteristics as Explainers of One-Sided Residuals

	Model	
	Half-normal	**Exponential**
Intercept	.3145	.1186
	(2.53)	(2.34)
Steel frame	−.3742	−.1657
	(3.04)	(3.67)
Concrete frame	−.2227	−.1090
	(1.49)	(2.00)
Masonary frame	−.1632	−.1129
	(1.12)	(2.10)
Steel roof base	.1713	.0719
	(1.59)	(1.80)
Concrete roof base	.1725	.0552
	(1.45)	(1.26)
Air conditioned	.2017	.0772
	(1.66)	(1.79)
Heat type	.1633	.0507
	(2.12)	(1.86)
Roof cover type	−.3299	−.1044
	(2.29)	(2.04)
Concrete floor base	—	.0609
		(1.34)
R^2	.25	.27

are associated with less efficiency in both equations, using a 10 percent criterion for significance. Statistical significance of other attributes diverges between the two models at this point, though signs are consistent for the two models. Importantly, the estimated intercept is positive and significant in both equations. These intercepts represent the expected value of the inefficient component of the error, after netting out the influence of building characteristics. The intercepts imply average proportional efficiency values of .73 and .89 for the half-normal and exponential models respectively.

6.5 Conclusions

This chapter provides a comparative analysis of the union–nonunion productivity differential using stochastic frontier and OLS estimation procedures. We believe that the frontier model is a more appropriate description of the theoretical definition of a production function. In addition, we find that the frontier model is supported empirically. Both approaches reveal a substantial union productivity premium, but the premium derived from the frontier model is 10 percentage points (36 percent) greater than the OLS estimate. Apparently, the most efficient unionized projects substantially outperform their nonunionized counterparts. Of course, some organizations or project managers are likely to be more efficient than others. Our estimates of average technical efficiency range from 73 to 89 percent.

REFERENCES

Addison, John, and Barry Hirsch (1989), "Union Effects on Productivity, Profits, and Growth: Has the Long Run Arrived?" *Journal of Labor Economics* 7(1)(January): 72–105.

Aigner, Dennis, Knox Lovell, and Peter Schmidt (1977), "Formulation and Estimation of Stochastic Frontier Production Function Models," *Journal of Econometrics* 6: 21–37.

Allen, Steven G. (1983), "Unionization and Productivity in Office Building and School Construction," Working Paper, National Bureau of Economic Research, Inc., June.

Allen, Steven G. (1984), "Unionized Construction Workers Are More Productive," *Quarterly Journal of Economics* 99(May): 251–274.

Allen, Steven G. (1986), "Unionization and Productivity in Office Building and School Construction," *Industrial and Labor Relations Review*, 39(2)(January): 187–201.

Allen, Steven G. (1987), "Can Union Labor Ever Cost Less" *Quarterly Journal of Economics* 102(May): 347–373.

Farrell, M.J. (1957), "The Measurement of Productive Efficiency," *Journal of the Royal Statistical Society* Series A (General) 120(3): 253–290

Freeman, Richard B., and James L. Medoff (1984), *What Do Unions Do?*, New York: Basic Books.

Greene, William. (1990), *Econometric Analysis*. New York: Macmillan Publishing Co.

Jondrow, James, Knox Lovell, Ivan Materov, and Peter Schmidt (1982), "On the Estimation of Technical Inefficiency in the Stochastic Frontier Production Function Model," *Journal of Econometrics* 19: 233–238.

Lewis, H. Gregg (1963), *Unionism and Relative Wages in the United States: An Empirical Investigation*. Chicago:University of Chicago Press.

Lewis, H. Gregg (1986), *Union Relative Wage Effects: A Survey*. Chicago:University of Chicago Press.

Meeusen, W., and J. van den Broeck (1977), "Efficiency Estimation from Cobb-Douglas Production Functions with Composed Error," *International Economic Review* 18(2) (June): 435–444.

Reynolds, Morgan O. (1986), "Trade Unions in the Production Process Reconsidered," *Journal of Political Economy* 94(April): 443–447.

Richmond, J. (1974), "Estimating the Efficiency of Production," *International Economic Review* 15: 515–521.

Schmidt, Peter. (1985–1986), "Frontier Production Functions," *Econometric Reviews* 4(2): 289–328.

Schmidt, Peter, and Tsai-Fen Lin, (1984), "Simple Tests of Alternative Specifications in Stochastic Frontier Models," *Journal of Econometrics* 24: 349–361.

7

DO PHYSICIANS MINIMIZE COST?

B. Kelly Eakin

7.1 Introduction

Uwe Reinhardt (1972), in a widely cited article, concludes that physicians under-employ aides and consequently produce only about 80 percent of the patient visits possible if physicians worked as much but employed twice the number of aides. The policy implication is obvious: the perceived physician shortage (of the time) could be alleviated if physicians would employ assistants in an economically efficient manner. Since Reinhardt's research many changes have occurred. The "physician shortage" has all but disappeared as an issue. Instead, there is often talk (particularly by physicians) of a "physician glut" and intense competition among physicians. Tightening reimbursement policies of third-party payers presumably has reduced physician profits. Also, health care inflation over this period has continued to hover well above the growth rate of the consumer price index. These conditions highlight the need to reinvestigate the issue of efficiency in the production of physician services.

Despite the attention given Reinhardt's findings and their importance to health care policy, surprisingly little interest has been shown in updating the study and in explaining the puzzle of seemingly uneconomic behavior. Reinhardt's study used a national cross section of physicians in 1965 and 1967. He estimated a production function that today appears esoteric, but at the time was relatively flexible and well suited to the problem. [1] Reinhardt calculated marginal products for physicians and aides from the estimated production function. He compared the ratio of marginal products to the ratio of their prices, which are data not used in estimation. Reinhardt concluded that aides are underemployed. Extrapolating from the production function

---

[1] Reinhardt (1972) preceded much of the work on flexible functional form such as the translog developed in Christensen, Jorgenson, and Lau (1973).

estimate, he also concluded that an approximate doubling of aides, *ceteris paribus*, would yield the ratio of marginal products equal to the ratio of input prices.

Brown and Lapan (1981) made a slight modification to Reinhardt's production function to overcome an inconsistency and bias in Reinhardt's model. They estimated the revised production function using a 1976 national cross section of physicians and compared the ratio of estimated marginal products to the ratio of input prices and also compared the value of the marginal product of inputs to their prices. They concluded that, on average, physicians employ aides efficiently. They also found physicians in group practices to be more productive.

Brown (1988) again addressed the issue of efficient employment of physician aides. Using the same methodology and data as Brown and Lapan, he focused on differences in the employment of physician assistants, nurses, and nonnurse aides. He concluded that the major inefficiency is overemployment of nonnurse (secretarial, administrative, and technician) aides.

All the studies have found evidence of scale economies in the production of physician services. The methodology of comparing production function estimates to data (input prices) outside the econometric model is also common to these studies. The results, however, differ considerably. The differences may result from changes in input prices between 1965 and 1976, a change in the production technology, differences in the specification of the production function, or unexplained changes in physician behavior. Regardless, the persistence of seemingly uneconomic behavior by physicians remains a puzzle.

I also address the issue of efficiency in the production of physician services. However, I do so using a methodology which has more economic grounding and content. I focus on efficiency differences between solo and group practice physicians and also on differences across specialties. The advantages of this study include more recent data, a choice-theoretic framework, and a more meaningful measure of the social cost of physician inefficiency.

The rest of this chapter is organized as follows. Section 7.2 presents a simple utility maximization model for the physician. The key result is that utility maximization may imply costs that are not minimized. Using this result along with cost and production theory, I develop the nonminimum variable cost function in Section 7.3. Section 7.4 covers data, estimation technique, and interpretation of the estimates. Section 7.5 concludes.

7.2 A Simple Utility Maximization Model for Physicians

Failure to minimize the cost of producing a given output is typically viewed as uneconomic behavior. This is because cost minimization is a necessary condition in the standard profit maximization model and cost minimization is also an implication of many alternative theories of the firm such as quantity-quality tradeoff models and output, revenue, and growth maximization models. Failure to minimize cost, however, may be rational behavior if inputs are direct arguments in the decision maker's utility function (or if the firm has some monopsony power in purchasing an input).

Assume the physician has the utility function

$$U(L, \Pi, X_2) \qquad U_L > 0 \quad U_\Pi > 0 \quad U_{X2} < 0 \tag{7.1}$$

where L is leisure, Π is profit or net income, and X_2 is the number of assistants hired. $U_{X2} < 0$ indicates that the physician gets disutility from being a supervisor. That is, in Reinhardt's term, there is a psychic cost to hiring assistants. Leisure is given by the identity

$$L = L_0 - X_1 - \tilde{X}_1 \tag{7.2}$$

where L_0 is the total time endowment, X_1 is the physician's own time in producing patient visits, and $\tilde{X}_1$ is the physician's outside income-producing activities (consulting). Profit or net income is given by the identity

$$\Pi = PY + \tilde{W}_1 \tilde{X}_1 - W_2 X_2 \tag{7.3}$$

where P is the price of a patient visit Y, $\tilde{W}_1$ is the wage the physician receives for outside consulting activities, and W_2 is the wage the physician pays to hired aides. That is, the physician is the residual claimant, but receives no direct wage from the practice. Finally, assume the production function for patient visits is

$$Y = f(X_1, X_2) \qquad f_1 > 0, f_2 > 0 \tag{7.4}$$

The problem facing the physician is to choose X_1, $\tilde{X}_1$, and X_2 to maximize Equation (7.1) subject to Equations (7.2), (7.3), and (7.4). The first-order conditions are

$$U_L = U_\Pi \tilde{W}_1$$
$$U_L = U_\Pi P f_1 \tag{7.5}$$
$$U_\Pi W_2 - U_{X2} = U_\Pi P f_2$$

which can be manipulated to give

$$\frac{f_2}{f_1} = \left(\frac{W_2}{\tilde{W}_1}\right)\left(\frac{U_\Pi P f_2}{U_\Pi P f_2 + U_{X2}}\right) \tag{7.6}$$

Equation (7.6) collapses to the cost minimization condition only if $U_{X2} = 0$. If $U_{X2} < 0$ and $U_\Pi > 0$, then this constrained optimization implies less than the cost-minimizing amount of X_2 is employed for any given output level. The right-hand side of Equation (7.6) can be interpreted as the physician's shadow or perceived price of X_2 relative to the price of X_1.

Another implication from this model should be pointed out. Assuming $\tilde{X}_1$, X_1, and $X_2 > 0$, the physician's leisure-labor decision does not affect the cost minimization incentive in producing patient visits. The leisure-labor tradeoff affects the optimal number of patient visits Y and $\tilde{X}_1$, but whatever these choices, the choices of X_1 and X_2 are a cost-minimizing bundle only if $U_{X2} = 0$. That is, the cost minimization incentive is independent of the value of U_L.

7.3 The Nonminimum Variable Cost Function

The primary result of the previous section shows that optimal choices by a utility-maximizing physician producing patient visits might not yield a cost-minimizing bundle of inputs. This suggests that physician behavior should be modeled in a manner that embodies the optimization, yet allows for systematic allocative inefficiency. The nonminimum variable cost function (NMVCF), developed below, provides such an approach.

The NMVCF follows the development and application of allocative inefficiency models found in Toda (1976), Atkinson and Halvorsen (1984), and Eakin and Kniesner (1988). Due to data limitations, a variable cost function plus an envelope condition are developed rather than the usual long-run cost function. The available data give information on total expenditures for supplies and capital, but no breakdown on prices and quantities for these inputs. Reasonable assumptions can be made that in a cross section these prices are constant. One price can be finessed this way without sacrificing parameters because a cost function is homogeneous to degree 1 in input prices. Consequently, the price of materials is assumed to equal 1 and is implicitly the numeraire.[2] By using a variable cost function treating capital as a "fixed" factor and simultaneously estimating the envelope condition, it is still possible to retrieve parameters associated with capital.

The NMVCF approach has at least three advantages over the production function approach employed by the previous studies of physician services. First, the NMVCF is based upon the economic problem of minimizing shadow cost, rather than merely a technical relation represented by a production function. Second, the traditional minimum variable cost function is nested in the NMVCF and therefore allocative efficiency is an easily tested hypothesis about parameter values. All data used in the efficiency hypothesis are used in the econometric model. Third, the NMVCF approach yields a more direct measure of the social cost of physician inefficiency. This point is discussed below when the measure of allocative inefficiency is presented.

---

[2] This assumption has also been employed in Cowing and Holtmann (1983) and Eakin and Kniesner (1988).

Physician services are modeled as a process involving four inputs, physician time (D), assistants (A), supplies (S), and capital (K), yielding one output, patient visits (Y). That is,

$$Y = f(D, A, S, K) \qquad (7.7)$$

It is assumed that the physician purchases inputs in competitive markets and can work outside the practice at a constant wage. The physician is assumed to minimize the shadow cost of producing patient visits. Shadow cost may differ from observed cost if the physician perceives some input prices to be different from their market prices, as suggested by Equation (7.6). Physician behavior, constrained by production technology and input market structures is embodied in the minimum variable shadow cost function

$$V^{sh} = V^{sh}(Y, W^{sh}; K) \qquad (7.8)$$

where W^{sh} is a vector of shadow prices for D, A, and S. Shephard's lemma gives the conditional input demands. In logarithmic form, these can be expressed as shadow share expressions

$$M_i^{sh}(Y, W^{sh}; K) = \frac{W_i^{sh} X_i}{V^{sh}} = \frac{\partial \ln V^{sh}}{\partial \ln W_i} \qquad i = D, A, S \qquad (7.9)$$

Rearranging Equation (7.9) gives the observed (and shadow) factor demands

$$X_i(Y, W^{sh}; K) = \frac{V^{sh} M_i^{sh}}{W_i^{sh}} \qquad i = D, A, S \qquad (7.10)$$

with which observed variable cost is obtained as

$$V^{obs}(Y, W^{sh}, W; K) = \sum_i W_i X_i(Y, W^{sh}; K) = V^{sh} \sum_i \frac{M_i^{sh} W_i}{W_i^{sh}} \qquad (7.11)$$

By letting $T_i = M_i^{sh} W_i / W_i^{sh}$ and $T = \sum_i T_i$, the variable cost function system of equations can be expressed as

$$\ln V^{obs} = \ln V^{sh} + \ln T \qquad (7.12a)$$

and

$$M_j^{sh} = \frac{T_j}{T} \qquad j = D, A, S \qquad (7.12b)$$

It is also assumed that capital is employed optimally. This condition is imposed by the envelope condition that

$$\frac{W_K K}{V^{sh}} = \frac{-\partial \ln V^{sh}}{\partial \ln K} \tag{7.13}$$

Recalling that $V^{sh}/V^{obs} = 1/T$, Equation (7.13) can be transformed into the ratio of observed capital expenses to observed variable cost, that is,

$$\text{KRATIO} = \frac{W_K K}{V^{obs}} = \frac{-(\delta \ln V^{sh}/\delta \ln K)}{T} \tag{7.14}$$

All that remains to implement the empirical model is choosing the functional form to represent shadow variable cost and shadow input prices. Shadow input prices are modeled multiplicatively as

$$W_i^{sh} = W_i \theta_i \tag{7.15}$$

Because efficient employment of assistants is the issue, only θ_A is estimated, while $\theta_D = \theta_S = 1$ is imposed. A translog shadow variable cost function,

$$\ln V^{sh} = \alpha_0 + \alpha_Y \ln Y + \frac{1}{2}\alpha_{YY}(\ln Y)^2 + \sum_i \beta_i \ln W_i^{sh}$$

$$+ \frac{1}{2}\sum_i \sum_j \beta_{ij} \ln W_i^{sh} \ln W_j^{sh}$$

$$+ \sum_i \beta_{ik} \ln W_i^{sh} \ln K + \frac{1}{2}\beta_{KK}(\ln K)^2$$

$$+ \sum_i \beta_{Yi} \ln Y \ln W_i^{sh} + \beta_{Yk} \ln Y \ln K \tag{7.16}$$

completes the model.[3] Using Equations (7.16) and (7.17) in Equations (7.12), (7.13), and (7.15) gives the system of equations estimated.

The NMVCF system along with the envelope condition allows long-run cost concepts to be evaluated. The long-run shadow cost function is

$$C^{sh} = V^{sh} + W_K K = V^{sh}(1 + T \text{ KRATIO}) \tag{7.17}$$

---

[3] Symmetry and homogeneity in shadow input prices are imposed by the usual parameter restrictions.

and the long-run observed cost function is

$$C^{obs} = V^{obs} + W_K K = V^{obs}(1 + \text{KRATIO}) \tag{7.18}$$

Evaluating C^{obs} with all shadow price divergence terms set equal to 1 gives an estimate of minimum long-run cost. That is,

$$\hat{C}^{min} = \hat{C}^{obs}(Y, W : \theta = 1) \tag{7.19}$$

Allocative inefficiency (AI) is measured as

$$\text{AI} = \frac{\hat{C}^{obs} - \hat{C}^{min}}{\hat{C}^{min}} \tag{7.20}$$

and is the proportion by which actual cost exceeds minimum cost. This is a better measure of the social cost of physician inefficiency than Reinhardt's foregone patient visits because AI is the opportunity cost of misallocated resources whose next best uses might or might not be to produce patient visits.

Finally, output-cost elasticities measure scale economies (SCE) and can be calculated using both the shadow and observed long-run cost functions. These measures are

$$\text{SCE}^{sh} = \frac{\partial \ln C^{sh}}{\partial \ln Y} \tag{7.21}$$

and

$$\text{SCE}^{obs} = \frac{\partial \ln C^{obs}}{\partial \ln Y} \tag{7.22}$$

Scale measures less (greater) than 1 imply economies (diseconomies) of scale.

7.4 Empirical Results

Estimating the nonminimum variable cost function system requires data on output, inputs, and input prices. The primary data source is the Physicians' Practice Costs and Income Survey conducted by the National Opinion Research Center between November 1984 and June 1885. Output is measured as total patient visits for the physician. Physician input is measured as total hours in the practice that produces these visits. Assistants are measured as the total nonphysician employees in the practice. Supplies are total medical supply expenditures divided by the number of physicians in the practice. The price of supplies is assumed constant across the sample. Capital expenditures are the sum of all rental and depreciation expenses for the practice, divided by the number of physicians. The price of physician's own time is calculated as the physician's net income from the practice divided by the annual hours put into the practice. Total variable cost is the sum of the physician's net income, total wages, and benefits paid to assistants per physician and total expenditures on medical supplies per physician.

I choose self-employed physicians specializing in general practice, family practice, internal medicine, pediatrics, and obstetrics and gynecology. Selecting physicians in these specialties with all the necessary cost function data leaves a sample of 347, of which 177 have solo practices and 170 are part of a group practice. There are 54 general practice, 97 family practice, 94 internal medicine, 47 pediatric, and 55 obstetric and gynecological physicians.

The NMVCF system consists of five equations—the variable cost function, three shares, and the envelope condition. A four-equation system is estimated as only any two of the three cost shares are independent. Capital is modeled as a choice variable, but shows up on the right-hand side of the equations. Consequently, the estimation technique used is iterative nonlinear three-stage least squares. Instruments include the exogenous input prices and output, and several predetermined variables such as age, race, and community variables.

The NMVCF system and the traditional variable cost function system are estimated for the entire sample, for solo and group practices, and also for each specialty subsample. Tables 7.1 to 7.4 present the parameter estimates for all models. Parameters associated with supplies are not estimated, but instead are retrieved by homogeneity restrictions. These retrieved parameters are not reported. Using a varying parameters framework with the pooled sample, a Chow-type test is performed which rejects the hypothesis of identical technologies.[4] This implies different production functions for solo and group practices. For the NMVCF presented in Table 7.2, rejecting identical cost functions implies technology and/or behavior differences.

An economic cost function, dual to the underlying production function, has several properties which I call regularity conditions. Implied by theory, these conditions must be satisfied for inference about technology to be legitimate. Conditions such as homogeneity and symmetry can be imposed by parameter restrictions and nonnegative cost is guaranteed by choice of functional form. With a flexible form, such as the translog chosen here, some theoretical properties cannot be easily imposed. Instead, they must be verified at the means of the data and at every data point.

Regularity conditions needing to be verified are that the shadow variable cost function is increasing in output, increasing in input prices, concave in input prices, and decreasing in the fixed factor. Fifteen of the sixteen estimated models satisfy all regularity conditions at the sample means and for the vast majority of observations. The exception, the NMVCF for pediatrics, fails regularity at the means and for most

---

[4] The test of identical minimum cost function parameters for group and solo physicians yields a chi-square test statistic of 38.23 with 15 degrees of freedom which is significant at the .001 level.

Table 7.1 Minimum Variable Cost Function Estimates for Solo and Group Practices

	Pooled	Solo	Group
α_O	−.004	−.002	−.011
	(.026)	(.039)	(.031)
α_Y	.342	.294	.409
	(.039)	(.056)	(.056)
α_{YY}	.194	.197	.198
	(.051)	(.066)	(.090)
β_D	.547	.532	.561
	(.008)	(.011)	(.010)
β_A	.360	.363	.359
	(.006)	(.009)	(.009)
β_K	−.157	−.167	−.135
	(.009)	(.011)	(.013)
β_{DD}	.136	.146	.136
	(.012)	(.018)	(.015)
β_{DA}	−.121	−.106	−.133
	(.011)	(.016)	(.014)
β_{DK}	.038	.474	−.117
	(.011)	(.013)	(.012)
β_{AA}	.131	.115	.141
	(.015)	(.023)	(.017)
β_{AK}	.002	−.003	.017
	(.011)	(.013)	(.012)
β_{KK}	−.101	−.104	.092
	(.017)	(.018)	(.019)
β_{YD}	−.018	−.028	−.010
	(.014)	(.018)	(.019)
β_{YA}	.012	.014	.011
	(.011)	(.014)	(.017)
β_{YK}	.030	.047	.014
	(.014)	(.017)	(.024)
Regularity	311/347	152/177	161/170

Standard errors in parentheses.

observations. No inferences on behavior or technology should be drawn from this model. The last line in Tables 7.1 to 7.4 reports the fraction of observations satisfying all regularity conditions.

Allocative inefficiency is captured by the shadow price divergence parameter, θ_A, reported in Table 7.2 and Table 7.4. All the NMVCF models have estimates of θ_A greater than 1, indicating the shadow price of aides exceeds the market price. This implies the physician underemploys assistants. However, by specialty, this result is statistically significant at the .10 level only for obstetrics and gynecological specialists. θ_A in the general practice NMVCF is significant at the .13 level.

Allocative inefficiency estimates are calculated as defined in Equation (7.20). Tables 7.5 and 7.6 present these estimates at the sample means. The "typical" solo practice physician underemploys assistants resulting in about 17 percent inefficiency while the estimate for the "typical" group practice doctor is 7.5 percent. Similar results occur across specialties. Allocative inefficiency is about 16 percent for obstetrics and gynecological physicians, while it is only about 7 percent for general, family, and internal medicine practices. Standard error estimates are also presented for the AI estimates, but the usefulness of these standard error estimates is unclear. The AI measure is nonnegative and follows no obvious distribution. The complexity and nonnormal distribution of the AI measure are criteria for using the the bootstrap

Table 7.2 Nonminimum Variable Cost Function Estimates for Solo and Group Practices

	Pooled	**Solo**	**Group**
α_O	−.052	−.115	−.065
	(.033)	(.066)	(.042)
α_Y	.350	.305	.413
	(.037)	(.051)	(.054)
α_{YY}	.194	.174	.197
	(.047)	(.061)	(.086)
β_D	.509	.433	.509
	(.019)	(.038)	(.027)
β_A	.420	.508	.435
	(.028)	(.052)	(.034)
β_K	−.119	−.097	−.107
	(.017)	(.020)	(.015)
β_{DD}	.150	.135	.146
	(.010)	(.018)	(.014)
β_{DA}	−.143	.117	.149
	(.010)	(.015)	(.014)
β_{DK}	.029	.012	−.015
	(.013)	(.009)	(.009)
β_{AA}	.146	.120	.155
	(.013)	(.021)	(.016)
β_{AK}	.004	.007	.019
	(.012)	(.010)	(.010)
β_{KK}	−.058	−.064	−.061
	(.020)	(.016)	(.016)
β_{YD}	−.021	−.024	−.012
	(.013)	(.013)	(.018)
β_{YA}	.016	.019	.013
	(.012)	(.014)	(.018)
β_{YK}	.022	.027	.009
	(.012)	(.010)	(.016)
θ_A	1.962	3.517	2.638
	(.532)	(1.094)	(.740)
Regularity	319/347	157/177	155/170

Standard errors in parentheses.

Table 7.3 Minimum Variable Cost Function Estimates by Specialty

	General	Family	Internal	Pediatric	Obgyn
α_O	.029	−.060	−.001	−.025	−.008
	(.083)	(.051)	(.057)	(.048)	(.056)
α_Y	.402	.244	.234	.415	.565
	(.125)	(.086)	(.140)	(.073)	(.094)
α_{YY}	−.066	.487	.019	.070	.377
	(.197)	(.177)	(.203)	(.093)	(.075)
β_D	.511	.548	.574	.590	.513
	(.019)	(.014)	(.023)	(.021)	(.019)
β_A	.368	.366	.337	.320	.407
	(.018)	(.012)	(.018)	(.019)	(.016)
β_K	−.158	−.172	−.139	−.148	−.140
	(.029)	(.022)	(.011)	(.012)	(.020)
β_{DD}	.174	.170	.171	.074	.138
	(.028)	(.024)	(.030)	(.032)	(.021)
β_{DA}	−.156	−.140	−.136	−.089	−.132
	(.025)	(.020)	(.024)	(.027)	(.019)
β_{DK}	−.014	.015	.051	.031	.033
	(.017)	(.014)	(.017)	(.015)	(.014)
β_{AA}	.174	.152	.030	.117	.154
	(.040)	(.023)	(.027)	(.037)	(.026)
β_{AK}	.018	−.010	.011	.011	−.012
	(.017)	(.013)	(.017)	(.016)	(.014)
β_{KK}	−.125	−.094	−.090	−.102	−.115
	(.025)	(.023)	(.021)	(.013)	(.020)
β_{YD}	−.017	.020	.034	−.089	−.044
	(.035)	(.027)	(.039)	(.033)	(.024)
β_{YA}	.028	−.013	−.023	−.052	.037
	(.032)	(.024)	(.030)	(.030)	(.021)
β_{YK}	.076	.068	.018	.067)	.029
	(.052)	(.040)	(.019)	(.019)	(.027)
Regularity	42/54	80/97	78/94	44/47	46/55

Standard errors in parentheses.

technique to establish empirical confidence intervals [Eakin, McMillen, and Buono (1990)].

The output-cost elasticities, SCE^{obs} and SCE^{sh}, also reported in Tables 7.5 and 7.6 indicate strong scale economies facing both solo and group physicians. This result suggests merger of practices could yield significant cost savings. The similarity of SCE^{obs} and SCE^{sh} indicate that while the physician may have a distorted perception of the placement of the average cost curve, he has a fairly good perception of its shape.

Reinhardt, Brown and Lapan, and Brown also found scale economies, but not to the extent found here. Solo practices face greater economies than do group practices. Across specialties, internists face the greatest scale economies, while obstetrics and

Table 7.4   Nonminimum Variable Cost Function Estimates by Specialty

	General	Family	Internal	Pediatric	Obgyn
α_O	−.017	−.090	−.049	−.557	−.105
	(.099)	(.059)	(.082)	(.365)	(.070)
α_Y	.401	.260	.262	.443	.528
	(.121)	(.081)	(.136)	(.089)	(.086)
α_{YY}	−.049	.483	.032	.065	.370
	(.184)	(.169)	(.196)	(.087)	(.071)
β_D	.473	.508	.533	.246	.433
	(.056)	(.038)	(.046)	(.177)	(.040)
β_A	.443	.421	.412	.722	.510
	(.079)	(.047)	(.067)	(.202)	(.050)
β_K	.135	−.127	−.118	−.044	−.072
	(.031)	(.033)	(.018)	(.034)	(.021)
β_{DD}	.147	.163	.174	.048	.132
	(.032)	(.024)	(.029)	(.044)	(.020)
β_{DA}	−.153	−.148	−.157	−.053	−.135
	(.036)	(.019)	(.022)	(.049)	(.020)
β_{DK}	−.024	.008	.020	−.004	.007
	(.012)	(.013)	(.019)	(.003)	(.010)
β_{AA}	.167	.161	.150	.059	.149
	(.046)	(.022)	(.026)	(.055)	(.025)
β_{AK}	.034	−.006	.028	.007	.001
	(.017)	(.013)	(.012)	(.007)	(.010)
β_{KK}	−.078	−.073	−.060	−.013	−.161
	(.025)	(.023)	(.025)	(.015)	(.019)
β_{YD}	−.020	.017	.018	−.014	−.035
	(.025)	(.025)	(.036)	(.015)	(.022)
β_{YA}	.027	−.013	−.011	.012	.033
	(.033)	(.025)	(.033)	(.014)	(.022)
β_{YK}	.046	.049	.015	.009	.020
	(.029)	(.034)	(.014)	(.010)	(.016)
θ_A	3.330	2.021	2.414	20.467	3.661
	(1.484)	(.878)	(1.359)	(23.421)	(1.436)
Regularity	44/54	79/97	84/94	14/47	48/55

Standard errors in parentheses.

Table 7.5   Estimates of Allocative Inefficiency (AI), Observed Scale Economies (SCE^{obs}), and Shadow Scale Economies (SCE^{sh}) for Solo and Group Practices from the Minimum Cost Function (mincf) and the Nonminimum Cost Function (nmcf)

	Pooled		Solo		Group	
	mincf	nmcf	mincf	nmcf	mincf	nmcf
AI	—	.057	—	.170	—	.075
		(.043)		(.036)		(.048)
SCE^{obs}	.324	.332	.278	.280	.397	.405
	(.043)	(.039)	(.060)	(.051)	(.062)	(.056)
SCE^{sh}	—	.342	—	.306	—	.417
		(.042)		(.058)		(.062)

Standard errors in parentheses.

Table 7.6 Estimates of Allocative Inefficiency (AI), Observed Scale Economies (SCE^{obs}), and Shadow Scale Economies (SCE^{sh}) by Specialty from the Minimum Cost Function (mincf) and the Nonminimum Cost Function (nmcf)

	General		Family		Internal		Pediatric		Obgyn	
	mincf	nmcf	mincf	nmcf	mincf	nmcf	mincf	nmcf	mincf	nmcf
AI	—	.074	—	.066	—	.061	—	*	—	.158
		(.063)		(.063)		(.101)				(.055)
SCE^{obs}	.306	.339	.254	.288	.213	.239	.384	*	.478	.446
	(.161)	(.136)	(.106)	(.097)	(.102)	(.099)	(.071)		(.091)	(.078)
SCE^{sh}	—	.374	—	.279	—	.230	—	*	—	.493
		(.121)		(.104)		(.113)				(.093)

*Not reported due to irregular cost function.
Standard errors in parentheses.

gynecology have more moderate economies. Two competing explanations can be developed to explain the value and pattern of the scale measures reported here. The first explanation is based on profit maximization in monopolistic competition. Mc-Carthy (1985) provided evidence that metropolitan physicians are monopolistically competitive. Manipulating the marginal revenue equals marginal cost condition for profit maximization gives

$$\frac{1}{E_d} = \frac{\text{SCE}}{R/C} - 1 \qquad (7.23)$$

where E_d is the price elasticity of demand for a visit to a specific physician, SCE is the output-cost elasticity, and R/C is the ratio of revenue to cost. Equation (7.23) shows that for a given R/C, demand is more elastic as SCE is greater. Likewise, for a given SCE, demand is less elastic as R/C is greater. Figure 7.1 depicts long-run equilibrium in monopolistic competition. In this case profit equals 0 so R/C equals 1 and Equation (7.24) simplifies to

$$E_d = \frac{1}{\text{SCE} - 1} \qquad (7.24)$$

Table 7.7 presents the demand elasticities implied by the cost function models under the assumption of monopolistic competition. Through this exercise, it appears that the demand for a specific physician's services is relatively inelastic. The profit maximization assumption guarantees that the elasticity of demand has an absolute value greater than unity. Demand for the solo physician's services is less elastic than for group practice physician services. That is, the solo practice has a slightly more loyal clientele. Across specialties, we find demand to be most elastic for obstetrics and gynecology and least elastic for internal medicine.

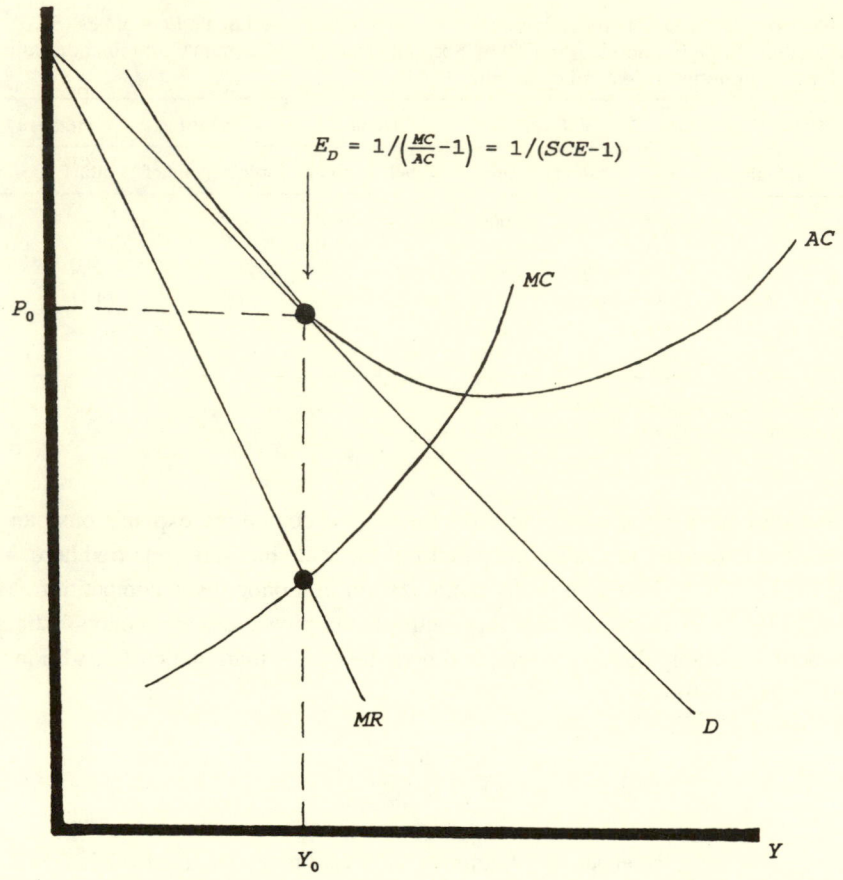

$$E_D = 1/\left(\frac{MC}{AC} - 1\right) = 1/(SCE-1)$$

Fig. 7.1 Relationship between cost and elasticity of demand in monopolistic competition equilibrium

Table 7.7 Demand Elasticities Derived Under the Assumption of Monopolistic Competition

Pooled		Solo		Group	
mincf	**nmcf**	**mincf**	**nmcf**	**mincf**	**nmcf**
−1.48	−1.52	−1.39	−1.44	−1.66	−1.72
(.094)	(.085)	(.115)	(.120)	(.171)	(1.82)

General		Family		Internal		Pediatric		Obgyn	
mincf	**nmcf**	**mincf**	**nmcf**	**mincf**	**nmcf**	**mincf**	**nmcf**	**mincf**	**nmcf**
−1.44	−1.60	−1.34	−1.39	−1.27	−1.30	−1.62	*	−1.92	−1.97
(.344)	(.245)	(.190)	(.200)	(.165)	(.190)	(.187)		(.344)	(.355)

*Not reported due to irregular cost function.

It is interesting to note that Hoerger (1990) found that internists tend to charge the same markup for new and established patient visits. He argues, but cannot show, that internists may face less elastic demand for new patients because of specialized illnesses and referrals. This may be the cause of his finding of less price discrimination between new and established patients of internists compared to pricing by general and family practices and obstetric and gynecological practices. The elasticity estimates presented in Table 7.7 provide evidence supporting Hoerger's conjecture.

Implied elasticity estimates range from -1.27 to -1.97. This range of estimates is lower in absolute value than found in previous studies. McCarthy found elasticities ranging from -3.07 to -3.32 while Lee and Hadley (1981) found a slightly broader range from -2.80 to -5.07.

An alternative explanation for the strong economies of scale found in this chapter can be non-profit maximization by the physician. The output inefficiency can result if the physician has a high utility value of leisure or receives disutility from producing output (separate from the leisure-labor tradeoff). This explanation suggests that underlying differences in utility functions likely lead to self-selection into solo and group practices. Evidence presented in this chapter on scale and behavior differences between solo and group practice physicians support this self-selection view.

7.5 Summary and Conclusions

This chapter has investigated efficiency in the production of physician services, which is both an important policy issue and an economic puzzle. I have deviated from previous studies by developing a cost function–based methodology which embodies more of the economic problem than does the previous production function approach. Besides the methodological advantages, the cost function approach, under certain assumptions, can be used to derive elasticities of demands across specialty and organization of practice.

The major finding of this chapter is that physicians underemploy assistants. Allocative inefficiency for solo practice physicians is about 17 percent of minimum cost, which is more than twice the estimate for group practice physicians. Among specialties, underemployment of assistants is statistically significant for obstetrics and gynecology, but not for other specialties. The evidence on scale and inefficiency suggests self-selection by both doctors and patients into group and solo practices.

REFERENCES

Atkinson, S., and R. Halvorsen (1984), "Parametric Efficiency Tests, Economies of Scale, and Input Demand in U.S. Electric Power Generation," *International Economic Review* 25(October): 643–662.

Brown, D. (1988), "Do Physicians Underutilize Aides?" *Journal of Human Resources* 23: 342–355.

Brown, D., and H. Lapan (1981), "Analysis of Physicians' Input Decisions," in N. Greenspan, ed., *Issues in Physician Reimbursement*, HCFA Pub. No. 03121, (August): 131–145.

Christensen, L., D. Jorgenson, and L. Lau (1973), "Transcendental Logarithmic Production Functions," *Review of Economics and Statistics* 55(February): 28–45.

Cowing, T., and A. Holtmann (1983), "The Multiproduct Short-Run Hospital Cost Function: Empirical Evidence and Policy Implications from Cross-Section Data," *Southern Economic Journal* 49(January): 637–653.

Eakin, B. K., and T. Kniesner (1988), "Estimating a Non-Minimum Cost Function for Hospitals," *Southern Economic Journal* 54(January): 583–597.

Eakin, B. K., D. P. McMillen, and M. J. Buono (1990), "Constructing Confidence Intervals Using the Bootstrap: An Application to a Multi-Product Cost Function," *Review of Economics and Statistics* 72(May): 339–344.

Hoerger, T. J. (1990), "Two Part Pricing and the Mark-Ups Charged by Primary Care Physicians for New and Established Patient Visits," *Journal of Health Economics* 8(February): 399–417.

Lee, R. H., and J. Hadley (1981), "Physician Fees and Public Medical Care Programs," *Health Services Research* 16: 185–203.

McCarthy, T. R. (1985), "The Competitive Nature of the Primary-Care Physician Services Market," *Journal of Health Economics* 4: 93–117.

Reinhardt, U. (1972), "A Production Function for Physician Services," *Review of Economics and Statistics* 54(February): 55–66.

Toda, Y. (1976), "Estimation of a Cost Function When Cost Is Not Minimized: The Case of Soviet Manufacturing Industries 1958–1971," *Review of Economics and Statistics* 58(August): 259–268.

8

A PRODUCTION FRONTIER MODEL WITH FLEXIBLE TEMPORAL VARIATION IN TECHNICAL EFFICIENCY

Young Hoon Lee and Peter Schmidt [1]

8.1 Introduction

Stochastic frontier models originated with Aigner, Lovell, and Schmidt (1977) and Meeusen and van den Broeck (1977). These models were intended for cross-sectional applications, and they rested on strong assumptions about the errors. Statistical noise was assumed to be normally distributed, while technical inefficiency was assumed to be distributed according to a specific one-sided distribution, such as exponential or half-normal. Furthermore, statistical noise and technical inefficiency were assumed to be independent of each other and of the explanatory variables (inputs). This line of research has been continued, with an emphasis on alternative distributional assumptions for technical inefficiency. For examples, see Stevenson (1980) and Greene (1990). Surveys are given by Schmidt (1986), Lovell and Schmidt (1988), and Bauer (1990), and by Greene in Section 2.4 of this book. It is now well understood that the basic parameters (regression coefficients) of the model can be estimated under weaker assumptions, but the separation of technical inefficiency from statistical noise [as in Jondrow, Lovell, Materov, and Schmidt (1982)] intrinsically requires strong distributional assumptions.

A more recent literature, into which this chapter fits, deals with frontier models in the context of panel data. Surveys of this literature are given by Lovell in Section 1.4.3 and by Greene in Section 2.5. Pitt and Lee (1981) and Schmidt and Sickles (1984) applied a standard model from the literature on panel data, in which inter-firm differences in time-invariant individual effects were interpreted as measures of technical inefficiency. Thus the strong distributional assumptions that are necessary

[1] The second author gratefully acknowledges the financial support of the National Science Foundation.

in a cross-sectional setting were replaced by the single (also strong) assumption that technical inefficiency is time-invariant.

An obvious question raised by these papers is the extent to which the assumption that technical inefficiency is time-invariant can be relaxed, without losing the advantages of panel data. Cornwell, Schmidt, and Sickles (1990), Kumbhakar (1990), Battese and Coelli (1991), Battese (1990), and Ivaldi, Monier-Dilhan, and Simioni (1991) have proposed panel data models that allow technical inefficiency to change over time, but in rather structured ways. In this chapter we allow more flexibility in the way that technical inefficiency changes over time. Specifically, we allow any arbitrary pattern of temporal change, subject to the restriction that the pattern (though not the magnitude) of the change is the same for all firms. This is a fairly direct relaxation of Kumbhakar's model, and it allows his model (or other similar models) to be tested against a flexible alternative.

Our model is suitable for applications in which the number of firms is large and the number of time-series observations per firm is relatively small. Here we apply the model to a data set previously analyzed by Erwidodo (1990), consisting of six observations on each of 171 Indonesian rice farms. We obtain plausible results.

8.2 The Model

We will consider a linear production frontier. To consider a cost frontier we would only have to change a few signs. Allowing for nonlinearity might introduce computational difficulties, but it would not introduce conceptual problems. Let there be N firms, indexed by $i = 1, \ldots, N$, and T time-series observations per firm, indexed by $t = 1, \ldots, T$. Let y_{it} be output for firm i at time t, and let X_{it} be the corresponding $k \times 1$ vector of explanatory variables (inputs). Let v_{it} be statistical noise, and let $u_{it} \geq 0$ represent technical inefficiency of firm i at time t. Then we will consider models of the general form

$$y_{it} = \alpha_t + X_{it}'\beta + v_{it} - u_{it} = \alpha_{it} + X_{it}'\beta + v_{it} \qquad (8.1)$$

Here $\alpha_{it} = \alpha_t - u_{it}$ is the intercept for firm i at time t. Correspondingly, α_t is the frontier intercept; that is, it is the maximum possible value of α_{it}. Empirically, we seek to estimate α_{it}, say by $\hat{\alpha}_{it}$, which leads to $\hat{\alpha}_t = \max_j \hat{\alpha}_{jt}$ (the maximum is taken over $j = 1, \ldots, N$; that is, over the firms in the sample), and correspondingly $\hat{u}_{it} = \hat{\alpha}_t - \hat{\alpha}_{it}$. This is a standard setup [e.g., Cornwell, Schmidt, and Sickles (1990, pp. 191–193)], and different models emerge as different choices for the form of α_{it} (or, equivalently, u_{it}).

The earliest treatments of frontiers with panel data, such as Pitt and Lee (1981) and Schmidt and Sickles (1984), assumed time-invariant technical inefficiency. This corresponds to α_{it} depending on i but not t, in which case α_t and u_{it} also do not depend on t. In this case we have the standard econometric panel data model with time-invariant individual effects (that is, the analysis of covariance model). Schmidt and Sickles discuss fixed effects models, in which no assumptions whatever beyond time-invariance are made about technical inefficiency, and random effects models, in which technical inefficiency is assumed to follow an unspecified distribution and to be uncorrelated with the inputs. Like Pitt and Lee, they also discuss the case in which a specific distribution is assumed for technical inefficiency. Thus there is considerable choice about what assumptions beyond time-invariance one wishes to impose on technical inefficiency.

Cornwell, Schmidt, and Sickles (1990) considered the model in which $\alpha_{it} = W_t'\delta_i$, where W_t is a vector of observed functions of time. They considered the specific case that α_{it} is quadratic in t, so that $W_{it} = [1, t, t^2]$ and $\alpha_{it} = \delta_{i0} + \delta_{i1}t + \delta_{i2}t^2$. Thus the intercept for each firm is quadratic in time, but the form of the quadratic varies over firms. The maximal (frontier) intercept is not necessarily quadratic, and therefore neither is the pattern of technical inefficiency for a given firm. However, the assumption that the intercept is quadratic in time is necessarily restrictive, and while there is no necessity to limit the choice to a quadratic, a precise specification of W_t is required. Note also that the number of individual-specific parameters (δ_{i0}, δ_{i1}, and δ_{i2} above) is greater than 1. As regards estimation of the model, Cornwell, Schmidt, and Sickles allowed for essentially the same set of specifications as Schmidt and Sickles. They considered fixed and random effects (δ's), and they allowed for correlation between the effects and the inputs. However, they did not allow for specific distributional assumptions about the effects. Some additional results for this model are given by Ivaldi, Monier-Dilhan, and Simioni (1991).

Kumbhakar (1990) specified a model in which $\alpha_{it} = \gamma(t)\delta_i$, where $\gamma(t)$ is specified up to some parameters. This allows the level of technical inefficiency to be nonconstant, but its temporal pattern is the same for all firms, since it is determined by the form of the function $\gamma(t)$. He suggested the particular form $\gamma(t) = [1 + \exp(bt + ct^2)]^{-1}$, which contains the two unknown parameters b and c. Battese (1990) and Battese and Coelli (1991) suggested some other forms for $\gamma(t)$. Estimation is by maximum likelihood, with a distributional assumption made for δ. A random effects treatment that did not assume a particular distribution for the effects would also be feasible. However, a fixed effects treatment (estimating the δ's as parameters) is problematical. The number of parameters is then dependent on sample size, and standard asymptotic results do not apply in such a case. [This is the so-called "incidental parameters problem" discussed by Chamberlain (1980).] The asymptotic properties of the estimates could perhaps be worked out directly, as we do below for our model.

Both the model of Cornwell, Schmidt, and Sickles and the model of Kumbhakar are generalizations of the simple model in which technical inefficiency is constant over time. The models are not directly comparable, in the sense that neither includes the other as a special case.

In this chapter we consider the model in which $\alpha_{it} = \theta_t\delta_i$, where the θ_t are parameters to be estimated. The simple panel data model obviously corresponds to $\theta_t = 1$ for all t. This model is a special case of Kumbhakar's model, corresponding to $\gamma(t)$ being represented by a set of dummy variables for time. Thus the temporal pattern of technical inefficiency is completely unrestricted, though again the pattern is assumed to be the same for all firms. We expect this to be an empirically useful specification when the number of time periods (T) is relatively small. If T is large, this specification probably introduces too many parameters into the estimation problem.

This specification requires a normalization, since the scale of the θ's is not identified until the scale of the δ's is set, or vice-versa. We choose the normalization $\theta_1 = 1$. The choice of normalization has no substantive implications.

Our model is a special case of the model of Holtz-Eakin, Newey, and Rosen [1988, eq. (2.2), p. 1373]. Unlike their model, our model does not contain lagged dependent variables, and it does not allow coefficients other than θ_t to vary over time. Our method of estimation (described below) will be quite different from their instrumental variables method, because the absence of lagged dependent variables is a considerable statistical simplification.

The model we consider can also be compared to the two-way analysis of co-variance model that includes both individual and time effects. That model effectively has $\alpha_{it} = \delta_i + \theta_t$. The number of parameters in the analysis of covariance model is exactly the same as in our model, but the models are different. Our interpretation of the analysis of covariance model is that it is suitable in cases in which there are relevant unobservable variables that vary over time but not over individuals; it does not handle the case that our model is designed for, in which the effects of unobservable individual components vary over time. Compared to the analysis of covariance model, our model is more difficult to estimate, because it is nonlinear. However, unlike the analysis of covariance model, our model allows for inclusion of observables that are time invariant or invariant over individuals, a considerable advantage in many applications.

Our model includes Kumbhakar's model as a special case, but it is not directly comparable to the model of Cornwell, Schmidt, and Sickles. However, although we will not pursue it in this chapter, our model can be extended in such a way that it also includes their model as a special case. Our model is a one-component model, in the sense that there is one unobservable effect (δ_i) per person. Models with multiple components are identified and could be estimated. Specifically, we could write $\alpha_{it} = \sum_{j=1}^{g} \theta_{tj}\delta_{ij}$, a model with g components. With $g = 3$, the model of Cornwell, Schmidt, and Sickles (1990) corresponds to $\theta_{t1} = 1, \theta_{t2} = t$, and $\theta_{t3} = t^2$ for all t. This is a testable hypothesis. Hypotheses about the number of components are also testable. For further discussion, see Lee (1991, secs. 2.3 and 3.3).

8.3 Estimation

The model under consideration is

$$y_{it} = X_{it}'\beta + \theta_t\delta_i + v_{it} \tag{8.2}$$

The v_{it} are assumed to be independently and identically distributed with mean zero and variance σ_v^2. Normality is not assumed. We write the T observations for firm i as

$$y_i = X_i\beta + \xi\delta_i + v_i, \tag{8.3}$$

where $y_i = (y_{i1}, \ldots, y_{iT})'$, $X_i = (X_{i1}, \ldots, X_{iT})'$, $v_i = (v_{i1}, \ldots, v_{iT})'$, and where

$$\xi' = (1, \theta') \qquad \theta' = (\theta_2, \ldots, \theta_T) \tag{8.4}$$

We write all NT observations as

$$y = X\beta + (I_N \otimes \xi)\delta + v \tag{8.5}$$

where y is the $NT \times 1$ vector with ith block y_i, and similarly for X and v, and where $\delta' = (\delta_1, \ldots, \delta_N)$. The parameters to be estimated are $\beta, \theta, \sigma_v^2$, and either δ (in a fixed effects treatment) or σ_δ^2 (in a random effects treatment).

The estimation of this model is nontrivial, and a rigorous treatment would be a lengthy distraction in the present context. Here we will provide a brief summary of enough results to understand how the model can be applied empirically in a production frontier setting. More details can be found in Lee (1991).

8.3.1 Fixed Effects

We first consider the fixed effects case, in which δ is treated as a vector of parameters to be estimated. This case is considered in detail in Lee (1991, chap. 2). The basic complication is that the number of parameters depends on sample size (the "incidental parameters problem"), so that we cannot confidently assert the basic results (consistency and asymptotic normality) for least squares or maximum likelihood estimators. Rather, they must be established directly.

Using standard notation for projections, define

$$P_\xi = \xi(\xi'\xi)^{-1}\xi' \qquad M_\xi = I_T - P_\xi \tag{8.6}$$

In particular note that M_ξ is the $T \times T$ idempotent matrix such that $M_\xi\xi = 0$. Therefore

$$\begin{aligned} M_\xi y_i &= M_\xi X_i\beta + M_\xi v_i \\ (I_N \otimes M_\xi)y &= (I_N \otimes M_\xi)X\beta + (I_N \otimes M_\xi)v \end{aligned} \tag{8.7}$$

and the effects (δ's) have been removed. We also define the sum of squared errors (SSE) associated with (8.7):

$$\mathrm{SSE}_F(\beta, \xi) = \sum_i (M_\xi y_i - M_\xi X_i\beta)'(M_\xi y_i - M_\xi X_i\beta)$$

$$= [(I_N \otimes M_\xi)y - (I_N \otimes M_\xi)X\beta]'[(I_N \otimes M_\xi)y$$
$$-(I_N \otimes M_\xi)X\beta] \qquad (8.8)$$

If ξ (equivalently, θ) were known, least squares applied to Equation (8.7) would have simple and desirable properties. The estimate of β would be consistent and asymptotically normal, by standard results. Under normality of the errors, least squares would be the MLE, and also it would be the conditional MLE that would follow from conditioning on the sufficient statistic for δ_i, which is $\xi'(y_i - X_i\beta)$.

Since ξ is not known, such simple results are not available. However, proceeding by analogy to least squares in the case of known ξ, we will define our estimates of β and ξ, say $\hat{\beta}$ and $\hat{\xi}$, as the values that minimize SSE_F as given in Equation (8.8). There is no closed form expression for these estimates. However, there is an expression for $\hat{\beta}$ in terms of $\hat{\xi}$, and vice-versa. Lee (1991, pp. 12–13) shows that $\hat{\beta}$ is given by least squares applied to Equation (8.7), with M_ξ evaluated at $\xi = \hat{\xi}$; that is,

$$\hat{\beta} = \left(\sum_i X_i' \hat{M}_\xi X_i \right)^{-1} \sum_i X_i' \hat{M}_\xi y_i$$
$$= [X'(I_N \otimes \hat{M}_\xi)X]^{-1} X'(I_N \otimes \hat{M}_\xi)y \qquad (8.9)$$

with $\hat{M}_\xi$ indicating that M_ξ is evaluated at $\xi = \hat{\xi}$. Furthermore, $\hat{\xi}$ is the eigenvector of $\sum_i (y_i - X_i\hat{\beta})(y_i - X_i\hat{\beta})'$ corresponding to the largest eigenvalue. Using these results it is relatively easy to calculate $\hat{\beta}$ and $\hat{\xi}$ iteratively.

Since our estimates are obtained by minimization of a criterion function, we can evaluate their asymptotic properties directly, using results on optimization estimators from Amemiya (1985). Throughout the chapter we will consider asymptotic properties of our estimates as $N \to \infty$ with T fixed. This reflects our view that the model is applicable to data sets in which N is large but T is not. Lee (1991, pp. 12–14) shows, under certain regularity conditions, that the estimates are consistent and asymptotically normal. The nonstandard nature of this case shows up in the form of the covariance matrix of the estimates. We have

$$\sqrt{N}[(\hat{\beta}', \hat{\theta}')' - (\beta', \theta')'] \to N(0, A_F^{-1} B_F A_F^{-1}) \qquad (8.10)$$

where A_F is the probability limit of the matrix of second-order derivatives of SSE_F with respect to β and θ, and B_F is the probability limit of the matrix of sums of squares and cross products of first derivatives. In standard cases we would have $A = B$, but here we do not.

Once β and ξ have been estimated, we still need to obtain estimates of the α_{it} so that technical inefficiency can be estimated (as in Section 8.2). The estimate of δ_i is $\hat{\delta}_i = \hat{\xi}'(y_i - X_i\hat{\beta})/\hat{\xi}'\hat{\xi}$, and then $\hat{\alpha}_{it} = \hat{\theta}_t \hat{\delta}_i$.

8.3.2 *Random Effects*

We now consider the random effects case, in which the δ's are treated as random draws from a probability distribution. This case is treated in detail in Lee (1991, chap. 3).

Specifically, let $E(\delta_i) = \mu$, define $\delta_i^* = \delta_i - \mu$, and assume that the $\delta_i^*, i = 1, \ldots, N$ are independently and identically distributed with mean zero and variance σ_δ^2. Furthermore, assume that the δ^* are uncorrelated with the v and with the regressors (inputs); the latter is a very strong assumption, since a firm might be expected to know its intercept, and this would likely affect its input choices. Then the T observations for firm i can be written as

$$y_i = X_i\beta + \xi\mu + \epsilon_i \qquad \epsilon_i = \xi\delta_i^* + v_i \qquad (8.11)$$

and all NT observations can be written as

$$y = X\beta + (c \otimes \xi)\mu + \epsilon \qquad (8.12)$$

where c is an $N \times 1$ vector of ones. The error ϵ has mean zero and is uncorrelated with the regressors, but it has a complicated covariance matrix:

$$\text{cov}(\epsilon) = \Omega = \sigma_v^2 I_{NT} + \xi'\xi\sigma_\delta^2(I_N \otimes P_\xi) \qquad (8.13)$$

When the error has mean zero and is uncorrelated with the regressors, but has a nonscalar covariance matrix, we would expect ordinary least squares (OLS) to be inefficient, and the efficient estimator should be of the form of generalized least squares (GLS). This is so in the present case. The OLS estimators of β, ξ, and μ are defined as the values that minimize the criterion function

$$\begin{aligned} \text{SSE}_O(\beta, \xi, \mu) &= \sum_i (y_i - X_i\beta - \xi\mu)'(y_i - X_i\beta - \xi\mu) \\ &= [y - X\beta - (c \otimes \xi)\mu]'[y - X\beta - (c \otimes \xi)\mu] \qquad (8.14) \end{aligned}$$

Denote these estimators by $\check{\beta}, \check{\xi}$, and $\check{\mu}$. Lee (1991, pp. 31–32) shows that there is an explicit solution for the OLS estimators, as follows:

$$\check{\beta} = \left[\sum_i (X_i - \bar{X})'(X_i - \bar{X})\right]^{-1} \sum_i (X_i - \bar{X})'(y_i - \bar{y}) \qquad (8.15)$$

where $\bar{X} = \sum_i X_i/N$ and similarly for $\bar{y}$. Define the mean residuals $\bar{e} = \bar{y} - \bar{X}\check{\beta}$, and let $\bar{e}_1$ be the first element of $\bar{e}$. Then

$$\check{\xi} = \frac{\bar{e}}{\bar{e}_1} \qquad \check{\mu} = \bar{e}_1 \tag{8.16}$$

The OLS estimators are consistent but inefficient. To get efficient estimates we need to perform GLS. To do so, note that the inverse of Ω is

$$\Omega^{-1} = \sigma_\epsilon^{-2}(M_\xi + q^2 P_\xi) \qquad q^2 = \frac{\sigma_\epsilon^2}{\sigma_\epsilon^2 + \xi'\xi\sigma_\delta^2} \tag{8.17}$$

Accordingly, we define the GLS estimators of β, ξ, and μ as the values that minimize the criterion function

$$\begin{aligned}
\text{SSE}_G(\beta,\xi,\mu) &= \sum_i (y_i - X_i\beta - \xi\mu)'(M_\xi + q^2 P_\xi)(y_i - X_i\beta - \xi\mu) \\
&= [y - X\beta - (c \otimes \xi)\mu]'[(I_N \otimes M_\xi) + q^2(I_N \otimes P_\xi)] \\
&\quad [y - X\beta - (c \otimes \xi)\mu]
\end{aligned} \tag{8.18}$$

Let the GLS estimators be denoted by $\tilde{\beta}, \tilde{\xi}$, and $\tilde{\mu}$. Then $\tilde{\beta}$ and $\tilde{\xi}$ can be expressed in terms of each other, as follows:

$$\tilde{\beta} = \{X'[(I_N \otimes \tilde{M}_\xi) + q^2(M_c \otimes \tilde{P}_\xi)]X\}^{-1}X'[(I_N \otimes \tilde{M}_\xi) + q^2(M_c \otimes \tilde{P}_\xi)]y \tag{8.19}$$

where $M_c = I_N - c(c'c)^{-1}c' = I_N - cc'/N$, and where $\tilde{M}_\xi$ and $\tilde{P}_\xi$ indicate M_ξ and P_ξ evaluated at $\xi = \tilde{\xi}$. Letting $e_i = y_i - X_i\tilde{\beta}$ and $\bar{e} = \sum_i e_i/N$, $\tilde{\xi}$ is the eigenvector corresponding to the largest eigenvalue of

$$\begin{aligned}
\sum_i \{(1 - q^2)^{-1/2}e_i &+ [1 - (1 - q^2)^{-1/2}]\bar{e}\}\{(1 - q^2)^{-1/2}e_i \\
&+ [1 - (1 - q^2)^{-1/2}]\bar{e}\}'
\end{aligned} \tag{8.20}$$

Finally, $\tilde{\mu} = (c \otimes \tilde{\xi})'(y - X\tilde{\beta})/(N\tilde{\xi}'\tilde{\xi})$.

The GLS estimators are consistent and asymptotically normal. Similarly to the case for the fixed effects estimators, their asymptotic covariance matrix is of the form $A_G^{-1}B_G A_G^{-1}$, where A_G is made up of second derivatives of SSE_G with respect to the parameters, while B_G is made up of sums of squares and cross products of first derivatives. Lee (1991, pp. 36–38) shows that the GLS estimators are efficient relative to the fixed effects estimators, though the efficiency difference diminishes as T grows. For small T, the efficiency difference is potentially large. It reflects the fact that the fixed effects estimator uses only the "within" variation of the data (variation in M_ξ space) while the GLS estimator uses both the "within" and the "between" variation (variation in P_ξ space).

Feasible GLS estimation replaces q^2 above with an estimate based on OLS or within estimation of the model. Note that q^2 depends on σ_v^2 and on $(\sigma_v^2 + \xi'\xi\sigma_\delta^2)$. σ_v^2 can be estimated consistently as $\mathrm{SSE}_F/N(T-1)$, where SSE_F is given by Equation (8.8) above, evaluated using any consistent estimates of β and ξ (e.g., OLS). Similarly, if we define the "between" sum of squares SSE_B as

$$\mathrm{SSE}_B(\beta, \xi, \mu) = \sum_i (P_\xi y_i - P_\xi X_i \beta - \xi\mu)'(P_\xi y_i - P_\xi X_i \beta - \xi\mu)$$

$$= [(I_N \otimes P_\xi)y - (I_N \otimes P_\xi)X\beta - (c \otimes \xi)\mu]'$$

$$\times [(I_N \otimes P_\xi)y - (I_N \otimes P_\xi)X\beta - (c \otimes \xi)\mu] \quad (8.21)$$

then SSE_B/N, evaluated at any consistent estimates of β and ξ, is a consistent estimate of $(\sigma_v^2 + \xi'\xi\sigma_\delta^2)$.

The GLS estimator is efficient relative to the fixed effects estimator, but its consistency hinges on the assumption that the effects are uncorrelated with the regressors, while the fixed effects estimator is consistent without this assumption. It therefore follows that the hypothesis of no correlation between effects and regressors can be tested, along the familiar lines of Hausman (1978) and Hausman and Taylor (1981), by testing the significance of the difference between the fixed effects and GLS estimators.

Estimates of the intercepts α_{it} follow from estimates of the other parameters, much as in the previous section. We have $\tilde{\delta}_i^* = \tilde{\xi}'(y_i - X_i\tilde{\beta} - \tilde{\xi}\tilde{\mu})/\tilde{\xi}'\tilde{\xi}$, $\tilde{\delta}_i = \tilde{\delta}_i^* + \tilde{\mu} = \tilde{\xi}'(y_i - X_i\tilde{\beta})/\tilde{\xi}'\tilde{\xi}$, and $\tilde{\alpha}_{it} = \tilde{\theta}_t\tilde{\delta}_i$.

8.3.3 Tests of Hypotheses about ξ

Certain hypotheses about ξ are of interest. The most obvious is the hypothesis that ξ is a vector of ones, in which case the general model just presented reduces to the usual simple model of the panel data literature. Lee (1991, chap. 4) provides tests of this hypothesis, developed along the lines of Gallant (1985). These tests are generalizations of the usual Wald, LM, and likelihood ratio tests. Here we will present only the simplest of these tests, which is the generalized likelihood ratio (LR) test. It is based on the statistic

$$\mathrm{LR} = \frac{\mathrm{SSE_{RESTRICTED}} - \mathrm{SSE_{UNRESTRICTED}}}{\hat{\sigma}_v^2}, \quad (8.22)$$

where $\mathrm{SSE_{UNRESTRICTED}}$ can be either SSE_F of Equation (8.8) or SSE_G of Equation (8.18), and where $\mathrm{SSE_{RESTRICTED}}$ is the same SSE, but evaluated at the estimates calculated under the restriction that ξ is a vector of ones (i.e., from the simple model). The statistic is asymptotically distributed as chi-squared with $T-1$ degrees of freedom.

We can also test whether ξ takes the restricted form implied by a parametric specification like Kumbhakar's. Suppose that $g(\psi)$ is a $T \times 1$ vector of functions of t and of a $p \times 1$ vector of parameters, with $p < T - 1$, and suppose that $g(\psi)$ is normalized so that its first element equals 1. We wish to test the hypothesis that $\xi = g(\psi)$ for some (unkown) ψ. For example, to test Kumbhakar's specification we would set $g(t, \psi) = [1 + \exp(b + c)]/[1 + \exp(bt + ct^2)]$. The hypothesis that the $T - 1$ elements of $g(\psi)$ that are not normalized to unity depend on only p parameters embodies $T - 1 - p$ restrictions. The LR test described above is one way to test these restrictions, but its use requires fitting the restricted model, which may not be easy. An alternative minimum chi-square test is based on the unrestricted estimates, say $\hat{\xi}$. Let $\hat{V}$ be the (estimated) asymptotic covariance matrix of $\hat{\xi}$. Then we define

$$\mathrm{MCS} = \min_{\psi}[\hat{\xi} - g(\psi)]'\hat{V}^{-1}[\hat{\xi} - g(\psi)] \tag{8.23}$$

This calculation generally requires a numerical minimization, but only over the p parameters in ψ. The asymptotic distribution of the statistic is chi-squared with $T - 1 - p$ degrees of freedom.

8.4   Empirical Results

We will analyze a data set previously analyzed by Erwidodo (1990). The data consist of information on 171 rice farms in Indonesia, for six growing seasons. The data were collected by the Agro Economic Survey, as part of the Rural Dynamic Study in the rice production area of the Cimanuk River Basin, West Java, and obtained from the Center for Agro Economic Research, Ministry of Agriculture, Indonesia. Time periods are growing seasons, and there are two growing seasons per year; three of the six time periods are dry seasons and three are wet seasons. The data are collected from six different villages that contain 19, 24, 37, 33, 22, and 36 farm families, respectively.

The data set includes information on seed, urea, trisodium phosphate (TSP), labor, and land, all of which are regarded as inputs to the production of rice. It also includes some dummy variables, as follows. DP is a dummy variable equal to 1 if pesticides are used, and 0 otherwise. DV1 equals 1 if high-yielding varieties of rice are planted, while DV2 equals 1 if mixed varieties are planted; the omitted category represents traditional varieties. DSS equals 1 in the wet season and 0 otherwise. $DR1, \ldots, DR5$ are dummy variables representing the six villages, and are intended to control for differences in soil quality or other relevant factors across villages. For a further discussion of the data, see Erwidodo (1990).

We specify a Cobb-Douglas production function:

$$y_{it} = \beta_0 + \sum_{k=1}^{5} \beta_k X_{kit} + \beta_6 \mathrm{DP}_{it} + \beta_7 \mathrm{DV1}_{it} + \beta_8 \mathrm{DV2}_{it}$$

$$+\beta_9 \text{DSS}_t + \beta_{10}\text{DR1}_i + \beta_{11}\text{DR2}_i + \beta_{12}\text{DR3}_i$$
$$+\beta_{13}\text{DR4}_i + \beta_{14}\text{DR5}_i + \theta_t\delta_i + v_{it} \tag{8.24}$$

Here y = logarithm of total production of rough rice, in kilograms; $X1$ = logarithm of amount of seed, in kilograms; $X2$ = logarithm of amount of urea, in kilograms; $X3$ = logarithm of amount of TSP, in kilograms; $X4$ = logarithm of amount of labor, in labor-hours; $X5$ = logarithm of area planted with rice, in hectares; and the other variables are as defined above. This is the same specification used by Erwidodo, with one exception. He also included a dummy variable for firm size (large or small output), which we do not include because he found it to be insignificant, and also because of worries about its exogeneity. (Erwidodo also considered a translog production function, but it did not lead to efficiency measures that were very different from those generated by the Cobb-Douglas specification.)

Table 8.1 Estimates from the Simple Model (Time-Invariant Inefficiency)

Variable	OLS	Within	GLS
Constant	5.0811		5.0636
	(26.7)		(26.3)
Seed	.1358	.1208	.1327
	(5.06)	(4.46)	(4.93)
Urea	.1200	.0918	.1132
	(6.91)	(4.79)	(6.38)
TSP	.0718	.0892	.0761
	(6.31)	(7.71)	(6.66)
Labor	.2167	.2431	.2230
	(7.60)	(8.25)	(7.75)
Land	.4819	.4521	.4770
	(15.9)	(14.0)	(15.6)
DP	.0077	.0338	.0141
	(.27)	(1.15)	(.49)
DV1	.1755	.1788	.1772
	(4.60)	(4.75)	(4.66)
DV2	.1356	.1574	.1446
	(2.60)	(3.40)	(2.78)
DSS	.0489	.0533	.0492
	(2.26)	(2.73)	(2.35)
DR1	−.0500	—	−.0511
	(−1.16)		(−1.03)
DR2	−.0393		−.0442
	(−.73		(−.75)
DR3	−.0623		−.0724
	(−1.09)		(−1.17)
DR4	.0248		.0017
	(.47)		(.20)
DR5	.0818		.0750
	(1.48)		(1.25)

Table 8.1 gives the results obtained from the simple panel data model in which technical inefficiency is time-invariant, while Table 8.2 gives the results from the model of this chapter. We present OLS, within (fixed effects), and GLS estimates. The results in Table 8.1 are very similar to the results of Erwidodo (1990, table 5.3, p. 112), as would be expected. Note that in Table 8.1 the within estimator does not yield estimates of the coefficients of the time-invariant village dummy variables, because time-invariant variables cannot be included in a fixed effects treatment of the simple model. One of the advantages of the general model is the ability to include time-invariant regressors, such as village dummies, in the fixed effects model.

The results in Table 8.2 are qualitatively reasonable. Labor, land, seed, and both types of fertilizer are productive, and returns-to-scale are constant or slightly decreasing. High-yielding rice varieties have higher yields than traditional varieties, and productivity is higher in the wet season than in the dry season. Some villages

Table 8.2   Estimates from the General Model (Time-Varying Inefficiency)

Variable	Within	GLS
Constant	4.2065	4.7453
	(11.0)	(16.9)
Seed	.1241	.1286
	(3.86)	(3.89)
Urea	.1069	.1045
	(5.07)	(4.63)
TSP	.0303	.0421
	(2.27)	(3.16)
Labor	.2303	.2188
	(7.92)	(6.98)
Land	.4579	.4739
	(10.6)	(10.7)
DP	.0080	.0272
	(.29)	(.97)
DV1	.0805	.1040
	(2.28)	(2.95)
DV2	.1226	.1370
	(2.43)	(2.89)
DSS	.1580	.1684
	(3.21)	(2.67)
DR1	.0487	.0124
	(.35)	(.15)
DR2	.6292	.1621
	(2.40)	(1.79)
DR3	.4853	.0904
	(2.13)	(.96)
DR4	.2316	.0625
	(1.27)	(.60)
DR5	.6342	.2581
	(2.98)	(2.78)

are significantly more productive than others. (Whether they are more efficient is a question to which we will return below.)

Most of the results in Table 8.2 are not very different from the corresponding results in Table 8.1. That is, the general model does not lead to very different regression coefficients than the simple model. The biggest changes are in the coefficients of TSP, DV1, and DSS. The t-values change more than the regression coefficients, but again most of these changes are not substantial. Similarly, comparing the within and GLS estimates in Table 8.2, most of the results are quite similar.

From the point of view of efficiency measurement, however, we are more interested in the vector ξ than in the regression coefficients. Whether the general model will lead to substantially different efficiency calculations than the simple model depends on how far ξ is from a vector of ones. In fact, our estimates of ξ do not resemble vectors of ones. From within estimation we have $\hat{\xi} = (1, 1.171, .491, .680, 1.220, 1.385)$, while from GLS estimation we have $\tilde{\xi} = (1, 1.441, .323, .416, 1.199, 1.685)$. The deviations of elements of ξ from unity are both individually and jointly significant. For example, for the within estimates, the t-values for the hypothesis $\theta_t = 1$ are 1.48, -3.05, -2.47, 2.51 and 2.48 for $t = 2, 3, 4, 5$, and 6, respectively, and the t-values for the GLS estimates are similar. Similarly, the generalized likelihood ratio statistic given in Section 8.3.3 for the joint hypothesis that ξ is a vector of ones equals 238 for the within estimates and 288 for GLS, and these values obviously exceed any reasonable critical value for the chi-squared distribution with five degrees of freedom. Thus it is clear that our generalization of the simple model to allow time-varying technical inefficiency is supported by the data.

We can also reject the hypothesis that ξ is of the form proposed by Kumbhakar (1990). The MCS statistic given by Equation (8.23) equals 10.3, which exceeds the 5% critical value (7.81) for the chi-squared distribution with three degrees of freedom. It does not exceed the 1% critical value (11.3). Thus the restrictions implied by Kumbhakar's specification are rejected, though perhaps not too decisively.

We now turn to the calculation of efficiency measures. As a general statement, we have $\hat{\alpha}_{it} = \hat{\theta}_t \hat{\delta}_i$, $\hat{\alpha}_t = \max_j \hat{\alpha}_{jt}$, and $\hat{u}_{it} = \hat{\alpha}_t - \hat{\alpha}_{it}$. When all elements of $\hat{\xi}$ (i.e., all $\hat{\theta}_t$) are of the same sign, as they are in our estimates, these formulae simplify a little. We then have $\hat{\alpha}_t = \hat{\theta}_t [\max_j \hat{\delta}_j]$, and $\hat{u}_{it} = \hat{\theta}_t [(\max_j \hat{\delta}_j) - \hat{\delta}_i]$. Thus some simple facts emerge. Ordinal rankings of different firms will be the same in all time periods and will be determined by the ordinal rankings of the $\hat{\delta}$'s. The temporal pattern of efficiency will be the same for all firms; this is the maintained hypothesis of our model. However, the magnitude of the temporal change in efficiency will vary over firms, and it will vary more for firms that are less efficient. Furthermore, inefficiency levels will be larger for time periods when $\hat{\theta}_t$ is larger and smaller for time periods when $\hat{\theta}_t$ is smaller.

Using the fixed effect (within) estimates, we find average (mean) efficiency levels of .449, .396, .666, .574, .382 and .340 for t = 1, 2, 3, 4, 5, and 6, respectively.

The overall average efficiency level is .468. The GLS estimates yield somewhat higher efficiency levels of .601, .485, .845, .806, .545, and .432, with an overall average of .619. [Note that these efficiency levels are calculated as $1 - \hat{u}_{it}$. The alternative calculation $\exp(-\hat{u}_{it})$ will lead to slightly higher efficiency levels; for example, .626 instead of .468 for the within estimates.] The overall average efficiency levels from within and GLS are somewhat but not too much different from the average efficiency levels implied by the simple model, which are .567 for within and .571 for GLS. However, Erwidodo reports a rather different average efficiency level, .935, from the method of Battese and Coelli (1988), which assumes normal noise and time-invariant half-normal technical inefficiency. It is expected that the method of Battese and Coelli would generate higher efficiency levels than our calculations; the strength of the distributional assumptions allows statistical noise to be purged more effectively. However, it is not obvious how to extend this method to the current model. Furthermore, imposing the half-normal assumption changes the levels of inefficiency but not the efficiency rankings, at least in the case of time-invariant inefficiency.

Figure 8.1 displays the temporal pattern of technical efficiency for various firms. The most efficient firm automatically is at 100% efficiency for all time periods. The other firms for which technical efficiency is displayed are the second most efficient firm, the median firm, and the least efficient firm. As noted above, the temporal pattern of technical efficiency is the same for all firms, though the magnitude of the changes varies over time. There is no apparent trend to the observed pattern, but efficiency levels are slightly higher on average in wet seasons than in dry seasons. Presumably a reasonable next step is to try to account for the observed temporal pattern in terms of changes in weather or other relevant conditions over time. The basic empirical fact driving these results must be that, after correcting for measured inputs and some other variables, output is less dispersed across firms in time periods 3 and 4 than in other time periods, and this fact should have some agricultural or economic basis.

Alternative efficiency measures can be calculated if some of the explanatory variables in the production function are interpreted as indicators of inefficiency, as opposed to legitimate determinants of frontier output. Our production function includes inputs (labor, land, seed, and two types of fertilizer), and it also includes dummy variables for rice variety, season, and village. Some of these dummy variables may affect both frontier output and technical inefficiency. For example, traditional rice varieties yield less than high-yielding varieties, so that the type of rice grown affects the maximum possible output. However, it is possible that individuals who grow traditional varieties also use less modern and less efficient techniques in general, so that at least some of the apparent effect of rice variety on output is in fact a difference in technical efficiency. Similarly, village location may affect frontier output, perhaps because soil quality affects output. However, farmers in different villages may also differ in efficiency, perhaps because of differences in education, access to technology, or level of superstition.

Whether a particular variable affects frontier output or the level of efficiency

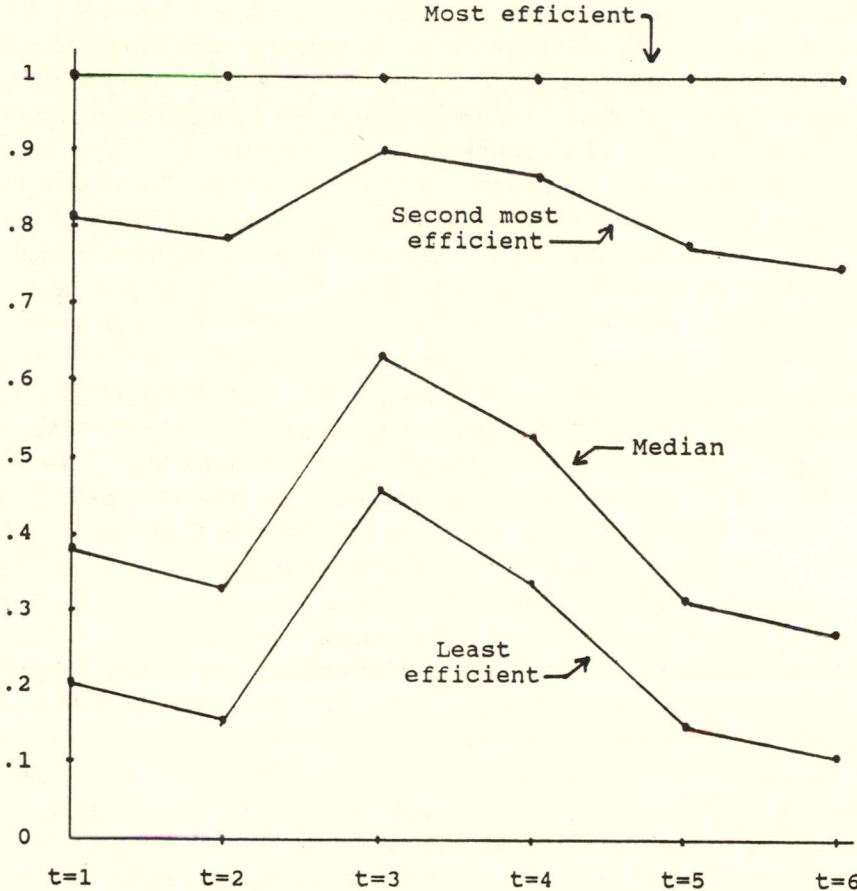

Fig. 8.1 Technical efficiency of some firms

is not a question we can expect to answer from the data, at least not in the present model. [This question can be addressed, under strong assumptions, in some other models, such as the model of Kumbhakar, Ghosh, and McGuckin (1991).] However, our answer to this question obviously affects the way that technical efficiency should be calculated. The calculations above assume that all the variables in the specification affect frontier output; we are controlling for all of them before efficiency is calculated. Alternatively, suppose that some variables Z_{it}, a subset of the variables X_{it} in the general specification (8.1), affect output only because they affect the level of technical inefficiency. Then in calculating efficiency levels it is appropriate to consider these variables as part of the intercept. Specifically, let $\hat{\gamma}$ be the estimated coefficients of these variables. Then the correct calculation is $\hat{\alpha}_{it} = Z_{it}\hat{\gamma} + \hat{\theta}_t\hat{\delta}_i$, $\hat{\alpha}_t = \max_j \hat{\alpha}_{jt} = \max_j(Z_{jt}\hat{\gamma} + \hat{\theta}_t\hat{\delta}_j)$, and $\hat{u}_{it} = \hat{\alpha}_t - \hat{\alpha}_{it}$. This is only roughly like not having included the variables Z in the specification in the first place; it differs because their inclusion may have changed the estimates of the coefficients of the other variables. Note also that, when variables Z_{it} are included in the intercept for purposes of efficiency calculations, the temporal pattern of technical efficiency will no longer necessarily follow the temporal pattern of the $\hat{\theta}_t$. Different firms may have different patterns of technical efficiency, and ordinal rankings may vary over time.

Of course, the question of whether to include regressors other than inputs in the production function, and of whether to then include them in the efficiency calculations, is not new to this model. In this model, however, their inclusion fundamentally changes the range of temporal patterns of technical efficiency that are possible.

The seasonal dummy DSS varies only over t, not over i, so its inclusion or noninclusion in the intercept would not affect the estimated efficiency levels of the firms. For the calculations about to be reported, we will regard the dummy variables for rice variety as affecting frontier output, but the dummy variables for village as affecting technical efficiency. Thus, in the notation above, $Z_{it} = [\mathrm{DR}1_i, \ldots, \mathrm{DR}5_i]$.

Based on the within estimates, we now find average levels of technical efficiency of .565, .536, .673, .629, .528, and .476 for $t = 1, 2, 3, 4, 5$, and 6, respectively, with an overall average of .568. These are somewhat higher levels of technical efficiency than we had previously. (This is perhaps surprising, since we are now effectively comparing the output of a given farm to the maximum over all farms, not just over the farms in the particular village.) For the GLS estimates, the average efficiency levels of .595, .509, .768, .741, .554, and .467 (with an overall average of .606) are not much different than we had previously.

Figure 8.2 displays the technical efficiency in all six time periods for various firms. The most efficient firm for $t = 1$ is also most efficient for all time periods except $t = 6$, when it is the third most efficient firm. The median firm for $t = 1$ and the least efficient firm for $t = 1$ have patterns of efficiency that are not very different from the pattern displayed in Figure 8.1. The least efficient firm for $t = 1$ is, incidentally, also least efficient for $t = 2, 5$, and 6, and it is the same firm that was least efficient (for all t) in Figure 8.1. The third most efficient firm for $t = 1$ is the most efficient firm for $t = 6$, and is the same firm that was most efficient (for all t) in Figure 8.1. Its pattern of technical efficiency is more or less the opposite of those of the other firms shown in Figure 8.2. Other more complicated patterns would also be possible in the case that Z_{it} varied over both i and t.

8.5 Concluding Remarks

In this chapter we have proposed a model for efficiency measurement in the presence of panel data for which the time-series dimension is not too large. We assume that the temporal pattern of technical inefficiency is the same for all firms, but is otherwise completely unrestricted. This is a plausible extension of previous models, and it is supported by the data to which we apply it.

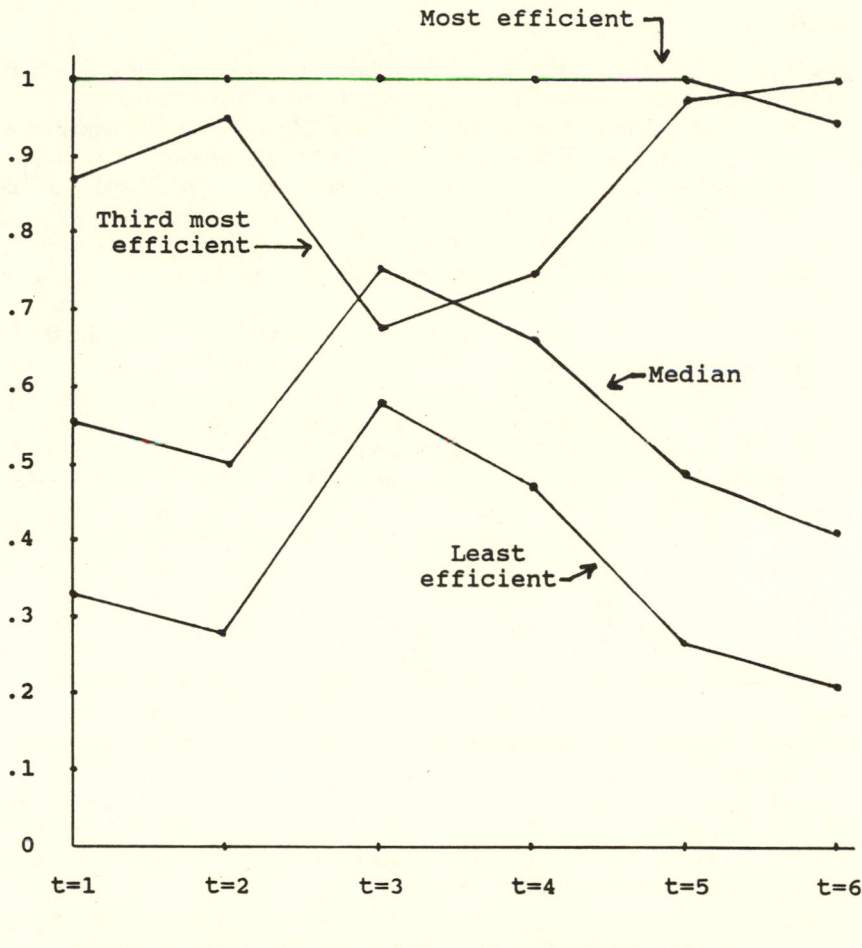

(Efficiency rankings are as determined at t=1.)

Fig. 8.2 Technical efficiency of some firms (dummy variables for village included in the intercept)

Our estimates of technical efficiency are essentially based on weighted averages of residuals (with the average taken over time, for a given firm), and an implication of a small time-series dimension of the data is that these averages may be rather noisy. This may tend to lead us to overestimate the differences between the intercepts of the firms, and therefore to underestimate technical efficiency levels. We could consider assuming a distribution for the effects, not for purposes of estimation of the regression coefficients, but just for the purpose of separating inefficiency from noise, as in Jondrow, Lovell, Materov, and Schmidt (1982) or Battese and Coelli (1988). This would appear to be a reasonable direction for future research.

REFERENCES

Aigner, D. J., C. A. K. Lovell, and P. Schmidt (1977), "Formulation and Estimation of Stochastic Frontier Production Functions," *Journal of Econometrics* 6(1) (July): 21–37.

Amemiya, T. (1985), *Advanced Econometrics*. Cambridge, Mass.: Harvard University Press.

Battese, G. E. (1990), "Frontier Production Functions, Technical Efficiency and Panel Data," Unpublished Paper, Department of Econometrics, University of New England, Armidale, Australia.

Battese, G. E., and T. J. Coelli (1988), "Prediction of Firm-Level Technical Efficiencies with a Generalized Frontier Production Function and Panel Data," *Journal of Econometrics* 38(3)(July): 387–399.

Battese, G. E., and T. J. Coelli (1991), "Frontier Production Functions, Technical Efficiency and Panel Data: With Application to Paddy Farmers in India," Unpublished Paper, Department of Econometrics, University of New England, Armidale, Australia.

Bauer, P. W. (1990), "Recent Developments in the Econometric Estimation of Frontiers," *Journal of Econometrics* 46(1/2)(October/November): 39–56.

Chamberlain, G. (1980), "Analysis of Covariance with Qualitative Data," *Review of Economic Studies* 47:225–238.

Cornwell, C., P. Schmidt, and R. C. Sickles (1990), "Production Frontiers with Cross-Sectional and Time-Series Variation in Efficiency Levels," *Journal of Econometrics* 46(1/2)(October/November): 185–200.

Erwidodo (1990), "Panel Data Analysis on Farm-Level Efficiency, Input Demand and Output Supply of Rice Farming in West Java, Indonesia," Unpublished Ph.D. Dissertation, Department of Agricultural Economics, Michigan State University, East Lansing.

Gallant, A. R. (1985), *Nonlinear Statistical Models*. New York: John Wiley and Sons.

Greene, W. H. (1990), "A Gamma-Distributed Stochastic Frontier Model," *Journal of Econometrics* 46(1/2)(October/November): 141–164.

Hausman, J. A. (1978), "Specification Tests in Econometrics," *Econometrica*, 46(6) (November): 1251–1272.

Hausman, J. A., and W. Taylor (1981), "Panel Data and Unobservable Individual Effects," *Econometrica* 49(6)(November): 1377–1399.

Holtz-Eakin, D., W. Newey, and H. S. Rosen (1988), "Estimating Vector Autoregressions with Panel Data," *Econometrica* 56(6)(November): 1371–1395.

Ivaldi, M., S. Monier-Dilhan, and M. Simioni (1991), "Heterogeneity and the Measurement of Efficiency," Unpublished Paper, Faculté des Sciences Economiques, Université de Toulouse, France.

Jondrow, J., C. A. K. Lovell, I. S. Materov, and P. Schmidt (1982), "On the Estimation of Technical Inefficiency in the Stochastic Frontier Production Function Model," *Journal of Econometrics* 23(2)(October): 269–274.

Kumbhakar, S. C. (1990), "Production Frontiers, Panel Data, and Time-Varying Technical Inefficiency," *Journal of Econometrics* 46(1/2)(October/November): 201–212.

Kumbhakar, S. C., S. Ghosh, and J. T. McGuckin (1991), "A Generalized Production Frontier Approach for Estimating Determinants of Inefficiency in U.S. Dairy Farms," *Journal of Business and Economic Statistics* 9(3)(July): 287–296.

Lee, Y. H. (1991), "Panel Data Models with Multiplicative Individual and Time Effects: Applications to Compensation and Frontier Production Functions," Unpublished Ph.D. Dissertation, Department of Economics, Michigan State University, East Lansing.

Lovell, C. A. K., and P. Schmidt (1988), "A Comparison of Alternative Approaches to the Measurement of Productive Efficiency," in Ali Dogramaci and Rolf Fare, eds., *Applica-*

tions of Modern Production Theory: Efficiency and Production. Boston, Mass. Kluwer Academic Publishers.

Meeusen, W., and J. van den Broeck (1977), "Efficiency Estimation from Cobb-Douglas Production Functions with Composed Error," *International Economic Review* 18(2) (June): 435–444.

Pitt, M., and L-F Lee (1981), "The Measurement and Sources of Technical Inefficiency in the Indonesian Weaving Industry," *Journal of Development Economics* 9(1): 43–64.

Schmidt, P. (1986), "Frontier Production Functions," *Econometric Reviews* 4(2): 289–328.

Schmidt, P., and R. C. Sickles (1984), "Production Frontiers and Panel Data," *Journal of Business and Economic Statistics* 2(4)(October): 367–374.

Stevenson, R. E. (1980), "Likelihood Functions for Generalized Stochastic Frontier Estimation," *Journal of Econometrics* 13(1)(May): 57–66.

9

TECHNICAL EFFICIENCY AND TECHNICAL PROGRESS IN SWEDISH DAIRY FARMS

Subal C. Kumbhakar and Lennart Hjalmarsson[1]

9.1 Introduction

In recent years panel data are increasingly used in the estimation of economic efficiency. Although one can estimate technical efficiency for each production unit using cross-sectional data, the estimates of technical efficiency can not control for individual-specific effects. One has to assume that these individual-specific effects are identical for all production units. On the other hand, when panel data are available one can separate technical (in)efficiency from individual-specific effects.

Panel studies can be classified into two groups in terms of their treatment of technical efficiency.

The most common procedure is to assume that technical efficiency is invariant over time. This assumption has the advantage of estimating technical efficiency without any distributional assumptions on it. This approach is applied in, for example, Battese and Coelli (1988), Pitt and Lee (1981), Kumbhakar (1987, 1988), and Schmidt and Sickles (1984). However, the main problem with this approach is that individual-specific effects are confounded with technical (in)efficiency of the production unit. Since individual-specific effects also capture the effects of inputs that are invariant over time (but vary across production units) and such effects are not inefficiency—it is inappropriate to label the individual-specific effects as technical inefficiency. Policy prescriptions based on such measures may be misleading unless one can disentangle the individual-specific effects from inefficiency.

[1] Paper presented at EURO XI, 11th European Congress on Operational Research, RWTH Aachen, Germany, July 16–19, 1991. Financial support from the SJFR, the Bank of Sweden Tercentenary Foundation, Jan Wallander's Research Foundation and Gothenburg Economic School Foundation is gratefully acknowledged.

The alternative procedure is to assume that technical efficiency is varying over time. This approach is applied in Cornwell, Schmidt, and Sickles (1990) and Kumbhakar (1990). However, in none of these studies technical inefficiency is separated from individual-specific effects.[2]

The purpose of this study is to develop a method that separates technical inefficiency from individual-specific effects. The proposed methodology has two steps. In the first stage, consistent estimates of the production function parameters (except for the individual-specific effects and parameters of the error components including technical inefficiency) are obtained. These estimates are used, in the second stage, to estimate individual-specific effects, parameters of the error components, and technical efficiency for each unit over time, that is, technical efficiency is assumed time-varying. Empirical implementation of this two-step procedure is much simpler than the ML method proposed in Kumbhakar (1991). The methodology is used to examine technical efficiency and technical progress of Swedish dairy farms. Since location or climate, and land quality are important farm-specific characteristics which should not be confounded with inefficiency the approach applied here is highly relevant. We use two panel data sets covering periods 1960–1967 and 1968–1976. The first set has 29 and the second 67 farms.

9.2 The Theoretical Model

Let the production function with technical inefficiency be written as

$$y = f(x)e^{\varepsilon} \tag{9.1}$$

where y is output, x is a vector of n inputs, $f(.)$ is the production technology, and ε is the error term which is composed of technical ineffciency τ and statistical noise ν. Using a translog production function to represent the underlying technology, the above relation can be written as

$$\ln y = \alpha_0 + \alpha' \ln x + \frac{1}{2} \ln x' B \ln x + \gamma_t t + \frac{1}{2} \gamma_{tt} t^2 + \delta' \ln x \, t + \varepsilon \tag{9.2}$$

where $\varepsilon = \tau + \nu$, α and δ are $n \times 1$ vectors and B is an $n \times n$ symmetric matrix of parameters. With panel data one can accommodate a richer specification of ε, viz.,

$$\varepsilon_{ft} = u_f + \tau_{ft} + \nu_{ft} \tag{9.3}$$

where subscripts f and t index farm ($f = 1, \dots, F$) and time ($t = 1, \dots, T$),

---

[2] Kumbhakar (1991) is an exception. He considered a model that separates technical inefficiency from individual- and time-specific effects. The maximum likelihood (ML) method proposed in the model is too complicated for empirical application.

respectively. u_f denotes farm-specific effects. Unlike the model using cross-sectional data, here we can disentangle farm-specific effects u_f from technical inefficiency τ_{ft}.

We assume that the objective of the farm is to maximize profit. Furthermore, in the present study we treat the inputs as exogenous. One can justify this assumption in terms of a two-stage decision process where input choice decision is made prior to output decision. In such a case maximizing profit with given (exogenous) input and output prices is equivalent to maximizing output. This argument is in accord to the textbook definition of the production function. Thus estimation of only the production function is consistent with the profit maximization hypothesis.

The production function specified in Equation (9.2) does not impose any restrictions on returns-to-scale (RTS) or, more specifically, the elasticity of scale function $\kappa(x)$ and technical progress. The elasticity of scale can be estimated from the sum of the marginal elasticities of output with regard to each input

$$\kappa(x) = \sum_{i=1}^{n} \frac{\partial \ln y}{\partial \ln x_i} = \sum_{i=1}^{n} \eta_i \tag{9.4}$$

where

$$\eta_i = \frac{\partial \ln y}{\partial \ln x_i} = \alpha_i + \sum_j \beta_{ij} \ln x_j + \delta_i t \tag{9.5}$$

Thus κ is not only farm-specific, it also varies over time unless the production function is homogeneous of degree one. [Equation (9.4) follows directly from the definition of the elasticity of scale as a directional elasticity of the production function; see Førsund and Hjalmarsson (1987, pp. 83–84).]

The rate of technical progress (RTP) is obtained as

$$\text{RTP} = \frac{\partial \ln y}{\partial \ln t} = \gamma_t + \gamma_{tt} t + \sum_j \delta_j \ln x_j \tag{9.6}$$

Technical progress is neutral if $\delta_j = 0, j = 1, \ldots, n$. If it is not neutral, we will measure the bias in the following way. Under perfect competition and profit-maximizing behavior

$$\eta_i = \frac{\partial \ln y}{\partial \ln x_i} = \frac{x_i}{y} \frac{\partial y}{\partial x_i} = \frac{w_i x_i}{py} = s_i \tag{9.7}$$

where p and w_i are output and input prices, respectively, and s_i the cost share for input i. From Equation (9.7) the bias in technical progress can be derived as follows:

$$\eta_t(x) = \frac{\partial \ln x_i}{\partial t} = \frac{\partial \ln s_i}{\partial t} + \frac{\partial \ln y}{\partial t} = \frac{1}{s_i} \delta_i + \text{RTP}. \tag{9.8}$$

Technical progress is input i using (saving) if

$$\eta_t(x) > 0 \quad (< 0) \tag{9.9}$$

9.3 The Econometric Model and Estimation

The specification of the error term in Equation (9.3) fits into the regular panel data model except for the presence of the technical inefficiency component τ_{ft} and the absence of time-specific components, λ_t.[3] Since τ_{ft} is one-sided (nonpositive), its parameters can be separately identified from those of ν_{ft} which is two-sided. Farm-specific components u_f are identified since they are time-invariant. From an estimation point of view one can treat u_f either fixed [the fixed effects (FE) model] or random [the random effects (RE) model]. The RE model has the advantage of estimating less parameters at the cost of assuming u_f independent of x_i. Such an assumption is not necessary in the FE model where u_f are parameters to be estimated along with the other parameters in the model. In this study we assume u_f to be fixed parameters thereby allowing correlations between u_f and x variables in the model.

Estimation of the parameters and technical efficiency are developed in two steps. In the first step we consider estimation of the parameters in α, δ, and B together with γ_t and γ_{tt}. Estimation of $(\alpha_0 + u_f)$ and parameters associated with τ and ν as well as farm- and time-specific technical efficiency are developed in the second step.

Step 1: Estimation of the parameters in α, δ, B, and γ_t, γ_{tt}
Consider the model outlined in Equations (9.2) and (9.3). The farm-effects u_f are eliminated from the model after within transformation. The resulting model becomes

$$
\begin{aligned}
\ln y_{ft} - \frac{1}{T}\sum_t \ln y_{ft} = {} & \sum_t \alpha_i \left(\ln x_{ift} - \frac{1}{T}\sum_t \ln x_{ift} \right) + \gamma_t \left(t - \frac{1}{T}\sum_t t \right) \\
& + \frac{1}{2}\left(\sum_i \sum_j \beta_{ij} \ln x_{ift} \ln x_{jft} \right) \\
& - \frac{1}{T}\sum_t \sum_i \sum_j \beta_{ij} \ln x_{ift} \ln x_{jft} \\
& + \frac{1}{2}\gamma_{tt}\left(t^2 - \frac{1}{T}\sum_t t^2 \right) + \omega_{ft} \tag{9.10}
\end{aligned}
$$

where

$$\omega_{ft} = \left(\tau_{ft} - \frac{1}{T}\sum_t \tau_{ft} \right) - \left(\nu_{ft} - \frac{1}{T}\sum_t \nu_{ft} \right) \tag{9.11}$$

[3] We have not introduced time-specific components since time is introduced as one of the variables in the production function.

It can be seen that $E(\omega_{ft}) = 0$, $\text{var}(\omega_{ft}) = \text{constant}$, and $\text{cov}(\omega_{ft}, \omega'_{ft}) = 0$ for $f \neq f', t \neq t'$ if

1. τ_{ft} and ν_{ft} are independently and identically distributed (iid) over f and t each with zero mean and constant variance.
2. τ_{ft} and ν_{ft} are independent among themselves for all i and t.

Thus one can use ordinary least squares (OLS) to obtain consistent estimates of the parameters in α, δ, B, and γ_t, γ_{tt}.

Step 2: Estimation of $(\alpha_0 + u_f)$ and τ_{ft}

Using the estimates of α, δ, B, and γ_t, γ_{tt} obtained from the first step, the residual from Equation (9.2) (including the intercept, α_0), e_{ft}, are calculated. These residuals also contain the following effects:

$$e_{ft} = \alpha_0 + u_f + \tau_{ft} + \nu_{ft} \tag{9.12}$$

The next problem is to estimate $(\alpha_0 + u_f)$ and the parameters associated with the distributions of τ_{ft} and ν_{ft}. To do so we make the following distributional assumptions on them. These are

ν_{ft} is i.i.d. $N(0, \sigma_\nu^2)$.

τ_{ft} is i.i.d. $N(0, \sigma_\tau^2)$ truncated at zero from below.

ν_{ft} and τ_{ft} are independent among themselves.

These assumptions are standard in the frontier models with cross-sectional data. We are using them in the panel data models also.

If one obtains estimates of the residuals corresponding to the stochastic frontier production function, z_{ft}, viz.,

$$z_{ft} = \alpha_0 + u_f + \nu_{ft} \equiv D_{ft}\mu_f + \nu_{ft} \tag{9.13}$$

where

$$\mu_f = \alpha_0 + u_f$$

and D_{ft} is a dummy variable corresponding to farm f $(f = 1, \ldots, F)$, technical inefficiency τ_{ft} can then be estimated by subtracting z_{ft} from e_{ft}. But z_{ft} is unobserved. So we need to estimate z_{ft} first. This is done by the EM algorithm; see Dempster, Laird, and Rubin (1977) and Huang (1984).

The EM algorithm has two steps. In the E step the unobserved variable z_{ft} is replaced by its expected value (conditional on e_{ft}). The likelihood function (obtained from the joint pdf of z_{ft} and e_{ft}) is maximized in the M step.

9.3.1 The EM Algorithm

To implement the EM algorithm, first we derive the conditional probability density function (pdf) of z_{ft} given e_{ft}, viz.,

$$f(z_{ft}|e_{ft}) = \frac{1}{\sqrt{2\pi}\sigma} \exp\left(\frac{-(z_{ft} - m_{ft})^2}{2\sigma^2}\right) \frac{1}{\Phi[(e_{ft} - m_{ft})/\sigma]} \qquad z_{ft} \geq e_{ft}$$

$$\tag{9.14}$$

where

$$m_{ft} = \frac{\sigma_\nu^2 e_{ft} + \sigma_\tau^2 D_{ft}\mu_f}{\sigma_\nu^2 + \sigma_\tau^2} \tag{9.15}$$

and

$$\sigma^2 = \frac{\sigma_\nu^2 \sigma_\tau^2}{\sigma_\nu^2 + \sigma_\tau^2} \tag{9.16}$$

Then the first two moments of z_{ft} given e_{ft} are calculated

$$E(z_{ft}|e_{ft}) = m_{ft} + \sigma\lambda_{ft} \tag{9.17}$$

and

$$E(z_{ft}^2|e_{ft}) = \sigma^2[1 + e_{ft}^*\lambda_{ft} - \lambda_{ft}^2] + (m_{ft} + \sigma\lambda_{ft})^2 \tag{9.18}$$

where

$$e_{ft}^* = \frac{e_{ft} - m_{ft}}{\sigma} \tag{9.19}$$

and

$$\lambda_{ft} = \frac{\phi(.)}{\Phi(.)} \tag{9.20}$$

$\phi(.)$ and $\Phi(.)$ are the standard normal density and the cumulative distribution function, respectively, evaluated at e_{ft}^*.

The EM algorithm works as follows. Let $\theta = (\mu', \sigma_\nu^2, \sigma_\tau^2)'$ and $\theta_{(p)}$ denote the estimate of θ at the pth iteration. In the E step of the algorithm the complete-data sufficient statistics

$$\left[\sum_f \sum_t e_{ft}^2, \sum_f \sum_t e_{ft} z_{ft}, \sum_f \sum_t z_{ft} D_{ft}, \sum_f \sum_t z_{ft}^2\right] \tag{9.21}$$

are estimated by

$$\left[\sum_f \sum_t e_{ft}^2, \sum_f \sum_t e_{ft} E(z_{ft}|e_{ft})_{(p)}, \sum_f \sum_t E(z_{ft}|e_{ft})_{(p)} D_{ft},\right.$$
$$\left.\sum_f \sum_t E(z_{ft}^2|e_{ft})_{(p)}\right] \tag{9.22}$$

The new estimate at the $(p + 1)$st iteration is obtained by maximizing the likelihood function, obtained from the joint pdf of e_{ft} and z_{ft}. (The joint pdf is the product of the marginal pdf of e_{ft} and z_{ft}.) These estimates are

$$\hat{\mu}_{f(p+1)} = \left(\sum_t D_{ft}\right)^{-1}\left[\sum_t D_{ft} E(z_{ft})_{(p)}\right] \qquad f = 1, \ldots, F \tag{9.23}$$

$$\hat{\sigma}_{\tau(p+1)}^2 = \frac{\sum_f \sum_t e_{ft}^2 - 2\sum_f \sum_t e_{ft} E(z_{ft})_{(p)} + \sum_f \sum_t E(z_{ft}^2)_{(p)}}{FT} \tag{9.24}$$

$$\hat{\sigma}_{\nu(p+1)}^2 = \frac{\sum_f \sum_t E(z_{ft}^2)_{(p)} - \sum_f \nu_{f(p+1)}^2 \sum_t D_{ft}}{FT} \tag{9.25}$$

The estimated variance of $\mu_{f(p+1)}$ is

$$\frac{\hat{\sigma}_{\nu(p+1)}^2}{\sum_t D_{ft}} \tag{9.26}$$

The estimates in each iteration are obtained from the OLS technique where the unobserved variable z is replaced by $E(z|e, \theta)$. Moreover, these estimates are the maximum likelihood (ML) estimates when convergence is achieved. Thus the main advantage of the EM algorithm is its simplicity in empirical implementation.[4]

Once the estimate of the parameters in θ [$\theta = (\mu', \sigma_\nu^2, \sigma_\tau^2)'$] is obtained, technical inefficiency specific to each farm over time is derived from the relation

---

[4] One can, in principle, use the EM algorithm to estimate all the parameters in one step. However, we used the EM algorithm in the second step because otherwise there are too many parameters to be estimated.

$$\hat{\tau}_{ft} = e_{ft} - E(z_{ft}|e_{ft}, \hat{\theta}) \qquad (9.27)$$

Technical efficiency can be derived from

$$\text{TE}_{ft} = \exp(\hat{\tau}_{ft}) \qquad (9.28)$$

9.4 Data

The data used in this study are taken from the annual survey of economic conditions of the farms in Sweden (JEU) handled by Statistics Sweden. The survey was used as a base for the price negotiations between the farmers and the government for the regulated part of Swedish agriculture. From this sample we have chosen those farms that concentrate on milk production. The selected group of farms has an average income from milk and meat that exceed 85 percent of total income. The data cover two periods, 1960–1967 and 1968–1975 with the same farms in each sample. Thus, we have two sets of panel data for two 8-year periods with 29 farms during the first period and 76 during the second. In 1976 definitions were changed so there are no comparable data after this point of time.

However, from an agricultural policy point of view, the chosen time periods are very interesting, since during the first period Swedish farming was exposed to a fairly strong profit squeeze, while the rate of return returned to more "normal" conditions during the second period. Moreover, the last period covers the industrial "productivity slowdown years" 1974–1975 after the first oil price shock, and our analysis will reveal if such a slowdown characterizes agriculture too.

Output y is measured by total sales per farm at constant prices. As regards factors of production we limit our production function analysis to four inputs: labor, capital, land, and material (other current inputs) denoted by L, K, A, and M, respectively.

Labor is measured as total number of hours worked, including management, family, and hired labor.

Capital input is measured as user cost of capital equipment (excluding buildings). User cost is defined as the sum of interest and depreciation on the stock of capital equipment at replacement value. We have used the same rates of user cost as those used in the JEU survey. The cost of repair and maintenance of the capital stock is not included here but is part of variable inputs.

Land input is measured as hectares of arable land with an adjustment for soil quality and climatic location. This quality adjustment might be crude, but is applied individually for each farm and should remove the largest part of land quality differences. Remaining quality differences are less of a problem within the framework applied here, within which farm-specific effects are included in the model.

The fourth factor, materials, is the aggregated value of cash expenditure items,

Table 9.1 Summary Statistics of the Data Set

Variable	Mean	Minimum	Maximum	No. of observations
1960–1967				
Output	71,096.74	7,976	16,8216	232
Labor	3,703.52	1,673	6,205	232
Material	129.71	35	378	232
Land	21.54	9	52	232
Capital	29,423.15	3,799	71,882	232
1968–1975				
Output	1,353.47	354	5,277	608
Labor	3,592.37	1,915	7,931	608
Material	303.39	75	1,048	608
Land	30.68	10	83	608
Capital	672.08	161	2,918	608

fuel, seed, pesticides, etc., as well as the costs of repair and maintenance of capital equipment. It is measured in constant prices.

Summary statistics of the data is presented in Table 9.1. Note that different base years are used in the two data sets so the monetary units (output, material, and capital) are not comparable.

During the studied periods the changes in absolute and relative prices have been considerable. Price indices for our inputs and output are presented in Table 9.2.

In the first period only capital had a slower price increase than the product, while in the second period both capital and materials had a slower rate of price increase than the product.

Table 9.2 Changes in Relative Prices of Inputs and Output, 1960–1967 and 1968–1975, Index

Year	Labor	Capital	Land	Material	Milk and meat (weighted)	Consumer price Index
1960	100	100	100	100	100	100
1967	193	125	167	111	130	133
1968	100	100	100	100	100	100
1975	257	147	208	157	194	161

Source: Statistics Sweden, official statistics.

9.5 Empirical Results

9.5.1 Specification tests

The model specified in Section 9.2 is estimated using two panel data sets on Swedish dairy farms. We used translog functions to represent the underlying production technology in both the data sets. The advantage of using a flexible function form such as translog to represent the production technology is that several restrictive functional forms can be statistically tested. Some of these forms are

1. Homogeneity of degree $\sum_i \alpha_i$. (This implies the following restrictions on the parameters: $\sum_i \beta_{ij} = 0, \sum_j \beta_{ij} = 0, \sum_i \delta_i = 0$.)
2. Neutral technical progress (which implies $\delta_i = 0$ for all $i = 1, \ldots, n$).
3. Homogeneity with neutral technical progress, that is, (1) and (2) combined.
4. Cobb-Douglas (CD) form with exogenous technical progress at the rate γ_t. (This requires the following restrictions: $\beta_{ij} = 0$ for all i and j, $\gamma_{tt} = 0$, $\delta_i = 0$.)

The above hypotheses are tested from the OLS estimates (after within transformation) using the standard F-tests.

In the first data set we failed to reject the restrictive forms implied by models (1) to (4). Since the model in (4) is the most restrictive form which is not rejected against the translog form, we used the CD production function for the data set covering 1960–1967. However, the second data set (1968–1975) rejected each of the above restrictions and, therefore, we used the translog function to represent the underlying production technology. The parameter estimates associated with these models are reported in Table 9.3. In both models the estimated parameters are of the right sign and in most cases the standard errors are small.

1960–1967

So far as the first data set (1960–1967) is concerned the estimated values of RTS and RTP are constant across farms and over time. Furthermore, technical progress is neutral. The elasticity of scale is found to be .78 indicating decreasing returns to scale in dairy farms. This is somewhat surprising given that the production function contains four inputs. The rate of technical progress is found to be increasing productivity by 3.45 percent per annum. This is less surprising and in accordance with earlier studies; see Hjalmarsson, Uhlin, and Carlsson (1985).

1968–1975

In the second data set (1968–1975), RTS, RTP, marginal elasticities, and measures of bias in technical progress are all farm-specific and also vary over time. However, to conserve space we report only the (sample) mean values of their estimates for each year in Table 9.4. The distribution of farms below and above technically optimal scale, that is, below and above RTS = 1, is reported in Table 9.5.

The proportion of suboptimal farms is very low and, except for one year, below 10 percent. The sample mean value of the elasticity of scale varies from about .70

Table 9.3 Parameter Estimates

Variable	1960–1968		1968–1975	
	Estimate	Standard error	Estimate	Standard error
Labor	.2697	.0889	.1986	.0446
Material	.1797	.0891	.1962	.0544
Land	.1248	.1199	.0010	.0471
Capital	.2073	.0485	.2964	.0249
Time	.0345	.0068	.0118	.0040
Labor × labor	—	—	.1271	.1146
Labor × material	—	—	.0437	.1254
Labor × land	—	—	−.2613	.1328
Labor × capital	—	—	.0708	.0867
Labor × time	—	—	−.055	.0111
Material × material	—	—	−.0198	.0790
Material × land	—	—	.1739	.1341
Material × capital	—	—	.0090	.0705
Material × time	—	—	.0129	.0124
Land × land	—	—	−.1335	.0837
Land × Capital	—	—	−.2373	.0821
Land × Time	—	—	.0006	.0106
Capital × Capital	—	—	.0941	.0325
Capital × Time	—	—	.0072	.0062

Table 9.4 Estimates of RTS, Elasticity of Scale, RTP, Rate of Technical Progress, Bias in Technical Progress, and Marginal Output Elasticities

	Year							
	1968	1969	1970	1971	1972	1973	1974	1975
RTS	.6979	.7145	.7281	.7391	.7528	.7492	.7801	.7951
RTP	.0313	.0254	.0197	.0137	.0076	.0006	−.0047	−.0103
	Bias in Technical Progress							
Labor	.0478	.0339	.0249	.0182	.0114	.0048	−.0007	−.0064
Material	−.0123	−.0227	−.0339	−.0387	−.0614	−.0764	−.0728	−.0609
Land	.1884	.1622	.2312	.2201	.2093	.1426	.1289	.1971
Capital	.0681	.0576	.0486	.0405	.0333	.0286	.0209	.0124
	Output Elasticities							
Labor	.1926	.1896	.1976	.1985	.2036	.1959	.2063	.2167
Material	.1706	.1653	.1605	.1573	.1553	.1505	.1479	.1450
Land	.0858	.0939	.0833	.0866	.0933	.1184	.1157	.0961
Capital	.2511	.2656	.2867	.2966	.3005	.2892	.3148	.3372

Table 9.5 Distribution of Farms by RTS*

	Year							
	1968	**1969**	**1970**	**1971**	**1972**	**1973**	**1974**	**1975**
RTS ≥1	5 (6.58)	6 (7.89)	6 (7.89)	7 (9.21)	5 (6.58)	6 (7.89)	8 (10.53)	7 (9.21)
RTS <1	71 (93.42)	70 (92.11)	70 (92.11)	69 (90.79)	71 (93.42)	70 (92.11)	68 (89.47)	69 (90.79)
Total	76 (100)	76 (100)	76 (100)	76 (100)	76 (100)	76 (100)	76 (100)	76 (100)

*Percent of total figures are in parentheses.

in the beginning of the period up to .80 at the end of the period, but the number of suboptimal farms remains about the same. Behind this development is an increasing marginal output elasticity of capital, which increases from about .25 to about .34 during the period. The rest of the marginal elasticities remain almost constant during the period. Compared to the first period 1960–1967, the marginal elasticity of labor is somewhat lower and that of capital somewhat higher during the second period 1968–1975.

The rate of technical progress starts at a fairly high level comparable and consistent with the rate during the first period. However, it decreases quite rapidly and turns into a technical regress from 1974. This is an indication that not only industry but also agriculture went into a productivity slowdown in the mid-1970s. One reason for this slowdown may be the in general higher profitability in Swedish agriculture during the 1970s decreasing the pressure toward increased efficiency in production.

Bias in technical progress turns out to be land and capital using during the whole period. The rate is fairly constant in the case of land but diminishes in the case of capital. Labor starts out with a positive bias, that is, labor-using bias, but ends with a negative one, that is, labor-saving bias. Bias is material-saving during the whole period and it increased over time (except for the last 2 years). In general, the bias pattern seems not to be induced by the development of relative prices; see Table 9.2. The increase in the relative price between land and material and between labor and all other inputs has not caused an expected bias in technical progress. However, one should expect the capital-using bias and the rapid increase in wages in 1974 and 1975 to be consistent with the change in bias from labor-using to labor-saving.

9.5.2 Technical efficiency

Now we look at the estimates of technical efficiency derived from the relation (9.28). This result is based on the residuals of the first-step estimation and parameters associated with the distribution of τ, $\nu - \sigma_\tau^2$, and σ_ν^2.

The estimates of σ_τ^2 and σ_ν^2 are obtained from the EM algorithm in step 2.[5] The estimated values of σ_τ^2 and σ_ν^2 are .030 and .005, respectively, for the first data set (1960–1967) and .018 and .004, respectively, for the second data set (1968–1975). Thus σ_τ^2 is quite large relative to σ_ν^2 in both the data sets. The efficiency distribution of farms during these periods are reported in Table 9.6.

A close look at the table shows remarkable similarity in the distribution of technical efficiency of farms during 1960–1967 and 1968–1975 except in the lowest and highest groups. The percentage of farms in the efficiency group 95 percent and above during 1968–1975 is about double of 1960–1967 figures. Similarly, the percentage of farms in the lowest efficiency group has declined from 10 percent to 3 percent over the period 1960–1967 to 1968–1975. Thus the general conclusion is that efficiency level of farms in the highest and lowest efficiency groups has improved substantially. This is also what one should expect during a period of slow progress at the frontier which makes it easier for nonfrontier units to catch up with or come closer to frontier technology.

We also examined the behavior of technical efficiency over time. To conserve space, we report only the mean values of technical efficiency, which is a measure of structural efficiency, in each year corresponding to both data sets. The results are reported in Table 9.7.

It can be seen from Table 9.7 that there is not much variation in the mean efficiency levels of farms over different years. This result is true for both samples. Thus we do not find any evidence of increase in efficiency levels of these farms over time. The mean efficiency of farms in the second sample (1968–1975) is somewhat smaller than that of the farms in the sample covering the period 1960–1967. However, there is no tendency of systematic improvement in the efficiency level of farms over time in the sample 1968–1975.

Table 9.6   Frequency Distribution of Technical Efficiency

Technical efficiency (percent)	1960–1967		1968–1975	
	Frequency	Percent of total	Frequency	Percent of total
95–100	22	9.48	105	17.27
92–95	60	25.86	170	27.96
89–92	39	16.81	119	19.57
83–89	61	26.29	140	23.03
78–83	26	11.21	58	9.54
Below 78	24	10.35	16	2.63
Total	232	100	608	100

[5] The estimates of farm-specific effects are not reported here to conserve space. These results can be obtained from the authors upon request.

Table 9.7 Estimates of Technical Efficiency by Year

1960–1967 Sample				1968–1975 Sample			
	Technical efficiency				Technical efficiency		
Year	Mean	Maximum	Minimum	Year	Mean	Maximum	Minimum
1960	85.61	96.89	51.66	1968	89.74	97.73	60.19
1961	87.35	96.51	65.45	1969	90.96	98.21	63.82
1962	90.32	97.56	74.02	1970	88.77	97.26	75.12
1963	87.86	96.69	76.78	1971	90.00	97.56	78.05
1964	87.69	97.31	74.29	1972	89.48	96.83	62.79
1965	88.53	97.21	67.90	1973	90.20	97.12	74.60
1966	87.11	97.00	60.07	1974	91.10	97.26	76.89
1967	86.20	94.86	74.06	1975	90.02	96.56	67.63

9.6 Conclusions

In this study we have presented a two-step method that separates technical inefficiency from individual-specific effects. The first step provides consistent estimates
of the production function parameters which are used, in the second step, to estimate individual-specific effects, parameters of the error components and technical
efficiency for each unit over time.

In the empirical implementation this two-step procedure is used to examine
technical efficiency and technical progress for two panel data sets of Swedish dairy
farms covering periods 1960–1967 and 1968–1976. The underlying technology was
assumed translog but in the first period a CD technology could not be rejected. The
parameter results in both models are of the correct sign, reasonable and with small
standard errors.

During the first period, 1960–1967, characterized by low profitability in Swedish
agriculture, technical progress at the frontier was rapid, about 3.5 percent per year.
During the second period, 1968–1975, with higher profitability, technical progress
starts at about the same level but decreases and turns into technical regress in the mid
1970s.

The efficiency distribution of farms shows remarkable similarity during 1960–
1967 and 1968–1975 except in the lowest and highest groups. The efficiency level of
farms in the highest and lowest efficiency groups has improved substantially between
the periods. This is also what one should expect during a period of slow progress
at the frontier which makes it easier for nonfrontier units to catch up with or come
closer to frontier technology. We do not, however, find any evidence of increase in
efficiency levels of these farms over time.

References

Battese, G. E., and T. J. Coelli (1988), "Prediction of Firm-Level Technical Efficiencies with a Generalized Frontier Production Function and Panel Data," *Journal of Econometrics* 38: 387–399.

Cornwell, C., P. Schmidt, and R. C. Sickles (1990), "Production Frontiers with Cross Sectional and Time Series Variation in Efficiency Levels," *Journal of Econometrics* 46: 185–200.

Dempster, A. P., N. M. Laird, and D. B. Rubin (1977), "Maximum Likelihood from Incomplete Data Via the EM Algorithm," *Journal of Royal Statistical Society,* Series B 39: 1–22.

Førsund, F. R., and L. Hjalmarsson (1987), *Analyses of Industrial Structure. A Putty-Clay Approach*, Stockholm, Sweden: IUI, Almqvist & Wiksell International.

Hjalmarsson, L., H-E. Uhlin, and E. Carlsson (1985), "Technical Progress and Productive Efficiency in Swedish Dairy Farms." Working Paper.

Huang, C. J. (1984), "Estimation of Stochastic Frontier Production Function and Technical Inefficiency Via the EM Algorithm," *Southern Economic Journal* 50: 847–856.

Kumbhakar, S. C. (1987), "Production Frontiers and Panel Data: An Application to U.S. Class 1 Railroads," *Journal of Business and Economic Statistics* 5: 249–255.

Kumbhakar, S. C. (1988), "On the Estimation of Technical and Allocative Inefficiency Using Stochastic Frontier Functions: The Case of U.S. Class 1 Railroads," *International Economic Review* 29: 727–743.

Kumbhakar, S. C. (1990), "Production Frontiers, Panel Data, and Time-Varying Technical Inefficiency," *Journal of Econometrics* 46: 201–211.

Kumbhakar, S. C. (1991), "Estimation of Technical Inefficiency in Panel Data Models with Firm- and Time-Specific Effects," *Economics Letters* 36: 43–48.

Pitt, M., and L. F. Lee (1981), "The Measurement and Sources of Technical Inefficiency in the Indonesian Weaving Industry," *Journal of Development Economics* 9: 43–64.

Schmidt, P., and R. C. Sickles (1984), "Production Frontiers and Panel Data," *Journal of Business and Economic Statistics* 4: 367–374.

10

TECHNICAL EFFICIENCY IN NEW JERSEY SCHOOL DISTRICTS

Therese A. McCarty and Suthathip Yaisawarng[1]

10.1 Introduction

Expenditure per pupil in U.S. public schools has risen dramatically in recent years. Between 1960 and 1983, expenditure per pupil for current services rose by 135 percent in real terms [Hanushek (1986, p. 1146)]. At the same time, achievement levels, as measured by test scores, have not risen proportionally, suggesting that resources are not being allocated to schools or utilized by them as productively as possible. Recent concern about the achievement of U.S. students and concern about the size of public budgets underline the importance of using resources allocated to public education effectively. This chapter explores one possible source of inefficiency in the operation of public schools, namely, productive or technical inefficiency.

Our interest in measuring technical efficiency is motivated by questions that have been raised recently in the public policy arena about the efficiency of some New Jersey school districts. Such questions have arisen primarily in two contexts. First, in response to the most recent challenge to New Jersey's school finance system, *Abbott v. Burke*, the state claimed that "deficiencies in education are primarily related to mismanagement in certain districts rather than to expenditures per pupil" [*Abbott v. Burke* (1989, p. iii)]. Second, the New Jersey Department of Education has implemented an evaluation procedure to monitor districts' performance. Districts found to be deficient under this procedure may eventually be "taken over" by the state. To date, two districts, Jersey City and Paterson, have been taken over [Hanley (1989) and *The New York Times* (1991)].

[1] We are indebted to the participants in the Union College Efficiency Workshop Series for their assistance and encouragement. We also would like to thank Cynthia Silverio for excellent research assistance.

In computing measures of technical efficiency for school districts, we pay particular attention to the role of inputs over which districts have little or no control. Ineffective use of inputs such as labor and capital may be characterized properly as technical inefficiency. However, inputs beyond districts' control, such as students' talent and socioeconomic status, may create the appearance of technical inefficiency. The appropriate administrative staff should be responsible for the former type of inefficiency but not the latter. Given that student background is a very important determinant of educational achievement,[2] appropriate treatment of it is of special concern.

We model public school districts as multiinput, multioutput decision-making units (DMUs) or "firms," which attempt to maximize their outputs for given inputs and technology. We argue that this is a more appropriate behavioral assumption in the context of public schools than cost minimization. As such, our models take an "output-oriented" rather than an "input-oriented" approach. These approaches are illustrated and compared in Figure 1.1, and are discussed in detail in Section 3.3. We measure a DMU's technical efficiency, that is, how well a DMU converts its inputs to outputs, based on its available technology. We offer two alternative measures of technical efficiency which take the effects of factors beyond the control of a DMU into consideration in different ways.

Our first model, Model 1, for measuring technical efficiency is a two-stage procedure. In the first stage, we use a data envelopment analysis (DEA) model in which only factors under a DMU's control are included as inputs in computing efficiency scores. In the second stage, we regress these efficiency scores on factors beyond a DMU's control, using a Tobit model. We then predict a DMU's efficiency for a given set of these uncontrollable factors. The difference between the computed efficiency score from the first stage and its predicted value from the second stage, the residual, is used as an index for measuring "pure" technical efficiency, which could be attributable to mismanagement. This approach allows us to disentangle the effects of uncontrollable inputs, such as students' socioeconomic status, from the efficiency scores. The second-stage residuals enable us to observe how a district's efficiency score compares with the score that an average district with the same uncontrollable input values would have.

Our second model, Model 2, is an all-in-one procedure. This approach takes uncontrollable inputs directly into account in computing efficiency scores. All factors that might affect outputs, whether or not they are controllable by management, are included in the DEA model. This model incorporates the effect of uncontrollable inputs into the DEA measure of technical efficiency. We use both models to measure the technical efficiency of New Jersey school districts, using data from the 1984–1985

---

[2] Hanushek (1986, p. 1163) surveyed studies of the relationship between socioeconomic status and achievement.

school year, and compare their results. We then identify circumstances under which each model might be more appropriate.

We organize the chapter as follows. Section 10.2 reviews previous efforts to measure technical efficiency in public schools, Section 10.3 describes the procedures we use to measure technical efficiency and Section 10.4 discusses our data set and results. We conclude the chapter with a discussion of the relative merits of each model and with a discussion of the implications of our results for school policy in Section 10.5.

10.2 Measurement of Technical Efficiency in Public Education

A number of studies have considered the possibility that technical inefficiency exists in public schools. These studies have used a variety of empirical techniques to identify technically efficient schools and to compare them with technically inefficient schools. These studies have in common the fact that they focus attention on schools that produce the highest levels of achievement given their inputs, or, in other words, they focus on schools on the production frontier.

Levin (1974, 1976) made one of the first attempts to account for technical inefficiency in educational production. He catalogued reasons that we might not expect schools to be technically efficient. These include a lack of managerial knowledge of the complex technical education production process and the absence of a competitive market environment [Levin (1976, p. 157)].

Levin used Aigner and Chu's (1968) parametric, nonstochastic linear programming model to compute the coefficients of the production frontier. He concluded that the parameters of the production function that characterizes schools on the frontier differ from those of the function that characterizes average schools, suggesting that ordinary least squares (OLS) regression analysis does not reveal accurately the relationship between inputs and output for technically efficient schools. Levin used his results to draw some conclusions about the presence of allocative inefficiency in schools, but did not attempt to compute the extent of their technical inefficiency.

Another early study of schools on the frontier [Klitgaard and Hall (1975)] examined the residuals from OLS regressions of the relationship between educational inputs and output in an attempt to identify schools that repeatedly produce unusually high levels of achievement. These schools were then compared with the other schools in the sample in a search for characteristics of schools that may account for high achievement. Fewer than 10 percent of the schools in Klitgaard and Hall's sample qualify as outliers or "outstanding" schools under their criteria. The "outstanding" schools had smaller classes, better-paid teachers, and more teachers with greater than 5 years' experience than the other schools in the sample.

Klitgaard and Hall's study was conducted in the spirit of production frontier analyses in the sense that it put heavy weight on outlying observations. However, it differed fundamentally by allowing the average relationship between inputs and output to determine the parameters of the production function, rather than considering the possibility that the production frontier may have a different shape. Given Levin's findings of different parameter estimates for the production frontier and average production function, it is indeed likely that OLS parameters may be misleading in this regard.

Most of the studies of technical efficiency in public schools have used DEA. The first such studies [Bessent and Bessent (1980) and Bessent, Bessent, Kennington, and Reagan (1982)] examined the relative efficiency of schools in one school district, Houston, Texas. These studies use the Charnes, Cooper, and Rhodes (1978) DEA model, which evaluates the efficiency of individual DMUs (i.e., schools) relative to a production frontier that exhibits constant returns-to-scale. The Bessent papers point out some advantages of DEA over previously used alternatives, namely, that multiple outputs can be accommodated easily, a parametric functional form does not have to be specified for the production function, and the sources of inefficiency for individual schools can be identified. These studies are noteworthy for the fact that they are not motivated solely by academic interest; rather, their results were used for actual evaluation of schools in Houston by that district's superintendent.

Several other DEA studies of schools have followed. Jesson, Mayston, and Smith (1987) used DEA to assess the performance of school districts in England. Färe, Grosskopf, and Weber (1989) used DEA to assess the performance of school districts in Missouri. The latter study is innovative in its use of "jackknifing," a technique designed to reduce the impact of outliers on efficiency measures. Also, they allowed for variable returns-to-scale in the construction of the production frontier.

Another DEA study, Lovell, Walters, and Wood (1990), used data from the High School and Beyond study to assess the performance of schools in producing educational opportunities, as well as intermediate and long-term educational achievement. One important way in which this study departs from the others discussed here is that it distinguishes between inputs that are subject to managerial control and inputs that are not. Only the former are included in the DEA model. Then, inputs beyond managerial control are used as independent variables in a "second-stage" regression analysis that attempts to explain the DEA efficiency scores. One of the main objectives of the present study is to compare this two-stage approach with the one-stage models used in most other DEA studies.

A few studies have used stochastic frontier methodology to study the nature of the educational production function and to measure efficiency in schools. Barrow (1991) used various forms of frontier estimation to estimate a cost frontier using data on English school districts. He found that the estimated level of efficiency is sensitive to the method of estimation used, and that average costs are calculated to lie between 4 and 16 percent of their frontier level. Wyckoff and Lavinge (1991) measured technical inefficiency for elementary schools in New York. They found average inefficiency estimates that range from 4 to 9 percent depending on the particular output measure used. Grosskopf, Hayes, Taylor, and Weber (1991) used a stochastic frontier and distance function methodology to study allocative and technical efficiency in Texas school districts. Their results suggest that school districts in the state are technically but not allocatively efficient.

Most studies of schools' productivity have to contend with some important data shortcomings. Schools produce a variety of outputs, some of which are not easily quantifiable, such as socialization. However, achievement test scores are normally the only output measure available. Hanushek (1986, pp. 1150–1155) discussed the drawbacks of test scores as a measure of educational output as well as some attempts to use alternative measures.

Some studies use a "value added" approach to measuring achievement, in which the difference between test scores at different ages is used in place of test score levels at a particular age as a measure of achievement produced by schools [see, e.g., Fox and Taylor (1991) and Grosskopf, Hayes, Taylor, and Weber (1991)]. The value added approach has the advantage of accounting for the effects of socioeconomic status on achievement by looking at changes in achievement brought about by schools. Unfortunately, our data do not permit us to take this approach.

10.3 Specifications of Efficiency Models

In this section, we present our models for measuring the productive efficiency of school districts. As mentioned in the introduction, we use DEA to compute efficiency scores in both our models.[3] The models differ in their treatment of uncontrollable inputs. Model 1 uses uncontrollable inputs as independent variables in a second-stage analysis, which attempts to disentangle the effect of uncontrollable inputs from the DEA measure of technical efficiency. Model 2 includes both controllable and uncontrollable inputs in the computation of DEA efficiency scores. In both models, DEA constructs a piecewise linear production surface using linear programs and computes an efficiency score for each DMU along the lines suggested by Farrell (1957) with modifications and extensions discussed in Färe, Grosskopf, and Lovell (1985).

Suppose that there are $k = 1, \ldots, K$ DMUs, which in the context of our empirical application are school districts. Each DMU produces $m = 1, \ldots, M$ outputs using inputs that are both under and beyond a district's control. Let y_k be an $(M \times 1)$ vector of M different outputs produced by DMU k and let Y be an $(M \times K)$ matrix of M different outputs used by K different DMUs. Let x_k be an $(N \times 1)$ vector of N different inputs under the kth district's control and let X be the corresponding $(N \times K)$ matrix of controllable inputs. Let z_k be a $(L \times 1)$ vector of L different inputs beyond the kth district's control. Let Z denote a $(L \times K)$ matrix of uncontrollable inputs.

---

[3] The DEA approach to constructing production frontiers is discussed in Section 1.5 and in Chapter 3.

The first stage of Model 1 uses DEA to compute efficiency scores for school districts. These efficiency scores reflect the extent to which each school district converts its controllable inputs to education outputs. In this case, our DEA model is formulated as

$$\mathrm{TE}_k = \max_{\Lambda,\theta} \quad \theta \tag{10.1}$$

subject to

$$Y\Lambda \geqq \theta y_k$$
$$X\Lambda \leqq x_k$$
$$I\Lambda = 1$$
$$\Lambda \in \Re_+^K$$

where Λ is a $(K \times 1)$ vector of weights or scale variables and I is a $(1 \times K)$ vector of ones. The fact that the weights sum to 1 indicates that the piecewise linear production surface can exhibit increasing, constant, or decreasing returns-to-scale. In other words, the DEA model gives a measure of technical efficiency of DMU k which reflects DMU k's transformation of controllable inputs to outputs, given DMU k's technology and its current scale of operation. Recall that our measure of technical efficiency uses an output orientation; that is, a DMU tries to increase its outputs proportionally given its inputs, while staying in the production set. Thus, the efficiency score takes on a value of at least one. If DMU k is technically efficient, its efficiency score is equal to one. If, however, DMU k is not technically efficient, its efficiency score is greater than one. The efficiency score reveals the extent to which DMU k could further increase its outputs proportionally without consuming additional resources. On the other hand, the efficiency score minus one is an index for the degree of inefficiency, which reveals the potential output loss due to not utilizing available resources to the fullest extent.

In the second stage, we attempt to disentangle the effects of factors beyond a DMU's control that might contribute to a DMU's efficiency. We use the efficiency scores computed from the DEA model as our dependent variable, which we regress on factors beyond the DMU's control. Since efficiency scores computed from the DEA model are truncated from below at one, an OLS regression would produce biased and inconsistent parameter estimates. Some researchers have attempted to deal with this problem. For example, Kalirajan and Shand (1985) use multiple classification analysis while Dusansky and Wilson (1990) used a truncated regression model to explain variations in their efficiency scores. Lovell, Walters, and Wood (1990) used a tie-breaking technique to generate unbounded efficiency scores which enabled them to use OLS. In this chapter, we use the truncated regression model, known as the

Tobit model, which provides unbiased and consistent parameter estimates. Our Tobit model is specified as follows:

$$\text{TE}_k = r_k\beta + u_k \quad \text{if } \text{TE}_k^* > 1 \tag{10.2}$$
$$= 1 \quad \text{if } \text{TE}_k^* \leqq 1$$

where TE_k is the technical efficiency of DMU k obtained from the first stage of Model 1, TE_k^* is the "true" but unobservable efficiency score[4] for DMU k, $r_k = [1 \quad z_k']$ is an $(1 \times (L + 1))$ vector of uncontrollable factors plus one, "$\prime$" signifies a transpose and β is an $((L + 1) \times 1)$ vector of parameters. u_k is a random term, identically and independently distributed with zero mean and constant variance σ^2. [See Amemiya (1985) or Judge, Hill, Griffiths, Lütkepohl, and Lee (1988).] This random term represents the "pure" technical efficiency after effects of uncontrollable factors have been disentangled.

Using the estimates of the parameters in the Tobit model, we compute the DMU's "pure" technical efficiency, $\hat{u}$, which is defined as

$$\hat{u}_k = \text{TE}_k - r_k\hat{\beta} \tag{10.3}$$

Note that $\hat{u}_k$ is not bounded from below at one. It can take on negative, zero, or positive values. If $\hat{u}_k$ is zero, then the DMU performs as well as the average DMU with the same set of uncontrollable factors. If $\hat{u}_k$ is not equal to zero, then its performance differs from the average DMU with the same set of uncontrollable factors. Recall that our DEA efficiency scores range from 1 to $+\infty$. The higher the value of the efficiency score, the poorer the performance of the DMU. By the same token, the smaller the value of $\hat{u}_k$, the better the performance of the DMU k. Therefore, the least inefficient DMU has the smallest $\hat{u}$ or the largest absolute value among those having $\hat{u} < 0$. The most inefficient DMU has the largest $\hat{u}$ among those having positive $\hat{u}$.

Model 2 addresses a slightly different research question than Model 1; namely, given factors both within and beyond a DMU's control, how efficient is the DMU? In this case, it is appropriate that factors beyond the control of the DMU which affect the outputs be built into the measure of technical efficiency.[5] The DEA model that

[4] Maddala (1983) pointed out that the Tobit model is appropriate when it is possible for the dependent variable to have values beyond the truncated point, yet those values are not observable. This is likely to be the case for our DEA efficiency scores. Given our sample, the best observable DMUs receive scores of one. We would argue that it is likely that some DMUs might perform better than the best DMUs in our sample. If these unobservable DMUs could be compared with a reference frontier constructed from the observable DMUs included in our sample, they would have efficiency scores, TE_k^*, less than one.

[5] Kumbhakar, Ghosh, and McGuckin (1991) incorporated all factors that affect DMUs' output in a stochastic production frontier model that specifies technical efficiency as a function of uncontrollable inputs.

incorporates both controllable and uncontrollable inputs, Model 2, is specified as follows:

$$TE_k = \max\nolimits_{\Lambda, \theta} \quad \theta \tag{10.4}$$

subject to

$$Y\Lambda \geqq \theta y_k$$
$$X\Lambda \leqq x_k$$
$$Z\Lambda \leqq z_k$$
$$I\Lambda = 1$$
$$\Lambda \in \Re_+^K$$

This DEA model is similar to that in Equation (10.1), except that it includes uncontrollable factors. Notation and interpretation of the numerical values of the efficiency scores are the same in Models 1 and 2.

10.4 The New Jersey School Districts

We use the two alternative models presented in Section 10.3 to measure technical efficiency in New Jersey school districts, using data from the 1984–1985 school year. Our choice of districts to be included in this study is motivated by the 1989 New Jersey Supreme Court decision in *Abbott v. Burke. Abbott v. Burke* was brought against the state by plaintiffs in four school districts: Camden, East Orange, Irvington, and Jersey City. Plaintiffs claimed that students in their school districts were being denied their right under the New Jersey Constitution to a "thorough and efficient" education on account of persisting differences among districts in expenditure per pupil. The state claimed in response that the schools in the plaintiffs' districts were poorly managed, and that increasing expenditure per pupil by itself was unlikely to improve matters much.

The New Jersey Supreme Court found that students in the plaintiffs' school districts are in fact denied a "thorough and efficient" education. The court then extended this finding to "poorer, urban" districts other than the four plaintiff districts. The court recommended 28 districts for legislative remedy and mandated that these districts receive "assured" funding at a level "substantially equal to that of property rich districts" [*Abbott v. Burke* (1989, p. 142)].

Our sample is made up of the 27 of these 28 court-identified districts for which we have complete data.[6] We limit our sample to this group of districts so that our

---

[6] We exclude Perth Amboy from the sample since we lack data on the socioeconomic status of its students.

Table 10.1 Descriptive Statistics for School Districts Designated by the New Jersey Supreme Court as Appropriate Targets of Legislative Remedy (Sample Size = 27)

	Mean	Std. Dev.	Minimum	Maximum
Outputs:				
MPCTPASS	32.85	14.44	8.0	60.0
RPCTPASS	47.22	16.84	21.0	74.0
WPCTPASS	33.26	14.67	13.0	64.0
Inputs:				
TPRATIO	.062	.007	.048	.075
QUALITY	.306	.093	.107	.474
OTHEREXP	2.238	.435	1.564	3.166
SESSCORE	−3.127	1.199	−6.526	−1.827

results will permit us to comment on policy decisions involving those districts. In particular, we wish to observe whether or not the four plaintiff districts in *Abbott v. Burke* are representative of the larger group of districts that the New Jersey Court recommended as candidates for substantially increased amounts of state aid. Our models, therefore, do not construct best-practice frontiers based on the performance of all districts in the state. A district on the frontier in our models might not be one of the most efficient districts in New Jersey. The efficiency scores that we compute are relative to the 27 court-identified districts and should be interpreted accordingly.

Table 10.1 presents descriptive statistics for our data set.[7] There are three outputs, the percentage of students in each district who pass each of three High School Proficiency Tests (HSPTs), in mathematics (MPCTPASS), reading (RPCTPASS), and writing (WPCTPASS). These scores can be interpreted as measuring the probability that a student in a given district will pass each HSPT. Our inputs that are under a district's control include the number of staff per pupil (TPRATIO), the proportion of staff with an M.A. or Ph.D. to the total number of staff (QUALITY), and expenditure per pupil excluding staff salaries (OTHEREXP) in thousands of dollars. TPRATIO and OTHEREXP are used as proxies of instructional inputs. The proportion of staff with higher degrees is used to control somewhat for differences in the quality of teachers across schools.

We also consider an input, students' socioeconomic status (SESSCORE), that is beyond the districts' control. This is a composite socioeconomic status score computed by the state of New Jersey.[8] Its value ranges from negative infinity to positive infinity, with zero indicating that the socioeconomic status of students in

---

[7] We use data that were collected by the New Jersey Department of Education. The data set is described in further detail in Walberg and Fowler (1987).

[8] "The SES (socioeconomic status) index consists of a factor-weighted composite of the educational level of adults in the district, their occupational status, number of persons per household, percentage of the district considered urban, median family income, percentage of the workforce receiving unemployment compensation, and the percentage of residents below the poverty line" [Walberg and Fowler (1987, p. 9)].

the given district is about average. Negative values of SESSCORE indicate that the socioeconomic status of students in the district is below average, while positive values of SESSCORE suggest the opposite. SESSCORE is negative for all districts included in our sample, suggesting that the socioeconomic status of students in our sample is relatively low. Given this low socioeconomic status, it is not surprising that average achievement levels, as measured by the probability that a student will pass each of the three HSPTs, are relatively low. Our data seem to be consistent with the general finding that socioeconomic status positively affects a student's achievement.

We now turn to discussion of our results. Table 10.2 presents efficiency scores for each district from Models 1 and 2. We begin our discussion with Model 1, which is a two-stage procedure. In the first stage, DEA efficiency scores are computed, using the three HSPTs as outputs and the three controllable inputs, TPRATIO, QUALITY, and OTHEREXP. In the group of 27 districts suggested by the court for remedy, three are identified, with scores of 1.0, as being efficient. They are Passaic, Pemberton, and Phillipsburg. Paterson has the highest score, 2.63, and hence apparently has the poorest performance of the 27 districts under consideration. This score indicates that a student who attends a school in Paterson would have a 16.3 percent higher chance of passing the HSPTs if the district were to utilize all inputs under its control efficiently.

The four plaintiff districts as a group have a relatively high degree of inefficiency, and thus are not representative of the group of districts identified by the court as likely candidates for legislative remedy. The average score for the plaintiff districts is 2.379, while the other 23 districts in this sample have an average score of 1.509. The plaintiff's average score differs in a statistically significant way from that of the other districts in the sample (at the 5 percent level). We refrain, however, from drawing conclusions from these results until we have completed the second stage of our procedure, which takes into account the socioeconomic status of the districts' pupils.

Districts identified in the first stage as being "inefficient" may not, in fact, exhibit waste and mismanagement. Rather, they may face a more difficult task in converting inputs to outputs given factors largely outside their control. To the extent that low socioeconomic status is associated with conditions that make learning more difficult, districts with low socioeconomic status pupils may be identified as being inefficient districts when in fact they are not engaging in behavior that we would wish to call inefficiency.

As discussed in Section 10.3, we isolate the component of efficiency scores that is not attributable to factors outside the districts' control in the second stage of Model 1. We consider students' socioeconomic status to be a factor outside the districts' control. We regress the efficiency scores on measures of socioeconomic status using a Tobit procedure.[9] We then examine the residuals from the Tobit. Districts with positive

---

[9] A Tobit model is available in the TSP software package. It provides maximum likelihood estimates of the Tobit model using the Newton-Raphson method.

Table 10.2 Efficiency Scores for School Districts Designated by the New Jersey Supreme Court as Appropriate Targets of Legislative Remedy

DMU	District	Model 1				Model 2	
		TE_k	Rank	$\hat{u}_k$	Rank	TE_k	Rank
1	Asbury Park City	2.176	16	.323	18	1.735	19
2	Bridgeton City	1.181	9	−.727	1	1.000	1
3	Burlington City	1.023	2	−.320	6	1.023	9
4	Camden City	2.265	18	−.120	11	1.000	1
5	East Orange	2.234	17	.720	19	2.169	20
6	Elizabeth City	1.585	12	.119	13	1.562	15
7	Garfield City	1.177	8	−.125	10	1.177	13
8	Gloucester City	1.119	6	−.474	4	1.022	8
9	Harrison Town	1.139	7	−.238	9	1.139	11
10	Hoboken City	2.044	15	.206	14	1.634	17
11	Irvington Town	2.426	21	1.013	23	2.417	24
12	Jersey City	2.592	23	.955	22	2.192	21
13	Keansburg Boro	1.054	3	−.580	2	1.000	1
14	Long Branch City	1.370	11	−.032	12	1.368	14
15	Millville City	1.021	1	−.303	7	1.021	7
16	New Brunswick City	1.609	13	.265	16	1.609	16
17	Newark City	2.408	20	.242	15	1.142	12
18	Orange City	2.387	19	1.051	24	2.387	23
19	Passaic City	*1.000	na	na	na	*1.000	na
20	Paterson City	2.628	24	.722	20	*1.000	1
21	Pemberton Twp	1.000	na	na	na	1.000	na
22	Phillipsburg Town	1.000	na	na	na	1.000	na
23	Pleasantville City	1.786	14	.268	17	1.653	18
24	Trenton City	2.497	22	.805	21	2.222	22
25	Union City	1.345	10	−.416	5	1.000	6
26	Vineland City	1.058	4	−.294	8	1.058	10
27	West New York Town	1.103	5	−.493	3	1.000	1
	Overall average	1.638		.107		1.390	
	Minimum	1.000		−.727		1.000	
	Maximum	2.628		1.051		2.417	
	Plaintiff average	2.379		.642		1.944	
	Nonplaintiff average	1.509		−.00006		1.293	

Notes:

1. An "*" indicates that the district is productively efficient by default, that is, the district has a unique combination of inputs and outputs relative to the others in the sample, and thus is compared only to itself in measuring the degree of productive efficiency.

2. Plaintiff districts include Camden City, East Orange, Irvington Town, and Jersey City.

3. $\hat{u}_k$ defined as in Equation (10.3) is computed by

$$\hat{u}_k = TE_k - .88 + .23s_k$$
$$\quad\quad\quad (.327)\,(.097)$$

   The numbers in parentheses are standard errors of the respective parameter estimates. The estimate of $\sigma = .59$ with standard error = .087.

4. DMUs 19, 21, and 22 were excluded from rank orderings because their residual values are not computed by the Tobit procedure. As a consequence, the $\hat{u}$ averages were computed from the remaining 24 districts.

residuals can be said to exhibit more inefficiency than the average district with the same socioeconomic status. On the other hand, districts with negative residuals are more efficient than the average district with the same socioeconomic status.

The estimated Tobit model is included in note 3 of Table 10.2. The coefficient of the socioeconomic status variable is statistically significant at the 5 percent level. Examination of the Tobit residuals gives us a somewhat different picture of districts' efficiency than do the efficiency scores alone. The rank orderings change substantially for some districts. For example, Paterson, which is the least efficient district in our sample according to the first-stage efficiency scores, turns out not to be the worst when effects of socioeconomic status are eliminated. Looking at the efficiency score alone would have suggested that Millville is relatively close to the best-practice frontier. However, when socioeconomic status is taken into account, we see that Millville's achievement levels are not substantially higher than we would expect given its inputs and its socioeconomic status.

Camden provides an example of a district that is better than the average inefficient district in spite of having an efficiency score that indicates a relatively high degree of inefficiency (2.26). A substantial part of Camden's "inefficiency," therefore, can be attributed to its students' socioeconomic status, which is beyond the Camden district's control. In terms of management, Camden does better than the average district with its socioeconomic status.

Most of the districts with efficiency scores that indicate high levels of inefficiency also have relatively large, positive residuals. Asbury Park, East Orange, Hoboken, Irvington, Jersey City, Newark, Orange, Paterson, and Trenton all have efficiency scores above 2.0. Their residuals, $\hat{u}$, range from .206 to 1.051. Asbury Park's poor ranking is of interest in light of the fact that it was threatened by state takeover in the mid-1980s. Subsequently, the district improved its performance, and was not taken over [Jannarone (1988)].

When we account for socioeconomic status in the second stage, the plaintiff districts' positions are relatively unchanged, except for Camden. The mean value of their residuals, .642, differs at the 95 percent confidence level from the mean of the other districts' residuals, $-.00006$. This calls into question the court's extrapolation from evidence regarding the plaintiff districts in calling for a remedy that applies to all 27 of these urban districts. It also suggests that mismanagement may in fact be at least part of the reason for low HSPT passing rates in three of the four plaintiff districts. Other poor, urban districts do better.

Jersey City is close to being the least efficient district, even when we consider the effects of the low socioeconomic status of its students. This poor score lends empirical support to former Governor Kean's assertion that Jersey City is, "arguably, the worst school district in the state" [Sullivan (1987)], and to former Education Commissioner Saul Cooperman's characterization of the Jersey City school district as "a public enterprise that has reached a state of managerial bankruptcy" [Hanley

(1988)]. In fact, the Jersey City school district was taken over by the state in 1989.[10]

The last two columns of Table 10.2 present efficiency scores and their rank orderings from Model 2, in which both controllable and uncontrollable inputs are included. The magnitude of efficiency scores is slightly lower than those obtained from the DEA model which includes only factors under the districts' control. On average, districts in our sample are 39 percent inefficient, meaning that a student attending a school in the district would have a 39 percent higher chance of passing the HSPTs, on average, if that district utilized its other inputs efficiently, given the socioeconomic status of its students.

Ordering these districts from the most efficient to the least efficient, we find that Bridgeton ranks first while Irvington ranks last. These rank orderings are quite similar to those based on residual values, $\hat{u}$, from Model 1. The Pearson correlation coefficient, .789, indicates that the two rank orderings are positively correlated at the 1 percent level. Comparing individual rankings between the two models, the most striking difference is the change in Paterson's rank from twentieth to first. In Model 2, Paterson appears to be technically efficient, that is, it receives a score of one. Investigation of DMUs that are used as benchmark DMUs in calculating efficiency scores for other inefficient districts reveals that Paterson is efficient by default. In other words, it uses a unique combination of inputs and outputs such that it is compared only to itself when its efficiency score is computed. A district that is efficient by default should not be considered as a role model in attempts to improve performance of inefficient districts. Another striking result is the dramatic change in Camden's rank. Camden turns out to be efficient in Model 2, with a change in rank from eleventh to first. Unlike Paterson, Camden was used as part of the reference set in measuring the efficiency scores of Hoboken, Newark, and Union, and hence is not efficient by default.

Table 10.3 presents a summary of slack and surplus variables[11] in both Models 1 and 2. Slack variables represent amounts of excessive input use. They reveal the extent to which use of particular inputs could be reduced given that a district has already reached the frontier of the production set. Analysis of slack variables from Model 1 suggests that districts that have positive slack, on average, could use .007 fewer teachers, 8.1 percent lower staff quality, and $606 less other expenditures per pupil. More than half of school districts in our sample have positive slack values for all inputs. Their excessive use of inputs accounts for 10 to 26 percent of total

---

[10] The State Department of Education has taken over the Jersey City school district as a result of its program of monitoring and evaluating districts. The department evaluates districts' performance in the following areas: finance, planning, community relations, curriculum and instruction, student attendance, facilities, professional staff, mandated programs, affirmative action, and performance in basic skills. Jersey City failed to meet the department's standards in all areas except community relations. [Gardner (1987)].

[11] The slack and surplus values may not be unique if there are alternative or multiple solutions to linear programming problems. This is not the case here; we do not find any alternative solutions for our results.

Table 10.3   Analysis of Slack and Surplus Variables (Sample Size = 27)

SLACK VARIABLES

	No. of DMUs with positive slack	Average	Total slack as Percent of total inputs
Model 1			
TPRATIO	14	.007	10.07
QUALITY	16	.081	23.08
OTHEREXP	23	.606	26.15
Model 2			
TPRATIO	12	.007	11.16
QUALITY	12	.086	24.17
OTHEREXP	18	.533	22.34
SESSCORE*	7	.249	†12.53

SURPLUS VARIABLES

	No. of DMUs with positive surplus	Average	Total surplus as % of total outputs
Model 1			
MPCTPASS	20	11.356	36.16
RPCTPASS	8	6.125	13.88
WPCTPASS	20	13.933	47.47
Model 2			
MPCTPASS	15	9.397	29.25
RPCTPASS	6	5.542	12.22
WPCTPASS	16	8.822	30.95

*Since values of SESSCORE are negative for all districts in our sample, their absolute values are used in computing the sum of SESSCORE slack values as a percentage of the total SESSCORE value.

inputs. Of particular concern is the excessive use of other expenditure per pupil (OTHEREXP). New Brunswick and Trenton spent $1300 and $1432, respectively, more than they should. If these excessive expenditures per pupil were incorporated into our measure of efficiency, their efficiency scores would be worse. Values of slack variables in Model 2 are relatively similar to those in Model 1; however, Model 2 has fewer DMUs with positive slack. New Brunswick and Trenton again have the most excessive use of other expenditure per pupil, with slack values of $1300 and $1125, respectively. These values are remarkably similar in the two models. The slack values of SESSCORE in Model 2 reveal that, on average, districts should be able to produce the maximum output levels with socioeconomic status that is lower by a SESSCORE value of .414.

In contrast, surplus variables reveal how much a district on the production frontier could further increase its outputs without consuming additional inputs. This, in effect, will change the mix of the district's outputs. The surplus values from Model 1 suggest that a student attending a district that has positive surplus could, on average, potentially increase the probability of passing HSPTs in mathematics, reading, and writing further by 11.4, 6.1, and 13.9 percent, respectively. The surplus values from Model 2 suggest a similar conclusion, except that the probabilities increase at lower rates. Model 2 has fewer DMUs with positive surplus and smaller average surplus values for all outputs than those in Model 1.

10.5 Conclusions and Policy Implications

The technical efficiency of certain New Jersey school districts has been questioned in recent years by the New Jersey Department of Education. Two districts, Jersey City and Paterson, have been found by the department to have performed deficiently, and consequently, they have been "taken over" by the department. Several other districts have been threatened with take over. Also, in contesting the *Abbott v. Burke* school finance reform case, the department claimed that low achievement levels in the plaintiff districts are largely attributable to mismanagement.

We have used two DEA models to compute technical efficiency scores for a group of 27 poor, urban New Jersey school districts. These are districts that the New Jersey Supreme Court identified in its *Abbott v. Burke* decision as candidates for legislative remedy, that is, increased state aid. Our results suggest that Jersey City and Paterson do, in fact, exhibit higher levels of technical inefficiency than would the average district whose students have the same socioeconomic status. Also, it appears that the plaintiff districts have higher than average levels of inefficiency among the group of 27 districts. These findings lend some support to the Department of Education's claim of inefficient management in the plaintiff districts as well as in the districts it has taken over. It appears, then, that achievement levels in these districts could be improved with more effective use of the districts' resources.

In computing our measures of technical efficiency, we pay particular attention to the role of factors beyond the control of school district managers, or "uncontrollable inputs." We explore two ways of incorporating such factors, in this case, students' socioeconomic status, into a DEA model. Our first model uses a two-stage approach in which Tobit analysis is used to eliminate the effects of socioeconomic status on districts' DEA efficiency scores. The second model incorporates both controllable and uncontrollable inputs in the DEA computation of efficiency scores.

Our two models produce similar results in the sense that the rankings of their efficiency scores are positively and significantly correlated. However, there are notable differences between the two approaches. The two-stage model enables us to remove the effects of socioeconomic status from DEA efficiency scores, which reflect the effects of controllable inputs only. On the other hand, the one-stage model takes socioeconomic status into account when the scores are computed.

When some factors affect outputs indirectly, these factors should be included in the second stage of a two-stage approach. However, the two-stage approach can be problematic when there is strong correlation between the first-stage inputs and the second-stage independent variables. If these variables were strongly correlated, then the claim that the two stages incorporate fundamentally different types of inputs, controllable and uncontrollable, becomes untenable. In this case, the DEA scores computed in the first stage are likely to be biased in the sense that they would actually reflect the effects of both categories of inputs. In the case of our empirical application, this is not a concern as the first- and second-stage variables are not significantly correlated.[12]

Results of the one-stage approach can be misleading when districts are found to be "efficient by default" if those districts are viewed as role models for inefficient districts. The two-stage approach may facilitate more meaningful evaluation of the performance of such districts. For example, we found Paterson to be efficient (by default) in the one-stage model; however, in the two-stage model it has a large, positive residual, indicating that its performance is poorer than the average district with the same socioeconomic status. In summary, each model has advantages and disadvantages. Either or both may be appropriate depending on the particular research questions being investigated.

REFERENCES

Abbott v. Burke (1989), Supreme Court of New Jersey No. A-63 (September term).

Aigner, D. J., and S-F. Chu (1968), "On Estimating the Industry Production Function," *American Economic Review* 58(4)(September): 826–839.

Amemiya, T. (1985), *Advanced Econometrics*. Cambridge, Mass.: Harvard University Press.

Barrow, M. M. (1991), "Measuring Local Education Authority Performance: A Frontier Approach," *Economics of Education Review* 10(1): 19–27.

Bessent, A., and W. Bessent (1980), "Determining the Comparative Efficiency of Schools Through Data Envelopment Analysis," *Educational Administration Quarterly* 16(2): 57–75.

Bessent, A., W. Bessent, J. Kennington, and B. Reagan (1982), "An Application of Mathematical Programming to Assess Productivity in the Houston Independent School District," *Management Science* 28(12)(December): 1355–1367.

Charnes, A., W. Cooper, and E. Rhodes (1978), "Measuring the Efficiency of Decision Making Units," *European Journal of Operational Research* 2(6): 429–444.

Dusansky, R., and P. W. Wilson (1990), "Technical Efficiency in the Decentralized Care of the Developmentally Disabled," Working Paper, Department of Economics, University of Texas, Austin.

Färe, R., S. Grosskopf, and C. A. K. Lovell (1985), *The Measurement of Efficiency of Production*. Boston: Kluwer-Nijhoff Publishing.

Färe, R., S. Grosskopf, and W. Weber (1989), "Measuring School District Performance," *Public Finance Quarterly* 17(4)(October): 409–428.

Farrell, M. J. (1957), "The Measurement of Productive Efficiency," *Journal of the Royal Statistical Society* Series A, General 120(3): 253–281.

---

[12] The Pearson correlation coefficients between SESSCORE and TPRATIO, QUALITY, and OTHEREXP are .15, .14, and −.21, respectively. None of these is significantly different from zero at the 95 percent confidence level.

Fox, B. J., and L. L. Taylor (1991), "Grading Texas Schools," *The Southwest Economy*, Federal Reserve Bank of Dallas, (July/August): 1–5.

Gardner, J. (1987), "Jersey City Schools Face State Action," *The New York Times* (September 17).

Grosskopf, S., K. Hayes, L. Taylor, and W. Weber (1991), "Teacher Salaries and Teacher Productivity," Paper Presented at Western Economic Association Meetings.

Hanley, R. (1988), "Bid for Takeover of School District Is Begun by Jersey," *The New York Times* (May 25), A1.

Hanley, R. (1989), "New Jersey Seizes School District in Jersey City, Citing Total Failure," *The New York Times* (October 5), sec. I, p. 1.

Hanushek, E. (1986), "The Economics of Schooling: Production and Efficiency in Public Schools," *The Journal of Economic Literature* 24 (September): 1141–1177.

Jannarone, T. R., Jr. (1988), "Turning a School District Around," *The New York Times* (April 24), sec. 12, p. 32.

Jesson, D., D. Mayston, and P. Smith (1987), "Performance Assessment in the Education Sector: Educational and Economic Perspectives," *Oxford Review of Education* 13(3): 249–266.

Judge, G. G., R. C. Hill, W. E. Griffiths, H. Lütkepohl, and T-C. Lee (1988), *Introduction to the Theory and Practice of Econometrics*, 2d ed., New York: John Wiley & Sons.

Kalirajan, K. P., and R. T. Shand (1985), "Types of Education and Agricultural Productivity: A Quantitative Analysis of Tamil Nadu Rice Farming," *Journal of Development Studies* 21(2)(January): 232–243.

Klitgaard, R., and G. Hall (1975), "Are There Unusually Effective Schools?" *Journal of Human Resources* 10(1)(Winter): 90–106.

Kumbhakar, S. C., S. Ghosh, and J. T. McGuckin (1991), "A Generalized Production Frontier Approach for Estimating Determinants of Inefficiency in U.S. Dairy Farms," *Journal of Business and Economic Statistics* 9 (July): 279–286.

Levin, H. (1974), "Measuring Efficiency in Educational Production," *Public Finance Quarterly* 2(1): 3–24.

Levin, H. (1976), "Concepts of Economic Efficiency and Educational Production," in J. Froomkin, D. Jamison and R. Radner, eds., *Education as an Industry*. Cambridge, Mass.: Ballinger.

Lovell, C. A. K., L. C. Walters, and L. L. Wood (1990), "Stratified Models of Education Production Using DEA and Regression Analysis," Working Paper No. 90-5, Department of Economics, University of North Carolina, Chapel Hill, N.C.; in A. Charnes, W. W. Cooper, A. Y. Lewin, and L. M. Seiford, eds., *Data Envelopment Analysis: Theory, Method and Process*. IC^2 Management and Management Science series. New York: Quorum Books (forthcoming).

Maddala, G. S. (1983), *Limited-Dependent and Qualitative Variables in Econometrics*. Cambridge: Cambridge University Press.

The New York Times (1991), "New Jersey Takes Over Schools in Paterson," (August 8).

Sullivan, J. F. (1987), "School Takeover Bill Gains in New Jersey," *The New York Times* (December 22), B2.

Walberg, H., and W. Fowler (1987), "Expenditure and Size Efficiencies of Public School Districts," *Educational Researcher* 16(7) (October): 5–13.

Wyckoff, J. H., and J. Lavinge (1991), "The Relative Inefficiency of Public Elementary Schools in New York," Working Paper, State University of New York, Albany.

11

SHARE TENANCY AND EFFICIENCY IN U.S. AGRICULTURE

Hyunok Lee and Agapi Somwaru

11.1 Introduction

Since the time of Adam Smith, economists have argued that share tenancy is inefficient. Because outputs are shared with the landlord, a share tenant gets only a portion of what he or she produces. Hence, the tenant does not have the incentive to cultivate efficiently on share-rented land and the tenant can be expected to undersupply resources [Bardhan and Srinivasan (1971), Bell and Zusman (1976), Braverman and Srinivasan (1981), Braverman and Stiglitz (1982)]. The result is Paretian inefficiency. Share tenancy, however, has survived the modern land reform era in developing as well as developed economies. This persistence has led many economists to attempt an economic explanation of share tenancy.

Several have questioned the classical argument of share tenancy inefficiency. Starting by observing that if share tenancy were inefficient as claimed it would have died out, Johnson (1950) and later Cheung (1969) argued that efficiency can be achieved with effective monitoring of share tenants. Johnson argued that short-term contracts could be used to ensure that tenant farmers use resources efficiently. If the tenant does not deliver an adequate share of output to the landlord he or she may be penalized by contract termination.

The Johnson-Cheung hypothesis of efficient resource use under share tenancy presumes contracts are enforceable. If share contracts are enforceable by explicit stipulation or implicit penalty of contract termination, the observed outcome should be efficient. However, if share contracts are not enforceable, tenant farmers maximize their own share of income and inefficiency results. Which hypothesis is correct is an empirical question. Previous attempts to address the efficiency issue empirically include Huang (1975) and Nabi (1986), who used Malaysian and Indian data, respectively. Neither found share tenancy to be inefficient. Both studies thus support the Johnson-Cheung hypothesis. Contrary results were obtained by Shaban (1987), whose test using Indian data rejected the Johnson-Cheung hypothesis.

All these tests, unfortunately, rely on the assumption that if inefficiency exists inputs will be used less intensively with share-rented land than with owned or cash-rented land. Input intensity is a valid measure of the relative efficiency of share tenancy only under restrictive conditions.[1] Shaban's test assumed a constant returns-to-scale technology to justify the input intensity approach. However, constant returns-to-scale is a restrictive assumption, that should be validated empirically. This seems particularly true for developing countries where the scope of land variation is limited relative to other inputs.

This study revisits the efficiency issue. Share tenancy inefficiency arises from the very nature of sharing by altering the relative "effective" prices faced by the tenant. Thus, we examine directly the empirical evidence of allocative inefficiency for share farmers. Since this study uses a profit maximization framework, following Lovell and Schmidt (1988) and Färe, Grosskopf, and Lee (1990), allocative efficiency in this context requires efficient allocation of inputs as well as outputs.[2] In light of this, we decompose allocative efficiency into cost and size efficiencies. Thus, the overall efficiency, that is, technically as well as allocatively efficient, can be broken down into the components of technical, cost, and size efficiencies. Finally, this study focuses on U.S. share tenancy.[3] Few analytical studies have recognized share tenancy as a phenomenon arising in an economic system beyond the agrarian context. In the United States one-third of total agricultural land is operated under share contracts. The implications of share tenancy in developing countries may differ from those in developed economies where property rights are better defined and credit and land markets are better developed.

11.2 Competing Hypotheses

This section gives a brief overview of the inefficiency and monitoring hypotheses within a profit maximization framework. The starting point is a production possi-

---

[1] To demonstrate this, assume two inputs: a single purchased input (x) and land (L). Let (x^s, L^s) and (x^o, L^o) denote the observations on the share tenant and the owner operator, respectively. According to the input intensity approach, (x^s/L^s) < (x^o/L^o) implies the existence of inefficiency. With some manipulation and assuming $L^o > L^s$, this inequality can be rewritten as $1 < [(x^o - x^s)/x^s]/[(L^o - L^s)/L^s]$. The expression on the right side of the inequality measures the elasticity of input x with respect to the land input between the two points (x^s, L^s) and (x^o, L^o). Therefore, whether this inequality holds or not is determined not only by the tenant's underuse of x (if inefficiency exists) but also technology. Technology becomes irrelevant to determining this inequality only under two circumstances, the constant returns to scale and obviously the case of $L^o = L^s$.

[2] Recently Färe, Grosskopf, and Lee (1990) introduced a nonparametric alternative to the expenditure-constrained profit maximization problem by Lee and Chambers (1986).

[3] Previous share tenancy studies on developed countries include: United States during the nineteenth and early twentieth centuries [Reid (1979)], United States during the Civil War [Alston and Higgs (1972)], southern region of the United States during 1930–1960 [Alston (1981)], Georgia cotton belt using 1911 data [Alston, Datta, and Nugent (1984)], and early France during the eighteenth century [Hoffman (1984)].

bility set $T = \{(y, L, x): (L, x) \text{ can produce } y\}$, where y is a vector of outputs, L is land, $x \in \Re_+^N$ is a vector of purchased inputs. Now consider a tenant farmer operating on share-rented land. Assuming y is a scalar,[4] the landlord specifies the tenant's output share $\alpha, 0 < \alpha < 1$, and the tenant's cost shares for each input, $\beta = (\beta_1, \ldots, \beta_i, \ldots, \beta_N), 0 < \beta_i \leq 1, \forall i$. When all β_i's $= 1$, share tenancy only involves output sharing and with any $\beta_i < 1$ the share contract involves cost as well as output sharing. Under the inefficiency hypothesis, the tenant chooses x and y to maximize his or her own share of profit:

$$\max_{x,y} \left\{ \alpha p y - \sum_{i=1}^{N} \beta_i w_i x_i : (y, x, L) \in T \right\} \tag{11.1}$$

where p is the output price and $w = (w_1, \ldots, w_i, \ldots, w_N)$ is a vector of input prices. The "effective" output and input prices faced by the tenant are αp and βw rather than p and w. Thus, when $(\alpha p, \beta w)$ are used in the maximization process the resulting x and y are in general lower than those maximizing $\{py - wx\}$. An insufficient incentive for input use comes from the maximization conditions for (11.1): the tenant equates the marginal value product of the ith input to $\beta_i w_i / \alpha$ instead of w_i. In other words, price-related allocative inefficiency may exist. The consequence of inefficiency is that:

$$\left(\alpha p \tilde{y} - \sum_{i=1}^{N} \beta_i w_i \tilde{x}_i \right) + [(1 - \alpha) p \tilde{y} - \sum_{i=1}^{N} (1 - \beta_i) w_i \tilde{x}_i] \leq \max\{py - wx\} \tag{11.2}$$

where $\tilde{x}$ and $\tilde{y}$ solve (11.1). The left side of the above inequality represents the total income produced under share tenancy, the sum of the returns to the tenant and landlord, which cannot exceed maximum profit on the right side.

According to the monitoring hypothesis, efficient input use which maximizes $\{py - wx\}$ can be stipulated contractually and can be monitored by the landlord. If true, share tenancy is as efficient as cash-renting or owner farming with no allocative inefficiency. Therefore, to determine which hypothesis describes reality one can equivalently examine the allocative inefficiency of share-tenant farms relative to that of the cash-tenant or owner farm. As an empirical reality, allocative inefficiency will be found even with owner farming or cash-rent farming, at least to the degree that perfect modeling is not possible. However, if share rented farms are found to be allocatively inefficient relative to the other tenancy forms, we may conjecture that share tenancy does indeed create allocative inefficiency.

Allocative inefficiency, if it exsits, varies with share arrangements. Under Equa-

---

[4] This will be the case when either a single output is considered or the technology is such that the output vector is separable from the input vector.

tion (11.1) if all inputs were shared in the same proportion as output ($\alpha = \beta_1 = \cdots = \beta_N$), relative "effective" prices would remain unaltered and Pareto optimality will be preserved under share tenancy [Heady (1947)]. On the other hand, if the share arrangement involves only output sharing (all β_i's = 1) or if all $\beta_i = \hat{\beta}$, relative input prices are unaltered, implying that no input distortions result for given output levels. Allocative inefficiency results then from the tenant's size decision. According to survey information conducted by the U.S. Department of Agriculture, landlords often share costs in the United States.[5] The coexistence of output sharing and out-put/cost sharing is particularly interesting because these have different implications for allocative inefficiency, which will be further examined later.

11.3 Decomposition of Allocative Efficiency

Allocative efficiency can be decomposed into cost efficiency and size efficiency. At given input prices, cost efficiency minimizes cost and the cost frontier $C(y : w)$ identifies the cost-minimizing surface for all possible output. Once cost efficiency is achieved, size efficiency maximizes profit, $\{py - C(y : w)\}$, by choosing y. The mathematical expressions of various efficiency measures are relegated to the next section. This section illustrates some basic notions of these efficiencies graphically.

Consider the input requirement set $V(y^T)$ in Figure 11.1. Tangent lines at B and A depict the market input price ratios and those faced by the cost-sharing tenant $(\beta_1 w_1 / \beta_2 w_2)$, respectively. The tenant's input choice at A is cost-inefficient and

[5] Survey information is obtained from the 1984 National Special Crop Survey on rice farms. The phenomenon of cost sharing in the United States contrasts with the previous finding by Adams and Rask (1968), who observed that cost-sharing arrangments were uncommon in developing countries.

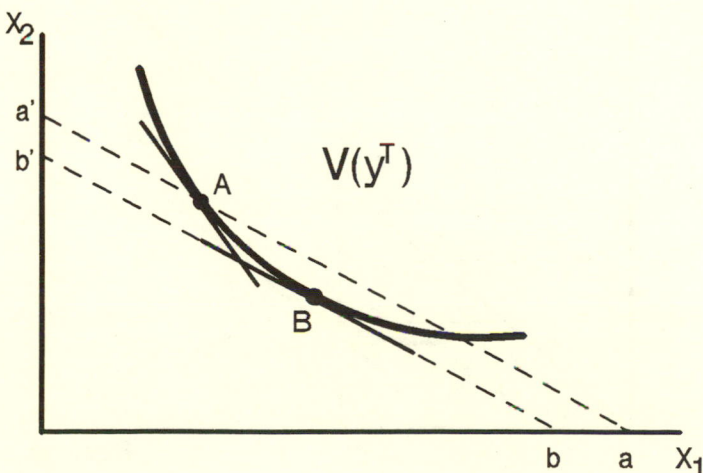

Fig. 11.1 Cost efficiency

potential cost reduction by moving from A to B will be measured by the difference in costs aa' and bb'. Note that under uniform cost sharing cost efficiency is preserved under share tenancy because uniform cost sharing creates no distortions in relative input prices ($\beta w_i / \beta w_j = w_i / w_j$).

Once cost efficiency is identified size efficiency can be computed by locating the allocatively efficient outcome. A pictorial representation of size efficiency expressed in revenue and cost space is found in Figure 11.2. The convex curve in Figure 11.2 represents the minimal production cost, $C(y : w)$ derived from the cost-efficient surface in Figure 11.1. Reproducing A and B from Figure 11.1 in Figure 11.2, cost-efficient point B lies on the curve and point A lies above the curve because A is cost-inefficient. [Note that $C(y : w)$ is a usual cost function with the output augmented by the output price.] By adding a 45° revenue line, allocative efficiency is achieved at point C where the distance between the revenue line and $C(y : w)$ is maximized. So, allocative efficiency measured by the movement $A \to C$ has two components: cost efficiency $A \to B$ and size efficiency $B \to C$.

Profits at A, B, and C are measured as the vertical distance, AF, BF, and CD, respectively, and various efficiencies can be expressed using a common measure, namely, foregone profit. The allocative efficiency measure (E^A) can be constructed as a proportion of profit at A to the maximum profit obtainable when production is allocatively efficient. By analogously defining cost efficiency (E^C) and size efficiency (E^S), the decomposition can be written: $E^A = E^C \cdot E^S = (AF/BF) \cdot (BF/CD) = AF/CD$.

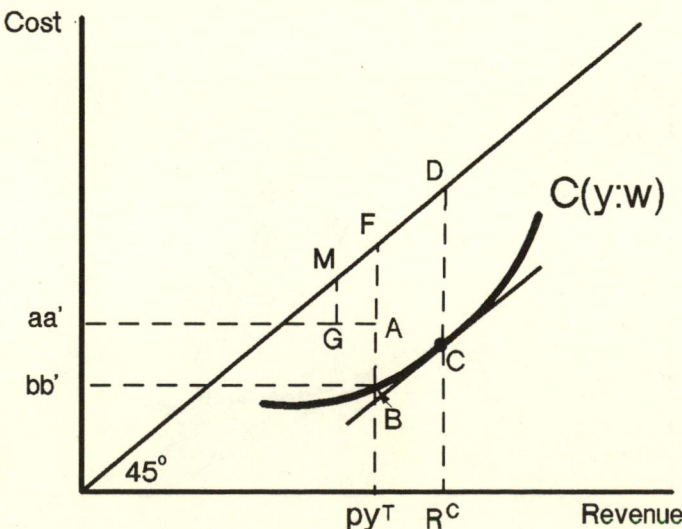

Fig. 11.2 Efficiency decomposition

11.4 Nonparametric Frontier Model

Given the definitions of various efficiencies, the next step is to compute the corresponding profits, namely, cost-efficient profit (π^C) and allocatively efficient profit (π^A). This involves devising an empirically tractable framework for which a nonparametric frontier method will be adopted. Since the frontier method identifies the frontier or best technology for given observations, we can also obtain information on technical efficiency as a byproduct.

Suppose a data set S consists of K $(k = 1, \ldots, K)$ observations of the input vector $x^k = (x_1^k, \ldots, x_n^k, \ldots, x_N^k) \in \Re_+^N$, output y^k, and land L^k. The production possibility set can be formed from the observed inputs and output:

$$
T = \left\{ (y, x, L) : \sum_{k=1}^{K} z^k y^k \geq y \right.
$$

$$
\sum_{k=1}^{K} z^k x_n^k \leq x_n, \quad n = 1, \ldots, N
$$

$$
\left. \sum_{k=1}^{K} z^k L^k \leq L, \quad z \in \Re_+^K, \quad \sum_{k=1}^{K} z^k = 1 \right\} \tag{11.3}
$$

where $z = (z^1, \ldots, z^k, \ldots, z^K)$ is a vector of intensity variables used to construct a free disposal convex hull. When the observed inputs are not employed with best practice, the observation lies inside T and is said to be technically inefficient. This implies that loss of profit may result from technical inefficiency as well as allocative inefficiency. Thus, we must first isolate loss of profit due to technical inefficiency from the maximum potential, allocatively efficient profit.

Various methods of measuring technical inefficiency exist: input measures, output measures, and radial measures [for a detailed discussion, see Färe, Grosskopf, and Lovell (1985)]. We adopt an output orientation. Under the assumption of identical p^k and w_n^k to all producers, technical efficiency (E^T) can be examined as a ratio of observed profit ($\hat{\pi}$) to technically efficient profit (π^T) : $E^T = \hat{\pi}/\pi^T$. Notice that the profit measure of technical efficiency is valid only under identical prices. This is particularly relevant to our study because our data are in value terms rather than prices and quantities. Färe, Grosskopf, and Lee (1990) have shown that under the assumption of identical prices, profit maximization problems like (11.4) modified in terms of revenue (py^k) and input costs ($w_n x_n^k$) instead of y^k and x_n^k yield the same solutions. We proceed with our model development in this section in terms of p and w, which is more general.

Technically efficiency profit π^T for farm j can be computed as

$$\pi^T(x^j, L^j : p, w) = \max_y \left\{ py - wx^j : \sum_{k=1}^K z^k y^k \geq y \right.$$

$$\sum_{k=1}^K z^k x_n^k \leq x_n^j, \quad n = 1, \ldots, N$$

$$\left. \sum_{k=1}^K z^k L^k \leq L^j, \quad z \in \Re_+^K, \quad \sum_{k=1}^K z^k = 1 \right\} \quad (11.4)$$

In Figure 11.2, denoting technically efficient output as y^T, the actual output ($\hat{y}$) could be observed at a point like G because $\hat{y}$ cannot be greater than y^T. Subsequently, E^T will be measured by the ratio GM/AF.

Once y^T is identified, cost-efficient profit π^C can be obtained by finding the minimum cost of producing y^T (note that py^T is a constant). Analogous to (11.4), we can express this as a restricted profit maximization problem:

$$\pi^C(y^T, L^j : p, w) = \max_x \{py^T - wx : (y^T, x, L^j) \in T\} \quad (11.5)$$

[The linear programming expression of (11.5) is not presented here but is identical to (11.4) except for y and x_n^j replaced, respectively, by y^T and x_n.]

Finally, allocative efficieny requires size efficiency as well as cost efficiency. Thus, allocative-efficient profit (π^A) can be obtained by identifying the output level which maximizes $\pi^C(y, L^j : p, w)$. This is equivalent to

$$\pi^A(L^j : p, w) = \max_{x,y} \{py - wx : (y, x, L^j) \in T\} \quad (11.6)$$

Note that problem (11.6) is constrained only by land which is assumed to be fixed.

Introducing overall efficiency (E^O) defined as a product of E^T and E^A, our efficiency decomposition is complete:

$$E^O = E^T \cdot E^C \cdot E^S = \frac{\hat{\pi}}{\pi^T} \cdot \frac{\pi^T}{\pi^C} \cdot \frac{\pi^C}{\pi^A} = \frac{\hat{\pi}}{\pi^A}$$

As is obvious from the construction of Equation (11.4), (11.5), and (11.6), it is always true that $\pi^T \leq \pi^C \leq \pi^A$, which implies that efficiency for the observed farm increases as each efficiency measure approaches one.

11.5 Empirical Results

The data used in this chapter come from the 1984 National Special Crop Survey conducted over major rice producing farms by the U.S. Department of Agriculture.[6] For empirical analysis, we concentrated on only one geographical area, the Mississippi River Delta region. Focusing on one region should reduce the wide variation in rice-farming practices observed at the national level. More importantly, concentrating on one region reduces price variation, an important consideration given our assumption that all farms face the same prices. The Mississippi River Delta region has the largest subsample, consisting of 167 observations (45 pure owners, 49 pure cash renters, 31 pure share renters, 21 mixed tenants with no share-rented land, and 21 mixed tenants with some share-rented land). The primary purpose of the survey was to obtain information on costs and returns in rice production. Thus, the data on individual farms are largely in value terms rather than quantities.

To arrive at the variable input measures, the data from the survey were aggregated into seven variable and two fixed input categories. The seven variable inputs are (1) fertilizers, (2) pesticides, (3) seeds, (4) custom services, (5) hired labor, (6) drying inputs, and (7) capital consumption.[7] The fixed inputs are land and water. Water was treated as a fixed input because in this region water is usually supplied by the individual farm from the surface water sources and is seldom purchased. To compute revenues, rice production is multiplied by the harvest-month price for medium-grain rice.

Calculating the various efficiency measures involves running three linear programming programs (11.4), (11.5), and (11.6) for each of 167 farms. While the nonparametric programming method imposes fewer a priori restrictions than the parametric method, it is by no means without problems. One well-known problem arises from the fact that the frontier is solely supported by the data. As a result, its shape is highly sensitive to outliers and thus measurement errors. Timmer (1971) attempted to deal with the outlier problem by screening the outliers by discarding efficient observations until a certain percentage of the sample lie outside the recomputed frontier [Aigner and Chu (1968)]. We have adopted this data-screening method using the 94 percent criterion.

---

[6] The survey was a multiframe stratified survey composed of a list and an area frame. The list frame, made up of farmers known to have previously grown rice, was stratified by size. The area frame, aerial photographs of land segments, was stratified by land use. The survey covers the seven rice-producing regions: Mississippi River Delta, Southwest Louisiana, Grand Prairie, Northeast Arkansas, Upper Coast, Lower Coast, and California.

[7] Capital consumption is calculated as the sum of depreciation of capital equipment owned and expenses on capital equipment leasing. The survey has information on capital stock. In order to arrive at a depreciation amount, a depreciation rate of .08 was used. This depreciation rate was estimated by Hansen and Lee (1990) for farm tractors.

Table 11.1 reports the mean values of efficiency measures by land-holding status. The major findings can be summarized as follows:

1. The result on allocative efficiency is consistent with the hypothesis of share tenancy inefficiency: share-renting farms exhibit relative allocative inefficiency.
2. Regardless of tenure status, allocative inefficiency is the major cause of loss of profit. Furthermore, cost inefficiency is more pervasive than size inefficiency.
3. Cash-rented farms are less allocatively efficient than owner-operated farms, which differs from the conventional presumption that cash tenants would be as efficient as owner operators.
4. Share tenants tend to be most technically efficient while cash rent tenants have the lowest technical efficiency.
5. Share tenants are found to be most overall inefficient, indicating that their allocative inefficiency is high enough to offset their relative technical efficiency.

Our data are consistent with the inefficiency hypothesis and do not support the monitoring hypothesis. The results on allocative inefficiency indicate that share tenant farms are least allocatively efficient among all tenure types considered, which strongly suggests that there exist incentive distortions with the share tenancy practice. From the perspective of our study, this conjecture is also supported by the fact that the most allocatively efficient group is that of owner farmers who have no reason for incentive distortion. On the other hand, the conventional inefficiency argument often presumes that cash-rent farming is as allocatively efficient as owner operation because a lump-sum cash payment does not distort incentives for input use. However, our empirical results suggest that cash-rent tenants are less allocatively efficient than owner operators. This may be true if cash-rent contracts involve provisions other than cash payments for land: landlords may provide machinery inputs or some provisions controling land quality may be included to prevent the cash tenant from abusing land.

Table 11.1 Calculated Efficiency Measures

| | Pure Holding | | | |
	Owner operator	Cash-rent tenant	Share-rent tenant	Mixed Holding
Technical (E^T) efficiency	.83	.80	.86	.85
Allocative (E^A) efficiency	.60	.55	.48	.57
Cost (E^C)	.70	.62	.56	.67
Size (E^S)	.86	.89	.85	.86
Overall efficiency (E^O)	.50	.46	.43	.49

Given the real possibility of such provisions being included in the cash-rent contract, our finding is not entirely surprising.

Allocative efficiency measures are far lower than the technical efficiency measure for all tenure types suggesting that potential loss of profit results primarily from allocative inefficiency and not from technical inefficiency. In turn, this suggests the possibility of a substantial gain from improving allocative efficiency. The existence of allocative inefficiency for owner operators deserves some discussion. As alluded to earlier, empirical findings on allocative inefficiency for owner operators can be attributed to a variety of reasons: no operator possesses a perfect knowledge of the technology and no model can reflect reality perfectly. For example, risk could be an important consideration in making production decisions, which, if true, may lead to systematic bias in our empirical results.

The finding that share tenants are more technically efficient than cash tenants is particularly interesting because it appears to contradict the so-called "screening model" of share tenancy [Hallagan (1978); Allen (1985); Brown and Atkinson (1981; Rao (1971)]. According to this model, the existence of different tenure contracts is a sorting mechanism for landlords in an environment of asymmetric information about the tenant's ability. The sorting mechanism induces high-ability tenants to choose cash-rent tenancy and low ability farmers to choose share tenancy. This screening argument, however, does not explain economic incentives of the landlord who supplies share rented land. Recent survey data on U.S. tenancy indicate that a substantial portion of the share-rent landlord population are retired farmers, who we may reasonably assume are equipped with good farming knowledge. Those landlords who think they can affect production decisions by providing land on a share basis may gain a return from providing farming expertise. This possibility by no means contradicts the screening model but rather can be considered as a corollary: share tenancy may explain a phenomenon of "merging firms" between the landlord and tenant. And our findings on technical efficiency may be the result of "merging technology."

Allocative inefficiency may vary for inputs. We examined whether any distinct pattern exists with different tenure status. Across all tenure types, a similar pattern of input misallocation was observed (with the exception of pesticides): overuse of fertilizer, custom work, and capital consumption and underuse of hired labor and drying inputs. However, pesticides are overused by owner operators, optimally used by cash-rent tenants, and underused by share-rent tenants. Interestingly, underuse of pesiticides unlike other input use may indicate the tenant's incentive to use less risk-reducing inputs like pesticides, further motivated by the additional risk-sharing aspect of share tenancy. This should be further investigated with a model incorporating risk. Among the share tenant farms, farms sharing cost and output are separated from the farms sharing only output, and their relative cost efficiency is examined. We find that the cost efficiency measure for the cost-sharing farms (.54) is lower than that of the noncost-sharing tenant farms (.57), which is consistent with our theory.

11.6 Conclusion

This chapter attempts to identify allocative inefficiency associated with share tenancy. A nonparametric approach to profit maximization under share tenancy was developed and applied to a cross-sectional data set on Mississippi rice farmers. The empirical results do not support the Johnson-Cheung hypothesis. Share tenant farms are found to be least allocatively efficient, which is consistent with the inefficiency hypothesis. However, for all tenure status, allocative inefficiency is the major cause of loss of profit. This fact may be particularly important given the common practice in production studies—the presumption of allocative efficiency.

Finally, the results on allocative efficiency should be interpreted with some caution. There likely are other behavioral considerations which are not incorporated here. Further analysis may be needed, perhaps by the inclusion of risk. Finally, the fact that share tenant farms are found to be more technically efficient merits further research.

References

Adams, Dale, and N. Rask (1968), "Economics of Cost-Share Leases in Less-Developed Countries," *American Journal of Agricultural Economics* 50(4)(November): 935–942.

Aigner, D. J., and S. F. Chu (1968), "On Estimating the Industry Production Function," *American Economic Review* 58(4)(September): 826–839.

Allen, F. (1985), "On the Fixed Nature of Sharecropping Contracts," *Economic Journal* 95 (March): 30–48.

Alston, L. (1981), "Tenure Choice in Southern Agriculture, 1930–1960," *Explorations in Economic History* 18(3)(July): 211–232.

Alston, L., S. K. Datta, and J. Nugent (1984), "Tenancy Choice in a Competitive Framework with Transactions Costs," *Journal of Political Economy* 92(6)(December): 1121–1133.

Alston, L., and R. Higgs (1982), "Contractual Mix in Southern Agriculture Since the Civil War: Facts, Hypothesis, and Tests," *Journal of Economic History* 42 (June): 327–352.

Bardhan, P., and T. N. Srinivasan (1971), "Cropsharing Tenancy in Agriculture: A Theoretical and Empirical Analysis," *American Economic Review* 61(1)(March): 48–64.

Bell, C., and P. Zusman (1976), "A Bargaining Theoretic Approach to Crop-Sharing Contracts," *American Economic Review* 66(4)(September): 578–588.

Braverman, A., and T. N. Srinivasan (1981), "Credit and Sharecropping in Agrarian Societies," *Journal of Development Economics* 9(3)(December): 289–312.

Braverman, A., and J. E. Stiglitz (1982), "Sharecropping and the Interlinking of Agrarian Markets," *American Economic Review* 72(4)(September): 695–715.

Brown, D. J., and J. H. Atkinson (1981), "Cash and Share Renting: An Empirical Test of the Link Between Entrepreneurial Ability and Contractual Choice," *Bell Journal of Economics* 12(1)(Spring): 296–299.

Cheung, S. N. S. (1969), *The Theory of Share Tenancy*. Chicago: University of Chicago Press.

Färe, R., S. Grosskopf, and H. Lee (1990), "A Nonparametric Approach to Expenditure-Constrained Profit Maximization," *American Journal of Agricultural Economics* 12(3) (August): 574–581.

Färe, R., S. Grosskopf, and C. A. K. Lovell (1985), *The Measurement of Efficiency of Production*. Boston: Kluwer-Nijhoff.

Hallagan, W. (1978), "Self Selection by Contractual Choice and the Theory of Sharecropping," *Bell Journal of Economics* 9(2)(Autumn): 344–354.

Hansen, L., and H. Lee (1991), "Estimating Farm Tractor Depreciation: Tax Implications," *Canadian Journal of Agricultural Economics* 39(3)(November): 463–479.

Heady, E. (1947), "Economics of Leasing Systems," *Journal of Farm Economics* 29: 659–678.

Hoffman, P. (1984), "The Economic Theory of Sharecropping in Early Modern France," *Journal of Economic History* 44(2)(June): 309–319.

Huang, Y. (1975), "Tenancy Pattens, Productivity, and Rentals in Malaysia," *Economic Development and Cultural Change* 23(4)(July): 703–718.

Johnson, D. G. (1950), "Resource Allocation Under Share Contracts," *Journal of Political Economy* 58(2)(April): 111–123.

Lee, H., and R. Chambers (1986), "Expenditure Constraints and Profit Maximization in U.S. Agriculture," *American Journal of Agricultural Economics* 68(4) (November): 857–865.

Lovell, C. A. K., and P. Schmidt (1988), "A Comparison of Alternative Approaches to the Measurement of Productive Efficiency," in A. Dogramaci and R. Färe, eds., *Applications of Modern Production Theory: Efficiency and Productivity*. Boston: Kluwer Academic Publishers, pp. 3–32.

Nabi, I. (1986), "Contracts, Resource Use and Productivity in Sharecropping," *Journal of Development Studies* 22(2)(January): 429–442.

Rao, H. (1971), "Uncertainty, Entrepreneurship, and Sharecropping in India," *Journal of Political Economy* 79(3)(May/June): 578–595.

Reid, J. (1979), "Sharecropping in American History," in J. Roumasset, J. Roumasset, J-M Boussard, and I. Singh, eds., *Risk, Uncertainty and Agricultural Development*. New York: Agricultural Development Council.

Shaban, A. (1987), "Testing Between Competing Model of Sharecropping," *Journal of Political Economy* 95(5)(October): 893–920.

Timmer, C. P. (1971), "Using a Probabilistic Frontier Production Function to Measure Technical Efficiency," *Journal of Political Economy* 79: 776–794.

12

COST EFFICIENCY IN BELGIAN MUNICIPALITIES

*Philippe Vanden Eeckaut, Henry Tulkens,
and Marie-Astrid Jamar*[1]

12.1 Introduction

In most countries, municipalities supply numerous services to the population. In the case of Belgium, in addition to the various forms of civil administration, they also provide police services, social services, educational services, and maintenance of municipal roads and infrastructure. The cost of these services appears, in an aggregate form, in the yearly accounts of each municipality.

The purpose of this chapter is to analyze the relation between this aggregate cost and the size of the services provided. The relation will first be viewed in terms of a usual total cost function, and then as a total cost "frontier," using in this case various techniques of efficiency analysis. Along the way some indications will be obtained on the nature of returns-to-scale in communal activities.

In the next section, we present our data and the measurement of a standard "average" parametric total cost function. In Section 12.3, we deal with two nonparametric methods of efficiency measurement, namely FDH and DEA: We present their respective results when applied to our data set and evaluate their respective merits. In Section 12.4 we briefly deal with returns-to-scale, and in Section 12.5, we turn to the question of identifying factors that might explain the observed inefficiencies; in particular, we explore the political factor. The concluding section summarizes our findings.

[1] This chapter was presented at the European Workshop on Productivity and Efficiency Measurement in the Service Industries held at CORE, October 1989. It reexamines and expands, on the basis of an updated data set, results that were presented earlier in Vanden Eeckaut and Tulkens (1989).

For this revision the first and their authors have benefited from the support of the Belgian Fonds de la Recherche Fondamentale Collective (under convention n° 2.4528.88), and of the Belgian Ministry of Scientific Policy (under its Programmed d'Actions Concertées n° 87–92); the second author achnowledges the sabbatical support of the Collège Interuniversitaire des Sciences du Management (CIM), Brussels, and the hospitality of GREGE, Marseilles.

12.2 THE DATA

12.2.1 The units

There are 596 municipalities or "communes" in Belgium. As statistical data sufficiently detailed for our purposes are only available from the regional authorities, we restrict our analysis to the communes located in the (french speaking) Région Wallone, which total 262. From this subset, we had to further discard 27 communes, because some key data were either missing (as appears from the *Note d'information* of the Ministere Charge des Pouvoirs Locaux quoted below), or verbally declared arbitrary by the officials supplying them (specifically, as far as educational data in many large cities are concerned). In brief, we deleted all municipalities with an expenditure level equal to or larger than 1 billion BFr, that is 11 of them, plus 16 whose expenditures are lower but lack some data. We shall in due course evaluate the possible effects that such deletions might have on our results. Our data set thus comprises a cross section of 235 municipalities.

12.2.2 Total cost

For measuring the aggregate total cost induced by the municipal services supplied, we take for each commune its total operating expenses, as registered in the "dépenses ordinaires" section of the municipal accounts. These are yearly figures for 1986. We take only operating expenses because investment outlays, registered as "dépenses extraordinaires," are too irregular over time in the various municipalities for a single cross section to be sufficiently homogeneous.

12.2.3 Output indicators

We do not have a direct measure to quantify the local public services provided in each municipality. In order to get an approximation of them, we identify observable factors which seem to be determining ones for the amount of such services. We call these factors "output indicators."

For each municipality, the retained indicators are the following (all data are for 1986, unless otherwise indicated):

- **The total population:** This indicator is chosen to reflect the basic administrative services provided to the local population (e.g., "état civil," i.e., maintaining the registers of births, marriages, and deaths; issuing identity cards, passports, and other certificates).
- The length of roads to be maintained by the municipality.
- **The number of senior citizens** (aged 65 and more): This indicator reflects the supply of social services to the elderly, such as retirement homes, general assistance, and medical assistance in public hospitals.

Table 12.1   Summary Statistics of the Data

	Tot. spend. (Mio Bfr)	Total Pop. (units)	Pop. > 65 (units)	Roads (kilometers)	Ben. sbs. grts (units)	Crimes (units)	Students (units)
Min	23	1362	256	34	1	9	0
Name	Tinlot	Herbeumont	Fauvillers	Martelange	Geer	Daverdisse	(6 mun.)
Max	750	31,070	4759	751	251	1237	2179
Name	Flemalle	Braine-l'A.	Courcelles	Bouillon	Manage	Ottignies	Herve
Med.	130	6504	924	168	22	116	326
Name	Rebecq	Anhée	Libramont	Sombreffe	Braives	Bütgenbach	Frasnes
Mean	182	8721	1227	205	39	180	461

- **The number of beneficiaries of minimal subsistence grants:** While the national authorities cover 50 percent of the cost of these grants, municipalities cover the rest. The amount of the grant varies with the characteristics of the recipient: people with or without dependents, age, etc.; being in charge of evaluating eligibility, the municipalities have some flexibility in this respect.
- **The number of crimes registered in the municipality:** This indicator is intended to reflect the importance of police services (the figures here are an average for the years 1984 and 1985).
- the number of students enrolled in local primary schools[2]

Our full data set is given in Appendix 1. We list here in Table 12.1 some summary statistics for each category of data.

12.2.4   Do the selected output indicators explain total costs?

To provide an answer to this question, we have estimated from the just described data a total cost function of the Cobb-Douglas type, by ordinary least squares. The dependent variable is the logarithm of current spending. The explanatory variables are the logarithmic values of the six indicators just described. The results of the parameters' estimation are presented in Table 12.2 (the *t*-statistics are in parentheses).

For all six indicators the estimated coefficients have the expected positive sign. They also are all significant, except for the one relating to the number of beneficiaries of subsistence grants.

The values of the coefficients represent the elasticities of expenditure with re-spect to each one of the indicators. For instance, if the population were to increase by 1 percent in any municipality, all other indicators remaining constant, total expen-

---

[2] These data are the updated ones announced in the first footnote. The source is Ministere Charge des Pouvoirs Locaux, des Travaux Subsidies et de L'eau (1989). The sources for the other data are indicted in Vanden Eeckaut and Tulkens (1989).

Table 12.2 Estimates of the Parameters of a Total Cost Function

Constant	Log Population	Log Pop. of age $\geq$ 65	Log Kilometers of Roads	Log Ben. sbs. grts	Log Crim.	Log Education	R^2
10.782	.514	.257	.156	.02	.122	.04	.91
	(5.20)	(2.70)	(6.84)	(0.754)	(3.94)	(2.59)	

diture in this municipality is predicted to increase by .514 percent, such an increase being meant to cover the cost of the increased amount of the general administrative services provided. Similarly, an increase of 1 percent of the senior citizens population would induce an increase in municipal spending of .257 percent, mostly in providing assistance. An analogous reasoning applies to the other explanatory variables.

The results of the specification attest to the significance and explanatory power of the chosen service indicators, with the sole exception of the number of beneficiaries of minimal subsistence grants. However, if we restrict the estimate of the total cost function to the subset of observations that will be declared "FDH-efficient" in Section 12.3, applying a technique described in Thiry and Tulkens (1992), we obtain better results that appear in Table 12.3.

All coefficients are more significant than in the previous estimate. Moreover, the coefficient relating to the minimum number of subsistence grants beneficiaries is now significant. We thus believe that this variable does play a role as an indicator of the welfare services provided by the municipalities. We shall consequently retain it in our measurements of cost efficiency.

12.2.5 Cost versus demand estimations

Some previous studies of expenditure patterns in Belgian municipalities, namely, Adnet, De Bucquois, Gevers, and Meunier (1987), Jurion (1987), and Moesen and Vanneste (1980), follow the approach of Bergstrom and Goodman (1973) and interpret local spending figures as expressions of the response of local authorities to the *demand* for local public services by the citizens. To this effect, they relate the mu-

Table 12.3 Estimates of the Parameters of a Total Cost Function from the FDH-Efficient Observations Only

Constant	Log Population	Log Pop. of Age $\geq$ 65	Log Kms of Roads	Log Ben. sbs. grts	Log Crim.	Log Education	R^2
4.53	.417	.313	.188	.04	.102	.144	.94
(32.4)	(4.19)	(3.53)	(9.05)	(1.64)	(3.55)	(5.32)	

nicipal expenses (broken down in broad categories such as education, public works, administrative services, etc.) to variables such as income, prices, and socioe co- nomic characteristics of the population. These demand-oriented analyses thus aim at explaining the magnitude reached by the various municipal services.

Our present cost analysis is a different one: We want to take as given the amount of services provided and wish to consider the total cost they induce. However, as we cannot measure directly the physical quantities of these services, we only have proxy indicators, that somehow evaluate the need for the various services. Now, one might argue that each commune may choose to act differently, given what these indicators are, depending upon the tastes and preferences, that is, demands, of its constituency. A serious limitation of our approach is thus to neglect this demand-based factor of differentiation between communes, by implicitly assuming that, for example, when two communes have the same value for some indicator, their respective demands for the municipal services involved are identical. This may be acceptable for services covering needs that are fairly uniform across municipalities (typically, standard ones such as, for instance, birth, marriage and death registration, or passport delivery). It definitely rules out the possibility of differences in tastes between municipalities (e.g., the quality or the variety of the services they decide to supply).

12.3 Cost-Efficiency Measurements

12.3.1 FDH Measure

(a) The Method

We introduce in this section a total cost-several outputs version of the FDH method originally proposed in Deprins, Simar, and Tulkens (1984) in a one input–several outputs context. As shown formally in this reference, no parametric function needs to be estimated, and no convexity property is assumed for the set in reference to which efficiency is gauged. As no other assumption is made on the reference cost-output relation than free disposability, the frontier associated with the data is called their "free disposal hull" (FDH).

The method is most easily understood by describing, in terms of the following steps, how it evaluates the cost efficiency of a given municipality:

1. A municipality is said to be *cost-inefficient* if it is *dominated* by one or more other municipalities, "domination" being taken in the sense that
   (a) These other municipalities have expenses lower than its own.
   (b) These other municipalities have all their output indicators greater than or equal to its own.
   A municipality is called *cost-efficient* if it is *undominated*.
2. If a municipality is cost-inefficient and dominated by more than one other municipality, the dominating one with the lowest expenses is called *most-dominating*.

3. If a municipality is cost-inefficient, its degree of cost efficiency is computed as the ratio, to its own expenditures, of the expenses of the municipality that dominates it most. By construction, this ratio is less than 1 and greater than 0. If the municipality is cost-efficient, its *degree* of cost efficiency is conventionally set equal to 1.

Complementarily to the computation of the cost-efficiency degree, one may further consider the following:

4. If a municipality is cost-inefficient, multiplying the complement to unity of its cost-efficiency degree by its total current expenses yields the *excess spending* of this municipality, that is, the amount of spending that it would have saved if it had behaved like the most dominating one.

We repeat this procedure for each one of the 235 municipalities in our data set. An example, where it is applied to the municipality of Herbeumont, is given in Table 12.4, whose figures are taken from the data in Appendix 1. Herbeumont is dominated by three municipalities: Stoumont, Lierneux, and Wellin which all have higher output indicators and spend less than Herbeumont. As amongst the three dominating municipalities, Stoumont is the most dominating one (it has indeed the lowest spending of all three), the degree of cost efficiency of Herbeumont, .89, is given by the ratio to its own expenses (64,258,012 francs) of the expenses of Stoumont (57,631,248 francs). This ratio is meant to suggest that Herbeumont could have reduced its cost to 89 percent of its actual level while continuing to produce the same level of outputs, since Stoumont shows that, with a so-reduced total cost, it is possible to produce even more. Finally, the excess spending of Herbeumont (over Stoumont) is computed as (1 – .89) times Herbeumont's expenses, yielding the amount of 6,626,764 francs mentioned in the last column.

(b.) Results

Table 12.5 and Figures 12.1 and 12.2 summarize the results obtained from applying the method to all 235 municipalities. In the table, results are ranked in increasing order of municipal spending.[3] Column (7) indicates the percentage of inefficient

Table 12.4 Computing FDH Efficiency for a Given Observation: An Example

Commune (Dominated or Dominating)	Current Spending, Francs	Pop.	Pop. >65	Roads, km	Subs. Grts. Ben.	Crim.	Educ.	Cost-Effic. Degree	Excess Spending, Francs
Herbeumont	64,258,012	1362	316	218	5	16	77	.89	6,626,764
Stoumont	57,631,248	2450	446	469	10	59	103		
Lierneux	63,665,677	3048	499	419	7	53	175		
Wellin	63,124,971	2656	402	246	10	64	98		

[3] The list with the detailed results (for the inefficient municipalities only) is given in Appendix 2.

Table 12.5 Summary Results of FDH Efficiency Computations

Municipality Expenses (mio BFr.) (1)	# Obs. in this Category (2)	Total Spendings (Mio BFr.) (3)	Efficient Municipalities		Inefficient Municipalities		Excess Spendings of Ineff. Mun.	
			# (4)	% [=(6)/(2)] (5)	# (6)	% [=(6)/(2)] (7)	(Mio BFr.) (8)	% [=(8)/(3)] (9)
0–99.9	88	5,939.3	70	79	18	21	167.4	2.8
100–199.9	82	11,858.3	63	77	19	23	443.7	3.7
200–299.9	25	6,306.0	20	80	5	20	135.8	2.2
300–499.9	23	8,818.1	21	91	2	9	52.6	0.6
500 and more	17	9,962.9	15	88	2	12	118.7	1.2
Total	235	42,878.6	189	80	46	20	918.2	2.1

municipalities in each expenditure class, and Figure 12.1 presents the frequency distribution of the efficiency degrees (for the inefficient municipalities only). Finally, column (8) gives the sum of the excess spendings for the inefficient municipalities in each expenditure class, and the frequency distribution of the excess spendings is given in Figure 12.2.

From these results we observe

1. That 20 percent of the total number of municipalities are declared inefficient, that is, are dominated by one or several other(s).
2. That the grand total of excess spendings amounts to 918 Mio BFr., that is, 2 percent of the total spendings of the municipalities of our data set.
3. That over the range 0 to 300 Mio BFr., the proportion of inefficient municipalities (column (7) of Table 12.5) is fairly constant, around 20 percent.
4. That about the same characterization applies to the proportion of excess spendings in each class (column (9) of Table 12.5). For larger municipalities, this proportion is much lower (about 10 percent).
5. That about half (443.7 Mio BFr.) of the total excess spendings concentrate in the 100 to 199.9 Mio BFr. bracket [column (8)].
6. That both frequency distributions exhibit a fairly typical decreasing shape.

(c) Discussion

—*Efficiency of large units and sparsity bias:* One observes from column (5) of Table 12.5 that the proportion of efficient units is noticeably higher for municipality classes with larger spendings (300 Mio. BFr. and more) than for those with lower spendings. This is due to a special kind of bias that we call the "sparsity bias." Recall that with the FDH methodology, "efficiency" simply means absence of observed better performance *with at least as large outputs*. Now in our data set, the number of large municipalities is small compared to the number of small ones; hence, for large

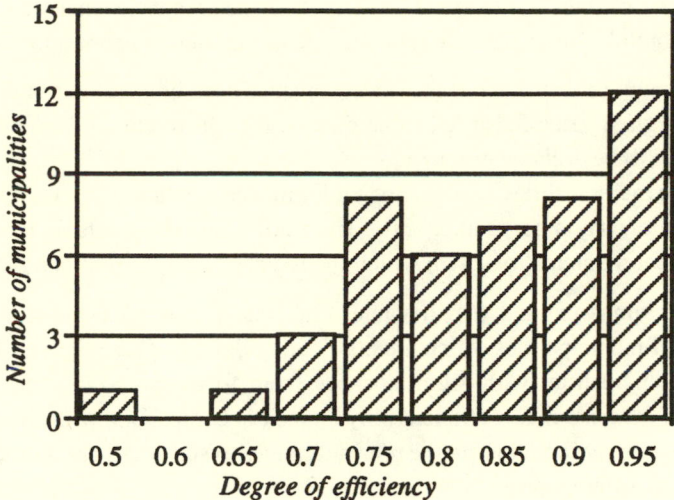

Fig. 12.1   Frequency distribution of the FDH efficiency degree (excluding efficient observations)

municipalities, one simply lacks the possibility of making many comparisons with similar ones. This induces a higher proportion of efficient units in this class. There is thus a bias in the method, *not* in favor of large units per se, but rather in favor of those units which lie in a range where other observations are scarce.

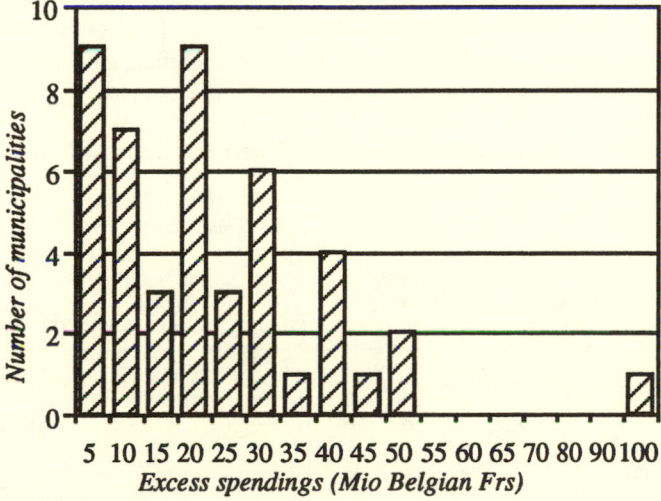

Fig. 12.2   Distribution of excess spendings

—Efficiency by default: An extreme form of the sparsity bias is what we call "efficiency by default." This expression refers to one of the following possible situations:

1. The municipality that has the lowest level of spending, as well as those with the highest value for at least one output. By construction of the procedure, they will be declared efficient.
2. Some municipalities, while being undominated and thus efficient, *do also not dominate* any other municipality. Their efficiency only rests on the absence of other municipalities with which the required comparisons can be made.

From columns (5) and (6) in Table 12.6, one can see the number and the proportions of municipalities which are efficient by default. These figures show that while the municipalities with high expenses seem to be more efficient, a higher proportion of them are in fact efficient only by lack of comparison with similar ones. If there were more observations in the relevant ranges, results for these municipalities might be quite different ones.

The two remarks just made suggest that the FDH method is perhaps better understood as one designed to identify the most obvious cases of *in*efficiency, rather than to characterize efficiency in itself.

—Outliers: With the FDH method, two categories of outliers can be identified: on the one hand, those observations that systematically appear as the most dominating one, and on the other hand, those observations that are dominated by many other ones. The results presented in Appendix 2 permit outliers of both kinds to be identified. As for the first one, Floreffe, for instance, is reported to be "most dominating" in nine cases [see column (6)]. This means that Floreffe has an important influence on the measure of efficiency. Indeed, when we removed Floreffe from our efficiency measure, five more municipalities were declared efficient. By contrast, Aubel— which is characterized by the lowest degree of efficiency (.54)—is dominated by 28 municipalities. "Outlying" here has however another significance: on the one hand,

Table 12.6 Number and Proportion of Communes Efficient by Default

Municipality Expenses (Mio B.Frs)	Observ. in this Category	Efficient Observ.	Efficient. and Dominating		Efficient by Default	
				% [(3)/(2)]		% [(5)/(2)]
(1)	(2)	(3)	(4)	(5)	(6)
0–99.9	88	70	33	47	37	53
100.0–199.9	82	63	16	25	47	75
200.0–299.9	25	20	4	20	16	80
300.0–499.9	23	21	1	5	20	95
500.0	17	15	1	7	14	93
Total	235	189	55	29	134	71

the result may cause some alarm in this commune, whose rulers may wish to identify the causes of such an overwhelming domination. On the other hand, removing Aubel does not, of course, influence the efficiency measure of any other municipalities (as the removal of Floreffe does).

12.3.2 DEA Measures

(a) Alternative Versions of the Method

For an efficiency study based on a reference cost frontier of the type used here, the DEA method of Charnes, Cooper, and Rhodes (1978), following Farrell (1957), proceeds by solving, for each observation, a linear program of the following form (below, $n = 235$ and denotes the number of municipalities; outputs are indexed by $r = 1, \ldots, s$, with $s = 6$, and k denotes a given observation):

Problem P:

$$\underset{\{\lambda_k, z_1, \ldots, z_n\}}{\text{Min}} \lambda_k$$

subject to

$$\lambda_k C_k - \sum_{j=1}^{n} z_j C_j \geq 0$$

$$\sum_{j=1}^{n} z_j y_{jr} \geq y_{kr} \qquad r = 1, \ldots, s$$

$$\lambda_k, z_j \geq 0 \qquad j = 1, \ldots, n$$

where C_k and C_j are the total spendings of municipalities k and j, respectively, and y_{kr} and y_{jr} are the amounts of the rth output indicator of these municipalities. The value of the objective function, λ_k, yields, at the optimum, the cost-efficiency degree of municipality k (comprised between 0 and 1), and the variables $z_j, j = 1, \ldots, n$ are weights associated with the municipalities in terms of which municipality k is evaluated. We shall label as "DEA-F" the efficiency measurement method that operates with the above linear program. It is understood to assume the reference frontier to be that of a cone issued from the origin of the cost-outputs space, implying constant returns to scale.

A subsequent version of the DEA method introduces in this program the following additional restriction:

$$\sum_{j=1}^{n} z_j \leq 1 \qquad (12.1)$$

a condition implying that the reference frontier is that of a convex set including the origin and satisfying free disposability. We call "DEA-CD" the measurement method resulting from condition (12.1) being added to Problem P. It is known to imply constant and decreasing returns-to-scale.

Alternatively, it has been proposed to introduce

$$\sum_{j=1}^{n} z_j = 1 \qquad\qquad (12.2)$$

a condition implying that the enveloping reference frontier is still convex, but not containing the origin, and satisfying free disposability. We call "DEA-V" the measurement resulting from computing efficiency by means of Problem P augmented with constraint (12.2). The added constraint induces "variable" returns-to-scale, in the sense of increasing returns for low values of the output variables and decreasing returns for high values.

An easy connection is made with the previous section by pointing out that one can show[4] that the FDH method described above also amounts to solving Problem P, augmented with the following additional conditions:

$$\sum_{j=1}^{n} z_j = 1 \qquad\qquad (12.3)$$

$$z_j \in \{0, 1\} \qquad j = 1, \dots, n \qquad\qquad (12.4)$$

(b) Results

In Table 12.7, columns (5) through (9) summarize the results obtained from the application to our data of the various forms of DEA just recalled. We observe

Table 12.7 Summary Results on Numbers of Efficient Municipalities with FDH and the Three DEA Methods

Category of expenses (Mio BFr)	Munic. in this cat.	Efficient with FDH		Efficient with DEA-V		Efficient with DEA-CD		Efficient with DEA-F	
		(#)	% [=(3)/(2)]	(#)	% [=(5)/(2)]	(#)	% [=(7)/(2)]	(#)	% [=(9)/(2)]
(1)	(2)	(3)	(4)	(5)	(6)	(7)	(8)	(9)	(10)
0–99.9	88	70	79	19	22	15	17	13	15
100–199.9	82	63	77	11	13	11	13	2	2
200–299.9	25	20	80	4	16	4	16	1	4
300–499.9	23	21	91	5	22	5	22	1	4
>500	17	15	88	7	41	7	41	0	0
Total	235	189	80	46	20	42	18	17	7

[4] See Tulkens (1993, sec. 2).

1. That for the municipalities in the first expenditure class, all three DEA methods, that is, DEA-V, DEA-CD, and DEA-F, yield fairly similar results in terms of the proportion of the observations that are declared efficient, and are thus spanning the reference cost frontier. This proportion lies in the range 15 to 22 percent.
2. That from the second expenditure class on, the results yielded by DEA-V and DEA-CD start diverging strongly from DEA-F .
3. That from this point on, DEA-V and DEA-CD yield identical results.
4. That overall, finally, only 7 percent of the observations are found efficient with DEA-F whereas this proportion rises to 20 percent with the two other DEA methods.

(c) Discussion

These findings strongly suggest that from the goodness-of-fit point of view, the DEA-F reference cost frontier is very inadequate. For the four upper expenditure classes, from 100 Mio BFr. and up, that is, for 147 observations (63 percent of the grand total), only 4 of them span the constant returns frontier.

Actually, one may notice that the data fit with DEA-F is worsening the larger the size of the municipalities, as appears from the numbers in the successive rows of column (9). This fact hints at a phenomenon of decreasing returns, that the constant returns imposed by DEA-F transforms in inefficiencies. The better data fit obtained with the DEA-CD results confirms this view: the reference cost frontier is now spanned by observations lying in the entire range of the total costs. (Note that in the higher percentage appearing in the top expenditure class there may perhaps be a sparsity bias at work, as defined above in the discussion of FDH.)

While allowing for decreasing returns thus substantially improves the goodness of fit of the reference frontier, introducing variable returns in the sense of DEA-V has a negligible effect on the number of efficient observations. This suggests that the decreasing returns phenomenon probably is already present from the first expenditure class on, and is fully so in all other classes.

12.3.3 Comparing FDH and DEA Results

With columns (3) and (4), Table 12.7 also provides a basis for comparing the results obtained with the FDH and DEA methodologies.

The table not only provides an illustration of the phenomenon that the reference frontiers constructed by FDH, DEA-V, DEA-CD, and DEA-F, respectively, are "nested" in one another, but it also permits one to evaluate quantitatively how far they each lie from the data, and consequently from one another: the FDH frontier lies closest and the DEA-F one the farthest, the degree of closeness being expressed by the number of observations that are declared efficient by the corresponding method.

Looking at the bottom line of the table, one difference is striking: the proportions between efficient and inefficient observations are simply reversed between FDH on the one hand (80 and 20 percent, respectively) and the DEA-V and CD methods on the other hand (20 and 80 percent, respectively).

We think that the data fit argument used before for questioning the acceptability of the DEA-F reference frontier vis-à-vis frontiers allowing for decreasing returns may now be used again to challenge the DEA frontiers vis-à-vis the FDH one. We present two arguments to support our claim.

Within the expenditure class of (100–199.9) Mio BFr., that comprises 82 observations, 52 (= 63 − 11) of them are FDH-efficient *and* not DEA-efficient. Goodness of fit is thus not very good there, since for these 52 undominated observations, their inefficiency, that is, their nonbelonging to the frontier entirely, results from the convexity assumption embedded in the DEA methods, of which FDH is free. Now our previous comments argued that there clearly are decreasing returns in these data, which is of course a convexity property. Are these two findings contradictory? The paradox is easily lifted by interpreting as local nonconvexities differences between FDH and DEA-CD/V results that appear *within a class*. As similar considerations can be made about the results obtained for the expenditure classes (200.0–299.9) and (300.0–499.9), our argument can be illustrated by the structure suggested on Figure 12.3. We conclude from this that DEA calls inefficient too many observations because of a formal assumption on the reference frontier that makes it fail to recognize local nonconvexities.

The truncated normal shape suggests the view that full efficiency is somehow the exception, with respect to which the standard cases distribute themselves normally with a single mode lying typically away from it. The plausibility of this view would hardly be questionable if it were confirmed by the shape of the distribution induced by FDH measures. But it is not, as Figure 12.4a shows. Moreover, experience teaches that it is repeatedly so. Indeed, results from both DEA and FDH efficiency computations were already provided and compared in Deprins, Simar, and Tulkens (1984) (along with a third method that we shall ignore here), on data bearing on a cross section of post office operations: a similar contrast was observed between the shapes of the frequency distributions of the efficiency degrees yielded by the two methods. And in Tulkens (1991, sec. 3), reporting on work done with Philippe Vanden Eeckaut on bank branches, this contrast was observed again.

It thus appears that with convexity—which is the key difference between FDH and the various DEA methods (and the only one with respect to DEA-V)—a systematic component is introduced in the characterization of behaviors vis-à-vis efficiency. Unless the convexity assumption can be given a strong a priori support—which is not the case with the data at hand—we see no reason to maintain it, and therefore reject the DEA results derived from it.

A second important argument, actually running more against DEA than in favor of FDH per se is provided by comparing the results obtained from computing excess

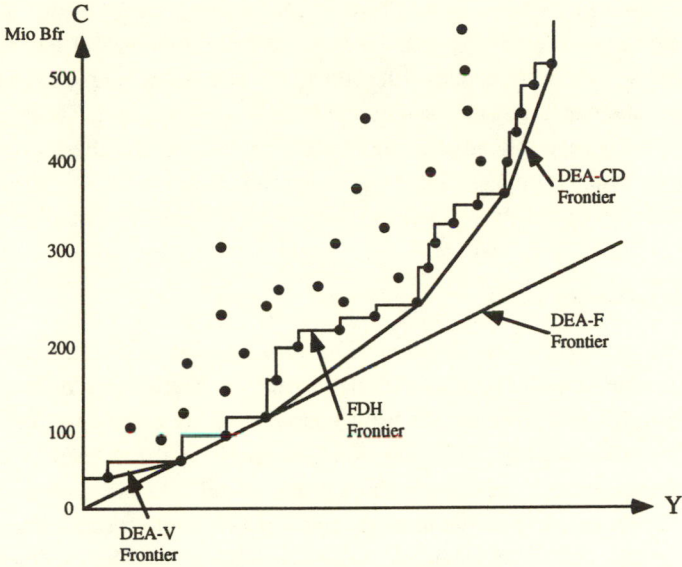

Fig. 12.3 An example of the data structure when local non-convexities are revealed by an FDH cost frontier and ignored by DEA cost frontiers

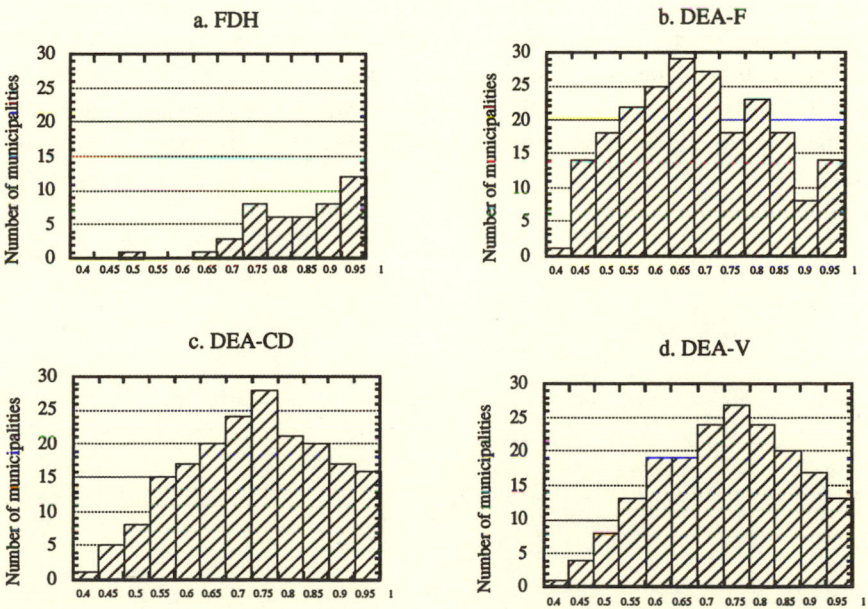

Fig. 12.4a–d Distributions of the efficiency degrees obtained with the alternative methods

spendings implied by each method. Table 12.8 provides these results. While with FDH the aggregate of excess spendings are claimed to represent 2.1 percent of the total spendings of the 235 municipalities (thus, 918 Mio Belgian Fr.), DEA-CD and V put this percentage at about 19 percent, and DEA-F at 33 percent. These differences are of course a logical implication of the "nested" property of the alternative reference frontiers from which the excess spending computations are made. We strongly think, however, that the credibility of these estimates varies inversely with their size.

12.4 Returns-To-Scale

With the Cobb-Douglas cost function estimated in Section 12.2, returns-to-scale are measured by the value of the sum of the estimated coefficients of the variables. This sum is 1.109, and when the function's parameters are estimated from the FDH-efficient observations only, their sum is 1.204. Both of these results indicate the presence of diseconomies of scale: a given proportional increase in all the indicators would induce an increase of the total expenditures in higher proportion. This confirms the remarks already made above, when the DEA-F and DEA-CD results were compared.

A further confirmation is the following. As suggested by Banker, Charnes and Cooper (1984), a quantification of the returns-to-scale phenomenon can be obtained within the DEA-F method by considering, for each observation, the value of Σz_j at the optimal solution of the linear programming problem P stated above: $\Sigma z_j > 1$ means that, locally, (i.e., for the observation under consideration), returns are decreasing; $\Sigma z_j < 1$ means that they are increasing; and $\Sigma z_j = 1$ implies constant returns.

An illustration of this computation for all 235 observations is provided in Figure 12.5, the units being ranked in increasing order of expenditure levels (the vertical axis is graduated in the logarithms of the $\Sigma z j$'s for convenience of the presentation only). It appears that increasing returns only hold (with very few exceptions) for communes

Table 12.8 Summary Results of Excess Spendings under the Alternative Methods

Municip. expenses (1)	Obs. in this category (units) (2)	Total spendings (Mio BFr.) (3)	Excess spendings (FDH) (Mio BFr) (4)	% [=(4)/(3)] (5)	Excess spendings (DEA-V) (Mio BFr) (6)	% [=(6)/(3)] (7)	Excess spendings (DEA-CD) (Mio BFr) (8)	% [=(8)/(3)] (9)	Excess spendings (DEA-F) (Mio BFr) (10)	% [=(10)/(3)] (11)
0–99.9	88	5,939	167	2.8	1154	19.8	1189	20.0	1,244	21.0
100–199.9	82	11,858	444	3.7	2607	22.0	2608	22.0	3,451	29.0
200–299.9	25	6,306	136	2.2	1401	22.2	1401	22.2	1,986	31.5
300–499.9	23	8,818	53	.6	1670	18.9	1670	18.9	3,217	36.5
>500	17	9,963	119	1.2	1370	13.7	1370	13.7	4,308	43.2
Total	235	42,884	918	2.1	8202	19.1	8238	19.2	14,206	33.13

[1] See Fulkens (1993, sec. 2)

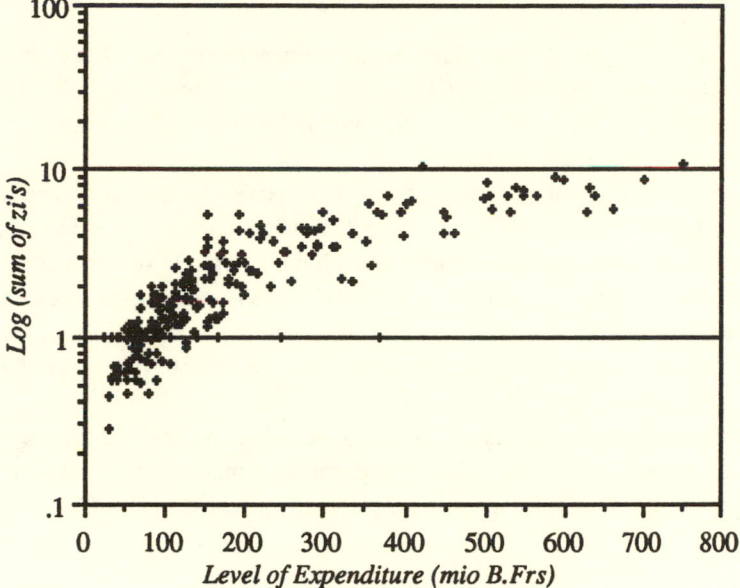

Fig. 12.5 Returns-to-scale with activity level measured by level of expenditure

with expenditure levels up to 100 Mio BFr., and that decreasing returns are already experienced by many communes with expenditures below that level. One can also find in Vanneste (1987), who made a study of administrative expenditures of all Belgian, municipalities, a confirmation of this diseconomies-of- scale phenomenon.

12.5 Political Majorities as an Explanatory Factor of the Observed Inefficiencies

In any attempt at explaining inefficiencies as computed above, two categories of arguments should be considered: methodological ones and behavioral ones. As far as methodology is concerned, we have already acknowledged in Section 12.5 the fact that the proxy character of our output "indicators" introduces a bias when quality variations are present. To appreciate the importance of this bias, and correct the efficiency evaluations accordingly, a natural way to proceed would be to compare qualitywise each FDH-inefficient municipality *with the one, or those, that dominate it,* in the same spirit that "peer groups" are examined in the DEA literature Some other methodology-related considerations will be made below.

As to behavioral aspects, we should like to devote this section to an investigation of the possible links between the political composition of the municipal authorities and the observed inefficiencies.

12.5.1 Political composition of the municipal authorities

There are in the Région Wallone three major political parties, which are represented in all municipalities: the Parti Socialiste (PS), the Parti Social Chrétien (PSC), and the Parti Réformateur Liberal (PRL). In some municipalities, there are in addition one or several purely local parties.

The various kinds of majorities that were observed in 1986 are listed in Table 12.9, with a code number in the left column. This code number is used in Appendix 3 for characterizing the political majority of each municipality. Note that such a characterization is not always a straightforward task: ours is based upon an examination of (i) the political affiliation of the mayor; (ii) the number of positions of "échevin" (deputy mayor) obtained by each party; and (iii) the number of votes obtained by each party in the elections.

We classify the majorities in 15 categories, that can then be regrouped in 6 classes, as presented in Table 12.9: "PS-dominated majorities," "PSC-dominated majorities," "PRL-dominated majorities," "anti-PS majorities," "PS-PSC-PRL coali-

Table 12.9 Number of Municipalities in Each Category of Political Majority—1986

Code Number	Political composition of the ruling majority	Number of municipalities in this category	
	PS-dominated majorities		
100	PS only	52	
102	PS associated to PSC	1	
103	PS associated to PRL	9	
105	PS associated to local parties	10	
	Total Socialist domination		72
	PSC-dominated majorities		
200	PSC only	12	
201	PSC associated to PS	11	
203	PSC associated to PRL	7	
205	PSC associated to local parties	22	
	Total PSC domination		52
	PRL-dominated majorities		
300	PRL only	2	
301	PRL associated to PS	15	
302	PRL associated to PSC	10	
305	PRL associated to local parties	15	
	Total PRL domination		42
250	"Anti-PS" majorities		25
400	PS-PSC-PRL coalitions		6
0	Local parties–dominated majorities		38
Total			235

tions," and "local parties–dominated majorities." By "anti-PS" majorities, we mean majorities obviously formed to exclude the socialists. The "local parties" category also comprises the communes for which we could not obtain reliable information.

To investigate possible links between the so-described political compositions of the local authorities and the observed inefficiencies, we proceed in two ways: in Section 12.5.2 we consider the results of the (FDH) efficiency measures according to the six classes of political majorities just defined; in Section 12.5.3 we consider both FDH and DEA efficiency results according to the number of parties that form ruling majorities, that is, according to the degree of homogeneity of the political power prevailing in the municipalities.

12.5.2 Efficiency results and dominating political parties

Table 12.10 presents FDH efficiency degrees and excess spendings in the municipalities according to the political composition of their majorities.

In terms of the proportion of inefficient municipalities within their class [column (3)], liberals and socialists are lowest (12 percent); they are followed by "anti-PS" and PSC-dominated majorities at about 25 percent, then by local parties–led communes (29 percent) and finally by tripartite coalitions, which fare worst with 33 percent.

The picture looks somewhat different when excess spendings are considered [columns (5) and (6)]. In proportion to the total expenditures they have to master [given in column (4)], socialist-dominated majorities fare least wasteful (.9 percent), followed closely by the liberal-dominated ones (1.6 percent), and by the PSC-led ones (2.2 percent), while the three other types of majorities appear to be much more criticizable from this point of view.

From Table 12.11 it should be noted, however, that municipalities with liberals and socialists in their majority also have the highest proportion of municipalities efficient "by default" (64 and 65 percent, respectively). This finding qualifies somewhat the superiority of their performance relative to the other parties.

Table 12.10 Political Majorities, FDH Efficiency Degrees and Excess Spendings

Categories of Political Majorities	Number of Municipalities in the Category	Inefficient Municipalities		Total Expend.	Excess Spendings	
	(1)	(#) (2)	%[=(2)/(1)] (3)	(Mio. Bfr) (4)	(Mio. Bfr) (5)	%[=(5)/(6)] (6)
Liberal domination	42	5	12	7,560.7	119.5	1.6
Socialist domination	72	9	13	16,785.7	153	.9
Cartels "anti-PS"	25	6	24	5,172.7	221.5	4.3
PSC domination	52	13	25	8,257.1	180.1	2.2
Local parties	38	11	29	4,525.6	197.5	4.4
Union	6	2	33	576.7	46.6	8.1
Total	235	46	20	42,878.6	918.3	2.1

Table 12.11 Number and Proportion of Municipalities Efficient by Default by Political Majorities

Political Majorities	Number of Munic. in the Category	% of Efficient Municip. in this Composition		% of Inefficient Municipalities
		Eff. & Dominating	Eff. by Default	
Liberal dominated	42	24	64	12
Socialist dominated	72	22	65	13
"Anti-PS" majorities	25	36	40	24
PSC dominated	52	25	50	25
Local parties dominated	38	18	53	29
PS-PSC-PRL coalitions	6	33	33	33
Total	235	24	56	20

12.5.3 Efficiency results and the number of parties in ruling majorities

The impact of the political factor can be further examined by considering the homogeneity of the political majorities. In this enquiry, we shall also see that the use of the FDH versus DEA methods appears to have a major impact on the findings.

We consider the following three types of majorities: (i)"strong" majorities, comprising the municipalities with essentially one ruling party; (ii) "dual" majorities, comprising the municipalities ruled by coalitions of two parties; and (iii) "multiple" majorities, comprising the remaining municipalities, all ruled by more than two parties.[5]

Table 12.12 presents the results of our previous efficiency analyses, aggregated by majority type. Starting with the last two columns on the right of the table, the DEA-F measure reveals nothing as to the number of inefficient observations in relation to the structure of political majorities: whatever this structure, it is always 92 to 93 percent of the municipalities that are inefficient. However, when moving toward the left of the table, one observes that the percentage of inefficient municipalities not only gets lower as the method changes (this is known from Section 12.52), but this percentage gets lower *more quickly* for stronger majorities: indeed, with DEA-CD and DEA-V, the percentage remains almost unchanged for the multiple majorities, but it decreases substantially for dual and strong majorities. This phenomenon appears as most pronounced when one reaches the FDH results in column (4): while only 12 percent of the municipalities with "strong" majorities are FDH-inefficient, this percentage rises to 24 percent for the municipalities with "dual" majorities, and to 30 percent for those with "multiple" majorities.

---

[5] Strong majorities are those of municipalities with code 100, 105, 200, 205, 300, 305; dual majorities are those municipalities with code 102, 103, 202, 203, 302, 303, 250; finally municipalities with code 400 and 0 are those with multiple majorities.

Table 12.12 Composition of Majorities and Efficiency Degrees According to the Various Methods

Type of Majority (1)	Mun. in the Category (2)	FDH Inefficient		DEA-V Inefficient	DEA-CD Inefficient		DEA-F Inefficient		
		(#) (3)	% [=(3)/(2)] (4)	(#) (5)	% [=(5)/(2)] (6)	(#) (7)	% [=(7)/(2)] (8)	(#) (9)	% [=(9)/(2)] (10)
Strong	113	14	12	87	77	91	80	105	93
Dual	78	19	24	62	79	62	79	72	92
Multiple	44	13	30	40	91	40	91	41	93
Total	235	46	20	189	80	193	82	218	93

Clearly, FDH identifies here a phenomenon that the other methods either conceal (as with DEA-F) or reveal only partially (as with DEA-CD and V). It is revealed by dominance, on which FDH is essentially based, rather than by the frontier concept, that is basic in DEA. The numerous observations in our data set that are DEA inefficient but also undominated are the reason why DEA fails to report it.

These observations are strongly confirmed when turning next to a similar analysis of excess spendings. Results on this are summarized on Figures 12.6 and 12.7. On Figure 12.6, one observes that the proportion of the total municipal expenses is largest for municipalities with strong majorities, and smallest for multiple-majority ones. Figure 12.7d, which is obtained from DEA-F, exactly reproduces that structure, but Figure 12.7a, obtained from FDH efficiency measures, considerably changes the picture: multiple-majority municipalities appear to account for a much larger share of total excess spendings (27 percent) than their share represents in the total expenses (12 percent, as seen from Figure 12.6); and the reverse is true for strong-majority municipalities. The other two figures, derived from the DEA-V and DEA-CD measures, suggest the same thing, but much less convincingly. Again, DEA would fail to report (as with DEA-F) or to stress sufficiently this characteristic of the excess spendings.

Table 12.13 provides a further illustration of the phenomenon, in terms of the proportion that the excess spendings represent in the total expenditures in each class of majority type.

As far as the substance of these findings is concerned, it is striking and probably of some interest to remark that they are of the same nature as those obtained by Roubini and Sachs 1989 at a macroeconomic worldwide level: these authors have indeed exhibited "a clear tendency for larger deficits in countries characterized by [. . .] the presence of many political parties in a ruling coalition."

12.6 Summary and Conclusions

In this chapter we have applied various efficiency and economies of scale measures to 235 municipalities in Belgium. A major difficulty arises with the measurement of the services provided to the population, for which we could only find proxy indicators. For these indicators, some justification is provided nevertheless by the significant

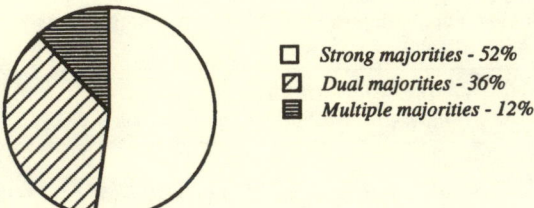

Fig. 12.6 Proportion of total expenses by majority type

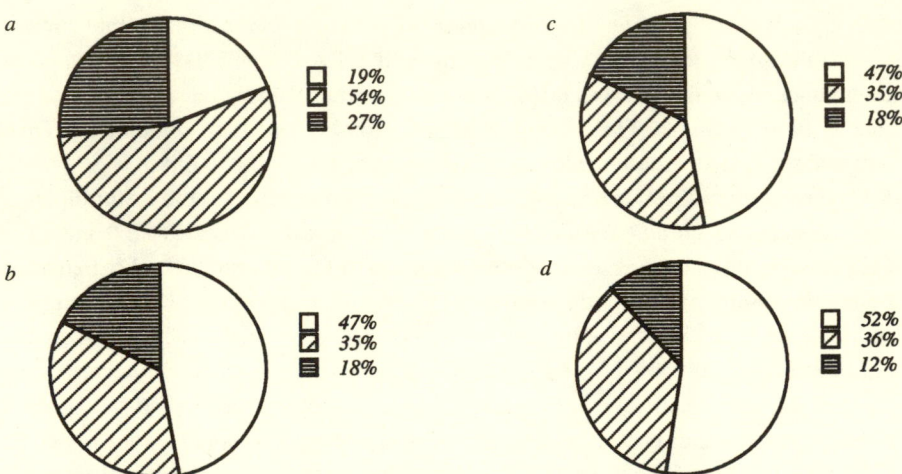

Fig. 12.7 (*a*) Proportion of FDH excess spendings by majority type. (*b*) Proportion of DEA-V excess spendings by majority type. (*c*) Proportion of DEA-C excess spendings by majority type. (*d*) Proportion of DEA-F excess spendings by majority type.

Table 12.13 Majority Composition and Excess Spendings

Type of Majority (1)	Total Spend. in this Category Mio. Bfr (2)	Excess Spendings	
		Mio. Bfr (3)	%[=(3)/(2)] (4)
Strong	22,465.9	179.6	.8
Dual	15,310.4	494.6	3.23
Multiple	5,102.3	244.1	4.78
Total	42,878.6	918.3	2.14

results we obtain from a preliminary econometric estimation of a cost-function based on them.

From the methodological point of view, DEA efficiency estimates are shown in this chapter to introduce too much convexity, because of resting on an insufficient data fit. This is revealed by the results provided by the FDH methodology which, overall, yield more credible results, especially in terms of the evaluation of excess spendings. For returns-to-scale, all methods yield convergent results on strongly decreasing returns in the large, with some sizeable local nonconvexities.

While FDH efficiency results (80 percent of total) are fairly generous, they also clearly identify the most obvious cases of inefficiency, which should inspire the inefficient municipalities to investigate by themselves which reasons might explain why their expenditures are so high relative to other municipalities providing at least as high a level of services. In this sense, the principal interest of the measure is to provide a diagnosis on the activities of the municipalities analyzed here. As to efficient municipalities, it was noted that a large number are efficient by default, so that little can be said as to their internal merits, because of lack of comparable units.

Finally, an examination of the possible role of political factors in explaining efficiency suggests first that municipalities run by nationwide parties lead to less inefficiencies than when other majorities are in power, and second that composite majorities, that is, multiple-party coalitions, more often induce inefficient behavior than homogeneous, that is, single-party, ones.

REFERENCES

Adnet, B., P. De Bucquois, L. Gevers, and B. Meunier (1987), "Eléments d'analyse comparative des dépenses sociales locales," in *Rapports préparatoires du Septième Congrès des Economistes de Langue Française,* Centre Interuniversitaire de Formation Permanente (CIFOP), Charleroi.

Banker, R., A. Charnes, and W. W. Cooper (1984), "Models for Estimating Technical and Scale Efficiency," *Management Science* 30: 1078–1092.

Bergstrom, T., and R. P. Goodman (1984), "Models for Estimating Technical and Scale Efficiency," *American Economic Review* 63 (July): 280–296.

Charnes, A., W. W. Cooper, and E. Rhodes (1978), "Measuring Efficiency of Decision Making Units," *European Journal of Operational Research* 1: 429–444.

Deprins, D., L. Simar, and H. Tulkens (1984), "Measuring Labour Efficiency in Post Offices," in M. Marchand, P. Pestieau, and H. Tulkens, eds., *The Performance of Public Enterprises: Concepts and Measurement.* Amsterdam, North-Holland, chap. 10, pp.243–267.

Farrell, M. J. (1957), "The Measurement of Productive Efficiency," *Journal of the Royal Statistical Society*, Series A, General, 120 (3): 253–281.

Jurion, B. (1987), "Externalités et dépenses des villes centrales," in P. Burgat and C. Jeanrenaud, eds., *Services Publics Locaux.* Paris:Economica, pp. 139–160.

Ministere Charge des Pouvoirs Locaux, des Travaux Subsidies et de L'eau (1989), *Note d'information*, Exécutif Wallon, Namur (janvier)

Moesen, W., and J. Vanneste (1980), "Determinanten van de gemeentelijke uitgaven," *Economisch and Social Tijdschrift* 5: 623–641.

Roubini, N., and J. Sachs (1989), "Political and Economic Determinants of Budget Deficits in the Industrial Democracies," *European Economic Review* 33 (May): 903–938.

Thiry, B., and H. Tulkens (1992), "Allowing for Technical Inefficiency in Parametric Estimates of Production Functions," *Journal of Productivity Analysis* 3, 1/2, 45–66.

Tulkens, H. (1993), "On FDH Efficiency Analysis: Some Methodological Issues and Applications to Retail Banking, Courts and Urban Transit," revised version of CORE Discussion Paper No. 9050, Center for Operations Research and Econometrics, Université Catholique de Louvain, Louvain-la-Neuve (forthcoming *Journal of Productivity Analysis* 4, 7/2).

Vanden Eeckaut, P., and H. Tulkens, (1989), "Une mesure de l'efficacité-coût dans 253 communes francophones," in H. Tulkens, ed., *Efficacité et management*, Travaux et Actes de la Commission no. 5 du Huitième Congrès des Economistes Belges de Langue Française, Centre Interuniversitaire de Formation Permanente (CIFOP), Charleroi, chap. 9, pp.177–207.

Vanneste, J. (1987), "L'offre de services administratifs dans les communes belges," in P. Burgat and C. Jeanrenaud, eds., *Services Publics Locaux*, Paris:Economica, pp. 161–179.

Appendix 1 Data Set: Spendings and Output Indicators

Municipality	Current spendings 1986 (Mio BFr.)	Population	Population of age > 65	Km of roads	Subs. grts benefic.	Crimes	Students in pr.sch.
Aiseau-Presles	221,256,848	10,815	1110	68	53	116	636
Amay	277,884,068	12,737	2041	148	127	284	721
Andenne	448,886,403	22,558	3260	266	119	480	828
Anderlues	193,076,680	11,313	1670	74	108	322	530
Anhée	125,260,849	6,504	1004	139	26	119	432
Ans	587,378,484	26,893	3511	133	120	801	1332
Anthisnes	52,322,431	3,385	470	134	12	36	228
Antoing	156,924,981	7,966	1369	74	30	137	278
Arlon	659,547,696	22,208	2851	325	55	755	1370
Assesse	90,451,462	5,341	580	226	21	83	339
Ath	638,998,390	23,535	3955	601	154	380	1219
Attert	84,232,528	3,133	492	197	8	24	356
Aubange	244,632,331	14,258	1907	144	79	219	350
Aubel	96,721,930	3,356	445	67	4	28	89
Awans	122,312,797	7,476	921	104	23	169	372
Aywaille	171,562,713	8,547	1172	437	45	405	423
Baelen	52,867,858	3,042	322	108	7	49	257
Bassange	92,691,657	7,782	1172	142	24	166	0
Bastogne	322,905,057	11,699	1385	544	36	293	381
Beaumont	114,099,057	5,985	828	326	50	110	323
Beauraing	161,364,949	7,857	1092	410	16	188	349
Berloz	33,227,156	2,386	394	50	8	17	135
Bernissart	192,255,670	11,167	1557	169	104	217	443
Bertogne	67,202,407	2,436	360	324	3	19	271
Bertrix	209,210,706	7,358	1111	502	31	121	267
Beyne-Heusay	152,415,894	11,398	1498	44	100	237	712
Bièvre	119,432,715	3,000	492	169	6	49	335
Blégny	155,006,390	11,324	1151	77	21	193	884
Bouillon	199,385,255	5,358	957	751	15	152	279
Braine-l' Alleud	596,446,917	31,070	3144	204	66	425	1190
Braine-le-Château	109,443,083	7,388	1047	49	14	169	267
Braine-le-Comte	366,109,837	16,716	2606	201	118	239	316
Braives	64,432,546	4,676	1015	149	22	56	221
Brugelette	52,912,359	3,111	439	63	18	50	145
Brunehaut	125,753,314	7,543	1343	155	13	53	453
Bülligen	140,489,500	5,176	702	446	2	42	500
Burdinne	32,955,598	2,196	444	121	7	30	36
Burg-Reuland	82,991,535	3,628	563	549	9	22	197
Bütgenbach	105,876,410	4,962	539	251	5	116	441
Celles	96,959,883	5,384	980	156	19	33	224
Cerfontaine	105,989,687	4,010	628	206	21	101	416
Chapelle-lez-H	293,894,966	14,041	1900	81	84	212	1138
Chastre	70,060,045	5,235	545	126	17	49	293
Chaudfontaine	451,459,488	19,949	2634	111	76	235	1461
Chaumont-Gisto	133,653,792	7,365	761	178	16	124	656
Chimay	237,007,328	9,360	1405	355	61	131	721
Chiny	114,256,384	4,563	791	210	17	49	156

Appendix 1 (continued)

Municipality	Current spendings 1986 (Mio BFr.)	Population	Population of age > 65	Km of roads	Subs. grts benefic.	Crimes	Students in pr.sch.
Ciney	372,090,282	13,476	1753	252	83	315	465
Clavier	63,207,151	3,616	561	193	13	69	218
Colfontaine	497,448,147	21,923	3434	87	120	375	1448
Comblain-au-Pont	92,024,159	5,019	757	72	20	148	349
Comines-Warneton	252,723,730	18,080	2792	204	83	367	192
Courcelles	700,157,184	29,044	4759	181	156	470	1767
Court-Saint-Etienne	135,436,357	7,332	989	62	22	139	482
Crisnée	30,713,978	2,256	300	48	6	65	0
Dalhem	97,685,972	5,494	552	104	9	42	569
Daverdisse	41,304,431	1,472	266	258	2	9	159
Dinant	333,858,066	11,961	1813	393	94	532	330
Dison	277,494,483	14,000	1979	62	90	247	1162
Doische	68,234,044	2,726	478	168	2	44	131
Donceel	42,238,344	2,256	300	48	5	28	113
Dour	250,322,010	17,089	3138	162	70	227	1207
Durbuy	184,276,611	8,207	1284	531	36	255	744
Ecaussinnes	194,826,154	9,356	1676	171	28	134	568
Eghezée	171,704,042	11,414	1612	323	38	162	270
Ellezelles	84,615,390	5,172	991	135	20	44	111
Enghien	139,089,315	9,970	1417	108	25	82	19
Engis	159,973,298	5,806	814	57	43	149	543
Erezée	88,188,333	2,239	342	228	7	72	110
Esneux	218,387,441	11,790	1873	144	48	401	361
Estaimpuis	137,941,955	9,583	1546	123	23	243	764
Estinnes	112,798,420	6,787	910	200	30	119	360
Etalle	90,763,592	3,719	553	179	12	50	245
Eupen	462,510,901	16,967	2589	84	138	395	682
Faimes	36,885,416	2,772	481	87	9	18	146
Farciennes	271,207,420	12,313	1468	39	60	158	1098
Fauvillers	53,941,726	1,630	256	182	5	17	130
Fernelmont	102,401,106	5,478	806	189	3	58	275
Ferrières	69,956,958	3,567	555	279	8	84	235
Fexhe-le-Haut-Clocher	41,087,925	2,567	402	82	8	45	287
Flémalle	750,843,322	27,260	4089	221	194	1052	2100
Fléron	312,581,350	15,889	1897	79	66	535	1232
Fleurus	547,720,961	22,432	3040	232	142	380	1132
Flobecq	41,127,305	2,981	632	54	8	39	0
Floreffe	88,959,463	6,290	826	380	27	160	296
Florennes	204,805,366	10,449	1237	373	74	182	520
Florenville	161,302,321	5,614	1091	349	30	122	216
Fontaine-l'Evêque	504,822,269	17,871	2516	91	155	432	0
Fosses-la-Ville	149,529,089	7,872	997	342	77	163	293
Frameries	394,665,042	21,516	3564	98	86	323	1225

Municipality	Current spendings 1986 (Mio BFr.)	Population	Population of age > 65	Km of roads	Subs. grts benefic.	Crimes	Students in pr.sch.
Frasnes-les-Anvaing	205,898,170	10,272	2060	350	24	75	326
Froidchapelle	77,861,947	2,700	432	210	9	64	206
Gedinne	116,285,021	4,083	667	215	15	95	272
Geer	40,001,015	2,381	329	62	1	33	241
Gernbloux	399,215,544	18,506	2513	258	80	348	790
Genappe	198,934,954	12,158	1693	399	26	215	511
Gerpinnes	197,078,636	11,052	1235	222	32	202	283
Gesves	93,018,727	4,594	708	198	10	79	149
Gouvy	108,634,948	4289	746	519	7	68	275
Grâce-Hollogne	408,085,950	22,067	2821	126	76	645	1402
Grez-Doiceau	177,708,303	9,485	1347	172	12	146	304
Habay	131,709,445	5,949	843	177	30	88	433
Ham-sur-Heure-Nalirines	283,968,678	11,923	1459	223	31	116	742
Hamoir	66,916,956	3,213	492	101	13	124	236
Hamois	105,586,336	5,634	612	300	50	74	641
Hannut	216,517,347	11,323	2094	286	39	217	447
Hastière	89,567,649	4,215	747	135	13	124	241
Hélécine	40,902,747	2,795	507	67	8	17	187
Hensies	133,927,744	7,030	852	63	38	38	131
Herbeumont	64,258,012	1,362	316	218	5	16	77
Héron	53,632,458	3,643	613	121	16	32	231
Herve	244,119,328	15,087	1502	234	34	319	2179
Hotton	98,713,856	4,264	498	128	9	59	84
Houffalize	143,239,193	4,134	731	460	10	100	248
Houyet	94,132,935	3,983	707	287	14	87	309
Incourt	52,223,681	3,186	538	134	5	39	204
Ittre	112,679,809	4,888	782	106	9	69	221
Jalhay	101,579,516	5,763	671	323	5	110	511
Jemeppe-sur-Sambre	353,813,545	16,860	2289	421	145	418	407
Jodoigne	147,748,408	9,418	1483	308	15	150	236
Juprelle	113,309,364	7,153	810	112	5	118	491
Jurbise	155,767,188	7,961	1091	172	25	27	412
La Bruyère	153,409,456	9,402	972	70	55	158	511
La Calamine	104,842,711	6,712	846	300	5	77	417
La Hulpe	165,695,681	7,087	912	43	6	206	209
La Roche-en-Ardenne	126,380,935	3,961	711	298	19	124	140
Lasne	151,178,624	11,709	1110	110	11	187	454
Le Roeulx	152,236,817	7,447	1131	95	38	176	151
Léglise	102,703,247	3,296	574	448	10	25	294
Lens	58,449,859	3,779	542	214	4	28	222
Les Bons Villers	130,601,513	8,053	1098	145	43	85	446
Lessines	316,347,738	16,017	3223	237	77	115	618

Appendix 1 (continued)

Municipality	Current spendings 1986 (Mio BFr.)	Population	Population of age > 65	Km of roads	Subs. grts benefic.	Crimes	Students in pr.sch.
Leuze-en-Hainaut	199,816,085	12,718	2164	215	60	143	323
Libin	127,344,853	4,050	566	502	11	66	321
Libramont-Chevigny	187,300,403	8,236	924	599	21	165	449
Lierneux	63,665,677	3,048	499	419	7	53	175
Limbourg	89,394,022	5,201	816	145	11	81	163
Lincent	41,064,301	2,619	443	51	9	13	145
Lobbes	86,848,810	5,305	806	62	24	94	314
Malmédy	292,743,569	10,101	1441	328	44	201	823
Manage	421,507,465	21,588	3316	50	251	606	1424
Manhay	80,207,087	2,622	428	426	9	56	220
Marche-en-Farnenne	334,954,725	15,240	1679	374	62	435	648
Marchin	96,646,169	4,615	627	151	38	53	387
Martelange	31,206,116	1,449	264	34	8	41	0
Meix-devant-Virton	77,638,887	2,578	413	156	9	25	139
Merbes-le-Château	70,601,421	3,910	624	91	30	33	91
Messancy	122,475,391	6,114	738	150	11	125	196
Mettet	171,152,679	10,020	1355	606	58	133	641
Modave	48,575,025	3,169	458	112	16	47	119
Mornignies	115,122,748	5,091	737	186	25	57	245
Mont-de-l'Enclus	50,586,421	3,068	640	69	3	41	16
Mont-Saint-Guibert	84,809,609	4,700	510	56	9	101	81
Montigny-le-Tilleul	259,297,473	9,852	1507	73	28	176	739
Morlanwez	353,468,625	17,610	2601	87	108	412	894
Musson	56,424,010	3,707	478	99	14	33	65
Nandrin	63,303,576	3,943	454	124	10	91	323
Nassogne	135,198,218	4,302	653	282	18	69	261
Neufchâteau	156,811,052	5,919	931	388	27	127	290
Neupré	150,939,795	8,431	753	93	18	127	475
Nivelles	627,639,545	22,130	2858	150	77	868	385
Ohey	60,764,005	3,546	508	158	17	38	395
Olne	34,843,633	3,251	297	68	6	52	181
Onhaye	68,137,867	2,796	402	202	16	42	249
Oreye	42,870,847	3,107	445	48	13	101	234
Orp-Jauche	83,273,990	6,140	1039	225	13	66	284
Ottignies-LLN	368,542,358	20,971	1696	130	58	1237	882
Oupeye	537,410,304	23,118	2543	129	83	492	1439
Paliseul	152,154,818	4,804	768	439	9	54	323
Pecq	85,781,188	5,214	808	61	14	200	233
Pepinster	134,116,883	8,996	1285	97	35	158	292
Péruwelz	297,912,687	16,480	2798	225	110	635	862

Municipality	Current spendings 1986 (Mio BFr.)	Population	Population of age > 65	Km of roads	Subs. grts benefic.	Crimes	Students in pr.sch.
Perwez	96,588,845	6,012	880	181	16	66	396
Philippeville	176,301,947	6,906	866	704	37	39	375
Plombières	160,124,055	8,443	1060	182	20	81	789
Pont-à-Celles	288,121,728	15,425	2013	223	55	185	980
Profondville	134,317,601	9,146	1326	112	42	193	374
Quaregnon	507,264,497	19,675	3026	72	114	351	1509
Quévy	132,102,106	7,246	1075	400	20	69	343
Quiévrain	93,934,300	6,914	1134	59	61	150	329
Ramillies	63,778,084	4,297	756	209	15	28	151
Rebecq	130,314,037	8,941	1422	139	32	124	533
Remicourt	65,667,366	4,409	717	74	6	71	195
Rendeux	66,009,716	2,005	381	191	4	59	150
Rixensart	402,234,055	20,012	2437	88	70	578	1018
Rochefort	292,042,259	11,089	1478	391	63	265	592
Rouvroy	54,624,529	1,838	292	88	4	20	216
Rurnes	69,665,100	5,227	842	38	19	38	71
Saint-Georges-sur-Meuse	111,730,567	6,201	912	125	28	68	0
Saint-Ghislain	564,407,609	22,001	3033	223	105	427	1485
Saint-Hubert	166,999,790	5,548	845	264	28	129	205
Saint-Léger	60,130,619	2,852	400	109	5	29	284
Saint-Nicolas	500,271,881	24,196	3433	82	161	341	1829
Saint-Vith	188,674,690	8,469	1043	472	24	91	611
Sainte-Ode	59,868,726	2,018	289	268	6	43	216
Sambreville	531,808,785	27,261	3721	130	180	1158	557
Silly	89,599,117	6,156	825	398	10	27	471
Sivry-Rance	83,907,624	4,430	623	209	45	41	361
Soignies	630,018,458	23,407	3353	316	129	314	1060
Sombreffe	90,543,593	6,365	962	168	16	92	202
Somme-Leuze	70,749,853	2,857	388	388	21	54	228
Sournagne	218,506,340	13,199	1458	113	64	262	906
Spa	310,948,642	9,645	1712	136	44	502	189
Sprimont	169,376,516	10,393	1382	150	35	248	641
Stavelot	121,346,608	6,122	924	278	29	238	133
Stoumont	57,631,248	2,450	446	469	10	59	103
Tellin	56,676,812	2,078	306	167	14	24	225
Tenneville	68,994,474	2,230	294	174	6	41	292
Thimister-Clermont	80,429,481	4,111	402	117	6	35	570
Thuin	379,379,305	14,198	1846	383	135	264	876
Tinlot	23,899,809	1,837	258	62	20	28	115
Tintigny	97,795,813	3,235	538	164	10	55	323
Trois-Ponts	81,303,060	2,114	361	273	5	36	139
Trooz	127,374,905	7,589	1056	75	40	166	580
Tubize	447,599,173	19,769	2418	81	76	342	571
Vaux-sur-Sûre	109,041,442	3,737	542	386	5	22	356
Verlaine	44,687,357	2,844	344	70	5	36	340
Veilsam	171,381,807	6,747	1125	483	25	132	267

Municipality	Current spendings 1986 (Mio BFr.)	Population	Population of age > 65	Km of roads	Subs. grts benefic.	Crimes	Students in pr.sch.
Villers-la-Ville	121,975,895	7,641	1126	206	13	52	648
Villers-le-Bouillet	72,303,401	4,823	743	121	51	139	193
Viroinval	151,316,820	5,615	990	358	28	171	277
Virton	233,529,987	10,449	1755	207	71	235	319
Visé	359,474,926	17,029	1896	112	108	719	740
Vresse-sur-Semois	84,613,265	2,633	597	266	5	88	192
Waimes	126,620,802	5,791	737	321	9	92	647
Walcourt	273,215,415	15,276	1838	440	40	181	732
Walhain	57,611,653	4,444	673	102	5	42	262
Wanze	193,103,852	11,271	1696	163	80	158	707
Waremme	241,340,233	12,386	1759	96	80	528	623
Wasseiges	31,845,213	1,789	347	71	9	18	215
Waterloo	549,123,610	25,232	2443	150	90	851	697
Wavre	529,013,353	26,495	3023	277	116	975	776
Welkenraedt	178,255,740	8,067	1032	81	13	105	423
Wellin	63,124,971	2,656	402	246	10	64	98
Yvoir	156,419,226	6,725	1011	231	25	18	673

Appendix 2 Dominated municipalities ranked according to excess spending

Municipality	Current spending (Mio BFr.)	Degree of efficiency	Excess spending	No. of dominant municip.	Most-dominant municipality
Vielsam	171,381,807	.9987	229,128	1	Mettet
Attert	84,232,528	.9961	324,904	1	Sivry-Rance
Limbourg	89,394,022	.9951	434,559	1	Floreffe
Hastière	89,567,649	.9932	608,186	1	Floreffe
Donceel	42,238,344	.9728	1,150,419	1	Fexhe-le-Haut-Clocher
Rouvroy	54,624,529	.9579	2,302,098	3	Anthisnes
Rendeux	66,009,716	.9575	2,802,565	1	Clavier
Gesves	93,018,727	.9564	4,059,264	1	Floreffe
Lincent	41,064,301	.8982	4,178,885	1	Faimes
Doische	68,234,044	.9263	5,026,893	2	Clavier
Hensies	133,927,744	.9511	6,552,839	2	Trooz
Herbeumont	64,258,012	.8969	6,626,764	3	Stoumont
Tintigny	97,795,813	.9249	7,344,351	2	Assesse
Etalle	90,763,592	.9175	7,489,602	3	Orp-Jauche
Court-Saint-Etienne	135,436,357	.9405	8,061,452	1	Trooz
Montigny-le-Tilleul	259,297,473	.9654	8,975,463	1	Dour
Mont-Saint-Guibert	84,809,609	.8525	12,506,208	1	Villers-le-Bouillet
Neupré	150,939,795	.9139	12,997,840	1	Estaimpuis
Spa	310,948,642	.9581	13,035,955	1	Péruwelz
Hotton	98,713,856	.8436	15,439,866	6	Orp-Jauche
Meix-devant-Virton	77,638,887	.7826	16,874,882	3	Ohey
Saint-Hubert	166,999,790	.8954	17,470,701	2	Fosses-la-Ville
Saint-Vith	188,674,690	.9071	17,522,011	1	Mettet
Trois-Ponts	81,303,060	.7831	17,637,383	4	Lierneux
Le Roeulx	152,236,817	.8823	17,919,216	1	Profondville
Erezée	88,188,333	.7933	18,231,375	1	Ferrières
Fernelmont	102,401,106	.8132	19,127,116	2	Orp-Jauche
Vaux-sur-Sûre	109,041,442	.8217	19,442,325	1	Silly
Waterloo	549,123,610	.9634	20,110,257	1	Wavre
Farciennes	271,207,420	.923	20,885,410	1	Dour
Ittre	112,679,809	.7895	23,720,346	1	Floreffe
Chiny	114,256,384	.7786	25,296,921	2	Floreffe
Mornignies	115,122,748	.7727	26,163,285	3	Floreffe
Gedinne	116,285,021	.765	27,325,558	2	Floreffe
La Hulpe	165,695,681	.8325	27,753,726	2	Estaimpuis
Aiseau-Presles	221,256,848	.8728	28,152,996	2	Wanze
Bièvre	119,432,715	.7573	28,981,253	5	Assesse
Messancy	122,475,391	.7263	33,515,928	1	Floreffe
La Roche-en-Ardenne	126,380,935	.7039	37,421,472	1	Floreffe
Bertrix	209,210,706	.8181	38,058,027	2	Mettet
Tubize	447,599,173	.9117	39,513,223	1	Grâce-Hollogne
Ham-sur-Heure-Nalinn	283,968,678	.8597	39,849,350	1	Herve
Aubel	96,721,930	.541	44,399,499	28	Anthisnes
Nassogne	135,198,218	.658	46,238,755	3	Floreffe
Welkenraedt	178,255,740	.7311	47,941,703	5	Rebecq
Nivelles	627,639,545	.8429	98,626,192	1	Wavre

Appendix 3 Political Composition of Ruling Majorities and Efficiency Degrees

Municipality	Coalition code	Efficiency degree
Andenne	100	1
Anderlues	100	1
Anthisnes	100	1
Antoing	100	1
Ath	100	1
Awans	100	1
Aywaille	100	1
Bernissart	100	1
Blégny	100	1
Braives	100	1
Burdinne	100	1
Chapelle-lez-Herlaimont	100	1
Chaudfontaine	100	1
Colfontaine	100	1
Courcelles	100	1
Crisnée	100	1
Dalhem	100	1
Donceel	100	.9728
Ecaussinnes	100	1
Eghezée	100	1
Eupen	100	1
Farciennes	100	.923
Fexhe-le-Haut-Clocher	100	1
Flémalle	100	1
Fleurus	100	1
Fontaine-l'Evêque	100	1
Fosses-la-Ville	100	1
Frameries	100	1
Geer	100	1
Juprelle	100	1
Lessines	100	1
Manage	100	1
Marchin	100	1
Martelange	100	1
Merbes-le-Château	100	1
Modave	100	1
Morlanwez	100	1
Quaregnon	100	1
Quévy	100	1
Remicourt	100	1
Rurnes	100	1
Saint-George-sur-Meuse	100	1
Saint-Ghislain	100	1
Saint-Nicolas	100	1
Sambreville	100	1
Sombreffe	100	1
Sournagne	100	1
Thuin	100	1
Tinlot	100	1

Municipality	Coalition code	Efficiency degree
Tubize	100	.9117
Waremme	100	1
Wasseiges	100	1
Bastogne	200	1
Celles	200	1
Enghien	200	1
Erezée	200	.7933
Estaimpuis	200	1
Habay	200	1
Jalhay	200	1
Lierneux	200	1
Lobbes	200	1
Rochefort	200	1
Rouvroy	200	.9579
Saint-Léger	200	1
Flobecq	300	1
Lasne	300	1
Arlon	105	1
Genappe	105	1
Nandrin	105	1
Neupré	105	.9139
Perwez	105	1
Silly	105	1
Trois-Ponts	105	.7831
Vielsam	105	.9987
Villers-la-Ville	105	1
Viroinval	105	1
Beaumont	205	1
Büllingen	205	1
Chimay	205	1
Durbuy	205	1
Esneux	205	1
Fauvillers	205	1
Ferrières	205	1
Gerpinnes	205	1
Harnoir	205	1
Hensies	205	.9511
Les Bons Villers	205	1
Leuze-en-Hainaut	205	1
Limbourg	205	.9951
Marche-en-Farnenne	205	1
Mettet	205	1
Musson	205	1
Ohey	205	1
Ottignies-LLN	205	1
Rendeux	205	.9575
Somme-Leuze	205	1
Verlaine	205	1
Vresse-sur-Semois	205	1
Dour	305	1

Municipality	Coalition code	Efficiency degree
Engis	305	1
Faimes	305	1
Gouvy	305	1
Grez-Doiceau	305	1
Hélécine	305	1
Jurbise	305	1
La Hulpe	305	.8325
Libramont-Chevigny	305	1
Montigny-le-Tilleul	305	.9654
Olne	30	1
Pepinster	305	1
Waimes	305	1
Wanze	305	1
Waterloo	305	.9634
Doische	102	.9263
Aubange	103	1
Beauraing	103	1
Bertrix	103	.8181
Braine-le-Comte	103	1
Brunehaut	103	1
Incourt	103	1
Philippeville	103	1
Saint-Vith	103	.9071
Sprimont	103	1
Bouillon	201	1
Cerfontaine	201	1
Comblain-au-Pont	201	1
Comines-Warneton	201	1
Floreffe	201	1
Gembloux	201	1
Lincent	201	.8982
Meix-devant-Virton	201	.7826
Mornignies	201	.7727
Tintigny	201	.9249
Walcourt	201	1
Aiseau-Presles	203	.8728
Court-Saint-Etienne	203	.9405
Dinant	203	1
Fernelmont	203	.8132
Grâce-Hollogne	203	1
Ham-sur-Heure-Nalinnes	203	.8597
Visé	203	1
Ans	250	1
Aubel	250	.541
Braine-le-Château	250	1
Chastre	250	1
Clavier	250	1
Estinnes	250	1
Fléron	250	1

Municipality	Coalition code	Efficiency degree
Hannut	250	1
Ittre	250	.7895
La Bruyère	250	1
Le Roeulx	250	.8823
Malmédy	250	1
Nivelles	250	.8429
Oreye	250	1
Oupeye	250	1
Péruwelz	250	1
Quiévrain	250	1
Ramilles	250	1
Rebecq	250	1
Saint-Hubert	250	.8954
Soignies	250	1
Vaux-sur-Sûre	250	.8217
Villers-le-Bouillet	250	1
Walhain	250	1
Wellin	250	1
Bassange	301	
Beyne-Heusay	301	1
Braine-l'Alleud	301	1
Ciney	301	1
Ellezelles	301	1
Florennes	301	1
Froidchapell	301	1
La Roche-en-Ardenne	301	.7039
Lens	301	1
Mont-de-l'Enclus	301	1
Stavelot	301	1
Thimister-Clermont	301	1
Trooz	301	1
Virton	301	1
Wavre	301	1
Amay	302	1
Chiny	302	.7786
Frasnes-les-Anvaing	302	1
Herve	302	1
Jemeppe-sur-Sambre	302	1
Jodoigne	302	1
La Calamine	302	1
Pecq	302	1
Pont-à-Celles	302	1
Stournont	302	1
Attert	400	.9961
Burt-Reuland	400	1
Nassogne	400	.658
Orp-Jauche	400	1
Profondville	400	1
Tellin	400	1
Anhée	0	1

Municipality	Coalition code	Efficiency degree
Assesse	0	1
Baelen	0	1
Berloz	0	1
Bertogne	0	1
Bièvre	0	.7573
Brugelette	0	1
Bütgenbach	0	1
Chaumont-Gistoux	0	1
Daverdisse	0	1
Dison	0	1
Etalle	0	.9175
Florenville	0	1
Gedinne	0	.765
Gesves	0	.9564
Hamois	0	1
Hastière	0	.9932
Herbeumont	0	.8969
Héron	0	1
Hotton	0	.8436
Houffalize	0	1
Houyet	0	1
Léglise	0	1
Libin	0	1
Manhay	0	1
Messancy	0	.7263
Mont-Saint-Guibert	0	.8525
Neufchâteau	0	1
Onhaye	0	1
Paliseul	0	1
Plombières	0	1
Rixensart	0	1
Sainte-Ode	0	1
Sivry-Rance	0	1
Spa	0	.9581
Tenneville	0	1
Welkenraedt	0	.7311
Yvoir	0	1

13

TECHNICAL EFFICIENCY IN VETERANS ADMINISTRATION HOSPITALS

James F. Burgess, Jr. and Paul W. Wilson[1]

13.1 Introduction

Local units of central government operations are subject to frequent changes in regimes of control. In many cases, new regimes are intended to induce greater efficiency in the local units; typically, however, evaluation of policy initiatives after the fact is not done systematically. One method for such efficiency evaluation is the mathematical programming approach described in Chapter 2. In particular, the efficiency of the network of federally operated veterans hospitals in the United States is evaluated over a short panel while the regime of control for setting the budgets of local units was changing. The presence of multiple outputs and the lack of good information on input prices are aspects of the hospital industry in general that make nonparametric approaches fruitful, as in Sherman (1984), Grosskopf and Valdmanis (1987), and Sexton et al. (1989). Specific theoretical problems addressed here include a method for assessing the significance of changes in average efficiency over time and a method for assessing the relative strength of outliers.

This study analyzes annual data collected by the U.S. Department of Veterans Affairs (VA) on VA hospitals from 1985 to 1987. The data contain information on inputs used by VA hospitals, including various measures of capital (infrastructure), labor, and supplies, as well as information on outputs, including totals for various

[1] Both authors wish to acknowledge financial and logistic support provided by their affiliations with the Management Science Group, U.S. Department of Veterans Affairs, 200 Springs Road, Bedford, MA 01730. We have benefited from comments by Hal Fried, Frank Holden, Knox Lovell, and Suthathip Yaisawarng. The collegial atmosphere of the Union College Efficiency Measurement Workshop Series was of invaluable aid to the first author in developing technical expertise. Conclusions and opinions expressed herein are those of the authors and do not necessarily reflect official positions of the U.S. Department of Veterans Affairs.

surgical procedures, patient-days, discharges, research and teaching activity, etc. A deterministic, nonparametric production frontier is constructed in order to measure the technical efficiency of each VA hospital relative to the performance of other hospitals in the VA system in both current and past time periods. The results of this study can be one step in the evaluation of several important policies implemented by the VA over the period covered by the data. For example, similar to reforms outside the VA, a prospective payment system for adjusting hospital budgets was implemented over the period represented by the data.

Several approaches for the measurement of technical efficiency in production have been developed since Farrell (1957) provided basic definitions for technical efficiency. When firms produce a single output from several inputs, stochastic parametric frontier production functions can be estimated using the methods of Aigner, Lovell, and Schmidt (1977) and Jondrow, Lovell, Materov, and Schmidt (1982). When firms produce multiple outputs, stochastic parametric frontier cost functions can be estimated using the same methodology, provided factor prices are known [e.g., Conrad and Strauss (1983)]. Unfortunately, in applications involving hospitals, nursing homes, government agencies, and production of local public goods by cities, factor prices typically are not available; either they are unknown or difficult to infer. In such settings, nonparametric linear programming methods often are employed to compute a deterministic, piecewise linear upper boundary for the production set. The upper boundary from observed data is used to compute a technical efficiency measure such as those described in Chapters 1 and 3 or by Charnes, Cooper, and Rhodes (1978, 1979), Färe and Lovell (1978), Burley (1980), Zieschang (1984), and Färe, Grosskopf, and Lovell (1985) [other nonparametric methods corresponding to alternative definitions of technical efficiency as derived by Deprins, Simar, and Tulkens (1984) also can be used].

In this study, the input weak technical efficiency measure described by Färe, Grosskopf, and Lovell (1985) which assumes inputs are strongly disposable is used (the implications of this assumption are discussed in the next section). In addition, decision-making units (DMUs) are assumed to take output as fixed while inputs are adjusted to produce the fixed output. DMUs identified as inefficient in the input weak technical sense presumably could produce the same output while making proportional reductions in all inputs. These assumptions reflect two important constraints faced by VA hospitals. First, all government agencies (including VA hospitals) may be viewed as budget maximizers; consequently, they face asymmetric incentives to exhibit dynamic optimizing behavior, especially when federal deficits are persistent [Niskanen (1971)]. In the presence of excess output capacity, VA hospitals are likely to avoid realizing savings in the current year budget, since underspending a budget is likely to result in budget reductions in subsequent years [Weitzman (1980)]. Input usage will increase over minimum feasible levels to meet the budget target. This could become problematic if VA hospitals are allowed to seek alternative sources of reimbursement as proposed. Second, VA hospitals are required to treat all veterans.

Those with service connected medical conditions or satisfy a means test are given highest priority and are treated with no direct patient cost. Others receive lower priority and may have to make some payments or file claims with insurers (although the means test is somewhat complicated, veterans with annual income less than $15,000 typically fall into the class with highest priority). Thus VA hospitals must choose inputs to produce a given output. Recently, hospitals in the sunbelt have been more likely to face excess demand for services than those in the north and east as the veteran population has migrated to some extent. In the presence of excess demand for output services, VA hospitals are likely to minimize input usage and appear to be relatively efficient, given the second behavioral constraint [see Burgess (1989) for further discussion of these incentives].

Efficiency scores derived from deterministic, nonstochastic frontiers such as the one used in this study are known to be susceptible to influence by outliers in the data. Outliers may be observations contaminated by measurement or other errors, or they may merely be observations with low probability of being observed (making them atypical among the observed data). Outliers of the second type are not a problem, but the former type may severely bias measured efficiency scores. When outliers which result from data errors lie on the computed production set frontier, efficiency scores of other DMUs are affected since efficiency is measured in a relative sense. The problem of outliers in the data is dealt with several ways in this study. First, the data were carefully checked to eliminate measurement errors, reporting errors, inconsistencies, etc. Second, several tests for outliers were conducted and are reported in Section 13.4. As discussed below, the efficiency scores reported in this study appear to be robust.

13.2 Methodology for Estimating Technical Efficiency

One of the first attempts at nonparametric efficiency measurement was by Boles (1966); Charnes, Cooper, and Rhodes (1978, 1979) provided extensions in an approach termed Data Envelopment Analysis. Their work has been extended by a number of authors and is described in detail in Chapter 3. This chapter uses the input weak technical efficiency specification of Färe, Grosskopf, and Lovell (1985), which is similar to the input orientation variable returns-to-scale model of Section 3.3.1. The Färe, Grosskopf, and Lovell specification used here assumes strong disposability of inputs and may be written in matrix notation as

$$\min \ \lambda_k \qquad\qquad (13.1)$$

subject to

$$Xu \leq \lambda_k x_k$$
$$Yu \geq \ y_k$$

$$\sum_{j=1}^{K} u_j = 1$$

$$u \in \Re_+^K$$

where K DMUs produce m outputs using n inputs, u is a $(K \times 1)$ vector of weights to be computed, $0 < \lambda_k \leq 1$ is a scalar, x_k is a $(n \times 1)$ vector of inputs for the kth DMU, y_k is a $(m \times 1)$ vector of outputs for the kth DMU, $X = (x_1, ..., x_K)$ is a $(n \times K)$ matrix of observed inputs, and $Y = (y_1, ..., y_K)$ is a $(m \times K)$ matrix of observed outputs. The production frontier surface represents the estimated best observed performance of the units across the space defined by the measured inputs and outputs. Efficient DMUs are those units that define the production set boundary; those units not on the frontier may be revealing managerial incompetence, incentives not to minimize inputs, or unmeasured factors. The minimand λ_k measures the input weak efficiency of the kth DMU. Constraining the weights in u to sum to one in (13.1) allows the reference technology to exhibit variable returns-to-scale [Färe, Grosskopf, and Lovell (1985, pp. 44–45)]. Note that product quality is difficult to measure in health care applications; hence caution is warranted when interpreting measured efficiency scores.

The efficiency scores obtained from (13.1) measure technical efficiency as the distance to the relevant isoquant, but do not consider where along the variable returns production frontier the DMU is situated. To measure scale efficiency, (13.1) must be recomputed for each DMU assuming first constant returns-to-scale and then nonincreasing returns-to-scale to produce technical efficiency scores λ_{CRS}, λ_{NIRS}, respectively. The λ_{CRS} score is computed by dropping the constraint that the weights u_j sum to one in (13.1). The λ_{NIRS} score is computed by requiring $\sum_{j=1}^{K} u_j \leq 1$ in (13.1). The scale efficiency score corresponding to (13.1) is then computed as $S_\lambda = \lambda_{\text{CRS}}/\lambda$. Clearly, $0 < S_\lambda \leq 1$. If $S_\lambda = 1$, then the DMU is scale-efficient; that is, the DMU is operating at the point of constant returns on the production frontier. If $S_\lambda < 1$, then the DMU is scale-inefficient due to either decreasing returns if $\lambda_{\text{NIRS}} = \lambda$, or increasing returns if $\lambda_{\text{NIRS}} \neq \lambda$.

The efficiency score calculated from (13.1) is independent of the units of measurement used for both inputs and outputs. This is important since units of measurement may always be defined arbitrarily. Färe, Grosskopf, and Lovell (1987) observe that some formulations do not share this property.

13.3 Data and Estimation of Efficiency

Data for this study were obtained from several sources covering the period 1985–1987: the VA financial accounting systems, the VA national patient discharge and outpatient data files, VA nursing home discharge files, and the annual survey of hospitals by the American Hospital Association (AHA). These files contain information on 159 VA hospitals and several independent VA outpatient clinics. For purposes of this study, data were limited to the 137 nonpsychiatric hospitals in the VA system, excluding independent outpatient clinics.

As noted above, data errors may bias efficiency measures since the technical efficiency of individual DMUs is measured relative to other DMUs. If the data errors are distributed inconsistently across observations, then in addition to the efficiency scores being biased, relative rankings of DMUs in terms of efficiency will be affected. Incentives to misreport information were examined to indicate possible sources of inaccuracy in the data. Within the VA system, individual hospitals are the primary unit of budget account, so data at the hospital level do not have to be approximated from other sources. Where incentive to underreport or overreport information occurs, it should be present uniformly across all hospitals. Summary statistics for each variable were examined for each of the 3 years under study; average values as well as the range and variance were checked, revealing several inconsistent or impossible values. This analysis was repeated several times, removing observations containing inaccurate values each time. Various consistency checks were run on the data to ensure that changes in the average values and distribution of values across time were plausible. After eliminating observations containing inaccurate values and observations for hospitals not represented across each of the 3 years, observations for 89 hospitals over the 3 years of study remain.

Data collected by the VA for its hospitals differ from data on non-VA hospitals collected by the AHA and used in other studies in several respects. First, all VA hospitals report information based on fiscal years beginning October 1; that is, fiscal year 1985 begins October 1, 1984, and runs to September 30, 1985. Reporting periods for non-VA hospitals run various cycles, requiring adjustments to realign the data so that the same time periods are represented for all hospitals. This problem is avoided in the VA data. Second, VA data are generated from actual operating accounts and patient records as opposed to the reliance on poorly audited survey information in non-VA studies. The VA data collection system is not without systematic flaws (e.g., ancillary tests are not always recorded on the patient files), but information entering the system is aggregated and checked more carefully than AHA and federal Medicare Cost Report files. In addition, the incentives faced by hospitals in reporting data are different. VA data are used to generate workload projections and set budgets, while the direct connection of AHA-reported data to resources garnered by a hospital is marginal at best. Hospitals, to some extent, view AHA reports as an unnecessary burden. Undoubtedly, some AHA data are little more than approximations, but there may be less incentive to misrepresent information intentionally. The same is not necessarily true for VA hospitals, and hence the various checks on the data described above were performed.

Most VA physicians are paid directly by the hospital, allowing their inclusion as inputs. Measures of physician time in studies of non-VA hospitals usually are not included as inputs because no reliable data exist; for example, see Conrad and Strauss (1983) and Sherman (1984). Others, such as Grosskopf and Valdmanis (1987), use counts of physicians associated with the hospital as an input, though many of the associated physicians may spend little time performing work directly related to outputs produced by the hospital.

Sexton et al. (1989) previously attempted to measure technical efficiency in the VA using data from 1985 and found that about one-third of VA hospitals were technically inefficient. Sexton et al. measure output by the number of outpatient visits and inpatient discharges weighted by bedsection (weights are derived from the VA weighted workload unit system). Unfortunately, the weighted workload unit measure is a sum of the resource utilization costs by bedsection rather than a measure of work performed. Since weighted workload units are summed across patients, it does not measure the number of patients served, but instead reflects an input quantity.

In order to estimate technical efficiency among VA hospitals using Equation (13.1), five separate direct hospital outputs were specified: inpatient days, including both long-term and acute-care patients (PDAY); number of inpatient discharges (DIS); number of outpatient visits (OPVIS); ambulatory surgical procedures (SAM); and inpatient surgical procedures (SIP). All five output measures can be identified precisely with minimal opportunity for measurement error. Summary statistics for these variables are shown in Table 13.1 for each year under study. Each of the variables has a good deal of variation within each year, reflecting the variety of sizes of VA hospitals in the sample. The surgical procedure variables SAM and SIP have minimum values of zero in each of the 3 years; some of the smaller hospitals in the sample perform no surgical procedures in one or more of the years represented in the data.

Inputs include the number of acute-care hospital beds (BDH); the number of long-term hospital beds (BDLT); clinical labor measured in full time equivalents (CFTE); nonclinical labor measured in full time equivalents (NCFTE); and physician hours (MDHRS). BDH and BDLT reflect capital used by the hospitals, while the remaining variables reflect different types of labor used in the production process. Grosskopf and Valdmanis (1987) use various measures of capital in their study of non-VA hospitals and suggest that the number of beds is a reliable measure of capital. The inputs listed here were chosen to reflect the input-output correspondence in VA hospitals, as well as to minimize any possible measurement error. Summary statistics for the input variables also appear in Table 13.1. Note that each of the inputs varies over time, indicating that hospitals adjust inputs to reflect changing conditions. Additional information regarding the construction of variables used in this study is available from the authors on request.

The VA instituted major changes in budgeting procedures over the sample period, intended to improve incentives for efficiency. A portion of each facility's budget was determined using the sum of resource utilization costs [used as an output by Sexton et al (1989)]. Despite improvements described by Stefos, LaVallee, and Holden (1991), this resource allocation method has been abandoned, partly because facilities were perceived to have added to inefficiency in pursuing standards that would increase

Table 13.1   Statistics on Outputs and Inputs (89 observations in each year)

	Mean	Standard Deviation	Minimum	Maximum
1985:				
PDAY	147,790.0	100,420.0	14,779.0	394,160.0
DIS	7,065.5	3,539.9	1,269.0	15,966.0
OPVIS	114,310.0	82,012.0	13,669.0	370,340.0
SAM	1,027.0	1,771.8	.0	9,803.0
SIP	2,443.2	1,594.2	.0	7,993.0
BDH	495.06	316.27	78.000	1,298.0
BDLT	118.19	127.71	10.000	959.00
CFTE	732.09	485.21	71.400	2,047.5
NCFTE	558.61	324.60	96.000	1,697.0
MDHRS	144,730.0	95,980.0	14,940.0	440,590.0
1986:				
PDAY	108,850.0	67,997.0	10,425.0	287,610.0
DIS	7,170.7	3,697.0	1,028.0	17,119.0
OPVIS	121,070.0	85,123.0	19,329.0	385,020.0
SAM	1,588.4	2,872.0	.0	15,142.0
SIP	2,292.3	1,707.5	.0	8,941.0
BDH	486.61	311.62	78.000	1,305.0
BDLT	116.26	116.23	10.000	959.00
CFTE	725.04	479.67	77.700	2,001.5
NCFTE	529.33	302.81	95.000	1,514.0
MDHRS	149,120.0	97,856.0	15,670.0	447,870.0
1987:				
PDAY	100,550.0	64,563.0	13,533.0	278,350.0
DIS	7,147.2	3,778.9	975.00	17,372.0
OPVIS	133,480.0	88,351.0	7,942.0	381,960.0
SAM	2,565.5	4,054.5	.0	18,820.0
SIP	3,447.7	2,955.3	.0	19,085.0
BDH	475.04	310.58	52.000	1,305.0
BDLT	126.43	135.21	10.000	959.00
CFTE	767.22	507.52	80.300	2,103.2
NCFTE	558.98	317.44	106.00	1,547.5
MDHRS	148,910.0	97,489.0	15,120.0	434,780.0

their budgets. For this reason, we are interested in whether or not the VA facilities became more or less efficient in the broad dimensions of the inputs and outputs used here over the 3 years covered by the data. In other words, did VA facilities expand their budgets in more or less productive ways under the new regime?

A summary of the results of using Equation (13.1) to estimate input weak efficiency for the 89 hospitals in the sample across the 3 years 1985, 1986, and 1987 is shown in Table 13.2. For observations from 1986 and 1987, efficiency is estimated using two different reference sets. First, efficiency is estimated relative to all hospitals in the sample in the current and previous years. Results of this are shown in the first three lines of Table 13.2. Mean efficiency declines from 1985 to 1986, and then rises

Table 13.2   Input Weak Efficiency Estimation (89 observations in each year)

Year	Reference Set	Mean	Std. Dev.	Minimum	Percent Efficient
1985	85	.9724	.05960	.7193	73
1986	85, 86	.9272	.1073	.6212	48
1987	85, 86, 87	.9332	.1056	.5961	58
1986	86	.9531	.08418	.6415	63
1987	87	.9568	.08711	.6371	69

in 1987, although not to the level in 1985. Next, efficiencies for 1986 and 1987 were estimated for all hospitals in the sample relative only to observations in the current year. Results of this are shown in the fourth and fifth lines of Table 13.2; the same pattern for changes in mean efficiency are observed, although the differences are not as large as when observations from previous years are included in the reference set. This approach is similar to the "window analysis" described in Section 1.7.2 and introduced by Charnes, Clark, Cooper, and Golany (1985). Including previous years in the reference set gives some idea of the relative movement in efficiency scores over these 3 years, but leaves differences between changes in technology and changes in technical efficiency unclear. Further research will investigate the decomposition of productivity change into technical change and efficiency change as described in Section 1.7.5 and Chapter 4, and implemented by Försund in Chapter 14.

Standard t-tests for differences in the mean efficiency scores shown in Table 13.2 cannot be employed here since the samples of scores are neither independent nor normally distributed. Hence a bootstrap procedure was employed by arranging the efficiency scores in vectors of length 89 corresponding to each year 1985 to 1987. To test for statistical significance of the difference in means from 1985 and 1986, pseudosamples were created by drawing 89 pairs (to preserve the contemporaneous correlation) of efficiency scores from the vectors for 1985 and 1986. Pairs were drawn such that each of the 89 pairs had equal probability of selection; draws were done with replacement. The resulting pseudosamples were then averaged and the difference in the means was computed. Repeating this process 10,000 times produced 9998 cases where the difference in the pseudomeans was greater than the observed difference for the original samples. Hence the largest sample difference in the means, between the first two lines of Table 13.2, is insignificantly different from zero. This bootstrap procedure was employed for each of the other nine possible pairs of means in Table 13.2, yielding no significant differences in the means [the bootstrap was initially examined by Efron (1979, 1982) and has been used in a variety of applications].

Though the change in means is small, the second moment change is quite striking. The standard deviation of scores in 1986 and 1987 with the expanded reference set is almost twice as large as that of 1985 and 50 percent larger when the reference set is just the current year. As the percentage of facilities measured to be efficient drops in a similar way, some of the increase in the variation of the scores is attributable to the reduction in efficiency, since one is the most common score by far. Other sources of the increase in variation could be changes in technology or changes in scale economies under the variable returns-to-scale formulation.

Additional insight can be gained by observing efficiency scores for individual hospitals shown in Table 13.3, numbered for anonymity. Efficiency scores are shown for each of the 89 hospitals for the 3 years under study, using each of the two alternative reference sets for 1986 and 1987. Typically, measured efficiency scores for those hospitals which are technically inefficient are larger when the reference set only includes current observations rather than both current and past observations. This fact is consistent with the means in Table 13.2 which decline in 1986 and 1987 relative to 1985 though, as indicated previously, the declines are insignificantly different from zero. Moreover, many hospitals appear to be technically efficient and many of those not on the frontier are close to it, with efficiency scores close to one. Nevertheless, measured efficiency scores are overstated to the extent that input slack wastes particular inputs and output slack forgoes particular outputs.

Table 13.4 shows summary statistics on the slack variables from the analysis using current and past observations as the reference set in estimating relative technical efficiency. For each input in each year, more than two-thirds of the hospitals in the sample show no slack; the other third have either input slack, output slack, or both as depicted in Figure 1.3 (Chapter 1). The slack should be viewed as an additional dimension of inefficiency. The largest slacks occur in the long-term bed input (BDLT) in 1985 and 1986; in 1987 the slack in BDLT is comparable to that in the other variables. One reason for this may be that, prior to measuring hospital inpatient output on a per case basis, strong incentives for VA facilities to distinguish between inpatients and long-term-care patients accurately did not exist. As a result, the length of stay in VA inpatient wards was very high. Once inpatient care was being measured on a per case basis, these long-term inpatients appeared as extreme outliers so VA hospitals reclassified both patients and beds toward long term care. Note that the average number of long term care beds per hospital increased from about 116 to 126 between 1986 and 1987. The more than doubling of average ambulatory surgical procedures between 1985 and 1987 also is the result of incentives in the budget determination process.

As noted in the previous section, the linear programming model in Equation (13.1) allows variable returns-to-scale; by modifying the constraints in (13.1), scale efficiency of VA hospitals can be examined. For 1985, 86 hospitals exhibit increasing returns-to-scale; one exhibits decreasing returns, while two are scale-efficient. For 1986 hospitals using 1985 and 1986 as the reference set, only one hospital is scale-efficient; all others show increasing returns-to-scale. For 1987 hospitals using 1985 to 1987 as the reference set, two hospitals appear scale-efficient, with the remaining 87 exhibiting increasing returns-to-scale. Average scale efficiency scores for the 3 years are .9727, .9686, and .9682, respectively. Therefore, although most hospitals

Table 13.3 Input Weak Efficiency Scores, by Hospital and Year

Hospital	1985 Rel. to 1985	1986 Rel. to 1985, 1986	1987 Rel. to 1985, 1986, 1987	1986 Rel. to 1986	1987 Rel. to 1987
1	.8709	.8007	.7459	.8699	.8588
2	1.0000	.9760	1.0000	.9952	1.0000
3	.9487	.9927	.9225	1.0000	.9323
4	.7949	.7507	.8265	.8857	.9551
5	.8948	.8230	.7127	.8469	.7624
6	.7919	.6866	.7849	.7446	.8086
7	1.0000	1.0000	1.0000	1.0000	1.0000
8	1.0000	1.0000	1.0000	1.0000	1.0000
9	1.0000	1.0000	1.0000	1.0000	1.0000
10	.7764	.6212	.6543	.6415	.7011
11	1.0000	.9680	1.0000	1.0000	1.0000
12	1.0000	.9981	1.0000	1.0000	1.0000
13	.9218	1.0000	1.0000	.9261	.9921
14	.9383	.8309	.7893	.8396	.7905
15	1.0000	1.0000	1.0000	1.0000	1.0000
16	.9909	.7811	.6506	.7835	.6700
17	1.0000	1.0000	1.0000	1.0000	1.0000
18	1.0000	.9629	1.0000	.9815	1.0000
19	.8895	.6216	.5961	.7145	.6371
20	.9526	.9294	1.0000	.9408	1.0000
21	1.0000	.7209	.6797	.7502	.6920
22	.9578	.8743	.8743	.9529	1.0000
23	1.0000	1.0000	1.0000	1.0000	1.0000
24	1.0000	1.0000	1.0000	1.0000	1.0000
25	1.0000	.8759	1.0000	.9115	1.0000
26	1.0000	.8906	.9254	.9484	.9405
27	.9901	.9105	.9273	.9412	1.0000
28	1.0000	1.0000	1.0000	1.0000	1.0000
29	.8900	1.0000	1.0000	1.0000	1.0000
30	1.0000	1.0000	1.0000	1.0000	1.0000
31	.9096	.9405	.9984	.9948	1.0000
32	1.0000	1.0000	.8945	1.0000	1.0000
33	1.0000	1.0000	1.0000	1.0000	1.0000
34	1.0000	.7512	.7433	.8370	.8154
35	1.0000	.8928	.8826	.9255	.9086
36	.8507	.7244	.7348	.7944	.7359
37	1.0000	1.0000	1.0000	1.0000	1.0000
38	1.0000	1.0000	1.0000	1.0000	1.0000
39	1.0000	.7298	.7871	.7754	.7885
40	1.0000	.6530	.7647	.8723	.9963
41	1.0000	1.0000	1.0000	1.0000	1.0000
42	1.0000	1.0000	1.0000	1.0000	1.0000
43	1.0000	1.0000	1.0000	1.0000	1.0000
44	1.0000	1.0000	.9730	1.0000	1.0000
45	1.0000	1.0000	1.0000	1.0000	1.0000
46	1.0000	.8869	1.0000	.9251	1.0000
47	1.0000	.7627	.7985	.8121	.8487
48	1.0000	1.0000	.8802	1.0000	.8843
49	1.0000	.9822	1.0000	1.0000	1.0000

Table 13.3   (continued)

Hospital	1985 Rel. to 1985	1986 Rel. to 1985, 1986	1987 Rel. to 1985, 1986, 1987	1986 Rel. to 1986	1987 Rel. to 1987
50	1.0000	.7018	.6488	1.0000	1.0000
51	1.0000	.8023	1.0000	1.0000	1.0000
52	1.0000	1.0000	1.0000	1.0000	1.0000
53	1.0000	1.0000	.9936	1.0000	1.0000
54	1.0000	.8902	.9317	1.0000	.9726
55	1.0000	1.0000	1.0000	1.0000	1.0000
56	1.0000	1.0000	1.0000	1.0000	1.0000
57	.9640	.9629	.9457	1.0000	1.0000
58	1.0000	.9818	1.0000	1.0000	1.0000
59	1.0000	.9925	1.0000	1.0000	1.0000
60	1.0000	1.0000	1.0000	1.0000	1.0000
61	1.0000	1.0000	1.0000	1.0000	1.0000
62	1.0000	.9047	1.0000	1.0000	1.0000
63	1.0000	.9943	.8391	1.0000	.9771
64	1.0000	1.0000	1.0000	1.0000	1.0000
65	1.0000	1.0000	1.0000	1.0000	1.0000
66	1.0000	1.0000	1.0000	1.0000	1.0000
67	.8841	.9640	.8425	1.0000	1.0000
68	1.0000	1.0000	1.0000	1.0000	1.0000
69	1.0000	1.0000	1.0000	1.0000	1.0000
70	1.0000	1.0000	1.0000	1.0000	1.0000
71	1.0000	.9624	.8506	.9745	.8711
72	1.0000	.9291	1.0000	.9922	1.0000
73	1.0000	1.0000	.9210	1.0000	.9300
74	.9589	.9284	.9535	.9331	.9782
75	1.0000	1.0000	1.0000	1.0000	1.0000
76	1.0000	1.0000	1.0000	1.0000	1.0000
77	1.0000	1.0000	1.0000	1.0000	1.0000
78	1.0000	1.0000	1.0000	1.0000	1.0000
79	1.0000	1.0000	1.0000	1.0000	1.0000
80	.8913	.9493	.9687	.9493	.9739
81	.8094	.8407	.8831	.8529	.8920
82	.9509	.8400	.8805	.8562	.9037
83	.9944	.9552	.9340	.9672	.9344
84	.7193	.6652	1.0000	.6885	1.0000
85	1.0000	1.0000	1.0000	1.0000	1.0000
86	1.0000	1.0000	1.0000	1.0000	1.0000
87	1.0000	1.0000	1.0000	1.0000	1.0000
88	1.0000	.9186	.9120	1.0000	1.0000
89	1.0000	1.0000	1.0000	1.0000	1.0000

operate on the increasing returns portion of the production frontier, they are relatively close to the point of constant returns. Given the wide scope of services offered by VA hospitals and the fact that their patients must come only from the population of veterans, it is quite plausible that most operate on the increasing returns portion of

Table 13.4 Slack Variable Analysis (89 observations for each year)

Year	Reference Set	Input	No. with Zero Slack	Total Slack as % of Total Input
1985	85	BDH	78	1.6
		BDLT	82	11.7
		CFTE	76	1.4
		NCFTE	77	1.5
		MDHRS	71	1.6
1986	85, 86	BDH	60	6.4
		BDLT	74	10.4
		CFTE	73	1.8
		NCFTE	65	2.6
		MDHRS	74	2.2
1987	85, 86, 87	BDH	71	3.9
		BDLT	82	3.7
		CFTE	74	1.8
		NCFTE	66	1.9
		MDHRS	78	1.0

the production frontier. Recall from Section 1.5.1, however, that the input orientation introduces a bias toward finding increasing returns-to-scale (see Figure 1.5).

A surprising number of VA hospitals in the sample have no measured inefficiency. Returning to Table 13.2, the percentage of hospitals lying on the estimated production set frontier is shown in the last column for each of the 3 years and the various reference sets. In all but one case, well more than half have no measured inefficiency. Furthermore, the distribution of efficiency scores for hospitals indicated as inefficient is skewed toward efficiency; that is, among hospitals with measured efficiency less than unity, most have efficiency scores near one. In any case, the prospective payment system implemented by the VA over the period of this study mentioned in the introduction seems to have had no significant effect on technical efficiency of VA hospitals over the period 1985 to 1987.

13.4 Outlier Analysis

By definition, nonparametric efficiency frontiers are determined by extreme values in the dimensional space created by the choice of inputs and outputs. Unlike parametric approaches that are nondeterministic, a single outlier can have much greater effects on measured efficiency. Efficiency scores obtained from a deterministic frontier, such as those summarized in Table 13.2 and enumerated in Table 13.3, should be evaluated for outliers through careful sensitivity analysis. Sexton, Silkman, and Hogan (1986) examine the effects of a single outlier in a model similar to Equation (13.1) and conclude that outliers can produce large biases in estimated efficiency scores, but formal diagnostic tests are needed. Seaver and Triantis (1989) discuss several diagnostic tests for outliers useful in models with a single output estimated by corrected ordinary least squares (COLS). All but one of these tests depend directly on ordinary least squares residuals, which are not available in linear programming models such as (13.1), and it is not clear how the tests would be applied in cases where there are multiple outputs (and where COLS cannot be used). Wilson (1992) extends the determinant-ratio method for detecting outliers introduced by Andrews and Pregibon (1978) (and used by Seaver and Triantis) to handle cases with multiple outputs.

Outliers are observations that "do not fit in with the pattern of the remaining data points and are not at all typical of the rest of the data" [Gunst and Mason (1980)]. Some outliers may result from recording or measurement errors and should be corrected (if possible) or deleted from the data; however, when outliers are detected in data, one should not automatically assume they result from such errors. If data are viewed as having come from a probability distribution, then it is quite possible (although unlikely) to observe points with low probabilities of occurring by chance. One would not expect to observe many such points given their low probability, and hence they may appear as outliers (i.e., dissimilar observations, if they appear at all). Cook and Weisberg (1982) observe that outliers of this type may lead to the recognition of important phenomena that might otherwise have gone unnoticed; in some cases such outliers may be the most interesting part of the data. In either case, removing outliers from the data may have a large impact on estimates obtained from various econometric models, and hence outliers also are referred to as "influential observations." Influential observations need not be and should not be removed if values for inputs and outputs are coded correctly, as they appear to be here. Nevertheless, they should be explainable so that sources of dispersion result from conditions the researcher desires to be endogenous.

In addition, it is well-known that when two or more outliers are present in a sample, one may mask the effect of another. Hence testing whether individual observations are outliers may fail to detect outliers that lie near other outliers. Consequently, one must also test whether pairs, triplets, etc. of observations might be outliers.

The methodology of Wilson (1992) not only identifies influential observations (either single observations or pairs, triplets, etc.), but also provides significance levels which may be used to rank the observations by the likelihood that they may be outliers. Further details on the derivation of the outlier statistic and computational techniques can be found in Wilson (1992).

In order of statistical significance, the four observations for each year that are most likely to be outliers are Hospitals 36, 68, 88, and 86 for 1985; Hospitals 36, 87, 30, and 86 for 1986; and Hospitals 86, 36, 23, and 30 for 1987. When data for the 3 years are pooled, the six most likely outliers in order of significance are Hospital 86 (1987), Hospital 36 (1985), Hospital 36 (1986), Hospital 36 (1987), Hospital 23 (1987), and Hospital 68 (1985). For 1985 and 1986, sequentially deleting observations produced significant values for the outlier statistic for all of these hospitals. For 1987, deleting the observation for Hospital 86 produced a significant value. When the observation for Hospital 36 was deleted the outlier statistic became insignificant; however, deleting two, three, and four observations simultaneously produced significant values of the outlier statistic. Similarly for the pooled data, sequential deletion of observations identified Hospital 86 in 1987 and Hospital 36 in 1985 and 1986 as possible outliers, but the statistic became insignificant when Hospital 36 in 1987 was deleted after deleting the first three observations. Simultaneously deleting four, five, and six observations produced significant values for the outlier statistic using the pooled data.

For each year 1985–1987, most observations were found to produce significant values for the outlier statistic when deleted from the sample. The observations discussed above are those which produced the most significant values of the outlier statistic and hence may be viewed as those which are most dissimilar to other observations in the sample. The group of hospitals that appear to be outliers shows remarkable consistency across the 3 years of the panel. Careful study of values for these hospitals indicates that while the observations are dissimilar, their values reflect actual conditions in the hospitals in those cities and are not the result of measurement error or some other type of data corruption. For instance, Hospital 36 has a disproportionate amount of long-term workload relative to other hospitals; so do Hospitals 23 and 86, although to a lesser extent. Note from Table 13.3 that Hospital 36 produces an efficiency score less than one for each of the 3 years under study and hence does not lie on the efficiency frontier (and consequently cannot affect other efficiency scores), whereas Hospital 86 is on the frontier in each of the years. Hospital 87 faces a large problem with homeless patients, and hence provides an atypical amount of outpatient care vis-à-vis other VA hospitals. All the outliers are relatively exceptional on the high end in some dimension of output, except Hospital 68 which has a very low psychiatric workload. Hospital 88, on the other hand, has a very high psychiatric workload. Sensitivity analysis for outliers should be part of any nonparametric efficiency measurement process. In this case, all outliers are reasonable and there is no need to delete any of them from the analysis; this result most likely is related to the careful checking for coding errors and other anomalies as the first step in the process.

Outliers in nonparametric efficiency measurement can be dissimilar either in outputs, in inputs, or both. Most of the outliers appear to be most dissimilar in outputs, perhaps as a result of complementarity in health care inputs. Since the nonparametric efficiency approach makes no assumption concerning the functional form of the production technology, output outliers on the high end have no effect on other efficiency scores, unless the outliers have a relatively efficient input mix that shifts the efficient frontier outward to make otherwise efficient hospitals inefficient. The latter does not appear to be the case in this situation. Some output slack appears in the estimated linear program as a result.

13.5 Conclusions

In this chapter we have provided a general efficiency analysis of a short panel of federally operated VA hospitals. Two techniques have been emphasized that are useful for doing general comparisons of nonparametric efficiency scores. First, mean efficiency scores for individual years are compared using a bootstrap procedure to test statistical significance. No significant difference in means is found, though the variance in the last 2 years of the sample is higher than in the first year. Second, an outlier statistic is used to rank outliers on a relative basis. The most influential observations are hospitals with relatively unusual mixes of outputs as we would expect; they do not appear to be the result of errors in the data.

Although efficiency scores for each hospital are reported, these should be used carefully. More detailed analysis is required to determine whether the measured efficiency scores reflect actual technical inefficiency or other factors. For instance, variations in quality of care provided by different hospitals may influence measured efficiency. General analysis of efficiency scores is more likely to be effective since Downs and Larkey (1986) suggest that administrators are more likely to respond to general conclusions as opposed to blatantly identifying winners and losers. The results obtained here do identify specific hospitals which deserve closer scrutiny than is possible to give to all hospitals in the sample; yet some may prove inefficient, while others may exhibit low measured efficiency for other reasons.

Recently, nonparametric efficiency scores such as the ones used in this chapter have been used as the dependent variable in regression models estimated in a second-stage analysis; for example, Register and Bruning (1987), Nyman and Bricker (1989), Aly, Grabowski, Pasurka, and Ranagan (1990), and Dusansky and Wilson (1992). These analyses attempt to explain variations in measured efficiency among DMUs. Future work using the VA data could employ quality and patient health status proxies as independent variables in a second-stage regression analysis to examine the extent to which these are responsible for the variations in measured efficiency reported above. Low efficiency scores in some hospitals could be due to higher quality of care being provided than in typical hospitals; low patient health status in some hospitals could also result in lower measured efficiency.

REFERENCES

Aigner, D., C. A. K. Lovell, and P. Schmidt (1977), "Formulation and Estimation of Stochastic Frontier Production Function Models," *Journal of Econometrics* 6(1)(July): 21–37.

Aly, H. Y., R. G. Grabowski, C. Pasurka, and N. Rangan (1990), "Technical, Scale, and Allocative Efficiencies in U. S. Banking: An Empirical Investigation," *Review of Economics and Statistics* 72(2)(May): 211–218.

Andrews, D. F., and D. Pregibon (1978), "Finding the Outliers that Matter," *Journal of the Royal Statistical Society B* 40(1): 85–93.

Boles, J. (1966), "Efficiency Squared: Efficient Computations of Efficiency Indexes," *Western Farm Economics Association Proceedings*, pp. 137–142.

Burgess, J. F., Jr. (1989), "A Principal-Agent Satisficing Model of VA Health Care," Working Paper, Graduate Management Institute, Union College, Schenectady, N.Y.

Burley, H. T. (1980), "Productive Efficiency in U. S. Manufacturing: A Linear Programming Approach," *Review of Economics and Statistics* 62(4) (November): 619–622.

Charnes, A., W. W. Cooper, and E. Rhodes (1978), "Measuring the Efficiency of Decision Making Units," *European Journal of Operational Research* 2(6) (November): 429–444.

Charnes, A., W. W. Cooper, and E. Rhodes (1979), "Measuring the Efficiency of Decision Making Units," *European Journal of Operational Research* 3(4) (July): 339.

Charnes, A., C. T. Clark, W. W. Cooper, and B. Golany (1985), "A Developmental Study of Data Envelopment Analysis in Measuring the Efficiency of Maintenance Units in the U. S. Air Forces," *Annals of Operations Research* 2: 95–112.

Conrad, R. F., and R. P. Strauss (1983), "A Multiple-Output Multiple-Input Model of the Hospital Industry in North Carolina," *Applied Econometrics* 15(3)(June): 341–352.

Cook, R. D., and S. Weisberg (1982), *Residuals and Influence in Regression.* New York: Chapman and Hall.

Deprins, D., L. Simar, and H. Tulkens (1984), "Measuring Labor Inefficiency in Post Offices," in M. Marchand, P. Pestieau, and H. Tulkens, eds., *The Performance of Public Enterprises: Concepts and Measurements.* Amsterdam, North-Holland: pp. 243–267.

Downs, G. W., and P. D. Larkey (1986), *The Search for Government Efficiency: From Hubris to Helplessness.* New York: Random House.

Dusansky, R., and P. W. Wilson (1992), "Technical Efficiency in the Decentralized Care of the Developmentally Disabled," *Review of Economics and Statistics* (forthcoming).

Efron, B. (1979), "Bootstrap Methods: Another Look at the Jackknife," *Annals of Statistics* 7(1) (March): 1–16.

Efron, B. (1982), "The Jackknife, the Bootstrap, and Other Resampling Plans," DBMS-NSF Regional Conference Series in Applied Mathematics, Monograph 38, Society for Industrial and Applied Mathematics, Philadelphia, PA.

Färe, R., and C. A. K. Lovell (1978), "Measuring the Technical Efficiency of Production," *Journal of Economic Theory* 19(1)(October): 150–162.

Färe, R., S. Grosskopf, and C. A. K. Lovell (1985), *The Measurement of Efficiency of Production.* Boston: Kluwer-Nijhoff Publishing.

Färe, R., S. Grosskopf, and C. A. K. Lovell (1987), "Some Observations on the New DEA," Working Paper no. 87–4, Department of Economics, University of North Carolina, Chapel Hill, N.C.

Farrell, M. J. (1957), "The Measurement of Productive Efficiency," *Journal of the Royal Statistical Society A* 120(3): 253–281.

Grosskopf, S., and V. Valdmanis (1987), "Measuring Hospital Performance: A Non-Parametric Approach," *Journal of Health Economics* 6(2)(June): 89–107.

Gunst, R. F., and R. L. Mason (1980), *Regression Analysis and its Application.* New York: Marcel Dekker, Inc.

Jondrow, J., C. A. K. Lovell, I. S. Materov, and P. Schmidt (1982), "On the Estimation of Technical Inefficiency in the Stochastic Frontier Production Function Model," *Journal of Econometrics* 19(2/3)(August): 233–238.

Niskanen, W. A. (1971), *Bureaucracy and Representative Government.* Chicago: Aldine Publishing Co., Inc.

Nyman, J. A., and D. L. Bricker (1989), "Profit Incentives and Technical Efficiency in the Production of Nursing Home Care," *Review of Economics and Statistics* 71(4) (November): 586–594.

Register, C. A., and E. R. Bruning (1987), "Profit Incentives and Technical Efficiency in the Production of Hospital Care," *Southern Economic Journal* 53(4)(April): 899–914.

Seaver, B. L., and K. P. Triantis (1989), "The Implications of Using Messy Data to Estimate Production-Frontier-Based Technical Efficiency Measures," *Journal of Business and Economic Statistics* 7(1)(January): 49–59.

Sexton, T. R., R. H. Silkman, and A. J. Hogan (1986), "The Methodology of Data Envelopment Analysis," in R. H. Silkman, ed., *Measuring Efficiency: An Assessment of Data Envelopment Analysis.* San Francisco, Calif.: Jossey-Bass.

Sexton, T. R., A. M. Leiken, A. H. Nolan, S. Liss, A. Hogan, and R. H. Silkman (1989), "Evaluating Managerial Efficiency of Veterans Administration Medical Centers Using Data Envelopment Analysis," *Medical Care* 27(12) (December): 1175–1188.

Sherman, H. D. (1984), "Hospital Efficiency Measurement and Evaluation: Empirical Test of a New Technique," *Medical Care* 22(10)(October): 922–938.

Stefos, T., N. LaVallee, and F. Holden (1992), "Fairness in Prospective Payment: A Clustering Approach," *Health Services Research* 27(2)(June): 239–261.

Weitzman, M. (1980), "The 'Ratchet Principle' and Performance Incentives," *The Bell Journal of Economics* 11(1)(Spring): 302–308.

Wilson, P. W. (1992), "Detecting Influential Observations in Frontier Models with Multiple Outputs," Working Paper, Department of Economics, University of Texas, Austin.

Zieschang, K. O. (1984), "An Extended Farrell Technical Efficiency Measure," *Journal of Economic Theory* 33(2)(August): 387–396.

14

PRODUCTIVITY GROWTH IN NORWEGIAN FERRIES

Finn R. Førsund

The field of economic index number theory is a veritable graveyard, so full is it of mathematically ingenious indices that are useless because they have no economic significance.

M. J. FARRELL (1957, p. 290).

14.1 Introduction

Key concepts when studying production over time are productivity, efficiency, and technical change. Productivity is defined as an index of outputs divided by an index of inputs. Efficiency is defined as a production unit's "success in producing as large as possible an output from a given set of inputs" [Farrell (1957, p.254)]. Technical change is the change in the transformation functions between inputs and outputs. When studying productivity change over time these concepts are related, as elaborated upon in Chapter 4.

Empirical studies show that a generic feature of production units at the micro level in the same business is that efficiency varies across units. A natural reference for technology is then *best practice* or the *frontier production function*. As pointed out in Chapter 4 change in productivity is the net effect of changes in efficiency and shift in the frontier production function. There is an old strand of literature based on embodiment of technology in micro units developing the notion of the average firm catching up with best practice, which points to this decomposition of productivity change [see Førsund and Hjalmarsson (1987, chap. 1) for a brief historical account].[1]

If the vintage assumption is not appropriate (there may be substitution possibilities ex post, or disembodied progress is possible, or we simply do not have enough information to support such a specific hypothesis about technology), then the focus is naturally on one micro unit at a time, and the question arises how to measure productivity change and its components for each unit.

The methods to be employed are presented in Chapter 4. In this chapter we will measure productivity change by using the Malmquist (1953) productivity index and its components introduced in Section 4.3.1. The data set is a panel of 135 ferries servicing the trunk roads of Norway for the five years 1984 to 1988.[2]

14.2 Methodology

Since the Malmquist index is treated extensively in Chapter 4, here we shall only expand on some points particular to our application and add some new perspectives.

In our application we shall study the same units over time. This does not mean that we have to restrict the study to a panel. The calculation of the best practice frontier for each period can be based on a varying set of units, but it is only with a panel that we can calculate the productivity indices for all periods. We have, in fact, excluded units not in the panel.

As pointed out in Chapter 4 the original definition of a Malmquist productivity index in Caves, Christensen, and Diewert (1982) makes use of the Shephard concept of distance function. However, for the ease of economic interpretation we prefer to make use of the efficiency measures introduced by Farrell (1957). The latter measures and distance functions are, of course, as pointed out in Chapter 4, identical.

When calculating total factor productivity change using the basic definition of an index of outputs divided by an index of inputs the key question is determination of the weights. Instead of using price information to calculate cost and income shares as weights, the idea of the Malmquist index is to reduce the multidimensionality

---

[1] Leif Johansen (1972) models production within the vintage framework, specifying ex ante frontier technology for new units and short-run production possibilities for the sector as a whole, which refines the distinction between short-run efficiency and shifts in technology when investing in new capacity. The distribution of capacity in input-output space in the short run shows the efficiency distribution. Technical change manifests itself by the change in the capacity distribution caused by addition of new capacity and scrapping of old. Productivity change can be studied by following the change in the capacity distribution over time. Johansen's "complete growth equation" (1972, sec. 7.8, pp. 170–175) captures the essence of the change by allowing identification of the effects of new capacity, scrapping of old, and input-saving and output-increasing technical change of existing capacity. The emphasis is on the dynamics of structural change rather than on a decomposition of productivity change for individual units.

[2] In Førsund and Hernæs (1992), using DEA, a comprehensive cross-sectional study of 1988 is made, and in Førsund (1992) a comparison of nonparametric frontier and parametric frontier is made for the same year.

when comparing productivities by keeping the observed proportions between outputs and inputs constant. Studying a unit at two different points in time there must be a common reference of technology, and unidimensionality is obtained by establishing distances to the common technology and measuring productivity change as the ratio of such distances. The relative distance from an observation to the frontier technology, keeping constant observed proportions between outputs on the one hand and inputs on the other, is the definition of the Farrell measure of technical efficiency. A condition on the path to the frontier must be added; we can move in the input-saving direction, keeping outputs constant, yielding a measure of relative savings of inputs of employing frontier technology, or in the output-increasing direction, keeping inputs constant, yielding a measure of relative increase in outputs employing frontier technology. We will move in an input-saving direction.[3]

The Malmquist index of productivity can then be expressed as the ratio of the corresponding Farrell efficiency measures for the two observations of a unit. The economic interpretation is straightforward: The index shows us the relative change in technical efficiency, that is, the change in the percentage saving of inputs possible if realizing frontier technology. Since output levels are constant and the same technology is the reference, this is the same as a change in total factor productivity when keeping observed factor proportions constant.

14.2.1 Farrell Efficiency Measures

Let the frontier technology be described by the following transformation function, with standard textbook properties:

$$F_i(y, x) = 0 \tag{14.1}$$

where y is the output vector and x the input vector, and the subscript i denotes the year of technology. It is assumed that observations from the same year as the frontier technology cannot show a better performance than that given by the technology, that is, a deterministic frontier is adopted [see, e.g., Førsund, Lovell, and Schmidt (1980)].

The Farrell input saving efficiency measure, E_{ij}, for a unit observed at time j with frontier technology $F_i(.) = 0$ as reference is:

$$E_{ij} = \min_{\alpha_{ij}} \{\alpha_{ij} : F_i(y_j, \alpha_{ij} x_j) \leqq 0\} \tag{14.2}$$

The inputs are reduced proportionally as much as possible to realize frontier technology. It is assumed that we have unique solutions for α_{ij}. When $i = j$ the measure

---

[3] The exposition in Chapter 4 is based on moving in the output-increasing direction.

must be between zero and one. When $i \neq j$ the measure may be greater than one if the observation is not feasible for period i frontier technology.[4]

The expression shows the direct connection between the Farrell measure and the Shephard (1953) concept of input distance function. The Shephard definition is the inverse of our definition of the Farrell input saving measure.

14.2.2 The Malmquist Productivity Index

As a convention the two observation periods for a unit will be termed 1 and 2, the latter being the most recent period. As a further convention we will compare 2 with 1, that is, expressions involving observation 2 will be in the numerator and expressions involving observation 1 will be in the denominator. The Caves, Christensen, and Diewert (1982) definition is generalized to have a technology base from a third period, i. The Malmquist input-based productivity index, $M_i(1, 2)$, with frontier technology, $F_i(.) = 0$, as reference is defined by[5]

$$M_i(1, 2) = \frac{E_{i2}}{E_{i1}} = \frac{\min_{\alpha_{i2}}\{\alpha_{i2}: F_i(y_2, \alpha_{i2}x_2) \leqq 0\}}{\min_{\alpha_{i1}}\{\alpha_{i1}: F_i(y_1, \alpha_{i1}x_1) \leqq 0\}} \tag{14.3}$$

The numerator shows the proportional adjustment of the observed input vector of unit 2 in order to be on the frontier function for period i with observed outputs, and the denominator shows the proportional adjustment of the observed input vector of unit 1 for observed outputs to be on the same frontier function, i. Both measures may be greater than one since frontier i is defined on a set not necessarily including observations 1 and 2. If $M_i(1, 2) > 1$, then unit 2 is more productive than unit 1. This holds irrespective of which technology is the reference.

Referring to the Farrell efficiency concepts the Malmquist index measures the relative change in either input-saving or output-increasing efficiency between two periods with reference to the same frontier technology. How does this index relate to total factor productivity change, defined as change in an index of outputs divided by an index of inputs? For a start we note that outputs are kept constant in definition (14.3). The numerator and denominator separately show the improvement in total

---

[4] The definition of the output-increasing measure is

$$E_{ij} = \min_{\beta_{ij}}\left\{\beta_{ij}: F_i\left(\frac{1}{\beta_{ij}}y_j, x_j\right) \leqq 0\right\}$$

The outputs are increased proportionally as much as possible to realize frontier technology using observed inputs. When using both types of measures at the same time they can be identified by indices 1 and 2, following Farrell's notion (1957, p. 259). When $i = j$ the efficiency measure is between zero and one, but can be greater when $i \neq j$. This Farrell measure is identical to the definition of output distance function, see Chapter 4.

[5] The output-based index is obtained by substituting the Farrell measures defined in footnote 4. This holds for all index formulae in this chapter.

factor productivity if output levels observed in periods 2 and 1, respectively, had been produced with frontier i technology. The ratio between them can therefore be interpreted as total factor productivity change between periods 1 and 2 with reference to frontier technology from period i.

How does productivity change measured by the Malmquist index (14.3) relate to efficiency and technology changes? By efficiency we understand the Farrell measure of technical efficiency of an observation relative to the frontier for the same period. Technology change is the shift in frontier technology between periods. Let us first restate the definition of the decomposition in Chapter 4, now based on the Caves, Christensen, and Diewert (1982) definition of the Malmquist index, and specify only two periods, 1 and 2. The Malmquist productivity index, M_i, can be multiplicatively decomposed into two parts:

$$M_i = \text{MC} \cdot \text{MF}_i \qquad i = 1, 2 \tag{14.4}$$

where MC is the *catching-up effect* and MF_i is the *frontier function shift effect*:[6]

$$\text{MC} = \frac{E_{22}}{E_{11}} \tag{14.5}$$

$$\text{MF}_i = \frac{E_{1j}}{E_{2j}} \qquad i, j = 1, 2, i \neq j \tag{14.6}$$

Notice that we need to know only one frontier technology, i, to calculate the productivity index, but knowledge about two frontiers, 1 and 2, to perform the decomposition.

The catching-up effect is the relative change in efficiency between the periods and shows the direction of change in the input-saving potential, as measured by relative distance to "own" frontiers. The frontier function shift effect measures the relative distance between technologies 1 and 2, in terms of relative efficiency for the same observation measured against two different frontiers. Using technology 1 as the base, the relative distance between frontiers is measured at output level of observation 2, and with input mix of observation 2, while using technology 2 as base, the distance is measured at observation 1, with input mix of observation 1. These measures will in general differ, even for constant returns technology.

14.2.3   The Chain Version of the Malmquist Index Decomposition

Before proceeding to the decomposition of the Malmquist index in a multiperiod setting we will address some basic index problems inherent in definition (14.3). In

---

[6] In Chapter 4 the Malmquist index is defined as the geometric mean of M_1 and M_2, implying that the distance between the frontiers is measured as the geometric mean of the distances measured at the two points of observation, that is, $\text{MF} = (\text{MF}_1 \cdot \text{MF}_2)^{1/2}$.

Caves, Christensen, and Diewert (1982) and in Chapter 4 only adjacent time periods are considered. In a more general setting of several time periods one has to face the choice of base of reference. Letting the base change according to the succession of periods as in the first applications in Färe, Grosskopf, Lindgren, and Roos (1989), and Färe et al. (1990), the bases change as in a Paasche index. Keeping the same reference, for instance the technology of the first year of the data series, gives the analogy of a Laspeyre index [see Klein, Schmidt, and Yaisawarng (1993) for an application]. The purpose of measuring productivity will be a guide to the choice. The idea of the first year technology as the fixed base is most natural when asking the question of productivity change. We most often want to know the productivity change from a certain year based on that year's technology rather than knowing how the present situation and technology performs looking backward in time. But when moving away from the base year we encounter the usual index problem of the base being more and more out of line with current practice.

One preferable property with an index over a longer period of time is that it is possible to chain it, that is, the index obeys the *circular relation* of Frisch (1936). We can then break down a total productivity change over a certain period on subperiods in a consistent way. Inspecting Equation (14.3) we see that the Malmquist index with fixed base technology does chain: $M_i(1, 3) = M_i(1, 2)M_i(2, 3)$, etc. Updating the reference technology successively results in losing this property: $M_1(1, 3) \neq M_1(1, 2)M_2(2, 3)$, etc.

The question is then how the chain version (14.3) can be decomposed. Generalizing to several time periods and keeping the fixed technology base, i, and one unit observed in two periods called 1 and 2, we have two measures of (input-saving) "own" efficency by setting $i = j = 1$, and $i = j = 2$ in (14.2). It still seems most appealing to define the catching-up effect as relative change in efficiency between periods 1 and 2, that is, maintain the definition (14.5). Concerning shifts in frontier technology we have now introduced three technologies; for the base year and for periods 1 and 2. Definition (14.6) cannot be applied since it only refers to the distance between technologies 1 and 2. One way of introducing the base technology i into the frontier shift term and keeping the multiplicative nature of the decomposition is to first measure the distances between technologies for period i and 2 and period i and 1, and then form the ratio of these distances. Applying Equation (14.6) with appropriate time indices we get the distances between technology i and the two technologies 2 and 1. These ratios measure the impact on relative input saving of changing technology at output levels observed in periods 2 and 1, respectively. Forming the ratio between them shows the relative change in the distance between the base technology i and the two technologies we are currently investigating, 2 and 1, or the impact on relative change in input saving, moving from technology 1 to technology 2, by measuring relative to the same base technology i. The measures based on the reference technology do not "cancel out" in general due to different output levels and input proportions at observation, 1 and 2.

The general expression for the Malmquist productivity index and its components for the development between two periods 1 and 2 with technology base i is then written [see Berg, Førsund, and Jansen (1992)]

$$M_i(1,2) = \text{MC} \cdot \text{MF}_i(1,2) = \frac{E_{22}}{E_{11}} \cdot \frac{E_{i2}/E_{22}}{E_{i1}/E_{11}} \qquad (14.7)$$

All the components of this version of the Malmquist index chain over time. We shall therefore call Equation (14.7) the *chain version* of the Malmquist productivity index. When the base technology, i, is 1 or 2 the frontier index (14.7) simplifies to (14.6).

An illustration of the Malmquist index and its components is provided in Figure 14.1 in the simple case of one input and output. Three constant returns-to-scale technologies and two observations of a unit are shown. The base technology i is more productive than technologies in either period 1 or 2.

Starting with the Malmquist productivity index (14.3) we have

$$M_i(1,2) = \frac{E_{i2}}{E_{i1}} = \frac{x_{i2}/x_2}{x_{i1}/x_1} = \frac{y_2/x_2}{y_1/x_1} \qquad (14.8)$$

using the simple geometric relationship $y_2/x_{i2} = y_1/x_{i1}$. In the case of one input and output and constant returns-to-scale technology the Malmquist index is identical to total factor productivity change between periods 1 and 2 independent of the base technology chosen.

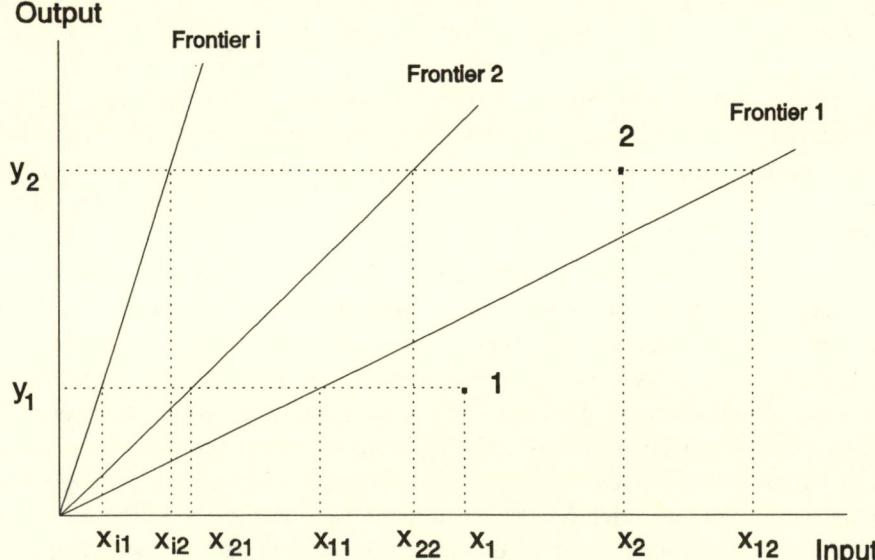

Fig. 14.1   The Malmquist productivity index and its components

On the right-hand side of Equation (14.7) we have the catching-up part:

$$\text{MC} = \frac{E_{22}}{E_{11}} = \frac{x_{22}/x_2}{x_{11}/x_1} = \frac{\frac{y_2/x_2}{y_2/x_{22}}}{\frac{y_1/x_1}{y_1/x_{11}}} \qquad (14.9)$$

The numerator in the last expression is the ratio between observed productivity in period 2 and the productivity at the frontier. The denominator shows the same ratio for period 1. The catching-up effect is the relative change in these ratios between observed and frontier productivities, that is, how average productivity catches up with frontier productivity.

The technology-shift component has a productivity interpretation, too:

$$\text{MF}_i(1,2) = \frac{E_{i2}/E_{22}}{E_{il}/E_{11}} = \frac{x_{i2}/x_{22}}{x_{il}/x_{11}} = \frac{y_2/x_{22}}{y_1/x_{11}} \qquad (14.10)$$

again utilizing the simple geometric relationship. The technology-shift component is simply the ratio of the potential productivities at the frontier technologies 2 and 1. Multiplying catching-up and frontier change terms we see that frontier productivities cancel out. We can easily verify in Figure 14.1 that technical progress has ocurred between periods 1 and 2, and that the Malmquist frontier measure has a value greater than one.

In this simple example the impact of choice of base technology disappears due to the relation $y_2/x_{i2} = y_1/x_{i1}$. In a multidimensional setting with generally different factor and output ratios for observations 1 and 2 the base technology will matter. But since all input-saving efficiency measure calculations are done keeping observed output levels constant, we are in general calculating changes in total factor productivities.

The equations above hold for a general definition of a frontier. For the empirical application we use the nonparametric procedure described in Chapter 4 consisting of enveloping the data with piecewise linear facets.

14.2.4 Calculating the Efficiency Scores

The linear programming models used to calculate the Farrell measures are discussed at some length in Chapter 4. Equation (14.7) shows us that four programs have to be solved for each calculation of the Malmquist index and its components. When calculating the "cross measures" it should be remembered that the observation we calculate for, k, is not a member of the set, $j = 1, \ldots, n$, on which the frontier technology is based. The programming problem yielding the efficiency scores and technology description in the form of weights, λ_{kj}, is:[7]

$$\min_{\lambda_k} E_k \tag{14.11}$$

subject to

$$y_{rk} \leq \sum_{j=1}^{n} \lambda_{kj} y_{rj} \qquad r = 1, \ldots, s$$

$$E_k x_{ik} \geq \sum_{j=1}^{n} \lambda_{kj} x_{ij} \qquad i = 1, \ldots, m$$

$$\lambda_{kj} \geq 0 \qquad j = 1, \ldots, n$$

The technologies are specified to be constant returns-to-scale. As pointed out in Chapter 4 this assumption ensures that solutions to the cross-measure programs exist. Since we measure change in efficiencies the assumption is not that restrictive, as illustrated in Chapter 4.

14.2.5 Intersecting Frontier Technologies

The frontiers calculated by the program above can only represent technology as revealed by the data. When technology changes over time parts of "old" technology may no longer be represented by the observations. We may then encounter technologies that intersect. An illustration is provided in Figure 14.2. Since we have specified CRS technologies they can be represented by unit isoquants in input coefficient space as in the original exposition in Farrell (1957). The technology in Figure 14.2 has shifted over time such that the new one, 2, is more efficient in utilizing factor 2, while being less efficient in utilizing factor 1. (In order to keep the figure simple technology i is not introduced.) Examples of this for the inputs energy (1) and labor (2) are found in Førsund and Hjalmarsson (1987, 1988). We shall consider observations 1 and 2 being located at points A, B, C, and D in different combinations (without exhausting the number of combinations) to bring out the importance of choice of base year.

Observation 1 located at point A and 2 at point D:

In this case both observations are outside the frontier from the opposite period. In such a case the direction of productivity change depends on which technology

---

[7] The interactive PC-software used for the calculations is developed at Centre for Research in Economics and Business Administration, Oslo.

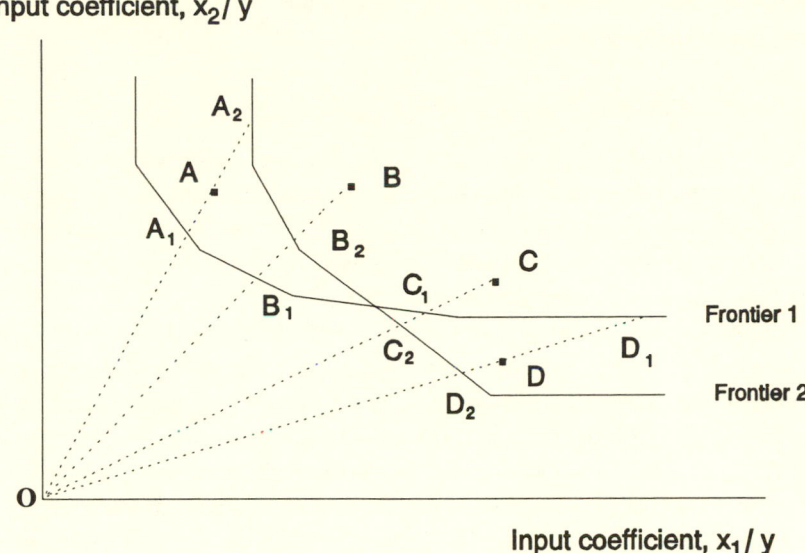

Fig. 14.2 Intersecting technologies

is chosen as the base. In the case of period 1 technology as the base we see that $E_{12} = OD_1/OD > 1$ and $E_{11} = OA_1/OA, E_{22} = OD_2/OD < 1$, resulting in $M_1(1, 2) > 1, MF_1(1, 2) > 1$, using Equations (14.3) and (14.7). Changing the base to 2 we have also $E_{21} = OA_2/OA > 1$, yielding $M_2(1, 2) < 1$ and $MF_2(1, 2) < 1$. Now, with period 1 as the base we ask what is the productivity change from A to D. It seems sensible to say that the technology shift should be measured at the new point, D; we ask what has technology shift contributed to the productivity observed at D. If period 2 is adopted as the base the technology shift is measured at the old point, A. But we have asymmetric information regarding technology: It is certain that the shift around point D is a real technology shift, but the apparent technology "regress" around point A may be due to the fact that no unit found it profitable (or generally in their interest) to operate in this part of the technology any more. Only inefficient units may be left in this region biasing the calculation of the period 2 frontier. Old technologies are usually not forgotten, but may be uneconomic to use.

Observation 1 located at A and 2 at B:

With this configuration we have $E_{12} = OB_1/OB, E_{22} = OB_2/OB < 1$ resulting in $MF_1(1, 2), M_2(1, 2)$, and $MF_2(1, 2) < 1$, but $M_1(1, 2)$ indeterminate. Since the technology shift is measured at the same side of the point of intersection the shift must have the same sign, that is, regress. The total productivity change is certainly showing regression in the case of the period 2 frontier as a base because observation 1 is outside technology 2. The indeterminateness in the case of frontier 1 as a base arises since there is less regression at the ray through B. The catching-up effect may then dominate the total change.

Observation 1 located at C and 2 at D:

This configuration illustrates the same point as above, but with both points located in the region with positive technology shift and observation 2 outside technology 1. We get a pattern with $M_1(1,2), MF_1(1,2), MF_2(1,2) > 1$, and $M_2(1,2)$ indeterminate. The technology shift is smallest when using period 2 as base, and the catching-up effect may then dominate the frontier shift effect.

Intersecting technologies occur when $M_1(1,2)$ and $M_2(1,2)$ are on the opposite side of one.[8] This happens if observation 2 is outside technology 1 and observation 1 is outside technology 2 at the same time. Regression may be expected to occur more frequently when the latest technology is used as the base. The conclusion we draw from the examples above is that in the case of intersecting technologies it makes most sense to have the first year as the technology base. Introducing another base technology i, as in Equation (14.7), gives two new possibilities for intersecting technologies, i may intersect both with 1 and 2. If we let i be the first year and let the unit isoquant intersect ray OA in front of A_1 and intersect ray OD behind D_1 in Figure 14.2 we have the same type of relationship as in the first configuration above. Switching between technologies i and 2 yields the same type of counterintuitive results as above.

If knowledge about technology does not get lost, one could say that observations should be *cumulated* over time when constructing the current frontier, or calculate what Tulkens (1990) calls *sequential efficiency*, as pointed out in Chapter 4. We leave this as a future exercise.[9]

14.3 Data

We have used two main sources for constructing the data. The most important is annual accounts over the years 1984 to 1988 of costs associated with the running of each ferry. All ferries (about 250) making up a part of the main road system of Norway, which is the responsibility of the government, are covered by the data. These data are reported by ferry companies to the authorities, as a basis for the support given to the companies.

The decision-making unit for operating the ferries is a ferry company. Subsidies are paid to 23 ferry companies for running the 150 ferry routes. It is up to the companies to determine what type of ferry to use and how to run them, as long as the

---

[8] Taking geometric means do not seem to be of any help in the economic interpretation of whether we have progression or regression.

[9] In Berg, Førsund, and Jansen (1992) the consequences of cumulating obervations were investigated for which units would appear on the frontier.

demand-based minimum requirements of the authorities are met. A company may run a ferry on several routes during a year. Most ferry transport runs at a loss,[10] which is covered by central authorities.

The other important data source is the ship register of ferries, containing information on the type, size, vintage, purchase price, speed, etc. of ferries. We linked the two data sets, obtaining times-series data for each ferry for the period 1984 to 1988.

14.3.1 Output

Output of a ferry is defined as the product of the total annual distance covered multiplied by the capacity (in standardised cars) of the ferry. We find it reasonable to assume that inputs (costs) are associated only with running a ferry of a given capacity, and not with the actual load.

14.3.2 Inputs

The data base allows us to identify four inputs: capital, labor, fuel, and maintenance. For each ferry in the cross section capital is, of course, given. However, since we want to study efficiency also with respect to capital, and companies may choose which ferry to run specific distances in the short run, we have found it relevant to include capital as a variable. The frontier is then of the ex ante type [see Johansen (1972), Førsund and Hjalmarsson (1987)].

Capital input can be measured in physical or value terms. We have found the value measures to be of variable quality and have therefore settled for a physical measure.[11] As a physical measure of capital we used capacity of the ferry, in number of standardized cars.

Due to data limitations total wages has to be used as a measure for labor. Wages are fairly uniform across ferries. A tentative test on some limited information on crew size indicated that wages as a proxy are acceptable [see Førsund and Hernæs (1992) for a more detailed discussion]. The current wages are deflated with the official index for sailors in inland waters (base year 1988).

Fuel costs constitute around 15 percent of total costs, excluding capital costs. Companies report cost of fuel per ferry. The current values are deflated by a price index for fuel oil (base year 1988).[12] One problem we should mention here is that the price varied considerably across companies for one year, 1988, investigated in detail in Førsund and Hernæs (1992). For the deflating procedure to give correct volume

---

[10] Only two ferry distances of the 150 run a surplus, and data for the ferries running the profitable distances are not reported to the authorities.

[11] See Førsund and Hernæs (1992) for a discussion of value measures of ferry capital and some results based on them.

[12] The data for rthe index were kindly provided by The Norwegian Petroleum Institute.

figures we are relying on the company fuel prices to keep a stable relationship to the mean price for each year.

Maintenance and repair vary considerably from year to year, since technical inspections of the ferries are required at fixed intervals, for example, every four years. Furthermore, repairs may occur lagged in relation to distance sailed. The current values are used in "raw" form only with the change of applying the price index for maintenance used in the National Accounts.

A summary view over the average values for each year is provided in Table 14.1. We notice that output has been quite stable for our panel. Labor input, measured by wages in deflated prices, has decreased steadily, while maintenance and fuel have increased. The large increase in 1986 for the latter input may be due to some extent to the deflating procedure. Fuel price dropped dramatically in that year, and companies may have used fuel in stock valued at a higher price in the accounts.

A careful screening of the data, weeding out units with missing observations and highly suspect ones, and concentrating on a panel, left us with 135 ferries.

14.4 Empirical Results

The strength of a micro approach is that you get information on a level that is recognizeable and relevant for real-world units, and not synthetic constructs like sectors. However, the amount of information poses a problem of presentation. After addressing the quality of the frontier calculations we shall first start with a "traditional" way of presenting results in the form of mean values of productivity change and then try to present results in a way that preserves the micro character of the analysis.

14.4.1 The Frontier Units

With a panel data set it is of great interest to study the stability of the efficient units. It strengthens the reliability of the approach if the same units appear on the frontier over

Table 14.1 Average Values for Output and Inputs (1988 Prices)

Variables	1984	1985	1986	1987	1988
Output					
Car-km in mill.	2.23	2.30	2.32	2.24	2.24
Input					
Labor wages, mill. NOK	4.47	4.02	3.79	3.49	3.19
Maintenance					
100,000 NOK	6.70	6.44	7.45	8.19	8.55
Fuel					
100,000 NOK	4.43	4.62	8.87	6.17	7.22
Capital					
car capacity	38.6	38.6	38.6	38.6	38.6

Table 14.2 The Frontier Units

Unit	Occurence in reference sets Efficiency score when not in set					Malmquist measures 1984–1988		
	1984	1985	1986	1987	1988	M_{84}	MC	MF_{84}
13	2	10	$E = .98$	95	$E = 1.0$	1.22	1.00	1.22
14	80	75	109	34	135	1.24	1.00	1.24
32	73	80	95	$E = .63$	$E = .71$	.75	.71	1.06
34	3	4	11	$E = .55$	$E = .40$	.61	.59	1.02
60	$E = .63$	7	$E = .65$	$E = .88$	$E = .87$	1.44	1.38	1.05
95	30	31	$E = .99$	85	$E = .97$	.96	.97	.99
103	$E = .98$	34	$E = .97$	9	$E = .85$	1.07	.87	1.24
104	18	24	37	31	$E = .98$	1.22	.98	1.24
106	$E = .28$	$E = .41$	$E = .34$	2	$E = .58$	2.55	2.06	1.21
129	53	$E = .98$	$E = .90$	$E = .66$	$E = .60$	.74	.60	1.24
132	$E = .36$	$E = .31$	$E = .34$	3	$E = .92$	3.12	2.53	1.24

time. In Table 14.2 the units appearing at least once as a frontier unit are entered with information on the frequency which it appeared in the reference sets, the efficiency score when not on the frontier, and the Malmquist measures for the total period. There are only two units, 13 and 14, that are efficient in all periods. Unit 13 was not, in fact, Pareto-efficient in 1988, but was dominated by unit 14.[13] The latter unit is the only one efficient in 1988. There are four more units that are either on the frontier or have high efficiency scores, and then three units starting out as efficient, but falling behind over time, and two units starting as inefficient and increasing performance over time.

This pattern is reflected in the productivity measures. The overall productivity change has been positive or improving over time for all but one of the efficient units, and negative for units with falling performance. The catching-up measure captures this development. The technology-shift term is positive (i.e. the measure is greater than one) for all units except one (marginally showing regression). Five of the units have the same value for the technology-shift term, this value being the maximal shift of the panel. All units have the same facet as the reference in 1988, but the facets differ in 1984, so there is no simple explanation why the same distance between frontiers is recorded in five-dimensional space.

The two units with the highest productivity increases have the highest of the panel. Productivity gains are due to catching up. The units are both quite small in output terms, while all other frontier units are the largest or among the largest.

14.4.2 Average Development

In order to see the various productivity measures for all years we have introduced the average (arithmetic) unit for each year. The results are set out in Table 14.3. Four

[13] A program testing for Pareto efficiency is run first in our software package, see Førsund and Hernæs (1992).

Table 14.3   The Chain Version of the Malmquist Index and its Components (Average Unit)

Period	Total productivity change				Catching-up	Frontier shift			
	M_{84}	M_{88}	$M_i(i,i+1)$	$M_{i+1}(i,i+1)$	MC	MF_{84}	MF_{88}	$MF_i(i,i+1)$	$MF_{i+1}(i,i+1)$
1984/85	1.024	.993	1.024	1.021	.992	1.033	1.002	1.033	1.030
1985/86	.946	.851	.923	.706	.986	.960	.863	.937	.716
1986/87	.974	.562	1.129	1.003	.995	.979	.565	1.135	1.008
1987/88	.997	1.715	.983	.998	.966	1.032	1.775	1.018	1.033
1984/88	.941	.815	.941	.815	.939	1.002	.868	1.002	.868

indices of total productivity change with varying reference technology are found in the first columns, then the catching-up index, and in the last four columns the frontier technology shift indices corresponding to the total indices. The main impression is one of productivity decline due to the average unit gradually falling behind the frontier. The technology-shift indices both show progression (at the start and end of the period), implying stationary technology over the total period. Even for this short span of periods the difference between the different productivity definitions is considerable, especially between having the first period as base and having the last period as base. Comparing the results for the two fixed base references we get one reversal as regards the direction of the technology shift for the total period, and two shifts for the productivity index for year-to-year changes. Changing base successively gives no reversals for either the total index or the frontier index except for the total period for the frontier shift index, when comparing using the first or second year, when measuring between one and two years. The results for the last year as base are in general more unstable than having the first year as base and calculating for adjacent periods with changing base. There are no reversals in the latter case. The difference in direction of the technical change transmitting over to total productivity change is between the periods 1986 and 1987, changing base showing progression and fixed base showing regression.

Based on the discussion in Section 14.2.5 we use the calculations with base fixed to the first year as the main alternative. The total decline in productivity for the average unit is then about 6 percent, with the first period showing progression and between 1985 and 1986 the largest decline. The frontier is approximately unchanged, with some small ups and downs over the periods.

14.4.3   Productivity Distributions

It would be a waste of information to stop at presenting results for the average unit. In Figures 14.3 to 14.5 the complete distributions for the 135 ferries are shown for the productivity change and its components between 1984 and 1988 with 1984 as the base. Each histogram in the figures represents a ferry, and the width of the histogram is proportional to the share of each ferry's output in total output in 1984.

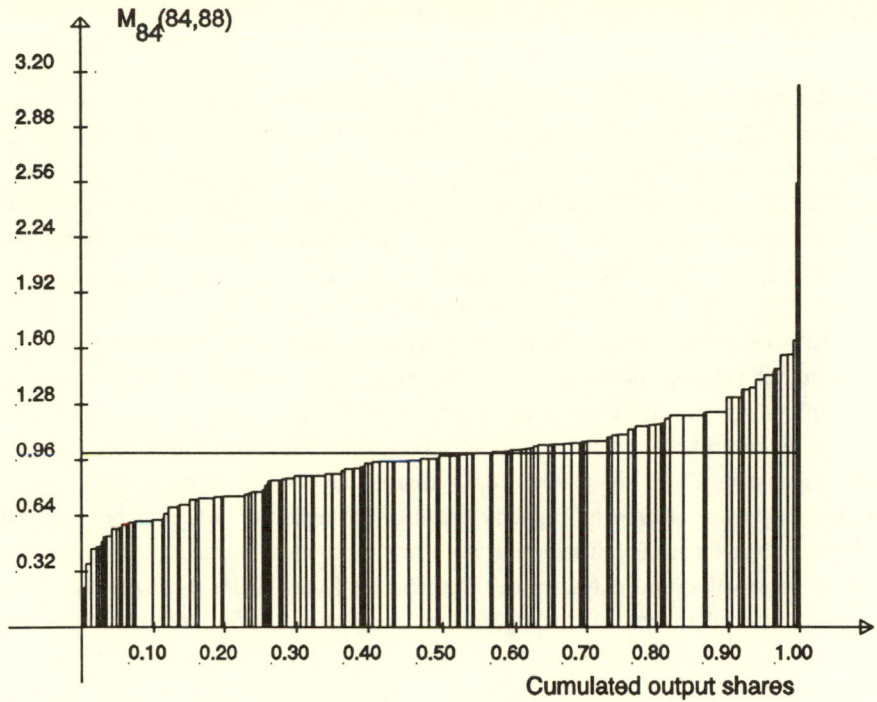

Fig. 14.3   Distribution of Malmquist productivity measure, 1984–1988

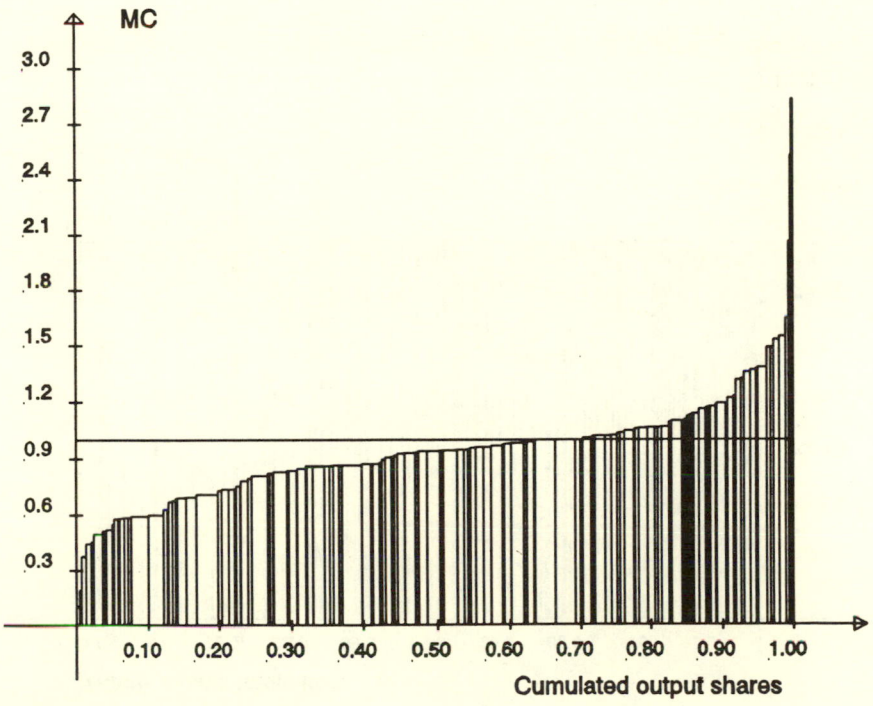

Fig. 14.4   Distribution of catching-up measure, 1984–1988

Starting with the total productivity distribution there is no apparent relationship between productivity change and size.[14] There is a thin tail of small units with much higher productivity change than the rest.

The distribution of the catching-up term shows a very similar picture with no relation between the term and size,[15] and the best performance tail is the same. The two largest units have catching-up values of one. This is because they are on the frontier in both periods. The units are 13 and 14 in Table 14.2.

The distribution for the technology-shift term looks quite different with a much more limited range of variation around one, and the largest units concentrated at the part with positive contribution of technology shift.[16]

In Figures 14.3 to 14.5 the productivity change values are sorted according to increasing values, and cumulated output shares can also be shown as frequencies to bring out more clearly the capacity share of the different values of productivity change. Such a frequency distribution is shown for the total measure in Figure 14.6. The ordinate values are output shares, but the total area under the distribution has been normalized to one, so the figures on the ordinate axis have no immediate

[14] The correlation coefficient is .05 and insignificant.
[15] The correction coefficient is .11 and insignificant.
[16] However, the correlation coefficient is only .09 and still insignificant.

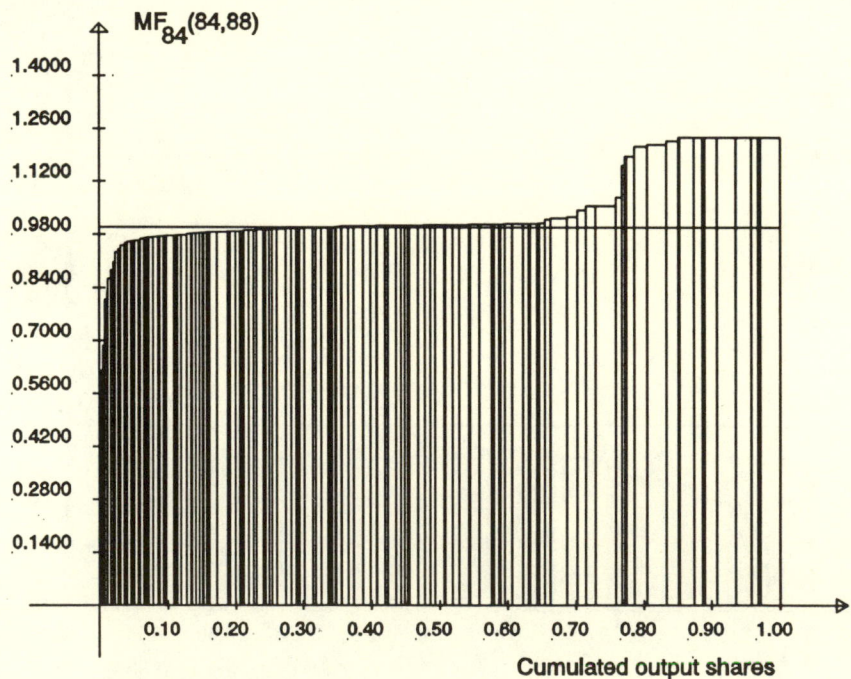

Fig. 14.5   Distribution of frontier function shift, 1984–1988

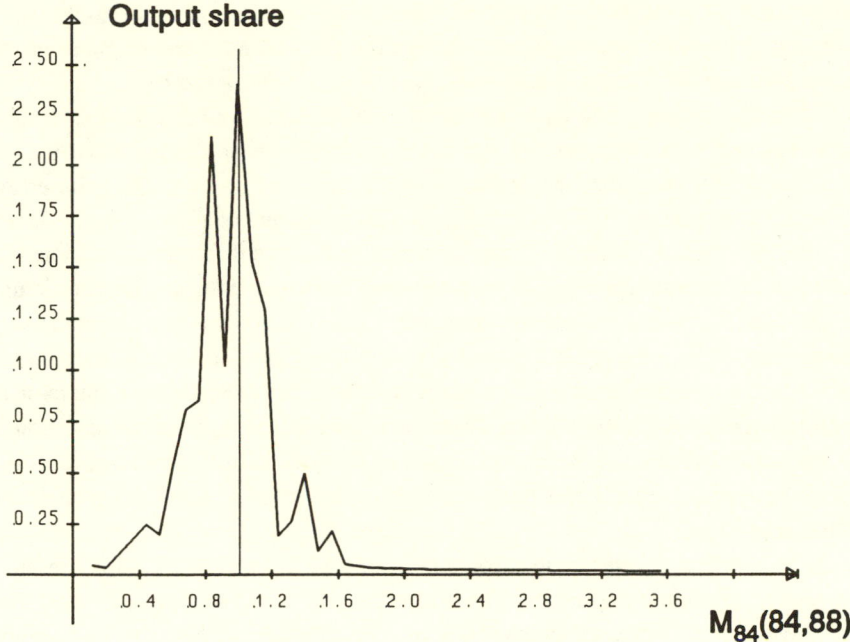

Fig. 14.6 Frequency distribution of Malmquist productivity measure, 1984–1988

interpretation. The units are aggregated over 50 intervals. The distribution has two marked peaks at values of about .8 and 1.0.

The connection between the measures can be visualized by showing two distributions on the same diagram. The catching-up distribution and the total productivity change distribution is shown in Figure 14.7. In order to avoid too much overlapping of the units we have aggregated within a 20 × 20 grid. Each square represents a (possibly aggregated) ferry, and the size of the square is proportional to production in 1984. There is a marked linear relationship between the measures. The correlation coefficient for the measures is .89 and significant. The horizontal and vertical lines at level one divide the units into units with both productivity changes positive and both negative. There are very few in the remaining quadrants with mixed results. We recognize the two small outliers 106 and 132 from Table 14.2 as the two furthest out in the northeast direction. The main share of capacity is located around the value one in both dimensions, as we should expect from the frequency (Figure 14.6).

The relationship between the technology shift and the total measure is quite different, as seen in Figure 14.8. There is no linear relation, but a grouping into two sets and a "tail" according to the value of the technology term. We recognize the two small units from Table 14.2 located furthest to the east in the first quadrant of the four formed by the horizontal and vertical lines through level one as members of the set with high values of the technology-shift measure, and the two large frontier units 13 and 14 are now aggregated into one square in the same quadrant. Since the catching-up measure is strongly correlated with the total measure a figure with the technology-shift measure and the former will be very like Figure 14.8.

Output is defined as the car capacity times the distance sailed. Since the former is our measure of capital a longer distance sailed will improve capital productivity. Labor productivity may also improve due to minimum crew regulations, and maintenance occurring at regular time intervals, while fuel and wear and tear maintenance depend on sailed distance. A closer investigation revealed that the technology-shift measure had no correlation with change in output between 1984 and 1988, but that the cathing-up, and thereby the total, measure had a strong linear relationship with output change. The connection is portrayed in Figure 14.9, which is of the same type as Figures 14.7 and 14.8. The relative change in output with values for 1988 in the numerator are on the abscissa. Within the four-quadrant system we have almost all observations in the first and third ones, meaning that units that experience output increase also have a positive catching-up effect. Change in output from 1984 to 1988 is not correlated with size in 1984.

The problem of intersecting frontiers discussed in Section 14.2.5 is present in our results. Looking at reversals of the frontier shift, we have 59 in total and 52 of them reversing a positive effect when having 1984 frontier as a base to a negative one

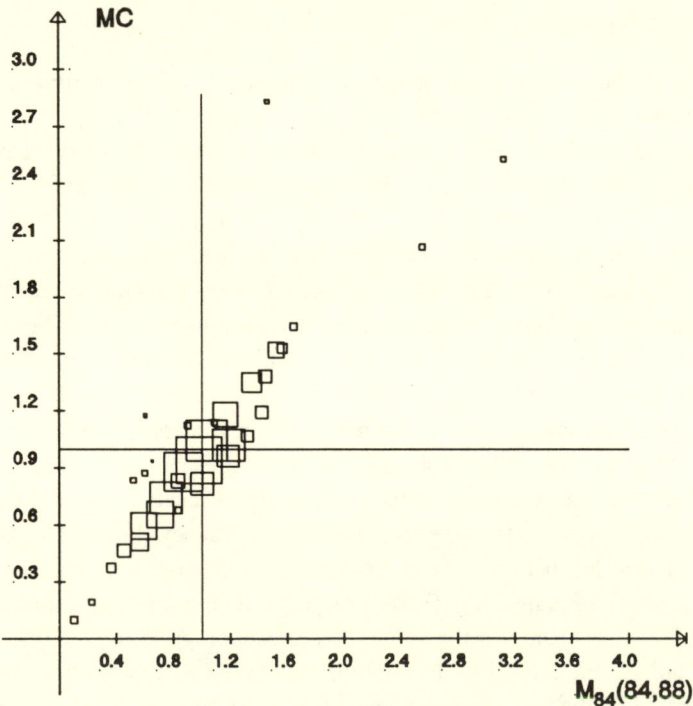

Fig. 14.7 Distribution of catching-up and total productivity change, 1984–1988

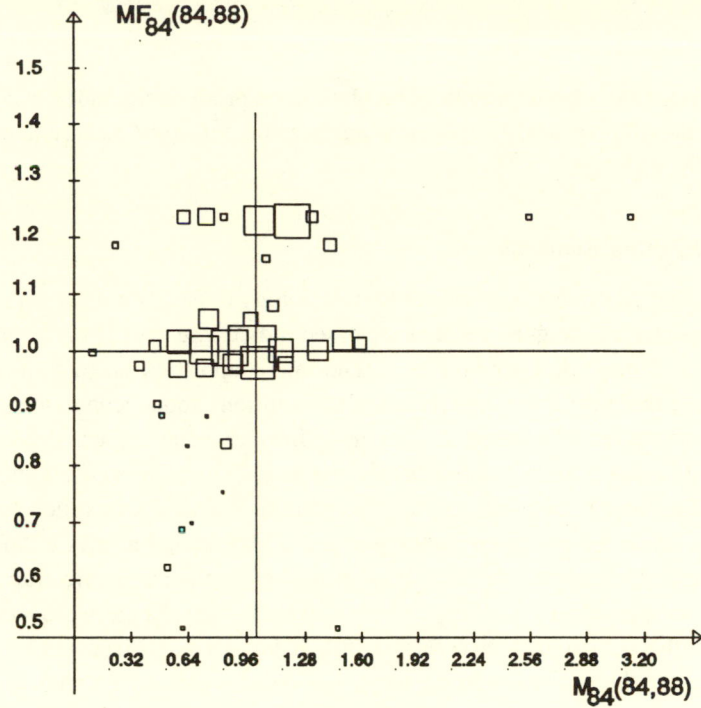

Fig. 14.8 Distribution of frontier function shift and total productivity change, 1984–1988

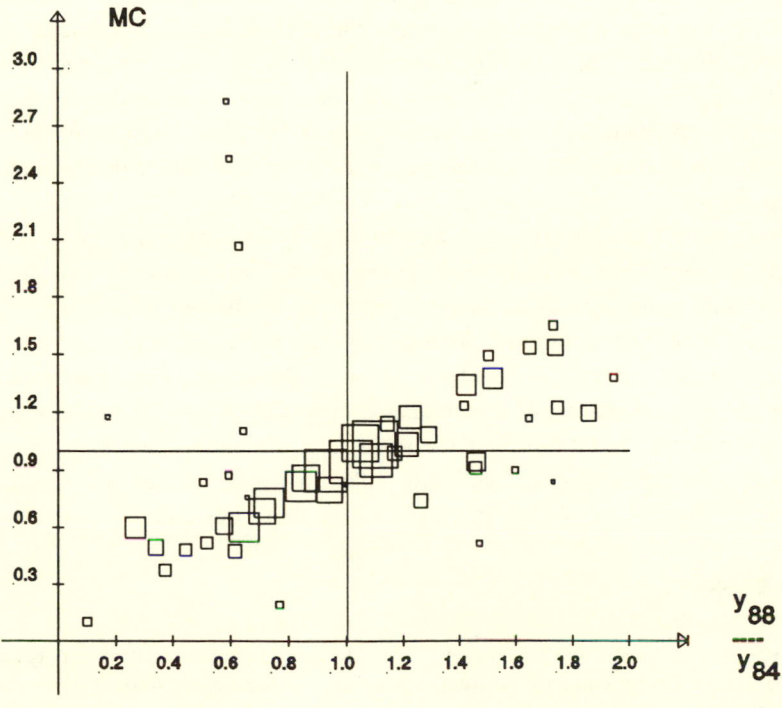

Fig. 14.9 Catching-up and output change, 1984–1988

when having 1988 frontier as base. The Malmquist productivity index was reversed 28 times, and all reversals changed from progression with 1984 as base to regression having 1988 as base.

14.5 Concluding Remarks

When calculating productivity indices the technology is usually not known and prices are used in forming weights. Technology-based indices are usually based on a sector as a unit, and price data are still used. The micro approach taken in this chapter does not use price data, nor does it require assumptions about economic behavior at all, rather it is essentially based on calculating frontier technologies. The Malmquist productivity index is ideally suited for this situation. Caves, Christensen, and Diewert (1982) point this out, but then they say, referring to the need for explicit production functions: "Thus the empirical usefulness of the Malmquist indexes is limited" (p. 1394). Hopefully, this statement has been proved wrong in our application.

The time period is rather short, 5 years, to expect much change in productivity in a business with fixed capital such as ferries. But, as pointed out in Section 14.3, the ferry companies are the decision-making units, and they can allocate ferries to different routes within their concession area, and even rent ferries from other companies. The overall impression is one of declining productivity. When decomposing productivity change into efficiency change (catching-up), and technology shift, it turns out that technology has been almost stationary, and the decline is due to a gradual falling behind in efficiency. The latter can be explained to a large extent by a decline in the distance sailed by ferries, and the ferries with declining distances dominating. The productivity distributions show the variation over the panel and do not show any systematic tendencies with respect to size, except for the frontiers being supported by large ferries.

In Chapter 4 the importance of the productivity decomposition for policy was pointed out. Our results clearly underline this point. The regression in productivity is due to sailing distances decreasing per ferry, and the frontier technology appears stagnant. The obvious policy recommendation is to reallocate ferries and get rid of some to increase distance sailed per ferry. However, the development of demand must be taken into consideration. If demand has declined there may be no other options than facing declining efficiency if the same ferry distances have to be serviced. Decreasing the sailed distance may also reflect a conscious policy of increasing capacity utilization when sailing in the face of declining demand.

REFERENCES

Berg, S. A., F. R. Førsund, and E. S. Jansen (1992), "Malmquist Indices of Productivity Growth During the Deregulation of Norwegian Banking," *Scandinavian Journal of Economics*, 94 (Supplement), 5211–5228.

Caves, D. W., L. R. Christensen, and W. E. Diewert (1982), "The Economic Theory of Index Numbers and the Measurement of Input, Output, and Productivity," *Econometrica* 50: 1393–1414.

Färe, R., S. Grosskopf, B. Lindgren, and P. Roos (1989), "Productivity Developments in Swedish Hospitals," Discussion Paper 89-3, Department of Economics, Southern Illinois University, Carbondale; also published in A. Charnes, W. W. Cooper, A. Y. Lewin, and L. Seiford, eds.; *Data Envelopment Analysis: The Theory, Applications and the Process* (forthcoming 1992).

Färe, R., S. Grosskopf, S. Yaisawarng, S. K. Li, and Z. Wang (1990), "Productivity Growth in Illinois Electric Utilities," *Resources and Energy* 12: 383–398.

Farrell, M. J. (1957), "The Measurement of Productive Efficiency," *Journal of the Royal Statistical Society,* Series A, General 120 (III): 253–281(290).

Førsund, F. R. (1992), "A Comparison of Parametric and Non-parametric Efficiency Measures: The Case of Norwegian Ferries," *Journal of Productivity Analysis*, 3, 25–43.

Førsund, F. R., C. A. K. Lovell, and P. Schmidt (1980), "A Survey of Frontier Production Functions and Their Relationship to Efficiency Measurement," *Journal of Econometrics* 13: 5–25.

Førsund, F. R., and L. Hjalmarsson (1987); *Analyses of Industrial Structure: A Putty-Clay Approach,* The Industrial Institute for Economic and Social Research. Stockholm. Almqvist and Wiksell International.

Førsund, F. R., and L. Hjalmarsson (1988), "Choice of Technology and Long-Run Technical Change in Energy-Intensive Industries," *Energy Journal,* 9: 79–97.

Førsund, F. R., and E. Hernæs (1992), "Ferry Transport in Norway: An Application of DEA Analysis," in A. Charnes, W. W. Cooper, A. Y. Lewin, and L. Seiford, eds., *Data Envelopment Analysis: The Theory, Applications and the Process* (forthcoming).

Frisch, R. (1936), "Annual Survey of General Economic Theory: The Problem of Index Numbers," *Econometrica* 4: 1–38.

Johansen, L. (1972), *Production Functions.* Amsterdam: North-Holland.

Klein, J. D., S. S. Schmidt, and S. Yaisawarng (1993), "Productivity Changes in the U.S. Electric Power Industry," in D. B. Audretsch and J. Siegfried, eds., *Empirical Studies in Industrial Organization: Essays in Honor of Leonard W. Weiss.* Dordrecht, The Netherlands: Kluwer Academic Publishers (forthcoming).

Malmquist, S. (1953), "Index Numbers and Indifference Surfaces," *Trabajos de Estadística* 4: 209–242.

Shephard, R. W. (1953), *Cost and Production Functions.* Princeton: Princeton University Press.

Tulkens, H. (1990), "Non-parametric Efficiency Analyses in Four Service Activities: Retail Banking, Municipalities, Courts and Urban Transit," CORE Discussion Paper 9050, Louvain-la-Neuve, Belgium.

15

EFFICIENCY AND COMPETITION IN O.E.C.D. FINANCIAL SERVICES

Fabienne Fecher and Pierre Pestieau[1]

15.1 Introduction

It seems widely accepted today that productivity growth in banking and insurance services, herein called financial services, is very low, if not negative. In a recent paper on the U.S. insurance industry, Baumol (1991) has argued that this is by no means attributable to managerial slack or "other form of misbehavior," but to what he calls the cost disease.[2] The cost disease plagues many other service industries, such as education, artistic performance, and police protection; it affects activities which are inherently resistant to technical change.

The purpose of this chapter is not to dispute Baumol's view but to put it in a slightly different perspective in which productivity growth consists of technical change, which indeed can be affected by cost disease, and of efficiency change, which is in contrast determined by factors pertaining to management quality and competitive conditions. We present estimates of multifactor productivity growth, technical progress, and efficiency change for the OECD financial services. We·then try to see to what extent efficiency change which is most often falling can be explained in part by the strength of regulation and the competitive conditions prevailing in each country. We also check whether or not there would be a competition-driven convergence in productivity growth of financial services.

[1] Financial support from the Belgian Science Foundation (FRFC n° 2.4537.90) and the Geneva Association are acknowledged. We wish to thank Shawna Grosskopf and Knox Lovell for helpful suggestions.

[2] The "cost disease" or the "unbalanced growth" hypothesis states that "differences in the rates of productivity growth in the pertinent sectors of the economy explain nearly all of the expansion of the services as a share of both the labor force and GNP, the latter being accounted for by a rise in the relative prices of the services at issue rather than by any expansion of their real outputs," [Baumol, Backman, and Wolff (1989, p. 116)]. See also Wolff (1991).

The chapter is organized as follows. In the next section, we sketch the methodology to be used to obtain the two components of multifactor productivity change. This amounts to estimating a sectoral production function using panel data consisting of financial services in a number of OECD countries over the period 1971 to 1986 with a time trend. This production function then allows for the construction of a "best practice" frontier to be used as a yardstick of efficiency across countries. Section 15.3 is devoted to the presentation of the OECD data and to the concept of financial services output. Section 15.4 presents the main results as to multifactor productivity changes in financial services. We will see that both the rate of multifactor productivity change as well as the level of efficiency vary quite a lot across countries and over time. Section 15.5 attempts to explain part of that variation with variables pertaining to the regulatory and competitive environment of financial services and to check whether or not one observes any convergence particularly among EEC countries.

15.2 Frontier Analysis and Multifactor Productivity Growth

The most important difference between the frontier approach and the traditional index number approach to productivity growth analysis lies in one assumption: the existence of an unobservable function, the production frontier, corresponding to the set of maximum attainable output levels for a given combination of inputs. We represent this so called "best practice" function $g[.]$, for production unit i and time t, as follows:

$$y_{it}^F = g[x_{it}, t] \tag{15.1}$$

where y_{it}^F is the potential output level on the frontier at time t for production unit (here country) i, and x_{it} is a vector of inputs. It is assumed that function $g[.]$ satisfies the usual regularity conditions and that an appropriate aggregate index of output exists.

Then, any observed output y_{it} using x_{it} for inputs may be expressed as

$$y_{it} = y_{it}^F e^{u_{it}} = g[x_{it}, t] e^{u_{it}} \tag{15.2}$$

where $u_{it} \le 0$ is the rate of technical efficiency $[0 < e^{u_{it}} = y_{it}/y_{it}^F \le 1]$ corresponding to observed output y_{it}.

The derivative of the logarithm of (15.2) with respect to time is then given by

$$\frac{\dot{y}_{it}}{y_{it}} = g_x \frac{\dot{x}_{it}}{x_{it}} + g_t + \dot{u}_{it} \tag{15.3}$$

where g_x and g_t denote, respectively, the output elasticities of $g[x_{it}, t]$ with respect to x_{it} and t and dotted variables indicate time derivatives.

As indicated by (15.3), output growth can be broken down into three components. The first corresponds to input growth weighted by output elasticities, the second is the rate of technological progress of the *"best practice"* frontier, and the last represents technical efficiency change.

Following Nishimizu and Page (1982), we define the rate of multifactor productivity growth (Δ MFP) as the growth in output not explained by input growth.[3] That is

$$\Delta\text{MFP}_{it} = g_t + \dot{u}_{it}, \tag{15.4}$$

the sum of technological progress measured at the frontier level, and the change in efficiency observed at the individual level.

In order to estimate this indicator of productivity growth, the starting point is the estimation of the unobservable production frontier indicated by Equation (15.1). From all methods proposed to build this frontier and based on observable data, parametric methods are employed for the estimation of functional forms. A stochastic approach is used.[4] For this purpose, let us write Equation (15.2) in the form:

$$y_{it} = g[x_{it}, t]e^{\epsilon_{it}} \tag{15.2a}$$

where $\epsilon_{it} = u_{it} + v_{it}$ is a composed error term combining technical efficiency u_{it} and a random term v_{it}, assumed to have the usual properties, that is, normal distribution, null mean, and standard error σ_v.

The major difficulty raised by the stochastic method is the decomposition of ϵ_{it} into the random and the inefficiency elements. We use "the time-varying effects approach"[5] proposed by Cornwell, Schmidt, and Sickles (1990). In this approach discussed in Chapter 2, the efficiency term is expressed as a parameterized function of time with parameters that vary across countries:

$$u_{it} = \theta_{i0} + \theta_{i1}t + \theta_{i2}t^2 \tag{15.5}$$

where θ_{i0} are the fixed effects pertaining to individual countries and θ_{i1} and θ_{i2} are other country related parameters allowing for variation in technical efficiency over time.

As to the specification of the function $g[.]$, we adopt a Cobb-Douglas form. Thus Equation (15.2a) becomes

---

[3] This approach is discussed in Chapter 4 of this volume.

[4] For a survey of alternative econometric approaches to efficiency measurement, see Lovell and Schmidt (1988) and Chapter 2.

[5] Barla and Perelman (1989) have used this method for airlines.

$$\ln y_{it} = \alpha + \sum_{k=1}^{K} \beta_k \ln x_{k,it} + \gamma t + \epsilon_{it} \tag{15.6}$$

where t, i, and k indicate, respectively, time, country, and production factor. There are two production factors: labor with coefficient β_1 and capital with coefficient β_2. With the notation Equation (15.5), Equation (15.6) can be written:

$$\ln y_{it} = \alpha + \sum_{k=1}^{K} \beta_k \ln x_{k,it} + \gamma t + \theta_{i0} + \theta_{i1} t + \theta_{i2} t^2 + v_{it} \tag{15.7}$$

The decomposition of the error term into its two components is implemented in two steps. In the first step one estimates (15.6) by OLS with estimated residuals denoted $\hat{\epsilon}_{it}$. In the second step one estimates θ_{i0}, θ_{i1}, and θ_{i2} by estimating the following equation by OLS:

$$\hat{\epsilon}_{it} = \theta_{i0} + \theta_{i1} t + \theta_{i2} t^2 + v_{it} \tag{15.8}$$

where $v_{it} \sim N(0, \sigma_v^2)$. The fitted values from (15.8) provide an estimate of u_{it} which is the efficiency indicator. This indicator $\hat{u}_{it}$ has to be normalized to satisfy the nonnegativity constraint. So in order to estimate the levels of technical efficiency $\hat{\mu}_{it}$ we calculate

$$\hat{\mu}_{it} = e^{(\hat{u}_{it} - \hat{u}_{\max})} \tag{15.9}$$

where $\hat{u}_{\max}$ indicates the most efficient observation in the panel that is assumed to lie on the production frontier.

Note that technical progress is assumed to be neutral and to occur at a constant pace. This means that second-order terms, allowing for accelerated or embodied technological progress, are neglected. As a consequence, differentiating Equation (15.7) with respect to time, we obtain multifactor productivity growth as a linear function of time and it consists of the rate of technical progress and the rate of change in technical efficiency.

$$\Delta \text{MFP}_{it} = \gamma + \theta_{i1} + 2\theta_{i2} t \tag{15.4a}$$

15.3 Variable Definitions and Data

The data used in this study have recently been made available from the OECD International Sectoral Data Base (ISDB) whose detailed description is given in Meyer-zu-Schlochtern (1988).

Output is value-added net of indirect taxes, at constant prices and in U.S. dollars corresponding to 1980 purchasing power parities. Note that this variable, like capital formation, is obtained on a national accounts basis and corresponds to sectoral aggregates in accordance with the International Standard Industrial Classification (ISIC).

Labor is defined as total employment, self-employed included, and is measured by the number of individuals. Capital is estimated by a perpetual inventory model. The data source for the estimation of the capital stock is gross fixed capital formation, assumed to have specific service lives and scrapping rates in each country considered.

Measuring the output with the national accounts value-added indicator is questionable in the particular case of financial services. Several authors have questioned the relevancy of such an indicator to assess the actual output of banks and insurance companies.[6] Focusing on the latter, two alternatives are often suggested: on the one hand, gross premiums or incurred losses, and, on the other hand, the number of policies contracted weighted by their value. The issue is obvious: considering that the objective of an insurance company is to provide risk coverage to its insurees and to invest their premiums, can we say that its value added, that is, wages plus capital consumption and profits, reflects the extent of those two activities? In the banking sector, studies of microunits rely on total deposits or on the number of accounts or transactions to proxy output.[7]

Using value added as a measure of output for banks and insurance companies is not entirely satisfactory. In financial services, where the main input is labor, the national accounts measure of production is in most countries no more than an index of labor, and hence, the calculation of labor productivity growth can be a tautological exercise. However, up to now, alternative comparable data on the real activities of financial services are not available.

15.4 Measures of Multifactor Productivity Growth and of Technical Efficiency

We use "the time-varying effects approach" presented above with two additional assumptions: the financial service branch is taken as a single service firm and the production set is homogeneous both across countries and over time, up to a trend term for the latter. We are thus able to obtain for each country the level of efficiency averaged over the whole period and the average annual rate of growth in efficiency. We further get a figure for technical progress, the same for all countries. Adding the rate of technical progress to the rate of growth in technical efficiency gives the rate of growth in multifactor productivity. Fecher and Perelman (1990) have proceeded with that decomposition as far as manufacturing sectors are concerned. We here apply it to financial services.

[6] See, for example, O'Brien (1991), Hornstein and Prescott (1991), and Hirshorn and Geehan (1977).
[7] See, for example, Ferrier and Lovell (1990).

Table 15.1 Stochastic Production Function for Financial Services

α	β_1	β_2	γ	R^2	σ_ϵ^2
−2.96*	.59*	.42*	.007*	.99	2.13
(−34.08)	(29.05)	(20.64)	(3.64)		

The *t*-tests are presented in parentheses.
*significant at the 1 percent level.

We turn first to the estimation of the production function (15.6) that constitutes the standard first stage in the estimation of technical efficiency. The estimated parameters, obtained by OLS, are presented in Table 15.1.

Elasticities of production illustrate the basic characteristics of production structure. Technological progress is estimated by the γ coefficient.

We also observe that the variance of the technical efficiency term, σ_u^2, which is obtained by estimating Equation (15.8) and is equal to 2.06, represents more than 90 percent of total variance, σ_ϵ^2. This confirms the importance of technical inefficiency.

The second step in the estimation of multifactor productivity growth consists in the estimation of technical efficiency for each observation. Summing up changes in efficiency and technological progress gives this measure. The results are given in Table 15.2. As the rate of technical progress is the same for all countries ($\gamma = .7$ percent), it is not presented but used to compute multifactor productivity change. It thus appears that there is some technical progress over the period covered and yet there is almost no growth in multifactor productivity.

Table 15.2 allows us to qualify Baumol's statement on the cost disease in financial services. Based on just multifactor productivity change, he is entirely right

Table 15.2 Financial Services Technical Efficiency, Annual Rate of Growth in Technical Efficiency and Multifactor Productivity, 1971–1986, 11 OECD Countries

Country	Mean Efficiency Level	Mean Efficiency Change	Mean Multifactor Productivity Change
Australia	.78	−.010	−.003
Belgium	.84	.002	.009
Canada	.85	−.002	.004
Germany	.88	.011	.018
Denmark	.67	−.009	−.002
France	.91	−.009	−.002
United Kingdom	.86	.002	.009
Japan	.98	.001	.008
Norway	.90	−.009	−.002
Sweden	.76	−.001	.005
United States	.71	−.008	−.001
All	.82	−.002	.004

to underline the poor performance of financial services: 5 countries (including the United States) out of 11 have negative growth. Where growth is positive, it is hardly significant. Only in (West) Germany does the estimated growth rate exceed 1 percent per annum. However, what Baumol has in mind is technical progress, which is low but positive. This positive technical progress is offset by poor performance in terms of technical efficiency change (negative in seven countries), and this can be imputed to poor management.

Indeed, Baumol makes an interesting distinction between what he calls "impersonal technical imperatives" as opposed to "villainous behavior." In his view, the former are only responsible for negative productivity growth. We show here that in a number of countries including the United States this could be the other way around.

15.5 Competition, Regulation, and Performance

15.5.1 The Conceptual Link

Recent theory in the economics of information shows that within a setting of uncertainty and asymmetric information, competitive pressures are the most effective way to foster productive efficiency.[8] Competition induces managers to operate as closely as possible to their production frontier and, further, it gives their principal, the owners or the state, the relevant information for better monitoring their activities. It also goes without saying that competition induces allocative efficiency.

In trying to eliminate managerial slack, shareholders, governments, or any other principals face difficulties arising from lack of information. Hence they cannot directly sort out the sources of inefficiencies: managerial weaknesses or the firm's true opportunities. Observations of the performance of competing firms in the same market, or of firms in similar environments, do provide relevant information for the development of more efficient incentive schemes.

Even without going into explicit incentive schemes, it is clear that competition fosters efficiency. If a management team performs poorly in competition to reduce costs, its utility is likely to suffer as a consequence. One of the issues one should raise in that respect is that the link between competition and deregulation, on the one hand, and efficiency, both allocative and technical, on the other hand, is not necessarily monotonic. One knows for sure that a firm operating in a setting without any competition and subject to heavy regulation is going to be less efficient than the same firm operating in a setting with competition and full deregulation. Yet, it is not clear that in the process of deregulating an economy and increasing its competitiveness, efficiency always increases monotonically.

In the wave of recent policies of deregulation and privatization,[9] a number of studies were issued showing that performance is positively related to the degree of

[8] Hayek (1945) and Hart (1983).

[9] Yarrow (1986) and Vickers and Yarrow (1988).

openness and competitiveness; in particular, they often show that for better performance, competition matters more than private ownership.

These studies call for two comments. First, they generally rely on a narrow set of data, for example, rather short time series of an industry before and after deregulation or privatization. Second, they use performance indicators which are not only partial but the meaning of which varies with the organizational form, the ownership regime, the market structure, and the regulatory intensity of the firms analyzed. The usual indicators are prices to evaluate allocative efficiency, labor productivity or the cost of capital to evaluate technical efficiency, and share prices or profit margins to assess profitability.

15.5.2 Empirical Findings

We would have liked to use readily available indicators of regulation and competition to control part of the variation in efficiency levels and efficiency changes found in the previous section. Unfortunately, there are no such indicators. We used all the information available for banks and insurance companies which pertain to the degree of concentration, the intensity of regulation, and the lack of openness to foreign competition.

Part of this information comes from surveys among practitioners (regulation in insurance); most of it comes from published data on concentration ratios and market shares. Depending on data availability, two variants are considered. The first includes five EEC countries (Belgium, Germany, Denmark, France and the United Kingdom) and the second seven countries, that is, those EEC countries plus Norway and Sweden. Both variants appear in Table 15.3.

To aggregate this heterogeneous data set, we use principal component analysis. Even though its limitations are known, this approach is useful in cases as here where one deals with a complex multidimensional process about which little known is a priori. For the two variants, we retain the first two components which explain most of the variance. In either variant, the first component is positively related to openness of the insurance market and negatively related to concentration in insurance and in banks. The second component is positively and strongly correlated with regulation in banks and insurance markets. Thus, one can use component I as an index of competition and component II as an index of regulation.

Table 15.4 gives partial correlation coefficients between those components and our indicators of efficiency level and efficiency change. They are positive in seven out of eight cases. Even though, our sample of countries is too narrow to draw any firm conclusions, the positive correlation between regulatory intensity and either the level or the change in efficiency is noteworthy. There are instances indeed where regulation can foster productive efficiency. A good example of this is the German insurance market. It is known for its rigid supervisory system which inhibits product

Table 15.3 Indicators of Regulation and Concentration. Principal Components Analysis

| | | | | | | | | Variant I (5 countries) | | Variant II (7 countries) | |
| | | | | Countries | | | | Comp I | Comp II | Comp I | Comp II |
Variables	Belgium	Germany	Denmark	France	United Kingdom	Norway	Sweden				
INSREG 1	1.45	2.35	1.66	2.15	1.40	—	—	.48	.26		
INSREG 2	1.25	2.25	1.25	1.75	1.50	.25	1.25	—	—	.50	.50
BANKREG	1	0	0	1	0	0	0	−.33	.53	−.52	.47
INSCOMP	20.25	39.25	8.00	18.75	30.50	4.50	5.00	.34	.56	.45	.54
BANKCOMP	.378	.740	.440	.574	.549	—	—	.59	.15		
INSMARKET	37.0	85.5	85.7	79.2	80.2	88.0	97.2	.42	−.55	.52	−.48
% variance explained								53	30	38	50
Variant I (5 countries)											
Comp I	−2.12	2.42	−.46	.17	−.003						
Comp II	1.26	.73	−1.76	.50	−.74						
Variant II (7 countries)											
Comp I	−1.90	1.93	.06	−.42	.88	−.81	.26				
Comp II	1.73	1.16	−.94	1.04	.32	−1.96	−1.34				

Sources

INSREG 1	Indicator of insurance regulation (obtained from a survey)	J. Finsinger (1991)
INSREG 2	Indicator of insurance regulation (obtained from a survey)	Andersen Consulting (1990, pp. 27–28).
BANKREG	Indicator of bank regulation (regulation of interest rates)	OECD (1989, p. 55).
INSCOMP	Indicator of competition in insurance (number of insurance companies accounting for 80% of premiums in 1990)	Andersen Consulting (1990, pp. 29–30).
BANKCOMP	Indicator of competition in banks (1 - threebank concentration ratio in 1973)	J. Revell (1987, p. 52).
INSMARKET	Indicator of foreign competition in insurance (market share of national insurance companies in 1990)	Andersen Consulting (1990, pp. 22–25).

Table 15.4   Correlation Coefficients

	Variant I		Variant II	
	Comp. I **Competition**	**Comp. II** **Regulation**	**Comp. I** **Competition**	**Comp. II** **Regulation**
Efficiency level	.30	.75	− .02	.37
Efficiency change	.45	.49	.52	.54

innovation and restricts certain types of investments. At the same time, it has been shown to exhibit a high technical efficiency but a low allocative efficiency.[10]

Quite clearly, the data are too preliminary and the number of countries too small to reach any definitive statement. This however shows that regulation and technical efficiency are not necessarily incompatible. On the other hand, competition as measured by the inverse of the concentration ratio is in general positively correlated with technical efficiency.

Finally, it is worth checking whether over the period 1971 to 1986, which coincides with that of the development of the European Community, one observes a trend toward converging changes in MFP. In Figure 15.1, the variation in MFP for our 11 countries is represented. One clearly sees that the EC member countries tend to

[10] See, on this, Finsinger, Hammond, and Tapp (1985).

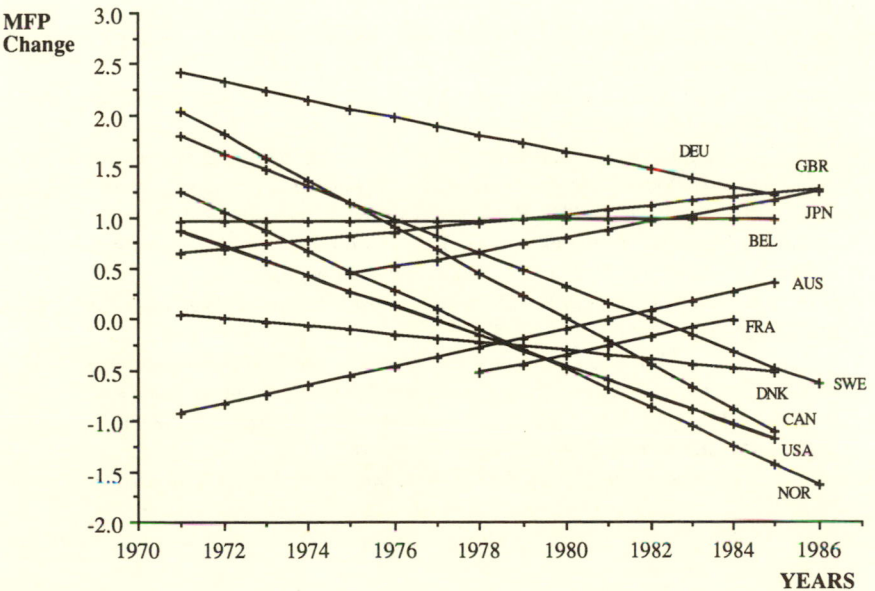

Fig. 15.1   MFP convergence

converge as opposed to the non-EC countries. This appears clearly when comparing the coefficients of variation in the beginning and at the end of the period. It falls for the EC countries and it increases for the non-EC countries.

15.6 Conclusion

The purpose of this chapter is to decompose the variation in multifactor productivity growth in financial services into technical progress and technical efficiency change to better understand the often observed low gains in productivity in banks and insurance companies. We have shown that most of that poor performance is imputable to slacks in technical efficiency.

We then tried to see whether regulation and lack of competition can explain differentials in MFP change across countries. Unfortunately the only available indicator of regulation is restricted to seven countries. On the basis of such a small sample the findings are rather mixed. Competition and regulation seem to favor both efficiency level and efficiency change. Further, one observes some convergence in the rate of productivity changes among EC countries.

REFERENCES

Andersen Consulting (1990), "Insurance in a changing Europe 1990–1995," Special Report n° 2068, pp. 27–28.

Barla, Ph., and S. Perelman (1989), "Technical Efficiency in Airlines Under Regulated and Deregulated Environments," *Annales de l'Economie Publique, Sociale et Coopérative* 1: 103–124.

Baumol, W. (1991), "Technological Imperatives, Productivity and Insurance Costs," *The Geneva Papers* 59: 154–165.

Baumol, W. J., S. A. Batey Backman, and E. N. Wolff (1989), *Productivity and American Leadership*. Cambridge, Mass.: The MIT Press.

Cornwell, C., P. Schmidt, and R. C. Sickles (1990), "Production Frontier with Cross-Sectional and Time-Series Variation in Efficiency Levels," *Journal of Econometrics* 46: 185–200.

Fecher, F., and S. Perelman (1990), "Productivity Growth, Technological Progress and R&D in OECD Industrial Activities," in G. Krause-Junk, ed., *Public Finance and Steady Economic Growth*. The Hague: The Public Finance Foundation.

Ferrier G., and C. A. K. Lovell (1990), "Measuring Cost Efficiency in Banking—Econometric and Linear Programming Evidence," *Journal of Econometrics* 46: 229–245.

Finsinger, J. (1991), "European Market Integration and the European Insurance Industry. Reasons for Trade, Barriers to Entry, Distribution Channels, Regulation and Price Levels," in G. Winckler, ed., *Tax Harmonisation and Financial Liberalisation in Europe*. Berlin: Verlag MacMillan Press (forthcoming).

Finsinger, J., E. Hammond, and J. Tapp (1985), *Insurance: Competition or Regulation*. London: IFS.

Hart, O. D. (1983), "The Market Mechanism as an Incentive Scheme," *Bell Journal of Economics* 14: 366–382.

Hayek, F. A. (1945), "The Use of Knowledge in Society," *American Economic Review* 35: 519–530.

Hirshorn, R., and G. Geehan (1977), "Measuring the Real Output of the Life Insurance Industry," *Review of Economics and Statistics* 59: 211–219.

Hornstein, A., and E. Prescott (1991), "Measures of the Insurance Sector Output," *The Geneva Papers* 59: 191–206.

Lovell, C. A. K., and P. Schmidt (1988), "A Comparison of Alternative Approaches to the Measurement of Productive Efficiency," in A. Dogramaci and R. Färe, eds., *Studies in Productivity Analysis. Applications of Modern Production Theory. Efficiency and Productivity*, Boston, Mass.: Kluwer Academic Publishers.

Meyer-zu-Schlochtern, F. J. M. (1988), "An International Sectoral Data Base for Thirteen OECD Countries," Working Paper 57, Department of Economics and Statistics, OECD.

Nishimizu, M., and J. M. Page (1982), "Total Factor Productivity Growth, Technological Progress and Technical Efficiency Change: Dimensions of Productivity Change in Yugoslavia, 1965–78," *Economic Journal* 92: 920–936.

O'Brien, C. D. (1991), "Measuring the Output of Life Insurance Companies," *The Geneva Papers* 59: 207–235.

OECD (1989), *La concurrence dans le secteur bancaire*, Paris.

Revell, J. (1987), "Mergers and the Role of Large Banks," Institute of European Finance, Research Monographs in Banking and Finance, 2.

Vickers, J., and G. Yarrow (1988), *Privatization. An Economic Analysis*. Cambridge, Mass.: MIT Press.

Wolff, E. N., (1991) "Productivity Growth, Capital Intensity and Skill Levels in the U.S. Insurance Industry, 1948–86," *The Geneva Papers* 59: 173–190.

Yarrow, G. (1986), "Privatization in Theory and in Practice," *Economic Policy* 1: 324–377.

16

EFFICIENCY AND PRODUCTIVITY GROWTH IN U. S. BANKING

Paul W. Bauer, Allen N. Berger, and David B. Humphrey [1]

16.1 Introduction

Until recently, bank cost studies focused almost exclusively on scale and product mix (scope) economies. While this has been useful, a potentially more important dimension of bank cost economies appears to be differences in efficiency. Recent studies have estimated inefficiencies of 20 percent or more of costs, even for banks of similar scale and product mix. These inefficiencies appear to dominate scale and product mix effects, which usually average 5 percent or less.

Our purposes in this chapter are twofold. First, we apply two methods of efficiency measurement that have been employed in extant efficiency literature and contrast the results across methodologies. Specifically, we compare the stochastic econometric frontier approach, first proposed by Aigner, Lovell, and Schmidt (1977), Meeusen and van den Broeck (1977), and Battese and Corra (1977), with the thick frontier approach of Berger and Humphrey (1991, 1992a). These methods are applied to a panel data set of 683 U.S. banks with over $100 million in assets in states that allow branch banking that were continuously in existence during 1977 to 1988. As these banks account for two-thirds of total banking assets, and all U.S. states allow some form of branching as of August 1991, our results may be considered reasonably representative of the industry as a whole. Since we have data for each year, we are also able to assess the variations in efficiency over time. Previous banking studies

[1] Federal Reserve Bank of Cleveland, Board of Governors of the Federal Reserve System, and Florida State University, respectively. The opinions expressed do not necessarily reflect those of the Board of Governors, the Reserve Banks, or their staffs. The authors would like to thank Knox Lovell and James Thomson for helpful comments and Alex Wolman and Fadi Alameddine for outstanding research assistance. Most of Humphrey's work was performed while he was at the Federal Reserve Bank of Richmond.

have not compared the results of alternative frontier methods [Ferrier and Lovell (1990) excepted], nor have they assessed efficiency at more than one point in time [Berger and Humphrey (1992a) excepted].

The second purpose of the chapter is the measurement of the growth of total factor productivity (TFP) in banking, which incorporates both technical change and scale economies. While some prior studies have investigated technical change in banking, they have done so using data for all banks, rather than for those on the efficient frontier. Such a procedure may confound technical change on the frontier with fluctuations in inefficiency that alter the average distance from the frontier. These prior studies also have determined average time trends for technical change, rather than specific year-to-year variations. This study breaks both of these molds. We estimate annual shifts for the efficient frontier, rather than for the universe of banks, and permit the size of these shifts to vary freely on a year-to-year basis. TFP growth is determined by combining our frontier measures of technical change with scale economy measures for frontier banks. In this way, productivity growth or movement *of* the frontier is considered separately from changes in inefficiency or average distance *from* the frontier. Productivity growth over 1977 to 1988 is of particular interest because of financial market innovation (cash management), regulatory change (deregulation of consumer deposit rates), and technical innovation (automated teller machines) during this interval.

16.2 A Brief Comparison of Frontier Efficiency Models

Inefficiency is assessed by measuring how far a firm's costs or input requirements are from a "best practice" set of firms or efficient frontier. The key methodological problem is that the true technically based frontier is unknown and must be estimated from levels found in the data set. The differences among techniques in the efficiency literature largely reflect differing maintained assumptions used in estimating these frontiers.

The stochastic econometric frontier approach modifies a standard cost (or production) function to allow inefficiencies to be included in the error term. A composite error term is specified which includes both random error and inefficiency, and specific distributional assumptions are made to separate these two components. Since inefficiencies only increase costs above frontier levels and random fluctuations can either increase or decrease costs, inefficiencies are assumed to be drawn from a one-sided distribution (usually the half-normal) and random fluctuations are assumed to be drawn from a symmetric distribution (usually the normal). This approach has been applied to banking by Ferrier and Lovell (1990). Berger (1993) used different techniques, described below, to identify the inefficiencies.

The thick frontier approach, instead of estimating a frontier *edge*, compares the average efficiencies of large groups of banks. Banks in the lowest average cost quartile are assumed to be of greater than average efficiency and form a thick frontier.

Similarly, banks in the highest average cost quartile are identified as likely having less than average efficiency. Differences in error terms within the highest and lowest cost quartiles are assumed to reflect random error, while the predicted cost differences between these quartiles are assumed to reflect inefficiencies plus exogenous differences in output quantities and input prices. Banks are stratified by size class before the quartiles are formed to ensure that a broad range of banks are represented in each quartile and to reduce the relationship between the quartile selection criterion and the dependent variable in the regressions.[2] The thick frontier approach has been applied to banking by Berger and Humphrey (1991, 1992a).

The data envelopment analysis (DEA) approach, which is not replicated here, assumes that random error is zero so that *all* unexplained variations are treated as reflecting inefficiencies. The DEA approach has been applied to banking by Rangan, Grabowski, Aly, and Pasurka (1988), Aly, Grabowski, Pasurka, and Rangan (1990), Elyasiani and Mehdian (1990), Ferrier and Lovell (1990), and Ferrier, Grosskopf, Hayes, and Yaisawarng (1991).

An illustrative comparison of the stochastic and thick frontier methods can be made using the raw data presented in Figure 16.1, which shows how average total costs per dollar of assets varies across eight bank size classes. The data are taken from the Federal Reserve Board's Reports of Condition and Income (Call Reports). The AC_{Q1} and AC_{Q4} lines are average costs for the lowest and highest quartiles, respectively, while the AC_{MIN}, AC_{MAX}, and AC_{MEAN} lines correspond to the overall minima, maxima, and means, respectively. The averages for all of these curves are taken over the 12-year period from 1977 to 1988, and so do not reflect the full variation in costs for any one year.[3] Mean average costs (AC_{MEAN}) are very flat across different sized banks—the range of variation is only 5 percent, suggesting very few scale economies or diseconomies. The average costs of the lowest and highest quartiles (AC_{Q1} and AC_{Q4}) are also relatively flat, with ranges of variation of 5 and 13 percent, respectively.

In the thick frontier approach, cost equations are estimated for the highest and lowest quartiles and the difference in predicted costs for a given set of output quantities and input prices is considered to be due to inefficiency. The raw-data approximation to this inefficiency is given in Figure 16.1 by the difference ($AC_{Q4} - AC_{Q1}$), which averages 23 percent. Measured inefficiency will differ from this because the cost equations control for and net out differences in output scale and product mix and input prices.

---

[2] The quartile selection criterion could bias the coefficient estimates if the dependent variable fluctuates too closely with the criterion variable (average costs by size class). This does not appear to be a problem here, since a regression of our dependent variable, log of total costs, on dummy variables for the cost quartiles yielded an R^2 less than .01. The R^2 is low because size is the main determinant of the dependent variable, and most of the effects of size are removed when the quartiles are formed separately by size class.

[3] For example, AC_{MIN} represents the costs of the bank with the lowest long-run costs in each size class, but in any one year, some other banks had short-run costs one-third to one-half as high.

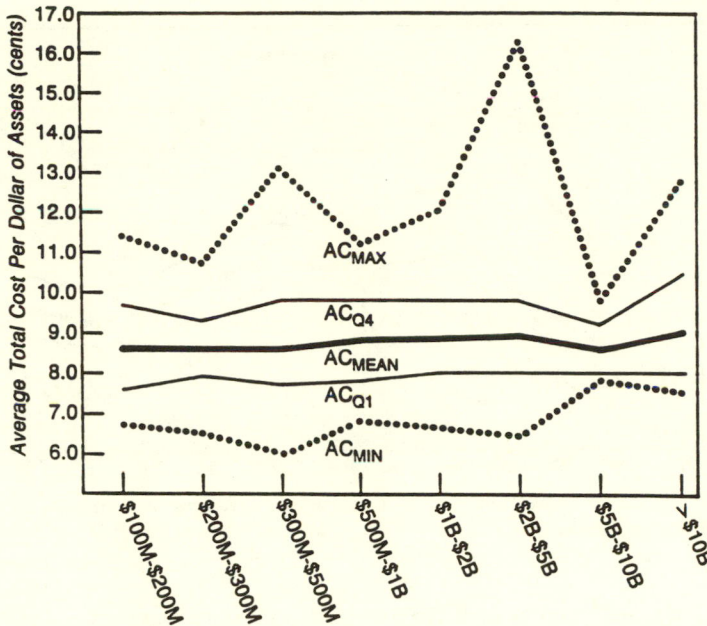

Fig. 16.1 Average costs by bank asset size class and cost quartile. (Averages over 1977–1988; M = million: B = billion; 683 panel banks.)

The stochastic econometric frontier will lie somewhere between the minimum costs and the mean of the data or approximately between AC_{MIN} and AC_{MEAN}. The precise location depends upon the actual shape of the distribution of the data and the assumed distribution for the inefficiencies. If the data are skewed toward the higher-cost banks, the stochastic econometric frontier will tend toward AC_{MIN}, while if the data are relatively unskewed, the frontier will lie closer to AC_{MEAN}. A raw-data estimate of the maximum average inefficiency under this method is given in Figure 16.1 by the difference ($AC_{MEAN} - AC_{MIN}$), which averages 29 percent. Note that the inefficiencies between the two approaches given here are not strictly comparable, since the thick frontier approach compares high- and low-cost banks, while the econometric frontier approach takes the average comparison of all banks to the frontier edge. However, these methods will be made comparable below.

Figure 16.2 presents a time series of average costs by bank quartile over time. Since the costs in the numerator and the assets in the denominator are both in nominal terms, the effects of inflation net out and the curves reflect the time trend of real average cost. The inverse of real average cost, corrected for changes in input prices, indicates the trend in bank technical change. Real average cost for Q1 banks (AC_{Q1}) rose by 34 percent over 1977 to 1988, while the growth in input prices was generally less than this amount, suggesting that technical change may be negative or very low over this period. This conclusion is unlikely to be altered by considering

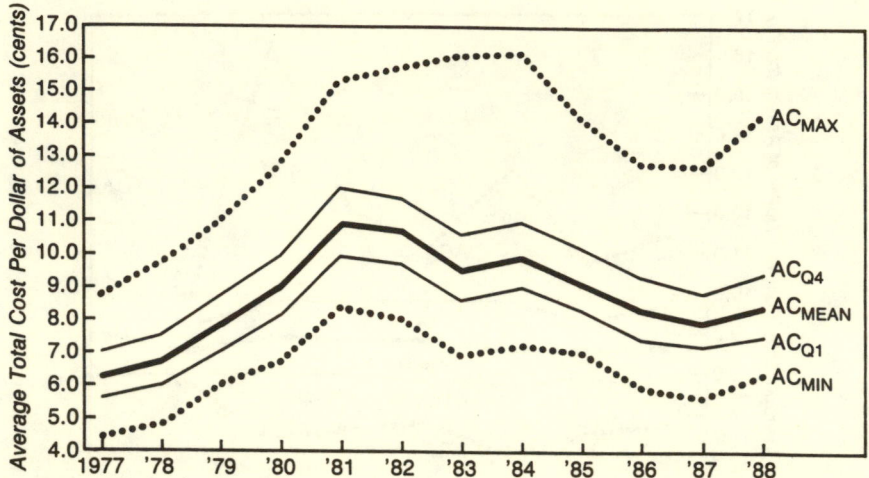

Fig. 16.2 Average costs over time and by cost quartile. (Averages over size-classes; M=million; B=billion; 683 panel banks.)

the effect of scale economies on TFP measurement, since these economies appear to be small. As discussed below, negative or low TFP growth may be associated with the peculiar nature of the banking industry's response to payments developments of the late 1970s and deposit rate deregulation and technical innovations of the 1980s.

The formal cost model underlying the stochastic econometric and thick frontier approaches used here can both be written as

$$\ln TC = \alpha + \sum_{i=1}^{5} \beta_i \ln Y_i + \frac{1}{2} \sum_{i=1}^{5} \sum_{j=1}^{5} \delta_{ij} \ln Y_i \ln Y_j + \sum_{k=1}^{4} \gamma_k \ln P_k$$

$$+ \frac{1}{2} \sum_{k=1}^{4} \sum_{n=1}^{4} \gamma_{kn} \ln P_k \ln P_n + \sum_{i=1}^{5} \sum_{k=1}^{4} \rho_{ik} \ln Y_i \ln P_k$$

$$+ \lambda_M M + \lambda_U U + \sum_{i=1}^{5} \theta_{iM} \ln Y_i M + \sum_{i=1}^{5} \theta_{iU} \ln Y_i U$$

$$+ \sum_{k=1}^{4} \phi_{kM} \ln P_k M + \epsilon \tag{16.1}$$

$$S_k = \alpha_k + \sum_{n=1}^{4} \gamma_{kn} \ln P_n + \sum_{i=1}^{5} \rho_{ik} \ln Y_i + \phi_{kM} M + \psi_k \qquad k = 1, 2, 3, 4 \tag{16.2}$$

where TC = real total cost (interest and operating costs deflated by the GNP deflator)[4]

Y_i = real value of output i, i equals (1) demand deposits, (2) small time and savings deposits, (3) real estate loans, (4) commercial and industrial loans, and (5) installment loans

P_k = real price of input k, k equals (1) labor, (2) physical capital, (3) interest rate on small time and savings deposits, and (4) interest rate on purchased funds

M = bank merger dummy variable, equals 1 for a bank in the year of its merger[5]

U = unit banking dummy variable, equals 1 when the bank was subject to unit laws (we include data from eight states that changed to branching laws during 1977–1988)

S_k = cost share of input k, which equals $\partial \ln TC / \partial \ln P_k$ from (16.1) plus an error term

ϵ, ψ_k = error terms[6]

The key to the stochastic econometric approach is the two-part composed error term, one part for inefficiency and one part for statistical noise. Thus, $\epsilon = \mu + \nu$, where $\mu \geq 0$ represents inefficiency and ν represents independent statistical noise. In our panel estimations, ν is allowed to follow a first-order serial correlation process. Unless panel data are available, one must assume that the regressors are independent of the inefficiency term as well as of the statistical noise. In addition, specific distributions for the noise and inefficiency terms must be imposed. However, if panel data are available, the latter two assumptions need not be imposed and can be tested. The stochastic econometric frontier is estimated several ways in order to test the sensitivity of the results to these assumptions.

The thick frontier model is estimated separately for the highest and lowest cost quartiles. Error terms within quartiles are assumed to represent mean zero, finite variance statistical noise which also have first-order serial correlation in the panel estimations. Measured inefficiencies are embedded in the difference in predicted costs

---

[4] As is standard in banking studies, cost figures do not include loan losses. They are instead effectively treated as declines in revenue, since the rates charged on loans include premiums to cover the expected value of these losses.

[5] In the year of a merger, the Call Report generally does *not* include the expenses incurred by acquired bank prior to the merger. This could create a bias, since the acquired bank's assets and liabilities are included generally.

[6] The standard symmetry and linear homogeneity in input prices restrictions are imposed in estimation, as are the Shephard's Lemma cross-equation restrictions. One of the share equations in (16.2) is dropped to avoid singularity. The number of branch offices is not specified in this model because cost efficiencies at the level of the banking firm are desired, rather than those for the average office [see Berger, Hanweck, and Humphrey (1987)]. The relatively unimportant interactions between the U term and the $\ln P_k$ and M terms are not specified in order to reduce the number of parameters to be estimated.

between the highest and lowest quartiles. The difference may occur in the intercepts or in the slope parameters.

The disturbance terms on the input share equations, ψ_k, are assumed to follow normal distributions with finite mean and variance for both frontier approaches. However, allowing ψ_k to have a nonzero mean in the stochastic econometric model allows for persistent allocative inefficiency over time [see Bauer, Ferrier, and Lovell (1987)]. These parameters are identified because the share equation intercepts remain identified through cross-equation restrictions.

16.3 Measures of Inefficiency and Total Factor Productivity

Within the stochastic frontier approach, four separate techniques are used to estimate individual bank inefficiencies, although all four use essentially the same cost function shown in Equations (16.1) and (16.2). Two panel estimation techniques are based on Schmidt and Sickles (1984). These techniques assume that bank inefficiencies are fixed over time.[7] The GLS panel estimator makes the further assumption that the inefficiency disturbances are uncorrelated with the regressors. The cost equations are estimated and a separate intercept α_i for each of the 683 banks is recovered as the mean residual for that bank. The most efficient bank in the sample is assumed to be fully efficient, and the inefficiency of bank i is given by the proportionate increase in predicted costs over the efficient bank, or $\hat{\alpha}_i - \min_j \hat{\alpha}_j$. The WITHIN panel estimator uses a fixed effects model to estimate α_i, where the variables are measured as deviations from individual bank means, eliminating the need to assume that inefficiency is uncorrelated with the regressors. Both of these estimators allow the statistical error terms to be correlated across equations and over time.

Some strong assumptions are required for these techniques to yield consistent estimates of inefficiency. First, inefficiency must be the only time-invariant fixed effect. Second, as the number of banks approaches infinity, the density of the inefficiency disturbances must be nonzero in the neighborhood of $(0, \omega)$ for some $\omega > 0$. That is, as the sample size increases, it must become more likely that firms on the estimated frontier are near the true frontier.

Two MLE estimation techniques are based on Bauer, Ferrier, and Lovell (1987). The composed error ϵ is the sum of the half-normally distributed inefficiency μ and the normally distributed statistical error ν. The measured inefficiency for an individual bank is the conditional mean $E(\mu|\epsilon)$.[8] The MLE (by year) technique allows the translog coefficients to vary over time, while the MLE (panel) technique holds the

---

[7] This assumption is not strictly necessary. Cornwell, Schmidt, and Sickles (1990) generalized the approach to allow inefficiencies to vary over time, but in a structured manner.

[8] The formula is $E(\mu|\epsilon) = (\sigma_\mu \sigma_\nu / \sigma) \cdot [\{\phi(\epsilon\lambda/\sigma)/[1 - \Phi(\epsilon\phi/\sigma)]\} - (\epsilon\lambda/\sigma)]$, where σ_μ and σ_ν are the variances of μ and ν, respectively, $\lambda \equiv \sigma_\mu/\sigma_\nu$ and $\sigma^2 \equiv \sigma_\mu^2/\sigma_\nu^2$. Clearly, this approach requires μ and ν to be independent of each other and of the regressors. An alternative is to use the conditional mode, which was found to be nearly the same here.

coefficients fixed over time. Unlike the other panel techniques, MLE (panel) does not allow for autocorrelation.

In the thick frontier approach of Berger and Humphrey (1991, 1992a), the difference in predicted average costs between cost quartiles is decomposed into explained and unexplained parts and the unexplained part is taken to be the inefficiency difference between the quartiles. The proportionate difference in predicted average costs is given by

$$DIFF = \frac{\widehat{AC}^{Q4} - \widehat{AC}^{Q1}}{\widehat{AC}^{Q1}} \qquad (16.3)$$

where $\widehat{AC}^{Qi} = \widehat{C}^{Qi}(X^{Qi})/TA^{Qi}$ is predicted average cost, $\widehat{C}^{Qi}$ incorporates the parameter estimates obtained using the Qi data, and X^{Qi} and TA^{Qi} are the vectors of mean regressors and the mean total assets, respectively, for the size class for the ith quartile (size class scripts suppressed for expositional ease). It is assumed that differences in output levels, output mix, and input prices are due not to inefficiencies, but to exogenous differences in the markets in which different banks operate. The part of $DIFF$ that cannot be attributed to the exogenous variables in the model constitute the measured inefficiency residual given by

$$INEFF = \frac{\widehat{AC}^{Q4} - \widehat{AC}^{Q4*}}{\widehat{AC}^{Q4}} \qquad (16.4)$$

where $\widehat{AC}^{Q4*} = \widehat{C}^{Q1}(X^{Q4})/TA^{Q4}$ is the predicted unit cost for Q4 data evaluated using the "efficient" Q1 technology. Thus, $INEFF$ captures only the unexplained difference in the estimated cost functions, holding the data constant at Q4. Included in $INEFF$ are overpayments of deposit and purchased funds interest, as well as operating cost inefficiencies.

For the thick frontier approach, as for the stochastic econometric approach above, both panel and cross-sectional methods by year are employed. First, a panel estimation is used in which the estimated cost function parameters are held constant over the entire time period and the average cost quartiles are formed on the basis of costs over the entire period as well (stable cost function, stable quartiles). This is analogous to the stochastic econometric frontier panel models [GLS, WITHIN, and MLE (panel)]. Second, separate cross-sectional estimates are made for each year of the sample, but the quartiles are based on the entire time period (varying cost function, stable quartiles). As discussed below, this is our preferred thick frontier method because it allows for changes over time in the technology and environment of banks that are reflected in changing slope parameters and yet eliminates much of the year-to-year noise for individual banks in choosing which are most and least efficient. This technique of basing the frontier on the entire time series panel, but allowing the parameters to vary over time, is practical only for the thick frontier approach and has no analog in the stochastic frontier approach. Finally, separate cross-sectional estimates are made for each year in a model in which the average cost quartiles are also formed by year (varying cost function, varying quartiles). This is analogous to the MLE (by year) stochastic econometric model.

Turning next to measurement of total factor productivity (TFP), this concept reflects technical change plus the scale economy effects on costs associated with variations in output levels over time. Measurement of the technical change component of TFP in a service industry like banking is difficult. Unfortunately, there is no unique indicator or proxy for measuring the effects of technical change, either for neutral or embodied technical progress. As a consequence, virtually all previous banking studies have chosen to model technical change as a simple time trend. However, studies of electric utilities have suggested that time trends may poorly reflect year-to-year variations in technical change when this process is not constant or smoothly increasing or decreasing [Kopp and Smith (1983), Nelson (1986)]. As a result, we adopt an index approach which allows technical change to vary freely over time. As developed by Caves, Christensen, and Swanson (1981) and Baltagi and Griffin (1988), the index approach is a generalization of Solow's index of technical change $A(t)$.

In the pooled models, time-specific intercept shift variables are specified to reflect neutral technical change. In cost equation (16.1), the intercept term α is replaced by $\sum_{t=1}^{12} \eta_t D_t$ where D_t equals 1 in period t and 0 otherwise ($t = 1, \ldots, 12$ over 1977–1988).[9] The growth rate of technical progress from t to $t+1$ is the common rate of input reduction holding outputs fixed:[10]

$$INDEX_{t+1,t} = -\left(\frac{\partial \ln TC}{\partial D_{t+1}} - \frac{\partial \ln TC}{\partial D_t} \right) = -(\eta_{t+1} - \eta_t) \qquad (16.5)$$

where the negative sign turns cost reductions into technical advances.

A more general technique, possible when there is sufficient cross-sectional variation, allows *all* cost function parameters to be affected by technical change, not just intercept shifts [e.g., Berger and Humphrey (1992a)]. This is equivalent to estimating equations (16.1) and (16.2) separately for each annual cross-section, and essentially nests the time-specific index model within it.[11] For the thick frontier

[9] This is a simplification of Caves, Christensen, and Swanson (1981) who allowed D_t to interact with the regressors. Baltagi and Griffin (1988) extended the Caves, Christensen, and Swanson specification by imposing a set of nonlinear restrictions on the D_t parameters to obtain the same $A(t)$ effect for neutral, nonneutral, and scale-augmenting technical change. When such nonlinear restrictions were used in Humphrey (1993), estimation was time-consuming and, importantly, the technical change estimates were almost identical without these restrictions. Similarly, the interactions of D_t with outputs and input prices did not greatly alter the technical change conclusions here.

[10] Technical change can alternatively be expressed as the common rate of output expansion holding inputs fixed. As shown in Caves, Christensen, and Swanson the two definitions are identical if there are no scale economies. They are close to each other here, since measured scale economies and diseconomies are small.

[11] One unnested difference between the cross-sectional and pooled techniques is that the unit banking dummy U was deleted from the cross-sectional estimations because of collinearity problems. Another difference is that the cross-sectional estimations do not account for autocorrelation.

approach, the growth rate of technical change is the proportional decline in predicted average costs using the estimated parameters from periods $t + 1$ and t but evaluated using data only from the base period t:

$$SHIFT_{t+1,t} = \frac{-(\widehat{AC}_{t+1}^{Q1*} - \widehat{AC}_t^{Q1})}{\widehat{AC}_t^{Q1}} \qquad (16.6)$$

where $\widehat{AC}_t^{Q1}$ is the predicted average cost for thick frontier banks in period t defined above, and $\widehat{AC}_{t+1}^{Q1*} = \hat{C}_{t+1}^{Q1}(X_t^{Q1})/TA_t^{Q1}$, the predicted average total cost for the same banks using period $t + 1$ technology. For the stochastic econometric frontier, the average costs in (16.6) refer to all banks rather than just those on the frontier, since the frontier consists of only one bank per year which might be significantly different from the adjacent years.

Scale economy effects are added to the technical change effects to yield TFP. These effects combine the overall cost elasticity, $SCE = \sum_{i=1}^{5} \partial \ln TC/\partial Y_i$, with the proportional change in the cost share (c_i) weighted average of the five outputs, $\dot{Y} = \delta \ln(\sum_{i=1}^{5} c_i Y_i)$, all in real terms.[12] As for $SHIFT, \dot{Y}$ uses the lowest cost quartile under the thick frontier approach and the overall average data under the stochastic econometric approach. Thus, TFP is expressed as

$$TFP = (INDEX \text{ or } SHIFT) + (1 - SCE)\dot{Y} \qquad (16.7)$$

Inefficiency can be incorporated into a TFP measure for all banks [Bauer (1990)] but in this application inefficiency is kept separate as our TFP applies only to frontier banks.[13]

16.4 Bank Inefficiency Estimates for 1977 to 1988

16.4.1 Stochastic Econometric Frontier Average Inefficiencies

Columns (1) to (4) of Table 16.1 show the average inefficiency estimates for the four stochastic econometric frontier techniques, which range from about 7 to 17 percent for the entire time period. Our preferred model is MLE (by year) in column (3), since the measured inefficiency is free to vary by year (unlike GLS and WITHIN), and the cost function parameters are also free to vary [unlike GLS, WITHIN, and MLE (panel)]. In this preferred model, bank inefficiency averages 15 percent. Despite the

---

[12] The c_i cost shares were taken from the Federal Reserve's *Functional Cost Analysis* (FCA) report and reflect the allocated operating and interest expenses to the five output categories for the set of large banks in the FCA report.

[13] Denny, Fuss, and Waverman (1981) attempt to measure other aspects of TFP, such as the effect of deviations of input prices from marginal outlays. However, such aspects are likely to be of little consequence here, since banks are reasonably competitive in most of their input markets.

Table 16.1 Estimated Inefficiency for the Stochastic Econometric and Thick Frontier Approaches by Year

	Stochastic Econometric Frontier Approach Average Inefficiencies				Thick Frontier Approach Interquartile Inefficiency Differences (Averaged across size classes)		
	GLS (1)	WITHIN (2)	MLE (by year) (3)	MLE (panel) (4)	Stable Function Stable Quartiles (5)	Varying Function Stable Quartiles (6)	Varying Function Varying Quartiles (7)
1977	7.2%	17.4%	15.0%	16.6%	19.0%	16.0%	12.9%
1978	7.2	17.4	16.2	17.0	21.4	10.8	24.4
1979	7.2	17.4	16.1	16.6	23.0	23.7	31.4
1980	7.2	17.4	15.3	16.6	22.4	24.8	30.8
1981	7.2	17.4	16.8	17.2	19.8	19.3	25.8
1982	7.2	17.4	13.5	16.4	15.1	19.3	10.7
1983	7.2	17.4	12.5	15.6	12.5	16.3	5.0
1984	7.2	17.4	15.0	16.0	12.4	19.8	14.7
1985	7.2	17.4	14.3	16.1	11.2	22.7	16.1
1986	7.2	17.4	14.5	16.5	10.7	22.0	15.3
1987	7.2	17.4	17.2	17.5	10.2	21.2	29.3
1988	7.2	17.4	17.2	17.8	10.7	26.5	33.0
Average	7.2%	17.4%	15.3%	16.6%	15.7%	21.0%	20.8%

Notes: For the stochastic econometric approach average inefficiencies, the GLS and WITHIN estimators are based on bank cost function intercepts and assume that bank inefficiency is fixed over time, while the MLE estimators are based on $E(\mu|\epsilon)$ and allow inefficiency to vary over time.

For the thick frontier approach interquartile inefficiency differences, the methods differ by whether the cost function parameters are assumed to be stable or vary over time, and by whether the average cost quartiles are based on average costs for the entire sample (stable) or for each year separately (varying).

The data are taken from the Federal Reserve's Reports of Condition and Income (Call Reports).

flexibility of this approach, the measured variation in inefficiency over time is rather small. The largest variation occurs in the early 1980s when inefficiency is seen to fall with the advent of deposit interest rate deregulation, that is, the establishment of new types of consumer accounts and the removal of interest rate ceilings on existing accounts. The measured fall in inefficiency may reflect a temporary disequilibrium in which the most efficient banks were the most aggressive in raising rates first and going after new funds. Examination of the pattern of inefficiencies by size class, shown in Table 16.2 for the MLE (by year) technique, suggests that larger banks at 19 percent average inefficiency may be slightly more inefficient than smaller ones.

Comparison among the stochastic econometric techniques finds about the same levels of average inefficiency for the three techniques other than GLS, raising suspicions about the GLS assumption that inefficiency is uncorrelated with the regressors. However, the correlations among the measures across banks are surprisingly high (not shown in tables). The R^2 between the GLS and WITHIN estimates is .89 and the R^2 between the two MLE methods is .93. The R^2 between each of GLS and WITHIN and each of the MLE methods is lower, between .38 and .50, in part because GLS and WITHIN force inefficiency to be time-invariant.

The assumption of a half-normal distribution for the inefficiencies is examined in Figure 16.3, which shows a histogram of the inefficiency estimates $E(\mu|\epsilon)$ for the preferred model, MLE (by year). The shape of this empirical distribution, as well as the distributions for the other three models (not shown), appears to be roughly consistent with the half-normal assumption. Previous studies have often used the half-normal assumption, but have not examined its consistency with the data.

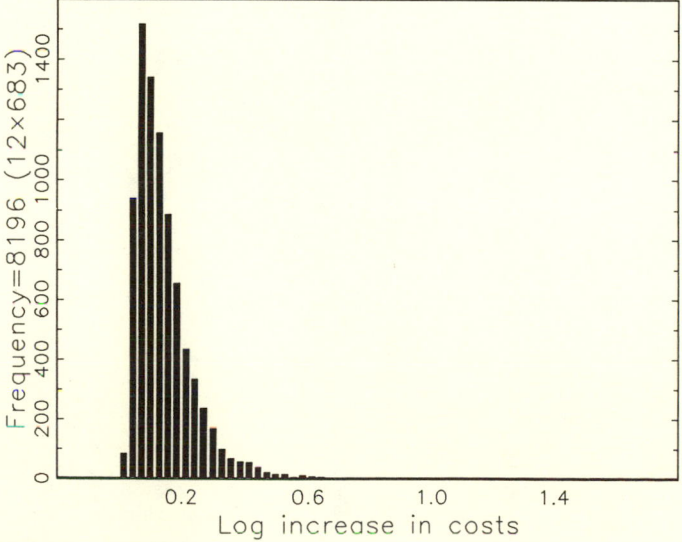

Fig. 16.3   Bank inefficiency (MLE by year)

Table 16.2 Inefficiency by Bank Size Class for the Preferred Models of the Stochastic Econometric and Thick Frontier Approaches by Year

	Bank Asset Size Classes *(M = million; B = billion)*								
	100M–200M	**200M–300M**	**300M–500M**	**500M–1B**	**1B–2B**	**2B–5B**	**5B–10B**	**>10B**	**Overall**
	Stochastic Econometric Approach Inefficiencies [MLE (by year)]								
1977	12.9%	13.8%	15.7%	15.5%	14.3%	15.9%	13.9%	20.5%	15.0%
1978	15.4	15.2	16.2	16.6	16.5	16.3	17.1	20.4	16.2
1979	15.6	14.9	16.2	16.1	16.7	16.7	17.9	17.8	16.1
1980	13.2	14.0	15.4	15.3	15.3	16.0	18.8	16.9	15.3
1981	14.6	15.1	16.9	17.1	16.9	19.1	20.0	18.0	16.8
1982	12.2	12.1	13.3	14.5	14.5	14.8	14.6	14.6	13.5
1983	12.2	11.5	12.0	12.5	13.9	13.2	13.2	16.1	12.5
1984	13.8	13.1	14.8	14.6	16.2	17.1	17.9	22.4	15.0
1985	14.4	12.5	13.9	14.6	15.4	15.8	16.2	18.8	14.3
1986	13.7	12.2	14.4	15.1	15.3	16.3	15.5	17.8	14.5
1987	14.5	13.6	17.9	19.4	19.3	17.9	16.3	21.1	17.2
1988	14.1	14.2	17.5	19.1	19.1	18.4	15.9	23.1	17.2
Overall	13.9%	13.5%	15.3%	15.9%	16.1%	16.4%	16.4%	19.0%	15.3%

Thick Frontier Approach Inefficiencies
(Varying Cost Function, Stable Quartiles)

1977	13.0%	1.0%	11.3%	12.9%	20.0%	16.6%	21.8%	31.1%	16.0%
1978	16.8	8.6	9.9	8.7	13.4	21.8	27.2	59.6	20.8
1979	18.6	10.6	12.7	8.0	13.8	24.6	30.9	70.2	23.7
1980	22.3	10.0	12.0	4.1	12.3	24.2	31.1	82.7	24.8
1981	15.5	12.0	11.7	9.4	13.8	17.6	20.5	54.1	19.3
1982	17.9	14.4	14.2	12.8	14.9	19.4	18.9	41.9	19.3

Bank Asset Size Classes
(M = million; B = billion)

	100M–200M	200M–300M	300M–500M	500M–1B	1B–2B	2B–5B	5B–10B	>10B	Overall
1983	19.7	15.1	16.2	13.6	15.9	16.8	13.6	19.8	16.3
1984	20.4	15.6	15.9	12.9	16.1	16.4	18.6	42.3	19.8
1985	20.4	18.3	18.9	18.5	16.4	17.7	19.1	52.1	22.7
1986	20.5	18.2	20.4	18.8	17.5	18.6	19.0	42.6	22.0
1987	22.7	18.0	22.3	19.3	17.5	19.4	16.9	33.3	21.2
1988	21.2	21.2	25.0	23.5	20.8	24.4	25.1	51.1	26.5
Overall	19.1%	13.6%	15.9%	43.5%	16.0%	19.8%	21.9%	48.4%	21.0%

16.4.2   Thick Frontier Interquartile Inefficiencies

Columns (5) to (7) of Table 16.1 show the interquartile inefficiency estimates for
the three thick frontier techniques, which range from about 16 to 21 percent for the
overall time period. Our preferred model is the varying cost function, stable quartiles
model shown in column (6), since all the frontier parameters are allowed to vary
across years, maximizing flexibility, but the cost quartiles are stable, minimizing the
effects of temporary or random fluctuations in costs. The results for the preferred
model indicate an average interquartile inefficiency of 21 percentage points of the
23 percent average difference in predicted and actual costs. Differences between
high- and low-cost banks in their output levels, input prices, and the other exogenous
variables explain the remaining 2 percentage points. In this model, inefficiency has
some year-to-year variation but no strong upward or downward trend is evident.
Again, the largest variation occurs in the early 1980s when inefficiency falls with the
advent of deposit interest rate deregulation.

A breakout of the inefficiencies by size class, shown in Table 16.2, suggests no
particular trend except that banks in the largest size class (assets > $10 billion) have
more than 48 percent inefficiencies, substantially more than the other size classes and
more than the actual or predicted cost differences for this size class. This suggests that
the cost function parameters, which are dominated by the observations on smaller
banks, may not extrapolate well to the relatively few large banks. If the largest size
class is deleted, average interquartile inefficiency is reduced from 21 to 17 percent.

As expected, the model in column (7) in which both the frontier parameters and
the cost quartiles are allowed to vary over time shows greater year-to-year variation
in the inefficiency estimates. However, the average results are very similar to those
for the preferred model, 20.8 versus 21.0 percent average interquartile inefficiency.
In contrast, when both the frontier parameters and the quartiles are held constant over
the entire period in column (5), the inefficiency estimates have a downward trend
starting in the early 1980s. Average interquartile inefficiency for this model is 15.7
percent, lower than in the other thick frontier models.

16.4.3   Comparison of Stochastic Econometric and Thick Frontier Inefficiencies

As noted above, the measured inefficiencies of the stochastic econometric and thick
frontier approaches are not strictly comparable because the former takes the average comparison of all banks to the frontier while the latter compares the average
banks in two different quartiles. Table 16.3, however, transforms these approaches
into comparable forms and compares the preferred MLE (by year) stochastic econometric approach with the preferred varying function, stable quartiles thick frontier
approach. Interquartile inefficiencies are first computed for both approaches using
quartiles based on the inefficiencies estimated using the stochastic econometric frontier approach [columns (1) and (2)]. The procedure is then repeated using actual

Table 16.3 Interquartile Inefficiency for Both Frontier Methods Using Stochastic Econometric Inefficiencies and Average Total Costs to Define the Quartiles

| | Stochastic Econometric Inefficiencies Define the Quartiles | | Average Total Costs Define the Quartiles | |
	Stochastic Econometric (1)	Thick Frontier (2)	Stochastic Econometric (3)	Thick Frontier (4)
1977	16.6%	26.7%	8.0%	16.0%
1978	20.0	30.8	7.2	20.8
1979	20.8	34.4	5.3	23.7
1980	18.4	33.9	3.2	24.8
1981	20.1	33.8	2.6	19.3
1982	14.8	28.6	2.5	19.3
1983	14.9	25.0	3.8	16.3
1984	20.6	25.2	4.0	19.8
1985	18.8	24.8	4.6	22.7
1986	17.2	23.0	5.0	22.0
1987	19.6	23.5	5.2	21.2
1988	18.3	22.8	5.3	26.5
Average	18.4%	27.7%	4.7%	21.0%

Notes: The preferred models are used for both approaches, that is, MLE (by year) for the stochastic econometric approach and varying cost function, stable quartiles for the thick frontier approach.

average costs to form the quartiles, that is, using the thick frontier quartiles. In all cases, the data are stratified by size class before the quartiles are obtained.

When each method uses quartiles based on its own approach, the stochastic econometric and thick frontier approaches yield similar interquartile inefficiencies of 18 and 21 percent in columns (1) and (4), respectively. These estimated inefficiencies become 5 and 28 percent in columns (3) and (2), respectively, when the other method is used to compute the quartiles, suggesting that there are important differences in the bank inefficiency rankings from the two approaches. Further examination reveals that, of the banks identified as being in the most efficient quartile in one method, only 38 percent are also identified as being in the most efficient quartile in the other method. If the two methods were totally unrelated, 25 percent would be expected to match. The matching percentage for the least efficient quartiles is 46 percent.[14] Thus, the data suggest that while the two methods find roughly the same level of inefficiencies, there are important differences between the methods in terms of which banks are identified as being the most and least efficient.

[14] The higher matching percentage for the least efficient banks may reflect the skewed nature of the inefficiencies, shown in Figure 16.3. The least efficient banks have much higher costs than other banks and may be easier to identify.

16.4.4   Comparison with Other Studies

The findings here of inefficiencies on the order of 15 to 21 percent of costs are similar to those found in the extant bank efficiency literature, although as noted, the results are not always strictly comparable. Of the stochastic econometric studies of banks, Ferrier and Lovell (1990) essentially applied the MLE (by year) method to a single year of data. They found average inefficiencies of 26 percent for a sample of small to medium sized banks for 1984. The similarity to the findings here is somewhat surprising, given the many differences between the studies. Ferrier and Lovell used smaller banks, used a different definition of bank output (number of accounts instead of dollar values), and excluded interest expenses, which make up the majority of bank costs. The MLE (by year) approach has also recently been applied to studies of corporate control [Piand Timme (1993)], savings and loans [Mester (1993)], and insurance [Cumming and Weiss (1993), Yuengert (1993)]. Our results are at the low end of Berger's (1991, 1993) range of about 10 percent to several hundred percent for samples of all sizes of banks in the 1980s. Berger applied techniques similar to the GLS and WITHIN frontier methods, but with parameters that vary by year and with some truncation of outliers. Berger's technique has recently been applied to studies of mergers [Berger and Humphrey (1992b)] and the profit function [Berger, Hancock, and Humphrey (1993)], and insurance [Gardner and Grace (1993)]. Our results are also within the range of findings of the previous thick frontier models of banking by Berger and Humphrey (1991, 1992), who found average interquartile inefficiencies of between 17 and 42 percent when examining banks of all sizes in the 1980s. The thick frontier approach has recently been applied to mergers [Rhoades (1993), Shaffer (1993)] and insurance [Yuengert (1993)].[15]

16.5   Total Factor Productivity and Scale Economies for Banks for 1977 to 1988

Total factor productivity combines the effects of technical change and changes in scale as output expands over time. Estimates of TFP for the four stochastic econometric frontier methods and the three thick frontier methods are shown in the top panel of Table 16.4. Negative growth rates are obtained for six of the seven estimations. These range from -3.55 percent to $+.16$ percent annually and represent a striking effect of unusual changes in the banking industry over this time period. Because the scale

---

[15] DEA frontier studies of banking find average inefficiencies of (in ascending order of magnitude) 12 percent by Elyasiani and Mehdian (1990), 21 percent by Ferrier and Lovell (1990), 43 percent by Rangan, Grabowski, Aly, and Pasurka (1988), 54 percent by Aly, Grabowski, Pasurka, and Rangan (1990), and 70 to 105 percent by Ferrier, Grosskopf, Hayes, and Yaisawarng (1991). DEA has recently been applied to credit unions, by Fried, Lovell, and Vanden Eeckant (1993). Our results may be less than most of these because of the upward bias in DEA from counting all random error as inefficiency.

economy estimates are so close to constant average costs (shown below), the TFP estimates almost exclusively reflect technical change.[16]

Although the negative TFP estimates are surprising, they are consistent with a number of other studies of bank TFP and technical change during this period. Negative technical change is found when (1) all banks in our panel are used (instead of only frontier banks) and (2) when technical change is alternatively represented by a time trend, a cost curve shift, or a more comprehensive set of time-specific shift variables than is specified here [see Humphrey (1993)]. Negative to small positive TFP growth rates were also found using aggregate bank data in a growth accounting model and in an estimated cost function over 1967 to 1987 [Humphrey (1991)]. While some studies of bank technical change [Hunter and Timme (1986), Evanoff, Israilevich, and Merris (1989), and Hunter and Timme (1991)], have reported larger positive growth rates, the underlying explanation may be methodological differences.[17]

There are several possible explanations for the measured poor productivity growth of banks over this time period. In the late 1970s, historically high interest rates greatly increased the use of cash management techniques by corporations. This reduced demand deposit balances which did not pay explicit interest and forced banks to rely more heavily on higher-cost funds.[18] Such an increase in real costs is measured as a reduction in TFP.

The increased interest costs from corporate cash management were extended to consumer deposit accounts with the deregulation of the early 1980s. Depositors were able to shift non-interest-earning demand deposits into interest-earning checking plans (NOW accounts) beginning in 1981 and were able to shift into variable-rate money market deposit accounts (MMDAs) by 1983. Interest rate ceilings on other deposits were phased out by 1986 as well. Competition among banks increased as regulatory impediments to such competition were reduced, raising bank costs and contributing to negative measured TFP growth.

Increased competition from outside of banking also increased during this time period, raising banks' costs of funds. Thrift institutions were given greater powers to compete for consumer funds, particularly the ability to offer checkable deposits, reducing the market power of banks. Similarly, nontraditional sources of competition, such as money market mutual funds that sold shares in portfolios of short-term Treasury securities, provided alternatives to federally insured deposits.

---

[16] To illustrate that TFP and technical change are nearly identical, the annual average technical change underlying the $-.39\%$, -2.28%, and -2.14% thick frontier TFP annual growth rates in Table 16.3 are $-.30\%$, -2.13%, and -1.97% respectively. The almost negligible effect of scale economies on TFP suggests that the use of alternative indices of the change in output (e.g., the Tornquist-Theil discrete approximation to a continuous Divisia index) would have little effect on the results.

[17] The former two studies cited used only operating costs, which reflect only around 25 percent of the total costs used here, and thus may not indicate technical change for the entire banking operation. The latter study cited used total costs, but contained a specification difficulty that, once adjusted for, turned their positive growth rate to negative [see Humphrey (1993), for details)].

[18] See Porter, Simpson, and Mauskopf (1979) for a description of this process.

Table 16.4 Total Factor Productivity and Scale Economies for the Stochastic Econometric and Thick Frontier Approaches by Year

| | *Stochastic Econometric Frontier Approach* | | | | *Thick Frontier Approach* | | |
	GLS (1)	WITHIN (2)	MLE (by year) (3)	MLE (panel) (4)	Stable Function Stable Quartiles (5)	Varying Function Stable Quartiles (6)	Varying Function Varying Quartiles (7)
	Indices of Total Factor Productivity (1977 = 100)						
1977	100.0	100.0	100.0	100.0	100.0	100.0	100.0
1978	101.9	90.2	103.5	103.8	97.8	97.8	101.3
1979	102.9	83.8	107.3	105.0	98.3	95.2	102.8
1980	98.5	75.6	103.7	101.7	94.2	91.0	98.7
1981	94.3	69.2	98.1	97.0	90.7	84.0	88.2
1982	91.0	65.4	96.5	89.9	90.1	77.3	75.5
1983	90.3	64.5	100.2	88.4	96.2	78.9	75.2
1984	91.2	64.6	108.2	91.2	92.7	78.3	75.4
1985	91.3	64.9	104.2	89.1	91.7	78.7	74.9
1986	92.5	66.0	102.5	89.2	92.8	80.3	78.1
1987	93.5	67.0	99.9	88.8	94.5	78.6	79.8
1988	93.9	67.2	101.8	88.9	95.8	77.6	78.8
Annual Growth Rate	−.57%	−3.55%	.16%	−1.06%	−.39%	−2.28%	−2.14%

Ray Scale Economies
(Averaged across size classes)

	GLS (1)	WITHIN (2)	MLE (by year) (3)	MLE (panel) (4)	Stable Function Stable Quartiles (5)	Varying Function Stable Quartiles (6)	Varying Function Varying Quartiles (7)
1977	.947	.936	1.035	1.017	1.025	1.054	1.022
1978	.962	.954	1.034	1.032	1.033	1.051	1.047
1979	.968	.963	1.023	1.047	1.038	1.052	1.058
1980	.979	.976	1.017	1.046	1.036	1.061	1.037
1981	.981	.978	1.028	1.049	1.033	1.079	1.056
1982	.961	.957	1.026	1.044	1.025	1.049	1.068

	Stochastic Econometric Frontier Approach				*Thick Frontier Approach*		
	GLS **(1)**	**WITHIN** **(2)**	**MLE** **(by year)** **(3)**	**MLE** **(panel)** **(4)**	**Stable Function** **Stable Quartiles** **(5)**	**Varying Function** **Stable Quartiles** **(6)**	**Varying Function** **Varying Quartiles** **(7)**
1983	.944	.938	1.019	1.033	1.018	1.052	1.053
1984	.948	.944	1.035	1.032	1.018	1.051	1.044
1985	.941	.936	1.024	1.026	1.016	1.032	1.041
1986	.939	.935	1.012	1.021	1.017	1.011	1.012
1987	.937	.932	1.000	1.020	1.017	1.011	1.013
1988	.937	.930	1.015	1.020	1.024	1.014	1.019
Average	.955	.950	1.022	1.032	1.025	1.043	1.039

Thus, over the late 1970s and the early 1980s, banks lost much of their monopsony power over their depositors, in part due to the actions of their corporate customers, in part due to the deregulation of consumer deposit rates, and in part due to increased nonbank competition. In all cases, banks' costs were driven up and measured TFP was driven down. Berger and Humphrey (1992a) estimated that as a net result of these changes, aggregate bank profits earned through the payment of below-market rates on deposits fell from $61 billion in 1980 to $4 billion in 1988 (in constant 1988 dollars).

It might have been possible for banks to offset these negative TFP factors by lowering operating costs, especially by closing branches. Indeed, a major technical innovation of the period, automated teller machines (ATMs), was predicted to facilitate the closing of many branches. However, to the contrary, the number of bank branches actually increased in the 1980s.[19] Part of the reason appears to be that the increased competition for depositors extended to providing convenient branches and ATMs for consumers, as well as higher interest rates. According to industry surveys, choice of bank by depositors is largely based on convenience. Part of the reason may also relate to enforcement of the Community Reinvestment Act, which encouraged banks to keep open some branches in certain local communities that might otherwise have been closed. In addition, the benefits of ATMs may have largely been captured by consumers, just as were the benefits of deposit rate deregulation. While the average cost of a single ATM transaction may be less than that of using a human teller, the added convenience of ATMs appears to increase the number of transactions substantially. For example, customers may withdraw less cash during a typical ATM transaction than during a typical human teller transaction, which increases the total number of transactions and operating costs absorbed by the bank [see Berger (1985)].

This analysis may explain why researchers have failed to observe much positive technical change or productivity growth in banking during the last one and one-half decades. All the important changes described here, cash management improvements, deregulation of deposit rates, increased nonbank competition, and the ATM innovation, in principle should have increased productivity in the banking sector, but not necessarily in its measured component. While measured productivity growth has been nonexistent, the users of banking services have benefited from higher deposit interest rates, added convenience of ATMs, and increased number of branches. These benefits, which constitute increases in the "quality" of banking output, are not captured in any measure of banking output. Thus, although there has been no measured productivity growth, it would be inappropriate to conclude that society as a whole

---

[19] Over the decade, banks closed about 6650 branches, but opened approximately 16,500.

has not benefited. Rather, there has been a substantial redistribution of productivity benefits in which users of banking services have gained at the expense of banks.[20]

We turn finally to the examination of the scale economy component of TFP, which has often been considered to be an important topic in banking of its own merit. Since most studies of bank scale economies have focused on smaller banks, it may be of particular interest to investigate the scale economies of the 12 annual samples of relatively large banks studied here. The scale economies derived from the seven stochastic econometric and thick frontier models are shown in the bottom panel of Table 16.4. The figures for the individual years are multiproduct ray scale economies, $\sum_{i=1}^{5} \partial \ln TC / \partial \ln Y_i$, averaged across size classes. A figure less than or greater than 1 indicates scale economies or diseconomies, respectively.

The estimates vary across estimation method from slight economies of about 5 percent to slight diseconomies of about 4 percent (that is, $.95 \leq \sum_i \partial \ln TC / \partial \ln Y_i \leq 1.04$). These results are also quite stable over time. Unlike the inefficiency and TFP results, the deregulation of the early 1980s does not appear to have affected scale economies significantly. A breakout by size class, shown in Table 16.5 for the preferred stochastic econometric and thick econometric models, indicates some minor variation by size of bank.

For the preferred stochastic econometric model, every size class shows scale diseconomies of 0 to 3 percent on average, except that the largest size class (assets > $10 billion) has average diseconomies of 5 percent. For the preferred thick frontier model, the scale diseconomies fall from an average 8 percent for the smallest size class ($100 million $\leq$ assets $\leq$ $200 million) to approximately constant average costs for the top two size classes (assets > $5 billion).

The small scale economy and diseconomy estimates found here on and off the frontier are consistent with most of the conventional studies of bank scale economies [see the surveys by Mester (1987), Clark (1988), and Humphrey (1990)].[21] An earlier study that compared frontier and nonfrontier scale economies [Berger and Humphrey (1991)] also found little difference, suggesting that the economies found here may well represent the universe of banks in branching states with assets over $100 million, rather than just the relatively efficient ones.

An additional conclusion is the average scale economies and diseconomies of about 5 percent or less found here and elsewhere appear to be dominated by

---

[20] An analogous situation occurred in the electric utility industry during the 1970s, when expensive pollution control restrictions were mandated. The measured output of this industry, kilowatt hours, did not rise commensurately with the increased costs, so that measured TFP fell (see Gollop and Roberts, 1983). However, society may still have benefited on net through improvements in air quality, but these are not incorporated in measured industry output.

[21] Studies finding larger scale economies typically have measured how operating costs, rather than total costs, vary with bank scale. The use of operating costs alone tends to bias the results toward finding scale economies, since banks typically substitute interest cost–intensive purchased funds for operating cost–intensive produced deposits as they increase scale, making operating costs per unit of output decline without any scale economics implications.

Table 16.5   Ray Scale Economies by Bank Size Class for the Preferred Models of the Stochastic Econometric and Thick Frontier Approaches by Year

| | Bank Asset Size Classes (M = million; B = billion) | | | | | | | | |
	100M–200M	200M–300M	300M–500M	500M–1B	1B–2B	2B–5B	5B–10B	>10B	Overall
	Stochastic Econometric Approach Ray Scale Economies [MLE (by year)]								
1977	1.005	1.006	1.016	1.023	1.035	1.045	1.061	1.089	1.035
1978	1.026	1.023	1.028	1.026	1.029	1.032	1.047	1.061	1.034
1979	1.033	1.031	1.024	1.019	1.014	1.010	1.023	1.026	1.023
1980	1.026	1.022	1.014	1.007	1.005	1.001	1.026	1.036	1.017
1981	1.044	1.039	1.034	1.022	1.017	1.009	1.021	1.035	1.028
1982	1.044	1.038	1.035	1.021	1.017	1.008	1.012	1.029	1.026
1983	1.031	1.026	1.024	1.011	1.011	1.004	1.012	1.031	1.019
1984	1.029	1.023	1.027	1.019	1.023	1.026	1.042	1.088	1.035
1985	1.031	1.024	1.022	1.014	1.011	1.012	1.024	1.057	1.024
1986	1.002	1.003	1.004	1.005	1.006	1.008	1.019	1.051	1.012
1987	.984	.988	.992	.993	.998	1.003	1.010	1.032	1.000
1988	.990	.985	1.002	1.011	1.018	1.024	1.032	1.055	1.015
Overall	1.020	1.017	1.018	1.014	1.015	1.011	1.027	1.049	1.022

Thick Frontier Approach Ray Scale Economies
[Varying Cost Function, Stable Quartiles]

	100M–200M	200M–300M	300M–500M	500M–1B	1B–2B	2B–5B	5B–10B	>10B	Overall
1977	1.056	1.048	1.065	1.052	1.053	1.052	1.049	1.054	1.054
1978	1.101	1.087	1.092	1.060	1.045	1.026	.988	1.009	1.051
1979	1.141	1.124	1.110	1.066	1.035	1.012	.958	.967	1.052
1980	1.168	1.152	1.132	1.071	1.031	1.000	.953	.977	1.061
1981	1.150	1.133	1.120	1.084	1.071	1.053	.994	1.029	1.079
1982	1.097	1.081	1.070	1.054	1.049	1.044	.995	.999	1.049
1983	1.080	1.074	1.065	1.050	1.042	1.045	1.020	1.041	1.052

Bank Asset Size Classes
(M = million; B = billion)

	100M–200M	200M–300M	300M–500M	500M–1B	1B–2B	2B–5B	5B–10B	>10B	Overall
1984	1.073	1.069	1.058	1.050	1.050	1.049	1.012	1.048	1.051
1985	1.041	1.043	1.029	1.039	1.048	1.038	1.011	1.005	1.032
1986	1.031	1.025	1.015	1.018	1.018	1.008	.999	.993	1.011
1987	1.024	1.018	1.012	1.013	1.012	1.009	.997	1.011	1.011
1988	1.031	1.027	1.020	1.019	1.012	1.010	.993	.996	1.014
Overall	1.083	1.073	1.066	1.048	1.039	1.029	.997	1.008	1.043

inefficiencies, which average about 15 to 20 percent here and are higher in some other studies.[22]

16.6 Conclusions

This chapter compares two general approaches to estimating inefficiency in banking, the stochastic econometric approach and the thick frontier approach, as well as comparing several specific techniques within each approach. We also employ these methods to obtain estimates of productivity growth and scale economies in the banking industry. The data set to which the analysis is applied is a panel of 683 large U.S. branching state banks that account for two-thirds of all U.S. banking assets. The data cover 1977 to 1988, a period of significant financial market innovation, deregulation, and technical innovation in banking.

The levels of bank inefficiency found here are reasonably consistent between the two approaches. Using the preferred models of each of the stochastic econometric and thick frontier approaches, the average difference in efficiency between the most and least efficient quartiles of banks is estimated to be 18 and 21 percent, respectively. Similarly, the average efficiency of all banks is estimated to be 15 percent using the preferred technique of the stochastic econometric approach. However, while the two approaches yield similar average efficiency findings, they rank individual banks quite differently.

The inefficiency estimates found here are consistent with those in the extant bank inefficiency literature, but are toward the low end of the literature's estimates. Nevertheless, these inefficiencies are sufficiently large to dominate the scale economy effects of 5 percent or less found here and elsewhere. This finding suggests that analyses which focus on the scale of bank operations may be misplaced. Further increases in competition in the banking industry are more likely to put pressure on inefficient banks of all sizes than to force banks of any particular size to exit the industry.

The stochastic econometric frontier and thick frontier approaches also give similar estimates for TFP growth and its two components—technical change and scale economies. Estimates of annual TFP growth ranged from negative to small positive values, from -3.55 percent growth per year to $+.16$ percent. These surprising results, which at first blush suggest technical retrogression, appear to be consistent with some

---

[22] The ray scale economy measure used here is a local, rather than global concept, and thus it could understate the gains-to-scale when exceptionally large changes in scale are involved [see Evanoff and Israilevich (1991)]. However, ray scale economies fairly accurately portray the cost effects of the changes in size that actually occur. Moreover, the relatively flat average cost curves shown in Figure 16.1, where the AC_{MEAN} curve varies by only 5 percent across all size classes, suggest that even very large changes in scale are not associated with large changes in average costs. In addition, Berger (1991, 1993), the only studies to compute both conventional efficiencies and scale efficiencies (comparisons of average costs for each bank to those for the scale-efficient bank of the same product mix), found conventional inefficiencies to dominate scale inefficiencies.

institutional events that occurred over this time period. In particular, over the late 1970s and the early 1980s, deposit interest costs rose sharply as banks lost much of their monopsony power over their depositors which had allowed them to pay below-market rates. This loss, which was the depositors' gain, was due to more sophisticated corporate cash management techniques, the deregulation of consumer deposit rates, and an increase in nonbank competition. The higher cost of funds is measured as a negative technical change because costs increased without a corresponding increase in measured output. The benefits of the key technical innovation of the period, ATMs, also appear to have been largely captured by consumers who got more convenient service without paying significantly more for it. Thus, despite the fact that *measured* productivity was reduced, the unmeasured extra product of the industry in the form of more favorable deposit rates and more convenient transactions for depositors implies that the true productivity of this industry may well have increased.

Turning to future implications, forthcoming increases in competitive pressure in banking will most likely come from bank mergers, both within and across markets. Several large banking organizations are in the process of, or have already completed, within-market mergers. In addition, if interstate banking legislation passes, substantially greater opportunities for across-market mergers will be created. In these next rounds of increased competition, there is considerably less room for depositor benefits than in the previous rounds, since most banks pay close to market rates already. However, the substantial inefficiencies cited above leave room for some *measured* increases in bank productivity if efficient banks take over inefficient banks and raise the efficiency of the latter group significantly.

REFERENCES

Aigner, D., C. A. K. Lovell, and P. Schmidt (1977), "Formulation and Estimation of Stochastic Frontier Production Function Models," *Journal of Econometrics* 86: 21–37.

Aly, H. Y., R. Grabowski, C. Pasurka, and N. Rangan (1990), "Technical, Scale, and Allocative Efficiencies in U.S. Banking: An Empirical Investigation," *Review of Economics and Statistics* 72: 211–218.

Baltagi, B. H., and J. M. Griffin (1988), "A General Index of Technical Change," *Journal of Political Economy* 96: 20–41.

Battese, G. E., and G. S. Corra, "Estimation of a Production Frontier Model with Application to the Pastoral Zone of Eastern Australia," *Australian Journal of Agricultural Economics* 21: 169–179.

Bauer, P. W. (1990), "Decomposing TFP Growth in the Presence of Cost Inefficiency, Nonconstant Returns to Scale, and Technological Progress," *Journal of Productivity Analysis* 1: 287–299.

Bauer, P. W., G. Ferrier, and C. A. K. Lovell (1987), "A Technique for Estimating a Cost System that Allows for Inefficiency," Working Paper, Federal Reserve Bank of Cleveland.

Berger, A. N. (1985), "The Economics of Electronic Funds Transfers," Outline, Board of Governors of the Federal Reserve System, Washington, D.C.

Berger, A. N. (1991), "The Profit-Concentration Relationship in Banking: Tests of Market-Power and Efficient-Structure Hypotheses and Implications for the Consequences of Bank Mergers," Finance and Economics Discussion Series (FEDS) No. 176, Board of Governors of the Federal Reserve System, Washington, D.C.

Berger, A. N. (1993), " 'Distribution-Free' Estimates of Efficiency in the U.S. Banking Industry and Tests of the Standard Distributional Assumptions," *Journal of Productivity Analysis*, 4.

Berger, A. N., G. A. Hanweck, and D. B. Humphrey (1987), "Competitive Viability in Banking: Scale, Scope, and Product Mix Economies," *Journal of Monetary Economics* 20: 501–520.

Berger, A. N., and D. B. Humphrey (1991), "The Dominance of Inefficiencies over Scale and Product Mix Economies in Banking," *Journal of Monetary Economics* 28: 117–148.

Berger, A. N., and D. B. Humphrey (1992a), "Measurement and Efficiency Issues in Commercial Banking," in Zvi Griliches, ed., *Output Measurement in the Service Sectors*, National Bureau of Economic Research. Chicago: University of Chicago Press.

Berger, A. N., and D. B. Humphrey (1992b), "Megamergers in Banking and the Use of Cost Efficiency as an Antitrust Defense, " *Antitrust Bulletin*, 33

Berger, A. N., D. Hancock, and D. B. Humphrey (1993), "Bank Efficiency Derived from the Profit Function, " *Journal of Banking and Finance*, 17.

Board of Governors of the Federal Reserve System (various years), *Reports of Condition and Income* and *Functional Cost Analysis*, Washington, D.C.

Caves, D. W., L. R. Christensen, and J. A. Swanson (1981), "Productivity Growth, Scale Economies, and Capacity Utilization in U.S. Railroads, 1955–1974," *American Economic Review* 71: 994-1002.

Clark, J. (1988), "Economies of Scale and Scope at Depository Financial Institutions: A Review of the Literature," *Federal Reserve Bank of Kansas City Economic Review* 73: 16–33.

Cornwell, C., P. Schmidt, and R. C. Sickles (1990), "Production Frontiers with Cross-Sectional and Time-Series Variation in Efficiency Levels," *Journal of Econometrics* 46: 185–200.

Cummins, J. D., and M. A. Weiss (1993), "Measuring Cost Efficiency in the Property-Liability Insurance Industry," *Journal of Banking and Finance*, 17.

Denny, M., M. Fuss, and L. Waverman (1981), "The Measurement and Interpretation of Total Factor Productivity in Regulated Industries with an Application to Canadian Telecommunications," in T. C. Cowing and R. E. Stevenson, eds., *Productivity Measurement in Regulated Industries*. New York: Academic Press, pp. 191-202.

Elyasiani, E., and S. M. Mehdian (1990), "A Non-Parametric Approach to Measurement of Efficiency and Technological Change: The Case of Large U.S. Commercial Banks," *Journal of Financial Services Research* 4: 157–168.

Evanoff, D. D., P. R. Israilevich, and R. C. Merris (1989), "Technical Change, Regulation, and Economies of Scale for Large Commercial Banks: An Application of a Modified Version of Shepard's Lemma," Working Paper, Federal Reserve Bank of Chicago.

Evanoff, D. D. and P. R. Israilevich (1991), "Scale Elasticity versus Scale Efficiency," *Issues in Financial Regulation*, Federal Reserve Bank of Chicago.

F. W. Dodge Division (various years) *Dodge Construction Potentials Bulletin*, Summary of Construction Contracts for New Addition and Major Alteration Projects. New York: McGraw-Hill.

Ferrier, G. D., and C. A. K. Lovell (1990), "Measuring Cost Efficiency in Banking: Econometric and Linear Programming Evidence," *Journal of Econometrics* 46: 229–245.

Ferrier, G. D., S. Grosskopf, K. Hayes, and S. Yaisawarng (1991), "Economies of Diversification in the Banking Industry: A Frontier Approach," Working Paper, Southern Methodist University, Dallas, Tex.

Fried, H. O., C. A. K. Lovell, and P. Vanden Eeckaut (1993), "Evaluating the Performance of U.S. Credit Unions," *Journal of Banking and Finance*, 17.

Gardner, L. A., and M. F. Grace (1993), "X-Efficiency in the U. S. Life Insurance Industry, " *Journal of Banking and Finance*, 17.

Gollop, F. M., and M. J. Roberts (1983), "Environmental Regulations and Productivity Growth: The Case of Fossil-Fueled Electric Power Generation," *Journal of Political Economy* 91: 654–674.

Humphrey, D. B. (1990), "Why Do Estimates of Bank Scale Economies Differ?," *Federal Reserve Bank of Richmond Economic Review* 76: 38–50.

Humphrey, D. B. (1991), "Flow Versus Stock Indicators of Banking Output: Effects on Productivity and Scale Economy Measurement," Working Paper, Federal Reserve Bank of Richmond.

Humphrey, D. B., (1993) "Cost and Technical Change: Effects of Bank Deregulation," *Journal of Productivity Analysis*, 4.

Hunter, W. C., and S. G. Timme (1986), "Technical Change, Organizational Form, and the Structure of Bank Productivity," *Journal of Money, Credit and Banking* 18: 152–166.

Hunter, W. C., and S. G. Timme (1991), "Technological Change and Production Economies in Large U.S. Commercial Banking," *Journal of Business* 64: 206–245.

Kopp, R., and V. K. Smith (1983), "An Evaluation of Alternative Indices of Technological Change," *Scandinavian Journal of Economics* 85: 127–146.

Meeusen, W., and J. van den Broeck (1977), "Efficiency Estimation from Cobb-Douglas Production Functions with Composed Error," *International Economic Review* 18: 435–444.

Mester, L. J. (1987), "Efficient Production of Financial Services: Scale and Scope Economies," *Federal Reserve Bank of Philadelphia Economic Review* 73: 15–25.

Mester, L. (1993), "Efficiency in the Savings and Loan Industry," *Journal of Banking and Finance*, 17.

Nelson, R. A. (1986), "Capital Vintage, Time Trends, and Technical Change in the Electric Power Industry," *Southern Economic Journal* 53: 315–332.

Pi, L., and S. G. Timme (1993), "Corporate Control and Bank Efficiency," *Journal of Banking and Finance*, 17.

Porter, R., T. Simpson, and E. Mauskopf (1979), "Financial Innovation and the Monetary Aggregates," *Brookings Papers on Economic Activity*, 1, The Brookings Institution, Washington, D.C., pp. 213–229.

Rangan, N., R. Grabowski, H. Aly, and C. Pasurka (1988), "The Technical Efficiency of U.S. Banks," *Economics Letters* 28: 169–175.

Rhoades, S. A. (1993), "Efficiency Effects of Horizontal (Within-Market) Mergers," *Journal of Banking and Finance*, 17.

Schmidt, P., and R. C. Sickles (1984), "Production Frontiers and Panel Data," *Journal of Business and Economic Statistics* 2: 367–374.

Shaffer, S. (1993), "Can Megamergers Improve Bank Efficiency?" *Journal of Banking and Finance*, 17.

Yuengert, A. M. (1993), "The Measurement of Efficiency in Life Insurance: Estimates of a Mixed Normal-Gamma Error Model," *Journal of Banking and Finance*, 17.

AUTHOR INDEX

Abramovitz, M., 43
Adams, D., 291n
Addison, J., 211, 212
Adnet, B., 303
Adolphson, D.L., 19, 54
Afriat, S.N., 22, 30, 184, 185
Aguilar, R., 74
Ahn, T., 8, 132n
Aigner, D.J., 36, 38, 71, 72, 73, 75, 76, 78, 82, 86, 198, 201, 210, 214, 237, 273, 295, 336, 386
Albriktsen, R.O., 36
Alchian, A.A., 5, 6
Ali, A.I., 9, 14, 29, 138, 146
Ali, M., 53
Allen, F., 297
Allen, S.G., 210n, 211, 212, 213, 214, 216, 218
Alston, L., 289n
Aly, H.Y., 349, 388, 402n
Amemiya, T., 38, 75, 242
Andrews, D.F., 347
Aoki, M., 18
Arnold, V., 8
Arrow, K., 68
Atkinson, J.H., 297
Atkinson, S.E., 43, 224
Averch, H., 6, 43

Baldwin, D., 210
Baltagi, B.H., 394
Banker, R.D., 8, 9, 19, 29, 37, 120, 134n, 139n, 148, 149, 150n, 314
Bardhan, P., 288
Barla, P., 376n

Barrow, M.M., 274
Barton, D.R., 6, 53
Battese, G.E., 20, 25, 26, 76, 77, 82, 86, 87, 100, 107, 109, 112, 116, 238, 239, 250, 253, 256, 386
Bauer, P.W., 19, 25, 45, 161, 188, 189, 237, 386, 392, 395
Baumol, W., 374, 379, 380
Becker, G.S., 197, 199, 202, 204
Beckers, D., 79, 80, 98n, 100
Bell, C., 288
Berg, S.A., 8, 50, 183, 358, 362n
Berger, A.N., 386, 387, 388, 392, 394, 402, 403, 406n, 407
Bergsman, J., 6
Bergstrom, T., 303
Bernstein, M.A., 6
Bessent, A., 8, 274
Bessent, W., 8, 274
Bhattacharyya, A., 96
Binswanger, H.P., 44
Bjurek, H., 23
Bloch, H., 6
Boehm, T.P., 17
Bol, G., 13, 14
Boles, J., 337
Borcherding, T.E., 7
Bowlin, W.F., 8
Braverman, A., 288
Breusch, T., 77n
Bricker, D.L., 349
Brown, D., 222, 231
Brown, D.J., 297
Brown, M., 43
Bruning, E.R., 9, 349

SUBJECT INDEX